Top 100

Health-Care Careers

Your Complete Guidebook to Training and Jobs in Allied Health, Nursing, Medicine, and More

THIRD EDITION

Dr. Saul Wischnitzer
and Edith Wischnitzer

jist Works
America's Career Publisher®

Top 100 Health-Care Careers, Third Edition
© 2011 by Dr. Saul Wischnitzer and Edith Wischnitzer

Published by JIST Works, an imprint of JIST Publishing
7321 Shadeland Station, Suite 200
Indianapolis, IN 46256-3923
Phone: 800-648-JIST   Fax: 877-454-7839
E-mail: info@jist.com   Web site: www.jist.com

Visit our Web site at **www.jist.com.** Find out about our products, get sample pages, and order a catalog.

Quantity discounts are available for JIST books. Please call 800-648-JIST or visit www.jist.com for a free catalog and more information.

Acquisitions Editor: Susan Pines
Development Editor: Dave Anderson
Interior Design: Marie Kristine Parial-Leonardo
Page Layout: Toi Davis
Proofreaders: Linda Seifert, Jeanne Clark
Indexer: Cheryl Lenser

Printed in the United States of America
15 14 13 12 11 10   9 8 7 6 5 4 3 2

Library of Congress Cataloging-in-Publication Data

Wischnitzer, Saul.
  Top 100 health-care careers : your complete guidebook to training and jobs in allied health, nursing, medicine, and more / Saul Wischnitzer and Edith Wischnitzer. -- 3rd ed.
      p. cm.
  Other title: Top one hundred health-care careers
  Includes index.
  ISBN 978-1-59357-809-1 (alk. paper)
  1. Medicine--Vocational guidance--Forecasting. I. Wischnitzer, Edith.
  II. Title. III. Title: Top one hundred health-care careers.
  [DNLM: 1. Health Occupations. 2. Vocational Guidance. W 21]
  R690.W565 2010
  610.69--dc22
                                                        2010025504

We have been careful to provide accurate information in this book, but it is possible that errors and omissions have been introduced. Please consider this in making any career plans or other important decisions. Trust your own judgment above all else and in all things.

Trademarks: All brand names and product names used in this book are trade names, service marks, trademarks, or registered trademarks of their respective owners.

ISBN 978-1-59357-809-1

Dedication and Acknowledgments

This book is dedicated to the memory of our parents,

Solomon and Ray Wischnitzer
and
Miksa and Gali Lefkovits,

who, through their devotion and by example, provided us with the ethical and spiritual values that have served as our guiding lights throughout life.

We are grateful to our son, Judah M. Wischnitzer, and our daughter Rachel L. Willig, who, in this edition, as in previous editions, applied their ample computer skills to incorporate the new material into the text.

Resume and Cover Letter Contributors

The following people contributed resumes and cover letters to this book. They are all professional resume writers. We appreciate their submissions.

Carol Altomare, MRW, ACRW, CPRW, CCMC, CJSS
World Class Résumés
P.O. Box 483
Three Bridges, NJ 08887
Phone: (908) 237-1883
E-mail: carol@worldclassresumes.com
www.worldclassresumes.com

Arnold G. Boldt, CPRW, JCTC
Arnold-Smith Associates
625 Panorama Trail, Building 1, Ste. 120C
Rochester, NY 14625
Phone: (585) 383-0350
Fax: (585) 387-0516
E-mail: Arnie@ResumeSOS.com
www.ResumeSOS.com

Beverley Drake, CEIP, IJCTC, CPRW
CareerVision Resume & Job Search Systems
1816 Baihly Hills Dr. SW
Rochester, MN 55902
Phone: (507) 252-9825
E-mail: careerexpertise@aol.com

Wendy Gelberg, CPRW, IJCTC
21 Hawthorn Ave.
Needham, MA 02492
Phone: (781) 444-0778
Fax: (781) 444-2778
E-mail: wgelberg@aol.com

Bill Kinser, MRW, CPRW, JCTC, CEIP, CCM
To The Point Resumes
4117 Kentmere Sq.
Fairfax, VA 22030
Phone: (703) 352-8969
Fax: (703) 991-2372
E-mail: bkinser@tothepointresumes.com
www.tothepointresumes.com

Janice M. Shepherd, CPRW, JCTC, CEIP
Write On Career Keys
Bellingham, WA 98226
Phone: (360) 738-7958
Fax: (360) 738-1189
E-mail: janice@writeoncareer-keys.com
www.writeoncareerkeys.com

Edward Turilli, MA
Director, Career Development Center
Salve Regina University
ARC—Anthem Résumé and Career Services
918 Lafayette Rd.
North Kingstown, RI 02852
Phone: (401) 268-3020
Fax: (401) 341-2994
E-mail: turillie@salve.edu
www.salve.edu/office_careerdev

Contents

PART 1
CHOOSING AND PLANNING A HEALTH-CARE CAREER 1

12 Rehabilitation Careers: Therapists, Therapy Assistants, and Aides 320

B Health-Care Professional Organizations 470

C Job Search Resources 476

Index 481

About This Edition

For centuries, health-care careers have long been considered admirable and attractive, and health care practitioners are always in need. If anything, the appeal of careers in health care only increases in times of economic uncertainty. The state of the national economy has a profound effect on the career interests and choices of prospective job seekers, including those considering health-care careers. Some areas, such as nursing, have a much greater need for employees than others. But overall, the demand for competent and well-trained people, directly or indirectly involved in health care remains strong. Advances in technology, expansion of benefits, and, of course, the vast numbers of baby boomers who will soon become senior citizens should lead to a substantial increase in the need for health-care services for the foreseeable future. This book is designed to help you explore and carefully consider your future and why a health-care career might be part of it.

The consistent demand for health-care professionals and paraprofessionals, combined with the changes in technology, work roles, and training requirements has prompted the need for a new edition. The contents of this new edition remain highly relevant and accurate. All school listings have been reviewed and updated. Job growth and salary projections are based on the most current data available. The information in this book will give you the most accurate overview possible for the top careers in a variety of health-care fields.

In addition, a considerable number of new topics have been added, including a section on historical landmarks in health care, additional names and descriptions of facilities and organization utilizing health-care personnel, new information outlining the desirable personal qualities of health care personnel, a discussion of the importance of teamwork for the health-care worker, and a discussion of self-awareness as a means of enhancing interpersonal relations. This new edition will help you to consider the impact of stress in health-care careers and the need for effective time-management. Discussions of such topics as the role of leadership, advanced patient directives, communication guidelines, professional standards, as well as problem solving skills, will provide readers with valuable new information that will assist in career planning. In addition, substantial new material has been added to help readers with the admissions process. The new contributions to this book will be an asset for your future, helping you to consider, train for, land, and succeed in your health-care career.

This book stems from the author's extensive background as a college prehealth professions advisor and private health career consultant. He is gratified to be able to assist you in this vital endeavor, and he wishes you well.

Introduction

The health-care professions represent one of the largest employment areas in the United States, annually absorbing thousands of newly trained workers. This field attracts people with a wide range of educational backgrounds, from high school through graduate school, because it offers such a variety of career options. The explosive growth of the health-care industry stems from a variety of factors:

- Our growing and aging population continually demands more health care. This translates into explosive growth in home health care and clinical outpatient services.
- Managed-care and cost-control efforts generate positions such as physician assistant and dental hygienist. These workers do many of the routine tasks doctors and dentists used to perform—at a much lower cost to patients and insurance companies.
- Technological advances create entirely new jobs, such as sonographer and nuclear medical technologist.
- Our society's increased health consciousness has placed a strong emphasis on the role of health advocates and counselors—in fields as diverse as enhancing nutrition and improving mental health.

This book is a complete career guide and directory. It will help you choose a health-care career, find the education or training you need for that career, and walk you through the job search process.

The book is divided into four parts.

Part 1 helps you determine whether you want to work in the health-care field and, if so, which career is best for you. Chapter 1 presents an overview of the field, listing the kinds of positions that are available and where you can find them. Chapter 2 offers several checklists and exercises to help you assess where your skills and interests lie. It also outlines the major categories of career options. Chapter 3 looks at where and how you can get the education and training you need for your chosen career—from finding the best program to financing your schooling.

Part 2 gives you a feel for what it's like to work in health care. Chapter 4 outlines the basic characteristics and skills a helping professional needs. Chapter 5 presents the professional's role from the *patient's* point of view and discusses several patient relations issues. Chapter 6 details the relationship between health-care professionals and patients.

Part 3 covers the job search process. Chapter 7 helps you define your career goals, target prospective employers, learn to network, and market yourself effectively. Chapter 8 teaches you to find job openings, create an effective resume, handle applications and examinations, and hone your interview skills.

Finally, Part 4 contains detailed descriptions of the top 100 allied health-care careers, outlining the basic characteristics of each. Each career description also lists schools that offer educational and training programs in the field. The career descriptions are organized into six categories and chapters:

- Diagnosing and treating practitioners
- Associated health-care workers
- Technologists, technicians, assistants, and aides
- Therapists, therapy assistants, and aides
- Health-care administrative workers
- Affiliated health-care workers

It may not be necessary to read this book from cover to cover. For example, you might skip Part 3 until you've done some research and discovered specific careers you are interested in. However, if you find you are ready to invest your time and money in a health-care career, all of the information in this book will be invaluable to you.

Historical Landmarks

The care of the body and mind are, in fact, ancient arts with a rich history of achievements and a pantheon of practitioners. By becoming a health-care professional, one joins a fellowship of individuals going back to the earliest of times. Following is a brief overview of the major landmarks of health care throughout history. An awareness of the milestones met by past members of the profession not only offers a sense of scope and progress, but can provide you with a sense of pride of joining such a fabled fellowship.

Ancient Times: 4000 BCE – 3000 BCE
Life span: 25–30 years

- Illness believed to arise by supernatural causes.
- Plant and herbal extracts were used as medicines.
- Trephining or boring a skull hole used as a treatment.

Early Egyptians: 3000 BCE – 300 BCE
Life span: 25–30 years

- Implored the assistance of their gods to heal the sick.
- Priests served as physicians.
- Medicinal plants and magic used for healing.

Early Chinese: 1500 BCE – 200 CE
Life span: 25–30 years

- Monitoring of pulse introduced to evaluate health status.
- Acupuncture introduced to relieve body pain.
- Concept of a medical basis for illness introduced.

Greek Era: 1200 BCE – 200 BCE
Life span: 25–35 years

- Hippocrates emphasized the importance of observing the ill and recording signs and symptoms as well as the need for professional ethics.

- Aristotle introduced science of comparative anatomy by dissection of various animal forms.
- Conceived of illness as being due to natural causes and used massage therapy.

Roman Era: 750 BCE – 400 CE
Life span: 25–35 years

- Galen, a prominent physician, postulated that the body's state is regulated by its innate "balance." He recognized the inflammatory process and analyzed infectious diseases.
- Introduction of sanitation and public health systems by building sewers to remove waste and aqueducts to bring water to cities.
- Diseases were treated by exercise and diet.

Dark Ages: 400 – 800 CE
Life span: 20–30 years

- Emphasis was placed on divine intervention to treat illness.
- Custodial care of the sick was in the hands of priests and monks.
- Herbal compounds were the medications most commonly used.

Middle Ages: 800 – 1400
Life span: 30–35 years

- Rhazes focused attention on the signs and symptoms of disease, thus distinguishing between small pox and measles.
- Suture material from animal gut introduced.
- Arab physicians required to pass licensing examination.

Renaissance: 1350 – 1450
Life span: 30–40 years

- Marks the rebirth of medicine after two stagnant eras.
- Vesalius publishes the first human anatomy book. This was made possible by the development of the printing press and a move toward the clinical application of anatomy.
- Roger Bacon furthered the use of chemical remedies to treat illness.

16th and 17th Century
Life span: 30–45 years

- Ambroise Pare laid the foundation for modern surgery.
- William Harvey reported on the closed circulation of blood with the heart as its pump.
- Anton Van Leeuwenhoek invented the microscope.
- The basic cause of disease remained unclear and infections were common.

18th Century
Life span: 35–50 years

- John Hunter developed scientific surgical procedures.
- Edward Jenner developed vaccination for small pox.
- James Lind recognized the use of Vitamin C–containing limes to prevent scurvy.

19th Century
Life span: 40–55 years

- James Blundell performed the first successful blood transfusion.
- Philippe Pinel introduced the concept of humane treatment of mentally ill people.
- Theodor Fliedner initiated the first formal training program for nurses; Florence Nightingale was one of his graduates.
- William Morton, a dentist, introduced ether as an anesthetic.
- Joseph Lister began using antiseptics prior to surgery to prevent infections.
- Elizabeth Blackwell became the first female physician in the United States.
- Paul Ehrlich, a German bacteriologist, uncovered laboratory procedures that permit differentiating between diseases. He used chemicals to destroy bacteria. He also laid the foundation for the study of immunity.
- Robert Koch, father of microbiology, developed the process that serves to identify and isolate bacteria.

20th Century
Life span: 65–75 years

- Karl Landsteiner identified the major blood groups.
- Sigmund Freud established the basis for psychology and psychiatry.
- Marie Curie isolated radium needed in radioactive procedures.
- Alexander Fleming discovered penicillin as a valuable antibiotic.
- Frederick Banting and Charles Best uncovered the potential of insulin as a treatment for diabetes.
- John Enders and Frederick Robbins discovered how to grow viruses in culture dishes.
- The kidney dialysis machine was created.
- Jonas Salk developed the polio vaccine.
- A heart-lung bypass machine was developed that permitted open heart surgery.
- Medicare and Medicaid were introduced.
- Heart and lung transplants were successfully performed.
- The CAT and MRI techniques were introduced for diagnostic purposes.
- The human genome project began.

Choosing and Planning a Health-Care Career

Recent years have witnessed an extensive debate on how best to ensure quality health care for everyone, delivered efficiently and cost-effectively. This issue is especially complex because our expanding and aging population needs, expects, and deserves adequate and competent health care. As a consequence, more and different types of health-care providers are needed to cope with both population increases and technological advances. As a result, the majority of positions being created in the health-care industry are in the allied health fields.

In order to meet these needs, professionals in many allied health-care fields now have direct patient contact in offices, clinics, and hospitals. These professionals educate and advise patients on illness prevention, proper nutrition, and therapeutic management of health-related problems. It's not just doctors and nurses directly treating patients—the health-care field is filled with professionals from a wide variety of backgrounds filling an equally wide array of roles.

As with other fields—from education to manufacturing—job growth varies from one occupation to the next. However, overall job growth for health-care professions is among the best. The following list, compiled by the U.S. Department of Labor, projects the percentage of anticipated increase in employment in a variety of health-care fields by occupation from 2010 to 2018.

Health Area	Percentage Increase
Home Health Aides	50
Medical Scientists	40
Physician Assistants	39
Athletic Trainers	37
Physical Therapist Aides	36
Dental Hygienists	36
Veterinary Technologists and Technicians	36
Dental Assistants	36
Medical Assistants	34
Physical Therapist Assistants	33

While these figures are encouraging, be aware that many people expect a major restructuring of the health-care industry over the next decade. As a result, it is difficult to project personnel needs with absolute certainty. In addition, rapid changes in technology can have a major impact on health-care jobs, both positive and negative. However, it is certain that our growing and aging population will require enormous health-care resources and that now is as good a time as any to embark on a health-care career.

The Health-Care Field: Where the Jobs Are

Until the turn of the 20th century, the United States had only three kinds of health-care practitioners: doctors, dentists, and nurses. Although many cities boasted hospitals, most doctors made house calls, treating patients in their homes. Today, health care is offered in offices, clinics, hospitals, and several other kinds of facilities. Nurses and health support personnel are much more involved in diagnosing and treating patients. Advances in science and technology have lead to an almost bewildering number of specialists focused on a particular aspect of human health. As a direct consequence of the revolutionary advances made in both prevention and treatment of illnesses, the life span of the average American increased by about 25 years in the 20th century—from 47 to 72 years.

Evidence of the growth in health-care services is all around you. Simply taking a walk through nearly any business district reveals the number and variety of health-care facilities at hand. You might be surprised by the number of people engaged in health-care services in your own community. Of course these include the skilled personnel working in the offices of doctors, dentists, podiatrists, optometrists, and chiropractors. But they also include allied health-care professionals employed at local hospitals, storefront clinics, nursing homes, rehab centers, and even small-animal care establishments. In addition to physicians and dentists, your neighborhood health-care offices and facilities employ technologists, technicians, therapists, assistants, administrative and office workers, and other support personnel.

The technological advances of the past century have created many new types of health-care careers, resulting in a huge industry that employs many millions of people. In fact, the health-care field is one of the largest employers in this country. Its broad spectrum of careers offers satisfying and rewarding jobs to people of all educational levels and abilities. These careers differ widely in complexity, variety of activities, and level of responsibility.

It is estimated that more than 12 million people work in health-care industries in the U.S. These include physicians, dentists, nurses, pharmacists, therapists, technologists, technicians, assistants, engineers, health support personnel, and others whose skills and knowledge are vital to the routine operations of the workplace. Government statistics indicate that health care is one of the largest and fastest-growing industries. These workers come from a wide variety of backgrounds, with education ranging from a high school diploma to a decade worth of postsecondary training.

As the title of this book suggests, there are at least one hundred (and, in fact, there are many more) occupations in the health-care industry to consider. At least one of these many challenging careers might be right for you.

Employment Sites

About 600,000 establishments make up the health-care industry. Three quarters of these are offices of physicians, dentists, or other health practitioners. Although hospitals constitute about one percent of all health-care establishments, they employ a third of all health-care workers.

Where you work is an important issue. Many different facilities provide services that are categorized as health care. Most private health-care facilities require a fee-for-services rendered. In some cases grants and contributions help provide financial support for these facilities. Most health-care careers are grouped according to the kind of services provided, which, in turn, is tied to the kind of facility that offers those services. Health service workers generally are employed in one of two kinds of facilities: inpatient or outpatient. Inpatient facilities include hospitals, senior residences, and other residential homes. Outpatient facilities vary widely in function and style.

Inpatient Facilities

Inpatient facilities that employ health-care workers include hospitals, senior residences, and other special residential facilities.

Hospitals

Hospitals are one of the major types of health-care facilities, and perhaps the most widely recognized. They vary in size and in type of services provided. Some hospitals serve the basic needs of a community; others are large complex centers offering a wide range of services including diagnosis, treatment, education and research. The greatest number of health-care workers are employed at hospitals. But not all hospitals are alike. They are categorized by the nature of their ownership and by the type of service they provide.

Hospital ownership is categorized in one of three ways: government, voluntary, or proprietary.

- **Government hospitals** are operated by federal, state, or local government agencies. The federal government operates the nationwide Veterans' Administration hospitals, states maintain psychiatric hospitals, and cities are responsible for municipal hospitals.
- **Voluntary hospitals** are local, private, not-for-profit institutions. Many are owned by religious organizations.
- **Proprietary hospitals** are operated for profit and are owned by either private individuals or companies.

Based on the type of service they provide, hospitals are further categorized as either acute-care or long-term care facilities:

- **Acute-care facilities** treat patients with sudden-onset illnesses and conditions (such as heart attacks and fractures). Patients typically stay in such facilities no more than a few days or weeks.

- **Long-term hospitals** treat patients with chronic and psychiatric illnesses. They also provide rehabilitative services, often extending over many months or even years.

University or college medical centers provide hospital services while also acting as sites for the education of medical students and physicians-in-training and for conducting basic and clinical medical research. These sites employ an especially wide array of health-care workers in order to meet their multiple missions.

Finally, some cities in the United States have *specialty hospitals,* which are devoted to caring for a specific population, such as children or patients suffering from one disease (such as cancer) as well as psychiatric and rehabilitation hospitals.

Senior Residences

The aging of the U.S. population and our increased mobility have led to a rapid increase in the number of senior residences (including nursing homes) that provide long-term care for the elderly. Today there are tens of thousands such facilities nationwide employing well over a million workers.

Some of these facilities provide short-term care for people of all ages who are convalescing from illness or injury. But most are geared toward the elderly, providing residents with services ranging from simple personal assistance to skilled nursing care.

- **Nursing (or geriatric) homes** are designed to provide basic physical and emotional care for individuals who are unable to do so for themselves. Such facilities are mandated to provide a safe and secure environment and suitable opportunities for social interaction.

- **Extended care facilities** are especially designed to provide skilled nursing care and rehabilitative care to help prepare patients for less specialized sites of care. Some extended care facilities have *subacute units* designed to provide services to patients who need short-term rehabilitation to recover from a major illness or surgery, treatment for cancer or kidney disease, or extended heart monitoring for diagnostic purposes.

- **Assisted living facilities** are becoming increasingly popular among senior citizens. These facilities are designed to enable residents to have a significant degree of freedom. Many individuals who can provide personal care for themselves find such accommodations attractive because the facility provides essential subsistence services including meals, housekeeping, laundry and routine medical care oversight, while still allowing for a relatively independent lifestyle. Many assisted living facilities are associated with nursing homes, extended care facilities, and or skilled care facilities. This allows individuals to be moved readily from one level of care to the next when changed health needs necessitate it.

Special Residential Facilities

In addition to senior residences, more than 7,000 inpatient facilities serve the special needs of those who require ongoing assistance but do not need to be hospitalized. These include residential homes for mentally retarded, emotionally disturbed, and physically handicapped people, as well as those who are impaired due to alcohol or substance abuse. Such facilities not only provide living accommodations but also arrange for the medical care of their clients, usually at outpatient sites.

Outpatient Facilities and Services

More than half a million people work in a wide variety of facilities that provide direct health-care services:

- **Ambulance services** transport patients to hospitals and other health-care facilities. These services are operated by both municipal and private agencies.

- **Blood banks,** located in hospitals or operated independently, draw, type, process, and store blood for medical use.

- **Clinics,** also called satellite clinics, are health-care facilities that offer many different types of services. Some clinics are composed of a group of physicians or dentists who share the same facility and personnel. Other clinics are operated by private groups who provide special care. Examples of these include surgical clinics that perform minor procedures; emergency care clinics; rehabilitation clinics offering physical, occupational, speech, and other therapies; and specialty clinics for monitoring and treating diabetes or cancer. Many hospitals operate clinics for outpatients that provide pediatric care, treatment for respiratory diseases, immunizations, and other special services. Clinic services are offered, usually free of charge, by medical schools in order to provide their students with supervised opportunities to gain clinical experience.

- **Clinical laboratories** usually are located in hospitals, but they can be operated privately. Workers in these labs draw blood and secure other body specimens for use in diagnosing illnesses.

- **Community mental health centers** offer 24-hour emergency assistance, inpatient or outpatient help, and counseling for mental health problems.

- **Dental laboratories** employ people to prepare crowns, bridges, and other dental appliances based on specifications submitted to them by dentists. Most are privately owned and operated.

- **Dental offices** vary in size, from those that are privately owned by one or more dentists to dental clinics that employ a large number of dentists. In some areas, retail or department stores operate dental or (podiatric) clinics. Dental services can include general care to all age groups or even specialty care.

- **Emergency care facilities,** both free-standing or at hospitals, provide special care for victims of accidents or sudden illness. These facilities are certified with ambulance services that rapidly transport patients to medical facilities for more intensive care.

- **Family planning centers** employ trained professionals who provide counseling on birth control, sterility, and questions concerning abortion.

- **Genetic counseling centers** usually are located in hospitals. Trained professionals counsel couples who are concerned about the possibility of birth defects—either because of hereditary problems or because the mother is especially at risk. These centers also arrange for fetal testing during pregnancy. Counselors interpret and clarify the meaning of the results of prenatal screening tests. They outline the possible medical options when a birth defect is uncovered and help the individuals cope with the psychological issues raised by the prospects of a genetic disorder. Couples frequently consult with genetic counselors if they are in their late childbearing years or where a family history or predisposition of genetic disease exists.

- **Government health agencies** are operated by all levels of government and promote and maintain public health. They employ scientists to determine whether standards are being observed in food preparation, water supply, and waste disposal facilities. They may also evaluate whether industrial health and safety standards are being met. In addition, they promote health education and offer inoculations and other health-care services to low-income people. Specific government health agencies are discussed later.

- **Health maintenance organizations (HMOs)** are prepaid insurance programs that provide medical coverage for office and hospital care at their own or affiliated institutions. They employ physicians, physician assistants, nurses, clinical laboratory workers, and others.

- **Health practitioner offices** are local sites in neighborhoods, city centers, or even private hospitals where physicians, dentists, and other practitioners render their services. These professionals may be engaged in solo or group practices and employ a variety of personnel.

- **Home health-care agencies** are public and private organizations that provide help (such as nursing or homemaker care) for those who are ill or disabled but don't need to be confined to a hospital or nursing home. The services of these agencies for the elderly and disabled is designed to provide care in a patient's home. Examples of such services include nursing care, personal care, rehabilitation therapy (physical, occupational, speech, and respiratory) and homemaking (food preparation, cleaning, etc.). Health departments, hospitals, private agencies, government agencies and nonprofit or volunteer groups can offer home care services.

- **Hospice agencies** provide care for terminally ill persons with life expectancies of six months or less. Care can be provided in the person's home or in a hospice facility. Care is directed toward allowing the person to die with dignity and in comfort. Aside from medical and nursing supervision, psychological, social, spiritual and financial counseling are provided for both the patient and their family.

- **Industrial health-care centers,** also known as occupational health clinics, are located at large companies or industries. Such centers provide health care for employees by performing routine medical examinations, teaching accident prevention and safety, and providing emergency care.

- **Industrial organizations** are involved in the research, development, and marketing of both prescription and over-the-counter drugs. They also produce medical devices—such as cardiac pacemakers and hearing aids—and sophisticated diagnostic and treatment equipment. They employ a variety of chemists, engineers, and marketing professionals.

- **Medical offices** vary from those that are privately owned by one doctor to large complexes that operate as corporations and employ many physicians and also other essential health-care professionals. Medical services obtained at these facilities can include diagnosis, examination, laboratory testing, minor surgery, and similar basic health care. Family physicians and internists treat a wide variety of diseases and a broad range of age groups. Others care only for certain restricted age groups, such as pediatricians and geriatricians. Most physicians are specialists, treating specific diseases associated with body organs or systems such as cardiologists, gastroenterologists, or orthopedic surgeons.

- **Mental health facilities** provide services to treat patients, suffering from mental diseases and disorders. Example of these facilities include guidance and counseling centers, psychiatric clinics and substance abuse, treatment centers.

- **Migrant health centers** provide essential health services to migrant and seasonal farm workers. Since migrant workers often don't have access to medical care because of their nonpermanent resident status, such centers employ many kinds of allied health workers.

- **Neighborhood health centers** provide residents in their areas with medical, dental, pharmaceutical, and counseling services. They provide both acute and preventive care.

- **Optical centers** usually are storefront businesses that are individually owned or belong to a chain. They provide eyeglasses or contact lenses, prepared according to an ophthalmologist's or optometrist's prescription. They employ a variety of workers who do vision testing, write prescriptions, and prepare and fit glasses and lenses.

- **Poison control centers** are state- or city-supported agencies that provide both general and specific information on the hazards of and treatments for poisons.

- **Professional health associations** are organized on the national, state, and local level. They represent the members of specific health professions or types of health facilities. They work to improve standards of practice or operations, enhance the professional education of their members, and perform research. They employ members of their profession to help meet their commitments; for example, the American Physical Therapy Association employs physical therapists as administrative personnel.

- **Rehabilitation centers** may be hospital-affiliated or independently operated. They serve patients who have been disabled because of accidents, injuries, strokes, or birth defects. They employ a variety of therapists who help patients recover as much of their functional abilities as possible. Health center facilities are located in hospitals, clinics and/or private centers. They provide care to help patients with physical or mental disabilities. Services include physical, occupational, recreational, speech and hearing therapy.

- **School health services** are found in schools and colleges. These services provide emergency care for victims of accidents and sudden illness; perform routine tests to check for health conditions such as speech, vision and hearing problems; promote health education; and seek to maintain the safe and sanitary school environment. Many school health services also provide some psychological counseling.

- **Voluntary health promotion agencies** function on all three government levels to address specific health problems or services. They provide health education, make health services more available, and support research (usually through grants).

In addition to the government health-care facilities noted earlier, other health services are offered at international, national, or state and local levels. Governmental services are tax supported institutions. These agencies also employ a wide variety of health-care personnel.

- **Agency for Health-Care Policy and Research (AHCPR)** is involved in evaluating the quality of health-care delivery and identifying the standards of treatment that should be provided by health-care facilities. It employs specialists in certain health-care areas.
- **Food and Drug Administration (FDA)** is the federal agency responsible for regulating food and drug products sold to the public. Health-care personnel are employed to meet this agencies important and challenging mission.
- **Occupational Safety and Health Administration (OSHA).** This is a federal agency established to enforce standards that protect workers from job-related injuries and illnesses.
- **U. S. Department of Health and Human Services (USDHHS)** is the national agency that deals with the health problems in the United States. A major division of the USDHHS is the *National Institutes of Health (NIH)* that employ numerous individuals engaged intensively in biomedical research. Another division, the *Center for Disease Control and Prevention,* employs health-care personnel who seek to determine the causes, spread, and control of diseases in populations. *Health departments* provide services on a state, city or local level as directed by USDHHS.
- **World Health Organization (WHO)** is the international organization, sponsored by the United Nations. It compiles statistics and information on diseases, publishes health information, and investigates and addresses serious health problems throughout the world.

Employment Opportunities

The Bureau of Labor Statistics—a division of the U.S. Department of Labor—makes 10-year employment projections for most job categories, including those in the health field (see Figure 1.1). Their data shows that many of the fastest-growing occupations are found in health services, which are expected to increase more than twice as fast as the economy as a whole. In fact, the health-care industry will generate well over a million new jobs between 2008 and 2018, more than any other industry.

Be aware, however, that the validity of the data depends on the state of the economy, government support, geographic location, technological advances, and changes in existing facilities to meet population changes. Depending on when you are reading this, the figures for some jobs could have changed substantially.

Government Funding

The government, at all levels, is a major source of funds for health-care services. The extent of such support is worked out between the current administration and Congress. This has been the subject of intense debate in recent years, with strong pressures holding down expenditures. Thus, the availability of future funding is uncertain.

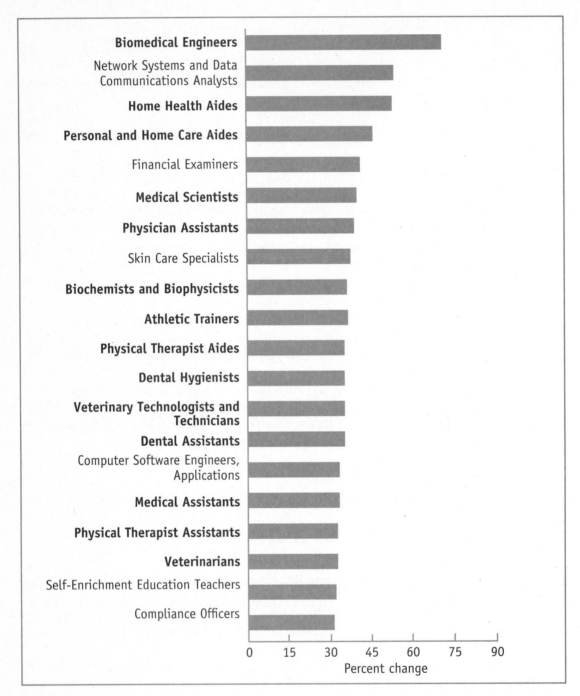

Figure 1.1: The fastest-growing occupations reflect growth in health-care services, 2008–2018. Health-care careers are shown in bold. The numbers at the bottom represent the percentage increase anticipated.

Geographic Location

Health services employers are unevenly distributed in this country. As a result, there are job opportunities in some areas and scarcities in others. Thus, there is a shortage of health-care professionals in both rural and inner-city areas—even though rural areas are underpopulated and inner-city areas are overpopulated.

Population shifts due to changes in economic opportunities also greatly affect the number of job opportunities. For example, when people began flocking to the West Coast and Sun Belt states, thousands of new job openings were created for health-care workers.

Expanding Careers

The time of diagnosing and treating practitioners is both valuable and costly. Thus, there has been a drive to reassign certain routine tasks to suitably trained and qualified allied health workers. As a result, workers such as physician assistants and dental hygienists are in high demand. With the restructuring of the medical profession under managed care, the use of physician assistants in a wide variety of settings is increasing significantly.

Technological Advances

Modern technology has created many career opportunities for health-care personnel. Early in the 20th century, for example, the use of X rays for diagnostic purposes virtually created the field of radiology and the need for qualified technologists and technicians. In the later part of the 20th century, the development of CAT scans, MRIs, and ultrasound equipment resulted in even more new career opportunities. Today's advances in genetic screening could lead to new careers down the road.

Facility and Service Expansion

Health care is undergoing a major restructuring because of the expansion of HMOs. HMOs put an increased emphasis on primary care and preventive medicine. As a consequence, the family practice specialty has grown, creating the need for support personnel. On the other hand, cost-cutting efforts on the part of the federal government and HMOs will hold down job opportunities in other fields. However, increased pressure for services by the growing population of elderly has generated a strong demand for home-care services in various categories. The lower cost of providing health care at home rather than at inpatient facilities has driven the need for personnel qualified to provide such services. The overall outlook for future funding in this field, however, is uncertain.

Women and Minorities

There has been a significant increase in the number of women and minorities in the health services field in recent years. Hospitals, medical schools, and other institutions have made concerted efforts to increase participation by these groups as health professionals, with some significant, positive results. For example, around 50 percent of students entering freshman medical school classes today are women, and more than 15 percent are minorities.

Other health professions in which these groups traditionally have been underrepresented—such as dentistry, optometry, podiatry, veterinary medicine, and health services administration—have also seen increases. These sustained advances should serve as encouragement to women and minority students who are contemplating careers in the health professions.

Trends in Health Care

When considering a career in health care, it is prudent to look ahead to the future and note the overall direction that this field is taking. Health care has seen many changes during the past several decades, and one can anticipate many more in the years to come.

Perhaps the most significant concern in the area of health care is *cost containment*. This refers to the attempt to control the rising cost of health care while maintaining and enhancing its services. The increase of health-care costs stems from technological advances and costly clinical procedures (e.g., organ transplants) that are increasingly commonplace. The technological and clinical advances, however, have served to extend life, especially in an aging population. In addition, the increase in the elderly population, with the greater need for medications to treat chronic illnesses, has raised health-care expenditures even further. Thus cost containment remains the most pressing health-care issue for our society. Revision of Social Security, Medicare, and Medicaid programs are related social challenges facing this country in the twenty-first century. With approximately 50 million Americans without health insurance, it is clear that the burden of paying for health care is everyone's to bear.

In addition to the above, there are a number of other factors that are strongly influencing the direction of the provision of health care, including

- **Greater demand for services.** The baby-boomers are nearing retirement. They will largely be eligible for Medicare, potentially driving up the cost for medical services across the board. On the plus side, the increased demand for services is, in large part, responsible for the enormous job growth in many sectors of the health-care industry.

- **Increased longevity.** Over the past several decades, and for a variety of reasons, longevity of senior citizens has markedly increased, meaning a greater need for services over a longer period of time.

- **Expansion of eligibility.** Government legislation has already broadly expanded Medicaid to include an additional 36 million people. The push for further health-care reform could lead to even more legislation that expands eligibility as well.

- **Improved medical services.** In recent years, remarkable and dramatic events in health-care research and technology have occurred. For example introducing implants into a variety of limb joints, replacement of heart valves, organ transplants and insertion of stents in blocked blood vessels. Such life-saving procedures occur with even greater frequency and often with high costs for both the patient and the health-care provider.

Many of the trends mentioned are a double-edged sword, often bringing with them better job opportunities for those in the profession, but at an increased financial cost. The future of health care in America will depend a great deal on our ability to balance innovation and patient needs with increasing government regulations and rising costs.

Choosing the Best Health-Care Career for You

Your choice of career is one of the most important decisions you will make. Why is it such a big deal? Well, assuming that your professional life lasts from age 25 to age 65 (and these days, retirement at 65 seems optimistic), you'll spend 40 years on the job. If you average 40 hours a week at work, you'll devote around 80,000 hours of your life to your career. Add to that the time and money you spend getting the right education and training, and you've got a large chunk of your life—and your resources—invested in your career choice.

Additionally, your career choice determines, to a large degree, the number of hours you'll work, the kinds of people you'll meet, and the lifestyle you'll be able to maintain. All of this points to why it's so important to spend some time and effort choosing a career that suits your personal needs, abilities, and goals, rather than simply "falling into" a job or letting someone else decide for you. This chapter helps you make your decision for yourself.

Choosing a health-care career that's right for you involves a four-step process:

1. You must prove *to your own satisfaction* (not just to your parents, your friends, or your teachers) that you *want* to focus your attention on possible employment in the health professions.
2. You must determine which of six health occupational groups, discussed later, is most interesting to you.
3. You must decide which of the career options in that occupational group you want to investigate further.
4. You should explore those specific career options in more detail to determine which ones are most worth pursuing.

The following sections discuss each of these steps in more detail.

Step 1: Choosing to Pursue a Career in Health Care

Your first step is deciding whether you are well-suited to a career in health care. To do this, it's helpful to match the characteristics of your "ideal job" to those commonly found in health-care careers. In the following list, mark with an X each of the characteristics that *must* be a component of your future career.

Characteristics of Your Ideal Career

_____**Using instruments.** You enjoy using your manual dexterity or skills and working with your hands.

_____**Teaching others.** You like instructing or showing people how to do or understand things.

_____**Being precise.** You expect to meet high standards of accuracy in your work.

_____**Complex tasks.** You enjoy jobs with many specific details and steps.

__✗__**Frequent public contact.** You enjoy working with people—for example, clients seeking services.

_____**Evident results.** You want to see your progress or tangible results of your work.

_____**Team effort.** You like working as part of a group.

__✗__**Ample employment.** You want to work in a field with lots of job opportunities.

_____**Problem-solving capacity.** You enjoy pinpointing problems and determining how to solve them.

_____**Routine.** You want a job with repetitive activities that does not present many challenges.

_____**Working outdoors.** You would like to work primarily outside.

_____**Fixed location.** You want to stay in one site for most of the workday.

_____**Creativity.** You like taking the initiative; devising original or novel concepts, products, or programs; and acting on them.

_____**Independence.** You want the flexibility to work on your own without a high degree of supervision.

_____**Competition.** You want a high-achievement position in which your success is based on reaching tough goals.

Reviewing a wide variety of jobs shows that the first nine characteristics are associated with many health-care positions. If you checked five or more of these characteristics, we encourage you to explore health-care careers in greater depth by proceeding to Steps 2 and 3.

Naturally, this list is only a simplified self-assessment profile, designed primarily to encourage further career investigation. Your initial assessment will be either reinforced or weakened as you explore. As you focus on choosing an occupation cluster and then on specific health-care careers, your interests may or may not be validated.

	Problem-solving ability	Uses instruments	Instructs others	Repetitious work	Hazardous	Outdoors	Physical stamina	Generally confined	Precision	Works with detail	Frequent public contact	Part-time	Can see results	Creativity	Influences others	Competition on the job	Is part of a team	Jobs widely scattered	Initiative
Diagnosing and Treating Practitioners																			
Chiropractors	•	•	•				•		•	•	•	•	•		•		•	•	•
Optometrists	•	•	•				•		•	•	•	•	•		•		•	•	•
Podiatrists	•	•	•				•		•	•	•		•		•		•	•	•
Veterinarians	•	•	•		•		•		•	•	•		•		•		•	•	•
Associated Health Careers																			
Dental hygienists		•	•	•			•			•	•	•					•	•	
Licensed practical nurses		•	•		•		•		•	•	•	•	•		•		•	•	
Pharmacists	•		•					•	•	•	•						•	•	•
Registered nurses	•	•	•		•		•		•	•	•	•	•		•		•	•	•
Technologist, Technician, Assistant, and Aide Careers																			
Dental assistants		•	•	•						•	•	•					•	•	
Dental laboratory technicians	•	•		•				•	•				•				•	•	
EEG technologists and technicians		•	•	•						•	•	•					•	•	
Electrocardiograph technicians		•	•	•						•	•	•	•				•	•	
Emergency medical technicians	•	•	•		•	•	•			•	•	•					•	•	
Medical laboratory workers		•		•	•				•	•	•						•	•	
Nursing aides, orderlies, and attendants		•	•	•	•		•			•	•	•					•	•	
Operating room technicians		•	•		•					•	•	•					•	•	
Optometric assistants		•	•							•	•	•					•	•	
Radiological (X-ray) technologists		•	•		•					•	•	•	•					•	
Respiratory therapy workers		•	•							•	•	•					•	•	
Rehabilitation Careers																			
Occupational therapists	•	•	•							•	•			•	•		•	•	•
Occupational therapy assistants		•	•					•		•	•	•	•				•	•	
Physical therapist assistants and aides		•	•								•		•				•	•	
Physical therapists	•	•	•				•			•	•			•	•		•	•	•
Speech pathologists and audiologists	•	•	•						•	•	•			•	•		•	•	•
Other Health Careers																			
Health services administrators	•										•					•	•	•	•
Medical records administrators	•								•	•							•	•	•
Medical records technicians and clerks				•					•	•	•						•	•	

Figure 2.1: Desirable personal characteristics for various health careers.

> **Tip:** For a more in-depth inventory of your career interests and values, see one or more of the following assessments (available at www.jist.com): *Career Exploration Inventory*, *O*NET Career Values Inventory*, and *O*NET Career Interests Inventory*.

Next, compare your own assessment of desirable job characteristics to those that are associated with health-care positions in general (see Figure 2.1).

Now that you have confirmed your interests, you are ready to choose a health occupation group to explore. The group you select will, in turn, point you toward a number of specific professions to consider.

Step 2: Choosing a Health Occupation Group

Step 2 in your career assessment process involves deciding which of six health occupation clusters best fits your interests. Each of these groups consists of a number of specific professions that have a variety of similar characteristics.

Part 4 of this book outlines 101 different allied health-care careers. These careers are grouped into six different occupational clusters:

- Diagnosing and treating practitioners (7 careers)
- Associated health careers related to medicine and dentistry (12 careers)
- Adjunctive health careers: technologists, technicians, and assistants (36 careers)
- Rehabilitation careers: therapists and therapy assistants (19 careers)
- Health-care administrative careers (7 careers)
- Affiliated health careers: medical scientists, educators, and information workers (20 careers)

The first four groups are organized primarily by education and training requirements, the nature of job responsibilities, and the type of work. The first of these characteristics—career preparation time—is especially important, because it affects the total cost of your education—both in terms of time and money. Because this is such a decisive issue, let's look at career preparation time in more detail.

High School Preparation

A key part of preparing for a successful career is completing high school. Your work here provides the foundation on which you'll build your advanced education and training. While you are in high school, you should work at improving your oral and written communication skills and get a solid grounding in the sciences (including mathematics). Your high school diploma is an essential prerequisite for advanced training programs, technical institutes, apprenticeships, and college. A good high school record is one of the keys that unlocks the door to a bright career in health care.

Having decided to attend college and possibly become a health-care professional, you should select your high school program to include courses that at least meet the minimum requirements for admission to a liberal arts college. The program should include the following:

- English: 4 years
- Laboratory science: 2 years
- Foreign languages: 2 years
- Mathematics: 3 years
- Social studies: 2 years

These are just the bare bones for college-readiness. You should go beyond these requirements when possible by taking electives to obtain a well-rounded academic background.

Post–High School Preparation

Once you have your high school diploma securely in hand, it's time to consider your next move: You must decide how much time you want to invest in your education and training. Careers in the allied health professions vary widely in their educational requirements. Some require as little as nine months of post–high school training; others require as much as nine years of schooling. These varying educational requirements are shown in Figure 2.2, which lists all the health-care careers discussed in this book and the minimum time needed to train for each. Keep in mind that within some categories there are multiple jobs with varying educational requirements. For example, some mental health workers only require a certification while others require a Master's degree.

The length of time you invest in your education determines the cost of your education: The more education a job requires, the greater the cost. (Keep in mind, however, that, in general, the more education you have, the more you are likely to earn.)

Depending on the career you choose, you can prepare for work in one of the following ways:

- Secure on-the-job training.
- Join an apprenticeship program and secure classroom and/or on-the-job training.
- Enroll in a vocational-technical school.
- Complete a training program at a hospital, medical center, or blood bank.
- Attend an accredited college and, if necessary, graduate school.

Take a moment to look over your preferences from Figure 2.1 and your desired education level from Figure 2.2 and choose one or two occupational groups that seem to match your ideal career characteristics and future educational goals (and resources). Keep in mind—you aren't married to this choice; it simply gives you a starting point for considering more specific health-care careers.

Confirming Your Group Choice

Choosing a suitable occupational group is a key element in determining the specific health-care career you want. Now that you've decided on an occupational group, it's a good idea to confirm your choice. To do this, you use an approach called *categorization*. This involves seeing in which of four groupings your personal attributes best fit.

People's occupational interests vary widely—all the way from actor to zoologist. Generally, career interests can be subdivided into four categories. Associated with each of these categories are four sets of attributes related to personal interests, behavior patterns, personality, and preferred social environment. The characteristics of these four categories are described on pages 21 and 22.

	On-the-job training	1 year of college	Associate degree (2 years)	3 years of college	Bachelor's degree (4 years)	Master's degree (2 years)	Doctorate (4 years)
PRACTITIONERS CAREERS							
Audiologists							
Chiropractors							
Dentists							
Optometrists							
Physicians							
Podiatrists							
Veterinarians							
ASSOCIATED HEALTH-CARE CAREERS							
Dental Hygienists							
Dietitians							
Genetic Counselors							
Licensed Practical Nurses							
Nurse Anesthetists							
Nurse-Midwives							
Nurse Practitioners							
Nutritionists							
Pharmacists							
Physician Assistants							
Registered Nurses							
Surgeon Assistants							
ADJUNCTIVE HEALTH-CARE CAREERS							
Anesthesiologist Assistants							
Blood Bank Technologists and Specialists							
Cardiovascular Technology Personnel							
Certified Nurse Assistants							
Clinical Laboratory Technicians							
Clinical Laboratory Technologists							
Cytotechnologists							
Dental Assistants							
Dental Laboratory Technicians							
Diagnostic Medical Sonographers							
Dietetic Technicians							
Electroneurodiagnostic Technologists							
Emergency Medical Technicians							
Food Technologists							

Figure 2.2: Preparation time for health-care careers.

	On-the-job training	1 year of college	Associate degree (2 years)	3 years of college	Bachelor's degree (4 years)	Master's degree (2 years)	Doctorate (4 years)
Histology Technicians	■	■	■	■	■		
Medical Assistants	■	■	■				
Mental Health Assistants	■	■	■				
Nuclear Medicine Technologists	■	■	■				
Nurse's Aides	■						
Ophthalmic Assistants	■	■					
Ophthalmic Laboratory Technicians	■	■					
Ophthalmic Technicians	■	■	■				
Ophthalmic Technologists	■	■	■				
Opticians	■	■	■				
Optometric Assistants	■						
Optometric Technicians	■	■					
Orthoptists	■	■	■	■	■	■	
Orthotists and Prosthetists	■	■	■	■	■		
Perfusionists	■	■	■				
Pharmacy Technicians	■	■					
Phlebotomists	■						
Pulmonary Function Technologists	■	■	■				
Radiation Therapy Technologists	■	■	■				
Radiological Technologists	■	■	■				
Surgical Technologists	■	■	■				
Veterinary Assistants	■						
REHABILITATION CAREERS							
Art Therapists	■	■	■	■	■		
Dance/Movement Therapists	■	■	■	■	■	■	
Home Health Aides	■						
Horticultural Therapists	■	■	■	■	■	■	
Massage Therapists	■	■	■	■	■		
Music Therapists	■	■	■	■	■		
Occupational Therapists	■	■	■	■	■	■	
Occupational Therapy Assistants	■	■	■	■			
Patient Representatives	■						
Physical Therapists	■	■	■	■	■	■	
Physical Therapy Assistants	■	■	■				
Psychiatric Aides	■	■					
Recreational Therapists	■	■	■	■	■		

(continued)

(continued)

	On-the-job training	1 year of college	Associate degree (2 years)	3 years of college	Bachelor's degree (4 years)	Master's degree (2 years)	Doctorate (4 years)
Rehabilitation Counselors	▓	▓	▓	▓	▓	▓	
Respiratory Therapists	▓	▓	▓				
Respiratory Therapy Aides	▓	▓	▓				
Respiratory Therapy Technicians	▓	▓					
Social Service Aides	▓						
Speech-Language Pathologists	▓	▓	▓	▓	▓	▓	
Substance Abuse Counselors	▓	▓	▓				
ADMINISTRATIVE HEALTH-CARE CAREERS							
Admitting Officers	▓						
Coordinators of Health Wellness	▓	▓	▓	▓	▓		
Directors of Hospital Public Relations	▓	▓	▓	▓	▓		
Directors of Nursing Home Activities	▓	▓	▓	▓	▓		
Directors of Quality Assurance	▓	▓	▓	▓	▓		
Directors of Volunteer Services	▓	▓	▓	▓			
Geriatric Care Managers	▓	▓	▓	▓	▓		
AFFILIATED HEALTH-CARE CAREERS							
Biomedical Engineers	▓	▓	▓	▓	▓		
Biomedical Equipment Technicians	▓	▓	▓				
Biomedical Photographers	▓						
Biomedical Writers	▓	▓	▓	▓	▓		
Certified Athletic Trainers	▓	▓	▓	▓	▓		
Child Life Specialists	▓	▓	▓	▓	▓		
Dietary Managers	▓	▓	▓	▓	▓		
Environmental Health Scientist	▓	▓	▓	▓	▓		
Geriatric Social Workers	▓	▓	▓	▓	▓		
Health Educators	▓	▓	▓	▓	▓		
Health Information Technicians	▓	▓	▓	▓	▓		
Health Sciences Librarians	▓	▓	▓	▓	▓	▓	
Health Services Administrators	▓	▓	▓	▓	▓		
Health Sociologists	▓	▓	▓	▓	▓		
Instructors for the Blind	▓						
Medical and Psychiatric Social Workers	▓	▓					
Medical Illustrators	▓	▓					
Medical Secretaries	▓	▓					
Medical Scientists	▓	▓	▓	▓	▓	▓	▓
Mental Health Workers	▓						

Category A: Practitioners and Administrators

Interests	Behavior	Personality	Environment
Organizing	Objective	Authoritative	Hierarchical
Creating	Forceful	Resourceful	Self-structured
Solving practical problems	Competitive	Logical	Pressured
Seeing completed product	Practical	Practical	Achievement-oriented
Working with people	Cooperative	Personable	Competitive

Sample careers in this category:

Chiropractor	Physician assistant
Dentist	Anesthesiologist assistant
Surgeon assistant	Pharmacist
Nurse-midwife	Emergency medical technician
Optometrist	Nurse practitioner
Physician	Health-care administrator
Podiatrist	Engineer

Category B: Therapists and Counselors

Interests	Behavior	Personality	Environment
Influencing	Personable	Spontaneous	Innovative
Motivating	Independent	Enthusiastic	Team-oriented
Persuading	Determined	Outgoing	Informal
Consensus building	Outspoken	Talkative	Competitive
Delegating authority	Welcomes challenge	Risk-assuming	Tolerant

Sample careers in this category:

Dietitian	Genetic counselor
Therapist	Medical and psychiatric social worker

Category C: Inventors, Teachers, and Writers

Interests	Behavior	Personality	Environment
Abstract thinking	Reflective	Reflective	Informal
Planning	Conscientious	Imaginative	Self-motivated
Innovating	Creative	Thoughtful	Low-key
Conceptualizing	Perceptive	Sensitive	Long-term goal-oriented
Implementing ideas	Cautious	Emotional	Challenging

Sample careers in this category:

Biomedical writer	Certified athletic trainer
Health educator	Instructor for the blind
Nurse	Medical photographer
Environmental health scientist	

Category D: Engineers, Researchers, and Office Managers

Interests	Behavior	Personality	Environment
Ordering	Orderly	Methodical	Controlled
Doing detailed work	Cooperative	Organized	Established
Working with systems	Consistent	Solitary	Orderly
Employing numbers	Careful	Systematic	Measurable
Keeping tight control	Sociable	Self-reliant	Predictable

Sample careers in this category:

Dietary manager   Medical librarian

Biomedical engineer   Environmental health scientist

Step 3: Identifying Your Specific Career

Step 3 in the career assessment process consists of identifying the specific careers that merit detailed exploration within the occupational cluster you've chosen. The number of careers encompassed by a group varies.

In the following worksheet, check all the careers that appeal to you from the occupational groups you chose in Step 2. Then read the detailed descriptions of those careers in Part 4 of this book and select those that are of special interest to you. Finally, list these in the worksheet on page 25. The listing should be in order of your interest. If none of the careers checked off are especially appealing to you, read up on some others in the same category and then identify those of special interest to you. With several specific career options available, you should now explore your first and second choices more thoroughly to affirm the suitability of your selections. If you lose interest in your initial choices, proceed to the other careers that are farther down on your interest list.

The Six Groups of Career Options

Group 1: Practitioner Careers

____ Audiologist

____ Chiropractor

____ Dentist

____ Optometrist

____ Physician

____ Podiatrist

____ Veterinarian

Group 2: Associated Health Careers

____ Dental hygienist

____ Dietitian

____ Genetic counselor

____ Licensed practical nurse

____ Nurse anesthetist

____ Nurse–midwife

____ Nurse practitioner

____ Nutritionist

____ Pharmacist

____ Physician assistant

____ Registered nurse

____ Surgeon assistant

Group 3: Adjunctive Health Careers: Technologists and Technicians

___ Anesthesiologist assistant

___ Blood bank technologist and specialist

___ Cardiovascular technology personnel

___ Certified nurse assistant

___ Clinical laboratory technician

___ Clinical laboratory technologist

___ Cytotechnologist

___ Dental assistant

___ Dental laboratory technician

___ Diagnostic medical sonographer

___ Dietetic technician

___ Electroneurodiagnostic technologist

___ Emergency medical technician

___ Food technologist

___ Histology technician

___ Medical assistant

___ Mental health assistant

___ Nuclear medicine technologist

___ Nurse's aide

___ Ophthalmic assistant

___ Ophthalmic laboratory technician

___ Ophthalmic technician

___ Ophthalmic technologist

___ Optician

___ Optometric assistant

___ Optometric technician

___ Orthoptist

___ Orthotist and prosthetist

___ Perfusionist

___ Pharmacy technician

___ Phlebotomist

___ Pulmonary function technologist

___ Radiation therapy technologist

___ Radiological technologist

___ Surgical technologist

___ Veterinary assistant

Group 4: Rehabilitation Careers: Therapists and Therapist Assistants

___ Art therapist

___ Dance/movement therapist

___ Home health aide

___ Horticultural therapist

___ Massage therapist

___ Music therapist

___ Occupational therapist

___ Occupational therapy assistant

___ Patient representative

___ Physical therapist

___ Physical therapy assistant

___ Psychiatric aide

___ Recreational therapist

___ Rehabilitation counselor

___ Respiratory therapist

___ Respiratory therapy aide

___ Respiratory therapy technician

___ Social service aide

___ Speech-language pathologist

___ Substance abuse counselor

Group 5: Administrative Health Careers

___ Admitting officer

___ Coordinator of health wellness

___ Director of hospital public relations

___ Director of nursing home activities

___ Director of quality assurance

___ Director of volunteer services

___ Geriatric care manager

(continued)

(continued)

Group 6: Affiliated Health Careers

___ Biomedical engineer

___ Biomedical equipment technician

___ Biomedical photographer

___ Biomedical writer

___ Certified athletic trainer

___ Child life specialist

___ Dietary manager

___ Environmental health scientist

___ Geriatric social worker

___ Health educator

___ Health information technician

___ Health sciences librarian

___ Health services administrator

___ Health sociologist

___ Instructor for the blind

___ Medical and psychiatric social worker

___ Medical illustrator

___ Medical scientist

___ Medical secretary

___ Mental health worker

Exploring Careers of Interest

There are at least four ways to explore a career: reading in depth, visiting facilities, gaining volunteer experience, and securing work experience. These options are not mutually exclusive; rather, they reinforce each other. The following sections discuss each of these approaches.

In-Depth Reading

Once you've read the preliminary overview of your prospective career in Part 4 of this book, write to the professional organizations listed at the end of the description or to one of the training programs in your area, or check out their Web sites for more information. In addition, your local library has a wide selection of career books, where you can find more detailed information. Appendix C, "Job Search Resources," also suggests reference sources.

Visiting Facilities

Getting a close-up look at a health-care institution or professional office can be very helpful in making your decision. Most facilities give tours to prospective students. Obviously, you should call for an appointment before visiting. Contact the administrative center, public relations department, or manager to arrange such a visit. The value of your visit will be enhanced if you come prepared with a list of questions you would like answered and knowing specifically what you want to see. If, at a later date, you focus your career plans on one specific choice, you may want to make a return visit to clarify or get more details on the information you received or even ask for an informational interview.

If your visit reinforces your career choice, your next step is to visit a school that trains students for that profession. Training facilities welcome prospective students, and their admissions officers usually will be happy to arrange for a site visit. To get the most from such a visit, plan to speak with both teachers and students. You should ask about admissions requirements, tuition, quality of instruction, adequacy of the facilities and equipment, and the school's job placement policy. Also ask about job prospects in your community.

Career Interest List

Career Selection	Training	Education Level	Income	Prospects
1.				
2.				
3.				
4.				
5.				

Volunteer Experience

You can benefit greatly—both personally and professionally—by volunteering at a facility that employs people in the career you are contemplating. For example, if the career involves working in a hospital, volunteering at one can give you great experience, even if you are not assigned to the department or duty in which you are interested. While you are there, you may find an opportunity to get at least some exposure in your specific area of interest. When asking for a position with a facility's volunteer office, inform them of your special interests, but be prepared to accept something other than your first choice.

Work Experience

In some special situations, you may be able to secure part-time or summer work in the field of your choice. Obviously, if you have only limited knowledge and experience, getting a paid job can be quite difficult. To a large extent, this depends on the general employment situation in the field and in your area. In addition, the type of jobs for which you can apply obviously will be restricted if you don't yet have training. Yet, being employed in almost *any* capacity in a health-care facility can help you get a realistic view of your eventual career activities.

Using several of these exploratory approaches—and, when necessary, applying them to more than one career option—you should be able to arrive at a sound decision about one or more health-care careers.

Step 4: Confirming Your Career Choice

The road to becoming an allied health professional is challenging. It requires a substantial expenditure of time, effort, and money. You should stop to assess the extent of your motivation, abilities, and determination to succeed. Take a moment to consider the following questions:

- Do you find information on how the body functions especially interesting?
- Is gaining knowledge meaningful to you beyond rewards of good grades?
- Is your desire for knowledge such that you seek information beyond what is taught?
- Are you excited to read about the many current advances in health care?
- Do you feel a sense of satisfaction and gratification from helping others and are you willing to put their needs before your own?
- Are you determined to get the education and training required for a career in health care?
- Do you respond well to challenges?

If you answered yes to most of these questions then you have some supporting evidence favoring your desire to become a health-care professional. However, to find personal satisfaction as a health-care professional, you must objectively determine your own unique abilities, interests, and temperament. Once you have done this and focused on an appropriate career goal, your next step is to get the right education or training for your field. We'll cover that in Chapter 3, "Planning Your Education."

Having tentatively identified one or two possible health careers, you must now evaluate how reasonable your choices are. You can do this by matching your personal attributes with those essential for the careers in question. To gain insight into your personal attributes, you must engage in some serious self-evaluation. This is helpful in confirming your career choices; it also encourages you to proceed further in pursuing your goal.

Self-evaluation can also be useful for enhancing your future job employment prospects (as discussed in Chapter 7, "Preparing for Your Job Search"). Knowing and understanding your own blend of interests, capabilities, and potential allows you to better market yourself to prospective employers. This knowledge also can help you compensate for any deficiencies you may have so that you can put your best foot forward in interviews. Being aware of your ultimate goal allows you to focus precisely on the right education and training for your career. If you do your homework, ultimately you will find the right match between your personality and career.

The Self-Evaluation Process

The key to meaningful self-evaluation is being fully honest with yourself. The actual procedure is straightforward; you simply consider several aspects of your personality and experience as realistically and honestly as possible. Using the following worksheet, outline your responses in all the categories defined.

Self-Evaluation Protocol

1. **Strengths.** Describe your personal attributes that an employer would find attractive, such as determination, organization, ambition, intelligence, effective leadership, or dependability.

   _____

   _____

   _____

   _____

2. **Weaknesses.** Describe your personal attributes that an employer might find unattractive, such as overly aggressive, abrasive, impatient, lazy, confrontational, or sloppy.

   _____

   _____

   _____

   _____

3. **Skills.** List all the things you can do well, even if you don't consider them marketable, such as computer literacy, foreign language skills, good handwriting, speed reading, or retentive memory.

   _____

   _____

   _____

   _____

(continued)

(continued)

4. **Hobbies.** Identify the things you enjoy and at which you excel, such as building model ships, playing a musical instrument, reading, or traveling.

_____

_____

_____

_____

5. **Education courses.** List courses you have taken that are either marketable or enjoyable.

_____

_____

_____

_____

6. **Experience.** List any work positions you have held on a full- or part-time basis.

_____

_____

_____

_____

7. **Personal preferences.** Provide information in areas not covered in the preceding items. This may include your choice for working indoors or outside, in large or small cities, at a fast- or slow-paced activity, for small or large companies, or being lightly or heavily supervised.

_____

_____

_____

_____

8. **Personal dislikes.** Provide information on types of places, activities, and people you would find unacceptable.

_____

_____

_____

_____

9. **Education/training commitment.** Decide how much time you are willing to invest in education and training activities. Check the time commitment you are prepared to make.

    ___ 2 years   ___ 4 years

    ___ 6 years   ___ More than 6 years

Your next step in self-evaluation is completing the following worksheet, which identifies 25 characteristics that may be relevant to you. Simply place a check in the column that represents how much you value that characteristic in your work. Completing this form will help you discover the match (or maybe the mismatch) between your career choice and your personal characteristics. You also might want to review this worksheet with your parents, spouse, or a friend to get an objective opinion of your responses and additional insight.

Personal Self-Assessment				
Attribute	**High**	**Average**	**Low**	**Unknown**
Responsible				
Efficient				
Resourceful				
Flexible				
Cooperative				
Objective				
Neat				
Self-confident				
Sincere				
Compassionate				
Outgoing				
Persevering				
Realistic				
Mature				
Ethical				
Self-centered				
Hardworking				
Quick thinking				
Competitive				
Emotional				
Self-reliant				
Thorough				
Calm under stress				
Communicate well				
Analytical				

Matching Your Career Choices and Personal Attributes

You have already identified the specific careers that especially interest you, and (presumably) you followed this up by investigating them further. The result should be that you have narrowed down your choice to one or two careers. In the following worksheet, you match the attributes for the career(s) you set your sights on with your own personal attributes.

Profession characteristics. In Part 4 of this book, you'll find profession characteristics for each of the 100 fields listed. These are located in the "Prerequisites" section of each career description. List the five most important ones in column 1 (and 2, if you've chosen more than one career) of the following worksheet.

Your personal attributes. These are the qualities you checked in the Personal Self-Assessment worksheet. Now list the five that are most important to you in column 3 of the following worksheet. Then check these attributes against the features listed for the specific careers you've chosen.

Defining Your Career Choices

Profession's Characteristics		Personal Characteristics
Career 1	Career 2	You
_____	_____	_____
_____	_____	_____
_____	_____	_____
_____	_____	_____

By matching columns 1 and 2 with column 3, you can achieve three goals:

1. Determine whether you are on the right track in your career choice. You can see whether you have selected career choices from the most appropriate grouping of the five.
2. Determine which of the two careers you just outlined is best suited for you, as reflected by how it matches your personal attributes.
3. Determine how close your favored career choice is to your attributes.

Once you have attained a close match between your personal attributes and a prospective career, you should gather as much information about it as possible using the strategies for career research discussed earlier in the chapter. Be sure to write to the professional organization associated with the career—addresses are listed at the end of each career description. Also research the number of prospective job openings in your area. You can do this by visiting a medical library at a hospital or medical school and scanning the want-ad section of journals published by professional organizations. Be sure to look through several recent issues.

For those still uncertain about a direction for their career, both school and private career counselors use formal interest assessments whose more objective results can serve to reinforce one's current subjective views or serve to dissuade one way from them. In addition, such tests may bring to light hidden areas of interest that can serve to expand a person's career horizon. The results of such tests, however, should not be taken as a definitive judgment, independent of your own personal viewpoint.

Facing the Future

The most important step to become a health-care professional is to decide that at all times you will be realistic and honest with yourself. Before you reach the stage of applying to a college or training program you should once again reevaluate your abilities and your conviction. You should determine if you possess the intelligence, scientific aptitude, personality, and inner strength-that are essential for success as a health-care provider.

Planning Your Education

After you have decided which health-care career is right for you, your next decision is vitally important. You must choose the most appropriate educational institution—one that provides the training you need for your professional responsibilities.

Sources of Health-Care Education

Where you get your professional training has a strong impact on your future success. Training programs for health-care careers are offered at a variety of trade schools, private vocational schools, technical institutes, colleges (both two- and four-year), universities, professional schools, and hospitals, as well as in the armed forces. In most cases, your career choice determines the kind of institution you choose.

Very few health-care jobs require *only* on-the-job training or an apprenticeship. Almost all positions require college-level work. Some of these programs are offered by vocational-technical schools and community and junior colleges; others are offered only at universities and professional schools.

> **TIP:** Upon entering high school, it is not essential to be committed to a specific career goal. Having a sense of direction toward a possible health-care career is enough. The next few years of study will often reinforce or more clearly define one's aspirations.

Vocational-Technical Schools

Vocational-technical schools offer a variety of health-care programs, including dental assistant and medical technology. If you opt for a vo-tech school, you receive classroom instruction and real-world training. When you complete such a program, you are awarded a certificate of achievement. At this point you are qualified to begin work, provided that no license is required for your chosen career. Your first employer may ask that you receive some on-the-job training when you begin.

Before enrolling in a vocational-technical school, you should make sure it is accredited. Two organizations offer accreditation: the National Association of Trade and Technical Schools (NATTS) and the Association of Independent Colleges and Schools (AICS). You might also get the names of some alumni from different schools. Call these people and ask them about the schools: How well were they were prepared for their jobs? How interested were prospective employers in hiring them? The more you know about each program, the easier it will be to decide on one.

Hospital Programs

Many hospitals, medical centers, and blood banks also offer health-care programs in a variety of technologist and technician fields. They provide both classroom and on-the-job training and award a certificate upon completion. Often, it is easier to get a job with a certain facility if you are a graduate of its educational program.

Community Colleges

Many community colleges offer health-care programs. Most of these programs can be completed in two years, at the end of which you receive an associate degree. Most programs have a limited number of required general courses. The bulk of your course work is specialized in the area for which you are training.

An associate degree can serve as an intermediate step toward a bachelor's degree. So, for example, if you have completed two years of training as a licensed practical nurse, your training can be credited toward a four-year degree in a registered nurse program.

Four-Year Colleges and Universities

The more advanced and complex health careers (for example, dietitian and physician assistant) require a bachelor's degree. Many people seeking such jobs enroll directly in a four-year program at a college or university. These schools require you to complete a variety of basic courses—including English composition, history, math, and others—as well as advanced courses in your major field of study. The courses in your major are designed to prepare you for your future work activities.

Graduate Schools

Quite a few associated health-care careers, such as nursing, nutrition, and rehabilitation careers require master's degrees (an additional two years of study) and some even a doctorate (an additional four years). Securing a graduate degree requires completing a prescribed number of courses as well as research work. A graduate degree often leads to increases in salary and enhances one's potential for career advancement.

Professional Schools

A number of health-care careers, such as medicine, dentistry, podiatry, and optometry, require education and training beyond a bachelor's degree. To enter these professions, you must earn a doctorate degree. These degrees are awarded to students who complete three to four years of highly specialized study and clinical training. An internship usually follows, and licensure is required in order to practice.

Selecting an Educational Institution

Postsecondary education and training is a considerable investment in time and money. You should seek an institution (a) where you feel comfortable, (b) that you can afford, and (c) whose program can help you succeed in your future career.

One of the best ways to choose an institution is to speak to people who are already working in the field you have chosen. Ask them which schools they recommend. This will give you some initial leads.

Once you have gotten the names of several appropriate schools, write to their admissions offices and ask for catalogs, applications, and financial aid forms. The catalogs should provide you with much of the basic information you need to become familiar with the school. Finally, arrange to tour the school, sit in on classes, and get the feel of the campus.

It is essential to get as detailed an assessment as possible of any prospective institution you are seriously considering. To do this requires considerable effort. It is important to obtain data from reliable sources (such as upper-level students) and record your information for comparative purposes. As part of the evaluation process, the following need to be considered very seriously: accreditation, admission prerequisites, school characteristics, and impressions from a site visit. These factors are considered in more detail below.

Accreditation

Make sure the school you're considering is accredited. A statement to this effect usually appears near the front of a school's catalog or on its Web site. *Accreditation* means that an independent agency has sent a team of professionals to the school to evaluate its program. These teams focus on a variety of issues, including the quality of the faculty, the nature of the curriculum, and the adequacy of the classrooms, laboratories, and library. They then submit a report to the accreditation agency, which decides whether to accredit the school.

The issue of accreditation is vital. In order to take the qualifying exams for your certification or license, you must provide proof that you have graduated from an accredited school. If you are unable to do so, your career will be seriously impaired. Additionally, many facilities do not hire graduates of unaccredited institutions.

Prerequisites

The prerequisites for admission into a program should be listed in the school's catalog or on its Web site. Read through these to make sure that the classes you are taking in high school will help you meet the requirements.

Find out whether the school requires you to take a special admissions test, such as the Allied Health Professions Admissions Test. If it does, you'll need to find out which test you must take and arrange to take it. (For more information, see Appendix A, "Health-Care Education Admissions Tests.")

School Characteristics

The school catalog should give detailed information about tuition, fees, curriculum, and the course of study in your major. It probably also will list the names of the faculty and their educational background, and the overall requirements for graduation. You should become familiar with these so that you don't run into difficulties as you near graduation.

The catalog might also give specific information on the layout of the campus, student organizations, school services, and extracurricular options. If time is an issue, you should also see if the schools you are interested in have evening classes or distance learning options.

Site Visit

If possible, you should make a personal visit to the schools you are seriously considering. That way, you can see for yourself whether the facilities measure up to those described in the institutions' literature. While you're on campus, try to accomplish several objectives:

- Meet with several students and ask about the quality of teaching and the dedication of the instructors.
- Visit the library and note its computer resources. Also check to see that its books and journals are up-to-date.
- Chat with the dean and other faculty members to get an idea of how demanding the school's program really is. See whether the "official" view matches the impressions you get from the students.
- Meet with admissions personnel and guidance counselors. Ask for information on class makeup; faculty-student ratios for lectures, laboratories, and clinical classes; and the school's job placement record.
- Try to sit in on a lecture or see a laboratory class in operation.
- Find out if the school offers the appropriate courses needed as prerequisites for admission to the type of institution you plan to apply to.
- Inquire of the school has a helpful advisory program. A knowledgeable and dedicated advisor can provide useful academic guidance and assistance in many aspects of career planning.
- Seek to determine the success rate of the schools graduates.

At the end of your visit you should have a sense whether the school is right for you. Above all, you should come away with the firm impression that the school will adequately prepare you for your chosen professional career. If you don't get that impression, you should look for another school.

Don't hesitate to investigate two or more institutions and compare them. Obviously, each school has its strengths and weaknesses, and some of your considerations in choosing a school will be highly subjective. Thus, some students prefer a large campus that offers several disciplines, while others prefer the unique atmosphere of a small school.

> **TIP:** There is some value in attending an institution that offers multiple career tracks. Consider the case of a student who discovers halfway through a program that the field he has chosen is not appropriate for him. At a large institution, he might transfer to another discipline without losing all the credits he has earned.

Your education involves a huge investment of time, effort, and financial resources. So it is worthwhile to do all you can to make sure the program you choose is the right one for you. Copy the following worksheet to record information about each school you investigate. Then, when it's time to make a choice, you can simply compare the facts.

After you've completed your school evaluations and arrived at your decision, it's time to submit an application. The next section describes the admissions process.

School Information Worksheet

School: _____ Application deadline: _____

Accredited by: _____

Cost of tuition: _____

Cost of room and board (if you will live on campus): _____

Cost of books and supplies: _____

Transportation costs: _____

Financial aid available? yes no   Application deadline: _____

Length of program: _____

Prerequisites: _____

_____

Dropout rate: _____

Placement rate for graduates: _____

Job placement assistance? yes no

Other comments: _____

_____

_____

_____

Securing Admission

Competition for school programs varies by discipline and by school. Some are more competitive than others. So how many schools should you apply to? That depends on how strong a candidate you are and how many applications your chosen schools receive in an average year. Obviously, the more institutions you approach, the better your chances of getting accepted. But remember, you have to pay a fee with each application, which means the process can become costly, especially if you have to visit out-of-town schools.

If you did not receive an application for admission when you requested a school catalog, you should call and ask for one or download the materials from the school's Web site. Find out the deadline for submission. Remember, *this usually is a firm date;* missing it makes you ineligible until the next admission cycle—often a full year away. Read the application carefully and see what supplementary materials you must submit: These might include transcripts; letters of recommendation; and SAT, ACT, or other test scores. Copy the following worksheet and keep a log for each school to which you are applying so that you have a permanent record of all the information and dates associated with each.

Application Tracking Record Worksheet

Name of school: _____

Address: _____

City: _____ State: _____ ZIP: _____

Phone: _____ Application deadline: _____

Admissions office contact person: _____

Check when completed

___ Catalog received   ___ Application received

___ Financial aid information received

___ Facility visited   Date: _____

___ Application filed   Date: _____

___ Transcript sent   Date: _____

___ Aptitude test scores sent   Date: _____

___ Recommendations sent

Name: _____   Date: _____

Name: _____   Date: _____

Name: _____   Date: _____

___ Financial aid application filed   Date: _____

The Need for a Fair Evaluation

It is widely recognized by admissions officers that academic standards vary widely between high schools. Thus, the level of achievement shown on a student's transcript may not accurately reflect his or her actual ability. Students with modest grades from more-demanding schools may have the same potential as those with impressive grades from less-demanding ones. Moreover, a grade point average alone does not reflect special circumstances a student may face, such as the need to hold a part-time job while going to school, the absence of a positive study environment, or other personal problems. Add to this the trend towards higher grades being awarded, leading to the overall inflation of grade point averages.

In light of these factors, admissions officers handle the issue of fair evaluations in two ways. First, they usually are well aware of the academic standards of most of the schools from which their applicants come. Thus, they can more fully appreciate the real meaning of a student's academic performance and realistically estimate his or her potential for college. Second, they ask students to take an aptitude or admission test, discussed later in this chapter.

Understand that some issues that impact admission potential are outside of your control. These include the number of applicants, your high school's reputation, and the section of the country you come from.

Admission Considerations

There are several important areas relative to your application for admission to college that *are* in your control. These include your academic profile (including transcript), test scores, essay or personal statement, references, extracurricular activities, and an interview. Each of these areas will be discussed separately.

Academic Profile

Your academic profile provides a picture of your educational accomplishments and thus may indicate possible future academic potential. Schools seek students who are capable of successfully meeting the challenge that their curriculum presents, as well as other significant factors. It should be noted that each school follows its own procedure for screening applicants.

Most schools will ask for an official copy of your *transcript*. This document provides a list of courses taken in the past, or presently, and the grades assigned to those you have completed. The two elements, courses and grades, provide a picture of your effort and achievement. This information is a key ingredient in the college admission assessment process.

However, the nature of your transcript is not always taken at face value. While a predominance of As on your record is obviously very desirable, it is clear that what is especially impressive are those grades in challenging courses. Taking such courses and earning superior grades in them makes the most favorable impression on admissions personnel. Your choice of courses is therefore a significant factor in setting the "tone" of your transcript. Most schools offer honors work such as Advanced Placement (AP) classes. Where this is the case, admissions committees would expect you to enroll in several of these, preferably balanced between the sciences and non-sciences. Admissions personnel have a reasonably good perspective of a school's course offerings; thus they are likely aware of the difficulty of courses that appear on your transcript.

> **TIP:** In viewing your transcript, special attention is frequently given to your most recent level of performance, namely, your junior and senior year grades. Also, the consistent direction of the level of your work is a significant factor. Consistent superior work over the years, or a marked upward trend from a mediocre start, can prove helpful in advancing your case toward acceptance.

Admission/Aptitude Tests

Aptitude tests are widely used to provide a nationally standardized measure of academic ability and achievement. Such tests have no established passing or failing grades; scores are rated by means of a scale, with the percentile or ranking in each subtest given. This kind of scoring allows comparison of applicants independent of academic background or school record. The extent to which these test results are used in deciding whether an applicant is admitted to a program varies from one school to another. Following are the most common tests for admission to various postsecondary programs.

College Admission Tests

High school vary in size, character, and the quality of their education. The use of standardized tests "levels the playing field," because it provides for uniformity in judging performance. It therefore makes it possible for candidates who come from different high schools to be compared in an objective manner.

There is a consensus among admission officers that the combination of both transcript and standardized test scores is a better predictor of performance than the use of the transcript by itself. Because of this enhanced predictive value, most colleges mandate taking either the SAT or ACT as a prerequisite for applying for admission. Some require specific achievement tests.

- **Scholastic Aptitude Test (SAT)**: This standardized exam measures verbal and mathematical reasoning abilities that are relevant to college performance. The verbal section emphasizes critical reading, while the math section requires students to produce some of their own results (with the aid of a calculator). There is also a standard written English test that reflects your familiarity with its usage. A copy of your scores is sent to you and each college specified on your application. The scale for the verbal and math tests is 200–800 and the written component has a 20–80 scale. In addition, the College Board provides students with several percentile rankings. These indicate how your scores compare with all other high school students, other college-bound students, and high school students in your state. Each college has its own score requirements, and the average scores of their incoming students is usually available on the Internet.

- **American College Testing Program Assessment (ACT):** This test is required for admission to many schools in some parts of the country. It consists of English, mathematics, reading, and science reasoning components. Scoring on this exam involves separate subtest scores in the 1–56 range and a composite score, representing the average of the four subtests. Scores are also provided for specific content areas within English, math, and reading.

- **Achievement Tests:** These are also sponsored by the College Board and they measure knowledge in specific subjects. They are curriculum-based and intended to assess outcomes of courses that you have recently completed. Therefore, if you are aware of the achievement tests you will need to take, it is best to do so as soon as possible after you have completed those subjects. By this means you can maximize your performance, since your knowledge base in the subject will be optimal.

The impact of your scores on your admission chances varies widely and is dependent on the particular school's admissions policy. Larger institutions place considerable weight on the results of standardized tests. In general, the scores are commonly considered in the context of the student's transcript. While the test scores may be indicators of academic ability, their validation is determined by whether the scores are consistent with one's grade point average in high school. A wide discrepancy between the two will raise concerns.

Professional and Graduate Tests

Four major aptitude tests are relevant to students seeking enrollment in health career training programs. These tests are used in the admissions process for specific professions:

- **Medical College Admission Test (MCAT)** for admission to medical, veterinary, and podiatry schools
- **Dental College Admission Test (DAT)** for admission to dental schools
- **Optometry Admission Test (OAT)** for admission to optometry schools
- **Pharmacy College Admission Test (PCAT)** for admission to pharmacy schools

Data relevant to these four professional school tests are summarized in Table 3.1. There are also three additional tests that are utilized in the graduate school admission process for a number of fields, though usually not for health-care-related programs. These are

- Graduate Record Examination (GRE)
- Graduate Management Aptitude Test (GMAT)
- Miller Analogies Test (MAT)

These three tests, as well as the four major ones noted previously, are discussed in detail in Appendix A.

Table 3.1: Summary of Data Relevant to Major Exams for Health Science Schools

Exam	Number of Times Offered	Exam Fee	Length of Exam (in hours)	Special Accomodations	For More Information
MCAT	Multiple	$225	5.5	YES	www.aamc.org/mcat/
DAT	Multiple	$225	5	YES	www.ada.org/dat.aspx
OAT	Multiple	$213	4.5	YES	www.ada.org/oat/
PCAT	4 (Saturdays)	$150	4.5	YES	www.pcatweb.info

Preparing for the Tests

It is vital that you allow yourself adequate time to study for an aptitude test. The following general guidelines should help you in your preparation:

- Familiarize yourself with the major topics for each of the subtests. This provides you with an overview of areas you should study.
- Start your studies with the subject you are most knowledgeable about or comfortable with. This helps boost your confidence as you prepare for more challenging segments of the exam.
- Do a preliminary review of the material before starting intensive study. Then, if you spot areas of weakness, you can start working on them right away. This will lessen your anxiety.
- When you're learning new facts, try to put them into a logical framework rather than simply memorizing them. Understanding how a fact relates to the whole helps you remember it better.
- Decide which study techniques work best for you, and stick with those. For example, try repeated readings of the material, outlining the subject, writing a summary of the text, or reciting the information out loud.
- Before memorizing information, be sure you fully understand it. Remember, it's harder to unlearn erroneous material than to learn it right the first time.
- Study when you are alert, and only for as long as you stay alert. If you get tired, take a break or stop. You won't retain information if you're exhausted.

- Repetition is a key to retention. Frequent short, intense review periods help you incorporate the information into your memory base.
- Get a good night's sleep after your study session—and especially the night before the test!

The Essay

As part of the application procedure you may be expected to write an essay. While it is true that in the screening of applicants priority is given to your high school record and aptitude test scores, your essay can have a pivotal influence on the admissions process. This is especially important in borderline situations, such as when an applicant is on the threshold of being accepted, wait-listed, or rejected.

> **TIP:** The essay has a critical role that may not always be appreciated by students who often rely too heavily on their academic achievements. While grades and test scores can open up the admission gates, the essay may serve to tilt the balance in your favor.

The essay you write may need to respond to a specific topic proposed by the school to which you are applying, or you may have the option of writing on a topic of your own choice. Where a school requests a response to a specific question, it naturally will vary from one institution to another. Moreover, the same school can change the topic periodically. Therefore, reading an essay written for a prior year may not always prove directly helpful.

While every school is different, there are several conventional essay topics that appear on applications every year, such as (1) why you wish to attend college; (2) more specifically, why you are applying to this college; (3) how you define success; (4) a story about yourself; (5) who you are; (6) what life issues are of importance to you. Most of these conventional questions serve as vehicles to bringing your personal attributes to the reader's attention.

References

References in support of your application are usually expected by colleges. It is *your* obligation to arrange for them to be sent to the schools to which you are applying. The usual sources for recommendations are current or former teachers. The expectation is to receive an evaluation of your academic skills in the teacher's subject and an assessment of your level of maturity as well as other personal assets. The college will commonly ask the applicant to arrange that specific recommendation forms be given to the individuals to be completed.

You need to take care when selecting teachers to recommend you. You should realize that the comments provided should enhance the impression generated by your transcript and related data. To do so, the teacher should know enough about you to speak intelligibly and specifically about your strengths and performance. There are situations that provide teachers with an opportunity to get to know you better, such as when you are a member of a small class where individual student interaction with the instructor is high, if you've taken more than one course with the teacher, or if the teacher also serves as a coach in some area and knows you also in that context. All of the aforementioned assume that you have performed will in courses whose instructors are writing your recommendation.

A recommendation from one (or two) of the traditional courses in the social or physical sciences is commonly expected—the more recent the better. Where you have special interests that you wish to pursue at a college, a solid letter from a teacher in the same field may strengthen your admission chances. Finally, a recommendation from an instructor of an advanced course is usually more effective at indicating your intellectual assets in that field.

Another potential source for a recommendation is a guidance counselor who knows you well—meaning he or she has had contact with you over an extended length of time. Such individuals should be able to write in-depth about your abilities and your academic progress and personnel growth over the years.

The Interview

An interview is a frequent requirement to school admissions; however, most colleges interview only a small number of applicants. While an interview does provide an opportunity to establish your strengths as a candidate, it should not be construed as a way to get the committee to overlook significant defects in your record. Nevertheless, if you are very anxious to gain admission to a specific school, can afford the expense, and are a presentable and articulate individual, you should try to set up an appointment. You can then take that opportunity to personally "sell" yourself.

It is essential that you adequately prepare for any interview. Your initial source of information should be the institution's catalog and Web site. Dress professionally for the interview—just as you would for a job interview—so that you make a positive impression from the start.

You will probably be allotted only about a half-hour for the interview so it is important to prepare a personal message that presents your personality and potential, and fit it in somewhere in the course of the interview. You might use a well-placed question to move the interview in a direction that is in your favor and allows you to come across most effectively.

Remember that the basic goal of the interview is for the admissions personnel to get to know you better and exchange thoughts about getting an education at their school. Your responses should be in this context. Be sure to respond to questions in a thoughtful and accurate manner. Following are a few other tips for succeeding in your admissions interview:

- Maintain eye contact throughout the session.
- Avoid brisk, one-word, or one-sentence answers.
- Get involved and demonstrate interest, thereby generating a dialogue.
- Ask about school strengths, but don't ask for comparisons.
- Don't try to explain deficiencies in your record (unless specifically asked).
- Have a transcript and test score reports with you, but do not present them unless requested.

Creating a Complete Package

The stark reality is that you will be but one out of hundreds or thousands of applicants competing for a place in freshman classes. You should also be aware that since each applicant applies to several schools, the initial screening process rejects some individuals outright and ranks others for further action, determining if they merit consideration at a later date. It is important to realize at the outset that in addition to your intellectual achievements and potential, the mechanics of the admission process itself are critical. Knowing which schools and how many to apply to, presenting your qualifications, writing your essay, and handling yourself well at interviews are all critical elements in achieving your goal.

The admission process is the culmination of your efforts to become a health-care professional. It involves marketing your personal assets to the maximum extent possible. It is up to you to get to know your strengths and minimize or, if possible, even eliminate weaknesses. The image that you indirectly project by means of your application materials will determine the success of your attempt to secure a place in an allied health professional school, and thus, achieve your goal of a health-care career.

Financing Your Education

A post-secondary education can be quite expensive. Tuition and related costs have been rising faster than inflation for a long time. Yet this problem has not deterred students from entering the allied health-care professions. This is because students can receive financial aid from a variety of different sources, including federal and state governments, large corporations, philanthropic foundations, and colleges and universities themselves. In recent years, more than $97 billion has been distributed annually to U.S. students, mostly in the form of grants, scholarships, and low-interest loans. In fact, 75 percent of all undergraduate students receive some form of financial aid.

You've probably heard a number of myths about financial aid. Many students think aid is available only to the poor; that applying for aid is a difficult, complex process; that eligibility requirements are hard to meet; and that there is a social stigma in accepting financial aid. In reality, although some federal programs are designed for students from low-income families, many others are not. Many students from middle- and even upper-income families also receive financial aid. In fact, the vast majority of students attending college in this country receive some kind of financial aid.

Applying for financial aid is a time-consuming but straightforward process. Before you begin, you have to gather data on your family's financial status. The application form shows you how to add up your own and your family's assets and then use the total to calculate how much you can afford to pay for your education. You then deduct that amount from the total cost of attending a specific school. The amount left over typically is what you qualify for in financial aid. The amount you actually receive, however, is determined by a variety of factors, including your grade-point average and test scores.

Government regulations impose strict guidelines on financial aid distribution, but colleges have much greater flexibility with their own institutional aid, such as tuition discounts. Such assistance amounts to about 25 percent of what the government dispenses. While some schools use the government formula in granting aid, others use financial aid to entice good students to enroll in their programs. So, if you are at the top of your class and your test scores are good, you may have some leverage in how much aid you receive.

Forms of Financial Aid

Financial aid grants vary from a few hundred to several thousand dollars a year. This money may be applied to tuition, fees, or personal expenses, although the terms of its use usually are clearly stipulated. Financial aid is offered in various forms, including scholarships, grants, loans, and stipends. Frequently more than one form is offered to make up a "financial aid package." Following are the most common forms of aid.

Scholarships

Scholarships are awarded for *prior achievement* in areas such as academic performance, leadership activities, athletic ability, and community service. You don't have to repay this money, and the amount usually is fixed by the terms of the scholarship fund. But, in some cases, financial need can be the determining factor.

Grants

Grants also do not have to be repaid. These are awarded for *potential ability*, as reflected by previous accomplishments. They usually are based on a student's financial need.

Loans

Student loans must be repaid. However, they usually carry low interest rates, and you don't have to repay them until your education is completed. Moreover, some loans offer deferment or cancellation of the debt in return for special services, such as working at a nonprofit facility in a low-income area.

Stipends

Stipends typically are *fixed amounts of money paid to students for their services;* a good example is a work-study program. Occasionally a school offers free room and board in lieu of or in addition to a stipend.

Work

Taking a part-time job can also help you fund your education. Some schools have placement offices that will help you find a part-time job. Many colleges offer work-study programs as well. However, before you take a job, be sure it will not seriously interfere with your course of studies. Remember, your first priority is your education.

Sources of Financial Aid

Your first step in learning more about financial aid sources is to visit the financial aid officer at your chosen school. He or she can give you the forms you need, help you determine your eligibility, tell you about the school's aid packages, and direct you to other potential aid sources.

Your high school guidance counselor and your school or public librarian can also direct you to information about government and private sources of financial aid.

The following is a list of the major sources of financial aid in this country:

- **Schools.** Many schools offer financial aid in various forms. Look through your chosen school's catalog for information about the packages it provides.
- **Government.** Federal and state governments are major sources of financial aid. Some of the biggest federal programs and sources of state aid are listed in Tables 3.2 and 3.3 (on pp. 45–46).
- **Private organizations.** A variety of local and national businesses (especially health-related facilities), as well as fraternal, civic, and service organizations, offer financial assistance to young people. Your local librarian (and the reference sources listed in Tables 3.2 and 3.3) can provide further information. In addition, many professional health organizations have financial aid programs in their areas of interest. You should contact them directly for more information.

- **Foundations.** Many foundations and charitable organizations offer aid for educational purposes. Some labor unions also provide assistance to members and their families.
- **Banks.** Most banks and other lending institutions loan money to students, but this assistance can be costly because their interest rates are often high. So check out your other options before approaching the bank.

Table 3.2: Financial Aid Programs—General Education

Program	Financial Aid Available	Eligibility Requirements	For More Information
Federal Pell Grant	Grants up to $5,550 per academic year	Financial need, as well as school costs and status as full-time or part-time student.	Contact your high school's guidance office or your post-secondary institutions financial aid office, or visit http://ed.gov/programs/fpg.
College Work-Study	Provides financial aid in the form of part-time employment. Jobs are limited to 40 hours per week. The hourly rate varies.	Financial need. You must be enrolled at least half-time as an under-graduate, vocational, or graduate student in an approved institution.	Contact your school's financial aid office or office of student employment.
FFEL/Direct Loan Programs (Stafford and Plus Loans)	Varies. Undergraduate: Usually between $3,500 and $12,500/year. Graduate: Up to $20,500/year. Interest rates are fixed. Subsidizing and deferment available.	Must be enrolled in or accepted as at least a half-time student in an eligible college, university, vocational, trade, technical, or business school. Amounts and types of loans vary based on year in school, dependency status, and financial need.	Contact your high school's guidance office or your post-secondary institutions financial aid office, or visit http://studentaid.ed.gov.
Federal Supplemental Education Opportunity Grant	Between $100 and $4,000/year	Exceptional financial need.	Contact your high school's guidance office or your post-secondary institutions financial aid office, or visit www2.ed.gov/programs/fseog/.
Veterans' Administration Program	Amount varies. Offers loans and grants.	Benefits for veterans and their children who meet specific requirements. Other eligibility requirements vary.	Contact the Veterans' Administration at www.gibill.va.gov.

NOTE: This financial aid chart should be used only as a general guideline. Financial aid programs, the dollars available, and eligibility requirements change annually. You should contact the programs directly for the most current information available.

Table 3.3: Financial Aid Programs—Health Careers

Program	Financial Aid Available	Eligibility Requirements	For More Information
Armed Forces Health Professions Scholarship	All educational expenses, excluding room and board, plus a $1,900/month stipend.	Must enroll in graduate level program full time. Must serve a number of years of active duty equal to the number of years you receive aid.	Contact a local recruiter or visit http://www.goarmy.com/amedd/hpsp.jsp.
Health Professions Student Loans	Varies. Deferment and federal loan repayment are available.	Graduate students in dentistry, optometry, pharmacy, podiatry, or veterinary medicine.	Contact your school's financial aid office, or visit http://bhpr.hrsa.gov/dsa/hpsl.htm.
National Health Service Corps Scholarships (NHSC)	Tuition and fees, plus a $1,300/month stipend.	Full-time students enrolled in the professional study of medicine, dentistry, nurse practitioner, nurse midwife, or physician's assistant. Must serve 2-4 years with the NHSC upon graduation.	Contact your school's financial aid office, or visit http://nhsc.hrsa.gov/scholarship/.
Nursing Scholarship Program	Tuition and fees, plus a $1,300/month stipend.	Enrolled in an eligible nursing program. Financial need. Two year commitment to working in an area with a nursing shortage.	Contact your school's financial aid office, or visit www.hrsa.gov/loanscholarships/scholarships/Nursing/.
Primary Care Loan Program	Varies. Usually covers all tuition and fees. Low cost Federal loan with fixed interest.	Full time student in allopathic or osteopathic medicine with demonstrated financial need. Must work in primary care for the life of the loan.	Contact your school's financial aid office, or visit http://bhpr.hrsa.gov/dsa/pcl.htm.
Nursing Student Loans	Varies. Usually covers all tuition and fees. Low interest, long-term loans.	Full time nursing student with demonstrated financial need.	Contact your school's financial aid office, or visit http://bhpr.hrsa.gov/dsa/nsl.htm.

NOTE: *This financial aid chart should be used only as a general guideline. Financial aid programs, the dollars available, and eligibility requirements change annually. Readers are urged to contact the programs directly for the most current information available.*

Applying for Aid

As soon as possible after you've chosen a school, call the financial aid office and ask for a financial aid form and information about any other aid programs the school offers.

- Read the application carefully and be sure you understand what it asks for.
- Use the school's application materials to determine how much the program will cost *in total*. Include tuition, room and board, book and supply fees, and any other costs.
- Gather all the financial data you need to complete the application. Remember to include all your own assets as well as your family's.
- Carefully and neatly complete the entire application and securely attach any necessary documents.
- Review the application to make sure you have answered all the questions accurately and completely; then obtain all the needed signatures.
- Make a photocopy of the completed application for your files.
- Send the application well before the deadline (by certified mail, if possible) to ensure it arrives on time.
- Set up a folder to keep accurate records about the applications and all relevant correspondence.

Are You Eligible?

Eligibility for financial aid usually depends on three factors: the type of aid you're seeking, the individual program requirements, and your financial status.

Most schools use the government's standardized formula to determine how much financial aid you can receive and how much you will be expected to pay yourself. The financial aid office probably will give you one of two forms to record your family's financial information. These forms are then sent to the appropriate service—either the College Scholarship Service (CSS) or American College Testing (ACT)—for need analysis. Schools use this analysis to determine whether you qualify for aid, and how much they will offer.

The responses you receive will vary from school to school. You may be offered different aid packages for different schools. You should not base your decision on which school to attend solely on the aid package you are offered, although this is a significant consideration. You should also take into account each school's location, its quality of instruction and facilities, its reputation, and its job placement record.

You must submit a new financial aid application each year. You can also reapply next year if you do not qualify this year.

Remember, if you don't qualify for financial aid, you can always ask about merit scholarships, student stipends, work-study programs, and low-interest student loans. If you are really determined, you can almost always find a way to finance your education. Keep in mind that your education will pay off later when you land the health-care job you've trained so hard for.

HEALTH PROFESSIONALISM

Working as a health-care professional means living between two worlds: the healthy and the infirm. The atmosphere, attitude, and attributes of these two worlds are essentially opposite. The world of the healthy is characterized by energy and activity, a broad focus, and plans for the future. The world of the ill is usually sedentary and narrowly focused on recovery or adjustment and other short-term goals.

Potential workers in the field of health care must be aware of the impact of the profession on their own lives. This will help them understand the role they play and what it means to be a patient, which, in turn, will help them to succeed. Knowing what would be required of you in your profession will also help you to make sound career choices from the start. The following three chapters explore these areas.

The Health-Care Professional

In electing a career ~~care professional~~, your goal should be to become the best caregiver possible. To achieve this aim, it is essential to master the necessary knowledge, develop your interpersonal skills, and learn how to accommodate your personal and professional activities so that they can coexist harmoniously. This chapter will deal with each of these important issues.

Characteristics of the Health-Care Professional

Although health-care workers are employed in many different career areas and in a variety of facilities, certain personal and professional characteristics and attitudes apply to all health-care personnel. Recognizing the need for these qualities will not only help you to decide if a health-care career is right for you, it can help you to succeed once you begin.

For starters, consider the following:

- Can you communicate concisely and accurately in a well-modulated voice?
- Would you dress appropriately and neatly as is suitable for a professional?
- Do you maintain a healthy lifestyle?
- Do you have a genuine interest in people's welfare?
- Do you seek to understand others and their needs?
- Are you tactful and courteous when dealing with others?
- Can you keep your composure under pressure?
- Do you assume responsibility for your actions at all times?
- Do you persevere to complete tasks and meet your goals?
- Are you willing and able to follow directions, both written and verbal?

- Do you gracefully accept criticism that is warranted?
- Do you constantly seek to improve your performance over time?
- Do you maintain ethical conduct in all of your professional and personal activities?
- Do you promptly meet responsibilities competently?
- Do you understand and respect the limits of your abilities?

Affirmative answers to the majority of these questions is a sign that you are ready for the responsibilities of a health-care career. The following sections will discuss some of the required characteristics in more depth.

Personal Qualities

There are many personal attributes and attitudes that are required of those entering the health-care professions. While many of these are positive traits to exhibit in any job (such as dependability), others are especially important in a health-care setting (such as empathy). It is important for you to continue to cultivate these personal qualities throughout your career.

Empathy: This means being able to identify with and remain sensitive to another person's feelings, situation, and state of being. Health-care practitioners frequently have professional contact with individuals of varying ages, ranging from the newborn to the elderly. A prerequisite for employment in health care is being sincerely interested in working with people, being able to communicate with them, and being sympathetic to their needs. Good interpersonal skills, then, are the primary vehicle to developing and expressing empathy.

Honesty: Having integrity is essential for a successful career in any field. People must feel confident that they can place their trust in you. In the health-care profession, especially, people seeking care need to feel secure about the information they are given and the level of care they are being provided. A corollary of being honest is a willingness to promptly acknowledge an error so that it can be rectified without delay. In health-care professions, such errors can sometimes be matters of life or death.

Dependability: This personal quality is essential since employers and patients place their trust in the health-care workers providing services. Being dependable means being prompt when reporting for work and responding to assignments. It also requires that all tasks be completed as is expected and required. While much of the work of health-care professionals is routine, new situations, information, and approaches often arise. One must be ready to adapt to these changes. Employers and patients alike will count on you to deal with obstacles and overcome frustrations of various types.

Open to criticism: Realize at the outset that no person is perfect and that experience will enhance performance. Almost any situation in a health-care setting can be a learning experience. This being the case, one should be prepared to accept constructive criticism gracefully. The source of the criticism can come from your supervisor, coworker, or even a client or patient. Be gracious in your reaction and response, and try to see the situation from the other's point of view. This advice assumes that criticism is offered respectfully, of course.

Enthusiasm: The manner in which one meets their responsibilities is important. Your enthusiasm can have a positive effect on fellow coworkers as well as clients or patients. It shows you care about and are invested in your work, which in turn will make those around you more confident in your abilities.

Self-motivation: While your job description provides overall guidance as to your responsibilities, it is essential that you fill the roles that aren't necessarily spelled out in a formal document. That means taking the initiative to learn new skills and accept additional responsibilities. Such actions will reflect positively on your sincerity, creativity, and commitment to the position.

Competence: Supervisors, coworkers, and especially patients, rely on you to do your job to the best of your ability and to meet your responsibilities. If you are ever uncertain about an assigned task, it is essential to seek clarification early on, rather than after a mistake is made.

Discretion: It is essential that you be discrete with regard to what you say to patients or clients to ensure that they not become too upset or discouraged. Information that is clearly relevant to the patient's well-being (positive or negative), should be noted in the record, and if critical, should be reported orally to one's superior.

Responsibility: This implies a willingness to be held accountable for one's actions. Acting responsibly will encourage others to put their trust in you and believe you will carry out your duties faithfully.

Team-player: In any health-care field, success depends on the combined efforts of many. It is thus vital that you work well as part of team. Doing so allows you to be a greater asset to your patients and can enhance your position in the eyes of your other team members and superiors.

Personal Health

Working in health care means having an obligation to promote good health and prevent disease. To further this goal, it is essential to maintain one's own health. After all, it is hard to convince patients or clients to take care of themselves if you aren't providing a positive model. Following are the five main factors contributing to personal good health:

- *Diet:* Planning well-balanced meals and eating nutritious foods provides the body with the resources needed to maintain optimal health. Foods from each of the five major groups—milk, meat, vegetables, fruits, and grains—should be eaten daily to meet one's dietary needs.

- *Rest:* Adequate rest and sleep help to restore energy and combat stress. While sleep can be harder to come by for some health-care professions, and each individual has their own essential level of sleep requirements, generally 7 to 8 hours are recommended per day.

- *Exercise:* Exercise maintains proper blood circulation and improves muscle tone. Exercise also improves one's mental attitude and facilitates restful sleep. It's a good idea to exercise daily and to create a regimen designed to fit your specific needs.

- *Good posture:* Good posture helps prevent fatigue and lowers tension on the body's muscles.
- *Avoid substance abuse:* Using alcohol, drugs, or tobacco, can seriously impact your health. Most substances can impair mental function and lower one's ability to make decisions.

Personal Appearance

When serving as a health-care worker it is important to become familiar with the required standards of dress and appearance. These are set by your place of employment, though the overall goal is usually to make a clean, neat, and professional appearance. While most of the requirements for personal appearance are similar to any field or job, some are more specific to the health-care professions. Be sure to consider the following:

- *Uniform:* Many health occupations require a uniform. This should conform to the type customarily used at the institution of employment. The uniform should be clean and pressed so that it is wrinkle-free and fits properly. Appropriate jewelry, such as a wedding ring, watch, small pierced earrings, etc., is usually acceptable.
- *Name badge:* For security reasons, most health-care facilities require that their personnel wear name-badges or photo identification tags at all times.
- *Shoes:* Some health-care occupations and specific facilities favor wearing white shoes. Irrespective of color, it is important is that your shoes fit well, provide strong foot support, and have low heels. This will serve to diminish foot fatigue and prevent accidents. After all, many health-care professions require workers to be on their feet most of the day.
- *Personal grooming:* Health-care workers usually come into close physical contact with patient/clients. Thus, it is essential that workers be clean and odor-free. Nails should be kept short and clean, since long and painted fingernails can both injure patients and be sites for carrying germs. Long nails also can tear or puncture elastic gloves, commonly used in many procedures. Hair should be kept clean and easy to care for.

Making the Most of Your Education

Becoming a health-care professional is a formidable challenge. It involves much more than merely accumulating the required number of course credits to graduate from a program. Rather, it is an experience in intellectual and personal growth and maturation. Thus, the educational phase of this endeavor should involve mastering basic theoretical knowledge, acquiring specific professional skills, and developing a positive attitude toward working in the healing arts.

Theoretical Knowledge

The foundation of providing health-care service is solid science skills. These include the basic sciences—biology, chemistry, and physics—and the behavioral sciences of psychology and sociology. These courses provide a framework for understanding the human body's form and function and how people behave. Supplementing this background, it is helpful to learn about legal concepts, economics, statistics, and computers. Knowledge of the liberal arts also can broaden your perspective. Finally, understanding the theoretical basis of techniques facilitates their proper application.

Professional Skills

Before you undertake a program of professional training, your formal education takes place mostly in the classroom and laboratory. This continues in professional school, but a new learning site is introduced: namely, the clinic. This is the essential learning environment for gaining professional practice experience. During your training, you will acquire skills in the following four key areas.

> **Technical Skills:** Technical skills include the ability to properly apply given techniques to evaluate, diagnose, and treat illnesses. These skills may include reading lab results, giving inoculations, or using sophisticated lab equipment.

> **Communication Skills:** Health professionals must interact with a wide variety of people. This means being able to accept responsibility and criticism from your supervisor while being constructively critical of those you are supervising. In essence, you must develop the interpersonal and communication skills that allow you to function in a responsible, challenging, and stress-filled environment.

> **Instruction and Management Skills:** Health-care professionals frequently are called on to instruct patients or their families. They also may have to be innovative and design practical solutions to health-care problems. Workers with administrative skills and obligations may be asked to develop short- or long-term goals for their facilities and to supervise the allocation of equipment and supplies.

> **Research Skills:** As part of your health-care activities, you may be called on to design an investigative project, which includes formulating a hypothesis and collecting data to test it. The results could be invaluable.

Many of these skills—especially the technical and research skills—require practice and patience to master. Achieving competency is a multistep process:

- Secure detailed knowledge about the skill.
- When possible, have the skill applied to yourself.
- Observe a professional using the skill.
- When possible, assist the professional in using the skill.
- Initially, use the new skill only under close supervision.
- When possible, employ the skill in a variety of situations without direct supervision.
- Take a test to demonstrate your capability with the skill.

Your Attitude

If you hope to succeed in the health-care (or any other) field, you must develop a positive attitude. This is especially true for the following:

- **Learning** is *always* a positive experience. You should look upon learning as a challenge to your intellect and pursue it throughout your professional life.
- **Inquisitiveness** implies a sense of adventure, because it involves venturing into the unknown as you move forward toward developing professional expertise.
- **Commitment** implies a willingness to put forth your best effort to obtain results—whether you are mastering a subject, providing therapy to a patient, or carrying out a procedure.

The Clinical Component

Your clinical education is an introduction to the core of your future work. The key element in this critical educational phase is *refinement*. You expand your basic knowledge and skills by broadening your exposure. The ultimate goal is developing professional competence. Clinical work may include several components:

- Working with several patients who have varied medical problems
- Observing different manifestations of a single pathological condition
- Working under time limitations
- Having multiple responsibilities

Starting off properly in a clinical context helps ensure you will have a meaningful learning experience. There are several steps you can take to get off on the right foot:

- Introduce yourself to your coworkers.
- Keep your eyes open to get an idea of how things are done in the work setting.
- Ask questions politely and try to determine what is expected of you.
- Don't be offended by questions others ask because of your student status.
- Assume that those around you will work to enhance your clinical abilities.
- Try to act as if you are a member of the team by contributing to the group's activities in a meaningful way.

Remember that the beginning awkwardness will dissipate soon, as your responsibilities, independence, and self-confidence increase. If you find yourself having trouble on tests or mastering skills, you may experience some self-doubt and anxiety. Learning and mastering new skills will help alleviate the inherent difficulties your new situation presents.

> **TIP:** Sometime during your clinical training, you may be struck by the reality that you can have a positive impact on the lives of others. This should be a strong motivator during this challenging time.

Here are some other points to remember when you experience anxiety:

- The admissions people at your educational program based your admission on their confidence that you are capable of achieving your goals.
- Most people have periodic episodes of anxiety, especially when facing new situations.
- Mild anxiety usually is temporary. It *will* pass.
- Anxiety can be a positive force if you take it as wake-up call. It can stimulate your emotional reserves so that you can better face the challenges of school.
- Finally, always keep in mind the rewards of attaining your goal.

If you find yourself facing long-term anxiety, try to find the underlying issues generating the anxiety and then seek to remedy the situation. Maybe you can do this by improving your study habits. If you can't get on top of the situation, don't be afraid to seek the help of a school advisor or faculty member.

Managing Your Professional Life

The Professional as a Helper

Almost every adult has had the opportunity to serve as a helper for others at some time in life. This may involve teaching a skill, guiding an activity, or rendering a service. Consequently, you may have experienced the satisfaction that comes from being a helper.

There are two types of helping relationships: social and therapeutic. A *social* relationship is defined as providing a personal act of service

- When a wide variety of resources are used
- When the service is not goal-oriented
- When the service may foster dependence
- When the relationship may not prove constructive

A *therapeutic* relationship is defined as providing a professional act of service

- Using established professional skill
- Providing service that is goal-oriented
- Providing service that does not foster dependence
- When the relationship should prove constructive

From this brief comparison, you can see that therapeutic help is characterized by the professional nature of the services, which are aimed at both the patient's short- and long-term benefit.

TIP: Traditionally health professionals have been viewed as providing direct patient assistance (such as nurses and therapists). While this is true for many professionals, others provide services that help patients only indirectly (such as biomedical engineers and hospital administrators). Nevertheless, professionals in the latter category also work for patients' well-being, and their services are vital to the proper functioning of health-care institutions.

Professional help may be provided by means of two other approaches. The first involves the use of assistants, and the second involves referrals. *Professional assistant* programs (see Chapters 11 and 12) were introduced to help provide lower-cost health care without diminishing quality, to create employment possibilities for those unable to take extensive programs, and to reduce a shortage of personnel. These positions involve the appropriate division of responsibilities and skills between the professional and assistant. This may involve the professional delegating some responsibilities and assuming a supervisory role.

Referral to another professional helper may be mandated under certain conditions, most often when the professional lacks the experience or equipment to provide the appropriate service.

Teamwork

Many people believe that overall health care is best provided using a team approach. A team approach requires that each member skillfully apply his or her professional abilities, while bearing in mind the supplementary and complementary activities of other team members. This approach allows patients to be viewed from multiple perspectives, ensuring the best possible care.

Teamwork consists of a group of personal sharing diverse areas of expertise working towards a common goal. Teamwork helps ensure continuity of care and improves communication between all concerned. Patients cared for by a team are more likely to respond positively to their treatment and therapy. They feel more reassured that they are receiving comprehensive care, which usually elevates their spirits and motivates them to be cooperative and get well faster.

Contributing significantly to the success of a team are the managerial skills of the team leader. She needs to coordinate activities and make sure that all appropriate personnel are actively involved in planning and providing the necessary services. The team leader sees to it that goals are set and monitors the patient/client's progress in meeting them. The team leader will, if necessary, arrange to modify existing treatment/therapy plans. She will aim to facilitate good communication and relationships between team members. Another responsibility of the team leader is familiarizing the members of the team with the patient's background and any special personal issues.

To be effective, a health-care team must be able to accommodate its members' personal and professional differences. A team may function based on a hierarchical arrangement, with both power and responsibility resting heavily on top to maximize efficiency. An alternative approach is a community structure, in which power is far less centralized, and mutual support is paramount. Think about what level of responsibility, interaction, and teamwork you would work best at, and try to find jobs or work environments that cater to those preferences.

The following tips well help you to work well as part of a health-care team:

- Act courteously and carefully consider the points of view of others.
- Have a positive attitude even in the face of unforeseen difficulties.
- Keep an open mind and be ready to consider and even try a new approach.
- Share your ideas and knowledge with others on the team.
- Offer to assist other team members when and where your knowledge and training allows.
- In the event your ideas are turned down, do not feel personally rejected.

Finally, it should be emphasized that when team members are committed, patient, and thorough in meeting their *individual* responsibilities, the chances for a favorable outcome greatly increases.

Leadership

The successful operation of a health-care facility requires employees to contribute their services at a wide variety of levels. As noted above, teamwork is the most essential factor in coordination of activities between personnel from various levels, and a team leader is essential for the effective performance of the team. Because the potential for advancement is high in many jobs and responsibilities are numerous and varied, anyone entering the health-care professions should consider if they have what it takes to be an effective leader.

Leadership implies having the innate potential to stimulate people to work together in a cooperative manner to achieve a common goal. Holding a leadership position presents a personal challenge, but not an insurmountable one. Should you take on a leadership role (or have one thrust upon you), the following guidelines may prove helpful in meeting your responsibilities:

- Lead the group in a democratic manner, treating all equally.
- Guide the group to accept common goals favored by the majority.
- Determine the strengths and weaknesses of the members of your group.
- Evaluate your own abilities and deficiencies and bear them in mind.
- Demonstrate self-confidence and a sense of integrity in all of your actions.
- Communicate with others clearly and make sure you are fully understood.
- Avoid public criticism of individuals; do so privately and confidentially.
- Personally maintain high standards as an example for others to follow.
- Demonstrate optimism so as to create a congenial working atmosphere.
- Demonstrate open-mindedness and consider new ideas and differing viewpoints.
- Be willing, when reasonable, to compromise on suggestions offered by others.
- While setting high standards, be sure that they are attainable.
- Give credit when it is due and acknowledge good work by praising others.

Finally, one should be aware that leadership can prove personally satisfying when carried out effectively, thoughtfully, and by securing the cooperation of all involved.

Networking for Support

Self-preservation is not enough as a work ethic. Career satisfaction involves sharing with your coworkers the joys and frustrations of your job. You'll find a commonality of interest with your colleagues. Expressions of appreciation from coworkers also contribute to your sense of belonging within the professional network. These factors can enhance your working environment and foster opportunities for securing support during difficult periods. You should also consider your friends and family when you are seeking support sources.

Accountability

It is obviously important to maintain high standards of practice for health-care professionals. This is achieved primarily by *peer review*. This term refers to the formal procedure for evaluating a colleague's work. A written evaluation is a means of constructive criticism that enhances self-awareness. It also is a basis for judging competency, thus providing protection for patients.

One should be aware that there are legal limits that define the extent of one's professional level of operation. Going beyond one's range of duty can incur serious liability; for example, distributing drugs to patients without proper authorization is illegal. If you detect incompetent or unethical behavior outside the realm of peer review, *you need to act*, even if you find it difficult to do so. Follow your institution's policies for reporting the situation to the proper authorities.

Critical Thinking

It is well established that critical thinking is a most essential skill for health-care practitioners. Critical thinking involves the ability to think creatively, make decisions, solve problems, visualize options, and digest information. Critical thinking allows you to effectively consider the possible consequence of your actions and determine if these are in the best interest of the patient or client. Your critical thinking skills can be enhanced by correctly evaluating the results of actions taken in the past and learning from those experiences.

Because health-care practitioners are faced with innumerable and often unexpected challenges, it is a good idea to develop a step-by-step approach for resolving problems. Such an approach might look like the following:

1. Recognize that a problem exists. Such awareness may come from various sources, including personal observation, observations of coworkers, or feedback directly from the patient or client.
2. Gain a thorough understanding of the nature of the problem. Determine the specific issues involved, namely, how, when, and where the problem arose, its nature, and its ramifications.
3. Consider and weigh several possible options to resolving the issue at hand and their possible consequences.
4. Determine the best method to resolve the problem and then properly implement it.
5. Evaluate the results of the implementation and modify the method used if necessary.

Time Management

While not true of all health-care professions, many jobs in health care require workers to juggle several responsibilities at once, sometimes under fast-paced or chaotic circumstances. For that reason, time management skills are critical. Such skills can help you from being overwhelmed by your responsibilities, increase your productivity, and lead to greater job satisfaction.

The first step in time management involves keeping an activity record for a period of several days. This allows you to determine how you actually use the time that is available to you. By regularly noting activities as they are performed, observing the amount of time each activity takes, and recording the results, you can detect emerging patterns. During certain periods of the day you may show higher energy levels and an improved quality of work. Wasted or otherwise underproductive time will also become apparent. Having analyzed how your hours are spent, you can begin to better organize your time. For example, important projects can be scheduled during the periods of the day when your energy levels are high.

Time management can be used to ensure success in meeting established goals. To do this properly, you need a daily planner or calendar (electronic or otherwise) to keep a record of activities, organize all your information, recognize time conflicts, and establish a prioritized schedule to achieve your goals.

An effective time management plan involves the following steps:

1. Analyze the list of established goals as to their achievability and urgency.
2. Identify your work habits and preferences and determine the most suitable time intervals to achieve maximum results.
3. Schedule tasks using the daily planner and calendar by noting all activities, break times, and personal need periods (e.g., exercise sessions, meal times).
4. Formulate a daily 'must do' list of activities. As each item is completed, cross it off your list. This can serve as an incentive to further stimulate your activities as you move along toward completing your work load.

Goal Setting

Properly managing your team can help you to complete your goals. Doing so will lead to greater career satisfaction and success. Goals are like maps that help you find your direction and reach your destination. Attaining goals can prove to be satisfying and are often a motivating force to further achievement. When setting goals, the following guidelines should be considered:

• Write down your goals. This gives them a sense of reality and attainability.
• Goals should be formulated in positive terms (avoid the word "don't").
• Define goals clearly and precisely and, where feasible, set a time limit.
• Prioritize multiple-goals.
• Set realistic goals that you are capable of attaining with a reasonable amount of effort and within a practical time frame.

Once you've set your goals, the next obvious step is to focus on achieving them. Start by determining the essential skills, information, and resources you need and the potential problems that you can anticipate along the way. Set a reasonable pace for properly executing your goals. To further ensure success, focus on one task at a time, unless you are interrupted by an urgent challenge. Avoid sources that can be distractions to the momentum of the work in progress. And most importantly, when a significant goal has been completed, reward yourself before proceeding to the next one.

As mentioned before, achieving one's goals can be quite satisfying. However, be aware that even with the best of plans, complications may arise. It then becomes necessary to reevaluate the situation and make adjustments and revisions. Also, due to circumstances both within and outside of your control, some goals may not be achieved. Failure to complete a goal is disappointing, naturally, but it also provides an opportunity to reevaluate the situation. Determine if your plans were unrealistic or uncover what elements were missing (e.g., skills, training, resources, time, etc.). Failure can and should motivate one to do better, if it is treated as a positive learning experience.

Managing Your Personal Life

Health-care careers are often challenging and both mentally and physically draining. In fairness to yourself and your patients or clients, you must stay healthy, be job-satisfied, and keep an optimistic view of life.

Caring for Yourself

When you maintain your good health, you feel, look, and function better. Good health refers to your physical *and* psychological well-being—both of which need to be maintained for you to function optimally.

It seems obvious that health professionals should maintain sound lifestyles. Unfortunately, this is not always the case. This may be because professional helpers sometimes subconsciously develop a sense of invincibility to illness and thus do not practice preventive health care. You can overcome the tendency to feel invulnerable in two ways:

- **Establish periods of "aloneness."** The principal function of a health-care professional is being a helper. This means that one-sided demands are constantly being placed on you, which automatically generates stress. You'll have a strong need at times for a respite that is more than a mere coffee break. When this happens, you should seek time to be alone with yourself. A short period of self-imposed solitude can have a rejuvenating effect on your mental and physical faculties.
- **Develop good work habits.** This means seeking an approach that values efficient decision making and competence while being open to innovation and experimentation. The optimal balance between these opposing goals serves to avoid burnout on one hand and ineffectiveness on the other.

Coping with Stress

Stress can be defined as the body's reaction to any stimulus that requires a person to adjust to changing circumstances in some manner. Stress causes the body to go into an alarm or warning mode. This mode is generated automatically and is called the 'fight or flight' response. If the body is subjected to stress with frequent "ups" and "downs," the normal function of the nervous system may be disrupted. Prolonged stress can lead to serious illness or disease. Many diseases have stress related origins, including migraine headaches, anxiety reactions, depression, allergies, asthma, some digestive disorders, hypertension (elevated blood pressure), insomnia and heart disease.

Everyone experiences some stress on a daily basis. The amount of stress felt is relative to the individual's innate nature and their personal perception of the situations that are generating the stress. A small amount of stress can prove beneficial; it makes individuals more alert to their environment and enhances their energy level. In fact, many health-care professionals thrive in the fast-paced, high stress environments they work precisely because they react well to such circumstances. Still, too much stress is dangerous if unchecked, so it is important to learn how to control it. The following tips can help minimize stress in and outside of the workplace:

- Maintain a healthy lifestyle, which includes a balanced diet, adequate periods of relaxation and sleep, and regular exercise.
- Don't ignore the onset of the feelings of stress. Immediately cease what you are doing. If possible, sit in a comfortable chair and take deep breaths to relieve the tension.
- If possible, listen to soothing music.
- Relax by taking a brief nap or, if possible, a warm bath.
- Meditate.
- Close your eyes and imagine you are somewhere relaxing.
- Take time out to engage in a distracting, pleasurable activity.
- Develop interests outside of your work activities. Get involved in sports, hobbies, clubs, or other recreational activities.
- Talk to someone who you feel comfortable with about the causes of your stress.
- Try to look at the situation generating the stress from a more positive perspective and see if it changes your feelings and attitude.
- Change the environment you are in to less stressful one, for example, by taking a walk.
- Don't face challenges alone, but seek help and delegate tasks to make your workload easier and thus avoid feeling overwhelmed.
- Avoid accepting multiple responsibilities at one time, this could generate additional and unnecessary stress.

Health-care careers come with their own specific rewards and demands. It is important to balance your professional and personal needs at all times in order to stay satisfied and successful in your career. Professionals who feel confident and accomplished, who work well as part of a team, who understand their strengths and weaknesses, who are determined to meet their goals, and who find satisfaction in their work will ultimately provide the best possible care to their patients or clients.

Chapter 5

Understanding
the Patient

We can usually manage our own well-being by maintaining a healthy lifestyle. However, illness and injury are often unavoidable. Even under the best of circumstances, people become sick, and some cases are serious enough to require hospitalization. This chapter focuses on patients who must be hospitalized for some reason. However most of the following discussion of patients' rights, needs, and attitudes applies to healthcare professionals in any setting.

The Impact of Hospitalization

An individual's hospitalization may be voluntary—for example, resulting from a decision to have elective surgery such as knee replacement—or it may be mandated by an acute illness such as appendicitis. Regardless of the cause, hospitalization significantly disrupts an individual's personal life. It can negatively affect family, coworkers, and even friends. The effect varies, depending on each person's circumstances. When the patient is the family breadwinner or a single parent and the illness is prolonged, its impact can be far-reaching and severe.

Admission to a hospital obviously implies that an illness requires more sophisticated treatment than is available at home or at a local clinic. This naturally raises a patient's level of anxiety; after all, placing one's well-being largely in the hands of strangers is unnerving.

Hospitalized patients suddenly are exposed to multiple losses—including a loss of the ability to live at home and a sense of privacy. In addition, they experience a loss of independence. In the hospital, their activities are determined by staff routine and their own specific medical problems. Even their diets are not fully under their control and may be altered dramatically at a physician's request. The necessary hospital procedure of monitoring vital signs day and night can prove the most disturbing. This loss of independence compounds an already difficult situation, which can lead to frustration or even depression.

Another consideration associated with hospitalization is the patient's loss of self-image. A significant change in how we think we look because of the impact of an illness or injury can have a strong influence on our psyches. If a change in appearance or function looks like it may be prolonged, it can induce a stage of denial that can even inhibit recovery.

On top of it all, all these losses and changes occur at the same time patients feel most vulnerable and inadequate because of their illnesses. This can generate considerable inner emotional turmoil—turmoil to which the health-care professional must respond in a reassuring and thoughtful manner. This is why health-care professionals must know how to reassure patients, helping them to maintain a positive attitude with the hopes of speeding the healing process.

Patient Status

Serious illness can stigmatize a person as markedly different from healthy members of society. This is more severe when the illness is compounded by a disability. A patient facing disability may feel that he or she has been diminished as a person by having lost an essential element of humanity.

When a physical loss is permanent, and especially when it is evident (such as in the case of amputation), the potential impact is much greater. Thus, the visual response of others must be carefully and tactfully managed by health-care professionals. Those working with disabled patients would do well to advise their patients to seek help from support groups. Simply seeing how others with similar conditions have succeeded in spite of their problems is helpful. Encouraging families to be supportive also contributes to a patient's sense of well-being.

Patient Privileges

Those who are sick enough to be hospitalized are granted certain amenities to make them more comfortable and encourage their recovery. Among these is a release from obligations to work or to care for themselves to the extent that is medically justified.

Increasingly today, people are becoming more conscious of their health and more involved in managing their own treatment. Naturally, this depends on the state of a patient's illness. When treatment options exist, patients deserve to be consulted; most patients and their families appreciate this courtesy. In fact, consulting with patients actually increases their momentum toward recovery.

Privileges, however, are not rights; rather, they are amenities that should be given only when they are warranted. For example, some patients may find it advantageous to remain "sick," for this status protects them from the outside world. It may also provide financial and social gain. If you suspect such a situation, you should document it before drawing any conclusions. If the situation is established as valid, you should cooperate with the institution's mental health personnel to resolve the issue with minimum embarrassment to the patient.

Patient Rights

In addition to certain privileges, patients have specific rights, such as the rights to life, health care, respect, and autonomy. These rights are defined in greater detail by the American Hospital Association and usually are given to the patient upon admission to the hospital. The following are just some of the items from the *Patient's Bill of Rights*. Patients have the right to

- Confidential treatment of all medical records and communication.
- Obtain complete, current information concerning diagnosis, treatment, and prognosis (expected outcome).
- Receive information necessary to provide informed consent prior to the start of any procedure or treatment.
- Reasonable response to a request for services from the staff.
- Be advised of and have the right to refuse to participate in any research project.
- Expect reasonable continuity of care (e.g., in the event a physician is absent).
- Review medical records and examine bills and receive explanations of all care provide and charges incurred.

In addition, residents in long-term care facilities are guaranteed certain rights under the Omnibus Budget Reconciliation Act of 1987. Every long-term care facility must inform residents or their guardians of these rights and copy must be posted at each facility.

The *Resident's Bill of Rights* protects, among other things, the rights to

- Privacy and confidentiality of personal and clinical record.
- Free choice regarding physician treatment, care, and participation in research.
- Accommodation of needs and choice regarding activities, schedules, and health-care services.
- Express grievances without fear of retribution or discrimination.
- Manage personal funds and utilize all personal possessions.
- Participate in social and religious and community activities.
- Unlimited access to immediate family or relatives.
- Remain in the facility and not be transferred or discharged, except for medical reasons, to protect the welfare of the resident or others, failure to pay, or if the facility cannot meet the resident's needs.

All states have adopted these rights. Health-care workers violating or denying these rights may face loss of their positions, fines, and even imprisonment. It is the obligation of all health-care workers to at all times provide for the well-being, safety, and care of the patients and residents that they are responsible for. Such responsibility is not to be taken lightly, of course, and should be a key consideration for anyone thinking about pursuing a career in health care.

Advanced Directives

Advanced directives, stipulate what hospitalized patients want or do not want in the event they become incapacitated and are unable to express their wishes regarding the nature of medical care on their behalf. Health-care practitioners must be aware of, respect, and honor advanced directives. Two major advanced directives exist, namely, a living will and durable power of attorney.

- *Living wills* are documents that allow an individual to state what measures should or should not be taken to prolong life when their condition is terminal (death is expected). This document must be signed by the individual, only when competent to do so, and also by two witnesses (who cannot benefit from the person's death). A living will commonly result in assuming the issuance of a do not resuscitate (D.N.R.) order for a terminally ill individual. Most states now have laws that allow withholding of life-sustaining measures and honor the contents of living wills.

- *Power of Attorney* is a durable document that permits another individual to make all decisions regarding health care if the patient or client is unable to do so themselves. This includes providing or withholding specific medical care or surgical procedures, spending or withholding funds for health care, and having access to the patients' medical records. Power of Attorney can be awarded to any legal-aged adult and must be signed by the individual as well as one or two witnesses.

Health-care personnel should be aware of these types of documents and, where pertinent, bear them in mind and respect their contents.

Post-hospitalization Anxiety

Upon a patient's discharge from the hospital, he or she may face uncertainties about the future. This is especially true for patients who must adjust to a disability or chronic condition. But even for those who have made a full recovery, concerns about future health may arise. They may have experienced some disappointment with how their treatment was handled, with the manner in which they were treated by the hospital personnel, or with the length of time it took to recover. Of special concern to such individuals is the possibility of a reoccurrence of their illness, or some other illness, that may necessitate another hospitalization.

This all points to the vital need for health-care professionals to be sensitive to the long-term impact they have on patients. Indeed, this is exactly why you must always be tactful and sensitive in what you say and do when you are in earshot of patients. Being sensitive means reassuring patients of your genuine interest in their welfare and your intent to do what you can to be helpful. Above all, avoid giving incorrect information or raising false hopes. If a patient asks questions that lie beyond your competence to answer, suggest that he or she be referred to someone who can answer them, such as the attending physician.

Patient Adjustment

Hospitalized patients who respond to medical care and are fully recovered can proceed with their lives upon discharge. But those whose illnesses leave them vulnerable to future illness (such as heart attack victims) and permanently disabled individuals are in a far different situation. These people may end up reassessing their most basic values to cope with their new circumstances.

Health-care professionals who deal with such patients—both those who are hospitalized and those receiving post-discharge therapy—must be sensitive in helping them acquire these new values. This process can take weeks or even months. The success of this process is critical to patients' rehabilitation; it is achieved when patients realize that, although their former potentials are no longer attainable, they can set new, more realistic goals.

When they receive medical treatment or therapy, patients may develop an unhealthy dependency on their care providers. In this case, it is critical that the health-care provider direct the relationship so that it is constructive rather than detrimental. Thus, as a patient proceeds from the acute stage to the recovery process, he or she should be encouraged to become more independent.

The Outpatient

To reduce costs, many HMOs and other facilities make strenuous efforts to treat patients on an outpatient basis. This applies even to some surgical operations.

While not stigmatized as "sick," outpatients may nevertheless suffer from a loss of self-image. This is because they view themselves in comparison with a society of healthy individuals and therefore feel deficient. Inpatients, who live in an environment of sick people, may feel this loss of self-image less intensely. On the other hand, outpatients do not feel the various losses associated with hospitalization. Finally, remember that the outpatient typically is on the road to recovery, as opposed to the permanently disabled individual, who is only on the road to adjustment.

Health-care professionals are ultimately responsible for the physical, mental, and emotional well-being of their patients or clients, whether they are in a hospital, a clinic, or a resident care facility. Understanding how your patients or clients feel and what their expectations and anxieties are, and appreciating and respecting their rights and wishes is key to becoming an effective and professional care-giver. Also, knowing what will be required of you as a health-care professional can help you to decide whether this is the right career field for you.

The Professional-Patient Relationship

A health-care practitioner is most successful when he or she develops a good "bedside manner." Important components of developing a good relationship with patients include effective communication, understanding cultural differences, understanding the special needs of patients in different age groups, and at all times maintaining professionalism. This chapter addresses these various topics.

Communicating Effectively

Health professionals interact daily with people from all walks of life. Their basic needs may be similar, but their lifestyles, backgrounds, cultures, and values vary widely. So the health professional must be able to communicate effectively with a wide variety of people both verbally and nonverbally.

Verbal Skills

Verbal communication skills are essential to secure information on a patient's medical history, current condition, and therapeutic progress; to establish rapport with the patient; to provide instructions to the patient; and to relay information to other health-care team members.

Success with verbal communication depends on several factors:

- **Vocabulary.** Sometimes choosing the wrong words can result in a patient's misunderstanding her condition and treatment. For this reason, you should avoid using technical jargon when talking to patients. Speak, slowly, clearly and in a moderate and sympathetic tone of voice. Make a genuine effort to understand what your patients are saying and to ensure that they've understood you properly. To ensure good communication, you might try the echoing technique: Repeat what a patient says to be sure you have it right, and ask him to explain to you in his own words what you've said to him.

- **Organized presentation.** When a complex explanation *is* needed (for example, if you must explain a procedure), be direct, clear, and to the point. Again, avoid using technical jargon. Instead, try using a logical, step-by-step approach, and avoid overwhelming the patient with details.

- **Attitude.** To a large degree, your manner of delivery determines the effectiveness of your message. Convey genuine concern in your tone of voice and in the words you choose. If there is a conflict, don't be argumentative, but focus on its proper resolution. When appropriate, you might inject some humor (pun intended) to lighten the atmosphere.

- **Effective Listening.** It is not enough to ensure that patients hear what you say to them; you also must be sure that you are hearing what *they* say. Be sensitive to your patients' nuances of expression and avoid prejudging their responses. Be patient, allowing the other side to gather their thoughts and present their views.

Improper tone of voice or manner of speech, overt criticism, or a lack of interest can lead to a breakdown in communication or even a defensive response from the patient or client. To avoid such a response, one should

- Be descriptive rather than critical of observed behaviors.
- Speak in terms of one's viewpoint rather than absolutes.
- Communicate from the perspective of an equal rather than a superior.
- Speak in an empathetic manner as a demonstration of your concern for the other person.

Keep in mind that many of the strategies discussed above for communicating with patients apply when communicating with coworkers as well.

> **TIP:** A better understanding of one's own values and motives can lead to improved interpersonal relations. Patients or clients have good reason to expect certain positive attitudes and behaviors on the part of their health-care practitioners. If you recognize, upon self-analysis, that you are lacking some trait necessary to your profession, it can be well worth it to cultivate the missing characteristic. Self-improvement starts with self-awareness.

Nonverbal Skills

Your nonverbal communication skills can be as important as your verbal skills. These are manifested in several ways:

- The most common forms of nonverbal communication are gestures, facial expressions, and other signs. Eye contact is another major element of facial expression and is essential for positive communication.

- Your nonverbal communication can either put your patients at ease or make them uncomfortable. Remember, you can convey disapproval simply by raising an eyebrow or pointing at someone. Watch your body language!

- When you are dealing with patients who don't speak English or those with perceptual deficiencies, you might use the *demonstration approach,* in which gestures and posturing substitute for the spoken word.

- Another way we communicate nonverbally is through our personal appearance. This is best reflected by the practice of wearing a uniform. Some health-care professionals feel uniforms are important because they quickly establish one's credentials and position of authority.

Finally, remember that touch is a very powerful way of communicating. Studies have shown that touch can be tremendously comforting and even therapeutic.

Cultural Influences

Cultural variations and personal biases affect how people interpret both verbal and nonverbal messages. For example, different cultural groups have different definitions of comfortable *personal space*. In mainstream U.S. society, we define four interacting-distance zones: intimate, personal, social, and public. When performing a procedure, health professionals often must function within the first two zones. Outside the examining room, however, you should adhere to each patient's preference for acceptable distance. This helps patients feel more secure in the health-care facility.

Another culturally dependent variable is *time.* Some groups are highly conscious of punctuality, while others are very lax about such things. Being aware of such differences can help you improve the effectiveness of your interactions with patients. While maintaining a schedule is important, you should try to accommodate your patients' needs. Be conscious of the difference between a formal visit and a social-professional visit. In other words, take a few minutes to talk to your patients and answer their questions. Striking the proper balance is a valuable tool for professional success.

Above all, be aware of your own biases—and remember that patients have them, too. Avoid showing prejudice in any manner during the course of your professional activities.

The Nature of the Relationship

While it is important to maintain good relationships with your patients, remember that these relationships are *not* friendships. To get optimal results for your patients, you must understand the nature of the professional-patient relationship, which encompasses three distinct stages:

- First, there is an initial acquaintanceship phase, where you seek to understand patients' concerns and consider possible courses of action.
- Next, you enter the task implementation phase, where you choose a course of action and see it through.
- Finally, you go through a disengagement phase, where you evaluate the results of your actions, instruct patients on any health-related issues, and send them on their way.

These three phases are experienced no matter how long or short the relationship.

Both you and your patient will enter the relationship with your own needs, expectations, and perceptions. These background factors determine the nature of your relationship with each patient.

Remember that the element of *trust* is central to the professional-patient relationship. Because the interaction between you and your patients occurs in a public context, trust becomes the vehicle that converts casualness to caring. You build trust when you express genuine concern, respect, and feelings of responsibility.

Maintaining Professionalism

Being professional does not mean simply being competent, efficient, and aloof. On the other hand, moving from a totally impersonal to a highly personal relationship is equally inappropriate and not in the patient's (or your own) best interest. You must find a proper balance between the two and then fine-tune that balance for each case. A key factor in attaining this goal is establishing good social relationships in your personal life and being flexible in meeting the challenges of daily life. Then you will have the tools to be more effective in your therapeutic relationships.

Use the following guidelines to help you strike the right balance between acting in a cold, distant manner and being excessively casual.

- Consider your appearance and the messages it sends. Wearing a white coat does not necessarily generate a sense of aloofness; nor does casual dress imply greater caring. But how you dress does affect how you feel, so you should give some consideration to how you look.

- When dealing with a new patient, exercise good judgment in deciding whether to call him by his first name. As a general rule, address people older than you by their surnames unless they ask you to do otherwise.

- Try to appreciate the needs of family members when present. In many cases, they may be undergoing intense distress as well. While your primary responsibility is to the patient, maintaining a positive yet professional relationship with family can help those family members support the patient as well.

- Try to communicate a sense of caring in your relationship with patients. Avoid establishing rigid limits in your interactions, but do try to keep to a schedule.

Your goal should be to combine a friendly approach with professional competence. This means demonstrating respect for each patient's values, beliefs, and needs in the context of proper professional care.

Adhering to Professional Standards

Legal responsibilities, ethics, and patient rights—all of which were discussed in previous chapters—will help determine the type of care provided by health-care workers. In addition, by following certain standards of conduct, practitioners and employees will be protected from liability and patients will more likely receive more optimal personal care. The following basic standards should be observed:

- Perform only those procedures for which you have been trained and are legally permitted to do.

- Use established, proven, and proper methods of carrying out procedures. You should follow the guidelines that were provided during your training. If uncertain, contact a person who can provide guidance for the procedure in question or consult manuals that offer step-by-step instructions. For use of equipment, one should refer to the manufacturer's instructions if the need arises.

- Be sure to obtain the required authorization before any procedure is undertaken. In some situation's authorization to perform a procedure must come from the physician or therapist who is providing patient care. In other cases one must check the patient/client record to see if authorization is indicated. Under some circumstances, it may be necessary to ask your immediate supervisor for assistance in securing necessary authorization.

- Identify the patient with certainty and obtain the patient's consent before performing any procedure. Frequently patients will have an identification band on their arm to confirm their identity. Moreover, you should state the person's name and wait for an affirmative response or reaction before proceeding. Having identified the patient, indicate the procedure you wish to perform and (e.g., inject a regular dose of antibiotics). Secure patient consent, as reflected either by an affirmative response or voicing no objection. Should the patient decline, promptly report the event to your immediate supervisor and await further instructions.

- Observe all necessary safety precautions when using equipment to ensure your own and your patient's safety. You need also to be aware of safety hazards in the areas you are working in and act appropriately.

- Keep all appropriate information confidential. Protect the privacy of patient records or remove any information contained therein without authorization or patient consent. If discussing a patient with a supervisor, do so out of earshot of others. Avoid discussing patient affairs with anyone outside of your health-care facility.

- Treat all patients equally regardless of race, religion, social or economic status, sex, or nationality. It is the obligation of health-care practitioners to provide their services equally to all individuals and to the best of their ability.

- If any significant error occurs or you make a mistake report it immediately to your supervisor. Correct a negative situation as soon as possible and gracefully accept full responsibility for your actions.

- Be professional in dress, language, manners, and actions. You should take pride in your occupation and in the work you do. Present a positive outlook at all times—it's good for your spirits and for those you are committed to serve.

Of course, even when standards are followed, errors leading to legal action may occur. Liability insurance constitutes an additional form of protection in such cases. Many insurance companies offer policies at reasonable cost for health-care workers to cover negligence suits and most hospitals and many other facilities provide such coverage for their workers.

In summary, it is important to be aware that it is your responsibility to understand the legal and ethical implications of your specific health-care career. Do not hesitate to ask questions or to request copies of written policies, when appropriate, from your employer. Contact your State Board of Health or Education to obtain information on regulations and guidelines relative to your occupation. Following these guidelines will provide you, your employer, and your patients with peace of mind.

Understanding Special Needs

All patients or clients are unique. They come with their own specific needs, values, backgrounds, and expectations. However, it can be useful to consider how the professional-patient relationship changes based on certain broad categories of patients. Perhaps the most common way to categorize patients is by age. The following describes specific attitudes and behaviors that can be useful when treating different age groups.

Caring for the Young

Your young patients could be as young as newborn and all the way up to adolescents.

Infants

Some infants have medical problems from birth. These babies require continued, demanding, dedicated care. They cannot express their wants and needs clearly, other than by crying. The needs of the infant fall into two categories: material and psychosocial.

The infant's primary material consideration is the need to eliminate physical discomfort, which may be due to hunger, thirst, irritation from a soiled diaper, or pain. Environmental discomforts may be due to noise, bright lights, or an unpleasant smell. Because infants cannot talk, you must be perceptive to their typical behavior patterns so that you will recognize any unusual behavior when providing care. You also must address the infant patient's psychosocial needs. Above all, this means you must generate trust—for example, by acting in a consistent, gentle manner with your tiny patients.

If you work with infant patients, you should take advantage of the bridge that parents can provide between you and their babies. Parents can be invaluable in providing feedback on an infant's behavior so that the impact of treatment can be fully evaluated and the infant's real needs can be met.

Children

Children deserve the same respect you would give to any other patient. While they spend most of childhood learning to be independent, when they become ill, children tend to regress toward infancy and give up the independence they have worked so hard to acquire. You must recognize this situation and provide needed and tactful support in order to provide a sense of security.

When interacting with children, it is essential to enhance their self-esteem. Approaching the child-patient respectfully, as an individual, will maximize your chance of a successful outcome. Here, too, the family can facilitate a positive response. Remember, the sick child is not your only client—you must support the parents as well. Doing so enables them to support the child, which helps in the recovery process.

You must also be attentive to the sick child's siblings, especially when their relationship is close. A sudden separation between two (or more) such siblings, plus the special attention given to the sick child, can generate a hostile response from those who are well. You should make an effort, where feasible, to minimize the impact of illness on the relationships between siblings. In the long run, doing so will help in the therapeutic process.

Adolescents

It is hard to generalize about adolescents, because their development happens at such variable rates (a polite way of saying their behaviors and attitudes can be unpredictable). This is understandable: During the adolescent stage, the individual must establish his or her own identity, value system, and life philosophy.

You may face special challenges when dealing with adolescents, since they often seek to assert their autonomy in decision making even though they cannot legally do so. The most prominent viewpoint in this area is the *Mature Minors Doctrine*, which allows parents or the state to speak on behalf of a minor's interest only as long as the minor is unable to represent him- or herself. Consequently, an adolescent's maturity level is the essential decisive factor.

Because of this, you should try to assess the maturity of your adolescent patients and respect their autonomy as much as possible. At the same time, you cannot exclude the parents from the decision-making process.

It is important to realize that an adolescent's feelings may fluctuate between the desire for autonomy and a retreat to the submissive state of childhood. An assessment of family relationships will help you decide how to deal with the decision-making process.

Caring for Active Adults

Most health professionals have generally positive relationships with patients in their middle years, but beyond this point, interfacing may prove more difficult. This is because physical ailments during the prime of life are secondary to psychosocial issues, such as work, parenting, and relationships—all of which generate stress. The individual's lifestyle also influences his physical and mental well-being.

Most people in their middle years consider themselves invulnerable to the aches and pains of the elderly. So, if a middle-aged patient experiences these ailments, she may respond with anger or confusion at the disruption in her life. Thus, when a catastrophic illness or injury occurs at this life stage, you may have to help the patient contend with denial, depression, and hostility.

In treating active adults, therefore, you must consider their psychosocial as well as physical needs. If a patient is unable to meet his established responsibilities and life goals, he may feel a sense of estrangement, vulnerability, and frustration coupled with a devastating loss of self-image. All of this engenders stress, which can have profound physical manifestations. As a professional, you must distinguish these manifestations from the genuine physical pain the patient may be experiencing.

You can help diminish your adult patients' anxiety by listening carefully to their concerns and adjusting your treatment approach accordingly.

Caring for the Elderly

In general, treating the elderly is comparable to working with other age groups. However, there are some specific issues of direct relevance to elderly patients. To begin with, many older people experience diminished sensory capacity (such as poor eyesight or bad hearing). Being aware of these limitations will help you interact with your elderly patients effectively and respectfully.

In addition, many older people need routine and schedule to help orient themselves to the time of day. In other words, a stable and predictable lifestyle helps them maintain emotional stability. If you can avoid altering their treatment routines, you can help provide the security and stability they need to recover their health.

Finally, you should remember that elderly patients face a continuing series of devastating losses as they age: They lose friends and family members to death, they lose their work identities to retirement, and many lose their independence to illness and the ravages of age. Being sincere in your care, listening carefully to their concerns, and sometimes just sitting quietly with them can help your older patients more than you know.

As a society, we must recognize that health-care delivery to the elderly is deficient because of a negative bias in this country known as *ageism*. This is reflected in many aspects of seniors' treatment and typically results in elderly people receiving lower-quality care. Becoming cognizant of the problem is the first step toward combating it.

THE JOB SEARCH

Once you have elected to enter the health-care field, chosen your prospective career, and completed your education and training, you are ready to enter the last phase of your endeavor: finding a job.

Securing employment as a health-care professional requires the same approach as for any other position. This means you must network to find job leads and prepare a resume and cover letter to send to prospective employers. You must also hone your skills for the interview that follows if your resume is of interest to a prospective employer. You will find advice on all these aspects of the job search in this section.

Preparing for Your Job Search

Your job search should be directed at finding both the right job and the right employer. You should begin planning your search long before you start sending out resumes to prospective employers. Because your first job can have a big impact on your future success, your preparation is crucial. This chapter helps you avoid some common pitfalls and make good decisions as you proceed. To do this, we outline a series of sequential steps that are essential to your career success.

In fact, the preliminary steps of the search process were laid out in Chapter 2, "Choosing the Best Health-Care Career for You." If you haven't done so, complete the self-evaluation exercises there. If you completed them earlier, review your responses now so that you are in a better position to assess your suitability for openings that come your way.

Defining Your Goals

Before you begin contacting prospective employers, you should develop your own unique job profile. In the worksheet on the following page, list the preferable, acceptable, and unacceptable conditions of any position you would consider.

Characteristics of Your Ideal Position

1. Do you want to work in the United States?
   ___ Yes   ___ No   ___ Preferable, but not mandatory

2. Are you willing to relocate to secure your first job?
   ___ Yes   ___ No

3. Are you willing to relocate periodically if your employer asks you to?
   ___ Yes   ___ No

4. Are you willing to travel as part of your job?
   ___ Yes   ___ No

5. Which part of the country do you prefer? (Number your preferences, with 1 being the most desirable.)
   ___ Northeast   ___ Southeast   ___ Southwest
   ___ Upper Midwest   ___ Lower Midwest   ___ Northwest

6. What kind of location do you prefer? (Number your preferences.)
   ___ Large city   ___ Midsized city
   ___ Small town   ___ Rural/outdoors

7. What size of employer do you prefer? (Number your preferences.)
   ___ Large corporation   ___ Midsized company
   ___ Small company   ___ Self-employed

8. What kind of facility do you prefer? (Number your preferences.)
   ___ Hospital   ___ Residential facility   ___ Outpatient facility

9. If you find a position that meets your preferred working conditions, would you decline it solely because of
   (a) Salary?
   ___ Yes   ___ No

   (b) Benefits (such as health insurance, travel allowance, vacation days, tuition reimbursement, retirement benefits)?
   ___ Yes   ___ No

   (c) The absence of a formal training program?
   ___ Yes   ___ No

Once you have a profile of your "ideal" position, you can use it to judge potential jobs in your field. As you learn more about positions available in your area, you may want to revise your answers.

Identifying Prospective Employers

Your next step in the job search process is to target the potential employers that best meet your needs. If you are still enrolled in an educational program or have access to the program's resources, your first stop should be your school's job placement office. The staff there can help you put together an effective resume or portfolio. Often, they maintain lists of employers in your area and field. They may also direct you to other graduates who are working in the field. These contacts can be invaluable in your job search.

One of the best and most overlooked sources of job leads is your local yellow pages. Look through the listings of facilities in your field, check the ones that most interest you, and then call or visit them directly. Ask if you can tour the facility and meet the human resources staff. Even if they have no openings, they can give you valuable information about the field. They may even direct you to other organizations that do have openings.

Other sources of information on potential job openings are want ads, professional organizations and journals, employment agencies, and the Internet, and perhaps most importantly, networking.

Want Ads

Most newspapers carry employment ads in the Sunday classified ads section. You should recognize at the outset, however, that while these ads are sometimes helpful, they are more often frustrating. Because they generate so many responses, the competition for jobs listed in the want ads is intense. You may find yourself sending in resume after resume with no response. Some people do find jobs through the want ads, and the high demand for many health-care professions means that there are usually many listings available, so you probably should spend some time and effort following up on them—just not at the expense of other approaches that may be more productive.

Read each want ad carefully and see how well it matches your background and interests. If it matches well, you should write a cover letter for the particular position. Wait a week or so before sending this letter and your resume; this ensures that the initial wave of applicants has passed, and your letter will receive closer attention. For more on preparing and sending resumes and cover letters, see Chapter 8.

Professional Organizations and Journals

Professional organizations are great sources of possible job leads. You'll find complete listings of these organizations alphabetically in Appendix B.

You should also spend some time in a medical school or hospital library reviewing the classified ads in the professional journal for your field. For a complete list of professional journals, handbooks, and directories, see Appendix C.

Another valuable source of information on health-care trade magazines is the Magazine Industry Marketplace. This reference book is available at your local library and is revised annually. You can also find lists of openings with the federal government in two biweeklies: *Federal Career Opportunities* and *Federal Jobs Digest*.

Keep in mind that reading journals and joining organizations directly related to your field provides benefits well beyond a list of job openings. Keeping up to date with research and events in your chosen field makes you more knowledgeable and provides information that might come in handy during an interview. Joining professional organizations provides you with a vast network of people with similar career aspirations who can offer you advice or even point you in the direction of organizations that are hiring.

Employment Agencies and Executive Recruiters

With determination and a little luck, the use of an employment agency or an executive recruiter will probably prove unnecessary. However, if such a resource is needed, you should first identify agencies in your area that actively recruit health-care personnel. It is even more valuable if you can locate those that specialize in securing positions for people *in your field*. When you are checking out an agency, ask how many people it has placed in your field in the last two years. Contact local health-care agencies and ask whether they have hired employees from that agency. Finally, be sure to find out whether the agency is paid by the employer who hires you, or whether you must pay for services yourself. Doing your homework can save you from wasting time and money on the wrong agency.

Your next step is to meet with a counselor from your chosen agency. Try to work with only one counselor, and send all correspondence and queries to that person. That way, the counselor is more likely to remember you and to recommend you to potential employers. Treat each meeting with your counselor as you would a job interview. Dress neatly, have all your materials at hand, and focus on making a good impression. Remember, this is the person who will be recommending you (or *not* recommending you) for a job! After each meeting, send a thank-you note to your counselor for his or her time and help. Finally, every other week or so, call your employment counselor to check in and remind him or her of your continued availability.

Because some agencies are paid by the employers they recruit for, and some charge the job seeker for their placement services, you can expect different services from each.

- If you pay for an agency's services, that agency is working for *you*. The counselor's job is to find you a job, so he or she may be more willing to spend time helping you with your resume and cover letter. While this help obviously is valuable, it is not cheap. Many agencies charge as much as 10 percent of your first year's salary for placing you in a job.

- If an agency is paid by the employer to recruit workers, that agency is working for the *company*. You are not charged for their services, but their efforts on your behalf may be limited. The same is true for executive recruiters, who are paid by employers to find high-paid workers such as veterinarians, biomedical engineers, and therapists.

The Internet

Most new college graduates today do at least part of their job searching on the Internet. All the major online commercial services provide networking opportunities as well as job search capabilities in health care. Use bulletin boards to focus on your particular employment needs. Introduce yourself, clearly indicate what kind of position you are seeking, and mention any help you can offer to others. You then have to patiently wait for replies.

A more direct approach is to look for jobs directly on the Internet. Many organizations maintain Web sites listing their current employment opportunities. You can check out your target facility's Web site, learn more about the organization and its openings, and even apply directly online.

Another option is to locate Web sites that list job opportunities for allied health professionals or jobs in your specific area of interest. You can use commonly used sites such as Monster or Career Builder or sites specifically focused on health-care careers, such as Absolutely Health Care. In fact, many larger job posting sites have search engines specifically geared towards health-care positions, such as Monster's focused search at http://healthcare.monster.com. In addition, most job search sites let you post your resume online, and many include additional job search resources, from resume and cover letter help to networking and organizational tools. See Appendix C, "Job Search Resources," for a complete list of suggested health-care career Web sites.

> **TIP:** As with want ads, it's important not to rely solely on the Internet to find a job. Simply posting your resume on job boards and waiting for employers to contact you will yield few results. Use the Internet as a resource for locating potential employers and apply to positions you find online, but don't neglect the other, often more-productive means of finding a job.

Networking: Your Best Source of Job Leads

Securing a job, especially the right one, requires a strong, proactive approach. You need to take the initiative and establish your own web of family, friends, and acquaintances who can pass along relevant job information to you. This kind of activity is known as *networking*, and it is the single most effective way to find job leads. Networking involves contacting everyone you know and asking them whether they know of any job openings in your field, or whether they can refer you to someone else who might know of any openings. Chances are, if you keep at it, networking will lead you to a job interview—or at least to an informational interview.

Use your network of contacts to get names of people who are working in positions similar to the one you want. Then call these people and ask whether they will meet with you to talk about their jobs. These are not job interviews per se; you are simply gathering information at this stage.

During an informational interview, ask the person about the field you are interested in, the company he or she works for, and the position's responsibilities. Specifically, you should ask about three issues at this interview:

- **Training.** Ask whether the company has a training program and how long it lasts. Also ask whether the company provides training for updating or upgrading your skills. Some companies provide their employees with financial help to complete educational course work in their specialties.

- **Salary and benefits.** Ask about the industry standard of compensation for entry-level positions in your field. (Figure 7.1 can provide guidance in this area.) Also ask what benefits the company offers. For example, does it provide health and disability insurance? What about vacation days, stock options, and retirement plans? These are an important part of any compensation package. Be aware that salaries fluctuate dramatically—even for similar positions—based on the location, organization, experience of the applicant, and other factors.

- **Job Requirements.** Ask what the basic requirements are for the job, including education, skills, and experience. Also try to get a sense of what a typical day at that job looks like, what the person likes most and least about the work, and what general advice they would give to someone just entering the profession.

This information can give you a realistic picture of what to expect and what you might ask when you go to an actual job interview. Keep a record of the information you get during your informational interviews. You'll find it invaluable in preparing for job interviews.

When tapping into and expanding your network, don't forget to include clubs or organizations you belong to, professional or otherwise. Interacting with others in your chosen profession, whether in person during conferences or training sessions, or on the Internet through e-mail, blogs, and message boards, can help to generate job leads and perhaps lead to even more career opportunities down the road.

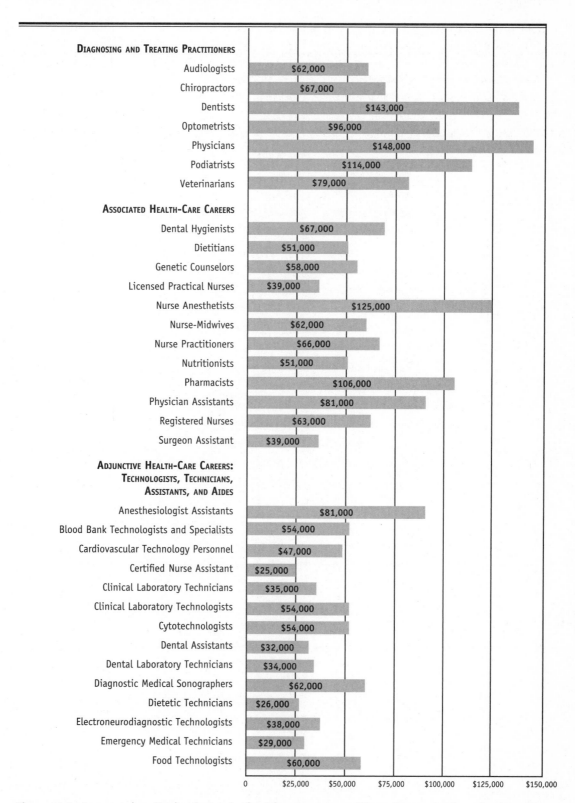

Figure 7.1: Average (median) salaries for health-care careers. These figures are based primarily on numbers released by the U.S. Department of Labor for 2010.

(continued)

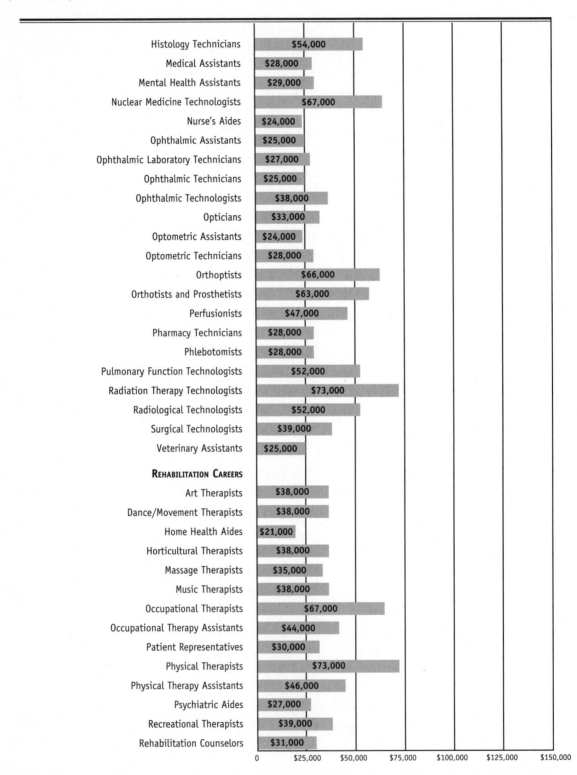

Job	Salary
Histology Technicians	$54,000
Medical Assistants	$28,000
Mental Health Assistants	$29,000
Nuclear Medicine Technologists	$67,000
Nurse's Aides	$24,000
Ophthalmic Assistants	$25,000
Ophthalmic Laboratory Technicians	$27,000
Ophthalmic Technicians	$25,000
Ophthalmic Technologists	$38,000
Opticians	$33,000
Optometric Assistants	$24,000
Optometric Technicians	$28,000
Orthoptists	$66,000
Orthotists and Prosthetists	$63,000
Perfusionists	$47,000
Pharmacy Technicians	$28,000
Phlebotomists	$28,000
Pulmonary Function Technologists	$52,000
Radiation Therapy Technologists	$73,000
Radiological Technologists	$52,000
Surgical Technologists	$39,000
Veterinary Assistants	$25,000
REHABILITATION CAREERS	
Art Therapists	$38,000
Dance/Movement Therapists	$38,000
Home Health Aides	$21,000
Horticultural Therapists	$38,000
Massage Therapists	$35,000
Music Therapists	$38,000
Occupational Therapists	$67,000
Occupational Therapy Assistants	$44,000
Patient Representatives	$30,000
Physical Therapists	$73,000
Physical Therapy Assistants	$46,000
Psychiatric Aides	$27,000
Recreational Therapists	$39,000
Rehabilitation Counselors	$31,000

0    $25,000 $50,000 $75,000 $100,000 $125,000 $150,000

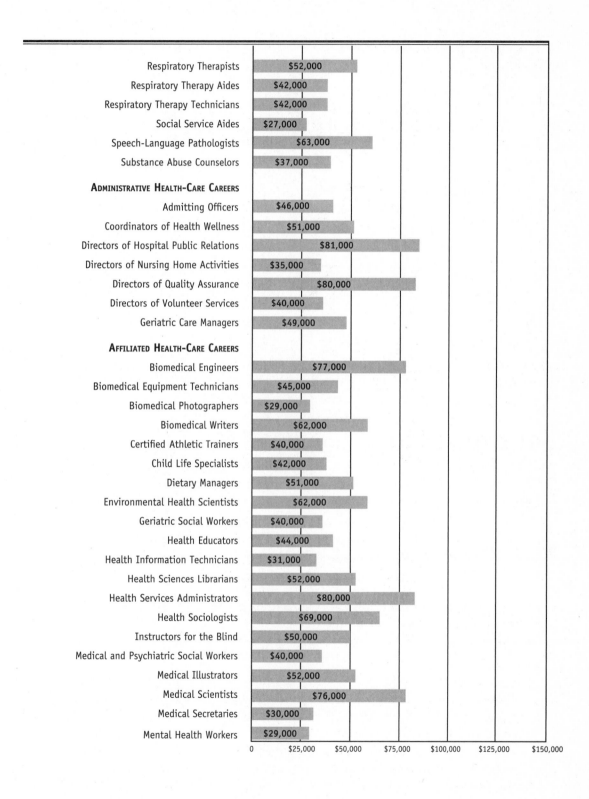

Respiratory Therapists	$52,000
Respiratory Therapy Aides	$42,000
Respiratory Therapy Technicians	$42,000
Social Service Aides	$27,000
Speech-Language Pathologists	$63,000
Substance Abuse Counselors	$37,000
ADMINISTRATIVE HEALTH-CARE CAREERS	
Admitting Officers	$46,000
Coordinators of Health Wellness	$51,000
Directors of Hospital Public Relations	$81,000
Directors of Nursing Home Activities	$35,000
Directors of Quality Assurance	$80,000
Directors of Volunteer Services	$40,000
Geriatric Care Managers	$49,000
AFFILIATED HEALTH-CARE CAREERS	
Biomedical Engineers	$77,000
Biomedical Equipment Technicians	$45,000
Biomedical Photographers	$29,000
Biomedical Writers	$62,000
Certified Athletic Trainers	$40,000
Child Life Specialists	$42,000
Dietary Managers	$51,000
Environmental Health Scientists	$62,000
Geriatric Social Workers	$40,000
Health Educators	$44,000
Health Information Technicians	$31,000
Health Sciences Librarians	$52,000
Health Services Administrators	$80,000
Health Sociologists	$69,000
Instructors for the Blind	$50,000
Medical and Psychiatric Social Workers	$40,000
Medical Illustrators	$52,000
Medical Scientists	$76,000
Medical Secretaries	$30,000
Mental Health Workers	$29,000

0    $25,000 $50,000 $75,000 $100,000 $125,000 $150,000

Finding a Job

Once you have identified job openings, the next challenge is to sell yourself to the employer. In this chapter you'll find suggestions for creating your marketing tools (your resume and cover letter), for handling applications and exams, and for interviewing effectively.

Your Resume

Your resume serves as a snapshot of your education, skills, and experience. To prepare it properly you have to be fully acquainted with the details of your career and the job you seek. An attractive resume is aimed at securing an invitation to come in for an interview. This is the next step in the job search process.

What Your Resume Should Include

Your resume should contain the following information:

- **Your contact information.** You should provide your full home address, phone number, and e-mail address.
- **Your career goal.** Carefully and precisely summarize the kind of job you are seeking.
- **Your education.** Beginning with the most recent educational institution you've attended, list all your completed degrees, diplomas, and certificates going back to high school. List the name and address of each institution, the years you attended, the degree or diploma your received, and (where appropriate) your major. You can also include any specialized training you've received or relevant workshops or conferences you've been a part of.
- **Honors, awards, and recognition.** List any recognition of special abilities or service you received during your school years. These may include specific awards, membership in honor societies, or being elected to school office.

- **Work experience.** List all the places you've worked, starting with the most recent. Include summer, part-time, and volunteer positions. Identify the length of time you were employed, your job title, and your major accomplishments on the job.
- **Qualifications.** As specifically as possible, list the skills you have to do the job you want. Include the names and types of software and equipment you can use.
- **Special abilities.** This section gives you an opportunity to promote yourself by identifying your special skills or unique achievements. If you set up a successful mini-business during school, list it here. If you held a job, ran track, belonged to a service club, and still managed to get good grades in school, that's something to list! Try to demonstrate your creativity, organizational skills, team spirit, and social/cultural activities. Indicate your special musical skills, community service activities, foreign language ability, and hobbies.

Using Information About the Target Position

Knowing the facts about the position you want allows you to demonstrate your suitability for it. After reviewing the job openings, identify the educational requirements and qualifications for each one. Make note of any prior experience required and the job's responsibilities. Then match these requirements and responsibilities to your personal assets. Now you can customize your resume to meet the prospective employer's needs.

Keep in mind that most employers receive many resumes for each job opening—sometimes hundreds. Frequently personnel managers expedite their review by simply scanning cover letters and resumes. That's why these marketing tools should be as attractive as possible. Your resume should be eye-catching (but still professional) and should focus the reviewer's attention on your candidacy and credentials.

Resume-Preparation Issues to Keep in Mind

You should focus on a number of issues in preparing your resume:

- **Brevity.** Don't assume that a longer resume is a better resume. Your resume should be no more than two pages. This means you must write in a brief, concise fashion. When presenting a project you successfully completed, list only the major elements of your activities rather than describing the protocol in detail. Try to get the basics across and leave the details for an interview.
- **Word choice.** Use action words that reflect accomplishment, such as *organized, designed,* and *implemented.* These imply intense personal involvement; they show that you have potential. Other words that leave a positive impression are *analyzed, created, developed, planned,* and *increased.* Whenever possible, use numbers or figures to document your achievements.
- **Presentation.** Make your resume as attractive as possible without resorting to gimmicks. The layout should be simple and clean. Proper spacing and use of margins, headings, and italics can make your information clear and more interesting. Your resume is like a commercial: The better it looks, the more likely your chances for success. Use a laser printer or have your resume

reproduced by a professional printer. In either case, use a high-quality paper in white, off-white, or pale gray with a contrasting ink.

- **Clarity.** Be sure the information you provide is accurate and as complete as possible for the reader to evaluate your abilities and potential. Don't exaggerate to enhance your appeal, and avoid being vague if you are trying to "cover up" information. Such a tactic may be a red flag that arouses the reader's attention. Have someone review your resume to ensure it has no grammatical errors, and use the computer spell-check for accuracy. Set aside the draft copy for a short while and then proofread it carefully before printing the final draft. Whenever possible, have someone else look over your resume as well.

> **TIP:** Some research positions and professional medical careers may request a *curriculum vitae* (or CV) rather than a resume. A CV emphasizes education and includes a more exhaustive listing of professional experience. It usually includes any publications, studies, or other academic achievements or credentials. Unlike resumes, CVs can run several pages long.

Sample Resumes

On pp. 91–96, you will find some sample resumes for various positions in the health-care field. These resumes were written by professional resume writers and originally appeared in *Expert Resumes for Health Care Careers*, Second Edition, by Wendy S. Enelow and Louise M. Kursmark (published by JIST Publishing).

❦ GINNY DIAZ, LPN ❦

822 Ely Avenue ◆ Bronx, NY 10466 ◆ 212-324-1934 ◆ gdiaz10@yahoo.com

LICENSED PRACTICAL NURSE

High-energy LPN with sound nursing skills; a pleasant, upbeat style; and a demonstrated commitment to service and performance excellence

❦ PROFILE ❦

- Well-regarded LPN with a wealth of diverse experience in family practice, triage, personal nursing, and other specialty nursing settings. Skilled in both direct service and supervisory roles.
- Highly perceptive individual with ability to quickly assess patient condition and determine appropriate escalations.
- Service-driven professional with top-notch communications skills. Able to build easy rapport with others, putting them at ease while building a sense of confidence and trust.
- Effective multitasker; a take-charge leader who thrives in busy, fast-paced environments.
- Respected team player known for willingness to go the extra mile to deliver the best care to both patients and family members.

❦ NURSING EXPERIENCE ❦

WOODLAWN RETIREMENT CENTER, Bronx, NY   2008 to present
Supervising Nurse
Lead team of 10 certified nursing aides in delivering both personal nursing and skilled nursing care to 60 residents/patients in retirement community with aging population. Supervise staff and manage scheduling issues. Handle medication rounds, verify physician orders, and provide wound care.

Patient Care
- Established record of success in providing patient services in absence of onsite doctor. Quickly and accurately assess patient condition, making sound judgments regarding need for advanced medical attention.
- Developed strong relationships with patients' on-call doctors, facilitating communications to ensure that patient care needs are clearly understood and appropriately met.
- Effectively establish rapport with family members, fostering a sense of confidence and professionalism. Built reputation as knowledgeable, trusted resource who readily goes "above and beyond" to help others.

Leadership & Supervision
- Brought new level of respect for staff to supervisory role, leveraging team-oriented, hands-on approach to reduce turnover while building sense of trust and loyalty.
- Raised team performance, placing renewed emphasis on quality assurance standards to ensure that patients consistently receive the best care.
- Took head-on approach to conflict resolution, stepping in to help parties explore issues and find mutually acceptable solutions while cultivating a collaborative, team-oriented work environment that promotes service excellence.

YONKERS CARDIOLOGY, Yonkers, NY   2004 to 2008
Triage Nurse
Provided telephone support to cardiology patients in busy medical practice while supporting doctors by checking vital signs, conducting EKGs, and providing face-to-face counseling in office.
- Earned praise from patients for service excellence despite challenges of working in very busy office.

Figure 8.1: A concise professional profile leads off this resume for an experienced LPN. It is followed by an extensive account of her work experience, with a heavy emphasis on her most recent position highlighting her supervisory skills as well as her patient care. Submitted by Carol Altomare, Three Bridges, NJ.

(continued)

(continued)

HEALTH SERVICE GROUP OF NEW YORK, Bronx, NY   2002 to 2004
Staff Nurse
Provided nursing support to detainees and inmates in jails in Westchester and Rockland counties.
- Effectively conducted medical screenings in challenging environment, leveraging strong communication skills to gain respect and set appropriate boundaries.
- Capably assessed new inmates to identify physical and mental conditions requiring medical attention.

WECARE DOCTORS GROUP, Tuckahoe, NY   2000 to 2001
Staff Nurse
Provided nursing support to all age groups, from infants to geriatrics, in extremely busy 10-physician medical practice. Conducted occupational health testing and phlebotomy. Administered injections.
- Built reputation for caring, compassionate style and ability to put patients at ease.

EMERGENCY CARE CENTER OF YONKERS, Yonkers, NY   1998 to 2000
Staff Nurse
Gained broad exposure to nursing in busy walk-in clinic.
- Quickly came up to speed in fast-paced environment, readily absorbing best practices from senior-level staff.
- Gained recognition for willingness to take on any challenge and success in anticipating doctor needs.

❧ LICENSURE & EDUCATION ❧

Licensed Practical Nurse, 1998
Completed Practical Nursing program at Westchester Technical School.

Currently enrolled in A.S. program in nursing (expected completion date May 2010), SUNY

ANDREW REEVES

833 Hillview Court • Fairfax, VA 22031
(703) 379-9201 • andrewr@email.com

PHYSICAL THERAPIST ASSISTANT

Three years of experience in a team-oriented, outpatient facility specializing in *orthopedics* and *sports therapy*. Accustomed to working with diverse patients, including professional athletes and the elderly. Contributed articles to a sports-related performance and injury-prevention newsletter. Experienced in conducting presentations on clinical practices and current research studies. Graduated with academic and clinical honors.

Licensure: Physical Therapist Assistant, Virginia

Affiliations: American Physical Therapy Association (APTA)
Member Fairfax County Runners Club, Northern Virginia Masters Swim Team

Certifications: Cardiopulmonary Resuscitation (CPR)/First Aid
Certified Fitness Instructor (CFI), National Strength Professionals Association (NSPA)

RELEVANT EXPERIENCE

DUNHILL ORTHOPEDICS AND SPORTS THERAPY, Manassas, VA   2007–Present
Physical Therapist Assistant (PTA)

Collaborate with Physical Therapists (PTs) in administering patient treatment plans in this outpatient orthopedic and sports therapy practice.
- Work independently with up to 20 patients per day, recovering from orthopedic and sports injuries.
- Work with five PTs with varied treatment styles and expertise and assist in supervising PTA students.
- Assist PTs in obtaining objective and subjective information and providing patient status for reevaluations and progress notes.
- Document problematic situations and collaborate with PTs to implement appropriate intervention.
- Instruct patients' family members in participating in patient treatment and discharge planning.
- Participate in biweekly Journal Club and in-service presentations among coworkers, including orthopedic surgeons, PTs, and athletic trainers.

POWERHOUSE GYM, Arlington, VA   2006–2008
Personal Trainer

Developed and implemented individual general fitness, weight loss, and sports-specific exercise programs for clients with a broad range of fitness levels and goals.

MONROE PHYSICAL & AQUATIC THERAPY ASSOCIATES, Rockville, MD   2005–2007
Physical Therapy Aide

Assisted patients with correct application of therapeutic exercises in the clinic and in aquatic therapy. Assisted PT in transferring patients in and out of the hydrotherapy pool. Provided immediate standby assistance to patients performing therapeutic exercises in an aquatic environment. Maintained patient records and scheduled and supervised maintenance of clinic modalities and equipment.

CLINICAL AFFILIATIONS

Performed the following eight-week rotations in acute care and outpatient settings:
- *Dunhill Orthopedics and Sports Therapy,* Silver Spring, MD, 2007
- *Johns Hopkins University Hospital,* Baltimore, MD, 2006
- *Steven Onslow* (Private Practice), Wheaton, MD, 2006

EDUCATION

A.A.S., Physical Therapist Assistant, George Mason University, Fairfax, VA, 2007
4.0 GPA • Outstanding Clinical Performance Award, Physical Therapist Assistant Program

Completed coursework and received CEUs covering a variety of techniques and pathologies of the lumbar spine, thoracic and cervical spine, shoulder, and geriatric knee.

Figure 8.2: In a concise one-page format, this resume showcases a wide range of personal abilities for a Physical Therapist Assistant who is also a Certified Fitness Instructor. Submitted by Bill Kinser, Fairfax, VA.

LISA A. MILLS, RT-M, LRT
414 St. John Place
Rochester, New York 14623
585-765-4321
millsla@earthlink.com

RADIOLOGIC TECHNOLOGIST / MAMMOGRAPHY TECHNOLOGIST
Healthcare ♦ Teaching ♦ Consulting / Private Industry

Accomplished healthcare professional with track record of acquiring and applying leading-edge technologies and procedures in clinical settings. Outstanding patient rapport and exceptional patient satisfaction. Superb teamwork skills, plus strong organizational/administrative capabilities. Excellent project management skills, encompassing sourcing and purchasing capital equipment and supplies, collaborating with engineers on facilities-construction issues, and developing written procedures for new clinical techniques.

PROFESSIONAL EXPERIENCE

ROCHESTER GENERAL HOSPITAL; Rochester, New York (1992–Present)

Mammography / Radiologic Technician—Women's Health Center   **2005–Present**

- See up to 30 mammogram patients daily.
- Assist physicians with various procedures, including stereotactic procedures and breast biopsies.
- Educate patients about procedures and train coworkers in new protocols.
- Ensure that quality standards, including Mammography Quality Standards Act (MQSA) inspection requirements, are maintained.

Key Accomplishments:

Chosen to serve on team that pioneered Women's Health Center at Rochester General Hospital, with specific accountability for setup and launch of Mammography Department.

- Conferred with clinical engineers and medical physicists on the physical layout of the department.
- Ensured that facilities met federal and state regulations for quality standards and environmental issues.
- Sourced and evaluated equipment and supplies; made purchase recommendations to decision-makers.
- Wrote manuals and policies for mammography, breast biopsies, and other related procedures.

Played a key role in introducing stereotactic breast biopsy procedures to the department.

- Evaluated equipment and reviewed facilities needs for this new technology.
- Established sterile processes and set up surgical procedures.
- Collaborated with other hospital departments to ensure that all clinical requirements were met.
- Coordinated administrative procedures with outpatient registration and nursing staff to facilitate processing of patients and proper charting/documentation.

Radiologic Technologist   **1992–2005**
Performed general radiography tests and procedures.
- Utilized portable radiography equipment and performed operating-room procedures.
- Conducted gastro-intestinal (GI) tract and vascular tests.
- Performed mammography tests until joining Women's Health Center in 2005.
- Maintained positive and productive rapport with emergency, nursing, and OR departments.

Key Accomplishment:

Pioneered introduction of mammography to RGH in 1986. Acquired specialized training, instructed colleagues in newly learned techniques, and ensured that strict quality standards were maintained. Functioned as in-house mammography specialist, leading to participation in setup of Women's Health Center.

Figure 8.3: This Radiologic/Mammography Technologist helped pioneer several new technologies, and her contributions are highlighted in the strong Key Accomplishments segments of her resume. Submitted by Arnold Boldt, Rochester, NY.

ADDITIONAL EXPERIENCE

FINGER LAKES COMMUNITY COLLEGE; Canandaigua, New York
Adjunct Instructor   **1993–Present**
Train and mentor college students majoring in Radiologic Technology.
- Follow three to four students during extensive clinical rotations.
- Provide hands-on training on various equipment and procedures.
- Conduct competency tests to establish students' speed and accuracy in performing tests.

EAST ROCHESTER UNION FREE SCHOOL DISTRICT; Rochester, New York
Mentor   **1996–1997**
Introduced middle school students to radiography as a potential career choice. Allowed students to observe day-to-day activities and responded to questions about radiography.

EDUCATION

FINGER LAKES COMMUNITY COLLEGE; Canandaigua, New York
Associate of Applied Science, Radiologic Technology   **1991**
GPA: 3.75; Honors Graduate

Associate of Applied Science, Secretarial Science (Medical)   **1989**
GPA: 3.5

PROFESSIONAL DEVELOPMENT

SLOAN-KETTERING CANCER INSTITUTE; New York, New York
—Breast Radiology, Chemotherapy & Radiation Therapy, Stereotactic Positioning (one-day program)

Numerous additional continuing education programs and professional conferences.

TECHNICAL PROFICIENCIES

Fisher Stereotactic Table; LoRad Mammography techniques; GE and Phillips radiology equipment.
Windows, Microsoft Office, online patient information systems.

LICENSURE

American Registry of Radiologic Technologists (1991–Present).
American Registry of Radiologic Technologists—Mammography (1998–Present).
NYS Department of Health—Diagnostic Radiology (1991–Present).

Priscilla K. Balding

3333 Tree Lane
Spokane, WA 99214
(509) 727-7347

Pharmacy — Medical Billing — Medical Office Administration

PROFILE

Team- spirited professional, patient and resourceful. Positive attitude, creative thinker/problem solver—effective in streamlining operations, improving productivity, and reducing costs.

Able to handle multiple responsibilities, set priorities, clearly communicate ideas to others, and respond positively to demanding situations. Recognized for speed, accuracy, quality of work, and outstanding customer service.

QUALIFICATIONS

- Insurance Billing—online and hand- billing experience for all insurances including Medicare and Medicaid—detailed working knowledge of insurance plans, overrides, and billing codes.
- 11 years of pharmacy experience—drug formulary, ingredients, compounding, analyzing prescriptions, inventory management, and recordkeeping.
- Outstanding customer service—recipient of numerous "Mystery Shopper" Customer Service Awards.

Added Value:

- 10+ years of experience in hospitality industry—catering, staff management, and event planning.

CAREER SUMMARY

Pharmacy Technician Level A, Rite- Aid, Spokane, WA, 2002–Present
Completed training program to become PTLA while working as cashier.

Main source of flow for prescriptions—analyze prescriptions; type prescriptions; count, compound, and dispense drugs. Order drugs and supplies. Provide extensive, caring, and informed Customer Service—established loyal customer base.

Access insurance company computers—set up prescriptions, calculate supply and quantity—utilize knowledge of limitations of different insurance plans. Maintain customer records and profiles on nationally linked proprietary computer system.

Assistant Manager, Wellington Yacht Club, Spokane, WA, 1996–1999
Answered to Board of Directors and General Manager of Catering and Fine Dining establishment.

Supervised up to 30 employees in all aspects of food and beverage area of Club. Assisted chef with menu planning and food- cost control. Instrumental in bringing about modernization of service styles. Initiated systems to improve efficiency and food service.

Food and Beverage/Catering Manager, Holiday Inn, Spokane, WA, 1995–2002 *(now Best Western Lakeway)*

Oversaw staff of 60+ people—purchasing, scheduling, event planning, and budgeting. Assisted chef with menu planning. Involved with entire remodel and re- imaging of hotel and lounge—participated in selecting and training staff, initiating new procedures, and implementing new computer system.

PROFESSIONAL DEVELOPMENT

Washington State Pharmacy Technician License—current
Pharmacy Training, Rite- Aid
Coursework in Accounting/General Business, City Community College

Figure 8.4: To cover a lot of ground for an experienced Pharmacy Technician who is considering other medical-related career options, this resume includes both pharmacy and business-management experience and achievements. Submitted by Janice Shepherd, Bellingham, WA.

Your Cover Letter

Every resume you send out should be accompanied by a cover letter. This provides employers with their first impression of you, and it should entice the reader to look carefully at your resume. The resume outlines your skills and experience; the cover letter ties these features to a future employer's specific needs. Thus, while the resumes you send out are fairly standardized, each cover letter should be modified to meet a potential employer's requirements.

A good cover letter accomplishes several things:

- It generates interest in your resume.
- It showcases your best skills and applies them directly to the job description.
- It provides a favorable indication of your written communication skills.
- It gives attractive, concrete facts about you and your background.

The Elements of a Cover Letter

The cover letter usually consists of four elements: the salutation, the opening, the body, and the closing:

- **Salutation.** If at all possible, address your letter to a specific individual. This may be someone in the personnel department, a department head, or a pro-spective supervisor. Be sure you spell the person's name correctly.
- **Opening.** Your focus should be to secure the reader's interest. If a mutual acquaintance suggested you write to this person, mention that acquaintance by name. If you are responding to an ad, note that in the letter.
- **Body.** Emphasize your special interest in the company by noting some of its favorable aspects, such as awards it has received, research breakthroughs, or a close match with your background and interest. You can secure this information from the business press, local newspapers, or the Internet. Also use this space to emphasize the two or three skills, accomplishments, or personal characteristics that make you an ideal candidate for the job.
- **Closing.** To close the letter, clearly emphasize your genuine interest in the position and ask to meet with the reader at his or her earliest convenience. Beneath the closing paragraph, type "Sincerely," and then leave three blank lines for your signature. Type your name beneath your signature. Make sure your phone number and e-mail address are listed on both your cover letter and your resume.

Print your letter on high-quality paper to match your resume. Be sure to keep a copy of each letter you send.

Sample Cover Letters

On pp. 98–100, you'll find some sample cover letters for positions in the health-care field. These letters were written by professional resume writers and originally appeared in *Gallery of Best Cover Letters* by David F. Noble (published by JIST Publishing).

March 21, 2010

Mr. William Babinski
Staffing Director
Chambers Medical Clinic
Duluth, Minnesota

RE: MEDICAL TRANSCRIPTIONIST

Dear Mr. Babinski:

Enclosed is a resume for the posted position.

Graduating with honors in 2009 from the medical transcription certification program at Manchester Community and Technical College, I am ready to begin the career for which I have worked so hard.

My medical records experience will be especially helpful in this position. Not only am I highly familiar with patient record management, but also I bring the following:

- ◆ Positive collaboration with physicians and other medical personnel
- ◆ Understanding of team concepts, legalities, confidentiality, hospital code and patient rights
- ◆ Experience working with pneumatic record transport systems
- ◆ Multicultural experience

General business skills complement my experience. This includes data entry, word processing, strong communication skills and accuracy, as well as the ability to monitor my own work. I've established a good track record for a positive attitude, initiative, organizational skills, pride in my work, confidence and team spirit.

I very much look forward to hearing from you regarding this position.

Sincerely,

Nina Altonson

NINA ALTONSON

Chauncey Court #16
Rochester MN 55555

(555) 555-5555

naltonson@yahoo.com

MEDICAL OFFICE PROFESSIONAL

◆◆◆

BUSINESS SKILLS

Data Entry 12,500 KPH
Telephone Skills
Pneumatic Record Transport System
Facilitation
Problem Solving
Customer Service
Filing (Numeric & Alpha)
Training of Staff

CULTURAL DIVERSITY & LANGUAGE

Four Years of Spanish
Extensive Travel–Western U.S.
Multicultural Experience

Figure 8.5: This letter for a Medical Transcriptionist uses a multicolumn format to produce good results. Submitted by Beverley Drake, Rochester, MN.

Frances C. MacSorley

1212 Juniper Circle
North Kingman, CT 66666

(000) 222-1111   francesmac@earthlink.com   Cell: (000) 222-3333

January 27, 2010

Philippe J. Desjardin
Director of Human Resources
New Haven Memorial Hospital
111 Brently Street
New Haven, CT 00000

Dear Mr. Desjardin:

This letter is in response to your advertisement in *The New Haven Sunday Times*, January 27, 2010, for a Licensed Practical Nurse to be employed at the Leone Mathieu Life Care Center.

I believe that my qualifications are strong for this position, for my 15 years in practical nursing have given me excellent professional experience in addition to my personal career objective of providing and maintaining the highest level of nursing care and quality of life to patients under my charge. My total nursing experience has been, and continues to be, full-time, direct patient care.

Always deeply committed to the nursing profession, I have striven to keep abreast of the latest data through in-service learning and reading various journals and selected publications. Courses taken in the liberal arts are in direct preparation for my Associate degree as a Registered Nurse. Moreover, they have broadened my capacity to deal with humanitarian issues that are so much a part of healing.

If you agree with me that my credentials are sound for this position at the Leone Mathieu Life Care Center, I would very much appreciate an opportunity to meet with you to discuss my candidacy for this opening at Memorial Hospital. I can be reached by e-mail, at my home after 5 p.m., or at any time by my cell phone to schedule an appointment at a time that is convenient to you.

Thank you for considering me for this position; I look forward to hearing from you soon.

Sincerely,

Frances C. MacSorley

Enclosures: résumé / application

Figure 8.6: After 15 years in practical nursing, this applicant wanted another LPN position while she worked on her registered nursing degree. The letter shows her commitment to nursing and humanitarian issues. Submitted by Edward Turilli, North Kingstown, RI.

Elizabeth Santiago

11 Riverside Drive   (555) 555-5555
New York, NY 10023   esantiago@xyz.com

April 23, 2010

Michael Kahn
Director of Human Resources
St. Luke's–Roosevelt Hospital Center
Roosevelt Division
1000 Tenth Avenue at 58 th Street
New York, NY 10019

Dear Mr. Kahn:

After reading about your organization's new health care initiatives, as described on the hospital's Web site, I was excited to learn of an opening for a Clinical Laboratory Scientist. My background in developing and implementing testing and instrumentation procedures can bring an immediate benefit to the hospital as it strives to improve patient care. I am enclosing my resume for your review.

With 15 years of experience in the hematology and pathology departments of two major teaching hospitals, I am able to prioritize workflow and resolve problems to ensure the efficiency and accuracy of department operations. In particular, I have reviewed and revised operating procedures to achieve regulatory compliance. Among my key accomplishments are the following:

- Managed installation and implementation of new coagulation system, including writing procedures and training staff. Coordinated with multiple departments for successful completion within a one-month time line.

- Integrated a standardized coagulation system across two hospital campuses to ensure better patient care and quality assurance.

- Established, wrote, and set up a preventative maintenance schedule for hematology instrumentation to ensure the quality of performance.

I look forward to the opportunity to talk with you in person about the contribution I can make to your hospital. You can reach me at (555) 555-5555.

Thank you for your consideration.

Sincerely,

Elizabeth Santiago

Enclosure

Figure 8.7: This Clinical Laboratory Scientist did background research on the prospective employer's Web site and links her accomplishments directly to the mission of the company. Submitted by Wendy Gelberg, Needham, MA.

Job Applications

Some large firms, government agencies, and hospitals use their own application forms rather than resumes (or in addition to them) to evaluate prospective candidates. The application's uniform structure helps the evaluator find the information he or she needs and allows for easy comparisons between candidates. Because applications don't let you present your qualifications the way *you* typically would, you should plan ahead of time how to present them under the categories most applications contain.

Job Application Tips

When completing an application, keep in mind the following tips:

- Ask for two copies of the application. That way, you can use one copy to prepare a first draft. And, if you make a mistake, you can use the second form.
- Read it before you complete it. Familiarize yourself with the form so that you can relate it to sections in your resume.
- When possible, complete the application at home and photocopy it.
- Print neatly in dark blue or black ink.
- When you are applying for several positions in the same company, you can leave the specific job title blank. Do not leave any other blanks on the application. If a question is not relevant to you, write N/A (not applicable) in the space provided.
- Sometimes you must fill out an application at the employment site, so be sure to take a copy of your resume with you. You might also find it useful to take a list of standard answers to commonly asked questions. Also take your complete list of references, along with their addresses and phone numbers.
- As with your resume, the answers you provide on an application form should be direct, accurate, and honest.

Bear in mind that more and more applications are being filled out online. Often employers will request that an electronic copy of your resume be sent alongside the application. When sending an electronic copy of your resume, format it simply and in a standard font (such as Arial or Times). Save it as a rich text file or PDF document, and be sure to send your cover letter as an attachment whenever possible.

Job Examinations

The most common job exams are those for civil service appointments. For these and similar tests you can and should prepare adequately. Government agencies usually provide samples of exams, and copies may be available at your local library. You can also find standardized test preparation books in a wide variety of fields at your local bookstore.

By practicing beforehand, you will improve your performance level, you'll be less nervous the day of the test, and you'll be familiar with the kinds of questions you'll have to answer.

Study Guidelines

Here are some general study guidelines for preparing for tests:

- Familiarize yourself with the major topics you must master.
- Begin your study sessions with your strongest area.
- Do a quick review of the material before beginning your intensive study.
- Determine the sequence of the information you must learn. Try to master it in a logical grouping rather than as isolated facts.
- Use your most successful study techniques to prepare for the exam.
- Before memorizing information, make sure you understand it.
- Keep your study sessions to a reasonable time limit, bearing in mind your physical and mental well-being.
- Remember that you will remember facts better if you can associate them with something you already know.
- Frequent, short, intense review periods are more useful than long study sessions.
- Getting a good night's sleep after intense evening study consolidates the material in your memory and thus enhances retention.

Test-Day Preparations

For the test day itself, make the following preparations:

- Prepare what you will need the night before (such as pencils, a calculator, and any reference materials you are allowed to bring).
- Get a good night's sleep the night before the exam. Avoid last-minute cramming.
- Arrive at the test center 5 to 30 minutes before the starting time.
- Use the restroom before the test begins.
- Before answering any questions, read through the instructions carefully and make sure you understand them.
- Do not spend too much time on any one question. Because you have only a limited amount of time, speed counts; a significant delay can prove costly if you don't have time to answer the questions you do know.

The Interview

The interview is probably the most critical element in securing any job. The goals of your cover letter and resume are to secure this opportunity to sell yourself.

Your interview goals are twofold:

1. **You want to show the employer you have the qualifications and the personality characteristics necessary for the job.** The interviewer will be looking for signs that you can do the work and that you will fit into the organization's social structure. He or she may also have unanswered questions about your records.

2. **You want to gather information** about working conditions, job responsibilities, and your compatibility with your potential supervisor. After all, *you* may discover that the job is not a good fit for you, even if the employer thinks otherwise.

Preparing for Interviews

To a large extent, your success in an interview depends on the amount of preparation you do *before* the interview.

- **Know your background.** Your resume is a "cold" outline of your professional life. During the interview, you can add the details that will enhance your chances. You might say, for example, "I had to work occasionally until late at night to meet the position's emergency needs." Or, "I recommended, ordered, and set up this piece of equipment that enhanced the efficiency of my workplace." Or, "I am especially proud of the following accomplishment...."

- **Take stock of your assets.** Make a list of your personal and professional abilities that will enhance your appeal to a prospective employer. On the personal side these might include punctuality, dependability, and good interpersonal relationship skills. Professionally you may want to emphasize a sense of commitment and dedication, loyalty, inquisitiveness, and a desire to take initiative.

- **Be informed about the position.** Get as much information about the job as you possibly can. Try to learn about its duties, responsibilities, and requirements. This will help you match your assets to the needs of the position so that you can present this match to your interviewer.

- **Do a mock interview.** It is natural to be nervous when facing an interview. You can ease this nervousness by practicing the interview experience. Have a friend pretend to be the interviewer. Prepare a list of questions you think will be asked. Have your friend ask them, and practice giving your answers until they come to you naturally and fluently. You can use the following questions as the basis for your mock interview:

  - How did you learn about this opening?
  - Why did you apply for this position?
  - What aspects of the position do you find most appealing?
  - What from your education or work experience is most relevant to this job?
  - Tell me about yourself.
  - What are your career goals?
  - What are your greatest assets and liabilities?
  - Describe a challenging situation you faced and tell how you handled it.
  - Where do you see yourself five years from now?
  - Were you ever terminated from a position? If so, why?
  - How do you deal with difficult patients?
  - Give me an example of when you took on a leadership role.

- Why should we hire you over other qualified candidates?
- Do you have any questions?

> **TIP:** Don't discuss salary during a first interview. If the interviewer brings it up, be as general as possible. For example, if you are asked what kind of salary you expect, you might say, "That depends on the work and on what kinds of opportunities are available." Wait until you have a job offer before you begin negotiating a salary.

Other Tips for Interview Success

In addition to practicing for the interview, there are some simple things you can do to increase your chances of success:

- Get a good night's sleep so that you are rested and alert.
- Shower in the morning; it will help you relax.
- Dress neatly and be properly groomed so that you make a good first impression.
- Arrive 15 minutes early for the interview so that you can adjust to the surroundings.
- Don't be upset if your interview session is delayed.
- When the interviewer arrives, greet him or her with a firm handshake.
- Stay as relaxed as possible. Try taking several deep breaths and exhaling slowly just before you enter the interviewer's office.
- Carry a copy of your resume with you.
- Make small talk at the beginning of the interview by commenting on the weather or something of interest in the person's office.
- Be courteous and friendly. Remember to smile.
- Maintain eye contact throughout the interview.
- Answer the questions honestly. Don't try to anticipate what the interviewer might want to hear.
- Be as straightforward and accurate as possible in your answers.
- If you respond poorly to a question, let it pass. Don't let it upset you for the rest of the interview.
- Try to be as natural as possible.
- Try to sell your assets by fitting them into the interview.

Questions to Ask

Once the interviewer has asked all his or her questions, it's your turn. The interviewer probably will ask if you have any questions. If not, seize the moment yourself by saying, "May I ask you some questions?" You will undoubtedly receive a positive response. Be sure to have some questions prepared ahead of time. Here are some good examples:

- What challenges does the position present?
- Would I be working alone, or will I be part of a group?

- To whom would I report? Would it be possible to meet that person?
- Would I supervise anyone? If so, could I meet them?
- Who will evaluate my performance? How, and how often?
- How can I advance in the company?
- What are this organization's plans for the future?
- How did this opening come about?
- What benefits does the company offer its employees?

Closing the Interview

At the end of the interview, thank the interviewer and ask about the next step in the hiring process. Ask whether you can provide any additional information. Express your genuine interest in the position (if that is the case), and say you are looking forward to hearing from the interviewer.

Following Up

As soon as you arrive home from the interview, sit down and write a brief note, thanking the interviewer for his or her time. Mention how much you enjoyed meeting the person, recap any pertinent things you have in common, and again emphasize that you'd like to talk again. Send the note the same day so that it arrives only a day or two after the interview.

Don't spend a lot of time and agony trying to judge your chances based on your interview performance. You may misjudge the impression you left. In any case, you don't know how many other candidates are being interviewed. Try to relax, knowing that you did your best.

HEALTH-CARE CAREER DESCRIPTIONS AND EDUCATION PROGRAMS

This part of the book contains detailed descriptions of 100-plus health-care careers. They are divided into six categories based on the nature of the professional activity:

- Diagnosing and treating practitioners
- Associated health-care personnel
- Adjunctive health-care personnel
- Rehabilitative personnel
- Administrative personnel
- Affiliated personnel

The form of presentation is the same for each of the careers:

- **Capsule.** A seven-category summary precedes each career description and provides an overview of the career's critical components. Following are brief descriptions of each:

  - *Principal activity.* This sums up the occupation's primary responsibilities and work tasks.
  - *Work Commitment.* Whether the job is primarily full- or part-time.

- *Preprofessional education.* This indicates the educational level that must be attained *prior* to admission to a training institution or professional school.
- *Program length.* This identifies the *average* amount of time needed to complete a training or educational program.
- *Work prerequisites.* This refers to both educational and licensing requirements needed prior to entering this career.
- *Career opportunities.* This categorizes the occupation's potential for growth and openings as Highly favorable, Favorable, Stable, or Limited.
- *Income range.* This represents what the middle 50% of people in this occupation earn, on average.

- **Scope.** This section introduces the career in broad terms, outlining the significance of the work, the general duties and responsibilities, and the patients or clients served.
- **Activities.** This section gives a detailed description of the actual work done by people in the field.
- **Work settings.** Health-care professionals work in a variety of situations—public, private, home, office, and several different kinds of institutions. This section lists the options commonly available to personnel in the field.
- **Advancement.** This section lists the prospects for moving up and assuming more-significant responsibilities in the field.
- **Prerequisites.** This section lists the educational prerequisites for career studies in the field. In addition, it lists the personal attributes that are natural, innate prerequisites for successfully carrying out the professional activities.
- **Education/training.** This section outlines the field's educational route, including the makeup of courses in the program leading to a certificate, diploma, or degree. It also lists training requirements that are specific to the career.
- **Certification/registration/licensure.** This section lists any professional certification or licenses needed to practice in the field.
- **Career potential.** This section discusses prospects for employment in the field.
- **For more information.** This section lists resources for those interested in learning more about the field, including the names and addresses of professional organizations. Also listed (when available) are agencies to contact regarding certification or registration.
- **Schools, colleges, and training programs.** These are listed by state. When writing for an application or catalog, address your request to the department at the school on the list (such as the Department of Physical Therapy). For some careers, hundreds of educational programs are available. In these cases, listings are not given. There are also fields for which a listing is inappropriate, because no formal education is required. In a few cases information could not be secured, so no lists are provided.

Be aware that the medical professions are constantly evolving. New technologies and research, as well as changes in health practices and national trends, can cause certain occupations to fluctuate in terms of pay, outlook, title, and scope. Once you have a sense of the careers you are most interested in, you should engage in further research using the resources suggested.

Diagnosing and Treating Practitioners

A physical health problem manifests itself in various ways, such as pain, swelling, color change, or some other disfigurement. Physicians and dentists who are involved in active practice and who are called on to treat patients exhibiting symptoms of illness and distress first need to diagnose the cause. This is the *diagnostic phase*, which is carried out by means of a history, physical examination, and various tests (such as X rays). Once a reliable diagnosis has been made, the next phase is to design a treatment plan. This is the standard approach used by physicians and dentists.

- **Physicians** provide preventive health care and treat both physical and mental illnesses. The scope of their expertise depends on the extent of their education and training.
- **Dentists** are concerned with problems of the oral cavity, especially the teeth and gums.

Other diagnosing and treating health practitioners employ the same methods of handling illnesses within the scope of their practices:

- **Audiologists** are specialists in evaluating problems with hearing.
- **Chiropractors** are specialists in the structural adjustment of the body skeleton, especially the vertebral column.
- **Optometrists** specialize in various aspects of eye care.
- **Podiatrists** are specialists in the care of the feet.
- **Veterinarians** specialize in the care of animals.

The education and training programs for these fields are quite rigorous, requiring between five and nine years of study and experience beyond high school. Students must secure a solid grounding in the natural sciences while in college, in the biomedical disciplines in professional school, and finally in intensive patient contact during their residency.

Before setting up a practice in any of these fields, you must also pass various exams to obtain licensure.

Audiologists

Principal activity: Diagnose and assist people with hearing, balance, and related sensory and neural problems.

Work commitment: Usually full-time

Preprofessional education: Bachelor's degree

Program length: 2 to 4 years

Work prerequisites: Master's degree

Career opportunities: Highly favorable

Income range: $51,000 to $79,000

Scope

Hearing disorders can result from a variety of causes, including trauma at birth, viral infections, genetic disorders, exposure to loud noise, certain medication, and aging. Audiologists assess individuals who are having hearing, balance, and related sensory and neural disorders. They evaluate the nature of the problems and where appropriate seek to coordinate them with relevant medical, educational, and psychological information to determine an appropriate course of treatment.

Activities

Audiologists use audiometers, computers, and other testing devices to measure an individual's ability to hear and distinguish between sounds. In addition, audiologists use computers to evaluate and diagnose balance disorders. Treatment may include examining and cleaning the ear canal, fitting and dispensing hearing aids, and fitting and examining cochlear implants.

Work settings

About half of all audiologists are employed in health-care facilities, which include physician offices, hospitals, and outpatient care centers. About 15% are employed in educational services, including elementary and secondary schools. Other positions are available at health and personal care centers, such as hearing aid stores, scientific and development research facilities, and state and federal government. A small number of audiologists are self-employed.

Advancement

Audiologists can advance to administrative and postsecondary teaching positions, especially once they secure a doctorate.

Prerequisites

A bachelor's degree from an accredited institution with courses in anatomy and physiology are needed. Desirable personal attributes include a friendly personality, a willingness to help people, and patience.

Education and Training

Individuals must have at least a master's degree; a doctoral degree is becoming much more common, and a number of states now require a doctorate to practice.

Certification/Registration/Licensure

Audiologists are certified by licensure in all 50 states. More than 40 states have continuing education requirements for licensure.

Career Potential

Though the number of openings may remain somewhat small, this job is growing much faster than average, and job prospects should be good, especially for those with doctorates. The rising number of senior citizens, a significant number of whom will develop hearing impairments, will contribute to this increased job growth.

For More Information

The professional organizations in this field are The American Academy of Audiology, 1130 Plaza of America Drive, Suite 300, Reston, VA 20190, (www.audiology.org) and the American Auditory Society, 19 Mantua Road, Mt. Royal, NJ 08061 (www.amauditorysoc.org).

Audiology Programs

Alabama
Alabama A&M University
4900 Meridian St.
Huntsville, AL 35811
www.aamu.edu

Auburn University at Montgomery
1199 Haley Center
Auburn, AL 36849
www.auburn.edu

University of Alabama
Tuscaloosa, AL 35487
www.ua.edu

University of Montevallo
Station 6720
Montevallo, AL 35115
www.montevallo.edu

University of South Alabama
2000 University Commons
Mobile, AL 36688
www.southalabama.edu

Arizona
Arizona State University
326 E Orange Street
Tempe, AZ 85287
www.asu.edu

Northern Arizona University
307 W Dupont Avenue
Flagstaff, AZ 86011
www.nau.edu

University of Arizona
Tucson, AZ 85721
www.arizona.edu

Arkansas
Arkansas State University
P.O. Box 1450
State University, AR 72467
www.astate.edu

University of Arkansas at
 Little Rock
2801 S. University Ave.
Little Rock, AR 72204
www.ualr.edu

University of Arkansas–
 Fayetteville
Fayetteville, AR 72701
www.uark.edu

University of Central Arkansas
210 Donaghey Ave.
Conway, AR 72035
www.uca.edu

California
California State University, Chico
400 W. First St.
Chico, CA 95929
www.csuchico.edu

California State University, Fresno
5241 N. Maple Ave.
Fresno, CA 93740
www.csufresno.edu

California State University,
 Fullerton
800 N State College Boulevard
Fullerton, CA 92834
www.fullerton.edu

California State University,
 Hayward
25800 Carlos Bee Blvd.
Hayward, CA 94542
www.csuhayward.edu

California State University,
 Long Beach
1250 Bellflower Blvd.
Long Beach, CA 90840
www.csulb.edu

California State University,
   Los Angeles
5151 State University Dr.
Los Angeles, CA 90032
www.calstatela.edu

California State University,
   Northridge
18111 Nordhoff St.
Northridge, CA 91330
www.csun.edu

California State University,
   Sacramento
6000 J St.
Sacramento, CA 95819
www.csus.edu

Loma Linda University
Nicholl Hall
Loma Linda, CA 92350
www.llu.edu

San Diego State University
5500 Campanile Dr.
San Diego, CA 92182
www.sdsu.edu

San Francisco State University
1600 Holloway Ave.
San Francisco, CA 94132
www.sfsu.edu

University of the Pacific
3601 Pacific Ave.
Stockton, CA 95211
www.uop.edu

University of the Redlands
1200 E. Colton Ave.
P.O. Box 3080
Redlands, CA 92373
www.redlands.edu

Colorado
Metropolitan State College of
   Denver
P.O. Box 173362
Denver, CO 80217
www.mscd.edu

University of Colorado
Box 425
Boulder, CO 80309
www.colorado.edu

University of Northern Colorado
Gunter 1000, Box 134
Greeley, CO 80639
www.univnorthco.edu

Connecticut
Southern Connecticut State
   University
501 Crescent St.
New Haven, CT 06515
www.southernct.edu

University of Connecticut
1392 Storrs
Storrs-Mansfield, CT 06269
www.uconn.edu

District of Columbia
Gallaudet University
800 Florida Ave. NE
Washington, DC 20002
www.gallaudet.edu

George Washington University
2121 1st Street
Washington, DC 20052
www.gwu.edu

Howard University
2400 6th St. NW
Washington, DC 20059
www.howard.edu

University of the District of
   Columbia
4200 Connecticut Ave. NW
Washington, DC 20008
www.ud.edu

Florida
Florida Atlantic University
777 Glades Rd.
P.O. Box 3091
Boca Raton, FL 33431
www.fau.edu

Florida State University
107 Regional Rehabilitation
   Center
Tallahassee, FL 32306
www.fsu.edu

Nova Southeastern University
3200 S. University Dr.
Fort Lauderdale, FL 33328
www.nova.edu

University of Central Florida
4000 Central Florida Blvd.
Orlando, FL 32816
www.ucf.edu

University of Florida
335 Dauer Hall
Gainesville, FL 32611
www.ufl.edu

University of South Florida
4202 E. Fowler Ave.
Tampa, FL 33620
www.usf.edu

Georgia
Georgia State University
33 Gilmer Street SE
University Plaza
Atlanta, GA 30303
www.gsu.edu

State University of West Georgia
1601 Maple St.
Carrollton, GA 30118
www.westga.edu

University of Georgia
Athens, GA 30602
www.uga.edu

Valdosta State University
1500 N. Patterson St.
Valdosta, GA 31698
www.valdosta.edu

Hawaii
University of Hawaii at Manoa
John A. Burns School of Medicine
   2500 Lower Campus Rd.
Honolulu, HI 96822
www.hawaii.edu

Idaho
Idaho State University
921 S. 8th Ave.
Pocatello, ID 83209
www.isu.edu

Illinois
Eastern Illinois University
600 Lincoln Ave.
Charleston, IL 61920
www.eiu.edu

Governors State University
College of Health Professions
1 University Pkwy.
University Park, IL 60466
www.govst.edu

Northern Illinois University
Department of Communications
DeKalb, IL 60115
www.niu.edu

Northwestern University
633 Clark St.
Evanston, IL 60208
www.nwu.edu

Rush University Medical Center
College of Health Sciences
600 S. Paulina St., Suite 440
Chicago, IL 60612
www.rush.edu

Saint Xavier University
3700 W. 103rd St.
Chicago, IL 60655
www.sxu.edu

Southern Illinois University
 Carbondale
Carbondale, IL 62901
www.siuc.edu

Southern Illinois University
 Edwardsville
Box 1600
Edwardsville, IL 62026
www.siue.edu

University of Illinois
901 W. Illinois St.
Urbana, IL 61801
www.uiuc.edu

Western Illinois University
1 University Circle
Macomb, IL 61455
www.wiu.edu

Indiana
Ball State University
2000 W. University Ave.
Muncie, IN 47306
www.bsu.edu

Indiana University
107 S. Indiana Ave.
Bloomington, IN 47405
www.indiana.edu

Purdue University
West Lafayette, IN 47907
www.purdue.edu

Iowa
Iowa State University
228 Gray Avenue
Ames, IA 50011
www.iastate.edu

University of Iowa
Iowa City, IA 52242
www.uiowa.edu

University of Northern Iowa
1227 W. 27th St.
Cedar Falls, IA 50614
www.uni.edu

Kansas
Fort Hays State University
600 Park St.
Hays, KS 67601
www.fhsu.edu

Kansas State University
Manhattan, KS 66506
www.ksu.edu

University of Kansas
School of Allied Health
3901 Rainbow Blvd.
Kansas City, KS 66160
www.kumc.edu

University of Kansas
Lawrence, KS 66045
www.ku.edu

Wichita State University
1845 N. Fairmount
Wichita, KS 67260
www.wichita.edu

Kentucky
Eastern Kentucky University
521 Lancaster Ave.
Richmond, KY 40475
http://w7.eku.edu

Murray State University
16th and Main Sts.
Murray, KY 42071
www.murraystate.edu

Spalding University
851 S. 4th St.
Louisville, KY 40203
www.spalding.edu

University of Kentucky
1028 S. Broadway, Ste. 3
Lexington, KY 40504
www.uky.edu

Western Kentucky University
1906 College Hts. Blvd.
Bowling Green, KY 42101
www.wku.edu

Louisiana
Grambling State University
100 Founder Street
Grambling, LA 71245
www.gram.edu

Louisiana State University
 423 Main Street
Baton Rouge, LA 70803
www.lsu.edu

Louisiana State University Health
 Sciences Center
1900 Gravier St.
New Orleans, LA 70112
www.lsuhsc.edu

Louisiana Tech University
305 Wisteral St.
Ruston, LA 71272
www.latech.edu

Southeastern Louisiana University
University Station, P.O. Box 879
Hammond, LA 70402
www.selu.edu

Southern University
P.O. Box 9888
Baton Rouge, LA 70813
www.subr.edu

University of Louisiana at Monroe
College of Health Sciences
Department of Communicative
 Disorders
Brown Hall
Monroe, LA 71209
www.ulm.edu

Maryland
Loyola College
4501 N. Charles St.
Baltimore, MD 21210
www.loyola.edu

Towson University
8000 York Rd.
Towson, MD 21252
www.towson.edu

University of Maryland at
 College Park
College Park, MD 20742
www.umd.edu

Massachusetts
Boston University
Sargent College of Health and
 Rehabilitation Sciences
685 Commonwealth Ave.
Boston, MA 02215
www.bu.edu

Bridgewater State College
131 Summer Street
Bridgewater, MA 02325
www.bridgew.edu

Elms College
291 Springfield St.
Chicopee, MA 01013
www.elms.edu

Northeastern University
10 Speare Pl.
Boston, MA 02115
www.northeastern.edu

Worcester State College
486 Chandler St.
Worcester, MA 01602
www.worcester.edu

Michigan
Eastern Michigan University
300 W Michigan Avenue
Ypsilanti, MI 48197
www.emich.edu

Wayne State University
5700 Cass Avenue
Detroit, MI 48202
www.wayne.edu

Western Michigan University
1903 W. Michigan Ave.
Kalamazoo, MI 49008
www.wmich.edu

Minnesota
Minnesota State University,
 Mankato
MSU 77-Elis and Stadium Rd.
Mankato, MN 56001
www.mnsu.edu

Minnesota State University
 Moorhead
1104 7th Ave. S.
Moorhead, MN 56563
www.mnstate.edu

St. Cloud State University
720 4th Ave. S.
St. Cloud, MN 56301
www.stcloudstate.edu

University of Minnesota
164 Pillsbury Dr. SE
Minneapolis, MN 55455
www.umn.edu

University of Minnesota–Duluth
1049 University Dr.
Duluth, MN 55812
www.d.umn.edu

Mississippi
Mississippi University for Women
1100 College St.
Columbus, MS 39701
www.muw.edu

University of Mississippi
University, MS 38677
www.olemiss.edu

University of Southern Mississippi
118 College Dr.
Hattiesburg, MS 39406
www.usm.edu

Missouri
Fontbonne College
6800 Wydown Blvd.
St. Louis, MO 63105
www.fontbonne.edu

Southeast Missouri State
 University
One University Plaza
Cape Girardeau, MO 63701
www.semo.edu

Southwest Missouri State
 University
901 S. National Ave.
Springfield, MO 65897
www.smsu.edu

St. Louis University
221 N. Grand Blvd.
St. Louis, MO 63103
www.slu.edu

Truman State University
100 E. Normal Street
Kirksville, MO 63501
www.truman.edu

University of Missouri–Columbia
Columbia, MO 65211
www.missouri.edu

Nebraska
University of Nebraska at Kearney
905 W. 25th St.
Kearney, NE 68849
www.unk.edu

University of Nebraska at Omaha
6001 Dodge St.
Omaha, NE 68182
www.unomaha.edu

University of Nebraska–Lincoln
Lincoln, NE 68588
www.unl.edu

Nevada
University of Nevada–Reno
1664 N. Virginia St.
Reno, NV 89557
www.unr.edu

New Hampshire
University of New Hampshire
Grant House, 4 Garrison Ave.
Durham, NH 03824
www.unh.edu

New Jersey
College of New Jersey
2000 Pennington Rd.
P.O. Box 7718
Ewing, NJ 08628
www.trenton.edu

Kean University
1000 Morris Ave.
Union, NJ 07083
www.kean.edu

Montclair State University
1 Normal Ave.
Montclair, NJ 07043
www.montclair.edu

Seton Hall University
School of Graduate Medical
  Education
400 S. Orange Ave.
South Orange, NJ 07079
http://gradmeded.shu.edu/

William Paterson University
300 Pompton Rd.
Wayne, NJ 07470
http://ww2.wpunj.edu/

New Mexico
Eastern New Mexico University
1200 W. University
Portales, NM 88130
www.enmu.edu

New Mexico State University
P.O. Box 30001
Las Cruces, NM 88003
www.nmsu.edu

University of New Mexico
Albuquerque, NM 87131
www.unm.edu

New York
Adelphi University
South Ave. P.O. Box 701
Garden City, NY 11530
www.adelphi.edu

Brooklyn College
The City University of New York
2900 Bedford Ave.
Brooklyn, NY 11210
www.brooklyn.cuny.edu

Buffalo State College
1300 Elmwood Ave.
Buffalo, NY 14222
www.buffalostate.edu

College of St. Rose
432 Western Ave.
Albany, NY 12203
www.strose.edu

The Graduate Center
365 Fifth Ave.
New York, NY 10016
www.gc.cuny.edu

Hunter College
695 Park Ave.
New York, NY 10021
www.hunter.cuny.edu

Ithaca College
201 Cerrache Center
Ithaca, NY 14850
www.ithaca.edu

Lehman College of CUNY
Bedford Park Blvd. W.
Bronx, NY 10468
www.lehman.cuny.edu

Long Island University
One University Plaza
Brooklyn, NY 11201
www.brooklyn.liu.edu

Long Island University
700 Northern Blvd.
Brookville, NY 11548
www.liu.edu

Marymount Manhattan College
221 E. 71st St.
New York, NY 10021
www.marymount.mmm.edu

Nazareth College of Rochester
4245 E. Ave.
Rochester, NY 14618
www.naz.edu

New York Medical College
School of Public Health
Valhalla, NY 10595
www.nymc.edu

New York University
The Steinhardt School of
  Education
82 Washington Sq. E.
New York, NY 10003
www.nyu.edu

Pace University
1 Pace Plaza
New York, NY 10038
www.pace.edu

Queens College
The City University of New York
65-30 Kissena Blvd.
Flushing, NY 11367
www.qc.edu

St. John's University
8000 Utopia Pkwy.
Jamaica, NY 11439
www.stjohns.edu

St. Joseph's College
155 W. Roe Blvd.
Patchogue, NY 11772
www.sjcny.edu

SUNY at Geneseo
One College Circle
Geneseo, NY 14454
www.geneseo.edu

SUNY at New Paltz
1 Hawk Drive
New Paltz, NY 12561
www.newpaltz.edu

SUNY Fredonia
280 Central Ave.
Fredonia, NY 14063
www.fredonia.edu

SUNY Plattsburgh State
101 Broad St.
Plattsburgh, NY 12901
www.plattsburgh.edu

Syracuse University
Syracuse, NY 13244
www.syr.edu

Teachers College of Columbia
  University
525 W. 120th St.
New York, NY 10027
www.tc.columbia.edu

University at Buffalo
The State University of New York
17 Capen Hall
Buffalo, NY 14260
www.buffalo.edu

North Carolina
Appalachian State University
Boone, NC 28608
www.appstate.edu

East Carolina University
School of Allied Health Sciences
Carol Belk Building
Greenville, NC 27858
www.ecu.edu

Elizabeth City State University
1704 Weeksville Rd.
Elizabeth City, NC 27909
www.ecsu.edu

North Carolina Central University
1801 Fayetteville St.
Durham, NC 27707
www.nccu.edu

University of North Carolina at
  Chapel Hill
Chapel Hill, NC 27599
www.unc.edu

University of North Carolina at
  Greensboro
1000 Spring Garden St.
Greensboro, NC 27403
www.uncg.edu

Western Carolina University
Hwy. 107
Cullowhee, NC 28723
www.wcu.edu

North Dakota
Minot State University
500 University Ave. W.
Minot, ND 58707
www.minotstate.edu

University of North Dakota
University Station
Grand Forks, ND 58202
www.und.nodak.edu

Ohio
Bowling Green State University
Bowling Green, OH 43403
www.bgsu.edu

Case Cleveland Western Reserve
  University
10900 Euclid Ave.
Cleveland, OH 44106
www.cwru.edu

Cleveland State University
2121 Euclid Ave.
Cleveland, OH 44115
www.csuohio.edu

Kent State University
Kent, OH 44242
www.kent.edu

Miami University
College of Arts & Science
E. High Street
Oxford, OH 45056
www.muohio.edu

Ohio State University
460 W 10th Avenue
Columbus, OH 43210
www.osu.edu

Ohio University
Athens, OH 45701
www.ohio.edu

University of Akron
302 E. Buchtel Ave.
Akron, OH 44325
www.uakron.edu

University of Cincinnati
2600 Clifton Ave.
Cincinnati, OH 45221
www.uc.edu

Oklahoma
Northeastern State University
600 N. Grand Ave.
Tahlequah, OK 74464
www.nsuok.edu

Oklahoma State University
324 Student Union
Stillwater, OK 74078
www.osu.okstate.edu

University of Central Oklahoma
100 N. University Dr.
Edmond, OK 73034
www.ucok.edu

University of Oklahoma
660 Parrington Oval
Norma, OK 73019
www.ou.edu

University of Tulsa
600 S. College Ave.
Tulsa, OK 74104
www.utulsa.edu

Oregon
Portland State University
P.O. Box 751
Portland, OR 97207
www.pdx.edu

University of Oregon
Eugene, OR 97403
www.uoregon.edu

Pennsylvania
Bloomsburg University
400 E. 2nd St.
Bloomsburg, PA 17815
www.bloomu.edu

California University of
  Pennsylvania
250 University Ave.
California, PA 15419
www.cup.edu

Clarion University of Pennsylvania
Clarion, PA 16214
www.clarion.edu

East Stroudsburg University of
  Pennsylvania
200 Prospect St.
East Stroudsburg, PA 18301
www.esu.edu

Edinboro University of
  Pennsylvania
 115A Compton Hall
Edinboro, PA 16444
www.edinboro.edu

Indiana University of
  Pennsylvania
1011 South Dr.
Indiana, PA 15705
www.iup.edu

Marywood University
2300 Adams Ave.
Scranton, PA 18509
www.marywood.edu

Temple University
1801 Broad St.N
Philadelphia, PA 19122
www.temple.edu

University of Pittsburgh
School of Health and
  Rehabilitation Sciences
4020 Forbes Tower
Pittsburgh, PA 15260
www.shrs.pitt.edu

West Chester University
Carter Drive
West Chester, PA 19383
www.wcupa.edu

Rhode Island
University of Rhode Island
Kingston, RI 02881
www.uri.edu

South Carolina
South Carolina State University
Taylor Hall
300 College St. NE
Orangeburg, SC 29117
www.scsu.edu

University of South Carolina
Columbia, SC 29208
www.sc.edu

South Dakota
University of South Dakota
414 E. Clark St.
Vermillion, SD 57069
www.usd.edu

Tennessee
University of Memphis
101 Wilder Tower
Memphis, TN 38152
www.memphis.edu

Vanderbilt University
2201 West End Ave.
Nashville, TN 37235
www.vanderbilt.edu

Texas
Baylor University
1311 S 5th Street
Waco, TX 76798
www.baylor.edu

Lamar University
4400 Martin Luther King Blvd.
P.O. Box 10009
Beaumont, TX 77705
www.lamar.edu

Our Lady of the Lake University
411 SW 24th St.
San Antonio, TX 78207
www.ollusa.edu

Stephen F. Austin State
  University
SFA Station
1936 North Street
Nacogdoches, TX 75962
www.sfasu.edu

Texas A&M University–Kingsville
700 University Blvd., MSC 114
Kingsville, TX 78363
www.tamuk.edu

Texas Christian University
2800 S. University Dr.
Fort Worth, TX 76129
www.tcu.edu

Texas State University–San
  Marcos
601 University Dr.
San Marcos, TX 78666
www.txstate.edu

Texas Tech University
18th Street & Boston Ave
Lubbock, TX 79409
www.ttu.edu

Texas Woman's University
P.O. Box 425589
Denton, TX 76204
www.twu.edu

University of Houston
4800 Calhoun Rd.
Houston, TX 77204
www.uh.edu

University of North Texas
P.O. Box 311277
Denton, TX 76203
www.unt.edu

University of Texas at Austin
Austin, TX 78712
www.utexas.edu

University of Texas at Dallas
1966 Inwood Rd.
Dallas, TX 75235
www.utdallas.edu

University of Texas at El Paso
500 W. University Ave.
El Paso, TX 79968
www.utep.edu

University of Texas–Pan American
1201 W. University Dr.
Edinburg, TX 78541
www.panam.edu

Utah
Brigham Young University
Provo, UT 84601
www.byu.edu

University of Utah
201 S. Presidents Circle,
  Room 201
Salt Lake City, UT 84112
www.utah.edu

Utah State University
Logan, UT 84322
www.usu.edu

Vermont
University of Vermont
Burlington, VT 05405
www.uvm.edu

Virginia
Hampton University
Hampton, VA 23668
www.hamptonu.edu

James Madison University
800 S. Main St.
Harrisonburg, VA 22807
www.jmu.edu

Old Dominion University
202 Rollins Hall
Norfolk, VA 23529
www.odu.edu

Radford University
E. Main St.
Radford, VA 24142
www.radford.edu

University of Virginia
1300 Jefferson Park Avenue
Charlottesville, VA 22903
www.virginia.edu

Washington
Eastern Washington University
101 Sutton Hall
Cheney, WA 99004
www.ewu.edu

University of Washington
1959 NE Pacific St., Box 356490
Seattle, WA 98195
www.washington.edu

Washington State University
Lighty 307 Box 641269
Pullman, WA 99164
www.wsu.edu

Western Washington University
516 High St.
Bellingham, WA 98225
www.wwu.edu

West Virginia
Marshall University
One John Marshall Dr.
Huntington, WV 25755
www.marshall.edu

West Virginia University
P.O. Box 6201
Morgantown, WV 26506
www.wvu.edu

Wisconsin
Marquette University
P.O. Box 1881
Milwaukee, WI 53201
www.mu.edu

University of Wisconsin–Eau
Claire
105 Garfield Ave.
P.O. Box 4004
Eau Claire, WI 54702
www.marquette.edu

University of Wisconsin–Madison
1975 Willow Dr.
Madison, WI 53706
www.wisc.edu

University of Wisconsin–
Milwaukee
2200 E. Kenwood Blvd.
P.O. Box 413
Milwaukee, WI 53201
www.uwm.edu

University of Wisconsin–Oshkosh
800 Algoma Blvd.
Oshkosh, WI 54901
www.uwosh.edu

University of Wisconsin–
River Falls
410 S. Third St.
River Falls, WI 54022
www.uwrf.edu

University of Wisconsin–Stevens
Point
2100 Main St.
Stevens Point, WI 54481
www.uwsp.edu

University of Wisconsin–
Whitewater
800 W. Main St.
Whitewater, WI 53190
www.uww.edu

Wyoming
University of Wyoming
1000 E. University Ave.
Laramie, WY 82071
www.uwyo.edu

Chiropractors

Principal activity: Practicing chiropractic medicine—a nonmedication, nonsurgical approach to healing

Work commitment: Full-time

Preprofessional education: 2 years of college

Program length: 3 to 4 years

Work prerequisites: Doctor of Chiropractic (DC) degree and license

Career opportunities: Favorable

Income range: $46,000 to $97,000

Scope

Chiropractors are health-care professionals who are trained to perform structural adjustments, especially to the vertebral column, as a means of treatment. The word *chiropractor* is derived from two Greek words: *cheir,* which means hand, and *praktikos,* meaning practical or operative. Taken together, they mean "done by hand." This healing approach is based on the hypothesis that misalignment of the spine results in neurological dysfunction and consequently a disturbance in various parts of the body. By manual adjustment or use of other nonsurgical or nonmedicinal methods, chiropractors restore the body to a healthy state.

Activities

Chiropractors diagnose patients' problems by obtaining a medical history, performing a physical examination involving spinal postural analysis, taking and evaluating X rays and measurements, and ordering laboratory tests. Patients treated by chiropractors may have either acute or chronic problems, including headaches, stiff neck, backaches, and fatigue. After arriving at a diagnosis, chiropractors seek to correct any structural problems found by reducing or immobilizing the abnormality. Many chiropractors supplement their standard manual adjustment methods by using traction, diathermy, galvanic currents, ultraviolet light, ultrasound, massage, paraffin baths, hot or cold compresses or baths, and sole or heel lifts. They may treat injuries of the limbs with first aid, strapping, or casting. They use supportive collars and braces to treat neck, lower back, elbow, knee, and ankle injuries. In addition to performing structural adjustments, chiropractors may make recommendations for dietary regimes and nutritional supplements to improve health. Some specialize in such areas as orthopedics, sports medicine, and nutrition. These fields require specialized postgraduate education programs.

Work Settings

The principal work sites are private chiropractic offices. Other locations include alternative health-care centers, health spas, and chiropractic colleges.

Advancement

Chiropractors may advance by moving to a bigger or more prestigious facility, opening a private practice, or specializing.

Prerequisites

Two years of college education are required for this field, including courses in general biology, chemistry, and physics.

Desirable personal attributes for the field include empathy for the sick, manual dexterity, good interpersonal skills (especially in communication), a detail-oriented personality, above-average intelligence, and superior observation skills.

Education/Training

The chiropractic educational program extends over eight semesters, which may be completed in three or four years, depending on the school's curriculum. The first half of the program emphasizes the basic sciences: anatomy, physiology, microbiology, biochemistry, pathology, and public health. This is followed by classes in physical, clinical, and laboratory diagnosis; gynecology and obstetrics; pediatrics; geriatrics; dermatology; otolaryngology; roentgenology; dietetics; orthopedics; physical therapy; emergency procedures; spinal analysis; and principles and practices of chiropractic and adjustive techniques. Clinical experience is incorporated into the curriculum.

Certification/Registration/Licensure

A written and practical examination taken under a state board of examiners is the standard route to licensure.

Career Potential

The increasing acceptance of chiropractic medicine as a healing approach strongly suggests that more practitioners will be needed over the next decade. The expanding older population of the United States, with their increased likelihood of structural problems, will also increase demand for chiropractors.

For More Information

The professional organization is the American Chiropractic Association, 1701 Clarendon Blvd., Arlington, VA 22209 (www.acatoday.org). Additional information can be secured from the Council on Chiropractic Education, 8049 N. 85th Way, Scottsdale, AZ 85258 (www.cce-usa. org).

Colleges of Chiropractic Medicine

California

Cleveland Chiropractic College
590 N. Vermont Ave.
Los Angeles, CA 90004
www.clevelandchiropractic.edu

Life Chiropractic College West
25001 Industrial Blvd.
Hayward, CA 94545
www.lifewest.edu

Los Angeles College of
 Chiropractic
16200 E. Amber Valley Dr.
Box 1166
Whittier, CA 90609
www.scuhs.edu

Palmer College of Chiropractic-
 West
90 E. Tasman Dr.
San Jose, CA 95134
www.palmer.edu

Pasadena College of Chiropractic
1505 N. Marengo Ave.
Pasadena, CA 91101

Connecticut

University of Bridgeport
College of Chiropractic
126 Park Ave.
Bridgeport, CT 06604
www.bridgeport.edu/chiro/

Florida

Palmer College of Chiropractic
4777 County Center Parkway
Port Orange, Florida 32129
www.naturalhealers.com/schools/

Georgia

Life University College of
 Chiropractic
1269 Barcley Circle
Marietta, GA 30060
www.life.edu

Illinois

National University of Health
 Sciences
200 E. Roosevelt Rd.
Lombard, IL 60148
www.nuhs.edu

Iowa

Palmer College of Chiropractic
1000 Brady St.
Davenport, IA 52803
www.palmer.edu

Minnesota

Northwestern College of
 Chiropractic
2501 W. 84th St.
Bloomington, MN 55431
www.nwhealth.edu

Missouri

Cleveland Chiropractic College
6401 Rockhill Rd.
Kansas City, MO 64131
www.clevelandchiropractic.edu

Logan College of Chiropractic
2501 Schoettler Rd.
P.O. Box 1065
Chesterfield, MO 63006
www.logan.edu

New York

New York Chiropractic College
P.O. Box 800
2360 St. Rte. 89
Seneca Falls, NY 13148
www.nycc.edu

Oregon

Western States Chiropractic
 College
2900 NE 132nd Ave.
Portland, OR 97230
www.wschiro.edu

South Carolina

Sherman College of Straight
 Chiropractic
P.O. Box 1452
Spartanburg, SC 29304
www.sherman.edu

Texas

Texas Chiropractic College
5912 Spencer Hwy.
Pasadena, TX 77505
www.txchiro.edu

Parker College of Chiropractic
2500 Walnut Hill Ln.
Dallas, TX 75229
www.parkercc.edu

Canada

Canadian Memorial Chiropractic
 College
1900 Bayview Ave.
Toronto, Ontario M4G 3E6
www.cmcc.ca

University of Quebec at Trois
 Rivieres
P. 500, Trois-Rivieres
Quebec G9A 5H7
www.uqtr.uquebec.ca

Dentists

Principal activity: Providing health care for teeth and gums

Work commitment: Full-time

Preprofessional education: Bachelor's degree

Program length: 4 years

Work prerequisites: Doctor of Dental Science (DDS) or Doctor of Dental Medicine (DMD) degree and license

Career opportunities: Favorable

Income range: $101,000 to $166,000

Scope

The basic goals of dentistry are to encourage good oral health, especially of the teeth and gums; to correct defects in teeth alignment; and to replace missing teeth. Prospective practitioners receive a wide range of training in both primary dental care and the dental specialties. But in complex situations, practitioners refer patients to specialists to secure appropriate treatment. Table 9.1 describes areas of dental specialization.

Table 9.1: Dental Specialties

Specialty	Nature of the Work
Endodontics	Diagnosing and treating diseases of the nerve (pulp) using root canal therapy
Oral pathology	The study of the causes and effects of dental diseases
Oral surgery	Utilizing surgical procedures to treat defects and diseases of the teeth, cheekbones, and jaw
Orthodontics	Involves correcting irregular and abnormally positioned teeth
Pedodontics	Providing dental care for children, adolescents, and young adults
Periodontics	Diagnosing and treating diseases of the tissues that surround the teeth and supporting gums
Prostodontics	Preparing full and partial dentures to replace lost teeth
Public health	Promote the development of good oral health in communities

Specialty training is offered at dental schools and usually takes about two years beyond dental school. The number of specialists in each of these fields varies widely. The overwhelming majority of dentists, however, are general practitioners. Naturally, some dentists are administrators or full-time dental faculty members or engage in research at dental colleges or in industry.

Activities

General dentists are trained to offer a wide array of professional services. These include treating gum inflammation (gingivitis) and infected, impacted, chipped, and broken teeth and eliminating decay. They instruct patients on proper dental care, including brushing and flossing. Dentists are qualified to perform less-challenging root-canal procedures, minor oral surgery, and extractions. They also prepare crowns and permanent or removable dentures. Some are trained to replace teeth with implants.

Work Settings

The principal work sites for dentists are private offices or hospitals and dental colleges. Some commercial companies manufacturing dental equipment or material also may employ dentists.

Advancement

Recent graduates who form a group practice may start off as associates and over time may move on to become partners. Others join a group temporarily while they are waiting to open a private practice of their own. Some dentists are employed in hospitals or public clinics or by HMOs.

Prerequisites

The minimum overall educational requirements are three years of undergraduate studies, although most accepted applicants have a bachelor's degree by the time they initiate their dental studies. The required course prerequisites are one year of biology and physics and two years of chemistry (inorganic and organic). Additional courses such as English, mathematics, psychology, and advanced biology may be required or recommended. In addition, it is mandatory to take the Dental Aptitude Test (DAT), and an interview is a common component of the admission process.

Desirable personal attributes for work in this field are strong communication skills, a favorable personality, well-organized work habits, diagnostic skills, superior manual dexterity, good vision, eye-hand coordination, a light touch, and creativity.

Education/Training

The four-year dental education program of training is standard for all professional schools. Essentially the curriculum is divided into one year of basic sciences and three years of clinical sciences. The basic sciences taken during the first year are anatomy, biochemistry, and physiology. The second year usually includes courses in endodontics, complete and partial dentures, and operative dentistry. The third year commonly includes oral diagnoses, periodontics, and crown and bridge work. The last year involves advanced courses in some of the dental specialties. Clinical experience under supervision starts early on and extends throughout dental school training. An internship is common, and specialty training for some may follow graduation from dental school.

Certification/Registration/Licensure

Dentists are required to be licensed in the state in which they want to practice. To be licensed, you must graduate from an accredited dental school and pass written and practical examinations.

Career Potential

Employment prospects are favorable overall. Fluoridation of water has drastically improved the quality of the teeth of the younger generation. However, greater emphasis on oral health, the increased longevity of the population, and advances in dentistry such as implants have created a greater need for dental care.

For More Information

The professional organization for dentists is The American Dental Association, 211 E. Chicago Ave., Chicago, IL 60611 (www.ada.org).

Schools and Colleges of Dental Medicine

Alabama
University of Alabama at
  Birmingham
School of Dentistry
1919 Seventh Ave. S.
University Station, SDA 125
Birmingham, AL 35294
www.dental.uab.edu

Arizona
Arizona College of Dental
Medicine of Midwestern
  University
19555 North 59th Avenue
Glendale, Arizona 85308
www.midwestern.edu

Arizona School of Dentistry and
  Oral Health
5850 E. Still Circle
Mesa, AZ 85206
www.atsu.edu

California
Loma Linda University
Loma Linda, CA 92350
www.dentistry.llu.edu

University of California–
  Los Angeles
10833 LeConte Ave.
Los Angeles, CA 90095
www.dent.ucla.edu

University of California–
  San Francisco
513 Parnassus Ave.
San Francisco, CA 94143
www.dentistry.ucsf.edu

University of Southern California
Norris Dental Science Center
School of Dentistry
1925 W. 34th St.
Los Angeles, CA 90089
www.usc.edu/dental

University of the Pacific
Arthur A. Dugani
School of Dentistry
2155 Webster St.
San Francisco, CA 94115
www.dental.uop.edu

Colorado
University of Colorado at Denver
School of Dental Medicine
Mail Stop F 833
4200 E. 9th Ave.
Aurora, Colorado 80045
www.uchsc.edu/sod

Connecticut
University of Connecticut
School of Dental Medicine
263 Farmington Ave.
Farmington, CT 06030
http://sdm.uchc.edu/

District of Columbia
Howard University
College of Dentistry
600 W St. NW
Washington, DC 20059
www.howard.edu/dentistry

Florida
Nova Southeastern University
College of Dental Medicine
3200 S. University Dr.
Ft. Lauderdale, FL 33328
www.nova.edu/dental

University of Florida
College of Dentistry
P.O. Box 100445
Gainesville, FL 32610
www.dental.ufl.edu

Georgia
Medical College of Georgia
School of Dentistry
1459 Laney Walker Blvd.
Augusta, GA 30912
www.mcg.edu/sod/

Illinois
Southern Illinois University
Building 273
2800 College Ave.
Alton, IL 62002
www.sdm.edu

University of Illinois at Chicago
College of Dentistry
801 S. Paulina St.
Chicago, IL 60612
www.uic.edu/dentistry

Indiana
Indiana University
School of Dentistry
1121 W. Michigan St.
Indianapolis, IN 46202
www.iusd.iupui.edu

Iowa
University of Iowa
College of Dentistry
311 N. Dental Building
Iowa City, IA 52242
www.dentistry.uiowa.edu

Kentucky
University of Kentucky
College of Dentistry
800 Rose St.
Medical Center
Lexington, KY 40536
www.mc.uky.edu/dentistry

University of Louisville
School of Dentistry
501 S. Preston St.
Louisville, KY 40202
www.louisville.edu/dental/

Louisiana
Louisiana State University
School of Dentistry
1100 Florida Ave., Box 101
New Orleans, LA 70119
www.lsusd.lsuhsc.edu

Maryland
University of Maryland
Baltimore College of Dental
  Surgery
650 W. Baltimore St.
Baltimore, MD 21201
www.dental.umaryland.edu

Massachusetts
Boston University Goldman
School of Dental Medicine
100 E. Newton St.
Boston, MA 02118
http://dentalschool.bu.edu/

Harvard School of Dental
  Medicine
88 Longwood Ave.
Boston, MA 02115
www.hsdm.med.harvard.edu

Tufts University
College of Dentistry
One Kneeland St.
Boston, MA 02111
www.tufts.edu/dental/

Michigan
University of Detroit
Mercy School of Dentistry
  2700 Martin Luther King Junior
  Blvd.
Detroit, MI 48219
www.udmercy.edu/dental/

University of Michigan
School of Dentistry
1011 N University
Ann Arbor, MI 48109
www.dent.umich.edu

Minnesota
University of Minnesota
School of Dentistry
515 Delaware St. SE
Minneapolis, MN 55455
www.dentistry.umn.edu

Mississippi
University of Mississippi
School of Dentistry
2500 N. State St.
Jackson, MS 39216
www.umc.edu

Missouri
University of Missouri–Kansas City
School of Dentistry
650 E. 25th St.
Kansas City, MO 64108
www.umkc.edu/dentistry/

Nebraska
Creighton University
School of Dentistry
2500 California St.
Omaha, NE 68178
www.creighton.edu

University of Nebraska
  College of Dentistry
40th and Holdredge Sts.
P.O. Box 830740
Lincoln, NE 68583
www.unmc.edu/dentistry/

Nevada
University of Nevada–Las Vegas
School of Dentistry
1001 Shadow Lane MS 7410
Las Vegas, NV 89104
http://dentalschool.unlv.edu/

New Jersey
University of Medicine and
  Dentistry of New Jersey
110 Bergen St.
Newark, NJ 07101
www.dentalschool.umdnj.edu

New York
Columbia University
School of Dental and Oral Surgery
630 W. 168th St.
New York, NY 10032
www.dental.columbia.edu

New York University
College of Dentistry
David B. Kriser Dental Center
345 E. 24th St.
New York, NY 10010
www.nyu.edu/dental/

State University of New York at
  Buffalo
School of Dental Medicine
327 Square Hall, South Campus
3435 Main St.
Buffalo, NY 14214
www.sdm.buffalo.edu

Stony Brook University
School of Dental Medicine
Rockland Hall
Stony Brook, NY 11794
www.hsc.stonybrook.edu/dental/

North Carolina
University of North Carolina
CB-7450 105 Brauer Hall
Chapel Hill, NC 27589
www.dent.unc.edu

Ohio
Case Western Reserve University
School of Dental Medicine
10900 Euclid Ave.
Cleveland, OH 44106
www.dental.case.edu

Ohio State University
College of Dental Medicine
305 W. 12th St.
Columbus, OH 43218
www.dent.ohio-state.edu

Oklahoma
University of Oklahoma
College of Dentistry
P.O. Box 26901
Oklahoma City, OK 73117
http://dentistry.ouhsc.edu/

Oregon
Oregon Health Science University
School of Dentistry
611 SW Campus Dr.
Portland, OR 972 39
www.ohsu.edu/sod/

Pennsylvania
Temple University
Maurice H. Kornberg
School of Dentistry
3223 N. Broad St.
Philadelphia, PA 19140
www.temple.edu/dentistry/

University of Pennsylvania
School of Dental Medicine
240 S. 40th St.
Philadelphia, PA 19104
www.dental.upenn.edu

University of Pittsburgh
School of Dental Medicine
3501 Terrace St.
Pittsburgh, PA 15261
www.dental.pitt.edu

South Carolina
Medical University of South
  Carolina
College of Dental Medicine
171 Ashley Ave.
Charleston, SC 29425
http://academicdepartments.
  musc.edu/dentistry/

Tennessee
Meharry Medical College
School of Dentistry
1005 D.B. Todd Blvd.
Nashville, TN 37208
www.mmc.edu

University of Tennessee
College of Dental Medicine
875 Union Ave.
Memphis, TN 38163
www.utmem.edu

Texas
Baylor College of Dentistry
Texas A&M University
Dallas, TX 75246
www.tambcd.edu

University of Texas
Dental Branch at Houston
6516 M.D. Anderson Blvd.
Houston, TX 77030
www.uthouston.edu

University of Texas
Health Science Center at San
  Antonio Dental School
7703 Floyd Curl Dr.
San Antonio, TX 78229
http://dental.uthscsa.edu/

Virginia
Virginia Commonwealth University
School of Dentistry
P.O. Box 980566
Richmond, VA 23298
www.vcu.edu/dentistry/

Washington
University of Washington
School of Dentistry
Health Science Building D 323
Box 356365
Seattle, WA 98195
www.dental.washington.edu

West Virginia
West Virginia University
School of Dentistry
P.O. Box 9400
Morgantown, WV 26506
www.hsc.wvu.edu/sod

Wisconsin
Marquette University
School of Dentistry
P.O. Box 1881
Milwaukee, WI 53233
www.marquette.edu/dentistry/

Canada
Dalhousie University
5981 University Ave.
Halifax, Nova Scotia B3H 1wz
www.dentistry.dal.ca

McGill University
Faculty of Dentistry
3640 University St.
Montreal, Quebec H3A 2B2
www.mcgill.ca/dentistry/

Universite Laval
Faculte de Medecine Dentaire
Quebec G1K 7P4
www.fmdulaval.ca/md

University de Montreal
Faculte de Medecine Dentaire
C.P. 6128, Succursale Centre-Ville
Montreal, Quebec H3C 3J7
www.umontreal.ca

University of Alberta
Faculty of Medicine and Dentistry
3028 Dentistry-Pharmacy Centre
Edmonton, Alberta T6G 2N8
www.dentistry.ualberta.ca

University of British Columbia
Room 278, 2199 Westbrook Mall
Vancouver, British Columbia V6T
  1Z3
www.dentistry.ubc.ca

University of Manitoba
Faculty of Medicine
780 Bannatyne Ave.
Winnipeg, Manitoba R3T 0W2
www.umanitoba.ca

University of Saskatchewan
College of Dentistry
Room B526, Health Sciences
  Building
107 Wiggins Rd.
Saskatoon, Saskatchewan S7N 5E5
www.usask.ca

University of Toronto
Faculty of Dentistry
124 Edward St.
Toronto, Ontario M5G 1G6
www.utoronto.ca/dentistry/

University of Schulich Dental
  School Western Ontario
1151 Richmond St.
London, Ontario N6A 5C1
www.schulichj.uwo.ca/dentistry

Optometrists

Principal activity: Providing corrective lenses and eye care	**Work prerequisites:** Doctor of Optometry (OD) degree and license
Work commitment: Usually full-time	**Career opportunities:** Highly favorable
Preprofessional education: College degree	**Income range:** $70,000 to $125,000
Program length: 4 years	

Scope

More than half the people in the United States wear glasses or contact lenses to help their vision. These lenses generally are prescribed and secured by optometrists or doctors of optometry (ODs). These professionals examine patients' eyes to determine whether they have any visual problems or eye diseases.

When necessary, optometrists prescribe eyeglasses and lenses and provide them for their clients.

Activities

Optometrists perform comprehensive examinations of the external and internal structures of the eye. They use both subjective and objective tests to evaluate a patient's vision. This evaluation includes determining visual acuity, depth and color perception, and the ability to focus and coordinate the eyes. The optometrist then forms a treatment plan based on an analysis of the eye examination and test results. Treatment may involve prescribing glasses or contact lenses or recommending vision therapy. In most states optometrists also treat certain eye diseases, such as conjunctivitis and corneal infections, and check eye pressure for signs of glaucoma. Optometrists may prescribe topical or oral drugs for certain eye problems. If they observe conditions that lie outside the scope of their practice (such as diabetes), they refer the patient to another eye care practitioner.

Work Settings

Most optometrists work in their own private offices in solo, partnership, or group practices. They also may be employed by chain vision care centers based in storefronts or by hospitals, HMOs, ophthalmologists, or other optometrists.

Advancement

Optometrists may move up to managerial positions in larger establishments. Those who seek to specialize in family practice, pediatrics, geriatrics, or vision therapy for ocular diseases may enroll in one-year postgraduate residency programs. In addition, those interested in teaching or research may seek a master's or Ph.D. degree in visual science, physiological optics, or neurophysiology of the eye.

Prerequisites

Students who want to enter optometry should seek admission to a college or university that offers courses in the basic pre-optometry requirements, including one year each of biology, chemistry (inorganic and organic), physics, math, and English. Individual schools require additional courses, which may include advanced biology (especially microbiology), psychology, speech, statistics, and business. Although prerequisites may be completed in two or three years, most applicants have a college degree when they enter optometry school. More than half of current optometry students are women.

Applicants seeking admission to an optometry school must take the Optometry Admission Test (discussed in Chapter 3 and Appendix A). The test measures general academic ability and science knowledge. The results—along with the student's undergraduate record, recommendations, and an interview—help determine admission to optometry school.

Optometry schools do not have a central application service. Applications must be secured from and returned to individual schools. Students must also make their own arrangements to have their OAT scores sent to their chosen schools. Competition for admission is keen.

Desirable personal attributes for a career in optometry include self-discipline, business skills, a talent for dealing with patients tactfully, a strong interest in helping people, good communication skills, and superior vision.

Education/Training

The program of studies for the Doctor of Optometry degree extends over four years. During the first two years, students take courses in the basic medical sciences (such as anatomy, biochemistry, pharmacology, and pathology) as well as in optics, visual sciences, and clinical techniques. During the third and fourth years, the emphasis is on patient care, with training in both primary eye care and specialty services. Training covers such areas of contemporary practice as contact lenses, binocular and low-vision therapy, and eye disease diagnosis and treatment.

Certification/Registration/Licensure

All U.S. states require a license to practice optometry. Licensure requires graduation from an accredited college of optometry and successful completion of both written and clinical examinations.

Career Potential

Employment prospects over the next ten years are expected grow at an above-average rate. As a substantial segment of the population passes the age of 45, they will need increased vision care. Greater awareness of the importance of vision, rising personal incomes, and the growth in employee vision care plans will also enhance employment opportunities for optometrists.

For More Information

The professional organization for optometrists is the American Optometric Association, 243 N. Lindbergh Blvd., St. Louis, MO 63141 (www.aoa.org).

You can get additional information from the Association of Schools and Colleges of Optometry, 6110 Executive Blvd., Suite 510, Rockville, MD 20852 (www.opted.org).

Schools and Colleges of Optometry

Alabama
University of Alabama at
  Birmingham
School of Optometry
UAB Station
Birmingham, AL 35294
www.uab.edu/optometry/

Midwestern University
Arizona College of Optometry
19555 N 59th Avenue
Glendale, Arizona 85303
www.midwestern.edu

California
Southern California College of
  Optometry
2575 Yorba Linda Blvd.
Fullerton, CA 92831
www.scco.edu

University of California, Berkeley
School of Optometry
390 Minor Hall
Berkeley, CA 94720
www.optometry.berkeley.edu

Western University of Health
  Sciences
College of Optometry
309 East 2nd Street
Pomona, California 91766
www.westernu.edu

Florida
Nova Southeastern University
College of Optometry
3200 S. University Dr.
Davie, FL 33328
optometry.nova.edu

Illinois
Illinois College of Optometry
3241 S. Michigan Ave.
Chicago, IL 60616
www.ico.edu

Indiana
Indiana University
School of Optometry
800 E. Atwater Ave.
Bloomington, IN 47405
www.opt.indiana.edu

Massachusetts
New England College of
  Optometry
424 Beacon St.
Boston, MA 02115
www.neco.edu

Michigan
Michigan College of Optometry
  at Ferris State University
1310 Cramer Circle
Big Rapids, MI 49307
www.ferris.edu/mco/

Missouri
University of Missouri–St. Louis
School of Optometry
1 University Boulevard
St. Louis, MO 63121
www.umsl.edu/~optomety/

New York
State University of New York
State College of Optometry
33 W. 42nd St.
New York, NY 10036
www.sunyopt.edu

Ohio
Ohio State University
College of Optometry
338 W. Tenth Ave.
Columbus, OH 43218
www.optometry.osu.edu

Oklahoma
Northeastern State University
College of Optometry
1001 N. Grand Ave.
Tahlequah, OK 74464
http://arapaho.nsuok.
  edu/~optometry/

Oregon
Pacific University
College of Optometry
2043 College Way
Forest Grove, OR 97116
www.opt.pacificu.edu

Pennsylvania
Pennsylvania College of
  Optometry
8360 Old York Rd.
Elkins Park, PA 19027
www.pco.edu

Tennessee
Southern College of Optometry
1245 Madison Ave.
Memphis, TN 38104
www.sco.edu

Texas
University of Houston
College of Optometry
505 J. Davis Armistead Building
Houston, TX 77204
www.opt.uh.edu

Canada
University of Montreal
School of Optometry
3744 Gean Brillant, Local 110
Montreal, Quebec H3T 1P1
www.umontreal.ca

University of Waterloo
School of Optometry
Faculty of Sciences
Waterloo, Ontario N2L 3G1
www.optometry.uwaterloo.ca

Physicians

Principal activity: Practicing medicine as generalists or specialists to treat patients

Work commitment: Full-time

Preprofessional education: Bachelor's degree

Program length: 4 years

Work prerequisites: Medical Doctor (MD) or Doctor of Osteopathy (DO) degree; residency license

Career opportunities: Vary depending on specialty

Income range: $117,000 to $166,000+

Scope

Physicians receive their basic education and initial clinical experience as medical students. While the curriculum of medical schools varies, the 125 traditional or allopathic ones have a common goal of preparing students so that they are qualified to be trained during their residency to become generalists (primary-care physicians), specialists, or subspecialists. The overwhelming majority of practitioners are allopathic physicians.

The general philosophy of the 20 osteopathic medical schools is as a healing modality—preparation of the generalist—with special emphasis on manipulation and treating the entire person. Osteopathic physicians are popular in a number of states, and some specialize. Many secure practice privileges at allopathic hospitals.

Toward the end of the 19th century, as healing knowledge increased, two distinct tracts developed—medicine and surgery. Most, but not all, areas of specialization developed from these two areas because of the complexity of treating the human body. The practice of medical science offers a wide range of opportunities, as summarized in Table 9.2. Note that the training period includes both internship and residency.

Nonmedical practice areas such as medical school education, administration, research, and medical writing offer additional opportunities for physicians with special interests and talents.

Table 9.2: Common Specialties and Subspecialties

Specialty	Training Period	Nature of the Work
Aerospace medicine	3 years	Health care for those involved in space travel
Allergy and immunology	5 years	Treatment of illnesses due to hypersensitivity to specific substances or conditions
Anesthesiology	4 years	Inducing a partial or total block of pain through the use of drugs or gases
Cardiovascular medicine	6 years	Diagnosis and treatment of heart and blood vessel diseases
Child and adolescent psychiatry	5 years	Treatment of emotional disorders in these groups of individuals

(continued)

(continued)

Specialty	Training Period	Nature of the Work
Colon and rectal surgery	6 years	Diagnosis and treatment of diseases of the lower bowel
Dermatology	4 years	Treatment of skin diseases
Diagnostic radiology	4 years	Use of specialized X ray techniques in the diagnosis of problems
Emergency medicine	3 years	Diagnosis and treatment of acute and life-threatening illnesses
Family practice	3 years	Providing preventive total health care for the entire family
Forensic pathology	4 years	Applying pathology in criminal investigations
Gastroenterology	5 years	Diagnosis and treatment of diseases of the digestive tract
Hand injuries	6 years	Treating injuries of the hand
Internal medicine	4 years	Diagnosis and treatment of diseases with medicines
Neonatal-perinatal medicine	6 years	Treatment of infants and high-risk newborns
Neuropathology	4 years	Diagnosis of pathological conditions of the nervous system
Nuclear medicine	6 years	Use of radioactive substances in the diagnosis and treatment of disease
Obstetrics/gynecology	5 years	Providing medical care during pregnancy and labor and for the female reproductive system
Ophthalmology	4 years	Diagnosis and treatment of eye diseases
Orthopedic surgery	4 years	Diagnosis and treatment of injuries to bones and joints
Otolaryngology	4 years	Treatment of ear, nose, and throat diseases
Pathology	4 years	Diagnosis of structural and functional changes in the body tissues due to disease
Pediatric cardiology	5 years	Diagnosis and treatment of heart diseases in children
Pediatric nephrology	5 years	Diagnosis and treatment of kidney diseases in children
Pediatrics	3 years	Care of infants and children and treatment of their diseases
Physical medicine and rehabilitation	4 years	Treatment by various techniques to permit maximum restoration of function
Plastic surgery	7 years	Surgery to repair or restore parts of the body
Preventive medicine	3 years	Individual and public disease prevention
Psychiatry	5 years	Diagnosis and treatment of emotional illnesses
Pulmonary medicine	5 years	Diagnosis and treatment of diseases of the respiratory tract
Rheumatology	4 years	Diagnosis and treatment of rheumatic diseases

Specialty	Training Period	Nature of the Work
Sports medicine	4 years	Treatment of sports-related injuries
Surgery	5 years	Treatment of disease by surgical means
Therapeutic radiology	4 years	Treatment of diseases by radiation therapy
Thoracic surgery	6 years	Surgical treatment of chest organ diseases
Urology	5 years	Treatment of kidney and bladder diseases
Vascular surgery	6 years	Surgery of blood vessels

Activities

Practicing physicians in essence are medical detectives. They seek to provide preventive health care, uncover the causes of illnesses, and determine the best protocols for treatment.

While the basic approach of taking a history and performing a physical examination is common to all clinical areas, a wide variety of testing procedures and therapeutic modalities are used in each of them. Thus, each specialty commonly uses its own diagnostic instruments for evaluation and treatment purposes. Some instruments, however, are common to several specialties. For example, internists and cardiologists use the electrocardiograph (EKG) to evaluate the patient's overall heart rhythm. Cardiologists also use echocardiography, which can evaluate the functional state of specific segments of the heart. The proper use of individual diagnostic tools and accurate interpretation of the results must be mastered to obtain the reliable information and data to facilitate forming a correct diagnosis. In addition, it is essential to know how to properly calculate the results of examination procedures. Based on data accumulated from a variety of sources, the physician chooses a course of action relative to treating the patient. These actions might include requesting further diagnostic tests to better formulate a definitive diagnosis, prescribing a medication to treat the presumed illness, or referring the patient to a more specialized practitioner for advanced care.

If hospitalization is required, the family physician or internist frequently coordinates patient care for the group of physicians and therapists treating the patient. Where appropriate, the patient may be transferred entirely to the care of a specialist or subspecialist.

Osteopathic physicians, who are especially popular in some sections of the country, have their own hospitals. However, they also frequently obtain privileges to train and practice in allopathic hospitals.

Work Settings

The activities of physicians focus on three theaters of practice: the office, the hospital/clinic, or both. The nature of the specialty's demands defines the principal work setting. For example, pediatrics is primarily an office-based specialty, with some hospital/clinic work required. Surgery, on the other hand, is largely a hospital-based activity, with some office time necessary. On the other hand, obstetrics/gynecology involves considerable time in both facilities to meet professional responsibilities.

Advancement

A physician can secure advancement after completing medical school in several ways. The first is to obtain training during residency to become a generalist or specialist. If this path is chosen, many areas also offer the option of pursuing subspecialty training by means of a fellowship. Some physicians gain part-time teaching appointments at medical schools as clinical faculty members. Over time, one of these individuals may move up the academic ranks and assume a full-time appointment as a member of a medical or surgical department at a hospital or medical center.

Prerequisites

Securing a degree from an accredited four-year college or university is the usual requirement for admission to medical school. There are a minimum number of science and non-science course requirements for admission to any U. S. medical school. These include one year of English, mathematics, biology, and physics and two years of chemistry (inorganic and organic). Individual schools may have some additional course requirements. Taking the Medical College Admission Test (MCAT) is a prerequisite for almost all allopathic and osteopathic medical schools. Securing an interview, which is by invitation only, is an essential part of the admission process. The choice of a major is optional, although traditionally many premedical students major in biology and chemistry. For those already holding a bachelor's degree who seek to become physicians but who lack the prerequisites, many institutions offer post baccalaureate programs that provide for the completion of the minimum course work in an accelerated fashion. Some schools offer combined baccalaureate-doctor of medicine degrees. These provide an accelerated program and assure early admission to medical school after the two years of undergraduate studies have been satisfactorily completed.

Desirable personal attributes for work in this field are intelligence, strong scientific interest, a favorable personality, physical and emotional strength, the ability to tolerate uncertainty and frustration, well-organized work habits, the capacity for self-education, social awareness, achievement, and creativity.

Education/Training

Both allopathic and osteopathic medical schools have a four-year program leading to a medical degree. While their curricula vary considerably, initially their focus is on the basic sciences, such as anatomy, physiology, biochemistry, pharmacology, and pathology. With mastery of the fundamental subjects, students are then exposed to the major clinical areas, such as internal medicine, surgery, obstetrics/gynecology, and psychiatry. Throughout the curriculum, and especially during the last year, students are offered opportunities to take electives. These may be in specialties (such as ophthalmology and anesthesiology) or subspecialties (such as cardiology and nephrology). Satisfactory completion of the curriculum and passing the necessary qualifying exams results in being granted an MD or DO degree.

Certification/Registration/Licensure

Medical students are expected to pass the "boards"—the United States Medical Licensing Examination (USMLE). It is given in three parts—the first after your initial two years of medical school, the second before you graduate, and the third after your first postgraduate year of training (internship).

Passing the three parts of the USMLE makes you eligible for licensure, but postgraduate training is still essential. Specialty organizations offer exams for certification in individual specialty areas after you satisfactorily complete a residency.

Career Potential

Overall, job prospects are expected to be very good. With an increasingly aging population, there is a greater need for physicians, especially in primary care. Many medical schools are increasing their enrollments based on perceived new demand for physicians. Openings will also result from the need to replace the relatively high number of physicians and surgeons expected to retire over the next decade. Job prospects should be particularly good for physicians willing to practice in rural and low-income areas. However, an imbalance exists in some specialties. You should take this into consideration when making a residency choice.

For More Information

The professional organizations for physicians are the American Medical Association, 515 N. State St., Chicago, IL 60610 (www.ama-assn.org); the American Osteopathic Association, 142 E. Ontario St., Chicago, IL 60611 (www.osteopathic.org); and the American Medical Women's Association, 801 N. Fairfax St., Alexandria, VA 22314 (http://jamwa.amwa-doc.org).

Additional good sources of information are the Association of American Medical Colleges, 2450 N St. NW, Washington, DC 20037 (www.aamc.org); the American Association of Colleges of Osteopathic Medicine, 5550 Friendship Blvd., Suite 310, Chevy Chase, MD 20815 (www.aacom.org); and the American Medical Student Association, 1902 Association Dr., Reston, VA 20191 (www.amsa.org).

Schools and Colleges of Allopathic Medicine

Alabama
University of Alabama
University Station
School of Medicine
A-100 Volker Hall
Birmingham, AL 35294
www.uab.edu/uasom/

University of South Alabama
College of Medicine
Mobile, AL 36688
www.usouthal.edu

Arizona
University of Arizona
College of Medicine
P.O. Box 245075
Tucson, AZ 85724
www.medicine.arizona.edu

Arkansas
University of Arkansas
College of Medicine
4301 W. Markham St.
Little Rock, AR 72205
www.uams.edu

California
Keck School of Medicine of the
  University of Southern California
1975 Zonal Ave.
Los Angeles, CA 90089
www.usc.edu/schools/medicine/

Loma Linda University
School of Medicine
Loma Linda, CA 92350
www.llu.edu

Stanford University School of
  Medicine
251 Campus Drive
Stanford, California 94305
www.med.stanford.edu/md

UCLA David Geffen School of
  Medicine
10833 Le Conte Avenue
Los Angeles, CA 90095
www.dgsom.healthsciences.ucla.
  edu

University of California–Davis
One Shields Ave.
Davis, CA 95616
http://som.ucdavis.edu/

University of California–Irvine
College of Medicine
Irvine, CA 92697
www.ha.ucl.edu

University of California–San Diego
School of Medicine
9500 Gilman Avenue
La Jolla, CA 92093
www.medicine.ucsd.edu

University of California–
  San Francisco
School of Medicine
C200, Box 0408
San Francisco, CA 94143
www.medschool.ucsf.edu

Colorado
University of Colorado
School of Medicine
Anschutz Medical Campus
P.O. Box 6508
Aurora, CO 80045
www.uchsc.edu/som

Connecticut
University of Connecticut
School of Medicine
263 Farmington Ave.
Farmington, CT 06030
www.medicine.uchc.edu

Yale University
School of Medicine
367 Cedar St.
New Haven, CT 06510
http://medicine.yale.edu/

District of Columbia
George Washington University
Health Sciences
2300 I Street NW
Washington, DC 20037
www.gwumc.edu/smhs/

Georgetown University
School of Medicine
Box 571421
Washington, DC 20007
http://som.georgetown.edu/

Howard University
College of Medicine
520 W Street NW
Washington, DC 20059
www.med.howard.edu

Florida
Florida International University
College of Medicine
1200 SW 8th Street
Miami, Florida 33199
www.fiu.edu

Florida State University
College of Medicine
Tallahassee, Florida 32306
http://medicine.fiu.edu/

University of Central Florida
College of Medicine
2201 Research Parkway
P.O. Box 60116
Orlando, Florida 32816
www.ucf.edu

University of Florida
College of Medicine
P.O. Box 100216
Gainesville, FL 32610
www.med.ucf.edu

University of Miami
Miller School of Medicine
P.O. Box 016159
Miami, FL 33101
www.med.miami.edu

University of South Florida
College of Medicine
12901 Bruce B. Downs Blvd.
Tampa, FL 33612
http://health.usf.edu/medicine/

Georgia
Emory University School of
 Medicine
1648 Pierce Drive NE
Atlanta, GA 30322
www.med.emory.edu

Medical College of Georgia
1120 15th St.
Augusta, GA 30912
www.mcg.edu

Mercer University
1550 College St.
Macon, GA 31207
http://medicine.mercer.edu/

Morehouse School of Medicine
720 Westview Dr. SW
Atlanta, GA 30310
www.msm.edu

Hawaii
University of Hawaii at Manoa
John A. Burns School of Medicine
965 Ollalo Street
Honolulu, HI 96813
http://jabsom.hawaii.edu/

Illinois
 Rosalind Franklin University of
 Medicine
3333 Green Bay Rd.
North Chicago, IL 60064
www.rosalindfranklin.edu/cms

Loyola University–Chicago
Stritch School of Medicine
2160 S. First Ave.
Maywood, IL 60153
www.meddean.luc.edu

Northwestern University
Feinberg School of Medicine
303 E. Chicago Ave.
Chicago, IL 60611
www.feinberg.northwestern.edu

Rush Medical College of
 Rush University
600 S. Paulina St.
Chicago, IL 60612
www.rushu.rush.edu/medcol/

Southern Illinois University
School of Medicine
P.O. Box 19624
Springfield, IL 62794
www.siumed.edu

University of Chicago
Pritzker School of Medicine
924 E. 57th St., BLSC 104
Chicago, IL 60637
http://pritzker.bsd.uchicago.edu/

University of Illinois at Chicago
College of Medicine
808 S Wood Street
Chicago, IL 60612
www.medicine.uic.edu

Indiana
Indiana University
School of Medicine
1120 South Dr., Fesler Hall 302
Indianapolis, IN 46202
www.medicine.iu.edu

Iowa
University of Iowa
The Roy J. and Lucille A. Carver
 College of Medicine
200 CMAB
Iowa City, IA 52242
www.medicine.uiowa.edu

Kansas
University of Kansas
School of Medicine
3901 Rainbow Blvd.
Kansas City, KS 66160
www.kumc.edu/som.html

Kentucky
University of Kentucky
College of Medicine
138 Leader Avenue
Lexington, KY 40507
www.mc.uky.edu/medicine/

University of Louisville
School of Medicine
323 Chestnut
Louisville, KY 40262
www.louisville.edu/medschool

Louisiana
Louisiana State University School
  of Medicine in New Orleans
1901 Perdido St.
New Orleans, LA 70112
www.medschool.lsuhsc.edu

Louisiana State University School
  of Medicine in Shreveport
P.O. Box 33932
Shreveport, LA 71130
www.lsuhscshreveport.edu

Tulane University
School of Medicine
1430 Tulane Ave.
New Orleans, LA 70112
www.tmc.tulane.edu

Maryland
Johns Hopkins University
School of Medicine
733 Broadway
Baltimore, MD 21205
www.hopkinsmedicine.org

Uniformed Services University of
  the Health Sciences
F. Edward Herbert
4301 Jones Bridge Rd.
Bethesda, MD 20814
www.usuhs.mil

University of Maryland
685 W. Baltimore St.
Baltimore, MD 21201
www.medschool.umaryland.edu

Massachusetts
Boston University
School of Medicine
715 Albany St.
Boston, MA 02118
www.bumc.bu.edu

Harvard Medical School
25 Shattuck St.
Boston, MA 02115
www.hms.harvard.edu

Tufts University
School of Medicine
136 Harrison Ave.
Boston, MA 02111
www.tufts.edu/med/

University of Massachusetts
Medical School
55 Lake Ave. N.
Worcester, MA 01655
www.umassmed.edu

Michigan
Michigan State University
College of Human Medicine
A239 Life Sciences
East Lansing, MI 48824
www.humanmedicine.msu.edu

University of Michigan
Medical School
4303 Medical Science Building
Ann Arbor, MI 48109
www.med.umich.edu/medschool/

Wayne State University
School of Medicine
540 E. Canfield Ave.
Detroit, MI 48201
www.med.wayne.edu

Minnesota
Mayo Clinic School
Mayo Medical School
200 First St. SW
Rochester, MN 55905
www.mayo.edu

University of Minnesota–Duluth
10 University Dr.
Duluth, MN 55812
www.d.umn.edu

University of Minnesota
Medical School
420 Delaware St. SE
Minneapolis, MN 55455
www.med.umn.edu

Mississippi
University of Mississippi
School of Medicine
2500 N. State St.
Jackson, MS 39216
www.som.umc.edu

Missouri
Saint Louis University
School of Medicine
Grand Blvd.14025
St. Louis, MO 63104
www.slu.edu

University of Missouri–Columbia
One Hospital Dr.
Columbia, MO 65212
www.som.missouri.edu

University of Missouri–Kansas City
School of Medicine
2411 Holmes
Kansas City, MO 64108
www.umkc.edu

Washington University
School of Medicine
660 S. Euclid Ave.
St. Louis, MO 63110
www.medicine.wustl.edu

Nebraska
Creighton University
School of Medicine
2500 California Plaza
Omaha, NE 68178
http://medicine.creighton.edu/

University of Nebraska
986585 Nebraska Medical Center
Omaha, NE 68198
www.unmc.edu

Nevada
University of Nevada
School of Medicine
Mail Stop 357
Reno, NV 89557
www.medicine.nevada.edu

New Hampshire
Dartmouth Medical School
3 Rope Ferry Rd.
Hanover, NH 03755
www.dartmouth.edu/dms/

New Jersey

New Jersey Medical School
University of Medicine &
 Dentistry of New Jersey
185 S. Orange Ave.
Newark, NJ 07103
www.umdnj.edu

Robert Wood Johnson Medical
 School
University of Medicine and
 Dentistry of New Jersey
675 Hoes Lane
Piscataway, NJ 08854
www.rwjms.umdnj.edu

New Mexico

University of New Mexico
School of Medicine
Albuquerque, NM 87131
www.unm.edu

New York

Albany Medical College
Office of Admission
47 New Scotland Ave.
Albany, NY 12208
www.amc.edu/academic/

Albert Einstein College of
 Medicine of Yeshiva University
1300 Morris Park Ave.
Bronx, NY 10461
www.aecom.yu.edu

Columbia University
College of Physicians and
 Surgeons
630 W. 168th St.
New York, NY 10032
www.cumc.columbia.edu/dept/ps/

Mount Sinai School of Medicine
 of the University of New York
One Gustave L. Levy Place
New York, NY 10029
www.mssm.edu

New York Medical College
Valhalla, NY 10595
www.nymc.edu

New York University School of
 Medicine
550 First Ave.
New York, NY 10016
www.med.nyu.edu

State University of New York
Upstate Medical University
College of Medicine
766 Irving Avenue
Syracuse, NY 13210
www.upstate.edu/com

State University of New York at
 Buffalo
School of Medicine and
 Biomedical Sciences
131 Biomedical Education
 Building
Buffalo, NY 14214
www.smbs.buffalo.edu

State University of New York
Downstate Medical Center
450 Clarkson Ave.
Brooklyn, NY 11203
www.downstate.edu

Stony Brook University
School of Medicine
Health Sciences Center
Stony Brook, NY 11794
www.hsc.stonybrook.edu/som/

University of Rochester
School of Medicine and Dentistry
601 Elmwood Ave.
Rochester, NY 14642
www.urmc.rochester.edu/smd/

Weill Medical College
Cornell University
445 E. 69th St.
New York, NY 10021
www.med.cornell.edu/

North Carolina

Brody School of Medicine at East
 Carolina University
600 Moye Blvd.
Greenville, NC 27834
www.ecu.edu/med/

Duke University
School of Medicine
DUMC 3710
Durham, NC 27710
www.dukemed.duke.edu

University of North Carolina at
 Chapel Hill
School of Medicine
CB#9500 1001 Bondurant Hall
Chapel Hill, NC 27599
www.med.unc.edu

Wake Forest University
School of Medicine
Medical Center Boulevard
Winston-Salem, NC 27157
www.wfubmc.edu/school/

North Dakota

University of North Dakota
School of Medicine & Health
 Sciences
501 N. Columbia Rd.
Grand Forks, ND 58203
www.med.und.nodak.edu

Ohio

Case Western Reserve University
School of Medicine
10900 Euclid Ave.
Cleveland, OH 44106
http://casemed.case.edu/

University of Toledo
College of Medicine
3000 Arlington Ave.
Toledo, OH 43614
www.mco.edu

Northeastern Ohio Universities
 College of Medicine
P.O. Box 95
Rootstown, OH 44272
www.neoucom.edu

Ohio State University
College of Medicine
370 W. Ninth Ave.
Columbus, OH 43210
www.medicine.osu.edu

University of Cincinnati
College of Medicine
P.O. Box 670552
Cincinnati, OH 45267
www.med.uc.edu

Wright State University
School of Medicine
P.O. Box 1751
Dayton, OH 45401
www.med.wright.edu

Oklahoma
University of Oklahoma
College of Medicine
P.O. Box 26901
Oklahoma City, OK 73126
www.medicine.ouhsc.edu

Oregon
Oregon Health Sciences University
School of Medicine
3181 SW Sam Jackson Park Rd.
Portland, OR 97239
www.ohsu.edu/som

Puerto Rico
Ponce School of Medicine
P.O. Box 7004
Ponce, Puerto Rico 00752
www.psm.edu

San Juan Batista
School of Medicine
Caguas, Puerto Rico
P.O. Box 4968
Caguas, Puerto Rico 00726
www.sanjuanbautista.edu

Universidad Central de Caribe
School of Medicine
P.O. Box 60-327
Bayamon, Puerto Rico 00960
www.uccaribe.edu

University of Puerto Rico
School of Medicine
P.O. Box 365067
San Juan, Puerto Rico 00936
www.md.rcm.upr.edu

Pennsylvania
Drexel University
College of Medicine
2900 W. Queen Ln.
Philadelphia, PA 19129
www.drex.med.edu

Jefferson Medical College
Thomas Jefferson University
1015 Walnut St.
Philadelphia, PA 19107
www.jefferson.edu/jmc

Pennsylvania State University
College of Medicine
P.O. Box 850
500 University Dr.
Hershey, PA 17033
www.hmc.psu.edu/md/

Temple University
School of Medicine
3340 N. Broad St.
Philadelphia, PA 19140
www.temple.edu/medicine

University of Pennsylvania
School of Medicine
3620 Hamilton Walk
Philadelphia, PA 19104
www.med.upenn.edu

University of Pittsburgh
School of Medicine
Pittsburgh, PA 15261
www.medschool.pitt.edu

Rhode Island
Brown University
Alpert Medical School
97 Waterman St. Box G-A213
Providence, RI 02912
http://bms.brown.edu

South Carolina
Medical University of South
  Carolina
College of Medicine
96 Jonathan Lucas St.
Charleston, SC 29425
www.musc.edu/com1/

University of South Carolina
School of Medicine
Columbia, SC 29208
www.med.sc.edu

South Dakota
Sanford School of Medicine of the
  University of South Dakota
414 E. Clark St.
Vermillion, SD 57069
www.med.usd.edu

Tennessee
East Tennessee State University
James H. Quillen College of
  Medicine
P.O. Box 702580
Johnson City, TN 37614
https://com.etsu.edu/

Meharry Medical College
School of Medicine
1005 Dr. D.B. Todd, Jr. Blvd.
Nashville, TN 37208
www.mmc.edu

University of Tennessee
Health Science Center
College of Medicine
910 Madison Avenue
Memphis, TN 38163
www.utmem.edu/medicine/

Vanderbilt University
School of Medicine
215 Light Hall
Nashville, TN 37232
www.mc.vanderbilt.edu

Texas
Baylor College of Medicine
One Baylor Plaza
Houston, TX 77030
www.bcm.edu

Texas A&M University System
Health Science Center
College of Medicine
159 Joe Reynolds Medical
  Building
College Station, TX 77843
www.medicine.tamhsc.edu

Paul L. Foster School of
  Medicine
Texas Tech University Health
  Science Center at El Paso
4800 Alberta Avenue
El Paso, Texas 79905
www.ttuhsc.edu/fostersom/

Texas Tech University
Health Science Center
3601 4th St.
Lubbock, TX 79430
www.ttuhsc.edu

University of Texas
Medical School at Galveston
5301 University Boulevard
Galveston, TX 7755
www.som.utmb.edu

University of Texas
Medical School at Houston
6431 Fannin St.
Houston, TX 77030
www.med.uth.tmc.edu

University of Texas
Medical School at San Antonio
7703 Floyd Curl Dr.
San Antonio, TX 78229
www.som.uthscsa.edu

University of Texas
Southwestern Medical Center at
 Dallas
Southwestern Medical School
5323 Harry Hines Blvd.
Dallas, TX 75390
www.utsouthwestern.edu

Utah
University of Utah
School of Medicine
30 N 1900 East Room
Salt Lake City, Utah 84132
www.med.utah.edu/som/

Vermont
University of Vermont
College of Medicine
E-126 Given Building
89 Beaumont Ave.
Burlington, VT 05405
www.med.uvm.edu

Virginia
Eastern Virginia Medical School
700 W Olney Road
Norfolk, VA 23507
www.evms.edu

University of Virginia
 School of Medicine
P.O. Box 800725
Charlottesville, VA 22908
www.healthsystem.virginia.edu/
 internet/som

Virginia Commonwealth University
School of Medicine
P.O. Box 980565
Richmond, VA 23298
www.medschool.vcu.edu

Washington
University of Washington
School of Medicine
Box 356340
Seattle, WA 98195
www.uwmedicine.org

West Virginia
Marshall University
Joan C. Edwards School of
 Medicine
1600 Medical Center Dr.
Huntington, WV 25701
www.musom.marshall.edu

West Virginia University
School of Medicine
P.O. Box 9111
Morgantown, WV 26506
www.hsc.wvu.edu/som/

Wisconsin
Medical College of Wisconsin
8701 Watertown Plank Rd.
Milwaukee, WI 53226
www.mcw.edu

University of Wisconsin
 School of Medicine
 & Public Health
750 Highland Avenue
Madison, WI 53706
www.med.wisc.edu

Canada
Dalhousie University
Faculty of Medicine
Halifax, Nova Scotia B3H 4H7
www.medicine.dal.ca

McGill University
Faculty of Medicine
3655 Promenade Sir William Osler
Montreal, Quebec H3G 1Y6
www.med.mcgill.ca

McMaster University
Faculty of Health Sciences
1200 Main St. W.
Hamilton, Ontario L8N 3Z5
www.fhs.mcmaster.ca

Memorial University of
 Newfoundland
Faculty of Medicine
Prince Phillips Dr.
St. John's, Newfoundland
 A1B 3V6
www.med.mun.ca/med

Queen's University
School of Medicine
68 Barry Street
Kingston, Ontario K7L 3N6
www.meds.queensu.ca/medicine/

Universite de Montreal
 School of Medicine
P.O. Box 6128, Station
 Centre-Ville
Montreal, Quebec H3J 3J7
www.med.umontreal.ca

Universite de Sherbrooke
Faculty of Medicine
Sherbrooke, Quebec J1H 5N4
www.usherb.ca

Universite Laval
Faculty of Medicine
Sainte-Foy, Quebec G1K 7P4
www.fmed.ulaval.ca

University of Alberta
Faculty of Medicine
2-45 Medical Sciences Building
Edmonton, Alberta T6G 2H7
www.med.ualberta.ca

University of British Columbia
Faculty of Medicine
317-2194 Health Sciences Mall
Vancouver, British Columbia
 V6T 1Z3
www.med.ubc.ca

University of Calgary
Faculty of Medicine
3330 University Dr. NW
Calgary, Alberta T2N 4N1
www.medicine.ucalgary.ca

University of Manitoba
School of Medicine
260-727 McDermot Ave.
Winnipeg, Manitoba R3E 3P5
www.umanitoba.ca/faculties/
 medicine/

University of Ottawa
Faculty of Medicine
451 Smyth Rd.
Ottawa, Ontario K1H 8M5
www.medicine.uottawa.ca/eng/

University of Saskatchewan
College of Medicine
B103 Health Sciences Building
107 Wiggins Rd.
Saskatoon, Saskatchewan S7N 5E5
www.usask.ca/medicine/

University of Toronto
Faculty of Medicine
1 Kings College Circle
Toronto, Ontario M5S 1A1
www.utoronto.ca

University of Western Ontario,
  Schulich
Faculty of Medicine & Dentistry
London, Ontario N6A 5C1
www.schulich.uwo.ca

Schools and Colleges of Osteopathic Medicine

Arizona
Arizona College of Osteopathic
  Medicine of Midwestern
  University
19555 N. 59th Ave.
Glendale, AZ 85308
www.midwestern.edu/azcom/

California
Touro University
College of Osteopathic Medicine
1310 Johnson Ln.
Mare Island
Vallejo, CA 94592
www.tucom.edu

Western University of Health
  Sciences
College of Osteopathic Medicine
  of the Pacific
309 E. Second St.
Pomona, CA 91766
www.westernu.edu

Colorado
Rocky Vista University
College of Osteopathic Medicine
8401 Chambers Road
Parker, Colorado 80134
www.rockyvistauniversity.org

Florida
Lake Erie College of Osteopathic
  Medicine
Brandenton Campus
5000 Lakewood Branch
Brandenton, Florida 34211
www.lecom.edu

Nova Southeastern University
College of Osteopathic Medicine
3301 College Avenue
Fort Lauderdale, FL 33328
www.nova.edu

Georgia
Philadelphia College of
Osteopathic Medicine
625 Old Peachthree Road NW
Suwanee, Georgia 30024
www.pcom.edu

Illinois
Chicago College of Osteopathic
  Medicine
Midwestern University
555 31st St.
Downers Grove, IL 60515
www.midwestern.edu/ccom/

Iowa
Des Moines University
College of Osteopathic Medicine
3200 Grand Ave.
Des Moines, IA 50312
www.dmu.edu/coms/

Kentucky
Pikeville College School of
  Osteopathic Medicine
214 Sycamore St.
Pikeville, KY 41501
http://pcsom.pc.edu/

Maine
University of New England
College of Osteopathic Medicine
11 Hills Beach Rd.
Biddeford, ME 04005
www.une.edu/com/

Michigan
Michigan State University
College of Osteopathic Medicine
A306 East Fee Hall
East Lansing, MI 48824
www.com.msu.edu

Missouri
A.T. Still University
Kirksville College of Osteopathic
  Medicine
800 W. Jefferson St.
Kirksville, MO 63501
www.atsu.edu/kcom/

Kansas City University of
  Medicine & Biosciences
College of Osteopathic Medicine
1750 Independence Ave.
Kansas City, MO 64106
www.kcumb.edu

Nevada
Touro University-Nevada
College of Osteopathic Medicine
874 American Pacific Drive
Henderson, Nevada 89014
www.touro.edu/med

New Jersey
University of Medicine and
  Dentistry of New Jersey
School of Osteopathic Medicine
1 Medical Center Dr.
Stratford, NJ 08084
www.som.umdnj.edu

New York
New York College of Osteopathic
  Medicine
Institute of Technology
P.O. Box 8000
Old Westbury, NY 11568
www.nyt.edu

Touro College
School of Osteopathic Medicine
230 W 125th Street
New York, NY 10027
www.touro.edu/med/

Ohio
Ohio University College of
  Osteopathic Medicine
102 Grosvenor Hall
Athens, OH 45701
www.oucom.ohiou.edu

Oklahoma
Oklahoma State University
College of Osteopathic Medicine
1111 W. 17th St.
Tulsa, OK 74107
www.healthsciences.okstate.edu

Pennsylvania
Philadelphia College of
  Osteopathic Medicine
4170 City Ave.
Philadelphia, PA 19131
www.pcom.edu

Lake Erie College of Osteopathic
  Medicine
LECOM at Seton Hall
1 Seton Hall Drive
Greensburg, Pennsylvania 15601
www.lecom.edu

Tennessee
Lincoln Memorial University
DeBusk College of Osteopathic
  Medicine
6965 Cumberland Gap Parkway
Harrogate, Tennessee 37752
www.lmunet.edu

Texas
University of North Texas
Texas College of Osteopathic
  Medicine at Forth Worth
3500 Camp Bowie Blvd.
Forth Worth, Texas 76107
www.hsc.unt.edu

Virginia
Edward Via Virginia College of
  Osteopathic Medicine
2265 Kraft Dr.
Blacksburg, VA 24060
www.vcom.vt.edu

Washington
Pacific Northwest University
Of Health Sciences
College of Osteopathic Medicine
111 South 3rd Street
Yakoma, Washington 98901
www.pnwu.org

West Virginia
West Virginia School of
  Osteopathic Medicine
400 N. Lee St.
Lewisburg, WV 24901
www.wvsom.edu

Podiatrists

Principal activity: Providing medical and surgical foot care

Work commitment: Usually full-time

Preprofessional education: Bachelor's degree

Program length: 4 years

Work prerequisites: Doctor of Podiatry Medicine (DPM) degree and license

Career opportunities: Stable

Income range: $75,000 to $166,000+

Scope

Doctors of podiatry specialize in the prevention, diagnosis, and treatment of diseases, injuries, and disorders of the foot and ankle. They use medical, surgical, mechanical, and physical treatment methods, and they may prescribe corrective footwear and shoe insert devices. The profession traces its origins as far back as ancient Egypt. The first practitioner in the United States was Julius Davidson, who set up an office in Philadelphia in 1841.

Activities

The typical podiatry practice covers the full range of podiatric problems, including corns, calluses, warts, ingrown toenails, bunions, and the treatment of foot injuries. Podiatrists use computerized machines to determine the exact size, shape, and dimensions for corrective shoes and inserts. Some specialize in such areas as pedopodiatrics (the care of children's feet), podogeriatrics (foot care for the aged), podiatry sports medicine (diagnosis and treatment of sports-related problems), and podiatric surgery. A newer specialty is diabetic and disease-related foot care.

Work Settings

Traditionally, podiatrists have worked in solo practices, often establishing offices in their homes or in professional buildings, but today group practices are more common. Podiatrists also serve on the staffs of clinics, hospitals, and nursing homes; in municipal health departments; at sports health facilities; and on the faculty of podiatry schools. Many also serve professionally as members of the U.S. armed forces.

Advancement

Podiatrists can advance by joining the staffs of prestigious facilities, by moving into a private practice, or by specialization.

Prerequisites

The initial goal of a pre-podiatry student is to secure a high school diploma or its equivalent with good grades in the sciences. The next step is to gain admission to an accredited college or university, where the basic science courses should be completed. These courses include one year of biology, chemistry, and physics, as well as mathematics and English composition. Other courses may be recommended by individual schools. A minimum of three years of college (90 semester hours) is required for admission to podiatry schools, but most applicants have graduated by the time they begin their professional studies.

Applicants to podiatry schools must take the Medical College Admission Test (MCAT) and arrange for official transcripts and letters of recommendation to be sent to their chosen schools. A single application can be used to apply to any or all of the six podiatry schools belonging to the American Association of Colleges of Podiatric Medicine Application Service (AAPMAS), as discussed in the section "For More Information."

Desirable personal attributes of those planning to enter this field include good interpersonal and business skills, proficiency in science, and superior manual dexterity.

Education/Training

Podiatry involves four years of study followed by one to three years of residency training. There are some differences in curriculum content among schools; however, the general pattern involves two years of basic medical science courses and two years of clinical course work. The curriculum's overall pattern is arranged so that students move from learning fundamental knowledge about the normal structure and function of the human body to a mix of basic and preliminary clinical science work in the second year. The third year is devoted primarily to clinical learning experience, with advanced seminars and electives. During this time students gain proficiency in the treatment of podiatric patients suffering from various problems.

Certification/Registration/Licensure

Podiatrists must be licensed by the state in which they will work. Licensing requirements differ from state to state, but they generally involve earning a DPM degree, passing written and/or oral proficiency exams, and satisfactorily completing at least a year of residency training, which is arranged through a matching program. In some states, exams administered by the National Board of Podiatric Examiners substitute for written state examinations. The Board exams are taken in two parts. The first, at the end of a student's second year of podiatry school, covers the basic sciences. The second, taken in the spring of the fourth year, covers the clinical areas. Podiatrists also may be certified in one of three specialty areas: primary medicine, orthopedics, or surgery.

Career Potential

Podiatrists' income potential has increased as a result of the rise in fitness, sports, and exercise programs, all of which may cause foot problems or injuries. An aging population also has resulted in a greater need for treatment for the elderly, and an increase in the number of Americans diagnosed with diabetes has lead to a need for more podiatrists as well. Their level of income, which increases with experience, is quite high. Unfortunately the occupation is relatively small, and most podiatrists continue to practice until retirement.

For More Information

The professional organization for this field is the American Podiatric Medical Association, 9312 Old Georgetown Rd., Bethesda, MD 20814 (www.apma.org). You can get additional information from the American Association of Colleges of Podiatric Medicine, 15850 Crabbs Branch Way, Rockville, MD 20855 (www.aacpm.org). The certifying organization is the American Board of Podiatric Surgery, 3330 Mission St., San Francisco, CA 94110 (www. abps.org).

Applicants to podiatry schools must take the MCAT. Those applying for September admission must take the MCAT no later than April of the year of desired admission. For more information on the MCAT, contact the MCAT Program Office, P.O. Box 4056, Iowa City, IA 52243 (www.aamc.org/students/mcat/contact.htm).

Colleges of Podiatry

Arizona
Arizona Podiatric Medicine
   at Midwestern University
19555 North 59th Avenue
Glendale, Arizona 85308
www.midwestern.edu

California
California College of Podiatric
   Medicine
1210 Scott Street
San Francisco, CA 94115
www.footandankle.com/ccpm/
   cme

California School of Podiatric
   Medicine at Samuel Merritt
   College
370 Hawthorne Ave.
Oakland, CA 94609
www.samuelmerritt.edu

Florida
Barry University
College of Podiatric Medicine
11300 NE Second Ave.
Miami Shores, FL 33161
www.barry.edu/gms/podiatry/

Illinois
Dr. William M Scholl College of
   Podiatric Medicine at Rosalind
   Franklin University of Medicine
   & Science
3333 Green Bay Rd.
North Chicago, IL 60064
www.rosalindfranklin.edu

Iowa
Des Moines University
College of Podiatric Medicine and
   Surgery
3200 Grand Ave.
Des Moines, IA 50312
www.dmu.edu/cpms/

New York
New York College of Podiatric
   Medicine
53 East 124th Street
New York, NY 10035
www.nycpm.edu

Ohio
Ohio College of Podiatric
   Medicine
10515 Carnegie Ave.
Cleveland, OH 44106
www.ocpm.edu

Pennsylvania
Temple University School of
   Podiatric Medicine
Eighth and Race Sts.
Philadelphia, PA 19107
http://podiatry.temple.edu/

Veterinarians

Principal activity: Providing animal care to maintain and restore health

Work commitment: Usually full-time

Preprofessional education: Bachelor's degree

Program length: 4 years

Work prerequisites: Doctor of Veterinary Medicine (DVM) degree and license

Career opportunities: Highly Favorable

Income range: $62,000 to $104,000

Scope

Veterinarians provide care for pets, livestock, sporting animals, and laboratory animals. They contribute to animal health and human well-being. Some are engaged in research, food safety inspection, or teaching. The majority treat only small companion animals, such as dogs, cats, and birds. Others treat only large animals, such as cattle and horses. Still others (mostly in rural areas) deal with both small and large animals.

Activities

Veterinarians advise owners on both the care and breeding of animals. They have the skill and training to diagnose medical problems, dress wounds, set fractured bones, and perform surgery. They also are qualified to prescribe and administer medicines and to vaccinate animals against diseases. Some veterinarians work with physicians and scientists to prevent and treat disease in humans. Those involved in health safety work may serve as livestock inspectors, checking for diseased animals. Those engaged in meat inspection examine slaughtering and processing plants, checking both live animals and carcasses for disease to see whether standards and sanitation are adequate.

Work Settings

Veterinarians are employed in private clinics and hospitals and by federal, state, and local government agencies. Some work at teaching institutions, zoos, and aquariums. Horse racing farms need resident veterinarians. Research laboratories, pharmaceutical companies, and animal food manufacturers also employ them.

Advancement

Those employed by others can move on to solo or group practices. Those employed by government agencies can move up the civil service ladder. Specialized training in one of a variety of specialty areas enhances career status.

Prerequisites

If you want to be a veterinarian, you must first earn a high school diploma or its equivalent. The next phase is getting admitted to an accredited college or university where all the pre-veterinary requirements can be met. These include one year of biology, chemistry (both inorganic and organic), and physics and other courses taken by pre-health profession students. You also must take the Medical College Admission Test (MCAT) or the Graduate Record Examination (GRE), depending on each school's requirements (see Appendix A for more information). Admission to veterinary colleges is highly competitive.

Desirable personal attributes include a love of animals, superior manual dexterity, a pleasant personality, good reasoning abilities, quick thinking, keen observation skills, and the ability to soothe anxious animals.

Education/Training

A DVM degree requires four years of professional study. In a traditional curriculum, the first two years of school are devoted to basic sciences—including the study of anatomy and physiology of dogs, cats, horses, cows, and other representative animals—along with biochemistry. The second year is devoted to the pathology of animal diseases and pharmacology. The last two years are devoted to clinical veterinary medicine, including surgery, radiology, public health, and preventive medicine, as well as principles of outpatient and farm practice. The veterinary clinical experience includes diagnosing and treating animal diseases and performing surgery and various laboratory tests. Some schools use a core elective curriculum, which reduces the number of required courses while increasing the number of electives; this allows students to design a more personalized program of studies.

Certification/Registration/Licensure

Before practicing veterinary medicine, students must earn a DVM degree and successfully complete the National Board Examination to secure a license. Some states have additional board examinations of their own.

Career Potential

Employment prospects for veterinarians in the next decade should be excellent, especially for those with specialized training in laboratory animal medicine, toxicology, pathology, animal behavior, and farm animals. Employment in this field is expected to grow as the number of pet owners increases and current practitioners retire.

For More Information

The professional organization for veterinarians is the American Veterinary Medical Association, 1931 N. Meacham Rd., Suite 100, Schaumburg, IL 60173 (www.avma.org). Another good source of information about this field is the Association of American Veterinary Medical Colleges, 1101 Vermont Ave. NW, Washington, DC 20005 (www.avmc.org).

Schools and Colleges of Veterinary Medicine

Alabama
College of Veterinary Medicine
Auburn University
104 Greene Hall
Auburn, AL 36849
www.vetmed.auburn.edu

Tuskegee University
College of Veterinary Medicine
Tuskegee, AL 36088
www.tuskegee.edu

Arizona
Argosy University–Phoenix
2233 W Dunlap Avenue
Phoenix, AZ 85021
www.drf.veterinaryschools.com

California
University of California–Davis
School of Veterinary Medicine
1 Shields Avenue
Davis, CA 95616
www.vetmed.ucdavis.edu

Western University of Health
Sciences
306 Second St.
Pomona, CA 91766
www.westernu.edu/cvm.html

Colorado
Colorado State University
College of Veterinary Medicine
and Biomedical Sciences
Fort Collins, CO 80523
www.cvmbs.colostate.edu

Florida
University of Florida
College of Veterinary Medicine
215 SW 16th Ave.
P.O. Box 100125
Gainesville, FL 32610
www.vetmed.ufl.edu

Georgia
Argosy University-Atlanta
980 Hammond Drive
Atlanta, GA 30328
www.drf.veterinaryschools.com

University of Georgia
College of Veterinary Medicine
Athens, GA 30602
www.vet.uga.edu

Illinois
University of Illinois–Urbana
College of Veterinary Medicine
2001 S. Lincoln Ave.
Urbana, IL 61802
www.cvm.uiuc.edu

Indiana
Purdue University
School of Veterinary Medicine
625 Harrison Street
West Lafayette, IN 49707
www.vet.purdue.edu

Iowa
Iowa State University
College of Veterinary Medicine
2508 Veterinary Administration
Ames, IA 50011
www.vetmed.iastate.edu

Kansas
Kansas State University
College of Veterinary Medicine
101 Trotter Hall
Manhattan, KS 66506
www.vet.ksu.edu

Louisiana
Louisiana State University
School of Veterinary Medicine
Baton Rouge, LA 70803
www.vetmed.lsu.edu

Massachusetts
Tufts University
School of Veterinary Medicine
200 Westboro Rd.
North Grafton, MA 01536
http://vet.tufts.edu/

Michigan
Michigan State University
College of Veterinary Medicine
G-100 Veterinary Medical Center
East Lansing, MI 48824
www.cvm.msu.edu

Minnesota
University of Minnesota
College of Veterinary Medicine
1365 Gortner Ave.
St. Paul, MN 55108
www.cvm.umn.edu

Mississippi
Mississippi State University
College of Veterinary Medicine
Box 9825
Mississippi State, MS 39762
www.cvm.msstate.edu

Missouri
University of Missouri
College of Veterinary Medicine
321 University Hall
Columbia, MO 65211
www.cvm.missouri.edu

New York
Cornell University
College of Veterinary Medicine
S2005 Schurman Hall
Ithaca, NY 14853
www.vet.cornell.edu

North Carolina
North Carolina State University
College of Veterinary Medicine
4700 Hillsborough St.
Raleigh, NC 27606
www.cvm.ncsu.edu

Ohio
Ohio State University
College of Veterinary Medicine
601 Vernon L. Tharp Street
Columbus, OH 43210
www.vet.ohio-state.edu

Oklahoma
Oklahoma State University
College of Veterinary Medicine
205 McElroy Hall
Stillwater, OK 74078
www.cvm.okstate.edu

Oregon
Oregon State University
College of Veterinary Medicine
Corvallis, OR 97331
www.vet.orst.edu

Pennsylvania
University of Pennsylvania
School of Veterinary Medicine
3800 Spruce St.
Philadelphia, PA 19104
www.vet.upenn.edu

Tennessee
University of Tennessee
College of Veterinary Medicine
P.O. Box 1071
Knoxville, TN 37901
www.vet.utk.edu

Texas
Texas A&M University
College of Veterinary Medicine
College Station, TX 77843
www.cvm.tamu.edu

Virginia
Virginia-Maryland Regional
  College of Veterinary Medicine
Duckpond Dr.
Blacksburg, VA 24061
www.vetmed.vt.edu

Washington
Washington State University
College of Veterinary Medicine
P.O. Box 647010
Pullman, WA 99164
www.vetmed.wsu.edu

Wisconsin
University of Wisconsin–Madison
School of Veterinary Medicine
2015 Linden Dr. W
Madison, WI 53706
www.vetmed.wisc.edu

Canada

Universite de Montreal–Quebec
Faculte de Medicine Veterinaire
St. Hyacinthe, Montreal J2S 7C6
www.umontreal.ca

University of Guelph
Ontario Veterinary College
Guelph, Ontario N1G 2W1
www.ovc.uoguelph.ca

University of Prince Edward
  Island
Atlantic Veterinary College
550 University Ave.
Charlottetown, PEI C1A 4P3
www.upei.ca/avc/

University of Saskatchewan
Western College of Veterinary
  Medicine
52 Campus Dr.
Saskatoon, Saskatchewan S7N
  5B4
www.usask.ca/wcvm/

Associated Health-Care Careers

Physicians and dentists are highly educated and rigorously trained health-care professionals. Because their time is limited and costly, they often delegate some of their responsibilities to other health professionals. Although they have less training, these people are qualified to efficiently perform certain tasks and procedures. This allows physicians and dentists to focus on diagnoses and treatment.

This chapter outlines eight health-care careers, all involving direct patient contact and providing valuable services that enhance the public's health:

- **Dental hygienists** carry out oral-care procedures and educate patients on the daily care of their teeth.
- **Dietitians** prescribe appropriate diets to restore and maintain good health and prevent disease.
- **Genetic counselors** provide information and guidance about medical issues that have a hereditary basis.
- **Nurses** of various types (registered, licensed practical, practitioners, midwives, anesthetists) provide a wide variety of hands-on daily patient care and services.
- **Nutritionists** advise individuals and groups on proper nutritional practices that enhance health and prevent disease.
- **Pharmacists** compound and dispense medications prescribed by doctors.
- **Physician assistants** perform many routine and sophisticated medical and diagnostic tasks and procedures.
- **Surgeon assistants** help doctors and nurses in the surgical arena.

This field has grown rapidly as a result of major advances in medical care. While pharmacists may be self-employed, the other professionals in this field work in private offices or hospital settings. All eight careers require specialized education and some training, and all offer good long-term prospects for employment.

Dental Hygienists

Principal activity: Providing tooth and gum care

Work commitment: Part- or full-time

Preprofessional education: High school diploma

Program length: 2 years minimum

Work prerequisites: Degree and license

Career opportunities: Highly favorable

Income range: $55,000 to $79,000

Scope

Dental hygienists are important members of the dental health-care team. Their knowledge and training enhance the quality of care dental patients receive. Their work requires superior technical and interpersonal skills. The hygienist represents an extension of the dentist and provides both clinical treatment and education. The first school to train dental hygienists was founded by a dentist in 1917 in Bridgeport, Connecticut, to help improve the oral health of schoolchildren.

Activities

Each state licenses its own dental hygienists. The extent of their permissible activities varies in different states. Their major activity is cleaning teeth. This service usually is provided to patients on a regular basis and involves removing soft and hard deposits, which requires scraping and sometimes gumline curettage. Hygienists also apply fluorides and sealers to help retard the formation of cavities and the buildup of plaque. In addition to performing these duties (known as oral prophylaxis), hygienists teach patients good oral hygiene techniques to maintain the health of their teeth and gums by demonstrating the proper way to brush and floss. These measures enhance the chances of preventing oral disease. In the course of their work, hygienists note and report on abnormalities they observe (such as loose teeth and missing fillings). They also may assist the dentist by taking and developing patient X rays and helping identify problem or potential problem sites.

Some states permit dental hygienists to perform preliminary examinations, identifying and charting missing teeth, cavities, and any abnormal growths. In certain states, hygienists may even remove sutures, apply dressings, and administer anesthesia during surgeries.

Laws governing dental hygienists are changing in some states, and this will expand their duties significantly. Under these new laws, hygienists would be allowed to take impressions for making models of teeth, insert fillings, and polish existing restorations. This frees the dentist to provide the many services that require his or her specialized expertise. Finally, in some practices, hygienists serve as office managers.

Work Settings

Most dental hygienists work for dentists on a part- or full-time basis. They may find employment in private or group practices or at hospitals or clinics. They also may find employment opportunities in schools, where they educate students about oral health. Dental hygienists can secure appointments in the armed forces as commissioned officers. There is a big need for hygienists to work in nursing homes, extended-care facilities, and state health departments. Overseas service opportunities also exist in government or privately sponsored health-care projects.

Advancement

With experience, dental hygienists can be promoted to supervisory positions, especially in multi-practitioner offices.

Prerequisites

To enter a dental hygienist program, you must have a high school diploma or its equivalent. It is helpful to have above-average grades and a science background.

Those entering this field should enjoy working with people. They also should be meticulous and patient and have good manual dexterity.

Education/Training

To enter this field, you must complete an accredited dental hygiene program at a community college or university. The standard program involves courses in the liberal arts, basic sciences, and clinical sciences, as well as supervised patient care experiences. Training in oral health education techniques and community health education also are provided.

Three educational paths are offered in this field:

- **Certificate or associate degree.** This two- or three-year program prepares the student for dental office practice.
- **Bachelor's degree.** This is a four-year program. At this level, once a graduate has gained work experience, he or she is eligible for teaching, administrative, or public health positions.
- **Master's degree.** This two-year postgraduate program qualifies individuals for advanced positions in teaching, administration, and public health.

Certification/Registration/Licensure

Graduates with any of these degrees from an accredited program are eligible to take licensing examinations. Once they satisfactorily complete the exams, they can identify themselves as *registered dental hygienists.*

To secure a license, almost all states require candidates to earn a passing score on a comprehensive, written Dental Hygiene National Board Examination. In addition, they must pass a state-approved licensure exam that tests both knowledge and clinical skills.

Career Potential

With the introduction of fluorides, a strong emphasis was placed on preventive dentistry. As part of this program, regular dental checkups and cleanings are routinely prescribed. This and the increased life span of people in the United States have greatly increased the need for dental hygienists. Job opportunities are quite favorable, with positions available all across the country. Salaries vary considerably, depending on the hygienist's training, experience, and responsibilities, and the position's geographic location. Benefit packages are often provided.

For More Information

The American Dental Hygienists' Association is the professional organization for this field. It publishes a journal and has a students' counterpart. The association is located at 444 N. Michigan Ave., Ste. 3400, Chicago, IL 60611 (www.adha.org).

You may want to arrange a visit with your family dentist's hygienist to observe him or her at work. You also may arrange to speak with a counselor at a school that offers a dental hygiene program.

All of the schools listed here offer dental hygiene programs accredited by the American Dental Association.

Dental Hygienist Programs

Alabama
University of Alabama
1919 Seventh Ave. S.
Room 406
Birmingham, AL 35294
www.dental.uab.edu

Wallace State Community College
801 Main St.
P.O. Box 2000
Hanceville, AL 35077
www.wallacestate.edu

Alaska
University of Alaska–Anchorage
3211 Providence Dr.
Anchorage, Alaska 99508
www.uaa.alaska.edu

Arizona
Northern Arizona University
S. San Francisco St.
Flagstaff, AZ 86011
www.nau.edu

Phoenix College
1202 W. Thomas Rd.
Phoenix, AZ 85013
www.pc.maricopa.edu

Pima Community College
2202 W. Anklam Rd.
Tucson, AZ 85709
http://wc.pima.edu

Rio Salado College
2323 W. 14th St.
Tempe, AZ 85281
www.rio.maricopa.edu

Arkansas
University of Arkansas–Fort Smith
College of Health Sciences
5210 Grand Ave.
P.O. Box 3649
Fort Smith, AR 72913
www.uafortsmith.edu

University of Arkansas for
   Medical Sciences
4301 W. Markham St.
Little Rock, AR 72205
www.uams.edu

California
Cabrillo College
6500 Soquel Dr.
Aptos, CA 95003
www.cabrillo.edu

CDHA California Dental
Hygiene Program
29 Emmons Park Drive
Taft, CA 93268
www.cdha.org

Cerritos College
11110 Allondra Blvd.
Norwalk, CA 90650
www.cerritos.edu

Chabot College
25555 Hesperian Blvd.
Hayward, CA 94545
http://chabotweb.clpccd.cc.
   ca.us/

Cypress College
9200 Valley View St.
Cypress, CA 90630
www.cypresscollege.edu

Diablo Valley College
321 Golf Club Rd.
Pleasant Hill, CA 94523
www.dvc.edu

Foothill College
12345 El Monte Rd.
Los Altos Hills, CA 94022
www.foothill.fhda.edu

Fresno City College
Health Sciences Division
1101 E. University Ave.
Fresno, CA 93741
www.fresnocitycollege.com

Loma Linda University
School of Dentistry
Loma Linda, CA 92350
www.llu.edu

Oxnard College
4000 S. Rose Ave.
Oxnard, CA 93033
www.oxnard.cc.ca.us

Pasadena City College
1570 E. Colorado Blvd.
Pasadena, CA 91106
www.pasadena.edu

Riverside Community College
Moreno Valley Campus
16130 Lasselle St.
Moreno Valley, CA 92551
www.rcc.edu/morenovalley/

Sacramento City College
3835 Freeport Blvd.
Sacramento, CA 95822
www.scc.losrios.edu

San Joaquin Valley College
8400 W. Mineral King
Visalia, CA 93291
www.sjvc.edu

Santa Rosa Junior College
1501 Mendocino Ave.
Santa Rosa, CA 95401
www.santarosa.edu

Shasta College
11555 Old Oregon Trail
P.O. Box 496006
Redding, CA 96049
www.shastacollege.edu

Southwestern College
900 Otay Lakes Rd.
Chula Vista, CA 91910
www.swc.cc.ca.us

Taft College
29 Emmons Park Dr.
Taft, CA 93268
www.taft.cc.ca.us

University of California,
  San Francisco
School of Dentistry
513 Parnassus Ave.
San Francisco, CA 94143
http://dentistry.ucsf.edu/

University of Southern California
Health Sciences Campus
Los Angeles, CA 90033
www.usc.edu

University of the Pacific
School of Dentistry
3601 Pacific Ave.
Stockton, CA 95211
www.pacific.edu/dentalhygiene/

West Los Angeles College
9000 Overland Ave.
Culver City, CA 90230
www.wlac.edu

Colorado
Colorado Northwestern
  Community College
500 Kennedy Dr.
Rangely, CO 81648
www.cncc.edu

Pueblo Community College
900 W. Orman Ave.
Pueblo, CO 81004
www.pueblocc.edu

University of Colorado
Health Sciences Center
4200 E. Ninth Ave.
Denver, CO 80262
www.uchsc.edu

Connecticut
Tunxis Community College
271 Scott Swamp Rd.
Farmington, CT 06032
http://tunxis.commnet.edu/

University of Bridgeport
126 Park Ave.
Bridgeport, CT 06604
www.bridgeport.edu

University of New Haven
College of Arts and Sciences
300 Boston Post Rd.
West Haven, CT 06516
www.newhaven.edu

Delaware
Delaware Technical College
333 Shipley St.
Wilmington, DE 19801
www.dtcc.edu

District of Columbia
Howard University
2400 6th St. NW
Washington, DC 20059
www.howard.edu

Florida
Brevard Community College
1519 Clearlake Rd.
Cocoa, FL 32922
www.brevardcc.edu

Broward Community College
111 E. Las Olas Blvd.
Ft. Lauderdale, FL 33301
www.broward.edu

Daytona Beach Community
  College
1155 County Rd. 4139
Deland, FL 32724
www.dbcc.edu

Edison Community College
8099 College Pkwy. SW
Ft. Myers, FL 33919
www.edison.edu

Florida Community College
501 W. State St.
Jacksonville, FL 32202
www.fccj.cc.fl.us

Gulf Coast Community College
Health Sciences Department
5230 Hwy. 98 W.
Panama City, FL 32401
www.gulfcoast.edu

Hillsborough Community College
4001 Tampa Bay Blvd.
Tampa, FL 33614
www.hcc.cc.fl.us

Indian River Community College
3209 Virginia Ave.
Ft. Pierce, FL 34981
www.ircc.edu

Manatee Community College
Division of Health Sciences
5840 26th St. W.
Bradenton, FL 34207
www.mccfl.edu

Miami Dade College
Medical Center Campus
950 NW 20th St.
Miami, FL 33127
www.mdc.edu

Palm Beach Community College
4200 Congress Ave.
Lake Worth, FL 33461
www.pbcc.edu

Pasco-Hernando Community
  College
Department of Allied Health
10230 Ridge Rd.
New Port Richey, FL 34654
www.pasco-hernandocc.com

Pensacola Junior College
1000 College Blvd.
Pensacola, FL 32507
www.pjc.cc.fl.us

Santa Fe Community College
3000 NW 83rd St.
Gainesville, FL 32606
www.santafe.cc.fl.us

South Florida Community College
School of Applied Sciences &
 Technologies
600 W. College Dr.
Avon Park, FL 33825
www.sfcc.cc.fl.us

St. Petersburg College
7200 66th St. N.
Pinellas Park, FL 33781
www.spjc.edu/hec/dental/

Tallahassee Community College
444 Appleyard Dr.
Tallahassee, FL 32304
www.tcc.cc.fl.us

Valencia Community College
P.O. Box 3028
Orlando, FL 32802
www.valencia.cc.fl.us

Georgia
Armstrong Atlantic State
 University
11935 Abercorn St.
Savannah, GA 31419
www.armstrong.edu

Athens Technical College
Allied Health Sciences
800 U.S. Hwy. 29 N.
Athens, GA 30601
www.athenstech.edu

Central Georgia Technical College
3300 Macon Tech Dr.
Macon, GA 31206
www.centralgatech.edu

Clayton College and State
 University
5900 N. Lee St.
Morrow, GA 30260
www.clayton.edu

Columbus Technical College
928 Manchester Expwy.
Columbus, GA 31904
www.columbustech.edu

Darton College
2400 Gillionville Rd.
Albany, GA 31707
www.darton.edu

Floyd College
Health Sciences Division
3175 Hwy. 27 S.
Rome, GA 30162
www.floyd.edu/dental/

Georgia Perimeter College
555 N. Indian Creek Dr.
Clarkston, GA 30021
www.gpc.edu

Lanier Technical College
2990 Landrum Education Dr.
Oakwood, GA 30566
www.laniertech.edu

Macon State College
100 College Station Dr.
Macon, GA 31206
www.maconstate.edu

Medical College of Georgia
1120 15th St.
Augusta, GA 30912
www.mcg.edu

Middle Georgia Technical College
80 Cohen Walker Dr.
Warner Robins, GA 31088
www.middlegatech.edu

Valdosta Technical College
4089 Val Tech Rd.
Valdosta, GA 31603
www.valdostatech.org

West Central Technical College
4600 Timber Ridge Dr.
Douglasville, GA 30135
www.westcentral.org

Hawaii
University of Hawaii at Manoa
2445 Campus Rd.
Honolulu, HI 96822
www.hawaii.edu

Idaho
American Institute of Health
 Technology
1200 N. Liberty
Boise, ID 83704

Idaho State University
921 S. 8th Ave.
Pocatello, ID 83209
www.isu.edu

Illinois
Carl Sandburg College
Allied Health Division
2400 Tom L. Wilson Blvd.
Galesburg, IL 61401
www.sandburg.edu

College of DuPage
425 Fawell Blvd.
Glen Ellyn, IL 60137
www.cod.edu

College of Lake County
Biological & Health Sciences
19351 W. Washington St.
Grayslake, IL 60030
www.clcillinois.edu

Harper College
1200 W. Algonquin Rd.
Palatine, IL 60067
www.harpercollege.edu

Illinois Central College
Health Careers and Public Services
1 College Dr.
Peoria, IL 61635
www.icc.edu

John A. Logan College
Biological & Health Sciences
700 Logan College Rd.
Carterville, IL 62918
www.jal.cc.il.us

Kennedy King College
6800 S. Wentworth Ave.
Chicago, IL 60621
http://kennedyking.ccc.edu/

Lake Land College
5001 Lake Land Blvd.
Mattoon, IL 61938
www.lakeland.cc.il.us

Lewis and Clark Community
 College
Allied Health Division
5800 Godfrey Rd.
Godfrey, IL 62035
www.lc.edu

Parkland College
2400 W. Bradley Ave.
Champaign, IL 61821
www.parkland.edu

Prairie State College
202 S. Halsted St.
Chicago Heights, IL 60411
www.prairie.cc.il.us

Rock Valley College
Allied Health Division
3301 N. Mulford Rd.
Rockford, IL 61114
www.rockvalleycollege.edu

Southern Illinois University
 Carbondale
Carbondale, IL 62901
www.siu.edu

Indiana
Indiana University Northwest
School of Nursing and Health
 Professions
3400 Broadway St.
Gary, IN 46408
www.iun.edu

Indiana University South Bend
1700 Mishawaka Ave.
South Bend, IN 46634
www.iusb.edu

Indiana University–Purdue
 University Fort Wayne
2101 E. Coliseum Blvd.
Fort Wayne, IN 46805
www.ipfw.edu/denthy/

Indiana University School of
 Dentistry
1121 W. Michigan St.
Indianapolis, IN 46202
www.indiana.edu

University of Southern Indiana
8600 University Blvd.
Evansville, IN 47712
www.usi.edu

Iowa
Des Moines Area Community
 College
2006 S. Ankeny Blvd.
Ankeny, IA 50021
www.dmacc.edu

Hawkeye Community College
1501 E. Orange Rd.
P.O. Box 8015
Waterloo, IA 50701
www.hawkeye.cc.ia.us

Iowa Western Community College
2700 College Rd.
Council Bluffs, IA 51503
www.iwcc.edu

Kirkwood Community College
Health Science Department
6301 Kirkwood Blvd. SW
Cedar Rapids, IA 52404
www.kirkwood.cc.ia.us

University of Iowa
College of Dentistry
Iowa City, IA 52242
www.uiowa.edu

Kansas
Johnson County Community
 College
12345 College Blvd.
Overland Park, KS 66210
www.jccc.net

Wichita Area Technical College
324 N. Emporia
Wichita, KS 67202
www.wichitatech.com

Wichita State University
College of Health Professions
1845 N. Fairmont
Wichita, KS 67260
www.wichita.edu

Kentucky
Big Sandy Community & Technical
 College
Allied Health and Related
 Technologies
One Bert T. Combs Dr.
Prestonburg, KY 41653
www.bigsandy.kctcs.edu

Bluegrass Community and
 Technical College
470 Cooper Drive
Lexington, KY 40506
http://legacy.bluegrass.kctcs.
 edu/ah/dh/

Henderson Community College
2660 S. Green St.
Henderson, KY 42420
www.hencc.kctcs.edu

Hopkinsville Community College
720 North Dr.
P.O. Box 2100
Hopkinsville, KY 42240
www.hopcc.kctcs.edu

University of Louisville
School of Dentistry
501 S. Preston St.
Louisville, KY 40202
www.louisville.edu

Western Kentucky University
1 Big Red Way
Bowling Green, KY 42101
www.wku.edu

Louisiana
Louisiana State University
 Health Sciences Center
School of Dentistry
1100 Florida Ave., Box 228
New Orleans, LA 70119
www.lsusd.lsuhsc.edu

Southern University at Shreveport
Allied Health/Health Science
 Division
3050 Martin Luther King, Jr. Dr.
Shreveport, LA 71107
http://web.susla.edu/

University of Louisiana at Monroe
700 University Ave.
Monroe, LA 71209
www.ulm.edu

Maine
University of Maine at Augusta
Lincoln Hall, 29 Texas Ave.
Bangor, ME 04401
www.uma.maine.edu

University of New England
716 Stevens Ave.
Portland, ME 04103
www.une.edu

Maryland

Allegany Community College
12401 Willowbrook Rd. SE
Cumberland, MD 21502
www.allegany.edu/dental/

Baltimore City Community College
2901 Liberty Heights Ave.
Baltimore, MD 21215
www.bccc.state.md.us

Baltimore College of Dental
 Surgery
666 W. Baltimore St.
Baltimore, MD 21201
www.dental.umaryland.edu

Massachusetts

Bristol Community College
777 Elsbree St.
Fall River, MA 02720
www.bristol.mass.edu

Cape Cod Community College
2240 Iyanough Rd.
West Barnstable, MA 02668
www.capecod.mass.edu

Middlesex Community College
33 Kearney Square
Lowell, MA 01852
www.middlesex.mass.edu

Mount Ida College
777 Dedham St.
Newton Centre, MA 02459
www.mountida.edu

Quinsigamond Community College
670 W. Boylston St.
Worcester, MA 01606
www.qcc.mass.edu/dental/

Springfield Technical Community
 College
P.O. Box 9000, Ste. 1
Springfield, MA 01102
www.stcc.edu

Michigan

Baker College
3403 Lapeer Rd.
Port Huron, MI 48060
www.baker.edu

Delta College
1961 Delta Rd.
University Center, MI 48710
www.delta.edu

Ferris State University
200 Ferris Dr.
Big Rapids, MI 49307
www.ferris.edu

Grand Rapids Community College
143 Bostwick Ave. NE
Grand Rapids, MI 49503
www.grcc.edu

Kalamazoo Valley Community
 College
6767 W. O Ave.
Kalamazoo, MI 49003
www.kvcc.edu

Kellogg Community College
Allied Health Department
450 North Ave.
Battle Creek, MI 49017
www.kellogg.edu

Lansing Community College
P.O. Box 40010
Lansing, MI 48901
www.lcc.edu

Mott Community College
1401 E. Court St.
Flint, MI 48503
www.mcc.edu

Oakland Community College
7350 Cooley Lake Rd.
Waterford, MI 48327
www.oaklandcc.edu

University of Detroit Mercy
8200 W. Outer Dr.
Detroit, MI 48219
www.udmercy.edu/
 dentalhygiene/

University of Michigan
Ann Arbor, MI 48109
www.umich.edu

Wayne County Community College
8551 Greenfield
Detroit, MI 48228
www.wcccd.edu

Minnesota

Argosy University
1515 Central Pkwy.
Eagan, MN 55121
www.argosyu.edu

Century College
3300 Century Ave. N.
White Bear Lake, MN 55110
www.century.edu

Herzing College
Lakeland Medical Dental Academy
 Division
5700 W. Broadway
Minneapolis, MN 55428
http://us.herzing.edu/lakeland/

Lake Superior College
2101 Trinity Rd.
Duluth, MN 55811
www.lsc.edu

Minnesota State Community and
 Technical College–Moorhead
1900 28th Ave. S.
Moorhead, MN 56560
www.minnesota.edu

Minnesota State University,
 Mankato
Mankato, MN 56001
www.mnsu.edu/dentalhygiene/

Normandale Community College
9700 France Ave. S.
Bloomington, MN 55431
www.normandale.edu

Rochester Community and
 Technical College
851 30th Ave. SE
Rochester, MN 55904
www.roch.edu

St. Cloud Technical College
1540 Northway Dr.
St. Cloud, MN 56303
www.sctc.edu

University of Minnesota
School of Dentistry
Moos Health Sciences Tower
515 Delaware St. SE
Minneapolis, MN 55455
www.dentistry.umn.edu

Mississippi
Meridian Community College
910 Hwy. 19 N.
Meridian, MS 39307
www.mcc.cc.ms.us

Mississippi Delta Community
  College
Hwy. 3 and Cherry St.
P.O. Box 668
Moorhead, MS 38761
www.mdcc.cc.ms.us

Northeast Mississippi Community
  College
101 Cunningham Blvd.
Booneville, MS 38829
www.necc.cc.ms.us

Pearl River Community College
5448 U.S. Hwy. 49 S.
Hattiesburg, MS 39401
www.prcc.edu

University of Mississippi
  Medical Center
2500 N. State St.
Jackson, MS 39216
www.umc.edu

Missouri
Missouri Southern State University
3950 E. Newman Rd.
Joplin, MO 64801
www.mssu.edu

Ozarks Technical Community
  College
P.O. Box 5958
Springfield, MO 65801
www.otc.edu

St. Louis Community College
300 S. Broadway
St. Louis, MO 63102
www.stlcc.cc.mo.us

State Fair Community College
Allied Health and Physical
  Education Department
3201 W. 16th St.
Sedalia, MO 65301
www.sfcc.cc.mo.us

University of Missouri–Kansas City
School of Dentistry
650 E. 25th St.
Kansas City, MO 64108
www.umkc.edu/dentistry/

Montana
Montana State University
Great Falls College of Technology
  Health Sciences
2100 16th Ave. S.
Great Falls, MT 59405
www.msugf.edu

Nebraska
Central Community College
P.O. Box 1024
Hastings, NE 68902
www.cccneb.edu

University of Nebraska Medical
  Center
College of Dentistry
40th and Holdrege Streets
Lincoln, NE 68583
www.unmc.edu/dentistry

Nevada
Community College of Southern
  Nevada
6375 W. Charleston Blvd.
Las Vegas, NV 89146
www.ccsn.edu

Truckee Meadows Community
  College
Health Science
7000 Dandini Blvd.
Reno, NV 89512
www.tmcc.edu

New Hampshire
New Hampshire Technical
  Institute
31 College Dr.
Concord, NH 03301
www.nhti.edu

New Jersey
Bergen Community College
400 Paramus Rd.
Paramus, NJ 07652
www.bergen.edu

Camden County College
P.O. Box 200
Blackwood, NJ 08012
www.camdencc.edu

Middlesex County College
2600 Woodbridge Ave.
Edison, NJ 08818
www.middlesexcc.edu

University of Medicine &
  Dentistry of New Jersey
1776 Raritan Rd.
Scotch Plains, NJ 07076
www.umdnj.edu

New Mexico
San Juan College
Dental Department
4601 College Blvd.
Farmington, NM 87402
www.sjc.cc.nm.us

University of New Mexico
1 University of New Mexico
Albuquerque, NM 87131
www.unm.edu

New York
Broome Community College
907 Front St.
P.O. Box 1017
Binghamton, NY 13902
www.sunybroome.edu

Erie Community College
6205 Main St.
Williamsville, NY 14221
www.ecc.edu

Eugenio Maria de Hostos
  Community College
500 Grand Concourse
Bronx, NY 10451
www.hostos.cuny.edu

Farmingdale State University of
  New York
2350 Broadhollow Rd.
Farmingdale, NY 11735
www.farmingdale.edu

Hudson Valley Community College
80 Vandenburgh Ave.
Troy, NY 12180
www.hvcc.edu

Monroe Community College
1000 E. Henrietta Rd.
Rochester, NY 14623
www.monroecc.edu

New York College of Technology
300 Jay St.
Brooklyn, NY 11201
www.citytech.cuny.edu

New York University College of
Dentistry
345 E. 24th St.
New York, NY 10010
www.nyu.edu/dental/

Onondaga Community College
4941 Onondaga Rd.
Syracuse, NY 13215
http://sunyocc.edu/

Orange County Community College
115 South St.
Middletown, NY 10940
www.suny.orange.cc.ny.us

North Carolina
Asheville-Buncombe Technical
Community College
340 Victoria Rd.
Asheville, NC 28801
www.abtech.edu

Cape Fear Community College
Allied Health Department
411 N. Front St.
Wilmington, NC 28401
www.cfcc.edu

Catawba Valley Community
College
2550 Hwy. 70 SE
Hickory, NC 28602
www.cvcc.edu

Central Piedmont Community
College
P.O. Box 35009
Charlotte, NC 28235
www.cpcc.cc.nc.us

Coastal Carolina Community
College
444 Western Blvd.
Jacksonville, NC 28546
www.coastal.cc.nc.us

Fayetteville Technical Community
College
2201 Hull Rd.
P.O. Box 35236
Fayetteville, NC 28303
www.faytechcc.edu

Forsyth Technical Community
College
Dental Education Department
2100 Silas Creek Pkwy.
Winston-Salem, NC 27103
www.forsyth.tec.nc.us

Guilford Technical Community
College
P.O. Box 309
Jamestown, NC 27282
www.gtcc.edu

Halifax Community College
P.O. Drawer 809
Weldon, NC 27890
www.halifaxcc.edu

University of North Carolina
Manning Dr. and Columbia St.
CB #7450
Chapel Hill, NC 27599
www.dent.unc.edu

Wake Technical Community
College
Health Science Division
9101 Fayetteville Rd.
Raleigh, NC 27603
www.waketech.edu

Wayne Community College
3000 Wayne Memorial Dr.
Goldsboro, NC 27534
www.wayne.cc.nc.us

North Dakota
North Dakota State College of
Science
800 Sixth St. N.
Wahpeton, ND 58076
www.ndscs.nodak.edu

Ohio
Columbus State Community
College
Allied Health
550 E. Spring St.
Columbus, OH 43215
www.cscc.edu

Cuyahoga Community College
700 Carnegie Ave.
Cleveland, OH 44115
www.tri-c.edu

James A. Rhodes State College
4240 Campus Dr.
Lima, OH 45804
www.rhodesstate.edu

Lakeland Community College
7700 Clocktower Dr.
Kirtland, OH 44094
www.lakeland.cc.oh.us

Lorain County Community College
Allied Health and Nursing
1005 Abbe Rd. N.
Elyria, OH 44035
www.lorainccc.edu

Ohio State University
305 W. 12th Ave.
Columbus, OH 43210
www.dent.ohio-state.edu/dhy/

Owens State Community College
P.O. Box 10000
Toledo, OH 43699
www.owens.cc.oh.us

Shawnee State University
940 Second St.
Portsmouth, OH 45662
www.shawnee.edu

Sinclair Community College
444 W. Third St.
Dayton, OH 45402
www.sinclair.edu

Stark State College of Technology
Health Technologies Division
6200 Frank Ave. NW
North Canton, OH 44720
www.starkstate.edu

University of Cincinnati/Raymond
Walters College
9555 Plainfield Rd.
Cincinnati, OH 45236
www.uc.edu

Youngstown State University
One University Plaza
Youngstown, OH 44555
www.ysu.edu

Oklahoma
Rose State College
6420 SE 15th
Midwest City, OK 73110
www.rose.edu

Tulsa Community College
909 S. Boston Ave.
Tulsa, OK 74119
www.tulsacc.edu

University of Oklahoma
College of Dentistry
1001 Stanton L. Young Blvd.
Oklahoma City, OK 73117
www.ou.edu

Oregon
Lane Community College
4000 E. 30th Ave.
Eugene, OR 97405
www.lanecc.edu

Mt. Hood Community College
26000 SE Stark St.
Gresham, OR 97030
www.mhcc.edu

Oregon Health & Science
University
3181 SW Sam Jackson Park Rd.
Portland, OR 97239
www.ohsu.edu

Oregon Institute of Technology
3201 Campus Dr.
Klamath Falls, OR 97601
www.oit.edu

Portland Community College
12000 SW 49th Ave.
P.O. Box 19000
Portland, OR 97280
www.pcc.edu

Pennsylvania
Community College of
Philadelphia
1700 Spring Garden St.
Philadelphia, PA 19130
www.ccp.edu

Harcum College
Allied Health Sciences
750 Montgomery Ave.
Bryn Mawr, PA 19010
www.harcum.edu

Harrisburg Area Community
College
One HACC Dr.
Harrisburg, PA 17110
www.hacc.edu

Luzerne County Community
College
1333 S. Prospect St.
Nanticoke, PA 18634
www.luzerne.edu

Manor College
700 Fox Chase Rd.
Jenkintown, PA 19046
www.manor.edu

Montgomery County Community
College
340 DeKalb Pike
Blue Bell, PA 19422
www.mc3.edu

Northampton Community College
3835 Green Pond Rd.
Bethlehem, PA 18020
www.northampton.edu

Pennsylvania College of
Technology
1 College Ave.
Williamsport, PA 17701
www.pct.edu

Thomas Jefferson University
1020 Walnut St.
Philadelphia, PA 19107
www.jefferson.edu/main/

University of Pittsburgh
School of Dental Medicine
Salk Hall
3501 Terrace St.
Pittsburgh, PA 15261
www.dental.pitt.edu

Westmoreland County Community
College
400 Armbrust Rd.
Youngwood, PA 15697
www.wccc.pa.edu

Rhode Island
Community College of Rhode
Island
1762 Louisquisset Pike
Lincoln, RI 02865
www.ccri.edu

University of Rhode Island
Kingston, RI 02881
www.uri.edu

South Carolina
Florence Darlington Technical
College
2715 W. Lucas St.
P.O. Box 100548
Florence, SC 29501
www.fdtc.edu

Greenville Technical College
P.O. Box 5616
Greenville, SC 29606
www.gvltec.edu

Horry Georgetown Technical
College
2050 Hwy. 501 E.
Conway, SC 29526
www.hgtc.edu

Midlands Technical College
P.O. Box 2408
Columbia, SC 29202
www.midlandstech.edu

Trident Technical College
P.O. Box 118067
Charleston, SC 29423
www.trident.tech.edu

York Technical College
452 S. Anderson Rd.
Rock Hill, SC 29730
www.yorktech.com

South Dakota
University of South Dakota
Division of Health Sciences
East Hall 120
414 E. Clark St.
Vermillion, SD 57069
www.usd.edu/dhyg/

Tennessee
Chattanooga State Technical
Community College
4501 Amnicola Hwy.
Chattanooga, TN 37406
www.chattanoogastate.edu

East Tennessee State University
Box 70267
Johnson City, TN 37614
www.etsu.edu

Meharry Medical College
3500 John A. Merritt Blvd.
Nashville, TN 37209
www.tnstate.edu

Roane State Community College
701 Briarcliff Ave.
Oak Ridge, TN 37830
www.roanestate.edu

University of Tennessee Health
  Science Center
College of Dentistry
875 Union Ave.
Memphis, TN 38163
www.utmem.edu/dentistry/

Texas
Amarillo College
P.O. Box 477
Amarillo, TX 79178
www.actx.edu

Austin Community College
3401 Webberville Rd.
Austin, TX 78702
www.austincc.edu/hltsci/

Baylor College of Dentistry
3302 Gaston Ave.
Dallas, TX 75246
www.tambcd.edu

Coastal Bend College
3800 Charco Rd.
Beeville, TX 78102
www.coastalbend.edu

Collin County Community College
2200 W. University Dr.
McKinney, TX 75070
www.cccd.edu

Del Mar College
101 Baldwin Blvd.
Corpus Christi, TX 78404
www.delmar.edu

El Paso Community College
P.O. Box 20500
El Paso, TX 79998
www.epcc.edu

Howard College
1001 Birdwell Ln.
Big Spring, TX 79720
www.howardcollege.edu

Lamar Institute of Technology
P.O. Box 10061
Beaumont, TX 77710
www.lit.edu

Midwestern State University
3410 Taft Blvd.
Wichita Falls, TX 76308
www.mwsu.edu

Tarrant County College
828 Harwood Rd.
Hurst, TX 76054
www.tccd.edu

Texas State Technical College
  Harlingen
1902 N. Loop 499
Harlingen, TX 78550
www.harlingen.tstc.edu

Texas Woman's University
Box 425796
Denton, TX 76204
www.twu.edu/hs/dh/

Tyler Junior College
P.O. Box 9020
Tyler, TX 75711
www.tjc.edu

University of Texas
Health Science Center at Houston
6516 MD Anderson Blvd.
Houston, TX 77030
www.uthouston.edu

University of Texas
Health Science Center at San
  Antonio
7703 Floyd Curl Dr.
San Antonio, TX 78229
www.uthscsa.edu

Wharton County Junior College
911 Boling Hwy.
Wharton, TX 77488
www.wcjc.edu

Utah
Dixie State College of Utah
Health Sciences
225 S. 700 E.
St. George, UT 84770
www.dixie.edu

Salt Lake Community College
Jordan Campus
Department of Health Sciences
3491 W. Wights Fort Rd.
West Jordan, UT 84088
www.slcc.edu

Utah Valley State College
School of Science and Health
800 W. University Parkway
Orem, UT 84058
www.uvsc.edu

Weber State University
3850 University Circle
Ogden, UT 84408
www.weber.edu

Vermont
University of Vermont
School of Medicine
Burlington, VT 05405
www.uvm.edu

Vermont Technical College
P.O. Box 500
Randolph Court, VT 05061
www.vtc.edu

Virginia
Northern Virginia Community
  College
4001 Wakefield Chapel Rd.
Annandale, VA 22003
www.nvcc.edu

Old Dominion University
Gene W. Hirschfeld School of
  Dental Hygiene
4608 Hampton Blvd.
Norfolk, VA 23529
www.odu.edu/dental/

Virginia Commonwealth University
School of Dentistry
Box 980566
Richmond, VA 23298
www.dentistry.vcu.edu

Virginia Western Community
  College
P.O. Box 14007
Roanoke, VA 24038
www.virginiawestern.edu

Wytheville Community College
1000 E. Main St.
Wytheville, VA 24382
www.wcc.vccs.edu

Washington
Clark College
1800 E. McLoughlin Blvd.
Vancouver, WA 98663
www.clark.edu

Columbia Basin College
Health Science Division
2600 N. 20th Ave.
Pasco, WA 99301
www.columbiabasin.edu

Eastern Washington University
310 N. Riverpoint Blvd.
Spokane, WA 99202
www.ewu.edu

Lake Washington Technical
College
11605 132nd Ave. NE
Kirkland, WA 98034
www.lwtc.ctc.edu

Pierce College
9401 Farwest Dr. SW
Tacoma, WA 98498
www.pierce.ctc.edu

Shoreline Community College
16101 Greenwood Ave. N.
Shoreline, WA 98133
www.shoreline.edu

Yakima Valley Community
College
16th and Nob Hill Blvd.
Yakima, WA 98907
www.yvcc.edu

West Virginia
West Liberty State College
P.O. Box 295
West Liberty, WV 26074
www.wlsc.edu

West Virginia University Institute
of Technology
604 Davis Hall
Montgomery, WV 25136
www.wvutech.edu

West Virginia University
P.O. Box 6201
Morgantown, WV 26506
www.wvu.edu

Wisconsin
Madison Area Technical College
3550 Anderson St.
Madison, WI 53704
http://matcmadison.edu/

Marquette University
P.O. Box 1881
Milwaukee, WI 53201
www.marquette.edu

Milwaukee Area Technical College
700 W. State St.
Milwaukee, WI 53233
www.matc.edu

North Central Technical College
1000 W. Campus Dr.
Wausau, WI 54401
www.ntc.edu

Northeast Wisconsin Technical
College
2740 W. Mason St.
P.O. Box 19042
Green Bay, WI 54307
www.nwtc.edu

Waukesha County Technical
College
800 Main St.
Pewaukee, WI 53072
www.wctc.edu

Wyoming
Laramie County Community
College
1400 E. College Dr.
Cheyenne, WY 82007
www.lccc.wy.edu

Sheridan College
3059 Coffeen Ave.
Sheridan, WY 82801
www.sheridan.edu

Canada
Algonquin College
1385 Woodroffe Ave.
Nepean, Ontario K2G 1V8
www.algonquincollege.com

Collège François-Xavier-Garneau
1660 Boulevard de l'Entente
Sillery, Quebec G1T 2S3
www.cegep-fxg.qc.ca

Cegep St-Hyacinthe
Clinique D'Hygiene Dentaire
300 Rue Boulle
St. Hyacinthe, Quebec J2S 1H9
www.cegepsth.qc.ca

Collège de Maisonneuve
3800 Sherbrooke St. E.
Montreal, Quebec H1X 2A2
www.cmaisonneuve.qc.ca

Dalhousie University
Faculty of Dentistry
5891 University Ave.
Halifax, Nova Scotia B3H 3J5
www.dentistry.dal.ca

University of Alberta
114th St. and 89th Ave.
Edmonton, Alberta T6G 2E1
www.ualberta.ca

University of Manitoba
Winnipeg, Manitoba R3T 2N2
www.umanitoba.ca

Vancouver Community College
250 W. Pender St.
Vancouver, British Columbia
V6B 1S9
www.vcc.bc.ca

Dietitians

Principal activity: Planning nutritious diets and providing nutrition education

Work commitment: Part- or full-time

Preprofessional education: High school diploma

Program length: 4 years

Work prerequisites: Bachelor's degree in dietetics or a nutrition-related field

Career opportunities: Stable

Income range: $41,000 to $62,000

Scope

Dietitians provide advice on nutritious food selection and preparation. They plan and supervise the preparation and serving of foods suitable for specific dietary needs. After scientifically evaluating their clients' diets, dietitians offer suggestions for modifications and improvements. They are knowledgeable about the most appropriate diets to maintain health and prevent disease at different phases of life and about what dietary modifications improve certain health conditions.

Activities

There are seven distinct areas of dietetic practice:

- **Clinical dietitians** work in health-care institutions such as hospitals and nursing homes. They evaluate patients' nutritional needs, formulate and implement appropriate nutritional programs, and assess and report results. To coordinate medical and nutritional needs, dietitians confer with physicians and other health-care providers. They provide patients and their families with detailed instructions on maintaining a proper diet upon discharge from the hospital. Within this general area are several subspecialties. For example, some dietitians deal only with overweight or critically ill patients. In small hospitals or clinics, dietitians may be responsible for managing all food services.

- **Community dietitians,** also known as *nutritionists,* advise both individuals and groups about proper nutritional practices that enhance health and prevent diseases. Nutritionists who work for clinics, nursing homes, HMOs, hospitals, and home care agencies evaluate facilities, develop nutritional care plans, and teach clients and their families about nutrition. They also advise health-care agencies on grocery shopping and food preparation for the elderly and chronically ill. Because of the current public interest in nutrition, these professionals are now finding employment with food manufacturers and in advertising and marketing agencies, where they analyze foods and prepare literature on nutritional content and other health-related issues.

- **Management dietitians** supervise large-scale meal planning in long-term health-care facilities, restaurants, companies, hotels, schools, colleges, and prisons. Typically, they have a wide range of duties and responsibilities, including hiring and training food-preparation workers, purchasing food and equipment, enforcing safety and sanitary conditions, and developing budgets.

- **Dietetic educators** are primarily involved in teaching dietetic principles at colleges, health-care facilities, and community centers.
- **Research dietitians** typically hold advanced degrees (such as a master's degree or Ph.D.) that let them undertake research studies at medical centers, government agencies, and educational facilities. Their work may involve developing and evaluating new nutritional approaches to treating diseases.
- **Consulting dietitians** provide a variety of services for health-care facilities. Typically, they work in private practice or under contract for others. They perform nutrition screening and offer advice on weight loss, cholesterol reduction, and diabetes management.
- **Business dietitians** technically are not health-care providers, but they do work in dietary planning and so are worth mentioning here. They work in private industry, advising companies on purchasing, food development, marketing, advertising, and sales.

Work Settings

Dietitians can find employment in a broad range of places, especially in medical facilities such as hospitals, clinics, and nursing homes. In addition, federal, state, and local government agencies offer positions in health departments and other health-related sites. Other dietitians find work with social service agencies, residential care facilities, educational institutions, industrial food services, restaurants, catering services, and hotels. Some work for physicians with practices devoted to weight management.

Advancement

Advancement is possible in all dietetic areas and comes with experience and successful performance. Promotion typically involves assuming supervisory responsibilities. Earning a graduate degree helps you advance in this field.

Prerequisites

In the course of earning their high school diplomas, students who want to enter this field should take courses in biology, chemistry, mathematics, home economics, and business management.

Desirable personal attributes include strong interpersonal and communication skills. Those who want to be dietitians should have the ability to speak before a group, because occasional lectures in special settings and one-on-one teaching may be a big part of the job. Obviously, those entering the field should be interested in food preparation and its impact on the well-being of others.

Education/Training

The basic requirement for entering this field is a bachelor's degree from an accredited institution, with a major in dietetics, nutrition food science, food preparation, or food services management. Undergraduate course work should include general biology, inorganic and organic chemistry, biochemistry, anatomy, physiology, microbiology, diet therapy, advanced nutrition, food services systems, food services management, quality food production, accounting, data processing, business management, and statistics.

Certification/Registration/Licensure

Dietitians in most states must satisfy specific academic and experience requirements to meet the standards set by the Commission on Dietetic Registration. Most positions are open exclusively to *registered dietitians* (*RDs*). An RD degree reflects that a candidate has met a specified high standard of education and training.

Career Potential

The job outlook for dietitians for the foreseeable future is solid. There is a continuous demand for dietitians to meet the needs of an aging and more health-conscious population in the United States. The impact of health-care reforms on the field is still unclear. Nevertheless, as the public becomes increasingly aware of the need for good dietary habits, the services of professionals in this field should be increasingly stimulated at various community levels. Also, with increased public awareness of obesity and diabetes, Medicare coverage has been expanded to include medical nutrition therapy for renal and diabetic patients, creating job growth for dietitians and nutritionists specializing in those diseases. Demand may be tempered somewhat by the lack of general insurance coverage for dietetic and nutritional services, as well as the trend toward outsourcing this work to other services or workers with different job titles.

For More Information

The professional organization for this field is the American Dietetic Association, 120 S. Riverside Plaza, Ste. 2000, Chicago, IL 60606 (www.eatright.org).

Dietitian Programs

Alabama
Alabama A&M University
P.O. Box 908
Normal, AL 35762
www.aamu.edu

Auburn University
Auburn, AL 36849
www.auburn.edu

Jacksonville State University
700 Pelham Rd. N.
Jacksonville, AL 36265
www.jsu.edu

Oakwood College
7000 Adventist Blvd.
Huntsville, AL 35896
www.oakwood.edu

Tuskegee University
Tuskegee, AL 36088
www.tuskegee.edu

University of Alabama
P.O. Box 870158
Tuscaloosa, AL 35487
www.ches.ua.edu/departments/
  nhm/

University of Montevallo
UM Station 6720
Montevallo, AL 35115
www.montevallo.edu

Arizona
Northern Arizona University
S. San Francisco St.
Flagstaff, AZ 86011
www.nau.edu

Arkansas
Ouachita Baptist University
410 Ouachita St.
Arkadelphia, AR 71923
www.obu.edu

University of Arkansas at Pine
  Bluff
UAPB Box 17
1200 University Dr.
Pine Bluff, AR 71601
www.uapb.edu

University of Central Arkansas
210 Donaghey Ave.
Conway, AR 72035
www.uca.edu

California
California State Polytechnic
  University
3801 W. Temple Ave.
Pomona, CA 91768
www.csupomona.edu

California State University, Chico
400 W. First St.
Chico, CA 95929
www.csuchico.edu

California State University, Fresno
5241 N. Maple Ave.
Fresno, CA 93740
www.csufresno.edu

California State University,
Long Beach
1250 Bellflower Blvd.
Long Beach, CA 90840
www.csulb.edu

California State University,
Los Angeles
5151 State University Dr.
Los Angeles, CA 90032
www.calstatela.edu

California State University,
Northridge
18111 Nordhoff St.
Northridge, CA 91330
www.csun.edu

California State University,
San Bernardino
5500 University Pkwy.
San Bernardino, CA 92407
www.csusb.edu

Loma Linda University
School of Allied Health
Professions
Loma Linda, CA 92350
www.llu.edu/allied-health/
nutrition/

Pacific Union College
One Angwin Ave.
Angwin, CA 94508
www.puc.edu

Point Loma Nazarene College
3900 Lomaland Dr.
San Diego, CA 92106
www.ptloma.edu

San Francisco State University
1600 Holloway Ave.
San Francisco, CA 94132
www.sfsu.edu

San Jose State University
1 Washington Sq.
San Jose, CA 95192
www.sjsu.edu

University of California, Berkeley
Berkeley, CA 94720
www.berkeley.edu

University of California, Davis
One Shields Ave.
Davis, CA 95616
www.ucdavis.edu

Colorado
Colorado State University
Fort Collins, CO 80523
www.colostate.edu

University of Northern Colorado
Greeley, CO 80639
www.univnorthco.edu

Connecticut
St. Joseph College
1678 Asylum Ave.
West Hartford, CT 06117
www.sjc.edu

University of Connecticut
358 Mansfield Rd.
Storrs, CT 06269
www.alliedhealth.uconn.edu

University of New Haven
300 Boston Post Rd.
West Haven, CT 06516
www.newhaven.edu

Delaware
University of Delaware
Newark, DE 19716
www.udel.edu

District of Columbia
Howard University
2400 6th St. NW
Washington, DC 20059
www.howard.edu

Florida
Florida International University
11200 SW 8th St.
Miami, FL 33199
www.fiu.edu

Florida State University
Tallahassee, FL 32306
www.fsu.edu

Georgia
Georgia State University
P.O. Box 3965
Atlanta, GA 30302
www.gsu.edu

University of Georgia
Athens, GA 30602
www.uga.edu

Idaho
Idaho State University
921 S. 8th Ave.
Pocatello, ID 83209
www.isu.edu

University of Idaho
College of Agriculture
Moscow, ID 83844
www.uidaho.edu

Illinois
Benedictine University
5700 College Rd.
Lisle, IL 60532
www.ben.edu

Bradley University
1501 W. Bradley Ave.
Peoria, IL 61625
www.bradley.edu

Dominican University
7900 W. Division St.
River Forest, IL 60305
www.dom.edu

Eastern Illinois University
600 Lincoln Ave.
Charleston, IL 61920
www.eiu.edu

Finch University of Health
Sciences
Chicago Medical School
3333 Green Bay Rd.
North Chicago, IL 60064
www.rosalindfranklin.edu

Illinois State University
Normal, IL 61790
www.ilstu.edu

Northern Illinois University
P.O. Box 3001
DeKalb, IL 60115
www.niu.edu

Olivet Nazarene University
One University Ave.
Bourbonnais, IL 60914
www.olivet.edu

Southern Illinois University at
  Carbondale
Carbondale, IL 62901
www.siuc.edu

University of Illinois at Chicago
Chicago, IL 60612
www.uic.edu

University of Illinois at Urbana-
  Champaign
1206 S. 4th St.
Champaign, IL 61820
www.uiuc.edu

Western Illinois University
1 University Circle
Macomb, IL 61455
www.wiu.edu

Indiana
Ball State University
2000 W. University Ave.
Muncie, IN 47306
www.bsu.edu

Goshen College
1700 S. Main St.
Goshen, IN 46526
www.goshen.edu

Indiana State University
200 N. 7th St.
Terre Haute, IN 47809
www.indstate.edu

Indiana University
107 S. Indiana Ave.
Bloomington, IN 47405
www.indiana.edu

Indiana University–Purdue
  University Indianapolis
Cavanaugh Hall, Room 129
Indianapolis, IN 46202
www.iupui.edu

Purdue University
700 W. State St.
West Lafayette, IN 47907
www.cfs.purdue.edu

Iowa
University of Northern Iowa
1227 W. 27th St.
Cedar Falls, IA 50614
www.uni.edu

Kansas
Kansas State University
Justin Hall 119
Manhattan, KS 66506
www.humec.ksu.edu

Kentucky
Berea College
CPO 2344
Berea, KY 40404
www.berea.edu

Morehead State University
150 University Blvd.
Morehead, KY 40351
www.morehead-st.edu

Murray State University
P.O. Box 9
Murray, KY 42071
www.murraystate.edu

University of Kentucky
210C Erikson Hall
Lexington, KY 40506
www.uky.edu

Western Kentucky University
1 Big Red Way
Bowling Green, KY 42101
www.wku.edu

Louisiana
Grambling State University
100 Main St.
Grambling, LA 71245
www.gram.edu

Louisiana State University
Baton Rouge, LA 70803
www.lsu.edu

Louisiana Tech University
P.O. Box 3178
Ruston, LA 71272
www.latech.edu/

Nicholls State University
Thibodaux, LA 70310
www.lsu.edu/

University of Louisiana at
  Lafayette
104 University Circle
Lafayette, LA 70504
www.louisiana.edu/

Maryland
Hood College
401 Rosemont Ave.
Frederick, MD 21701
www.hood.edu

Johns Hopkins University
Bay View Medical Center
Food and Clinical Nutrition
  Department
4940 Eastern Avenue
Baltimore, MD 21224
www.hopkinsbayview.org

Massachusetts
Framingham State College
100 State St.
Framingham, MA 01701
www.framingham.edu

Michigan
Andrews University
Berrien Springs, MI 49104
www.andrews.edu

Central Michigan University
Mount Pleasant, MI 48859
www.cmich.edu

Eastern Michigan University
202 Welch
Ypsilanti, MI 48197
www.emich.edu

Madonna University
36600 Schoolcraft Rd.
Livonia, MI 48150
www.munet.edu

Marygrove College
8425 W. McNichols Rd.
Detroit, MI 48221
www.marygrove.edu

Michigan State University
East Lansing, MI 48824
www.msu.edu

Northern Michigan University
1401 Presque Isle Ave.
Marquette, MI 49855
www.nmu.edu

Wayne State University
Detroit, MI 48202
www.science.wayne.edu

Western Michigan University
1901 W. Michigan Ave.
Kalamazoo, MI 49008
www.wmich.edu

Minnesota
College of Saint Benedict/Saint
  John's University
37 S. College Ave.
Saint Joseph, MN 56374
www.csbsju.edu

College of St. Scholastica
1200 Kenwood Ave.
Duluth, MN 55811
www.css.edu

Concordia College
901 8th St. S.
Moorhead, MN 56562
www.cord.edu

Minnesota State University,
  Mankato
Mankato, MN 56001
www.mnsu.edu

University of Minnesota
225 Food Science and Nutrition
1334 Eckles Ave.
St. Paul, MN 55108
http://fscn.cfans.umn.edu/

Mississippi
Delta State University
1003 W. Sunflower Rd.
Cleveland, MS 38732
www.deltastate.edu

University of Southern Mississippi
118 College Dr.
Hattiesburg, MS 39406
www.usm.edu

Missouri
Central Missouri State University
P.O. Box 800
Warrensburg, MO 64093
www.cmsu.edu

Fontbonne College
6800 Wydown Blvd.
St. Louis, MO 63105
www.fontbonne.edu

Southeast Missouri State
  University
One University Plaza
Cape Girardeau, MO 63701
www.semo.edu

Southwest Missouri State
  University
901 S. National Ave.
Springfield, MO 65804
www.smsu.edu

University of Missouri–Columbia
Columbia, MO 65211
www.missouri.edu

New Hampshire
University of New Hampshire
Grant House
4 Garrison Ave.
Durham, NH 03824
www.unh.edu

New Jersey
Montclair State University
1 Normal Ave.
Montclair, NJ 07043
www.montclair.edu

Rutgers
Cook College
New Brunswick, NJ 08903
http://sebs.rutgers.edu/

University of Medicine &
  Dentistry of New Jersey
1776 Raritan Rd.
Scotch Plains, NJ 07076
http://shrp.umdnj.edu/

New Mexico
New Mexico State University
P.O. Box 30001
Las Cruces, NM 88003
www.nmsu.edu

New York
Buffalo State College
1300 Elmwood Ave.
Buffalo, NY 14222
www.buffalostate.edu

Cornell University
410 Thurston Ave.
Ithaca, NY 14850
www.cornell.edu

D'Youville College
320 Porter Ave.
Buffalo, NY 14201
www.dyc.edu

Lehman College
City University of New York
250 Bedford Park Blvd. W.
Bronx, NY 10468
www.lehman.cuny.edu

Marymount College
100 Marymount Ave.
Tarrytown, NY 10591
www.fordham.edu

New York University
22 Washington Sq.
New York, NY 10012
www.nyu.edu

Queens College
City University of New York
65-30 Kissena Blvd.
Flushing, NY 11367
www.qc.cuny.edu

Syracuse University
119 Euclid Ave.
Syracuse, NY 13244
http://humanecology.syr.edu/

North Carolina
Bennett College
900 E. Washington St.
Greensboro, NC 27401
www.bennett.edu

East Carolina University
E. 5th St.
Greenville, NC 27858
www.ecu.edu

North Carolina Agricultural &
  Technical State University
1601 E. Market St.
Greensboro, NC 27411
www.ncat.edu

University of North Carolina at
  Chapel Hill
Rosenau Hall, CB #74100
Chapel Hill, NC 27599
www.sph.unc.edu

University of North Carolina at
  Greensboro
1000 Spring Garden St.
Greensboro, NC 27403
www.uncg.edu

Western Carolina University
Cullowhee, NC 28723
www.wcu.edu

North Dakota
North Dakota State University
1301 12th Ave. N.
Fargo, ND 58105
www.ndsu.nodak.edu

University of North Dakota
Grand Forks, ND 58202
www.und.nodak.edu

Ohio
Bluffton University
1 University Dr.
Bluffton, OH 45817
www.bluffton.edu

Bowling Green State University
Bowling Green, OH 43403
www.bgsu.edu

Case Western Reserve University
10900 Euclid Ave.
Cleveland, OH 44106
www.cwru.edu

Kent State University
Kent, OH 44242
www.kent.edu

Miami University
Oxford, OH 45056
www.muohio.edu

Ohio State University
Atwell Hall
453 W. 10th Ave.
Columbus, OH 43210
http://ehe.osu.edu/

Ohio University
Athens, OH 45701
www.ohio.edu

University of Akron
302 Buchtel Mall
Akron, OH 44325
www.uakron.edu

University of Cincinnati
College of Allied Health Sciences
3202 Eden Avenue
Cincinnati, Oh 45267
www.uc.edu

Youngstown State University
1 University Plaza
Youngstown, OH 44555
www.ysu.edu

Oklahoma
Langston University
P.O. Box 728
Langston, OK 73050
www.lunet.edu

Oklahoma State University
Stillwater, OK 74078
http://ches.okstate.edu/nsci/

University of Oklahoma
801 NE 13th St.
Oklahoma City, OK 73190
www.ou.edu

Oregon
Oregon State University
Corvallis, OR 97331
http://oregonstate.edu/

Pennsylvania
Cheyney University of
  Pennsylvania
1837 University Circle
P.O. Box 200
Cheyney, PA 19319
www.cheyney.edu

Edinboro University of
  Pennsylvania
Edinboro, PA 16444
www.edinboro.edu

Gannon University
109 University Sq.
Erie, PA 16541
www.gannon.edu

Immaculata University
1145 King Rd.
Immaculata, PA 19345
www.immaculata.edu

Indiana University of
  Pennsylvania
1011 South Dr.
Indiana, PA 15705
www.iup.edu

La Salle University
School of Nursing
1900 W. Olney Ave.
Philadelphia, PA 19141
www.lasalle.edu

Mansfield University of
  Pennsylvania
Mansfield, PA 16933
www.mansfield.edu

Marywood University
2300 Adams Ave.
Scranton, PA 18509
www.marywood.edu

Mercyhurst College
501 E. 38th St.
Erie, PA 16546
www.mercyhurst.edu

Messiah College
One College Ave.
Grantham, PA 17027
www.messiah.edu

Saint Vincent College
300 Fraser Purchase Rd.
Latrobe, PA 15650
www.stvincent.edu

Seton Hill University
Division of Natural and Health
  Sciences
One Seton Hill Dr.
Greensburg, PA 15601
www.setonhill.edu

University of Pittsburgh
School of Health and
  Rehabilitation Services
4020 Forbes Tower
Pittsburgh, PA 15260
www.shrs.pitt.edu

Puerto Rico
Universidad Del Turabo
School of Health Sciences
P.O. Box 3030
Gurabo, PR 00718
www.suaqm.edu

Rhode Island
University of Rhode Island
Kingston, RI 02881
www.uri.edu

South Dakota
Mount Marty College
1105 W. 8th St.
Yankton, SD 57078
www.mtmc.edu

South Dakota State University
Administration 200
P.O. Box 2201
Brookings, SD 57007
www3.sdstate.edu

Tennessee
Carson-Newman College
2130 Branner Ave.
Jefferson City, TN 37760
www.cn.edu

David Lipscomb University
3901 Granny White Pike
Nashville, TN 37204
www.lipscomb.edu

Middle Tennessee State University
1301 E. Main St.
Murfreesboro, TN 37132
www.mtsu.edu

University of Tennessee
Knoxville, TN 37996
www.utk.edu

University of Tennessee at Martin
544 University St.
Martin, TN 38238
www.utm.edu

Texas
Abilene Christian University
Abilene, TX 79699
www.acu.edu

Lamar University–Beaumont
4400 Martin Luther King Blvd.
P.O. Box 10009
Beaumont, TX 77710
www.lamar.edu

Texas Christian University
2800 S. University Dr.
Fort Worth, TX 76129
www.tcu.edu

Texas Southern University
3100 Cleburne St.
Houston, TX 77004
www.tsu.edu

Texas Woman's University
P.O. Box 425589
Denton, TX 76204
www.twu.edu

University of Houston
4800 Calhoun Rd.
Houston, TX 77204
www.uh.edu

University of Texas
Southwestern Medical Center at
  Dallas
5323 Harry Hines Blvd.
Dallas, TX 75390
www.utsouthwestern.edu

University of Texas at Austin
1 University Station, A2700
Austin, TX 78712
www.utexas.edu

University of Texas
Health Science Center at Houston
7000 Fannin, Ste. 1200
Houston, TX 77030
www.uthouston.edu

University of Texas–Pan American
1201 W. University Dr.
Edinburg, TX 78541
www.panam.edu

Utah
Brigham Young University
Provo, UT 84602
www.byu.edu

University of Utah
College of Health
200 HPER N.
250 S. 1850 E., Room 200
Salt Lake City, UT 84112
www.health.utah.edu

Utah State University
Dept. of Nutrition and Food
  Science
Rogan, Utah 84322
www.usu.edu/dietetic

Vermont
University of Vermont
Burlington, VT 05405
www.uvm.edu

Virginia
James Madison University
800 S. Main St.
Harrisonburg, VA 22807
www.jmu.edu

Radford University
E. Main St.
Radford, VA 24142
www.runet.edu

Virginia Polytechnic Institute and
  State University
Department of Human Nutrition,
  Foods and Exercise
338 Wallace Hall (0430)
Blacksburg, VA 24061
www.hnfe.vt.edu

Washington
Central Washington University
Mitchell Hall
Ellensburg, WA 98926
www.cwu.edu

Washington State University
Department of Food Science and
  Human Nutrition
P.O. Box 646376
Pullman, WA 99164
http://sfs.wsu.edu/

University of Washington
305 Raitt Hall, Box 353410
Seattle, WA 98195
www.washington.edu

Washington State University-
  Spokane
310 North Riverpoint Boulevard
P.O. Box 1495
Spokane, WA 99210
http://spokane.wsu.edu/

West Virginia
Marshall University
One John Marshall Dr.
Huntington, WV 25755
www.marshall.edu

West Virginia Wesleyan College
59 College Ave.
Buckhannon, WV 26201
www.wvwc.edu

Wisconsin
Mount Mary College
2900 N. Menomonee River Pkwy.
Milwaukee, WI 53222
www.mtmary.edu

University of Wisconsin–
 Green Bay
2420 Nicolet Dr.
Green Bay, WI 54311
www.uwgb.edu

University of Wisconsin–
 Madison
1415 Linden Dr.
Madison, WI 53706
www.nutrisci.wisc.edu

University of Wisconsin–
 Stevens Point
2100 Main St.
Stevens Point, WI 54481
www.uwsp.edu

University of Wisconsin–
 Stout
Menomonee, WI 54751
www.uwstout.edu

Viterbo University
900 Viterbo Dr.
La Crosse, WI 54601
www.viterbo.edu

Genetic Counselors

Principal activity: Providing information and advice on hereditary disorders and risks

Work commitment: Usually full-time

Preprofessional education: Bachelor's degree with a biology major

Program length: Two years

Work prerequisites: Master's degree

Career opportunities: Favorable

Income range: $48,000 to $66,000

Scope

Genetic counselors are trained health-care professionals who help people seeking information about hereditary disorders. They have learned communication skills that help them serve patients in a variety of ways, including helping them put their concerns into perspective.

Activities

Genetics is the study of gene transmission from parents to their children. A fetus's genetic profile can be useful in predicting potential health problems. Over the past few decades, medical technology has made remarkable progress in this area. Today, a multitude of genetically transmitted conditions and diseases can be identified in fetuses, including Down's syndrome, muscular dystrophy, cystic fibrosis, Tay-Sachs disease, sickle cell anemia, and some forms of mental retardation. Diagnosing such diseases involves microscopic analysis of the number and appearance of chromosomes. Chromosome samples are obtained from fetal cells extracted from the amniotic fluid. Other techniques also are available for studying fetal chromosomes and proteins.

Complementing this cellular approach is *ultrasound imaging*, which can uncover anatomical malformations in the heart, lungs, and spine. In some situations, physicians can perform surgery on the developing fetus *in utero* (in the womb); in others, physicians can correct abnormalities after birth.

Genetic counselors get patient information from medical geneticists and other sources. They help potential and prospective parents by giving them information about prenatal screening tests and explaining test results and medical options. They deal with couples who have serious concerns about the well-being of future children. Such couples may include those of late childbearing age (in their late 30s and 40s), those belonging to certain races or nationalities (for example, Tay-Sachs disease is most prevalent in those of Eastern European Jewish origin), and those with a known family history of disease. Genetic counselors help such patients become better informed and help them cope with the psychological issues generated by the stresses of genetic disorders.

Work Settings

The majority of genetic counselors are employed by major medical centers. That's where both genetic screening and prenatal diagnosis take place. Genetic counselors may be affiliated with pediatric and obstetrics/gynecology departments at such medical centers. Some genetic counselors are employed by federal and state health-care agencies. Some professionals are in private practice.

Advancement

Supervisory positions are often available in centers that employ several counselors.

Prerequisites

To enter this field, you must earn a bachelor's degree with a major in biology. Required courses include general biology, developmental biology (vertebrate embryology), genetics, molecular genetics, general chemistry, psychology, and statistics. Recommended courses include organic chemistry, advanced psychology, and Spanish.

Desirable attributes for those planning a career in this field include empathy and superior communication and counseling skills.

Education/Training

Courses taken as part of a master's degree program include human anatomy and physiology, biochemistry, human genetics, clinical medicine, animal genetics, medical genetics, client counseling, and delivery of genetic services. As part of their fieldwork, students are placed in clinical settings (for several hundred hours) and are exposed to cytogenetics and laboratory work.

Certification/Registration/Licensure

Graduates of genetics counseling master's degree programs can take a certification examination offered by the American Board of Genetic Counseling.

Career Potential

Genetic counseling is a relatively new profession. But there is a definite demand for genetic counselors, as reflected by the fact that all those who have graduated from the educational programs in this field have secured employment in the field. While the total number of workers in the profession is relatively small, the increased use of genetic screening should prompt a need for a growing number of counselors.

For More Information

The professional organization for this field is the National Society of Genetic Counselors, 233 Canterbury Dr., Wallingford, PA 19086 (www.nsgc.org).

Genetic Counselor Programs

Alabama
University of South Alabama
  Medical School
Mobile, AL 36688
www.usouthal.edu

Alaska
Alaska Genetics Clinic
1231 Gambell St., Ste. 407
Anchorage, AK 99501

Arizona
Phoenix Children's Hospital
1919 E. Thomas Rd.
Phoenix, AZ 85016
www.phxchildrens.com

University of Arizona
Tucson, AZ 85721
www.arizona.edu

Arkansas
University of Arkansas for Medical
  Sciences
4301 W. Markham St.
Little Rock, AR 72205
www.uams.edu

California
California State University at
  Northridge
18111 Nordhoff St.
Northridge, CA 91330
www.csun.edu

Children's Hospital Central
  California
9300 Valley Children's Place
Madera, CA 93638
www.valleychildrens.org

Kaiser Permanente
2025 Morse Ave.
Sacramento, CA 95825
www.kaiserpermanente.org

San Francisco State University
Genetic Counseling Programs
Department of Biology
San Francisco, CA 94132
www.sfsu.edu

Stanford University
Genetic Counseling
300 Pasteur Drive H315
Stanford, CA 94305
www.med.stanford.edu/
  genetic-counseling

University of California, Berkeley
570 University Hall
Berkeley, CA 94720
www.berkeley.edu

University of California
Irvine Medical Center
101 The City Drive
Orange, CA 92868
www.ucihealth.com

University of California,
  Los Angeles
300 UCLA Medical Plaza
Los Angeles, CA 90024
www.ucla.edu

Colorado
University of Colorado Health
  Sciences Center
The Graduate School
4200 E. 9th Ave.
Campus Box C-296
Denver, CO 80262
www.ucdenver.edu

Connecticut
Yale University School of
  Medicine
333 Cedar St.
New Haven, CT 06510
http://info.med.yale.edu/ysm/

District of Columbia
George Washington University
2121 Eye St. NW
Washington, DC 20052
www.gwu.edu

Howard University
4th and College Sts. NW
Washington, DC 20059
www.gs.howard.edu

Florida
Arnold Palmer Hospital for
  Children & Women
92 W. Miller St.
Orlando, FL 32806
www.arnoldpalmerhospital.org

Georgia
Children's Healthcare of Atlanta
  at Scottish Rite
1001 Johnson Ferry Rd. NE
Atlanta, GA 30342
www.scottishritechildrens.org

Memorial Health
4700 Waters Ave.
Savannah, GA 31404
www.memorialhealth.com

Hawaii
Kapiolani Health
1319 Punahou St.
Honolulu, HI 96826
www.kapiolani.org

Idaho
St. Luke's Regional Medical Center
190 E. Bannock St.
Boise, ID 83712
www.stlukesonline.org

Illinois
Lutheran General Prenatal Center
1875 Dempster St.
Park Ridge, IL 60068

Northwestern University
Feinberg School of Medicine
303 E. Chicago Ave.
Chicago, IL 60611
www.feinberg.northwestern.edu

Rush University
College of Nursing
600 S. Paulina St.
Chicago, IL 60612
www.rush.edu

Indiana
Indiana University School of
  Medicine
975 W. Walnut St.
Indianapolis, IN 46202
www.iupui.edu

Iowa
University of Iowa Hospitals and
  Clinics
Center for Disabilities and
  Development
100 Hawkins Dr.
Iowa City, IA 52242
www.medicine.uiowa.edu/CDD

Kansas
University of Kansas Medical
  Center
3901 Rainbow Blvd.
Kansas City, KS 66160
www.kumc.edu

Kentucky
University of Kentucky Medical
  Center
Lexington, KY 40506
www.uky.edu

University of Louisville
Child Evaluation Center
Louisville, KY 40292
www.louisville.edu

Louisiana
Tulane University School of
  Medicine
1430 Tulane Ave.
New Orleans, LA 70112
www.som.tulane.edu

Maine
Foundation for Blood Research
8 Nonesuch Rd.
P.O. Box 190
Scarborough, ME 04070
www.fbr.org

Maryland
Genetic Counseling Training
  Program
10 Center Drive MSC 1852,
  Bldg.10
Bethesda, MD 20832
www.genome.gov/10001156

National Human Genome Research
  Institute
National Institutes of Health
Building 31, Room 4B09
31 Center Dr., MSC 2152
9000 Rockville Pike
Bethesda, MD 20892
www.genome.gov

University of Maryland
School of Medicine
655 W. Baltimore St.
Baltimore, MD 21201
www.medschool.umaryland.edu

Massachusetts
Beth Israel Deaconess Medical
  Center
330 Brookline Ave.
Boston, MA 02215
www.bidmc.org

Boston University
School of Medicine
Center of Human Genetics
715 Albany Street, W408
Boston, MA 02118
www.bumc.bu.edu/hg

Brandeis University
Waltham, MA 02454
www.bio.brandeis.edu/grad/gc/

Michigan
Michigan State University
East Lansing, MI 48824
www.msu.edu

Sinai-Grace Hospital
6071 W. Outer Dr.
Detroit, MI 48235
www.sinaigrace.org

University of Michigan Health
  System
1500 E. Medical Center Dr.
Ann Arbor, MI 48109
www.med.umich.edu

Wayne State University School of
  Medicine
Detroit, MI 48202
www.wayne.edu

Minnesota
University of Minnesota Hospital
  & Clinics
420 Delaware St. SE
Minneapolis, MN 55455
www.umn.edu

Mississippi
University of Mississippi Medical
  Center
2500 N. State St.
Jackson, MS 39216
www.umc.edu

Missouri
University of Missouri Hospital &
  Clinics
Columbia, MO 65211
www.missouri.edu

Montana
Shodair Children's Hospital
Department of Medical Genetics
P.O. Box 5539
Helena, MT 59604
www.shodairhospital.org

Nebraska
University of Nebraska Medical
  Center
42nd and Emile
Omaha, NE 68198
www.unmc.edu

New Hampshire
Dartmouth-Hitchcock Medical
  Center
One Medical Center Dr.
Lebanon, NH 03756
www.dhmc.org

New Jersey
Cooper University Hospital
One Cooper Plaza
Camden, NJ 08103
www.cooperhealth.org

Hackensack University Medical
  Center
30 Prospect Ave.
Hackensack, NJ 07601
www.humed.com

New Mexico
University of New Mexico
Albuquerque, NM 87131
www.unm.edu

New York
Binghamton University Genetic
  Counseling Program
P.O. Box 6000
Binghamton, NY 13902
www.binghamton.edu

Mount Sinai School of Medicine
One Gustave L. Levy Place
New York, NY 10029
www.mssm.edu

New York State Department of
  Health
WCLR Empire State Plaza
Albany, NY 12201
www.health.state.ny.us

New York University School of
  Medicine
550 First Ave.
New York, NY 10016
www.nyu.edu

Sarah Lawrence College
1 Mead Way
Bronxville, NY 10708
www.slc.edu

North Carolina
Carolinas HealthCare System
P.O. Box 32861
Charlotte, NC 28232
www.carolinas.org

University of North Carolina at
  Greensboro
Genetic Counseling
P.O. Box 26170
Greensboro, NC 27402
www.uncg.edu/gen/

Ohio
Akron Children's Hospital
One Perkins Square
Akron, OH 44308
www.akronchildrens.org

Case Western Reserve University
10900 Euclid Ave.
Cleveland, OH 44106
www.cwru.edu

University of Cincinnati
College of Allied Health Sciences
202 Goodman Dr.
Cincinnati, OH 45267
www.cahs.uc.edu

Oklahoma
Oklahoma State Department of
  Health
1000 NE 10th St.
Oklahoma City, OK 73117
www.health.state.ok.us

University of Oklahoma
Medical Center
CHO 2B 2418
940 NE 13th
Oklahoma City, OK 73104
www.ouhsc.edu

Oregon
Oregon Health & Science
  University
3181 SW Sam Jackson Park Rd.
Portland, OR 97239
www.ohsu.edu

Pennsylvania
Arcadia University
450 S. Easton Rd.
Glenside, PA 19038
www.beaver.edu

Penn State Hershey Medical
  Center
500 University Dr.
Hershey, PA 17033
www.pennstatehershey.org

Thomas Jefferson University
  Hospital
111 S. 11th St.
Philadelphia, PA 19107
www.jeffersonhospital.org

University of Pittsburgh
Pittsburgh, PA 15260
www.pitt.edu

Rhode Island
Women & Infants Hospital of
  Rhode Island
101 Dudley St.
Providence, RI 02905
www.womenandinfants.org

South Carolina
University of South Carolina
School of Medicine
2 Medical Park
Columbia, SC 29208
www.med.sc.edu

South Dakota
University of South Dakota
School of Medicine
Health Science Center
1400 W. 22nd St.
Sioux Falls, SD 57105
www.usd.edu

Tennessee
Vanderbilt University
2201 West End Ave.
Nashville, TN 37235
www.vanderbilt.edu

Texas
Baylor College of Medicine
One Baylor Plaza
Houston, TX 77030
www.bmc.edu

University of Texas Medical
  School at Houston
6431 Fannin St.
Houston, TX 77030
www.med.uth.tmc.edu

Utah
University of Utah Medical Center
201 S. Presidents Circle, Room
  201
Salt Lake City, UT 84112
www.utah.edu

Vermont
Vermont Regional Genetics Center
1 Mill St.
Burlington, VT 05401

Virginia
University of Virginia Health
 System
Department of Pediatric Genetics
P.O. Box 800386
Charlottesville, VA 22908
www.healthsystem.virginia.edu

Virginia Commonwealth University
 School of Medicine
Medical College of Virginia Campus
P.O. Box 980565
Richmond, VA 23298
www.medschool.vcu.edu

Washington
University of Washington Medical
 Center
1959 NE Pacific
Seattle, WA 98195
www.washington.edu

West Virginia
West Virginia University
Health Sciences Center
P.O. Box 6201
Morgantown, WV 26506
www.hsc.wvu.edu

Wisconsin
La Crosse Regional Genetics
 Service
P.O. Box 1326
La Crosse, WI 54602
www.gundluth.org

St. Vincent Hospital
835 S. Van Buren St.
P.O. Box 13508
Green Bay, WI 54307
www.stvincenthospital.org

University of Wisconsin
Laboratory of Genetics
445 Henry Hall
Madison, WI 53706
www.genetics.wisc.edu

Wyoming
Wyoming Department of Health
2300 Capitol Ave.
Room 117
Cheyenne, WY 82002
http://wdh.state.wy.us/

Canada
Hospital for Sick Children
The Rommens Lab
Program in Genetics & Genomic
 Biology
555 University Ave.
Room 11-109, Elm Wing
Toronto, Ontario M5G 1X8
www.genet.sickkids.on.ca

McGill University
1205 Av. Docteur Penfield, N5/13
Montreal, Quebec H3A 1B1
www.mcgill.ca/humangenetics/

University of British Columbia
Department of Medical Genetics
Provincial Medical Genetics
 Programme
4500 Oak St., Room C234
Vancouver, British Columbia
 V6H 3N1
www.medgen.ubc.ca

University of Toronto
Molecular Genetics & Molecular
 Biology Program
Toronto, Ontario M5S 1A1
www.utoronto.ca

Licensed Practical Nurses

Principal activity: Providing nursing care for the infirm and injured

Work commitment: Full-time

Preprofessional education: High school diploma

Program length: 1 to 1½ years

Work prerequisites: Certificate/diploma/license

Career opportunities: Highly favorable

Income range: $33,000 to $47,000

Scope

Licensed practical nurses (LPNs) provide bedside care to a wide variety of patients, including the injured, ill, convalescent, and disabled. They work under the supervision of a registered nurse (RN). Because LPNs have fewer responsibilities, their education and training are more limited than that of an RN. In a few states, they are called licensed vocational nurses (LVNs).

Activities

A major task for LPNs is taking and recording, at prescribed intervals during the day, patients' vital signs, including blood pressure, temperature, and pulse. They also help care for patients by feeding, bathing, and dressing them. They may dress wounds and prepare patients for exams. They also assist in medical examinations by physicians. They note any significant changes in their patients' conditions and record these; when appropriate, they report changes immediately to their supervisor.

In non-hospital settings such as doctors' offices, LPNs prepare patients for exams, change dressings, advise patients on home health care, and carry out a variety of administrative chores. Aside from serving on general hospital wards, LPNs may work in specialty areas such as obstetrics, pediatrics, or surgery.

Work Settings

The major work sites for LPNs are medical centers and hospitals. The second-largest employment field is nursing homes. Openings also are available in HMOs, clinics, physicians' and dentists' offices, rehabilitation centers, prison medical offices, sanitariums, industrial health clinics, long-term facilities, and even private homes.

Advancement

You can advance by getting a supervisory position with responsibilities over nursing assistants and nurse's aides. By completing additional course work, an LPN can become a registered nurse. Some LPNs receive salary advancements by seeking employment in larger or more prestigious health-care facilities.

Prerequisites

A high school diploma or its equivalent is usually required to become a licensed practical nurse.

Desirable personal attributes for work in this field include compassion, strength, good communication skills, the ability to follow instructions, concern for detail, and a desire to help the infirm and disabled.

Education/Training

Many institutions offer state-approved practical nursing programs, including technical, vocational, and trade schools; hospitals; and community and junior colleges. The basic curriculum includes courses in anatomy and physiology and medical, surgical, psychiatric, pediatric, and obstetric nursing. In addition, prospective LPNs are taught about nutrition and diet, first aid, administering medications, community development, and community health. They also learn various nursing concepts and basic nursing skills and techniques. Part of the training includes supervised clinical experience in a hospital. After candidates successfully complete the educational and training program, they are awarded a certificate or diploma.

Certification/Registration/Licensure

Earning a certificate or diploma from a state-approved practical nursing program qualifies a candidate to take the written state board licensing examination. After the candidate passes the exam, he or she is awarded a license to practice.

Career Potential

The employment outlook for LPNs appears favorable on the whole. Demand will be driven by the aging population and the need for more long-term health care. The increase in procedures performed in physicians' offices and in outpatient care centers will lead to a significant increase in the number of LPNs in these facilities.

However, recent history has seen marked cyclical fluctuations between surpluses and shortages of nurses. Changes in the U.S. health-care system also create uncertainty. Although the nursing needs for a growing population—especially the booming elderly population—are high, cost containment pressures will result in lowered nursing needs.

For More Information

More than a thousand state-licensed practical nursing programs exist in various educational settings in the United States—far too many to list here. For information about a program in your area, contact the National Federation of Licensed Practical Nurses, Inc., 605 Poole Dr., Garner, NC 27529 (www.nflpn.org).

You can receive additional information from the National Association for Practical Nurse Education and Service, Inc., P.O. Box 25647, Alexandria, VA 22313 (www.napnes.org), or the National League for Nursing, 61 Broadway, New York, NY 10006 (www.nln.org).

Nurse Anesthetists

Principal activity: Administering anesthesia to surgical and obstetric patients

Work commitment: Usually full-time

Preprofessional education: Licensed registered nurse

Program length: 2 years

Work prerequisites: Certified, registered RN status

Career opportunities: Favorable

Income range: $99,000 to $148,000

Scope

A nurse anesthetist is a registered nurse who is certified to administer anesthesia to patients. It is estimated that more than half of all anesthesia procedures are performed by nurse anesthetists. This is especially true in rural areas. Nurse anesthetists differ from anesthesiology assistants, who can work only under the direct supervision of an anesthesiologist.

Nurse anesthetists also can perform their responsibilities independently. They work under the general oversight of an anesthesiologist, who usually supervises the entire department.

Activities

Nurse anesthetists select the proper anesthetic and the appropriate dosage for the specific procedure to be performed. They may assist with surgical, obstetric, or dental procedures. During their activities they monitor patients' vital signs, note their conditions, and follow their postoperative course in the recovery room.

Work Settings

Nurse anesthetists work in hospital operating rooms, ambulatory surgery sites, and dentists' offices.

Advancement

In a facility that relies primarily on nurse anesthetists, gaining experience and having managerial skills may result in additional supervisory responsibilities.

Prerequisites

A bachelor's degree in nursing along with a license is required for admission to most nurse anesthetist programs.

Desirable personal attributes for those entering this field are an ability to work well under stress, superior talents in science, and the capacity to assume enormous personal responsibility.

Education/Training

Programs for nurse anesthetists last from 18 to 20 months. Course work includes anatomy, physiology, pharmacology, and anesthetic procedures. Practical experience in administering anesthesia also is provided.

Certification/Registration/Licensure

All states require nurse anesthetists to be licensed. To secure certification, candidates must pass an examination administered by the American Association of Nurse Anesthetists. Successfully passing this exam means the candidate may be designated as a certified registered nurse anesthetist (CRNA). To retain this status, nurses must undergo a biannual recertification process. This involves completing continuing-education courses.

Career Potential

Nurse anesthetists have many opportunities for general or specialty practice throughout the United States. This is one of the best-paid nursing specialties and has been ranked in the top 20 percent of income-earning professions.

For More Information

The professional organization for this field is the American Association of Nurse Anesthetists, 222 S. Prospect Ave., Park Ridge, IL 60068 (www.aana.com).

Nurse Anesthetist Programs

Alabama
Samford University
800 Lakeshore Dr.
Birmingham, AL 35229
www.samford.edu

University of Alabama at
  Birmingham
1530 3rd Ave. S.
Birmingham, AL 35294
www.uab.edu

Arizona
Midwestern University
Nurse Anesthesia Program
19555 North 59th Avenue
Glendale, AZ 85308
www.midwestern.edu

Arkansas

Arkansas State University
College of Nursing & Health
   Professions
P.O. Box 910
Jonesboro, AR 72467
www2.astate.edu/conhp/

California

Kaiser Permanente School of
   Anesthesia
California State University–
   Fullerton
100 S. Los Robles
Pasadena, CA 91188
www.kpsan.org

Samuel Merritt College
370 Hawthorne Ave.
Oakland, CA 94609
www.samuelmerritt.edu

University of California,
   San Francisco
San Francisco, CA 94143
www.ucsf.edu

University of Southern California
Keck School of Medicine
Department of Anesthesiology
1200 N. State St., Room 14-901
Los Angeles, CA 90033
www.usc.edu/schools/medicine/
   departments/anesthesiology/

Connecticut

Central Connecticut State
   University
Biology Department
Room 332 Copernicus Hall
New Britain, CT 06050
www.biology.ccsu.edu/Pro-
   grams/Grad/MA_Anesthesia.
   htm

Hospital of Saint Raphael
School of Nurse Anesthesia
1423 Chapel St.
New Haven, CT 06511
www.hsrsna.com

New Britain School of Nurse
   Anesthetist
100 Grand Street
New Britain, CT 06052
www.nbsna.org

Southern Connecticut State
   University and Bridgeport
   Hospital
Nurse Anesthesia Program
267 Grant St.
Bridgeport, CT 06610
www.bhnap.org

District of Columbia

Georgetown University
37th and O Streets NW
Washington, DC 20057
www.georgetown.edu

Florida

Barry University/Mount Sinai
   Medical Center
11300 NE Second Ave.
Miami Shores, FL 33161
www.barry.edu

Florida Gulf Coast University
MSN Nurse Anesthesia Program
10501 FGCU Boulevard South
Fort Myers, FL 33965
www.fgcu.edu/chp/nursing/
   anesthesia/

Florida Hospital College of Health
   Sciences
671 Winyah Drive
Orlando, FL 32803
www.fhchs.edu

Florida International University
College of Health and Urban
   Affairs
University Park, HLS 485
Miami, FL 33199
http://cnhs.fiu.edu/nursing/

Gooding Institute of Nurse
   Anesthesia
Bay Medical Center
615 N. Bonita Ave.
Panama City, FL 32401
www.baymedical.org

Wolford College
School of Nurse Anesthesia
4933 Tamiami Trail N., Ste. 201
Naples, FL 34103
www.nrwsna.org

Georgia

Mercer University School of
   Medicine
777 Hemlock Street
HB 185
Macon, GA 51201
www.mccg.org/crna

Medical College of Georgia
1120 15th St.
Augusta, GA 30912
www.mcg.edu

Illinois

Decatur Memorial Hospital
2300 N. Edward St.
Decatur, IL 62526
www.dmhhs.com

Evanston Northwestern
   Healthcare
2650 Ridge Ave.
Evanston, IL 60201
www.enh.org

Rosalind Franklin University of
   Medicine and Science
Nurse Anesthesia Program
3333 Greenbay Road
North Chicago, IL 60064
www.rosalindfranklin.edu

Rush University
College of Nursing
600 S. Paulina St.
Chicago, IL 60612
www.rush.edu

Southern Illinois University at
   Edwardsville
School of Nursing
Campus Box 1066
Edwardsville, IL 62026
www.siue.edu/nursing/

Iowa

Drake University
2507 University Ave.
Des Moines, IA 50311
www.drake.edu

University of Iowa
College of Nursing
200 Hawkins Dr.
Iowa City, IA 52242
www.anesth.uiowa.edu

Kansas
Newman University
3100 McCormick Ave.
Wichita, KS 67213
www.newmanu.edu

University of Kansas Medical
 Center
3901 Rainbow Blvd.
Kansas City, KS 66103
www.kumc.edu

Kentucky
Trover Foundation
435 N. Kentucky Ave.
Madisonville, KY 42431
www.troverfoundation.org

Louisiana
Louisiana State University Health
 Sciences
1900 Gravier St.
New Orleans, LA 70112
www.lsuhsc.edu

Our Lady of the Lake College
Nurse Anesthesia Program
7500 Hennessy Boulevard
Baron, rouge, LA 70808
www.ololcollege.edu

Xavier University of Louisiana
1 Drexel Dr.
New Orleans, LA 70125
www.xula.edu

Maine
Eastern Maine Medical Center
489 State St.
P.O. Box 404
Bangor, ME 04401
www.emmc.org

University of New England
11 Hills Beach Rd.
Biddeford, ME 04005
www.une.edu

University of New England
716 Stevens Ave.
Portland, ME 04103
www.une.edu

Maryland
Naval Medical Education and
 Training Command
Navy Nurse Corps Anesthesia
 Program
8901 Wisconsin Ave.
Bethesda, MD 20889
http://nshs.med.navy.mil/

Uniformed Services University of
 the Health Sciences
4301 Jones Bridge Rd.
Bethesda, MD 20814
www.usuhs.mil

University of Maryland School of
 Nursing
655 W Lombard Street, Suite 365
Baltimore, MD 21201
www.nursing.umaryland.edu

Massachusetts
Boston College
William F. Connell School of
 Nursing
140 Commonwealth Ave.
Chestnut Hill, MA 02467
www.bc.edu/schools/son/

Northeastern University
Bouve College of Health Sciences
Graduate School of Nursing
360 Huntington Ave.
Boston, MA 02115
www.northeastern.edu/bouve/

Michigan
Henry Ford Hospital
University of Detroit Mercy
2799 W. Grand Blvd.
Detroit, MI 48202
http://healthprofessions.
 udmercy.edu/programs/crna/

Oakland University–Beaumont
3601 W. 13 Mile Rd.
Royal Oak, MI 48073
www.beaumonthospitals.com/
 crna/

University of Detroit Mercy
4405 Woodward Ave.
Pontiac, MI 48341
www.udmercy.edu/crna/

University of Michigan–Flint
Hurley Medical Center
One Hurley Plaza
Flint, MI 48503
www.umflint.edu

Wayne State University
Eugene Applebaum College of
 Pharmacy and Health Sciences
Detroit, MI 48202
www.cphs.wayne.edu

Minnesota
Abbott Northwestern Hospital
800 E. 28th St.
Minneapolis, MN 55407
www.abbottnorthwestern.com

Mayo School of Health-Related
 Sciences
1108 Siebens Building
200 1st St. SW
Rochester, MN 55905
www.mayo.edu

Minneapolis School of Anesthesia
6715 Minnetonka Blvd.
St. Louis Park, MN 55426
www.nurseanesthesia.org

Minneapolis VA School of
 Anesthesia
One Veterans Drive, 112A
Minneapolis, MN 55417

Saint Mary's University of
 Minnesota
2500 Park Ave.
Minneapolis, MN 55404
www.smumn.edu

University of Minnesota
School of Nursing
5-160 Weaver-Densford Hall
308 Harvard Street SE
Minneapolis, MN 55455
www.nursing.umn.edu

Missouri
Goldfarb School of Nursing at
 Barnes Jewish College
MS-90-36-697
4483 Duncan Avenue
Saint Louis, MO 63110
www.barnesjewishcollege.edu

Southwest Missouri State
  University
College of Health and Human
  Services
Professional Building, Room 400
901 S. National Ave.
Springfield, MO 65804
www.smsu.edu/bms/programs/
  msna.html

Truman Medical Center
School of Nurse Anesthesia
2301 Holmes St.
Kansas City, MO 64108
www.trumed.org/crna/

Webster University
470 E. Lockwood Ave.
St. Louis, MO 63119
www.webster.edu

Nebraska
Bryan LGH Medical Center
1600 S. 48th St.
Lincoln, NE 68506
www.bryanlgh.org

New Jersey
Our Lady of Lourdes Medical
  Center
1600 Haddon Ave.
Camden, NJ 08103
www.lourdesnet.org

New York
Albany Medical College
43 New Scotland Ave.
Albany, NY 12208
www.amc.edu

Columbia University School of
  Nursing
630 W. 168th St.
New York, NY 10032
http://cpmcnet.columbia.edu/
  dept/nursing/

Harlem Hospital Center
506 Lenox Ave.
New York, NY 10037
www.ci.nyc.ny.us/html/hhc/
  html/harlem.html

SUNY Health Science Center
  at Brooklyn
Nurse Anesthesia Program
Harlem Hospital Center
Kings County Hospital Center
450 Clarkson Avenue Box 22
Brooklyn, NY 11203
www.downstate.edu

University at Buffalo
State University of New York
School of Nursing
1040 Kimball Tower
3435 Main St.
Buffalo, NY 14214
http://nursing.buffalo.edu/

North Carolina
Carolinas Health Care System
P.O. Box 32861
Charlotte, NC 28232
www.carolinasmedicalcenter.org

Duke University
School of Nursing
Trent Dr., DUMC 3322
Durham, NC 27710
www.nursing.duke.edu

East Carolina University
School of Nursing
Doctor's Park #5A
Brody School of Medicine
Greenville, NC 27834
www.ecu.edu

Wake Forest University
Baptist Medical Center
University of North Carolina at
  Greensboro
Medical Center Blvd.
Winston-Salem, NC 27157
www.wfubmc.edu

North Dakota
University of North Dakota
Grand Forks, ND 58202
www.und.nodak.edu

Ohio
Case Western Reserve University
Frances Payne Bolton School of
  Nursing
10900 Euclid Ave.
Cleveland, OH 44106
http://fpb.cwru.edu/

St. Elizabeth Health Center
1044 Belmont Ave.
Youngstown, OH 44504
www.hmpartners.org

United States Air Force
74th Medical Group/SGOSA
4881 Sugar Maple Dr.
Wright-Patterson AFB 45433
www.wpafb.af.mil

University of Akron College of
  Nursing
Anesthesia Program
509 Carroll Street
Akron, OH 44325
www.uakron.edu/nursing/

University of Cincinnati
College of Nursing and Health
3110 Vine St.
Cincinnati, OH 45221
www.nursing.uc.edu

Oregon
Oregon Health Science University
School of Nursing
Nurse Anesthesia Program
3455 SW US VETERANS hospital
  Road
Portland, OR 97239
www.ohsu.edu/son/

Pennsylvania
Allegheny Valley Hospital
La Roche College
School of Nurse Anesthesia
1301 Carlisle St.
Natrona Heights, PA 15065
www.laroche.edu

Altoona Hospital
620 Howard Ave.
Altoona, PA 16601
www.altoonahosp.org

Crozer Chester Medical Center
Villanova University
College of Nursing
800 Lancaster Ave.
Villanova, PA 19085
www.villanova.edu/nursing/

Drexel University
3141 Chestnut St.
Philadelphia, PA 19104
www.drexel.edu/cnhp/

Excela Health School of
 Anesthesia
813 Ligonier Street
Ligatrobe, PA 15650
www.excelahealth.org

Frank. J. Tornetta School at
 Montgomery Hospital
1301 Powell St.
Norristown, PA 19401
www.mhanesthesia.com

Geisinger Medical Center
100 N. Academy Ave.
Danville, PA 17822
www.geisinger.org

Hamot Medical Center
201 State St.
Erie, PA 16550
www.hamot.org

Lankenau Hospital
100 Lancaster Ave.
Wynnewood, PA 19096
www.mainlinehealth.org

Nazareth Hospital
2601 Holme Ave.
Philadelphia, PA 19152
www.nazarethhospital.org

Pennsylvania Hospital
800 Spruce St.
Philadelphia, PA 19107
www.pennmedicine.org/pahosp/

St. Francis Medical Center
La Roche College
400 45th St.
Pittsburgh, PA 15201
www.laroche.edu

Thomas Jefferson University
Jefferson College of Health
 Professions
Nurse Anesthesia Program
130 S. 9th Street
Suite 1130
Philadelphia, PA 19107
www.jefferson.edu/jchp/

University of Pennsylvania
Nursing Education Building
420 Guardian Dr.
Philadelphia, PA 19104
www.nursing.upenn.edu/nap/

University of Pittsburgh
School of Nursing
3500 Victoria St.
314 Victoria Building
Pittsburgh, PA 15261
www.pitt.edu

Washington Hospital
155 Wilson Ave.
Washington, PA 15301
www.washingtonhospital.org

Westmoreland–Latrobe Hospitals
La Roche College
532 W. Pittsburgh St.
Greensburg, PA 15601
www.westmoreland.org

Wyoming Valley Health Care
 System
575 N. River St.
Wilkes-Barre, PA 18764
www.wvhcs.org

York College of Pennsylvania
Nurse Anesthetists Program
605 S George Street
Loretta Clairborne Building
York, PA 17401
www.ycp.edu

Rhode Island
Memorial Hospital of Rhode
 Island
111 Brewster St.
Pawtucket, RI 02860
www.mhri.org/anesth/unitsch.
 htm

St. Joseph Hospital
200 High Service Ave.
North Providence, RI 02904
www.saintjosephri.com

South Carolina
Medical University of South
 Carolina
99 Jonathan Lucas St.
P.O. Box 250160
Charleston, SC 29425
www.musc.edu/nursing/

University of South Carolina
15 Medical Park
Columbia, SC 29203
www.sc.edu

South Dakota
Mount Marty College
3932 S. Western Ave.
Sioux Falls, SD 57105
www.mtmc.edu

Tennessee
Lincoln Memorial University
Caylor School of Nursing
6965 Cumberland Gap Parkway
Harrogate, TN 37752
www.lmunet.edu

Middle Tennessee School of
 Anesthesia
P.O. Box 6414
Madison, TN 37116
www.mtsa.edu

Union University of Nursing
Nurse Anesthesia Track
1050 Union University Drive
Jackson, TN 38305
www.uu.edu/academics/son/

University of Tennessee
Medical Center at Knoxville
1924 Alcoa Hwy.
Knoxville, TN 37920
www.utmedicalcenter.org

University of Tennessee at
 Chattanooga
Erlanger Medical Center
615 McCallie Ave.
Chattanooga, TN 37403
www.utc.edu

University of Tennessee Health
 Science Center
877 Madison Ave.
Memphis, TN 38163
www.utmem.edu/nursing/

Texas
Army Medical Department Center
 and School
2250 Stanley Rd.
Fort Sam Houston, TX 78234
www.cs.amedd.army.mil

Baylor College of Medicine
One Baylor Plaza
Houston, TX 77030
www.bcm.edu

Texas Christian University
School of Nurse Anesthesia
2800 W. Bowie St., Ste. 319
Fort Worth, TX 76109
www.crna.tcu.edu

Texas Wesleyan University
1201 Wesleyan St.
Ft. Worth, TX 76105
www.txwesleyan.edu

University of Texas
Health Science Center at Houston
7000 Fannin, Ste. 1200
Houston, TX 77030
www.uthouston.edu

U.S. Army Graduate Program in
    Anesthesia Nursing
2250 Stanley Rd.
Fort Sam Houston, TX 78234
www.dns.amedd.army.mil/crna/

Utah
Westminster College
School of Nursing
Nurse Anesthesia
1840 South 1300 East
Salt Lake City, Utah 84105
www.westminstercollege.edu

Virginia
Old Dominion University
School of Nursing
4608 Hampton Blvd.
Norfolk, VA 23529
www.odu.edu

Virginia Commonwealth University
P.O. Box 980226
MCV Campus
Richmond, VA 23298
www.vcu.edu

Washington
Sacred Heart Medical Center
Gonzaga University
101 W. 8th Ave.
Spokane, WA 99202
www.shmc.org

West Virginia
Charleston Area Medical Center
3110 MacCorkle Ave. SE
Charleston, WV 25314
www.camcinstitute.org/
    anesthesia/

Mountain State University
Nurse Anesthesia Program
609 S Kanawha Street
P O Box 9003
Beckley, WV 25802
www.mountainstate.edu

United Hospital Center
La Roche College
3 Hospital Plaza
P.O. Box 1680
Clarksburg, WV 26301
www.uhcwv.org

Wisconsin
Franciscan Skemp Healthcare
700 West Ave. S.
La Crosse, WI 54601
www.franciscanskemp.org

Nurse-Midwives

Principal activity: Providing obstetric care

Work commitment: Part- or full-time

Preprofessional education: Licensed RN

Program length: 9 months to 2 years

Work prerequisites: Certification and license

Career opportunities: Favorable

Income range: $35,000 to $80,000

Scope

Nurse-midwives are registered nurses who provide professional health care to women throughout pregnancy, labor, and delivery and for a short time after birth. They maintain consultative arrangements with obstetricians and other specialists to provide assistance when needed. Nurse-midwives serve only carefully screened women—those whose pregnancies and deliveries are not likely to present complications. Women with prior histories of pregnancy complications and those with existing health problems are referred to obstetricians or are cared for jointly. Currently more than 8% of all births in the United States are attended by midwives, a relatively dramatic increase from the past that is expected to continue. Most midwife-attended births today take place in hospitals. The growing popularity of nurse-midwives is evidenced by the fact that federal health insurance (such as Medicaid) now reimburses them for professional services. In addition, many state legislatures require that insurance coverage must include services rendered by certified nurse-midwives associated with physicians or hospitals.

Activities

The nurse-midwife performs complete physical examinations of her pregnant patients and monitors and records the progress of each pregnancy. To help increase the well-being of mother and child, she provides education on proper nutrition, exercise, breast-feeding, child care, and the baby's integration into the family. Family care during the birthing process is formulated with the parents. The nurse-midwife supervises the labor, provides pain-relief medication when necessary, and performs normal deliveries. If unexpected complications arise, an obstetrician is called in promptly.

The nurse-midwife examines and evaluates the baby upon birth and notes its state of health. She also provides the initial follow-up care for the new mother and child, after which a pediatrician assumes responsibility for the infant.

In addition to their other duties, nurse-midwives advise their patients on family planning and perform routine gynecological care.

Work Settings

Nurse-midwives typically are self-employed. They also may work in hospitals, HMOs, clinics, and obstetricians' offices.

Advancement

Nurse-midwives who work for institutions may elect to move into private practice, thus arranging their own employment conditions.

Prerequisites

The basic requirement for undertaking a nurse-midwife certification program is being a registered nurse. Candidates must have a bachelor's degree in nursing before starting a master's degree program. RNs who want to become certified nurse-midwives should have some prior experience in obstetrical nursing.

Desirable personal attributes in this field include satisfaction with nursing, the desire for a more challenging and responsible position, sensitivity (especially in interpersonal relations), dexterity, and quick thinking.

Education/Training

There are three routes to becoming a certified nurse-midwife. The first two are open to those who are already registered nurses, and the third option is for those who do not have an RN degree.

- **Certificate program:** This requires an intense period of 9 to 12 months of study and supervised clinical experience.
- **Master's degree program:** This extends for 16 to 24 months and leads to the simultaneous awarding of a certificate in nurse-midwifery and a master's degree.
- **Combined RN/master's degree program:** This three-year program has two parts. The first year is devoted to general nursing education courses that prepare candidates to take the RN license examination. Upon

choosing nurse-midwifery as a specialty, candidates spend the next two years in a master's degree program, which includes information on the essential medical aspects of pregnancy, labor, childbirth, and infant care. Gaining admission to a nurse-midwife program can be difficult, because the number of candidates far exceeds the number of program openings annually.

Certification/Registration/Licensure

Graduates of accredited nurse-midwife programs are eligible to take the national certification examination.

Career Potential

Estimates are that the need for nurse-midwives will increase substantially over the next decade. This makes the outlook for jobs excellent. This is likely the result of changing views of the birth process in the United States. An increasing number of prospective mothers today view the process as a natural event that requires more educational and emotional support and less medical intervention. So they are choosing a more personalized and empathetic birthing experience at a lower cost. That, combined with nursing shortages in places all across the country, make this a field with a lot of potential.

For More Information

The professional organization for nurse-midwives is the American College of Nurse-Midwives, 8403 Colesville Rd., Ste. 1550, Silver Spring, MD 20910 (www.midwife. org).

Nurse-Midwife Programs

California
Vanderbilt University
150 10th Street
Claremont, CA 91711
www.nursing.vanderbilt.edu

California State University-
  Fullerton
Nurse Midwifery
800 N State College Boulevard
Fullerton, CA
www.nursing.fulleton.edu

Charles R. Drew University of
  Medicine and Science
1731 E. 120th St.
Los Angeles, CA 90059
www.cdrewu.edu

San Diego State University
5500 Campanile Dr.
San Diego, CA 92182
www.sdsu.edu

University of California,
  Los Angeles
School of Nursing
Box 951702
Los Angeles, CA 90095
www.nursing.ucla.edu

University of California,
  San Francisco
Midwifery Educational Program
1001 Potrero Avenue, 6-D-14
San Francisco, CA 94110
www.nurseweb.ucsf.edu

Colorado
University of Colorado at Denver
Campus Box 167
P.O. Box 173364
Denver, CO 80217
www.cudenver.edu

Connecticut
Yale University School of Nursing
P.O. Box 9740
New Haven, CT 06536
http://nursing.yale.edu/

District of Columbia
Georgetown University
4000 Reservoir Rd. NW
Washington, DC 20057
http://gumc.georgetown.edu/

Florida
University of Florida
College of Nursing
653 W. 8th St.
Building 1, 3rd Floor
Jacksonville, FL 32209
http://con.ufl.edu/

University of Miami
5801 Red Rd.
P.O. Box 248153
Coral Gables, FL 33124
www.miami.edu

Georgia
Emory University
Woodruff School of Nursing
Atlanta, GA 30322
www.nursing.emory.edu

Illinois
University of Illinois at Chicago
845 S. Damen Ave.
Chicago, IL 60612
www.uic.edu/nursing/

Indiana
University of Indianapolis
School of Nursing
1400 E. Hanna Ave.
Indianapolis, IN 46227
http://nursing.uindy.edu/

Kansas
University of Kansas
School of Nursing
3901 Rainbow Blvd.
Kansas City, KS 66160
www2.kumc.edu/midwife/

Kentucky
Frontier School of Midwifery and
  Family Nursing
195 School St.
P.O. Box 528
Hyden, KY 41749
www.midwives.org

Maryland
University of Maryland
School of Nursing
655 W. Lombard St.
Baltimore, MD 21201
http://nursing.umaryland.edu/

Massachusetts
Baystate Health System
Midwifery Education Program
759 Chestnut St.
Springfield, MA 01199
http://baystatehealth.com/

Boston University
School of Public Health
715 Albany St.
Boston, MA 02118
www.bumc.bu.edu

Michigan
University of Michigan
School of Nursing
400 N. Ingalls
Ann Arbor, MI 48109
www.nursing.umich.edu

Minnesota
University of Minnesota
Academic Health Center
420 Delaware St. SE
MMC 735
Minneapolis, MN 55455
www.ahc.umn.edu

Missouri
University of Missouri–Columbia
Sinclair School of Nursing
Columbia, MO 65211
www.muhealth.org

New Jersey
University of Medicine & Dentistry of New Jersey
65 Bergen St.
Newark, NJ 07107
www.umdnj.edu

New Mexico
University of New Mexico
College of Nursing
Nursing/Pharmacy Building
Albuquerque, NM 87131
http://hsc.unm.edu/

New York
Clementine Midwifery
514 9th Street
Brooklyn, NY 11215
www.clementinemidwifery.com

Columbia University
School of Nursing
710 W. 168th St.
New York, NY 10032
www.columbia.edu

New York University
Steinhardt School of Education
Division of Nursing
246 Greene St.
New York, NY 10003
www.nyu.edu/nursing/

State University of New York at
  Stony Brook
School of Nursing
Stony Brook, NY 11794
www.nursing.stonybrook.edu

SUNY Downstate Medical Center
Health Science Center
450 Clarkson Ave.
Brooklyn, NY 11203
www.hscbklyn.edu

North Carolina
East Carolina University
Nurse-Midwifery Program
E. 5th St.
Greenville, NC 27858
www.nursing.ecu.edu

Ohio
Case Western Reserve University
Frances Payne Bolton School of
  Nursing
10900 Euclid Ave.
Cleveland, OH 44106
http://fpb.cwru.edu/

Ohio State University
College of Nursing
Newton Hall
1585 Neil Ave.
Columbus, OH 43210
www.con.ohio-state.edu

University of Cincinnati
College of Nursing
P.O. Box 210038
Cincinnati, OH 45221
www.uc.edu

Oregon
Oregon Health & Science
  University
3181 SW Sam Jackson Park Rd.
Portland, OR 97239
www.ohsu.edu

Pennsylvania
Midwifery Institute of
  Philadelphia University
222 Hayward Hall
Schoolhouse Ln. and Henry Ave.
Philadelphia, PA 19144
www.instituteofmidwifery.org

University of Pennsylvania
School of Nursing
Women's Health Care Studies
   Programs
Nursing Education Building
420 Guardian Dr.
Philadelphia, PA 19104
www.nursing.upenn.edu

Rhode Island
University of Rhode Island
College of Nursing
Kingston, RI 02881
www.uri.edu/nursing/

South Carolina
Medical University of South
   Carolina
College of Nursing
Nurse-Midwife Program
99 Jonathan Lucas St.
P.O. Box 250160
Charleston, SC 29425
www.musc.edu/nursing/

Tennessee
Vanderbilt University
School of Nursing
Godchaux Hall 226
461 21st Ave. S.
Nashville, TN 37240
www.nursing.vanderbilt.edu

Texas
Baylor College of Medicine
Department of Obstetrics &
   Gynecology
6550 Fannin, 9th Floor
Houston, TX 77030
www.bcm.edu/obgyn/

University of Texas at El Paso/
   Texas Tech University
School of Nursing
500 W. University Ave.
El Paso, TX 79968
www.utep.edu

University of Texas Medical
   Branch
School of Nursing
301 University Blvd.
Galveston, TX 77555
www.son.utmb.edu

University of Texas Southwestern
   Medical Center at Dallas
Nurse-Midwife Program
5323 Harry Hines Blvd.
Dallas, TX 75390
www.swmed.edu

Utah
University of Utah
Nurse Midwifery Program
10 S. 2000 E.
Salt Lake City, UT 84112
www.nursing.utah.edu

Virginia
Shenandoah University
Division of Nursing
1775 N. Sector Court
Winchester, VA 22601
www.su.edu/nursing/

Washington
University of Washington
School of Nursing
Box 357260
Seattle, WA 98195
www.son.washington.edu

West Virginia
Marshall University Medical Center
Nurse-Midwife Program
1600 Medical Center Dr.
Huntington, WV 25701
http://musom.marshall.edu/
   medctr/

Wisconsin
Marquette University
College of Nursing
P.O. Box 1881
Milwaukee, WI 53201
www.marquette.edu/nursing/

Nurse Practitioners

Principal activity: Providing primary-care medical services under a doctor's supervision

Work commitment: Full-time

Preprofessional education: Bachelor's degree in nursing

Program length: 1½ to 2 years

Work prerequisites: Master's degree and certification

Career opportunities: Stable

Income range: $50,000 to $96,000

Scope

Nurse practitioners (NPs) offer health services that enable primary care physicians to provide care to more patients and deliver services in areas where they are needed. Like physician assistants, they extend primary care physicians' potential by allowing them to focus on treating more critically ill and complex cases. However, although they have similar training and responsibilities as physician assistants, nurse practitioners have greater autonomy. Some states allow them to practice independently and even prescribe medications. Many have specialties in areas such as pediatric and geriatric care.

Activities

Nurse practitioners handle a wide range of problems. They take medical histories, conduct physical examinations, make diagnoses, and treat common minor injuries and illnesses. NPs can order and interpret laboratory tests, EKGs, and X rays. They also advise patients on health maintenance and perform such routine procedures as injections, immunizations, and wound care. They may help develop and implement patient treatment plans and write progress notes.

NPs assist physicians in acute, short-term hospitals and extended-care facilities. They educate families about disease prevention and family planning and refer them to other specialists and community health agencies.

Work Settings

Nurse practitioners work in clinics, nursing homes, hospitals, and their own offices.

Advancement

Nurse practitioners who work in hospitals and large clinics may be appointed to supervisory positions. Some open their own offices.

Prerequisites

To gain admission to a nurse-practitioner program, you must be a registered nurse and hold a bachelor's degree in nursing from an accredited program.

Desirable personal attributes include using good judgment under stress, strong communication skills, manual dexterity, and a pleasant personality.

Education/Training

The program of study lasts from 18 months to 2 years and involves both classroom and clinical exposure. Because most nurse practitioners have a more limited background in the basic sciences, these are not as intensively emphasized during the first year of study as they are for PAs. Health maintenance subjects, including proper nutrition, are an important element of the curriculum. In the second year of study, candidates gain supervised clinical experience under a physician.

Certification/Registration/Licensure

Nurse practitioners must be nationally certified by the American Nurses' Association or a specialty nursing organization.

Career Potential

The employment outlook for nurse practitioners is positive, mainly because of the need for medical care in underserved areas, where they play an important role in providing primary care. In addition, growing HMOs use more personnel such as NPs, who provide cost-effective care. Today, NPs are gaining wider acceptance by the medical community, the public, and the government.

For More Information

More than 450 educational institutions offer nurse practitioner programs—far too many to list here. Most of them confer master's degrees.

To get more information about this field, contact the American College of Nurse Practitioners, 1111 19th St. NW, Ste. 404, Washington, DC 20036 (www.acnpweb.org).

The National Organization of Nurse Practitioner Faculties sells a National Directory of Nurse Practitioner Programs that is updated annually. You can contact the organization at 1522 K St. NW, Ste. 702, Washington, DC 20005 (www.nonpf.com).

Nutritionists

Principal activity: Providing guidance on proper nutritional intake	**Program length:** 2 to 6 years
Work commitment: Part- or full-time	**Work prerequisites:** Vary with the position
Preprofessional education: High school diploma	**Career opportunities:** Stable
	Income range: $41,000 to $62,000

Scope

The science of food and how it affects the body is known as nutrition. Providing guidance to individuals on proper eating based on knowledge in this field is the function of a nutritionist. Nutritionists are sometimes called *dietitians* (see p. 160).

Activities

Proper nutrition is essential because it affects the body's health. To promote good health among individuals, nutritionists obtain information from their clients about any specific nutritional needs and current diet. They offer recommendations for improving someone's diet. This includes suggestions on the variety and amount of food that is optimal for the individual. Nutritionists also offer group programs of a general or specific nature (such as weight-loss, diabetic, and low-cholesterol diets) that are designed to improve the nutritional well-being of the attendees.

Nutritionists not only work with healthy people but also meet the special dietary needs of others, such as growing children, the obese or underweight, the elderly, and especially the infirm. These people need specially designed diets to meet their unique requirements.

The goal of the nutritionist is to design meals and menus that are healthy and tasty, meeting their clients' needs. To achieve this aim, they have to be familiar with their clients' personal situations. To do so, they interview the client and/or his or her family in detail. Medical charts or conferences with attending physicians or caregivers may be required to help the nutritionist become fully informed and thus make proper recommendations. After obtaining a comprehensive picture of a client's health and nutritional condition and requirements, the nutritionist can prepare a diet that provides variety, a balance of nutritional elements, and the appropriate caloric intake.

Nutritionists may find it necessary to motivate some of their clients to become concerned enough about their well-being to eat properly. Monitoring clients for an extended period after prescribing their diets will indicate whether the nutritionist's message of a close correlation between diet and health is being heeded.

Teaching clients about the nutritional value of various foods and the rationale behind their own diets is as important as designing the diet itself. This makes the clients feel that they are partners in the project. In addition, nutritionists need to instruct their clients how best to prepare their foods so that nutrition and taste are retained as fully as possible.

Work Settings

Nutritionists are employed in hospitals, nursing homes, extended-care centers, clinics, health clubs, weight-loss organizations, and sports training camps. Many are self-employed and provide counseling on a private basis. Those employed in health-care facilities may work various shifts, usually 40 hours a week. Those who are self-employed or who work for non-health-care facilities generally work traditional daytime hours.

Advancement

Advancement comes with experience and successful performance. Promotion typically involves assuming supervisory responsibilities. Earning a graduate degree can prove helpful to furthering one's career goals.

Prerequisites

Those who aspire to advance in this field need an advanced education. At a minimum, a high school diploma with emphasis on science and home economics is essential. This background is a necessary prerequisite for getting admitted to schools that offer associate or bachelor's degrees.

Desirable personal attributes for this profession are good communication and teaching skills. A strong belief in the value of proper nutrition and a desire to help people in this regard are essential. In addition, having a positive attitude about physical fitness and wellness, being interested in food science, and being tolerant and patient are valuable assets for working as a nutritionist.

Education/Training

The educational requirements for a nutritionist vary widely, depending on the position. Most require at least an associate degree, and better appointments require a bachelor's or master's degree. It is beneficial to demonstrate to prospective employers that you have attended seminars and symposia on nutrition as part of continuing your education in the field.

Certification/Registration/Licensure

Those acting as nutritional counselors need to be registered members of the American Nutritional Dietetics Association.

Career Potential

Although employment opportunities are only fair, your job potential increases the more education you have. Registration with the American Dietetic Association is another asset. When seeking a position, send your resume to the personnel director of hospitals, nursing homes, extended-care providers, and health and fitness clubs and spas. For the latter type of facilities, be sure to mention the value of having a nutritionist on staff. Newspapers may list openings for nutritionists in their employment section.

For More Information

Contact the American Dietetic Association, 120 S. Riverside Plaza, Ste. 2000, Chicago, IL 60606 (www.eatright.org) for more information on this profession and registration.

Nutritionist Programs

See program listings for Dieticians (p. 162).

Pharmacists

Principal activity: Dispensing medications

Work commitment: Part- or full-time

Preprofessional education: High school diploma

Program length: 5 years

Work prerequisites: Pharm.D. in pharmacy and license

Career opportunities: Favorable

Income range: $93,000 to $121,000

Scope

The pharmaceutical industry has made dramatic advances in recent decades, developing a wide variety of new drugs to enhance, extend, and even save lives. After they have been developed, tested, and approved by the U.S. Food and Drug Administration, these medicines are made available to the public. Dispensing them is the pharmacist's responsibility. Although remarkable advances in manufacturing pharmaceuticals have dramatically reduced the need for pharmacists to compound medications, new, complex responsibilities are associated with dispensing them. Community pharmacists are in the unique position of establishing personal relationships with the people in the neighborhoods they serve.

Activities

Pharmacists must carefully review and interpret prescriptions written by physicians and dentists. They have specialized knowledge of proper dosages, frequency of usage, and drug interactions, and they are qualified to discuss these issues with both doctors and patients. After securing the proper drugs, they must package them properly.

The elderly and the young are the largest consumers of medications. They frequently need guidance on handling their medications beyond what is written on the label. Pharmacists may tell patients what time of day to take a medication or what foods to avoid when taking a medication. Elderly patients frequently take multiple drugs simultaneously, some of which may be incompatible. They may be under the care of several physicians who write prescriptions for different ailments. With a computer, a pharmacist has ready access to a patient's prescription history and can warn the patient about possible drug interactions.

Pharmacists are also in a strategic position to provide advice on self-medication products (nonprescription items) that are used to prevent and treat a variety of common ailments, such as colds, flu, headaches, and muscle pain. They can offer comparative judgments on the effectiveness of medications. Some pharmacists also stock and sell surgical appliances.

While most don't employ full-time pharmacists, many nursing homes and extended-care facilities make arrangements with pharmacists to provide consultation services and various medications for their clients. In this way the institutions provide for their patients' prescription needs.

Work Settings

Pharmacists work in a variety of settings. Community pharmacies employ two-thirds of all pharmacists; 25% of pharmacists who work in this venue own their own pharmacies. Another work setting is a hospital pharmacy, which provides for inpatients and sometimes outpatients. Hospital pharmacists also are responsible for preparing some special intravenous solutions in bulk and for providing medications and drug information within their institutions. In this setting, pharmacists come into professional contact with physicians, nurses, and nutritionists; therefore, their impact is felt in many parts of the hospital.

Although community and hospital pharmacies employ the majority of pharmacy school graduates, others are employed in the armed forces, V.A. hospitals, the U.S. Public Health Service, and Indian health programs. Positions are also available in pharmaceutical industry laboratories and research firms. Because such specialized work involves research and development, an advanced degree (an M.S. or Ph.D.) is usually required. Teaching positions are also filled by pharmacists in schools offering such programs.

Advancement

In community and hospital pharmacies, pharmacists can advance to managerial positions. Pharmacists also can establish their own businesses. With an advanced degree (discussed in the "Education/Training" section), pharmacists can enter administration, teaching, or research.

Prerequisites

A high school diploma or its equivalent is needed to apply for admission to an accredited pharmacy program.

Desirable personal attributes include an interest in science in general and in the healing arts in particular, good communication and people skills, great attention to detail, and good math and business skills.

Education/Training

Pharmacy programs grant the degree of Doctor of Pharmacy (Pharm.D.), which requires at least six years of post-high school study. You need at least two years of college study before you are admitted to a pharmacy program, although most applicants have three. The first two or three years (the prepharmacy phase) include courses in biology, anatomy, physiology, chemistry (both general and organic), physics, and mathematics. This phase can be completed at a campus branch of a university or at a community college. The professional phase of the program must be taken at a college of pharmacy. Studies there include learning about natural drugs (pharmacognosy), synthetic drugs (medicinal chemistry), the effects of drugs on the body (pharmacology), and the effects of dosage on drug activity (pharmaceutics). Students also study the social, psychological, administrative, and professional aspects of the practice of pharmacy.

Those interested in teaching, administrative work, or laboratory research probably should secure a master's of science (M.S.) or doctor of philosophy (Ph.D.) degree. These degrees require additional study time.

Certification/Registration/Licensure

To begin practice, graduates of accredited programs must complete an internship under a licensed community or hospital pharmacist and pass a qualifying examination. Internships usually last one year, although some states now recognize shorter "externships" under the supervision of a school of pharmacy.

The exam, which is administered by a state board of pharmacy, takes three days and includes theoretical questions on pharmacy disciplines as well as a practical exam.

Most states offer reciprocity concerning licensure, which means if you've passed the exam in one state you can set up practice in another. But some states require all pharmacists to pass the state's own exam before setting up practice.

Career Potential

Because the elderly—who are the largest consumers of pharmaceuticals—constitute the fastest-growing segment of the U.S. population, the demand for pharmacists is expected to be strong across the country over the next decade.

For More Information

The following two organizations can provide useful additional information: the American Pharmacists Association, 2215 Constitution Ave. NW, Washington DC, 20037 (www.pharmacist.com), and the American Association of Colleges of Pharmacy, 1426 Prince St., Alexandria, VA 22314 (www.aacp.org).

For licensure information, contact the National Association of Boards of Pharmacy, 1600 Feehanville Dr., Mount Prospect, IL 60056 (www.nabp.net).

Colleges and Schools of Pharmacy

Alabama
Auburn University
Harrison School of Pharmacy
217 Walker Building
Auburn, AL 36849
www.pharmacy.auburn.edu

Samford University
McWhorter School of Pharmacy
800 Lakeshore Dr.
Birmingham, AL 35229
http://pharmacy.samford.edu/

Arizona
Midwestern University
College of Pharmacy
19555 N. 59th Ave.
Glendale, AZ 85308
www.midwestern.edu/cpg/

University of Arizona
College of Pharmacy
1703 E. Mabel
P.O. Box 210207
Tucson, AZ 85721
www.pharmacy.arizona.edu

Arkansas
University of Arkansas for Medical
 Sciences
College of Pharmacy
Education Building II/6-104
4301 W. Markham, #522
Little Rock, AR 72205
www.uams.edu/cop/

California
Loma Linda University
Loma Linda, CA 92350
www.llu.edu

Touro University
College of Pharmacy
Mare Island
1310 Johnson Lane
Valejo, CA
www.tu.edu

University of California, San
 Diego
Skaggs School of Pharmacy and
 Pharmaceutical Sciences
9500 Gilman Dr.
La Jolla, CA 92093
http://pharmacy.ucsd.edu/

University of California, San
 Francisco
School of Pharmacy
San Francisco, CA 94143
http://pharmacy.ucsf.edu/

University of Southern California
School of Pharmacy
1985 Zonal Ave.
Los Angeles, CA 90033
www.usc.edu/schools/
 pharmacy/

University of the Pacific
Thomas J. Long School of
  Pharmacy & Health Sciences
3601 Pacific Ave.
Stockton, CA 95211
http://web.pacific.edu/

Western University of Health
  Sciences
309 E. Second St.
Pomona, CA 91766
www.westernu.edu

Colorado
Regis University School of
  Pharmacy
3333 Regis Boulevard
Denver, CO 80221
www.regis.edu

University of Colorado
School of Pharmacy
4200 E. 9th Ave., C238
Denver, CO 80262
www.uchsc.edu/sop/

Connecticut
University of Connecticut
Storrs, CT 06269
www.uconn.edu

District of Columbia
Howard University
College of Pharmacy
2400 6th St. NW
Washington, DC 20059
www.howard.edu

Florida
Florida A&M University
College of Pharmacy
Tallahassee, FL 32307
www.famu.edu

Nova Southeastern University
College of Pharmacy
Health Professions Division
3200 S. University Dr.
Ft. Lauderdale, FL 33328
http://pharmacy.nova.edu/

Palm Beach Atlantic University
901 S. Flagler Dr.
P.O. Box 24708
West Palm Beach, FL 33401
www.pba.edu

University of Florida
College of Pharmacy
Box 100495
Gainesville, FL 32610
www.cop.ufl.edu

Georgia
Mercer University
Southern School of Pharmacy
3001 Mercer University Dr.
Atlanta, GA 30341
www.mercer.edu/pharmacy/

University of Georgia
College of Pharmacy
Athens, GA 30602
www.rx.uga.edu

Idaho
Idaho State University
College of Pharmacy
970 S. Fifth St.
Campus Box 8288
Pocatello, ID 83209
http://pharmacy.isu.edu/live/

Illinois
Midwestern University
555 31st St.
Downers Grove, IL 60515
www.midwestern.edu

University of Illinois at Chicago
College of Pharmacy
164 PHARM MC 886
833 S. Wood St.
Chicago, IL 60612
www.uic.edu

Indiana
Butler University
College of Pharmacy & Health
  Sciences
4600 Sunset Ave.
Indianapolis, IN 46208
www.butler.edu/cophs/

Purdue University
School of Pharmacy and
  Pharmaceutical Sciences
1330 Heine Pharmacy Building
West Lafayette, IN 47907
www.pharmacy.purdue.edu

Iowa
Drake University
College of Pharmacy and Health
  Sciences
2507 University Ave.
Des Moines, IA 50311
http://pharmacy.drake.edu/

University of Iowa
College of Pharmacy
115 S. Grand Ave.
Iowa City, IA 52242
http://pharmacy.uiowa.edu/

Kansas
University of Kansas
School of Pharmacy
2056 Mallott Hall
Lawrence, KS 66045
www.pharm.ku.edu

Kentucky
University of Kentucky
College of Pharmacy
Rose St./Pharmacy Building
Lexington, KY 40536
www.mc.uky.edu/pharmacy/

Louisiana
University of Louisiana at Monroe
College of Pharmacy
700 University Ave.
Monroe, LA 71209
http://rxweb.ulm.edu/
  pharmacy/

Xavier University of Louisiana
College of Pharmacy
1 Drexel Dr.
New Orleans, LA 70125
www.xula.edu

Maryland
College of Notre Dame
School of Pharmacy
4701 N Charles Street
Baltimore, MD 21210
www.ndm.edu

University of Maryland, Baltimore
School of Pharmacy
20 N. Pine St.
Baltimore, MD 21201
www.pharmacy.umaryland.edu

Massachusetts
Massachusetts College of
 Pharmacy and Allied Health
 Sciences
179 Longwood Ave.
Boston, MA 02115
www.mcphs.edu

Northeastern University
Bouve College of Health Sciences
School of Pharmacy
123 Behrakis Health Sciences
 Center
Boston, MA 02115
www.northeastern.edu/bouve/

Michigan
Ferris State University
College of Pharmacy
220 Ferris Dr.
Big Rapids, MI 49307
www.ferris.edu

University of Michigan
428 Church St.
Ann Arbor, MI 48109
http://pharmacy.umich.edu/
 pharmacy/

Wayne State University
Eugene Applebaum College of
 Pharmacy and Health Sciences
Detroit, MI 48202
http://cphs.wayne.edu/

Minnesota
University of Minnesota–Duluth
1117 University Dr.
Duluth, MN 55812
www.d.umn.edu

University of Minnesota
5-130 Weaver-Densford Hall
308 Harvard St. SE
Minneapolis, MN 55455
www1.umn.edu/twincities/

Mississippi
University of Mississippi
School of Pharmacy
Department of Pharmacy Practice
2500 N. State St.
Jackson, MS 39216
www.pharmd.org

Missouri
St. Louis College of Pharmacy
4588 Parkview Place
St. Louis, MO 63110
www.stlcop.edu

University of Missouri–Kansas City
School of Pharmacy
Kansas City, MO 64110
www.umkc.edu/pharmacy/

Montana
University of Montana
32 Campus Dr.
Missoula, MT 59812
www.umt.edu

Nebraska
Creighton University
School of Pharmacy & Health
 Professions
2500 California Plaza
Criss III Room G71
Omaha, NE 68178
http://spahp2.creighton.edu/

University of Nebraska
986000 Nebraska Medical Center
42nd and Emile
Omaha, NE 68198
www.unmc.edu/pharmacy/

Nevada
University of Southern Nevada
11 Sunset way
Henderson, NV 89014
www.usn.edu

New Jersey
Rutgers
The State University of
 New Jersey
College of Pharmacy
98 Brett Rd.
Piscataway, NJ 08854
www.rutgers.edu

New Mexico
University of New Mexico
Health Sciences Center
College of Pharmacy
MSC 09 5360
1 University of New Mexico
Albuquerque, NM 87131
http://hsc.unm.edu/pharmacy/

New York
Albany College of Pharmacy
106 New Scotland Ave.
Albany, NY 12208
www.acp.edu

Long Island University
Arnold and Marie Schwartz
 College of Pharmacy and Health
 Sciences
75 DeKalb Ave.
Brooklyn, NY 11201
www.brooklyn.liu.edu/
 pharmacy/

St. John Fisher College
Wegmans School of Pharmacy
3690 East Avenue
Rochester, NY 14618
www.uspharmd.com/school/
 Pharmacy

St. John's University
College of Pharmacy
8000 Utopia Pkwy.
Jamaica, NY 11439
http://new.stjohns.edu/

Touro College of Pharmacy
2090 7th Avenue #5
New York, NY 10027
www.touro.edu

University at Buffalo
State University of New York
School of Pharmacy
126 Cooke Hall
Buffalo, NY 14260
www.pharmacy.buffalo.edu

North Carolina
Campbell University
School of Pharmacy
P.O. Box 1090
Buies Creek, NC 27506
http://campbellpharmacy.net/

University of North Carolina
School of Pharmacy
Chapel Hill, NC 27599
www.pharmacy.unc.edu

Wingate University
School of Pharmacy
Wingate,NC 28174
www.pharmacy.wingate.edu

North Dakota
North Dakota State University
College of Pharmacy
Sudro Hall, Room 123
Fargo, ND 58105
www.ndsu.edu/pharmacy/

Ohio
Ohio Northern University
Rudolph H. Raabe College of
    Pharmacy
Ada, OH 45810
www.onu.edu/pharmacy/

Ohio State University
College of Pharmacy
Columbus, OH 43210
www.osu.edu

University of Cincinnati Medical
    Center
College of Pharmacy
231 Albert Sabin Way
Cincinnati, OH 45267
http://medcenter.uc.edu/

University of Findley
School of Pharmacy
1000 N Main Street
Findlay, OH 45840
www.uspharmd.com/school/
    pharmacy/

University of Toledo
College of Pharmacy
2801 W. Bancroft St.
Toledo, OH 43606
www.utpharmacy.org

Oklahoma
Southwestern Oklahoma State
    University
100 Campus Dr.
Weatherford, OK 73096
www.swosu.edu/pharmacy/

University of Oklahoma
College of Pharmacy
P.O. Box 26901
Oklahoma City, OK 73190
http://pharmacy.ouhsc.edu/

Oregon
Oregon State University
College of Pharmacy
203 Pharmacy Building
Corvallis, OR 97331
http://pharmacy.oregonstate.
    edu/

Pacific University
Pharmacy School
2043 College Way
Forest Grove, OR 97116
www.pacific.edu

Pennsylvania
Duquesne University
Mylan School of Pharmacy
Bayer Learning Center
600 Forbes Ave.
Pittsburgh, PA 15282
www.pharmacy.duq.edu

Lake Erie College of Osteopathic
    Medicine
1858 W. Grandview Blvd.
Erie, PA 16509
www.lecom.edu

Temple University of Higher
    Education
3307 N. Broad St.
Philadelphia, PA 19140
www.temple.edu/pharmacy/

University of Pittsburgh
School of Pharmacy
3501 Terrace St.
1104 Salk Hall
Pittsburgh, PA 15261
www.pharmacy.pitt.edu

University of the Sciences in
    Philadelphia
600 S. 43rd St.
Philadelphia, PA 19104
www.pcps.edu

Wilkes University-Nesbitt
School of Pharmacy
84 West South Street
Wilkes Barre, PA 18766
www.wilkes.edu

Rhode Island
University of Rhode Island
College of Pharmacy
Fogarty Hall
41 Lower College Rd.
Kingston, RI 02881
www.uri.edu/pharmacy/

South Carolina
Medical University of South
    Carolina
College of Pharmacy
280 Calhoun St.
Charleston, SC 29425
www.sccp.sc.edu

University of South Carolina
College of Pharmacy
514 Main Street
Columbia, SC 29208
www.cop.sc.edu

South Dakota
South Dakota State University
College of Pharmacy
Box 2202C
Brookings, SD 57007
www.sdstate.edu

Tennessee
East Tennessee State University
Gatton College of Pharmacy
Maple Avenue VA Bldg 7
Mountain Home, TN 37684
www.etsu.edu/Pharmacy/

University of Tennessee
Health Science Center
College of Pharmacy
Memphis, TN 38163
www.uthsc.edu/pharmacy/

Texas
Texas A & M University
Irma Rangel College of Pharmacy
1010 W Avenue B-MSC 131
Kingsville, TX 78363
www.pharmacy.tamhsc.edu

Texas Southern University
College of Pharmacy and Health
    Sciences
3100 Cleburne St.
Houston, TX 77004
www.tsu.edu

Texas Tech University
School of Pharmacy
1300 Coulter Avenue
Amarillo, TX 79106
www.ttuhsc.edu

University of Houston
College of Pharmacy
Room 141, Science & Research
  Building 2
Houston, TX 77204
www.uh.edu/pharmacy/

University of the Incarnate World
  Pharmacy
4301 Broadway, CPO #99
San Antonio, TX 78209
www.uiw.edu/pharmacy/

University of Texas at Austin
College of Pharmacy
1 University Station
Austin, TX 78712
www.utexas.edu/pharmacy/

Utah
University of Utah
College of Pharmacy
30 S. 2000 E.
Salt Lake City, UT 84112
www.pharmacy.utah.edu

Virginia
Shenandoah University
Bernard J. Dunn School of Pharmacy
1775 North Sector Ct.
Winchester, VA 22601
www.pharmacy.su.edu

Virginia Commonwealth University
School of Pharmacy
410 N. 12th St.
Richmond, VA 23298
www.pharmacy.vcu.edu

Washington
University of Washington
H-364 Health Sciences Building
P.O. Box 357631
Seattle, WA 98105
www.washington.edu

Washington State University
P.O. Box 646510
Pullman, WA 99164
www.pharmacy.wsu.edu

West Virginia
West Virginia University
Robert C. Byrd Health Sciences
  Center
School of Pharmacy
P.O. Box 9500
Morgantown, WV 26506
www.hsc.wvu.edu/sop/

Wisconsin
University of Wisconsin
School of Pharmacy
777 Highland Ave.
Madison, WI 53705
www.pharmacy.wisc.edu

Wyoming
University of Wyoming
College of Health Sciences
School of Pharmacy
Department 3375
1000 E. University Ave.
Laramie, WY 82071
http://www.uwyo.edu

Physician Assistants

Principal activity: Carrying out specific medical duties under a physician's supervision

Work commitment: Usually full-time

Preprofessional education: 2-year college-level program

Program length: 2 years

Work prerequisites: PA program, certificate, or degree

Career opportunities: Highly favorable

Income range: $68,000 to $97,000

Scope

Physician assistants (PAs) carry out diagnostic and treatment tasks that are assigned and supervised by physicians. These responsibilities must be consistent with the state's laws. They perform many of the routine jobs previously handled by family or primary care physicians. Studies have shown that a significant number of patients visiting such doctors can be successfully cared for by physician assistants. PAs thus allow physicians to apply their knowledge and skills to more complex cases. PAs may work in consultation with physicians or may be of direct personal assistance.

Activities

PAs are involved in a wide variety of activities. These may include taking medical histories, performing physical examinations, ordering common laboratory tests, and arriving at preliminary diagnoses. PAs may also be involved in treating medical emergencies such as bruises, cuts, and minor burns. They may handle certain phases of preoperative and postoperative patient care. When working for various specialists, PAs may administer injections, suture wounds, or apply casts.

Work Settings

With the wide acceptance of physician assistants by the medical community, positions are available in hospitals, HMOs, clinics, and physicians' offices.

Advancement

By obtaining additional education and experience, PAs can secure more prestigious appointments with larger facilities. Additional specialized education can qualify them to become involved in specialty work.

Prerequisites

PA programs offer certificates or degrees (associate, bachelor's, or master's) upon completion of a prescribed course of studies. The prerequisites are determined by the nature of the program. To apply for admission to a four-year program, a candidate must have a high school diploma or its equivalent. Those seeking to enter two-year programs should have at least two years of college or a bachelor's degree. They should also have been involved in health-care work for several years.

Desirable personal attributes for work in this field include a logical thinking style, a strong sense of compassion, good judgment, a willingness to follow instructions, and the ability to work well for and with others. Competition for admission to PA programs is intense. Thus, interested individuals should strive to earn good grades in high school and college.

Education/Training

Most PA programs last two years. The educational program is divided into two parts. The first lasts 6 to 12 months and covers basic and advanced clinical sciences, including courses in anatomy, physiology, biochemistry, pharmacology, pathology, microbiology, physical diagnosis, radiology, and electrocardiography. The second part of the program lasts 9 to 15 months and includes clinical rotations and preceptorships in a variety of clinical disciplines at hospitals, clinics, and physician's offices, with the most emphasis given to primary care.

Certification/Registration/Licensure

PA activities are regulated by individual states, and their requirements vary. In most states PAs must be certified by the National Commission on Certification of Physician Assistants. After completing an accredited program, candidates must pass an exam of written and skills assessment components. Those passing these tests are Physician Assistant-Certified. To retain this status, they must take at least 100 hours of continuing medical education every two years and retake the certification exam every six years.

Career Potential

Employment outlook for PAs is excellent as physicians and patients have become convinced they are effective health-care providers. Today, thousands of PAs are working throughout the United States, and a near-50% increase can be expected over the next decade.

For More Information

The professional organization for PAs is the American Academy of Physician Assistants, 950 N. Washington St., Alexandria, VA 22314 (www.aapa.org).

For certification information, contact the National Commission on Certification of Physician Assistants, 12000 Findley Rd., Ste. 200, Duluth, GA 30097 (www.nccpa.net).

Physician Assistant Programs

Alabama
University of Alabama at
  Birmingham
School of Health Related
  Professions
RMSB 481
1705 University Blvd.
Birmingham, AL 35294
www.uab.edu

University of South Alabama
307 University Blvd. N.
Mobile, AL 36688
www.southalabama.edu/allied-
  health/pa/

Arizona
Arizona School of Health Sciences
5850 E. Still Circle
Mesa, AZ 85206
www.ashs.edu

Midwestern University
Physician Assistant Program
19555 North 59th Avenue
Glendale, AZ 85308
www.mu.edu

California
Charles R. Drew University of
  Medicine and Science
College of Allied Health
1731 E. 120th St.
Los Angeles, CA 90059
www.cdrewu.edu

Loma Linda University
School of Allied Health
  Professions
Loma Linda, CA 92350
www.llu.edu

Riverside County
Riverside Community College
PA Program
16130 Lassalle Street
Moreno Valley, CA 92551
www.rcc.edu

Samuel Merritt College
370 Hawthorne Ave.
Oakland, CA 94609
www.samuelmerritt.edu

San Joaquin Valley College
8400 W. Mineral King Ave.
Visalia, CA 93291
www.sjvc.edu

Stanford University School of
  Medicine/Foothill College
Primary Care Associate Program
  (PCAP)
1215 Welch Rd., Modular G
Palo Alto, CA 94305
http://pcap.stanford.edu/

Touro University at Mare Island
College of Health Sciences
1310 Johnson Ln., Mare Island
Vallejo, CA 94592
www.tu.edu

University of California–Davis
  Health System
Medical Center
2315 Stockton Blvd.
Sacramento, CA 95817
www.ucdmc.ucdavis.edu

University of Southern California
Keck School of Medicine
Health Sciences Center
Los Angeles, CA 90033
www.usc.edu/keck

Western University of Health
  Sciences
309 E. Second St.
Pomona, CA 91766
www.westernu.edu

Colorado
Red Rocks Community College
13300 W. 6th Ave.
Lakewood, CO 80228
www.rrcc.edu

University of Colorado School of
  Medicine
4200 E. 9th Ave.
Denver, CO 80262
www.uchsc.edu

Connecticut
Quinnipiac University
275 Mount Carmel Ave.
Hamden, CT 06518
www.quinnipiac.edu

Yale University School of
  Medicine
333 Cedar St.
New Haven, CT 06510
http://medicine.yale.edu/

District of Columbia
George Washington University
900 23rd St. NW
Washington, DC 20037
www.gwumc.edu

Howard University
Division of Allied Health Sciences
Sixth Ave. and Bryant St. NW
Washington, DC 20059
www.howard.edu

Florida
Barry University
Graduate Medical Sciences
11300 NE Second Ave.
Miami Shores, FL 33161
www.barry.edu/pa/

Miami Dade College
Medical Center Campus
950 NW 20th St.
Miami, FL 33127
www.mdc.edu/medical/

Nova Southeastern University
3200 S. University Dr.
Fort Lauderdale, FL 33328
www.nova.edu

University of Florida
Gainesville, FL 32610
www.medicine.ufl.edu

Georgia
Emory University
School of Medicine
1440 Clifton Rd.
Atlanta, GA 30322
www.med.emory.edu

Medical College of Georgia
1120 15th St.
Augusta, GA 30912
www.mcg.edu

South University
709 Mall Blvd.
Savannah, GA 31406
www.southuniversity.edu

Idaho
Idaho State University
921 S. 8th Ave.
Pocatello, ID 83209
www.isu.edu

Illinois
Cook County Hospital
Malcolm X College
1900 W. Van Buren St.
Chicago, IL 60612
http://malcolmx.ccc.edu/

Finch University of Health
Sciences
Chicago Medical School
3333 Green Bay Rd.
North Chicago, IL 60064
www.rosalindfranklin.edu

Midwestern University
555 31st St.
Downers Grove, IL 60515
www.midwestern.edu

Indiana
Butler University
College of Pharmacy & Health
Sciences
4600 Sunset Ave.
Indianapolis, IN 46208
www.butler.edu/cophs/

University of Saint Francis
2701 Spring St.
Fort Wayne, IN 46808
www.sf.edu

Iowa
Des Moines University
Osteopathic Medical Center
3200 Grand Ave.
Des Moines, IA 50312
www.dmu.edu

University of Iowa College of
Medicine
5167 Westlawn
Iowa City, IA 52242
http://paprogram.medicine.
uiowa.edu/

Kansas
Wichita State University
College of Health Professions
1845 N. Fairmount
Wichita, KS 67260
www.wichita.edu

Kentucky
University of Kentucky
PA Program
900 S. Limestone St.
Lexington, KY 40536
www.uky.edu

Louisiana
Louisiana State University
Health Sciences Center
1501 Kings Hwy.
Shreveport, LA 71130
www.lsuhscshreveport.edu

Maine
University of New England
11 Hills Beach Rd.
Biddeford, ME 04005
www.une.edu

Maryland
Anne Arundel Community College
School of Health Professions
101 College Pkwy.
Arnold, MD 21012
www.aacc.edu

Towson University
8000 York Rd.
Towson, MD 21252
http://wwwnew.towson.edu/
chp/pa/welcome.html

University of Maryland Eastern
Shore
1 Backbone Rd.
Princess Anne, MD 21853
www.umes.edu

Massachusetts
Massachusetts College of
Pharmacy and Health Sciences
179 Longwood Ave.
Boston, MA 02115
www.mcphs.edu

Northeastern University
360 Huntington Ave.
Boston, MA 02115
www.northeastern.edu

Michigan
Central Michigan University
Mount Pleasant, MI 48859
www.cmich.edu

Grand Rapids Medical Education
Partners
1000 Monroe NW
Grand Rapids, MI 49503
www.grmep.org

University of Detroit Mercy
8200 W. Outer Dr.
P.O. Box 19900
Detroit, MI 48219
www.udmercy.edu

Wayne State University
Eugene Applebaum College of
Pharmacy and Health Sciences
Detroit, MI 48202
www.pa.cphs.wayne.edu

Western Michigan University
1903 W. Michigan Ave.
Kalamazoo, MI 49008
www.wmich.edu

Minnesota
Augsburg College
2211 Riverside Ave. S.
Minneapolis, MN 55454
www.augsburg.edu

Missouri
Southwest Missouri State
University
901 S. National Ave.
Springfield, MO 65804
www.smsu.edu

St. Louis University
School of Allied Health
Professions
221 N. Grand Blvd.
St. Louis, MO 63103
www.slu.edu

Montana
Rocky Mountain College
1511 Poly Dr.
Billings, MT 59102
www.rocky.edu

Nebraska
Union College
3800 S. 48th St.
Lincoln, NE 68506
www.ucollege.edu

University of Nebraska Medical
Center
42nd and Emile
Omaha, NE 68198
www.unmc.edu

New Hampshire
Massachusetts College of
Pharmacy and Health Sciences
1260 Elm St.
Manchester, NH 03101
www.mcphs.edu

New Jersey
Seton Hall University
400 S. Orange Ave.
South Orange, NJ 07079
www.shu.edu

University of Medicine &
Dentistry of New Jersey
Robert Wood Johnson Medical
School
675 Hoes Ln.
Piscataway, NJ 08854
www.umdnj.edu

New Mexico
University of New Mexico
School of Medicine
Albuquerque, NM 87131
www.unm.edu

University of St. Francis
Physician Assistant Program
4401 Silver Avenue SE
Albuquerque, NM 87108
www.stfrancis.edu

New York
Albany Medical College
43 New Scotland Ave.
Albany, NY 12208
www.amc.edu

Brooklyn Hospital Center/Long
Island University
121 DeKalb Ave.
Brooklyn, NY 11201
www.brooklyn.liu.edu

CUNY Harlem Hospital Center
The City College of New York
506 Lennox Ave.
WP Room 619
New York, NY 10037
www1.ccny.cuny.edu

Daemen College
4380 Main St.
Amherst, NY 14226
www.daemen.edu

Hofstra University
113 Monroe Lecture Hall
127 Hofstra University
Hempstead, NY 11549
www.hofstra.edu

Le Moyne College
Department of Biology
1419 Salt Springs Rd.
Syracuse, NY 13214
www.lemoyne.edu

Mercy College
555 Broadway
Dobbs Ferry, NY 10522
www.mercy.edu

New York Institute of Technology
Northern Blvd.
Old Westbury, NY 11568
www.nyit.edu

Pace University–Lenox Hill
Hospital
One Pace Plaza
New York, NY 10038
www.pace.edu

Rochester Institute of Technology
1 Lomb Memorial Dr.
Rochester, NY 14623
www.rit.edu

St. Vincent Catholic Medical
Center of New York
153 West 11th Street
New York, NY 10011
www.svcmc.org

Stony Brook University
State University of New York
School of Health Technology &
Management
Stony Brook, NY 11794
www.hsc.stonybrook.edu/shtm/

SUNY Downstate Medical Center
450 Clarkson Ave.
Brooklyn, NY 11203
www.downstate.edu

Touro College of Health Sciences
27-33 W. 23rd St.
New York, NY 10010
www.touro.edu

Wagner College-Staten Island
University Hospital
375 Seguine Ave.
Staten Island, NY 10309
www.wagner.edu/departments/
pa_program/

North Carolina
Duke University Medical Center
Trent Dr.
Durham, NC 27710
http://medschool.duke.edu

East Carolina University
School of Allied Health Sciences
Belk Building
Greenville, NC 27858
www.ecu.edu/ah/

Methodist College
5400 Ramsey St.
Fayetteville, NC 28311
www.methodist.edu

Wake Forest University Baptist
Medical Center
Medical Center Blvd.
Winston-Salem, NC 27157
www.wfubmc.edu

North Dakota
University of North Dakota School
of Medicine & Health Sciences
501 N. Columbia Rd.
Grand Forks, ND 58202
www.und.nodak.edu

Ohio
Cuyahoga Community College
PA Program
11000 Pleasant Valley Rd.
Parma, OH 44130
www.tri-c.edu/programs/
physicianassistant/

Kettering College of Medical Arts
3737 Southern Blvd.
Kettering, OH 45429
www.kmcnetwork.org

Marietta College
215 Fifth St.
Marietta, OH 45750
www.marietta.edu

Medical College of Ohio
School of Allied Health
3000 Arlington Ave.
Toledo, OH 43614
www.mco.edu

University of Findlay
1000 N. Main St.
Findlay, OH 45840
www.findlay.edu

Oklahoma
University of Oklahoma
Health Sciences Center
P.O. Box 26901
Oklahoma City, OK 73190
www.ou.edu

Oregon
Oregon Health & Science
University
3181 SW Sam Jackson Park Rd.
Portland, OR 97239
www.ohsu.edu

Pacific University
2043 College Way
Forest Grove, OR 97116
www.pacificu.edu

Pennsylvania
Arcadia University
Health Science Center
450 S. Easton Rd.
Glenside, PA 19038
www.arcadia.edu

Chatham College
Woodland Rd.
Pittsburgh, PA 15232
www.chatham.edu

DeSales University
2755 Station Ave.
Center Valley, PA 18034
www.desales.edu

Duquesne University
School of Health Sciences
323 Health Sciences Building
Pittsburgh, PA 15282
www.duq.edu

Gannon University
109 University Square
Erie, PA 16541
www.gannon.edu

King's College
133 N. River St.
Wilkes-Barre, PA 18711
www.kings.edu

Lock Haven University of
Pennsylvania
401 N. Fairview St.
Lock Haven, PA 17745
www.lhup.edu

Marywood University
2300 Adams Ave.
Scranton, PA 18509
www.marywood.edu

Pennsylvania College of
Technology
One College Ave.
Williamsport, PA 17701
www.pct.edu

Philadelphia College of
Osteopathic Medicine
4170 City Ave., Evans Hall
Philadelphia, PA 19131
www.pcom.edu

Philadelphia University
School House Ln. and Henry Ave.
Philadelphia, PA 19144
www.philau.edu

Saint Francis University
117 Evergreen Dr.
P.O. Box 600
Loretto, PA 15940
www.francis.edu

Seton Hill University
One Seton Hill Dr.
Greensburg, PA 15601
www.setonhill.edu

South Carolina
Medical University of South
Carolina
College of Health Professions
171 Ashley Ave.
Charleston, SC 29425
www.musc.edu

South Dakota
University of South Dakota
School of Medicine
414 E. Clark St.
Vermillion, SD 57069
www.usd.edu

Tennessee
Bethel University
325 Cherry Ave.
McKenzie, TN 38201
www.bethelu.edu

Trevecca Nazarene University
333 Murfreesboro Rd.
Nashville, TN 37210
www.trevecca.edu

Texas
Baylor College of Medicine
Department of Family &
   Community Medicine
One Baylor Plaza
Houston, TX 77030
www.bcm.edu

Midland College-Texas Tech
   University
Health Sciences Center
3600 N. Garfield
Midland, TX 79705
www.midland.edu

University of North Texas Health
   Science Center at Fort Worth
3500 Camp Bowie Blvd.
Fort Worth, TX 76107
www.hsc.unt.edu

University of Texas Health Science Center at San Antonio
7703 Floyd Curl Dr.
San Antonio, TX 78229
www.uthscsa.edu

University of Texas Medical
   Branch
School of Allied Services
301 University Blvd.
Galveston, TX 77555
www.utmb.edu

University of Texas Southwestern
   Medical Center at Dallas
5323 Harry Hines Blvd.
Dallas, TX 75390
www.utsouthwestern.edu

Utah
University of Utah
School of Medicine
201 S. Presidents Circle, Room 201
Salt Lake City, UT 84112
www.utah.edu

Virginia
Eastern Virginia Medical School
P.O. Box 1980
Norfolk, VA 23501
www.evms.edu

James Madison University
Department of Health Sciences
800 S. Main St.
Harrisonburg, VA 22807
www.jmu.edu

Jefferson College of Health
   Sciences
920 S. Jefferson St.
Roanoke, VA 24016
Shenandoah University
1460 University Dr.
Winchester, VA 22601
www.su.edu

Washington
University of Washington
Medex Northwest
Division of Physician Assistant
   Studies
4311 11th Ave. NE, Ste. 200
Seattle, WA 98105
www.washington.edu/medicine/
   som/depts/medex/

West Virginia
Alderson-Broaddus College
College Hill
Philippi, WV 26416
www.ab.edu

Wisconsin
University of Wisconsin–La Crosse
Gunderson Lutheran Medical
   Foundation/Mayo School of
   Health Science
1725 State St.
La Crosse, WI 54601
www.uwlax.edu/PAstudies/
   partnership.htm

University of Wisconsin–Madison
Medical Sciences Center,
   Room 1050
1300 University Ave.
Madison, WI 53706
www.wisc.edu

Uniformed Services
Interservice PA Program
Academy of Health Sciences
3151 Scott Rd.
Fort Sam Houston, TX 78234
www.cs.amedd.army.mil/ipap/

Naval Medical Education and
   Training Command
8901 Wisconsin Ave.
Bethesda, MD 20889
http://nshs.med.navy.mil/

Sheppard Air Force Base
3790 MSTW/MSM
Sheppard AFB, TX 76311
www.sheppard.af.mil

Registered Nurses

Principal activity: Providing skilled nursing care for sick patients	**Program length:** 2 to 4 years
Work commitment: Usually full-time	**Work prerequisites:** Diploma/degree/license
Preprofessional education: High school diploma	**Career opportunities:** Highly favorable
	Income range: $52,000 to $77,000

Scope

Patients often judge a hospital's quality by the nursing care they receive. This demonstrates the importance of this strongly people-oriented profession, which focuses on health recovery and maintenance. The field provides an opportunity for service in a wide range of settings and specialties and offers a high degree of career satisfaction. Registered nurses are directly responsible for carrying out treatment plans that have been ordered by physicians. This requires a combination of technical skills and knowledge of nursing procedures, along with an understanding of expected results.

Activities

Because nursing covers a broad spectrum of situations, we'll discuss its activities in terms of both hospital and nonhospital work settings.

In Hospitals

Hospital nurses determine patients' care needs in light of a physician's medical treatment plan. Based on their assessments, nurses formulate and execute care plans and then evaluate their effectiveness. These plans must provide for the patients' medical and physical needs. Nurses also lend emotional support that can facilitate the recovery and rehabilitation process. Because nurses are in close contact with patients for extended periods, they can provide valuable insights into their progress. Nurses document patients' charts and help prepare them for activities after discharge. A registered nurse may supervise LPNs and other junior nursing staff members.

- **Private-duty nurses** provide exclusive care for individual patients in a hospital or in their homes. These nurses are self-employed.
- **Operating room nurses** provide care before, during, and immediately after surgery. They help prepare patients for surgery, directly assist surgeons and other team physicians by providing them with needed instruments and supplies, and check on the postoperative state of patients. This area has various specialties, such as orthopedic, cardiac, and thoracic surgery nurses.
- **Critical-care nurses** care for patients who are in life-threatening situations. Their special training qualifies them to provide complicated nursing support services, recognize physiological changes in patients' conditions, and operate sophisticated medical equipment.
- **Rehabilitation nurses** serve both adults and children suffering from a reduction in their optimal functional potential due to accidents, birth defects, or

diseases. They provide a variety of treatments, exercises, and emotional support that help their patients regain lost function and adapt to permanent disabilities. To prepare for this specialty, candidates must complete a post-RN course or a master's degree in rehabilitation nursing.

- **Clinical nurse specialists** hold advanced degrees (usually a master's) with specialized training. Their areas of expertise may be cancer, cardiac, neonatal, or mental health care. They may be directly involved in the delivery of nursing services as well as in education, administrative, or consultative activities. They also work in nonhospital settings.

- **Advanced-practice nurses** are highly trained specialists with one of four professional titles: clinical nurse specialist (just described), nurse-anesthetist (p. 175), nurse practitioner (p. 185), or nurse-midwife (p. 181).

Outside Hospitals

- **Office nurses** work for physicians in all specialties as well as for dental surgeons, nurse-midwives, and nurse practitioners. They may perform routine laboratory tests and administrative functions.

- **School nurses** are engaged by boards of education to provide health and nursing services in individual schools or school districts. They provide emergency medical care, help administer physical exams, communicate with parents about students' physical and emotional problems, ensure that state health codes (especially regarding immunization) are implemented, and advise school constituencies on health issues.

- **Community health nurses** provide services to patients in nonhospital settings such as clinics, schools, and private homes. They teach groups about maintaining a healthy environment, proper nutrition, and preventive health measures. They also carry out physicians' plans and provide care for ambulatory patients. In addition, they initiate public-health programs that encourage immunization and provide information on alcohol, drugs, and infectious diseases.

- **Occupational health nurses** are engaged by corporations, factories, and government agencies to provide nursing care for their employees. This care may include treating minor diseases and injuries, providing physical examinations, and educating workers about health issues.

- **Nurse educators** typically are faculty members of nursing schools. They assist in the training of nurses and teach continuing education courses.

Work Settings

Registered nurses have a very wide choice of work settings and their services are in demand. These include hospitals of different types, nursing homes, schools, community health centers, public health offices, and industrial facilities.

Advancement

With additional experience and training, a registered nurse may move into a supervisory, management, or administrative position such as head nurse. Other potential directions for advancement include specialty training, especially in one of the advanced-practice nursing specialties.

Prerequisites

To gain admission to a nursing education program, candidates must have a high school diploma (or its equivalent) with a minimum C average.

Those entering this field should have good physical and emotional health, compassion, patience, a team-player mentality, and the ability to assume challenging medical responsibilities.

Education/Training

There are three educational routes to becoming a registered nurse:

- **Two-year associate degree programs** offered by community, junior, and technical colleges.
- **Three-year diploma programs** offered by hospitals.
- **Four-year bachelor's degree programs** offered by colleges and universities. These usually award the bachelor's of science in nursing (BSN) degree.

All three of these programs involve both classroom course work and supervised nursing practice. The basic curriculum is the same for each, but the programs vary in depth and scope, depending on the program's length. The basic courses cover anatomy, physiology, sociology, English, psychology, philosophy, microbiology, and nursing concepts and techniques. Those pursuing a bachelor's degree must also take courses in precalculus, chemistry (both general and organic), biology, anthropology, and epidemiology, as well as several advanced nursing courses. Within the bachelor's program there may be special tracks leading to specialty training, such as community health or school nursing. For some specialties, a master's degree is essential.

Certification/Registration/Licensure

A nursing license is required in every state. Candidates obtain their license by passing a written state board examination after graduating from an accredited nursing school.

Career Potential

Current projections are that employment of registered nurses is expected to grow faster than average for all occupations through the next decade, resulting in many new jobs. The major factor is the change currently underway in the health-care system, especially in light of the growing population of elderly citizens. In fact, employers in many parts of the country have expressed difficulty in filling nursing positions.

For More Information

More than a thousand educational institutions offer diplomas and degrees in nursing (from bachelor's to doctorate)—far too many to list here.

For more information, contact the American Nurses' Association, 8515 Georgia Ave., Ste. 400, Silver Spring, MD 20910 (www.nursingworld.org), or the National League for Nursing, 61 Broadway, New York, NY 10006 (www.nln.org).

Specialty Nursing Organizations

Air & Surface Transport Nurses
  Association
9101 E. Kenyon Ave., Ste. 3000
Denver, CO 80237
www.astna.org

American Academy of Nurse
  Practitioners
P.O. Box 12846
Austin, TX 78711
www.aanp.org

American Association of
  Critical-Care Nurses
101 Columbia
Aliso Viejo, CA 92656
www.aacn.org

American Association of
  Neuroscience Nurses
4700 W. Lake Ave.
Glenview, IL 60025
www.aann.org

American Association of Nurse
  Anesthetists
222 S. Prospect Ave.
Park Ridge, IL 60068
www.aana.com

American Association of Nurse
  Attorneys
7794 Grow Dr.
Pensacola, FL 32514
www.taana.org

American Association of
  Occupational Health Nurses
2920 Brandywine Rd., Ste. 100
Atlanta, GA 30341
www.aaohn.org

American Association of Spinal
  Cord Injury Nurses
75-20 Astoria Blvd.
Jackson Heights, NY 11370
www.aascin.org

American College of Nurse-
  Midwives
8403 Colesville Rd.
Silver Spring, MD 20910
www.midwife.org

American College of Nurse
  Practitioners
1111 19th St. NW,
Ste. 404
Washington, DC 20036
www.nurse.org/acnp/

American Nephrology Nurses'
  Association
E. Holly Ave., Box 56
Pitman, NJ 08071
www.annanurse.org

American Nurses' Association
8515 Georgia Ave.,
Ste. 400
Silver Spring, MD 20910
www.nursingworld.org

American Organization of Nurse
  Executives
Liberty Place
325 Seventh St. NW
Washington, DC 20004
www.aone.org

American Society of Ophthalmic
  Registered Nurses
P.O. Box 193030
San Francisco, CA 94119
http://webeye.ophth.uiowa.
  edu/asorn/

American Society of
  PeriAnesthesia Nurses
10 Melrose Ave., Ste. 110
Cherry Hill, NJ 08003
www.aspan.org

American Society of Plastic
  Surgical Nurses
3220 Pointe Pkwy., Ste. 500
Atlanta, GA 30092
www.aspsn.org

American Urological Association
1000 Corporate Blvd.
Linthicum, MD 21090
www.auanet.org

Association for Professionals
  in Infection Control and
  Epidemiology
1275 K St., Ste. 1000
Washington, DC 20005
www.apic.org

Association of Operating Room
  Nurses, Inc.
2170 S. Parker Rd., Ste. 300
Denver, CO 80231
www.aorn.org

Association of Rehabilitation
  Nurses
4700 W. Lake Ave.
Glenview, IL 60025
www.rehabnurse.org

Association of Women's Health,
  Obstetric and Neonatal Nurses
2000 L St. NW, Ste. 740
Washington, DC 20036
www.awhonn.org

Council on Cardiovascular Nursing
American Heart Association
7272 Greenville Ave.
Dallas, TX 75231
www.americanheart.org

Dermatology Nurses' Association
E. Holly Ave., Box 56
Pitman, NJ 08071
www.dnanurse.org

Emergency Nurses Association
915 Lee St.
Des Plaines, IL 60016
www.ena.org

International Nurses Society on
  Addictions
P.O. Box 10752
Raleigh, NC 27605
www.intnsa.org

National Association for Practical
  Nurse Education and Service,
  Inc.
P.O. Box 25647
Alexandria, VA 22313
www.napnes.org

National Association of
  Orthopaedic Nurses
401 N. Michigan Ave., Ste. 2200
Chicago, IL 60611
www.orthonurse.org

National Association of Pediatric
Nurse Practitioners
20 Brace Rd., Ste. 200
Cherry Hill, NJ 08034
www.napnap.org

National Association of School
Nurses
P.O. Box 1300
Scarborough, ME 04070
www.nasn.org

National League for Nursing
61 Broadway
New York, NY 10006
www.nln.org

Oncology Nursing Society
125 Enterprise Dr.
Pittsburgh, PA 15275
www.ons.org

Society of Otorhinolaryngology
and Head/Neck Nurses, Inc.
116 Canal St., Ste. A
New Smyrna Beach, FL 32168
www.sohnnurse.com

Surgeon Assistants

Principal activity: Assisting surgeons in various settings

Work commitment: Usually full-time

Preprofessional education: College-level program

Program length: 2 years

Work prerequisites: PA certification

Career opportunities: Highly favorable

Income range: $33,000 to $70,000

Scope

Surgeon assistants (SAs) are physician assistants (PAs) with specialized training that qualifies them to work under the supervision of surgeons. SAs make up about 15 percent of all physician assistants and usually are called PAs.

The scope of their activities is determined by their training, the arrangement they have with their supervising surgeons, and limitations imposed by state law. The job's basic responsibilities include securing preliminary information from patients and helping surgeons provide therapy to patients.

Activities

Commonly, SAs secure patients' medical histories, carry out physical examinations, and perform (or order) standard laboratory tests. They then organize the data and make a preliminary interpretation to present to the surgeon. SAs also perform preoperative procedures, assist during surgery, and participate in patients' postoperative care. SAs may also treat minor injuries under a surgeon's guidance.

Work Settings

The SA's usual work setting is a surgical office, hospital, or clinic. In hospitals, they may work in the operating, recovery, or emergency rooms and in outpatient clinics.

Advancement

Advancement is possible and comes with experience and successful performance. Promotion typically involves assuming supervisory responsibilities or relocating to a larger institution.

Prerequisites

The prerequisites for SA training programs range from a high school diploma to certification as a physician assistant.

Desirable personal attributes for this profession include a pleasant personality, good oral and written communication skills, the ability to make sound decisions under pressure, manual dexterity, and the capacity to work well with and for others.

Education/Training

There are three ways to secure training as an SA:

- Those who have completed a physician assistant training program and have been certified can secure on-the-job training with a surgeon or at a hospital surgical service. Such training may last 3 to 6 months.
- Those who have completed the prerequisites—namely, two years of basic science college course work—should seek admission to a PA program. Once they have completed the program and have been certified, they can get specialized training at a postgraduate program for surgeon assistants or with a surgeon or hospital.
- Candidates can seek admission directly into one of several accredited SA programs (see the last section). Like PA programs, these require two years of basic science course work. These programs are divided into didactic and clinical segments. The focus of the curriculum is to provide the clinical and technical skills relevant to surgical care in addition to basic medical training. The programs provide exposure to both general and specialized surgery and emergency room traumatic surgery.

A certificate is awarded upon completion of any SA program. The competition for places in these SA programs is intense.

Certification/Registration/Licensure

Certification for surgical assistants is available through the National Board of Surgical Technology and Surgical Assisting (www.nbstsa.org).

Career Potential

The need for SAs is growing as the demand for surgical services increases. With the changes currently taking place in health care, especially with regards to the aging population, SAs should be readily integrated into the personnel needed by HMOs.

For More Information

The professional organizations for SAs are the American Academy of Physician Assistants, 950 N. Washington St., Alexandria, VA 22314 (www.aapa.org) and the American Association of Surgical Physician Assistants (www.aaspa.com). Information about physician assistant programs can be found on page 197.

Surgeon Assistant Programs

Alabama

University of Alabama at
  Birmingham
School of Health-Related
  Professions
Webb Building, Room 407
Birmingham, AL 35294
www.uab.edu

New York

Cornell University Medical College
1300 New York Ave.
New York, NY 10021
www.cornell.edu

Ohio

Cuyahoga Community College
11000 Pleasant Valley Rd.
Parma, OH 44130
www.tri-c.edu

Virginia

Eastern Virginia Medical School
P.O. Box 1980
Norfolk, Virginia 23501-1980
www.evms.edu

Adjunctive Health-Care Careers: Technologists, Technicians, Assistants, and Aides

Physicians, dentists, and other diagnosing and treating practitioners are assisted in their work by a wide variety of technologists, technicians, and assistants. These health-care workers provide an invaluable service, performing complex laboratory tests and analyses, operating sophisticated equipment to monitor patients, and handling many routine duties. These people both directly and indirectly help save lives, ease pain, and improve patients' quality of life. Their activities are indispensable in maintaining an effective health-care system.

Most of the professions discussed in this chapter require an associate degree, while others need only about one year of training. A few even provide on-the-job training that counts toward qualification.

The 35 careers discussed here are quite varied, not only in the amount of education or training required, but also in terms of duties and responsibilities. Some careers are hospital-based, and others are based mainly in offices or clinics. Some are devoted to patient care, whether physical or mental, and others are exclusively diagnostic in nature. Thus, a wide range of options is available to those prepared to invest several months to a few years in training.

For example, there are a variety of personnel who provide basic patient care under the direction of an institution's nursing staff. These personnel have numerous job titles, including Certified Nurse's Assistant (CNA), Nursing Assistant, Psychiatric Attendant, Nurse's Aide, Patient Care Technician, Resident Assistant, Care Giver, Patient Care Assistant (PCA), or Home Health Aide. While only a few of these job titles are specifically addressed in this book, they will give you a sense of the kinds of work performed and information you can use to research related jobs. As you will soon find, a wide range of adjunctive health-care career options is available to those prepared to invest several months to a few years in training.

Anesthesiologist Assistants

Principal activity: Assisting anesthesiologists during surgery

Work commitment: Full-time

Preprofessional education: Bachelor's degree

Program length: 2 years

Work prerequisites: Master's degree and certification

Career opportunities: Highly favorable

Income range: $68,000 to $97,000

Scope

Anesthesiologist assistants (AAs) belong to a relatively new health-care profession. They are members of a surgical team, working under a physician's supervision to administer anesthesia to patients. A formal training program in this field was initiated in the mid-1970s. Individuals with a strong interest in medicine will find this position challenging and rewarding, both intellectually and financially.

Activities

Principally AAs are involved in maintaining patients under anesthesia and monitoring vital signs during operations. The anesthesiologist, who is the AA's immediate supervisor, usually is available somewhere on the floor or in the hospital to provide guidance. The AA is present when the anesthesiologist induces sleep at the onset of surgery and also at the completion of the operation. AAs also help the anesthesiologist review medical and surgical data prior to procedures.

Work Settings

Obviously, most AAs work in the operating and recovery rooms of hospitals, but they may also be involved in pre-anesthetic evaluation of patients on the other floors. They also may find employment in clinics and outpatient surgical facilities. AAs are eligible to work in all states that permit the use of physician assistants, because they are considered specialist practitioners in that field. Currently 18 states have legislation governing AAs.

Advancement

An anesthesiologist assistant who enjoys the work and has the academic potential, resources, and opportunity to do so may consider applying to medical school and becoming a physician.

Prerequisites

A college degree with a premedical, biology, or chemistry major is recommended. Applicants with backgrounds in other allied health fields, such as nursing, medical technology, and respiratory therapy, are also considered. Thus, some AA applicants may be just out of college, while others will have worked in a health-care field for some time.

Desirable personal attributes for those entering this field include a superior ability in science, an ability to function well under stress, and the capacity to assume enormous personal responsibilities.

Education/Training

The AA training program lasts two years and leads to a master's degree. The emphasis is on basic science studies in such areas as anatomy, physiology, and pharmacology, followed by clinical experience in various aspects of anesthesiology.

Certification/Registration/Licensure

A certification examination is given by the National Commission on the Certification of Anesthesiologist Assistants.

Career Potential

Current AA graduates are in high demand and receive attractive starting salaries. Future needs will depend, in part, on how widely this profession gains acceptance. The field also depends on the impact of managed health care, where the use of AAs can lower costs. The projected job growth for this profession over the next decade is much faster than average.

For More Information

The professional organization for this field is the American Academy of Anesthesiologist Assistants, P.O. Box 13978, Tallahassee, FL 32317 (www.anesthetist.org). For certification information, contact the National Commission for Certification of Anesthesiologist Assistants, P.O. Box 15519, Atlanta, GA 30333.

Anesthesiologist Assistant Programs

Florida
Nova Southeastern University
3301 College Avenue
Davie, FL 33328
www.nova.edu

Georgia
Emory University
617 Woodruff Memorial Building
Atlanta, GA 30322
www.emory.edu

South University
709 Mall Boulevard
Savannah, Georgia 31406
www.southuniversity.edu

Missouri
University of Missouri-Kansas City
2411 Holmes Street
Kansas City, MO 64108
www.med.umkc.edu

Ohio
Case Western Reserve University
11100 Euclid Avenue
Cleveland, OH 44106
www.case.edu

Blood Bank Technologists and Specialists

Principal activity: Securing and processing donated blood for transfusions

Work commitment: Full-time

Preprofessional education: Bachelor's degree and certification as a medical technologist

Program length: 1 year for technologist; 2 years for specialist

Work prerequisites: Completion of an accredited blood bank technology program

Career opportunities: Stable

Income range: $45,000 to $63,000

Scope

Although the first human blood transfusion occurred in the early 1800s, reliable success with this lifesaving technique did not occur until 1900. Then it was discovered that both the red blood cells and plasma of the donor must be compatible with those of the recipient. Over the years, blood transfusion has become a sophisticated technological activity. Blood bank technologists draw, process, and store blood that is used for accident victims, patients undergoing surgery, and those with chronic blood diseases such as hemophilia and leukemia.

Currently this field has two kinds of personnel: blood bank technologists and specialists in blood bank technology. Both are discussed in this section.

Activities

Blood bank technologists draw, process, test, type, and store donated blood. Those who acquire special education to become specialists in blood bank technology may be called on to serve as administrators and educators, technical consultants, and researchers. Their special skills help them select appropriate donors, carry out pretransfusion testing, and detect possible dangerous blood conditions.

Work Settings

Blood bank technologists are employed by medical centers and hospitals, as well as by community blood bank transfusion services, private laboratories, and blood banks.

Advancement

With experience, a blood bank technologist can assume supervisory responsibilities over other personnel or be appointed to administrative control over a facility's operations. This is most likely for specialists in blood bank technology, because they have more education and training.

Prerequisites

There are two common routes to accredited programs in blood bank technology:

- Being a certified medical technologist with a bachelor's degree
- Having a bachelor's degree with a major in the biological or physical sciences plus one year of full-time clinical laboratory experience

Desirable personal attributes include meticulous work habits, dependability, and the ability to work under stress.

Education/Training

One-year accredited programs in blood bank technology are offered by many hospital and community blood banks, many universities, and the American Red Cross. These programs involve courses and training in immunology, genetics, serology, physiology, transfusion practices, and laboratory operations. In addition, students receive practical experience in a blood bank setting and training in immunohema/biological concepts. Some programs offer a master's degree, which makes you eligible to apply for certification as a specialist in blood bank technology.

Certification/Registration/Licensure

Certification in this field is offered by the American Society of Clinical Pathologists in conjunction with the American Association of Blood Banks. Eligible candidates must satisfactorily complete a written generalist examination. Those passing are designated as certified blood bank technologists (BB-ASCP).

Those with this designation who also have five years of experience or a master's or doctorate degree in immunohematology or a related field may take a more advanced examination to become a certified specialist in blood bank technology (SBB-ASCP).

Career Potential

In the past, the demands for personnel in this field have exceeded the number of job candidates. However, this imbalance is starting to stabilize. Still, job prospects are generally positive, especially in hospitals.

For More Information

The professional organization for this field is the American Society for Clinical Pathology, 2100 W. Harrison St., Chicago, IL 60612 (www.ascp.org). You can obtain additional information from the American Association of Blood Banks, 8101 Glenbrook Rd., Bethesda, MD 20814 (www.aabb.org). For certification or registration information, contact the ASCP Board of Registry, P.O. Box 12277, Chicago, IL 60612.

Blood Bank Technologist/Specialist Programs

Alabama
University of Alabama at
  Birmingham
SBB Program
1714 9th Ave. S.
Birmingham, AL 35294
www.uab.edu

California
Sacramento Medical Foundation
Specialist in Blood Banking
  Technology
1625 Stockton Blvd.
Sacramento, CA 95816
www.smfbc.org

District of Columbia
U.S. Army Blood Bank Fellowship
  Program
Walter Reed Army Medical Center
6900 Georgia Ave.
Washington, DC 20307
www.militaryblood.dod.mil

Florida
Central Florida Blood Bank, Inc.
32 W. Gore St.
Orlando, FL 32806
www.cfbb.org

Transfusion Medicine Academic
  Center
Florida Blood Services
Specialist in Blood Banking
  Program
10100 9th St. N.
St. Petersburg, FL 33713
www.fbsblood.org

Georgia
American Red Cross Blood
  Services
Atlanta Specialist in Blood Bank
  Technology Program
1925 Monroe Dr. NE
Atlanta, GA 30030
www.redcross.org/atlanta/

Illinois
Rush University
Specialist in Blood Banking
  Technology Program
600 S Paulina Street, 1014-A-Aac
Chicago, IL 60612
www.rushu.rush.edu

University of Illinois at Chicago
School of Biomedical and Health
  Information Sciences
1919 W. Taylor St.
Chicago, IL 60612
www.uic.edu

Indiana
Indiana Blood Center
Specialist in Blood Banking
  Program
3450 N Meridian Street
Indianapolis, IN 46208
www.indianablood.org

Louisiana
Medical Center of Louisiana
Blood Bank –1st Fl.
2021 Perdido Street
New Orleans, LA 70112
www.lsuhsc.edu

Maryland
Johns Hopkins Hospital SBB
Carnegie Building #656
600 N. Wolfe St.
Baltimore, MD 21287
www.jhmi.edu

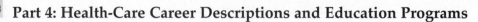

NIH Clinical Center Blood Bank
Specialist in BB Technology
  Program
NIH/CC/DTM, Building 10/1C711
10 Center Dr. MSC 1184
Bethesda, MD 20892
www.cc.nih.gov/dtm/

Massachusetts
Beth Israel Deaconess Medical
  Center
West Campus SBB Training Center
One Deaconess Rd.
Boston, MA 02215
www.bidmc.harvard.edu

Ohio
American Red Cross Blood
  Services–Central Ohio
995 E. Broad
Columbus, OH 43205

American Red Cross Blood
  Services
Northern Ohio Region
3747 Euclid Ave.
Cleveland, OH 44115
www.redcross-cleveland.org

Hoxworth Blood Center
University of Cincinnati Medical
  Center
3130 Highland Ave.
P.O. Box 67005
Cincinnati, OH 45267
www.hoxworth.org

Texas
Gulf Coast School of Blood Bank
  Technology
1400 La Concha Ln.
Houston, TX 77054
www.giveblood.org

University Health Systems
4502 Medical Dr.
San Antonio, TX 78229
www.sbbofsa.org

University of Texas Medical
  Branch
UTMB SBB Program
301 University Blvd.
Galveston, TX 77555
www.utmb.edu/sbb

University of Texas Southwestern
  Medical Center
Blood Bank Technology
  Program–Dallas
5323 Harry Hines Blvd.
Dallas, TX 75390
www.telecampus.utsystem.edu

Wisconsin
The Blood Center of Southeastern
  Wisconsin
638 N. 18th St.
Milwaukee, WI 53233
www.bcw.edu

Cardiovascular Technology Personnel

Principal activity: Carrying out non-invasive and invasive cardiovascular procedures

Work commitment: Full-time

Preprofessional education: High school diploma or the equivalent

Program length: On-the-job training (8 to 16 weeks) to 2 years

Work prerequisites: Experience and/or schooling

Career opportunities: Highly favorable

Income range: $33,000 to $62,000

Scope

Workers in this field record heart and circulatory function. They are also known as electrocardiograph (EKG) technicians and technologists. This field has a number of specialized areas, including the use of both noninvasive and invasive procedures. Their various activities are discussed below.

Activities

Cardiovascular Technicians

Cardiovascular technicians are entry-level workers who usually perform their duties at a cardiologist's office or at a hospitalized patient's bedside. They use an EKG machine to graphically detect and trace the electrical impulses transmitted by the heart musculature. This instrument records the minute electrical changes taking place during and between the contractions of the heart chambers. The technician readies the equipment, explains to the patient what the test procedure involves (such as attaching leads to appropriate areas of the body), and then makes a recording at various monitoring positions. The physician uses the resulting cardiogram as a diagnostic indicator of the heart and circulatory system's state of health. Doctors routinely order EKGs before any significant surgery, upon hospitalization, as part of an annual physical, and when monitoring patients with suspected or established cardiac or cardiovascular problems.

Specialized (Noninvasive) Cardiovascular Technicians

This category includes a variety of skilled EKG technicians who perform more sophisticated tests, including holter monitoring and stress testing. A holter monitor is a portable EKG unit that records electrical heart activity over an extended period (usually 24 hours). The technician fits the patient with the unit by placing the leads on designated sites on the chest and attaching the recording monitor to a belt around the patient's waist. When the patient returns in a day or so, the technician removes the cassette tape and either sends it out for analysis or places it in a scanner. After checking the tape's quality, the technician prints the information so that it can be evaluated by the cardiologist who ordered the test. For a stress test, the technician records a continuous EKG for a patient before and during treadmill exercise. This monitors and records the impact of increased exertion on the patient's heart function.

Other technicians who have special skills using ultrasound equipment such as echocardiographs, vectocardiographs, and cardiac Doppler units may devote all their time to operating this equipment.

Cardiovascular Technologists

Cardiovascular technologists are involved in invasive studies of the heart. They work in coronary care or in hospitals' surgical intensive care units. They help physicians introduce various dyes, probes, and catheters into patients' hearts and legs. This is done to determine whether a blockage exists or for other diagnostic purposes. Such technologists may assist cardiac surgeons during angioplasties (balloon procedures performed to open clogged arteries) or when they insert pacemakers under the chest wall to help the heart maintain a normal rhythm.

Work Settings

Noninvasive cardiovascular procedures are carried out in cardiologists' offices as well as in hospitals. Invasive procedures are almost always hospital-based activities.

Advancement

With additional training and experience, a cardiovascular technician can become a technologist and perhaps assume supervisory responsibilities. EKG technicians can attend school part-time and become technologists.

Prerequisites

A high school diploma or its equivalent is the essential starting point for securing a position in this field.

Desirable personal attributes for this field include manual dexterity, the ability to follow detailed instructions, dependability, and a pleasant and reassuring personality.

Education/Training

On-the-job training is the usual route to becoming an EKG technician. This training typically is given over a 6- to 16-week period by an EKG supervisor or cardiologist. Most hospitals prefer to train their own active hospital personnel. Many vocational-technical schools, junior and community colleges, and hospitals offer formal training programs. Programs for EKG technicians usually last one semester.

Prospective EKG technologists may secure on-the-job training (for one or two years), but they also can attend a formal program that usually lasts two years. In the latter case, the first year is devoted to academic instruction and the second to specialized training in noninvasive and invasive technology. Colleges award associate degrees to those who complete the program. Some qualified allied health personnel may receive credit for prior studies and thus shorten their training time.

Certification/Registration/Licensure

This field has an accreditation process, though it is currently voluntary. For more information, contact Cardiovascular Credentialing International, 4456 Corporation Ln., Virginia Beach, VA 23463 (www.cci-online.org).

Career Potential

Employment opportunities for cardiovascular personnel are expected to grow faster than average. This is due in large part to the rising prevalence of heart disease and the aging population. Opportunities for skilled technicians and technologists are expected to be more favorable than those for EKG technicians trained only in routine cardiography.

For More Information

The professional organizations for this field are the Alliance of Cardiovascular Professionals, Thalia Landing Offices, Building 2, 4356 Bonney Rd., #103, Virginia Beach, VA 23452 (www.acp-online.org); the Society for Vascular Ultrasound, 4601 President Dr., Lanham, MD 20706 (www.svunet.org); and the American Society of Echocardiography, 1500 Sunday Dr., Ste. 102, Raleigh, NC 27607 (www.asecho.org).

Cardiovascular Technology Programs

Alabama
Community College of the AF/AYH
130 W. Maxwell Blvd.
Maxwell AFB, AL 36122
www.maxwell.af.mil

California
Grossmont College
8800 Grossmont College Dr.
El Cajon, CA 92020
www.grossmont.net

Connecticut
Fox Institute-New Hampshire
99 South Stret
W Hartford, CT 06110
www.foxinstitute.com

Florida
Edison Community College
8099 College Pkwy. SW
P.O. Box 60210
Ft. Myers, FL 33906
www.edison.edu

National School of Technology–
  Kendall
9020 SW 137th Ave.
Miami, FL 33186
www.nst.edu

Santa Fe College
3000 NW 83rd St.
Gainesville, FL 32606
www.sfcollege.edu

St. Joseph's Hospital
3001 W. Dr. Martin Luther King
  Jr. Blvd.
Tampa, FL 33607
www.sjbhealth.org

Ultrasound Diagnostic School
5701 Hillsborough Ave.
Tampa, FL 33619
www.uds-tampa.com

Georgia
Cardiovascular Technology
  Program
Darton College
2400 Gillionville Road
Albany, GA 31707
www.darton.edu

Kentucky
Spencerian College-Louisville
4627 Dixie Highway
Louisville, KY 40216
www.spencerian.edu/Louisville/

University Health Care System
Cardiovascular Technologist
  Program
1350 Walton Way
Augusta, GA 30901
www.universityhealth.org

Illinois
Rush University
College of Health Sciences
600 S. Paulina St.
Chicago, IL 60612
www.rush.edu

Kansas
University of Kansas
School of Allied Health
3901 Rainbow Blvd.
Kansas City, KS 66160
www.alliedhealth.kumc.edu

Maine
Southern Maine Community
  College
2 Fort Rd.
South Portland, ME 04106
www.smccme.edu

Maryland
Howard Community College
10901 Little Patuxent Pkwy.
Columbia, MD 21044
www.howardcc.edu

Naval School of Health Sciences
8901 Wisconsin Ave.
Bethesda, MD 20889
http://nshs.med.navy.mil

Massachusetts
Northeastern University
360 Huntington Ave.
Boston, MA 02116
www.northeastern.edu

Michigan
Oakland Community College
7350 Cooley Lake Rd.
Waterford, MI 48237
www.oaklandcc.edu

Minnesota
Northwest Technical College–
  East Grand Forks
2022 Central Ave. NE
East Grand Forks, MN 56721
www.ntcmn.edu

New Jersey
Morristown Memorial Hospital
100 Madison Ave.
Morristown, NJ 07962
www.atlantichealth.org

University of Medicine &
  Dentistry of New Jersey
150 Bergen St. D-447
Newark, NJ 07107
www.umdnj.edu

New York
Molloy College
1000 Hempstead Ave.
Rockville Centre, NY 11571
www.molloy.edu

Rochester General Hospital
1425 Portland Ave.
Rochester, NY 14621
www.urmc.rochester.edu

Sanford-Brown Institute
Garden City
711 Stewart Avenue 11530
www.sanfordbrown.edu

Ohio
Cuyahoga Community College
11000 Pleasant Valley Rd.
Parma, OH 44130
www.tri-c.edu

University of Toledo
Community and Technical College
2801 W. Bancroft St.
Toledo, OH 43606
www.utoledo.edu

Pennsylvania
American Center for Technical
  Arts & Sciences
1930 Chestnut St., 1st Floor
Philadelphia, PA 19103
www.actas.net

Eastern University
1300 Eagle Rd.
St. Davids, PA 19087
www.eastern.edu

Geisinger Medical Center
Pennsylvania State University
100 N. Academy Ave.
Danville, PA 17822
www.geisinger.edu

Gwynedd-Mercy College
1325 Sumneytown Pike
Gwynedd Valley, PA 19437
www.gmc.edu

Lancaster Institute for Health
  Education
410 N. Duke St.
P.O. Box 3555
Lancaster, PA 17604
www.lha.org

South Dakota
Southeast Technical Institute
Cardiovascular Technology
  Program
2301 Career Place
Sioux Falls, SD 57107
www.southeasttech.edu

Texas
Advanced Health Education
  Center
8502 Tybor St.
Houston, TX 77074
www.aheconline.com

El Centro College
Main and Lamar Sts.
Dallas, TX 75202
www.elcentrocollege.edu

Houston Community College
3100 Shenandoah
Houston, TX 77021
www.hccs.edu

Virginia
Sentara Norfolk General Hospital
600 Gresham Dr.
Norfolk, VA 23507
www.sentara.com/hospitals/
  sentara_norfolk.html/

Washington
Spokane Community College
Cardiovascular Technology
  Program
1810 N. Greene St.
Spokane, WA 99217
www.scc.spokane.edu

Canada
British Columbia Institute of
  Technology
3700 Willingdon Ave.
Burnaby, British Columbia
  V5G 3H2
www.bcit.ca

Burwin Institute
P.O. Box 1029
Lunenburg, Nova Scotia
  B0J 2C0
www.burwin.com

CDI College
Toronto Central
117 Eglinton Ave. E., Third Floor
Toronto, Ontario M4P 1H4
www.cdicollege.ca

Certified Nurse Assistants

Principal activity: Assist with patient care in a nursing home

Work commitment: Usually full-time

Preprofessional education: High school diploma or GED certificate

Program length: 2 to 8 weeks (75 to 140 hours)

Work prerequisites: At least 75 hours training and passing an exam

Career opportunities: Highly favorable

Income range: $22,000 to $27,000

Scope

Certified nurse assistants are important members of the health-care team and are frequently the principal caregivers in nursing homes. They provide direct, personal patient care and assist higher level nurses (RNs and LPNs) as needed. Thus, CNAs are considered the backbone of the nursing home workforce in providing rehabilitative, restorative, and custodial care services to sick, disabled, and dependent residents.

Activities

Most CNAs work a 40 hour week. They help residents carry out the activities of daily living. These include eating, bathing, dressing, using the toilet, and getting around. They also assist with instructional components of daily living, provide emotional support, and help distribute medications when necessary.

A CNA's job can be difficult and at times hazardous. They have demanding workloads that can often be physically challenging as well. Additionally a CNA is accountable for on-going data collection and documentation relative to resident care. They also perform some medical procedures such as catheter care, specimen collection, recording vital signs, height and weight measurements, and supervising performance of range in motion exercise.

Work settings

The primary work site of CNAs, are nursing homes, but they also may be employed in hospitals and private households.

Advancement

Opportunities for advancement are limited. To advance further, additional formal education and training are required. Experience does serve to provide a basis to judge one's potential for advancement in health care.

Prerequisites

A high school diploma or its equivalent is required.

Desirable personal attributes for this job include good physical and emotional health, the ability to follow instructions and use good judgment, dependability, and a strong sense of compassion.

Education/Training

Federal law requires that institutions certified under Medicare and/or Medicaid use CNAs who have completed a minimum of 75 hours of training and pass a competency evaluation within four months of employment. About two-thirds of educational programs for CNAs are offered at hospitals, educational centers, and health agencies. Coursework generally includes medical terminology, basic mechanics of personal care, nursing skills, and infection control.

Certification/Registration/Licensure

Professional certification requirements for nursing assistants are very common. Most nursing homes require completion of state-mandated educational requirements. To receive state registration, a written competency exam, such as the National Nurse's Aide Assessment Program, must be passed (visit the National Council on the State Boards of Nursing's Web site at www.ncsbn.org/1721.htm for more information). A background check may also be required.

Career Potential

A recent survey found that well over 1.5 million nursing home residents are placed in approximately 1,800 nursing homes. A million nursing staff members have been employed to meet their needs. Federal law requires that nursing homes maintain a sufficient level of staffing. Given the increased aging of society and the demands for greater basic nursing services, the need for CNAs should increase substantially over the next decade. This is also reflected in the fact that some CNAs work a 60 hour-week and that the number of contingent and part-time CNAs is also growing.

For More Information

This field has no professional organization. Information can be secured from the American Health Care Association, 2001 L Street, NE, Washington, DC 2005 (www.ahca.org). You can also visit the National Network of Career Nursing Assistants' Web site at www.cna-network.org.

Clinical Laboratory Technicians

Principal activity: Carrying out clinical tests ordered by physicians

Work commitment: Usually full-time

Preprofessional education: High school diploma

Program length: 2 years

Work prerequisites: Associate degree or certificate and certification

Career opportunities: Favorable

Income range: $30,000 to $45,000

Scope

In their office practices and while making hospital rounds, physicians order many different laboratory tests. These tests determine a patient's state of health for diagnostic purposes and treatment outcomes. An average major hospital might perform more than 2 million tests a year. That's why clinical laboratory technicians, also known as medical laboratory technicians, are employed in such large numbers. They work under the supervision of certified laboratory technologists in a variety of settings to perform the thousands of lab tests required to treat patients.

Activities

Medical laboratory technicians perform the less-complex tests and carry out the routine procedures that are assigned to laboratories. Technicians perform blood counts, microscopically examine specimens, and inoculate cultures. They may work in several areas of the clinical laboratory or specialize in just one.

For example, histology technicians (see p. 262) preserve and process tissue specimens obtained from patients and then cut and stain them for microscopic examination by pathologists. Phlebotomists (see p. 308) are technicians who draw blood from patients for laboratory analysis. They are supervised by clinical laboratory technologists.

Work Settings

Clinical laboratory technicians may work in hospitals or private laboratories, physicians' offices, HMOs, clinics, or commercial organizations such as pharmaceutical companies. Federal and local health agencies also employ medical laboratory technicians.

Advancement

By gaining experience or enrolling in a bachelor's degree program, a technician can become a clinical laboratory technologist or attain a supervisory position.

Prerequisites

A high school diploma or its equivalent is essential for entry into a clinical laboratory technician training program.

Desirable attributes for this profession include solid abilities in biology and chemistry, excellent vision, organized and thorough work habits, maturity, attention to detail, and the ability to work under pressure and with others.

Education/Training

Clinical laboratory technicians generally have an associate degree from a junior college or community college. This is the most common educational pathway for this field. Another approach is to secure a certificate from a hospital, medical school, vocational training institute, or the armed forces. A few technicians receive on-the-job training at a hospital.

The Clinical Laboratory Improvements Act requires those who perform certain highly complex tests to have at least an associate degree. There are two nationally recognized accrediting agencies for training programs in medical laboratory science: the Accrediting Bureau of Health Education Schools (ABHES) and the National Accrediting Agency for Clinical Laboratory Sciences (NAACLS).

Certification/Registration/Licensure

Clinical laboratory technicians can be certified by the ASCP Board of Registry, by the ABHES or the NAACLS, or by one of the other agencies listed on p. 223. Achieving such recognition can lead to a better-paying position and greater advancement potential.

Career Potential

The job outlook for clinical laboratory technicians is generally favorable. However, it is subject to continuing changes in the health-care industry.

For More Information

The professional organization for this field is the American Society of Cytopathology, 400 W. Ninth St., Ste. 201, Wilmington, DE 19801 (www.cytopathology.org).

Laboratory Technician Programs

Hundreds of programs throughout the United States train people to become clinical laboratory technicians—far too many to list here. For information on an accredited training program in your area, contact ABHES, 7777 Leesburg Pike, Ste. 314, Falls Church, VA 22043 (www.abhes.org), or NAACLS, 8410 W. Bryn Mawr Ave., Ste. 670, Chicago, IL 60631 (www.naacls.org). For information on certification, contact the American Society for Clinical Pathology, 33 West Monroe Street, Suite 1600, Chicago, IL 60603 (www.ascp.org).

You'll find more accrediting agencies listed under Clinical Laboratory Technologists.

Clinical Laboratory Technologists

Principal activity: Performing clinical laboratory tests ordered by physicians

Work commitment: Usually full-time

Preprofessional education: High school diploma or associate degree

Program length: 4 years

Work prerequisites: Bachelor's degree in medical technology and certification

Career opportunities: Stable

Income range: $45,000 to $63,000

Scope

The work of clinical laboratory technologists is vital in the detection, diagnosis, and treatment of many different diseases. Technologists perform tests on a wide variety of specimens, including body fluids, tissues, and cells.

Activities

Clinical laboratory technologists frequently use computer-automated equipment to perform large series of tests (24 to 40) simultaneously. Using microscopes, technologists identify bacteria, parasites, and other microorganisms as well as abnormal cells in tissue fluids. They also analyze the chemical content of fluids and match blood types to determine the feasibility of transfusions. Cell counters are commonly used to determine into what numerical range specific types of cells fall. One of their key functions is to measure drug levels to judge how a patient is responding to a specific treatment. Their findings are relayed to physicians and become part of a patient's record. Thus, their laboratory services cover tests in a variety of fields, including cytology, histology, serology, and bacteriology.

Work Settings

Most clinical laboratory technologists are employed by hospitals, private laboratories, physicians' offices, or clinics. Some are employed by laboratory equipment manufacturers in product development, marketing, or sales.

Advancement

Clinical laboratory technologists with appropriate experience, graduate education (see the section "Education/Training"), and managerial skills can advance to supervisory positions such as chief technologist or laboratory manager.

Prerequisites

A high school diploma or associate degree lets you enroll in a bachelor's degree program in medical technology.

Desirable personal attributes for this field include a strong interest in and aptitude for the biological sciences, precision and attention to detail, superior vision, dependability, maturity, the capacity to work efficiently under pressure, and a desire to be part of a health-care team.

Education/Training

Two educational routes lead to a bachelor's degree in medical technology. One is a four-year program plus clinical experience at a college. The other involves three years of college course work followed by one year of practical training in a hospital setting. Course requirements in both programs include biology, chemistry, microbiology, hematology, immunology, and clinical chemistry, as well as clinical technology course work.

Graduate programs offering a master's degree in medical technology provide specialized training for careers in administration, teaching, and research.

Certification/Registration/Licensure

Certification, while voluntary, is a prerequisite for most jobs and is usually essential for advancement. Three agencies grant certification in this field (see the section "For More Information"), and each has different requirements. Many clinical laboratory technologists are certified by more than one agency.

Career Potential

Certified licensed technologists should find favorable job opportunities as the U.S. population grows larger and older. In addition, the number of available tests is always increasing, and physicians are making greater use of them for diagnostic purposes. Restraining factors include the effort by HMOs to contain costs and the automation of testing procedures.

For More Information

The professional organizations for this field are the American Society for Clinical Laboratory Science, 6701 Democracy Blvd., Ste. 300, Bethesda, MD 20817 (www.ascls.org), and American Medical Technologists, 710 Higgins Rd., Park Ridge, IL 60068 (www. amt1.com).

Agencies that certify clinical laboratory technologists are American Medical Technologists; the ASCP Board of Registry, P.O. Box 12277, Chicago, IL 60612 (www.ascp.org); the Credentialing Commission of the International Society for Clinical Laboratory Technology, 818 Olive St., St. Louis, MO 63101; and the National Accrediting Agency for Clinical Laboratory Sciences, 8410 W. Bryn Mawr Ave., Ste. 670, Chicago, IL 60631 (www.naacls.org).

Cytotechnologists

Principal activity: Preparing and studying cell smears for a microscopic evaluation	**Program length:** Usually 1 year, but sometimes more
Work commitment: Full-time	**Work prerequisites:** Graduating from an accredited cytotechnology program
Preprofessional education: 2 years of college; bachelor's degree preferred	**Career opportunities:** Stable
	Income range: $45,000 to $63,000

Scope

Our society is coming to recognize the importance of preventive medicine. This is reflected in the campaigns to vaccinate children and to discourage smoking, excessive drinking, and substance abuse. It is also reflected in the push to test for early warning signs of cancer by means of mammography, colonoscopy, and pap smears. Cytotechnologists are trained to prepare specimens for examination and evaluation to test for these and other conditions.

Activities

Cytotechnologists smear sample cells on slides and then stain them to enhance contrast and facilitate their evaluation. They are trained to identify abnormal cells on these slides, and they report their observations to pathologists, who review their work. More recently technologists have been using computers to help identify precancerous and cancerous cells. This technology will undoubtedly play a larger role in the future.

Work Settings

Cytotechnologists are employed by hospitals, private laboratories, and research institutes. A few teach in colleges and universities.

Advancement

In this profession, advancement comes by securing a degree and experience. Some employers identify three ascending ranks of technologists.

Prerequisites

Completing two years of college is a minimum criterion for entering a cytotechnology training program, and some schools require even more credits. Undergraduates should take courses in biology, bacteriology, anatomy, physiology, genetics, and parasitology, as well as a year of basic chemistry.

Desirable personal attributes for this field include superior vision, patience, dependability, precision, a strong sense of responsibility, and an interest in the biological sciences and medical diagnosis.

Education/Training

To become a certified member of this profession, you must graduate from an accredited cytotechnology program. It is preferable to complete a bachelor's degree before studying cytotechnology. For those with a degree, the training program lasts one year; for others it takes longer.

Accredited cytotechnology training programs include courses in clinical medicine, anatomy, histology, embryology, cytochemistry, cytophysiology, endocrinology, and cytology screening.

Certification/Registration/Licensure

Candidates must graduate from an accredited program before taking the certification exam administered by the American Society of Clinical Pathologists. After attaining certification and gaining three years of experience, cytotechnologists can be certified by the International Academy of Cytology. Several states require cytotechnologists to be licensed.

Career Potential

Employment prospects are positive overall. While the number of positions available may seem low compared to other health-care careers, constantly evolving technologies and a steady increase in the volume of laboratory tests should help to ensure some job growth over the next decade.

For More Information

The professional organization for this field is the American Society of Cytopathology, 400 W. Ninth St., Wilmington, DE 19801 (www.cytopathology.org). For information on certification as a cytotechnologist, write to the ASCP Board of Registry, P.O. Box 12277, Chicago, IL 60612.

Cytotechnologist Programs

Alabama
Samford University
800 Lakeshore Dr.
Birmingham, AL 35229
www.samford.edu

University of Alabama at
  Birmingham
UAB Station-SHRP 381K
Birmingham, AL 35294
www.uab.edu

Auburn University Montgomery
Program in Cytotechnology
School of Sciences
204B Moore Hall
P O Box 244023
Montgomery, AL 36124
www.aum.edu/cls

Arkansas
Arkansas State University
Jonesboro, AR 72467
www.astate.edu

University of Arkansas for Medical
  Sciences
4301 W. Markham St.
Little Rock, AR 72205
www.uams.edu

California
California State University
1000 E. Victoria St.
Carson, CA 90747
www.csudh.edu

California State University
18111 Nordhoff St.
Northridge, CA 91330
www.csun.edu

Charles R. Drew University of
  Medicine and Science
1731 E. 120th St.
Los Angeles, CA 90059
www.cdrewu.edu

Loma Linda University
School of Allied Health
  Professions
Department of Clinical Laboratory
  Science
Loma Linda, CA 92350
www.llu.edu

UCLA Medical Center
Center of Health Sciences
10833 Le Conte Ave., Mail Code
  173216
Los Angeles, CA 90095
www.pathology.ucla.edu

Connecticut
University of Connecticut
2131 Hillside Rd. U-88
Storrs, CT 06269
www.uconn.edu

University of Connecticut Health
  Center
263 Farmington Ave.
Farmington, CT 06030
www.uchc.edu

District of Columbia
George Washington University
2121 Eye St. NW
Washington, DC 20052
www.gwu.edu

Howard University
2400 6th St. NW
Washington, DC 20059
www.howard.edu

Florida
Barry University
11300 NE Second Ave.
Miami Shores, FL 33161
www.barry.edu

Georgia
Armstrong Atlantic State
  University
11935 Abercorn St.
Savannah, GA 31419
www.armstrong.edu

Columbus State University
4225 University Ave.
Columbus, GA 31907
www.colstate.edu

Grady Health System
80 Butler St. SE
Atlanta, GA 30303
www.gradyhealthsystem.org

Idaho
Boise State University
1910 University Dr.
Boise, ID 83725
www.boisestate.edu

Idaho State University
921 S. 8th Ave.
Pocatello, ID 83209
www.isu.edu

Illinois
Augustana College
639 38th St.
Rock Island, IL 61201
www.augustana.edu

Illinois College
1101 W. College Ave.
Jacksonville, IL 62650
www.ic.edu

Roosevelt University
430 S. Michigan Ave.
Chicago, IL 60605
www.roosevelt.edu

Satellite Program of
   University of Nebraska
Cytotechnology Program
Carle Clinic
602 West University Avenue
Urbana, IL 61801

Indiana
Indiana University
300 N. Jordan Ave.
Bloomington, IN 47405
www.indiana.edu

Indiana University
Department of Pathology and
   Laboratory Medicine
Van Nuys Medical Science
   Building
635 Barnhill Dr., Room A-128
Indianapolis, IN 46202
www.pathology.iupui.edu

Indiana University–Purdue
   University Fort Wayne
2101 E. Coliseum Blvd.
Fort Wayne, IN 46805
www.ipfw.edu

Indiana University School of
   Medicine
Cytotechnology Program
Clarian Pathology Laboratory
350 W 11th Street
Indianapolis, IN 46202
www.medicine.iu.edu

Indiana University School of
   Medicine
Building 24, Ste. 2401
5610 Crawfordsville Rd.
Speedway, IN 46224
www.iupui.edu

Iowa
Luther College
700 College Dr.
Decorah, IA 52101
www.luther.edu

Mercy Hospital School of
   Cytotechnology
Mercy Medical Center
1111 6th Ave.
Des Moines, IA 50314
www.mercydesmoines.org

University of Northern Iowa
1227 W. 27th St.
Cedar Falls, IA 50614
www.uni.edu

Kansas
Fort Hays State University
600 Park St.
Hays, KS 67601
www.fhsu.edu

Friends University
2100 W. University
Wichita, KS 67213
www.friends.edu

Newman University
3100 McCormick Ave.
Wichita, KS 67213
www.newmanu.edu

University of Kansas
126 Strong Hall
Lawrence, KS 66045
www.ku.edu

University of Kansas Medical
   Center
1600 Bell-Cytology Laboratory
3901 Rainbow Blvd.
Kansas City, KS 66103
www.kumc.edu

Kentucky
Bellarmine University
2001 Newburg Rd.
Louisville, KY 40205
www.bellarmine.edu

Eastern Kentucky University
521 Lancaster Ave.
Richmond, KY 40475
www.eku.edu

Pathology and Cytology
   Laboratories, Inc.
290 Big Run Rd.
Lexington, KY 40503

University of Louisville
Louisville, KY 40292
www.louisville.edu

Louisiana
Nicholls State University
Consortium for Cytotechnology
   Education
235 Civic Center Blvd.
Houma, LA 70360
www.nicholls.edu/
   cytotechnology/

University of Louisiana at Monroe
700 University Ave.
Monroe, LA 71209
www.ulm.edu

Maine
University of Maine
5713 Chadbourne Hall
Orono, ME 04469
www.umaine.edu

Maryland
Johns Hopkins Hospital
600 N. Wolfe St.
Baltimore, MD 21287
www.hopkinsmedicine.org

Massachusetts
Berkshire Medical Center
725 North St.
Pittsfield, MA 01201
www.berkshiremedicalcenter.net

Suffolk University
8 Ashburton Place
Boston, MA 02108
www.suffolk.edu

University of Massachusetts
   Dartmouth
285 Old Westport Rd.
North Dartmouth, MA 02747
www.umassd.edu

Michigan
Andrews University
Berrien Springs, MI 49104
www.andrews.edu

Baker College of Muskegon
1903 Marquette Ave.
Muskegon, MI 49442
www.baker.edu

Baker College of Owosso
1020 S. Washington St.
Owosso, MI 48867
www.baker.edu

Detroit Medical Center–University
  Laboratories
Program in Cytotechnology
4707 St. Antoine Boulevard
Detroit, MI 48201
www.harperhospital.org/univlab/

DMC University Laboratories
3990 John R St.
Detroit, MI 48201
www.dmc.org/univlab/

Ferris State University
901 S. State St.
Big Rapids, MI 49307
www.ferris.edu

Henry Ford Hospital
2799 W. Grand Blvd.
Detroit, MI 48202
www.henryfordhealth.org

Madonna University
36600 Schoolcraft Rd.
Livonia, MI 48150
www.madonna.edu

Northern Michigan University
1401 Presque Isle Ave.
Marquette, MI 49855
www.nmu.edu

Oakland University
Rochester, MI 48309
www.oakland.edu

Wayne State University
Detroit, MI 48202
www.wayne.edu

Minnesota
Mayo Clinic College of Medicine
Mayo School of Health Sciences
200 First St. SW
Rochester, MN 55905
www.mayo.edu/mshs/

Minnesota State University
  Moorhead
1104 7th Ave. S.
Moorhead, MN 56563
www.mnstate.edu

Saint Mary's University of
  Minnesota
700 Terrace Heights
Winona, MN 55987
www.smumn.edu

Winona State University
P.O. Box 5838
Winona, MN 55987
www.winona.edu

Mississippi
University of Mississippi Medical
  Center
2500 N. State St.
Jackson, MS 39216
www.umc.edu

Missouri
Avila College
11901 Wornall Rd.
Kansas City, MO 64145
www.avila.edu

Jewish Hospital College of
  Nursing and Allied Health
Mail Stop: 90-30-625
306 S. Kingshighway Blvd.
St. Louis, MO 63110
www.jhconah.edu

University of Missouri–Columbia
Columbia, MO 65211
www.missouri.edu

University of Missouri–St. Louis
One University Blvd.
St. Louis, MO 63121
www.umsl.edu

Saint Louis University
Cytotechnology Program
Doisy College of Health Sciences
3437 Caroline Street
St. Louis, MO63104
www.slu.edu

Nebraska
Clarkson College
101 S. 42nd St.
Omaha, NE 68131
www.clarksoncollege.edu

Dana College
2848 College Dr.
Blair, NE 68008
www.dana.edu

University of Nebraska Medical
  Center
42nd and Emile
Omaha, NE 68198
www.unmc.edu

Nevada
APL School of Cytotechnology
Associated Pathologists'
  Laboratories
4230 S. Burnham, Ste. 250
Las Vegas, NV 89119

New Jersey
Bloomfield College
467 Franklin St.
Bloomfield, NJ 07003
www.bloomfield.edu

College of St. Elizabeth
2 Convent Rd.
Morristown, NJ 07960
www.cse.edu

Fairleigh Dickinson University
Metropolitan Campus
1000 River Rd.
Teaneck, NJ 07666
www.fdu.edu

Felician College
262 S. Main St.
Lodi, NJ 07644
www.felician.edu

Kean University
1000 Morris Ave.
Union, NJ 07083
www.kean.edu

New Jersey City University
2039 Kennedy Blvd.
Jersey City, NJ 07305
www.njcu.edu

St. Peter's College
2641 Kennedy Blvd.
Jersey City, NJ 07306
www.spc.edu

University of Medicine &
  Dentistry of New Jersey
School of Health-Related
  Professions
1776 Raritan Rd.
Scotch Plains, NJ 07076
www.umdnj.edu

New York
Albany College of Pharmacy
106 New Scotland Ave.
Albany, NY 12208
www.acp.edu

College of St. Rose
432 Western Ave.
Albany, NY 12203
www.strose.edu

Long Island University
1 University Plaza
Brooklyn, NY 11201
www.brooklyn.liu.edu

Long Island University
700 Northern Blvd.
Brookville, NY 11548
www.liu.edu

Memorial Sloan-Kettering Cancer
  Center
School of Cytotechnology
1275 York Ave.
New York, NY 10021
www.mskcc.org

New York Medical College
Department of Pathology
Valhalla, NY 10595
www.nymc.edu

State University of New York
  Upstate Medical University
College of Health Professions
750 E. Adams St.
Syracuse, NY 13210
www.upstate.edu/chp/

Stony Brook University
State University of New York
School of Health Technology &
  Management
Stony Brook, NY 11794
www.stonybrook.edu

North Carolina
Central Piedmont Community
  College
P.O. Box 35009
Charlotte, NC 28235
www.cpcc.edu

East Carolina University
E. 5th St.
Greenville, NC 27858
www.ecu.edu

Greensboro College
815 W. Market St.
Greensboro, NC 27401
www.greensboro.edu

University of North Carolina at
  Chapel Hill
Department of Allied Health
  Professions
CB #7120, Medical School, Wing E
Chapel Hill, NC 27599
www.alliedhealth.unc.edu/

North Dakota
University of North Dakota
Box 8237
Grand Forks, ND 58202
www.und.nodak.edu

Ohio
Akron General Medical Center
400 Wabash Ave.
Akron, OH 44307
www.agmc.org

Kent State University
Kent, OH 44242
www.kent.edu

Mount Union College
1972 Clark Ave.
Alliance, OH 44601
www.muc.edu

Notre Dame College
4545 College Rd.
South Euclid, OH 44121
www.notredamecollege.edu

University of Akron
302 Buchtel Mall
Akron, OH 44325
www.uakron.edu

Ursuline College
2550 Lander Rd.
Pepper Pike, OH 44124
www.ursuline.edu

Oklahoma
University of Oklahoma
Health Sciences Center
1100 N. Lindsey
Oklahoma City, OK 73104
www.ouhsc.edu

Pennsylvania
Bloomsburg University
400 E. Second St.
Bloomsburg, PA 17815
www.bloomu.edu

College Misericordia
301 Lake St.
Dallas, PA 18612
www.misericordia.edu

Elizabethtown College
One Alpha Dr.
Elizabethtown, PA 17022
www.etown.edu

Gannon University
109 University Square
Erie, PA 16541
www.gannon.edu

Gwynedd-Mercy College
1325 Sumneytown Pike
Gwynedd Valley, PA 19437
www.gmc.edu

Holy Family College
9701 Frankford Ave.
Philadelphia, PA 19114
www.hfc.edu

Juniata College
1700 Moore St.
Huntingdon, PA 16652
www.juniata.edu/

La Roche College
9000 Babcock Blvd.
Pittsburgh, PA 15237
www.laroche.edu

Mansfield University of
  Pennsylvania
Mansfield, PA 16933
www.mansfield.edu

The University Health Center of
  Pittsburgh
Anisa I. Kanbour School of
  Cytotechnology
300 Halket Street
Pittsburgh, PA 15213
http://path.upmc.edu/cytotech

Slippery Rock University
1 Morrow Way
Slippery Rock, PA 16057
www.sru.edu

Thiel College
75 College Ave.
Greenville, PA 16125
www.thiel.edu

Thomas Jefferson University
Jefferson College of Health
  Professions
Department of Laboratory
  Sciences
130 S. 9th St.
Philadelphia, PA 19107
www.jefferson.edu/jchp/

University of Pittsburgh School
  of Medicine
Department of Pathology
S-417 BST
200 Lothrop St.
Pittsburgh, PA 15261
http://path.upmc.edu/

Rhode Island
Rhode Island School of
  Cytotechnology
University of Rhode Island
Feinstein Providence Campus
80 Washington Street
Providence, RI 02903
www.rischoolofcytotechnology.
  com

Salve Regina University
100 Ochre Point Ave.
Newport, RI 02840
www2.salve.edu

University of Rhode Island
Department of Cell and Molecular
  Biology
117 Morill Hall
45 Lower College Rd.
Providence, RI 02881
http://cels.uri.edu/cmb/

South Carolina
Charleston Southern University
9200 University Blvd.
Charleston, SC 29423
www.csuniv.edu

Francis Marion University
P.O. Box 100547
Florence, SC 29501
www.fmarion.edu

Medical University of South
  Carolina
College of Health Professions
151B Rutledge Avenue
Charleston, SC 29425
www.musc.edu

Tennessee
Austin Peay State University
601 College St.
Clarksville, TN 37044
www.apsu.edu

East Tennessee State University
P.O. Box 70267
Johnson City, TN 37614
www.etsu.edu

University of Tennessee–Knoxville
Knoxville, TN 37996
www.utk.edu

University of Tennessee–Memphis
Health Science Center
Cytotechnology Program
930 Madison Avenue
Memphis, TN 38163
www.uthsc.edu

Texas
Lamar University
4400 MLK Blvd.
P.O. Box 10009
Beaumont, TX 77710
www.lamar.edu

University of North Texas
P.O. Box 311277
Denton, TX 76203
www.unt.edu

University of Texas
M.D. Anderson Cancer Center
1515 Holcombe Blvd.
Houston, TX 77030
www.mdanderson.org

University of Texas Health
  Science Center at Houston
7000 Fannin, Ste. 1200
Houston, TX 77030
www.uth.tmc.edu

University of Texas Health
  Science Center at San Antonio
Graduate School of Biomedical
  Sciences
Department of Pathology
UTHSCSA Mail Code 7750
7703 Floyd Curl Dr.
San Antonio, TX 78229
www.uthscsa.edu

U.S. Army Medical Department
  Center & School
U.S. Army School of
  Cytotechnology
3851 Roger Brook Dr.
Fort Sam Houston, TX 78234
www.cs.amedd.army.mil

Utah
University of Utah Health Science
  Center
ARUP Laboratories
500 Chipeta Way
Salt Lake City, UT 84108
www.path.utah.edu

Weber State University
3850 University Circle
Ogden, UT 84408
www.weber.edu

Vermont
Fletcher Allen Health Care
111 Colchester Ave.
Burlington, VT 05401
www.fahc.org

University of Vermont
Burlington, VT 05405
www.uvm.edu

Virginia
Averett College
420 W. Main St.
Danville, VA 24541
www.averett.edu

Old Dominion University
Cytotechnological Program
2118 Health Sciences BLDG
Norfolk, VA 23529
http://hs.odu.edu/medlab/
  academics/cyto/

West Virginia
Alderson-Broaddus College
College Hill Rd.
Philippi, WV 26416
www.ab.edu

Marshall University
One John Marshall Dr.
Huntington, WV 25755
www.marshall.edu

Wisconsin
Edgewood College
1000 Edgewood College Dr.
Madison, WI 53711
www.edgewood.edu

Marshfield Clinic/St. Joseph
  Hospital
Cytotechnology Program
1000 North Oak Avenue
Marshfield, WI 54449
www.marshfieldclinic.org

University of Wisconsin-
  Milwaukee
ACL Cytology School
West Allis Memorial Hospital
8901 West Lincoln Avenue
West Allis, WI 53227
www4.uwm.edu

Wisconsin State Laboratory of
  Hygiene
School of Cytotechnology
465 Henry Mall
Madison, WI 53706
www.slh.wisc.edu

Dental Assistants

Principal activity: Directly assisting dentists in treating patients

Work commitment: Part- or full-time

Preprofessional education: High school diploma

Program length: 9 to 11 months

Work prerequisites: Certificate or degree

Career opportunities: Highly favorable

Income range: $27,000 to $40,000

Scope

Dental assistants have a wide variety of responsibilities that require both technical and interpersonal skills. Their activities are critical to the success of a dental practice.

The job involves retrieving patients' records; preparing the necessary instruments for different procedures; preparing patients for treatment and making them comfortable before, during, and after their treatment; and directly assisting the dentist during various procedures (such as clearing the mouth and handling instruments). In addition, dental assistants take and develop X rays, make teeth impressions, remove sutures and surgical dressings, and perform a variety of office management tasks.

Activities

Dental assistants perform a variety of patient care, office, and laboratory duties. They seek to make patients comfortable in the dental chair and in a position suitable for the dentist to perform his or her professional duties. Assistants sterilize instruments and prepare tray setups for dental procedures. They pass instruments and materials to the dentist as he or she works and they keep patients' mouths clear and dry by suction or other means. Assistants may also instruct patients in oral health care, prepare material for making impressions, and process dental X-ray films.

Work Settings

Dental assistants work in solo or group dental practices or in specialty offices such as orthodontics (teeth straightening) or endodontics (root canal treatment). Positions are also available in hospitals, clinics, schools, and even insurance companies.

Advancement

With increased experience and superior ability, a dental assistant can be assigned greater responsibilities and secure an appointment as an office manager.

Prerequisites

A high school diploma or its equivalent is required to apply for admission to a dental assistant program.

Desirable personal attributes for a career in this field include good communication skills, an outgoing personality, good manual dexterity, and a desire to help people.

Education/Training

Dental assistants can finish their academic training in 9 to 11 months. Some schools even offer accelerated programs. Dental assistant programs are offered by colleges, community colleges, vocational-technical schools, and dental schools.

Education involves course work in the biomedical sciences and dental assisting techniques and procedures.

Certification/Registration/Licensure

Dental assistants become certified by passing an exam administered by the Dental Assisting National Board. Before taking the exam, candidates must complete an accredited dental assisting program. Those graduating from nonaccredited programs and those who have only on-the-job training may take the certifying exam only after completing two years of full-time experience as dental assistants.

Some states require registration or licensure in addition to certification. These states offer their own tests for such licensure.

Career Potential

Dental assistants' salaries are determined by their qualifications, experience, specific duties, and geographic location. Benefit packages may be provided.

The need for dental assistants has increased significantly in recent years, and long-term employment prospects are quite good. This is due to two factors. First, recent emphasis on preventive care has led to an increased need for dental services. Second, most dentists today no longer work alone, but need an assistant who is an essential collaborator in treatment.

For More Information

The professional organization for this field is the American Dental Assistants Association, 35 E. Wacker Dr., Ste. 1730, Chicago, IL 60601 (www.dentalassistant.org).

For more information, you can speak with a dental assistant at your dentist's office and possibly arrange for an observational visit. An admissions officer at a school offering a program in this field will be glad to speak with you about the school's program and admissions issues.

Dental Assistant Programs

Alabama

Bessemer State Technical College
U.S. Hwy 11 S.
P.O. Box 308
Bessemer, AL 35021
www.bessemertech.com

Fortis College-Mobile
3590 Pleasant Valley Road
Mobile, AL 36609
www.fortis.edu

Calhoun Community College
P.O. Box 2216
Decatur, AL 35609
www.calhoun.cc.al.us

H. Councill Trenholm State
 Technical College
1225 Air Base Blvd.
Montgomery, AL 36108
www.trenholmtech.cc.al.us

James Faulkner State Community
 College
1900 Hwy. 31 S.
Bay Minette, AL 36507
www.faulkner.cc.al.us

Tri-State Institute
100 London Pkwy
Birmingham, AL 35211
www.tristateinstitute.com

University of Alabama
UAB Station
Birmingham, AL 35294
www.uab.edu

Wallace State Community College
801 Main St.
P.O. Box 2000
Hanceville, AL 35077
www.wallacestate.edu

Alaska

University of Alaska
3211 Providence Dr.
Anchorage, AK 99508
www.uaa.alaska.edu

Arizona

Apollo College-Phoenix
8503 N. 27th Ave.
Phoenix, AZ 85051
www.apollocollege.com

Apollo College-Tucson
3550 N. Oracle Rd.
Tucson, AZ 85705
www.apollocollege.com

Phoenix College
1202 W. Thomas Rd.
Phoenix, AZ 85013
www.pc.maricopa.edu

Pima Community College
4905 E. Broadway Blvd.
Tucson, AZ 85709
www.pima.edu

Arkansas

Pulaski Technical College
3000 W. Scenic Dr.
North Little Rock, AR 72118
www.pulaskitech.edu

California

Bryman College
18040 Sherman Way, Ste. 400
Reseda, CA 91335
www.bryman.edu

Cerritos College
11110 Alondra Blvd.
Norwalk, CA 90650
www.cerritos.edu

Chabot College
25555 Hesperian Blvd.
Hayward, CA 94545
http://chabotweb.clpccd.cc.ca.
 us/

Chaffey Community College
5885 Haven Ave.
Rancho Cucamonga, CA 91737
www.chaffey.edu

Citrus College
1000 W. Foothill Blvd.
Glendora, CA 91741
www.citrus.cc.ca.us

City College of San Francisco
50 Phelan Ave.
San Francisco, CA 94112
www.ccsf.cc.ca.us

College of Alameda
555 Atlantic Ave.
Alameda, CA 94501
http://alameda.peralta.edu/

College of Marin
835 College Ave.
Kentfield, CA 94904
www.marin.cc.ca.us

College of San Mateo
1700 W. Hillsdale Blvd.
San Mateo, CA 94402
http://gocsm.net/

College of the Redwoods
7351 Tompkins Hill Rd.
Eureka, CA 95501
www.redwoods.edu

Concorde Career Institute
12951 Euclid St., Ste. 101
Garden Grove, CA 92840
www.concordecareers.com

Contra Costa College
2600 Mission Bell Dr.
San Pablo, CA 94806
www.contracosta.cc.ca.us

Cypress College
9200 Valley View St.
Cypress, CA 90630
www.cypresscollege.edu

Diablo Valley College
321 Golf Club Rd.
Pleasant Hill, CA 94523
www.dvc.edu

Foothill College
12345 El Monte Rd.
Los Altos Hills, CA 94022
www.foothill.fhda.edu

Modesto Junior College
435 College Ave.
Modesto, CA 95350
www.mjc.edu

Monterey Peninsula College
980 Fremont St.
Monterey, CA 93940
www.mpc.edu

North-West College
2121 W. Garvey Ave. N.
West Covina, CA 91790
www.north-westcollege.edu

Orange Coast College
2701 Fairview Rd.
Costa Mesa, CA 92626
www.orangecoastcollege.edu

Palomar College
1140 W. Mission Rd.
San Marcos, CA 92069
www.palomar.edu

Pasadena City College
1570 E. Colorado Blvd.
Pasadena, CA 91106
www.pasadena.edu

Sacramento City College
3835 Freeport Blvd.
Sacramento, CA 95822
www.scc.losrios.edu

San Joaquin Valley College–Fresno
295 E. Sierra Ave.
Fresno, CA 93710
www.sjvc.edu

San Jose City College
2100 Moorpark Ave.
San Jose, CA 95128
www.sjcc.edu

Santa Barbara City College
721 Cliff Dr.
Santa Barbara, CA 93109
www.sbcc.cc.ca.us

Santa Rosa Junior College
1501 Mendocino Ave.
Santa Rosa, CA 95401
www.santarosa.edu

United Education Institute–
  San Diego
1323 6th Ave.
San Diego, CA 92101
www.uei-edu.com

Western Career College–
  Pleasant Hill
380 Civic Dr., Ste. 300
Pleasant Hill, CA 94523
www.westerncollege.com

Colorado
Emily Griffith Opportunity School
1250 Welton St.
Denver, CO 80204
www.egos-school.com

Front Range Community College
Boulder County Campus
2190 Miller Dr.
Longmont, CO 80501
www.frontrange.edu

Pikes Peak Community College
5675 S. Academy Blvd.
Colorado Springs, CO 80906
www.ppcc.edu

Pima Medical Institute–Colorado
  Springs
370 Printers Pkwy.
Colorado Springs, CO 80910
www.pmi.edu

T.H. Pickens Technical Center
500 Airport Blvd.
Aurora, CO 80011
www.aps.k12.co.us/pickens/

Connecticut
Briarwood College
2279 Mount Vernon Rd.
Southington, CT 06489
www.briarwood.edu

Tunxis Community–Technical
  College
271 Scott Swamp Rd.
Farmington, CT 06032
http://tunxis.commnet.edu/

District of Columbia
Margaret Murray Washington
  Career High School
Washington, DC 20001
www.k12.dc.us/schools/
  mmwashington/

Florida
Brevard Community College
1519 Clearlake Rd.
Cocoa, FL 32922
www.brevard.cc.fl.us

Broward Community College
111 E. Las Olas Blvd.
Fort Lauderdale, FL 33301
www.broward.edu

Charlotte Technical Center
18300 Toledo Blade Blvd.
Port Charlotte, FL 33948
http://charlottetechcenter.ccps.
  k12.fl.us/

Concorde Career Institute
7960 Arlington Expressway
Jacksonville, FL 32211
www.concordecareers.com

Daytona State College
1200 W. International Speedway
  Blvd.
Daytona Beach, FL 32114
www.dbcc.cc.fl.us

Florida State College
501 W. State St.
Jacksonville, FL 32202
www.fscj.edu

Fortis Institute
4081 East Olive Road
Pensacola, FL 32514
www.fortis.edu

Gulf Coast Community College
5230 W. Hwy. 98
Panama City, FL 32401
www.gulfcoast.edu

Indian River State College
3209 Virginia Ave.
Ft. Pierce, FL 34981
www.irsc.edu

Lindsey Hopkins Technical
  Educational Center
750 NW 20th St.
Miami, FL 33127
http://lindsey.dadeschools.net/

Manatee Technical Institute
5603 34th St. W.
Bradenton, FL 34210
www.manatee.k12.fl.us

Palm Beach State College
4200 Congress Ave.
Lake Worth, FL 33461
www.palmbeachstate.edu

Pensacola Junior College
1000 College Blvd.
Pensacola, FL 32504
www.pjc.edu

Pinellas Technical Education
  Center
901 34th St. S.
St. Petersburg, FL 33711
www.myptec.org

Robert Morgan Vocational-
Technical Institute
18180 SW 122nd Ave.
Miami, FL 33177
http://rmec.dadeschools.net/

Sanford-Brown Institute
5701 E Hillsboro in Tampa
Tampa, FL 33610
www.sbtampa.com

Santa Fe Community College
3000 NW 83rd St., P237
Gainesville, FL 32606
ww.sffccnm.edu

Southern College
111 Hollingsworth Dr.
Lakeland, FL 33801
www.flsouthern.edu

Ultimate Medical Academy
9309 N Florida Avenue
Tampa, FL 33612
www.ultimatemedical.edu

United Education Institute
3563 Philips Hwy., Building C
Jacksonville, FL 32207
www.ueicareers.com

Georgia
Albany Technical College
1704 S. Slappey Blvd.
Albany, GA 31701
www.albanytech.edu

Augusta Technical College
3200 Augusta Tech Dr.
Augusta, GA 30906
www.augustatech.edu

Gwinnett Technical College
5150 Sugarloaf Pkwy.
Lawrenceville, GA 30043
www.gwinnetttech.edu

Lanier Technical Institute
2990 Landrum Education Dr.
Oakwood, GA 30566
www.laniertech.edu

Medix School
2108 Cobb Pkwy.
Smyrna, GA 30080
www.medixschool.edu

Savannah Technical College
5717 White Bluff Rd.
Savannah, GA 31405
www.savannahtech.edu

United Education Institute
1564 Southlake Parkway
Morrow, GA 30260-3021
www.ueicareers.com

Idaho
American Institute of Health
Technology
1200 N. Liberty
Boise, ID 83704
www.aiht.com

Boise State University
1910 University Dr.
Boise, ID 83725
www.boisestate.edu

Illinois
Illinois Central College
1 College Dr.
East Peoria, IL 61635
www.icc.edu

Illinois Valley Community College
815 N. Orlando Smith Ave.
Oglesby, IL 61348
www.ivcc.edu

John A. Logan College
700 Logan College Rd.
Carterville, IL 62918
www.jal.cc.il.us

Lake Land College
5001 Lake Land Blvd.
Mattoon, IL 61938
www.lakelandcollege.com

Lewis and Clark Community
College
5800 Godfrey Rd.
Godfrey, IL 62035
www.lc.cc.il.us

Morton College
3801 S. Central Ave.
Cicero, IL 60804
www.morton.edu

Parkland College
2400 W. Bradley
Champaign, IL 61821
www.parkland.edu

Indiana
Indiana University
School of Dentistry
1121 W. Michigan St.
Indianapolis, IN 46202
www.iusd.iupui.edu

Indiana University Northwest
3400 Broadway
Gary, IN 46408
www.iun.edu

Indiana University–Purdue
University Fort Wayne
2101 E. Coliseum Blvd.
Fort Wayne, IN 46805
www.ipfw.edu

Indiana University–South Bend
1700 Mishawaka Ave.
P.O. Box 7111
South Bend, IN 46634
www.iusb.edu

Ivy Tech State College
1170 S. Creasy Ln.
Lafayette, IN 47905
www.ivytech.edu/lafayette/

Professional Careers Institute
7302 Woodland Dr.
Indianapolis, IN 46278
www.pcicareers.com

University of Southern Indiana
8600 University Blvd.
Evansville, IN 47712
www.usi.edu

Iowa
Des Moines Area Community
College
2006 S. Ankeny Blvd.
Ankeny, IA 50021
www.dmacc.edu

Hawkeye Community College
1501 E. Orange
Waterloo, IA 50701
www.hawkeye.cc.ia.us

Iowa Western Community College
2700 College Rd.
Council Bluffs, IA 51503
www.iwcc.cc.ia.us

Kirkwood Community College
6301 Kirkwood Blvd. SW
Cedar Rapids, IA 52404
www.kirkwood.edu

Marshalltown Community College
3700 S. Center St.
Marshalltown, IA 50158
www.iavalley.cc.ia.us/mcc/

Northeast Iowa Community
  College
10250 Sundown Rd.
Peosta, IA 52068
www.nicc.edu

Western Iowa Tech Community
  College
4647 Stone Ave.
Sioux City, IA 51106
www.witcc.edu

Kansas
Flint Hills Technical School
3301 W. 18th Ave.
Emporia, KS 66801
www.fhtc.edu

Kentucky
Kentucky Community and
  Technical College
300 N. Main St
Versailles, KY 40383
www.kctcs.edu

Louisiana
Remington College–New Orleans
321 Veterans Memorial Blvd.
Metairie, LA 70005
www.remingtoncollege.edu

Maine
University of Maine
5713 Chadbourne Hall
Orono, ME 04469
www.umaine.edu

Maryland
Allegany College
12401 Willowbrook Rd. SE
Cumberland, MD 21502
www.ac.cc.md.us

Medix School
700 York Rd.
Towson, MD 21204
www.medixschool.com

Massachusetts
C.H. McCann Technical School
70 Hodges Cross Rd.
North Adams, MA 01247
www.mccanntech.org

Massasoit Community College
900 Randolph St.
Canton, MA 02021
www.massasoit.mass.edu

Middlesex Community College
591 Springs Rd.
Bedford, MA 01730
www.middlesex.mass.edu

Mount Ida College
777 Dedham St.
Newton, MA 02459
www.mountida.edu

Northern Essex Community
  College
100 Elliott St.
Haverhill, MA 01830
www.necc.mass.edu

Springfield Technical Community
  College
One Armory Square
Springfield, MA 01102
www.stcc.edu

Worcester Polytechnic Institute
100 Institute Rd.
Worcester, MA 01609
www.wpi.edu

Michigan
Delta College
1961 Delta Rd.
University Center, MI 48710
www.delta.edu

Grand Rapids Community College
143 Bostwick Ave. NE
Grand Rapids, MI 49503
www.grcc.cc.mi.us

Kellogg Community College
450 North Ave.
Battle Creek, MI 49017
www.kellogg.cc.mi.us

Lake Michigan College
2755 E. Napier Ave.
Benton Harbor, MI 49022
www.lakemichigancollege.edu

Lansing Community College
P.O. Box 40010
Lansing, MI 48901
www.lansing.cc.mi.us

Mott Community College
1401 E. Court St.
Flint, MI 48053
www.mcc.edu

Northwestern Michigan College
1701 E. Front St.
Traverse City, MI 49686
www.nmc.edu

Olympia Career Training Institute
5349 W. Main St.
Kalamazoo, MI 49009
www.olympia-institute.com

Washtenaw Community College
4800 E. Huron River Dr.
P.O. Box D-1
Ann Arbor, MI 48106
www.wccnet.edu

Wayne County Community College
801 W. Fort St.
Detroit, MI 48226
www.wcccd.edu

Minnesota
Central Lakes College
501 W. College Dr.
Brainerd, MN 56401
www.clcmn.edu

Hennepin Technical College
9000 Brooklyn Blvd.
Brooklyn Park, MN 55445
www.hennepintech.edu

Herzing College–Minneapolis
5700 W. Broadway
Minneapolis, MN 55428
www.herzing.edu/minneapolis/

Hibbing Community College
1515 E. 25th St.
Hibbing, MN 55746
www.hcc.mnscu.edu

Minneapolis Community &
  Technical College
1501 Hennepin Ave.
Minneapolis, MN 55403
www.minneapolis.edu

Normandale Community College
9700 France Ave. S.
Bloomington, MN 55431
www.normandale.edu

Northeast Metro Career &
 Technical Center
3300 Century Ave. N.
White Bear Lake, MN 55110

Northwest Technical College
905 Grant Ave. SE
Bemidji, MN 56601
www.ntcmn.edu

Rochester Community & Technical
 College
851 30th Ave. SE
Rochester, MN 55904
www.rctc.edu

St. Cloud Technical College
1540 Northway Dr.
St. Cloud, MN 56303
www.sctc.edu

Mississippi
Hinds Community College
3925 Sunset Dr.
Jackson, MS 39213
www.hindscc.edu

Pearl River Community College
101 Hwy. 11 N.
Poplarville, MS 39470
www.prcc.edu

Missouri
East Central College
1964 Prairie Dell Rd.
Union, MO 63084
www.eastcentral.edu

Mineral Area College
5270 Flat River Rd.
P.O. Box 1000
Park Hills, MO 63601
www.mineralarea.edu

Missouri College
1405 South Hanley Road
Brentwood, MO 63144
www.missouricollege.com/dental/
 assistant

Nichols Career Center
605 Union St.
Jefferson City, MO 65101
www.nicholscareercenter.org

Montana
MSU–Great Falls College of
 Technology
2100 16th Ave. S.
Great Falls, MT 59405
www.msugf.edu

Salish Kootenai College
52000 Hwy. 93, P.O. Box 70
Pablo, MT 59855
www.skc.edu

Nebraska
Central Community College
E. Hwy. 6, P.O. Box 1024
Hastings, NE 68902
www.cccneb.edu

Kaplan University-Omaha
5425 North 103rd Street
Omaha, NE 68134
www.omaha.kaplanuniversity.edu

Metropolitan Community College
P.O. Box 3777
Omaha, NE 68103
www.mccneb.edu

Mid-Plains Community College
1101 Halligan Dr.
North Platte, NE 69101
www.mpcc.edu

Omaha College of Health Careers
225 N. 80th St.
Omaha, NE 68114

Southeast Community College
8800 O St.
Lincoln, NE 68520
www.southeast.edu

Nevada
Truckee Meadows Community
 College
7000 Dandini Blvd.
Reno, NV 89512
www.tmcc.edu

New Hampshire
New Hampshire Technical
 Institute
31 College Dr.
Concord, NH 03301
www.nhti.edu

New Jersey
Atlantic Cape Community College
5100 Black Horse Pike
Mays Landing, NJ 08330
www.atlantic.edu

Berdan Institute
265 Route 46 W.
Totowa, NJ 07512
www.berdaninstitute.edu

Camden County College
College Dr.
P.O. Box 200
Blackwood, NJ 08012
www.camdencc.edu

Technical Institute of Camden
 County
343 Berlin Cross Keys Rd.
Sicklerville, NJ 08081
www.ccts.tec.nj.us/ti/

University of Medicine &
 Dentistry of New Jersey
School of Health Related
 Professions
65 Bergen St.
Newark, NJ 07107
http://shrp.umdnj.edu/

New Mexico
Apollo College–Albuquerque
5301 Central Ave. NE, Ste. 101
Albuquerque, NM 87108
www.apollocollege.com

New York
New York University
College of Dentistry
345 E. 24th St.
New York, NY 10010
www.nyu.edu

University at Buffalo
The State University of New York
17 Capen Hall
Buffalo, NY 14260
www.buffalo.edu

North Carolina
Alamance Community College
1247 Jimmie Kerr Rd.
Graham, NC 27253
www.alamance.cc.edu

Asheville-Buncombe Technical
Community College
340 Victoria Rd.
Asheville, NC 28801
www.abtech.edu

Cape Fear Community College
411 N. Front St.
Wilmington, NC 28401
http://cfcc.edu/

Central Piedmont Community
College
P.O. Box 35009
Charlotte, NC 28235
www.cpcc.edu

Fayetteville Technical Community
College
2201 Hull Rd.
P.O. Box 35236
Fayetteville, NC 28303
www.faytech.edu

Guilford Technical Community
College
P.O. Box 309
Jamestown, NC 27282
www.gtcc.edu

Rowan-Cabarrus Community
College
1333 Jake Alexander Blvd. W.
Salisbury, NC 28147
www.rowancabarrus.edu

University of North Carolina
One University Heights
Asheville, NC 28804
www.unca.edu

University of North Carolina
School of Dentistry
Manning Dr. and Columbia St.
CB #7450
Chapel Hill, NC 27599
www.dent.unc.edu

Wake Technical Community
College
9101 Fayetteville Rd.
Raleigh, NC 27603
www.waketech.edu

Wayne Community College
3000 Wayne Memorial Dr.
Goldsboro, NC 27534
www.wayne.cc.edu

Wilkes Community College
1328 Collegiate Dr.
P.O. Box 120
Wilkesboro, NC 28697
www.wilkescc.edu

North Dakota
Interstate Business College
520 E. Main Ave.
Bismarck, ND 58501

North Dakota State College of
Science
Allied Dental Education
Department
800 6th St. N.
Wahpeton, ND 58076
www.ndscs.edu

Ohio
Cuyahoga Community College
2900 Community College Ave.
Cleveland, OH 44115
www.tri-c.edu

Jefferson Community College
4000 Sunset Blvd.
Steubenville, OH 43952
www.jcc.edu

Ohio Institute of Health Careers
631 Griswold Rd.
Elyria, OH 44035
www.ohiobusinesscollege.edu

Remington College–Cleveland
West
26350 Brookpark Rd.
North Olmstead, OH 44070
www.remingtoncollege.edu

Oklahoma
Rose State College
6420 SE 15th St.
Midwest City, OK 73110
www.rose.edu

Oregon
Apollo College–Portland
2004 Lloyd Center, 3rd Floor
Portland, OR 97232
www.apollocollege.com

Blue Mountain Community College
2411 NW Carden Ave.
Pendleton, OR 97818
www.bluecc.edu

Chemeketa Community College
4000 Lancaster Dr. NE
P.O. Box 14007
Salem, OR 97309
www.chemeketa.edu

Lane Community College
4000 E. 30th Ave.
Eugene, OR 97405
http://lanecc.edu/

Linn-Benton Community College
6500 Pacific Blvd. SW
Albany, OR 97321
www.linnbenton.edu

Portland Community Center
12000 SW 49th Ave.
P.O. Box 19000
Portland, OR 97280
www.pcc.edu

Pennsylvania
Community College of
Philadelphia
1700 Spring Garden St.
Philadelphia, PA 19130
www.ccp.edu

Harcum College
750 Montgomery Ave.
Bryn Mawr, PA 19010
www.harcum.edu

Harrisburg Area Community
College
1 HACC Dr.
Harrisburg, PA 17110
www.hacc.edu

Luzerne County Community
College
1333 S. Prospect St.
Nanticoke, PA 18634
www.luzerne.edu

Manor Junior College
700 Fox Chase Rd.
Jenkintown, PA 19046
http://manor.edu/

Median School of Allied Health
Careers
125 7th St.
Pittsburgh, PA 15222
www.medianschool.edu

Sanford-Brown Institute
E 777 Penn Center Blvd.
Pittsburgh, PA 15235
www.sandfordbrown.edu

Rhode Island
Community College of Rhode
  Island
Flanagan Campus
1762 Louisquisset Pike
Lincoln, RI 02865
www.ccri.edu

South Carolina
Aiken Technical College
2276 Jefferson Davis Hwy.
P.O. Box 400
Graniteville, SC 29829
www.aik.tec.sc.us

Florence-Darlington Technical
  College
2715 W. Lucas St.
P.O. Box 100548
Florence, SC 29501
www.fdtc.edu

Greenville Technical College
506 S. Pleasantburg Dr.
P.O. Box 5616
Greenville, SC 29607
www.gvltec.edu

Midlands Technical College
P.O. Box 2408
Columbia, SC 29202
www.midlandstech.edu

Spartanburg Technical College
Business I-85 and New Cut Rd.
P.O. Box 4386
Spartanburg, SC 29305
www.stcsc.edu

York Technical College
452 S. Anderson Rd.
Rock Hill, SC 29730
www.yorktech.com

South Dakota
Lake Area Technical Institute
230 11th St. NE
P.O. Box 730
Watertown, SD 57201
www.lakeareatech.edu

University of South Dakota
414 E. Clark St.
Vermillion, SD 57069
www.usd.edu

Tennessee
Chattanooga State Technical
  Community College
4501 Amnicola Hwy.
Chattanooga, TN 37406
www.chattanoogastate.edu

Concorde Career College
5100 Poplar Ave., Ste. 132
Memphis, TN 38137
www.concorde.edu

East Tennessee State University
P.O. Box 70267
Johnson City, TN 37614
www.etsu.edu

Remington College
441 Donelson Pike
Nashville, TN 37214
www.remingtoncollege.edu

Roane State Community College
701 Briarcliff Ave.
Oak Ridge, TN 37830
www.roanestate.edu

Tennessee Technology Center at
  Knoxville
1100 Liberty St.
Knoxville, TN 37919
www.ttcknoxville.edu

Tennessee Technology Center at
  Memphis
550 Alabama
Memphis, TN 38105
www.ttcmemphis.edu

Volunteer State Community
  College
1480 Nashville Pike
Gallatin, TN 37066
www.volstate.edu

Texas
Del Mar College
101 Baldwin Blvd.
Corpus Christi, TX 78404
www.delmar.edu

El Paso Community College
P.O. Box 20500
El Paso, TX 79998
www.epcc.edu

Grayson County College
6101 Grayson Dr.
Denison, TX 75020
www.grayson.edu

Houston Community College
  Southeast
3100 Shenandoah
Houston, TX 77021
www.hccs.edu

San Antonio College
1300 San Pedro Ave.
San Antonio, TX 78212
www.alamo.edu/sac/

School of Health Care Sciences
Dental Training Squadron
Sheppard AFB, TX 76311
www.sheppard.af.mil

Tarrant County College
Northeast Campus
828 Harwood Rd.
Hurst, TX 76054
www.tccd.edu

Texas State Technical College–
  Waco
3820 Campus Dr.
Waco, TX 76705
www.waco.tstc.edu

Utah
Provo College
1450 W. 820 N.
Provo, UT 84601
www.provocollege.edu

Virginia
J. Sargeant Reynolds Community
  College
P.O. Box 85622
Richmond, VA 23285
www.jsr.cc.va.us

Kee Business College–Chesapeake
825 Greenbrier Circle, #100
Chesapeake, VA 23320
www.keecollege.com

Old Dominion University
Gene W. Hirschfeld School of
  Dental Hygiene
Hampton Blvd.
Norfolk, VA 23529
www.odu.edu

Wytheville Community College
1000 E. Main St.
Wytheville, VA 24382
www.wcc.vccs.edu

Washington
Apollo College–Spokane
10102 E. Knox, Ste. 200
Spokane, WA 99206
www.apollocollege.com

Bates Technical College
1101 S. Yakima Ave.
Tacoma, WA 98405
www.bates.ctc.edu

Bellingham Technical College
3028 Lindbergh Ave.
Bellingham, WA 98225
www.beltc.ctc.edu

Bryman College–Lynwood
19020 33rd Ave. W., Ste. 250
Lynwood, WA 98036
www.bryman.edu

Clover Park Technical College
4500 Steilacoom Blvd. SW
Lakewood, WA 98499
www.cptc.edu

Highline Community College
2400 S. 240th St.
Des Moines, WA 98198
www.highline.edu

Lake Washington Technical
  College
11605 132nd Ave. NE
Kirkland, WA 98034
www.lwtc.ctc.edu

Renton Technical College
3000 NE 4th St.
Renton, WA 98056
www.rtc.edu

South Puget Sound Community
  College
2011 Mottman Rd. SW
Olympia, WA 98512
www.spscc.ctc.edu

Spokane Community College
1810 N. Greene St.
Spokane, WA 99217
www.scc.spokane.edu

Wisconsin
Fox Valley Technical College
1825 N. Bluemond Dr.
P.O. Box 2277
Appleton, WI 54912
www.fvtc.edu

Gateway Technical College
3520 30th Ave.
Kenosha, WI 53144
www.gtc.edu

Lakeshore Technical College
1290 North Ave.
Cleveland, WI 53015
www.gotoltc.com

Madison Area Technical College
3550 Anderson St.
Madison, WI 53704
http://matcmadison.edu/matc/

Northeast Wisconsin Technical
  College
2740 W. Mason St.
Green Bay, WI 54307
www.nwtc.edu

Western Wisconsin Technical
  College
304 Sixth St. N.
La Crosse, WI 54601
www.westerntc.edu

Wyoming
Sheridan College
3059 Coffeen Ave., P.O. Box 1500
Sheridan, WY 82801
www.sheridan.edu

Dental Laboratory Technicians

Principal activity: Preparing teeth replacement appliances such as crowns and bridges

Work commitment: Usually full-time

Preprofessional education: High school diploma

Program length: 2 years

Work prerequisites: Degree or certification

Career opportunities: Favorable

Income range: $26,000 to $45,000

Scope

Dental technicians serve patients indirectly and dentists directly by providing them with prostheses—replacement units for missing natural teeth. Being a dental laboratory technician means holding a position that requires creative skill, sound judgment, and manual dexterity.

Activities

Dental technicians receive impressions (molds) and written, detailed instructions from dentists on the prostheses they need to prepare. They design these prostheses in the form of full dentures for those lacking all their teeth; removable partial dentures or fixed bridges for those having one or several missing teeth; crowns, which are caps for teeth that need to be restored to their original shape and size; and orthodontics to help straighten teeth. The prostheses are prepared using a variety of materials, including precious metals and alloys.

Work Settings

Dental technicians work for commercial dental labs, which may employ a few to over a hundred individuals. On average, such labs employ five full-time technicians. Laboratories generally prepare the full range of prostheses, but some specialize in one kind.

Additional opportunities exist for work in dental schools and training institutions, hospitals, and companies that manufacture prosthetic materials.

Advancement

With some experience and management skills, a technician can attain a supervisory position. In addition, technicians who have business acumen can start their own laboratories or become salespeople—marketing instruments, equipment, and materials used in the profession.

Prerequisites

You need a high school diploma or its equivalent to apply to an accredited dental technology program. Contact the specific school to learn about its individual requirements.

Desirable personal attributes for work in this field include superior manual dexterity, originality, and thoroughness.

Education/Training

On-the-job training is the route taken by many prospective dental technicians. It usually takes several years to become highly skilled. Alternatively, two-year dental technology programs are offered by community colleges, technical-vocational schools, and even dental schools. Classroom and laboratory work is provided in subjects such as oral anatomy, dental materials science, and fabrication procedures. After you complete the program, you receive an associate degree.

Certification/Registration/Licensure

Certification is optional. Those with degrees in dental laboratory technology from an accredited program can become certified by passing an examination administered by the National Board for Certification in Dental Laboratory Technology. This exam evaluates both technical skills and knowledge. To be eligible for the exam, degree holders need two years of work experience, and nondegreed individuals with on-the-job training need five years.

Career Potential

Dental technicians may receive benefit packages and are paid on an hourly basis. Trainees receive near the minimum scale. Salary increases come with experience.

Although there has been a dramatic decline in the need for dentures and an increase in endodontic (root canal) therapy, which prolongs the usefulness of teeth, a strong demand for crowns and partials remains. Also, because trainee salaries are low, employers often have problems filling positions.

For More Information

For more information, contact the American Dental Association, 211 E. Chicago Ave., Chicago, IL 60611 (www.ada.org), or the National Association of Dental Laboratories, 1530 Metropolitan Blvd., Tallahassee, FL 32308 (www.nadl.org).

A useful means of gaining valuable insight into this career is visiting one or more dental laboratories and observing their technicians at work. Your observations can give you a better understanding of the issues involved and can facilitate your career decisions.

Dental Laboratory Technician Programs

Alabama
ITT Technical Institute
6270 Park South Drive
Bessemer, AL 35022
www.itt-tech.edu

H. Councill Trenholm State
Technical College
1225 Air Base Blvd.
Montgomery, AL 36108
www.trenholmtech.cc.al.us

Arizona
ITT Technical Institute
5005 S. Wendler Drive
Tempe, AZ 85282
www.itt-tech.edu

Pima Community College
4905 E. Broadway Blvd.
Tucson, AZ 85709
www.pima.edu

California
California Vocational College
3951 Balboa Street
San Francisco, CA 94121
www.cvc-dentaltech.com

City College of San Francisco
50 Phelan Ave.
San Francisco, CA 94112
www.ccsf.cc.ca.us

Diablo Valley College
321 Golf Club Rd.
Pleasant Hill, CA 94523
www.dvc.edu

Keating Dental Lab
15881 Hale Avenue
Irvine, CA 92606
www.keatingdentalarts.com

Los Angeles City College
855 N. Vermont Ave.
Los Angeles, CA 90029
www.lacitycollege.edu

Merced College
3600 M St.
Merced, CA 95348
www.mccd.edu

Newton International College
8762 Garden Grove Blvd.
Garden Grove, CA 92844
www.newtoninco.com

Pasadena City College
1570 E. Colorado Blvd.
Pasadena, CA 91106
www.pasadena.edu

Riverside City College
Moreno Valley Campus
16130 Lasselle Street
Moreno Valley, CA 92551
www.rcc.edu

Simi Valley Adult School
3192 Los Angeles Avenue
Simi Valley, CA 93065
www.simi.tec.ca.us

Colorado
ITT Technical Institute
500 E 84th Avenue
Thornton, CO. 80229
www.itt-tech.edu

Florida
Florida Southern College
111 Lake Hollingsworth Dr.
Lakeland, FL 33801
www.flsouthern.edu

Indian River State College
3209 Virginia Ave.
Fort Pierce, FL 34981
www.irsc.edu

Lindsey Hopkins Technical
Educational Center
750 NW 20th St.
Miami, FL 33127
http://lindsey.dadeschools.net/

McFatter Technical Center
6500 Nova Dr.
Davie, FL 33317
www.mcfattertech.com

Pensacola Junior College
1000 College Blvd.
Pensacola, FL 32504
www.pjc.edu

Georgia
Atlanta Technical College
1560 Metropolitan Pkwy. SW
Atlanta, GA 30310
www.atlantatech.org

Augusta Technical College
3200 Augusta Tech Dr.
Augusta, GA 30906
www.augustatech.edu

Gwinnett Technical College
5150 Sugarloaf Pkwy.
Lawrenceville, GA 30043
www.gwinnetttech.edu

Idaho
Idaho State University
921 S. 8th Ave.
Pocatello, ID 83209
www.isu.edu

Illinois
Southern Illinois University at
  Carbondale
Carbondale, IL 62901
www.siuc.edu

Triton College
2000 Fifth Ave.
River Grove, IL 60171
www.triton.edu

Indiana
Indiana University–Purdue
  University Fort Wayne
2101 E. Coliseum Blvd.
Fort Wayne, IN 46805
www.ipfw.edu

Iowa
Kirkwood Community College
6301 Kirkwood Blvd. SW
Cedar Rapids, IA 52404
www.kirkwood.edu

Kentucky
Lexington Community College
Cooper Dr. and Oswald Blvd.
Lexington, KY 40506
www.bluegrass.kctcs.edu/LCC/

Louisiana
Louisiana State University
1100 Florida Ave.
New Orleans, LA 70119
www.lsuhsc.edu

Maryland
Lewis Dental Laboratory, Inc.
2104 Trimble Road P O Box 888
Edgewood, MD 21040
www.lewisdental.com

Massachusetts
Middlesex Community College
33 Kearney Square
Lowell, MA 01852
www.middlesex.mass.edu

Michigan
Ferris State University
901 S. State St.
Big Rapids, MI 49307
www.ferris.edu

Minnesota
Northeast Metro Career &
  Technical Center
3300 Century Ave. N.
White Bear Lake, MN 55110
www.northeastmetrotech.com

Missouri
St. Louis Community College–
  Meramec
300 S. Broadway
St. Louis, MO 63102
www.stlcc.edu/mc/

Nebraska
Central Community College
East Hwy. 6
P.O. Box 1024
Hastings, NE 68902
www.cccneb.edu

New Jersey
Union County College
1033 Springfield Ave.
Cranford, NJ 07016
www.ucc.edu

New York
Erie Community College–South
  Campus
4041 Southwestern Blvd.
Orchard Park, NY 14127
www.ecc.edu

New York City Technical College
300 Jay St.
Brooklyn, NY 11201
www.citytech.cuny.edu

North Carolina
Durham Technical Community
  College
1637 Lawson St.
Durham, NC 27703
www.durhamtech.edu

Ohio
Columbus State Community
  College
550 E. Spring St.
Columbus, OH 43215
www.cscc.edu

Cuyahoga Community College
2900 Community College Ave.
Cleveland, OH 44115
www.tri-c.edu

Oregon
Portland Community College
12000 SW 49th Ave.
P.O. Box 19000
Portland, OR 97280
www.pcc.edu

Tennessee
Chattanooga State Technical
  Community College
4501 Amnicola Hwy.
Chattanooga, TN 37406
www.chattanoogastate.edu

East Tennessee State University
Box 70267
Johnson City, TN 37614
www.etsu.edu

Texas
School of Health Care Sciences
Dental Training Squadron
Sheppard AFB, TX 76311
www.sheppard.af.mil

University of Texas
Health Science Center at San
  Antonio
7703 Floyd Curl Dr.
San Antonio, TX 78229
www.uthscsa.edu

Washington
Bates Technical College
1101 S. Yakima Ave.
Tacoma, WA 98405
www.bates.ctc.edu

Wisconsin
Milwaukee Area Technical College
700 W. State St.
Milwaukee, WI 53233
www.milwaukee.tec.wi.us

Diagnostic Medical Sonographers

Principal activity: Taking ultrasound images of body organs for diagnostic purposes

Work commitment: Full-time

Preprofessional education: High school diploma

Program length: 1 to 4 years

Work prerequisites: Diploma or degree in ultrasound

Career opportunities: Favorable

Income range: $47,000 to $74,000

Scope

Using sound waves, ultrasound can provide doctors with critical visual information about the size, contour, and in some cases even the actions of various organs. Physicians use ultrasound to study the brain, heart, blood vessels, eyes, and abdominal and pelvic organs. It is also useful in detecting sites of fluid accumulation and tumors. It is a noninvasive procedure that is attractive because it provides clinical data without patient discomfort or risk.

Ultrasound is especially useful in obstetric practices, providing physicians with a view of the developing fetus and allowing them to assess its development and position. This is important when doctors are considering such procedures as amniocentesis or delivery by C-section. This procedure also establishes or confirms the presence of multiple fetuses.

Activities

Before beginning, the sonographer explains the procedure to the patient. He or she then smears the patient's skin surface to be scanned with a gel to ensure that the transducer is in direct contact with the skin without an intervening layer of air. After positioning the patient, the sonographer views the screen as the scanning proceeds. Evaluating the image's quality is critical to securing the essential information for the physician. This is achieved by recording the visual data. Sonographers also file the sonography results, evaluate new equipment, and maintain a reference library on ultrasound information. Working in this field requires special education and training.

Work Settings

Sonographers are employed by hospitals, clinics, obstetricians' offices, radiologists' offices, and research facilities.

Advancement

With experience and education, a sonographer can move into a supervisory position. Sonographers may specialize, using ultrasound in such areas as neurosonology (for brain examination), obstetrical/gynecological sonography (examination of the uterus), ophthalmic sonography (examination of the eye), or Doppler sonography (examination of near-surface arteries, such as carotids).

Prerequisites

The basic requirement for entering a training program is a high school diploma or its equivalent. Some programs require candidates to have an allied health science background.

Desirable personal attributes include attention to detail, patience, good rapport with patients and health professionals, good physical health, and excellent vision.

Education/Training

You can follow two routes to become a diagnostic medical sonographer: informal and formal. The first route, on-the-job training, is usually followed by people already working in health care, such as registered nurses or radiological and medical technologists. Their prior educational backgrounds qualify them for many in-hospital training programs. Securing a degree from an accredited program is preferable.

You can obtain formal training at various sites, depending on the program's length, the diploma or degree granted, and your background.

Three different kinds of formal training programs lead to different kinds of degrees, depending on their length and scope:

- Diploma programs typically last one year and are based in a hospital. These programs are best for those with a background in the health professions.
- Associate degree programs typically last two years and are offered by community colleges.
- Bachelor's degree programs last four years and are offered by colleges and universities.

Because the number of openings in most of these programs is limited, competition to secure admission is quite competitive.

The educational program consists of classroom work and supervised clinical experience. Topics include human anatomy and physiology, histology, major relevant clinical diseases, pathological anatomy, physics, principles of ultrasound, imaging and display techniques, instrumentation maintenance, ultrasound characteristics, image evaluation, patient psychology, and medical ethics.

Certification/Registration/Licensure

Candidates become certified as registered diagnostic medical sonographers by taking a two-day comprehensive written examination. There are five ways to become eligible for the exam. You can find more information on these different ways by contacting the Society of Diagnostic Medical Sonographers, whose address is listed in the section "For More Information."

Career Potential

Currently the demand for sonographers is excellent in both the short and long term. This high demand has resulted from the expansion of health care and the aging population.

As more institutions introduce sonography as a clinical diagnostic tool and significant advances are made in this field, its potential will be enhanced, and it will become an even more challenging and rewarding field.

For More Information

The professional organization for this field is the Society of Diagnostic Medical Sonographers, 2745 Dallas Pkwy., Plano, TX 75093 (www.sdms.org). The agency handling certification is the American Registry of Diagnostic Medical Sonographers, 51 Monroe St., Plaza East One, Rockville, MD 20850 (www.ardms.org).

Diagnostic Medical Sonography Programs

California
Loma Linda University
School of Allied Health
  Professionals
Loma Linda, CA 92350
www.llu.edu

Maric College
20700 Avalon Blvd.
Ste. 210
Carson, CA 90746
www.mariccollege.com

Florida
Barry University
School of Natural & Health
  Sciences
11300 NE 2nd Ave.
Miami Shores, FL 33161
www.barry.edu

Broward College
3501 SW Davie Rd.
Davie, FL 33314
www.broward.edu

Hillsborough Community College
Dale Mabry Campus
P.O. Box 30030
Tampa, FL 33630
www.hccfl.us

University of Miami–Jackson
Memorial Medical Center
1611 NW 12th Ave.
Miami, FL 33136
www.miami.edu

Georgia
Medical College of Georgia
1120 15th St.
Augusta, GA 30912
www.mcg.edu

Illinois
Rush University
College of Health Sciences
600 S. Paulina St., Ste. 440
Chicago, IL 60612
www.rushu.rush.edu

Triton College
2000 Fifth Ave.
River Grove, IL 60171
www.triton.edu

Wilbur Wright College
4300 N. Narragansett
Chicago, IL 60634
http://wright.ccc.edu/

Iowa
University of Iowa Hospitals and
  Clinics
200 Hawkins Dr.
Iowa City, IA 52242
www.uiowa.edu

Kansas
University of Kansas
School of Allied Health
3901 Rainbow Blvd.
Kansas City, KS 66160
http://alliedhealth.kumc.edu/

Kentucky
West Kennedy State Vocational
  Technical
4810 Alben Barkley Dr.
P.O. Box 7380
Paducah, KY 42002
www.westkentucky.kctcs.edu

Louisiana
Ochsner Clinic Foundation
Academic Division
1514 Jefferson Hwy.
New Orleans, LA 70121
www.ochsner.org/education/

Maryland
UMBC
Division of Professional Education
  and Training
1000 Hilltop Circle
Baltimore, MD 21250
www.continuinged.umbc.edu

Massachusetts
Middlesex Community College
591 Springs Rd.
Bedford, MA 01730
www.middlesex.mass.edu

Michigan
Henry Ford Health System
1 Ford Place
Detroit, MI 48202
www.henryfordhealth.org

Jackson Community College
2111 Emmons Rd.
Jackson, MI 49201
www.jccmi.edu

Marygrove College
8425 W. McNichols Rd.
Detroit, MI 48221
www.marygrove.edu

Oakland Community College
22322 Rutland Dr.
Southfield, MI 48075
www.oaklandcc.edu

Minnesota
Argosy University/Twin Cities
College of Health Sciences
1515 Central Pkwy.
Eagan, MN 55121
www.argosyu.edu

Mayo Clinic College of Medicine
Mayo School of Health Sciences
200 First St. SW
Rochester, MN 55905
www.mayo.edu/mshs/

Missouri
Coxhealth School of
  Medical Sonography
3801 S National Avenue
Springfield, MO 65807
www.coxhealth.com

St. Louis Community College at
  Forest Park
5600 Oakland Ave.
St. Louis, MO 63110
www.stlcc.edu/fp/

Nebraska
Nebraska Methodist College
8501 W. Dodge Rd.
Omaha, NE 68114
www.methodistcollege.edu

University of Nebraska Medical
  Center
School of Allied Health
  Professions
42nd and Emile
Omaha, NE 68198
www.unmc.edu

New Jersey
Bergen Community College
400 Paramus Rd.
Paramus, NJ 07652
www.bergen.cc.nj.us

University of Medicine &
  Dentistry of New Jersey
School of Health Related
  Professions
65 Bergen St.
Newark, NJ 07107
www.umdnj.edu

New York
New York University Medical
  Center
342 E. 26th St.
New York, NY 10016
www.nyu.edu

Rochester Institute of Technology
1 Lomb Memorial Dr.
Rochester, NY 14623
www.rit.edu

SUNY Downstate Medical Center
450 Clarkson Ave.
Brooklyn, NY 11203
www.downstate.edu

North Carolina
Caldwell Community College &
  Technical Institute
2855 Hickory Blvd.
Hudson, NC 28638
www.cccti.edu

Pitt Community College
P.O. Drawer 7007
Greenville, NC 27835
www.pitt.cc.edu

Ohio
Central Ohio Technical College
1179 University Dr.
Newark, OH 43055
www.cotc.edu

Kettering College of Medical Arts
3737 Southern Blvd.
Kettering, OH 45429
www.kcma.edu

Owens Community College
P.O. Box 10000
Toledo, OH 43699
www.owens.edu

Oklahoma
University of Oklahoma
Health Sciences Center
1100 N. Lindsey
Oklahoma City, OK 73104
www.ouhsc.edu

Pennsylvania
Community College of Allegheny
  County
Boyce Campus
595 Beatty Rd.
Monroeville, PA 15146
www.ccac.edu

Thomas Jefferson University
Jefferson College of Health
  Professions
Edison Building
130 S. 9th St.
Philadelphia, PA 19107
www.jefferson.edu

Texas
Alvin Community College
3110 Mustang Road
Alvin, TX 77511
www.alvincolleg.edu

Austin Community College
5930 Middle Fiskville Rd.
Austin, TX 78752
www.austincc.edu

Del Mar College
101 Baldwin Blvd.
Corpus Christi, TX 78404
www.delmar.edu

El Centro College
801 Main St.
Dallas, TX 75202
www.elcentrocollege.edu

El Paso Community College
P.O. Box 20500
El Paso, TX 79998
www.epcc.edu

Houston Community College
3100 Main Street
Houston, TX 77002
www.hccs.edu

Utah
Weber State University
3850 University Circle
Ogden, UT 84408
www.weber.edu

Washington
Bellevue Community College
3000 Landherholm Circle SE
Bellevue, WA 98007
http://bellevuecollege.edu/

Seattle University
901 12th Ave.
P.O. Box 222000
Seattle, WA 98122
www.seattleu.edu

West Virginia
West Virginia University
Robert C. Byrd Health Sciences
  Center
P.O. Box 9100
Morgantown, WV 26506
www.hsc.wvu.edu

Wisconsin
Chippewa Valley Technical College
620 W. Clairemont Ave.
Eau Claire, WI 54701
www.cvtc.edu

St. Francis Hospital
3237 S. 16th St.
Milwaukee, WI 53215
www.covhealth.org

St. Luke's Medical Center
2900 W. Oklahoma Ave.
Milwaukee, WI 53215
www.aurorahealthcare.org

University of Wisconsin Hospital
  and Clinics
600 Highland Ave.
Madison, WI 53792
www.uwhospital.org

Dietetic Technicians

Principal activity: Helping dietitians meet the food needs of their employers' facilities

Work commitment: Full-time

Preprofessional education: High school diploma or its equivalent

Program length: 2 years

Work prerequisites: Associate degree

Career opportunities: Favorable

Income range: $21,000 to $37,000

Scope

The tasks of a dietetic technician depend on the nature and size of the employer. They can cover a broad range of activities, though they all involve helping patients and clients maintain a healthy and appropriate diet.

Activities

At large hospitals or medical centers, dietetic technicians often work directly under a registered dietitian. They are qualified to create recipes, prepare menus, enforce safety and sanitary standards, train and manage dietary and clerical workers, and manage cafeterias. In small institutions, a dietetic technician can attain a management position under the supervision of a consultant dietitian.

Work Settings

Dietary technicians often work in large health-care facilities—such as medical centers, hospitals, and nursing homes—or in smaller facilities (either health-related or not) such as cafeterias or diners.

Advancement

With experience, dietetic technicians may be promoted to supervisory positions. However, it is difficult to transfer credits from a dietary technician program to a dietitian degree program unless you do so at the same institution.

Prerequisites

A high school diploma or its equivalent is essential for entry into a dietetic technician program. Courses in home economics and business are recommended.

Desirable personal attributes for those entering this field include an ability to work under pressure and superior decision-making skills.

Education/Training

Many junior and community colleges offer two-year associate degree programs for dietetic technicians. Course work includes classes in biology, chemistry, nutrition, diet therapy, and food services management.

Certification/Registration/Licensure

Graduates of accredited programs can take the National Registration Examination for Dietetic Technicians, which is offered by the Commission on Dietetic Registration.

To maintain status as a registered dietetic technician (DTR), you must complete at least 50 hours of approved continuing education every five years.

Career Potential

The job outlook for dietetic technicians in the coming decade is quite favorable because of the aging population. Consequently, more facilities for senior citizens (such as nursing homes) will require the services of dietetic technicians.

For More Information

The professional organization for this field is the American Dietetic Association, 120 S. Riverside Plaza, Ste. 2000, Chicago, IL 60606 (www.eatright.org).

Dietetic Technician Programs

Arizona
Chandler-Gilbert Community
  College
Dietetic Technician Consortium
Nutrition Faculty
2626 East Pecos Road
Chandler, AZ 85225
www.cgc.maricopa.edu

Central Arizona College
8470 N. Overfield Rd.
Coolidge, AZ 85228
www.centralaz.edu

Arkansas
Black River Technical College
P.O. Box 468
Pocahontas, AR 72455
www.blackrivertech.org

California
Chaffey College
5885 Haven Ave.
Rancho Cucamonga, CA 91737
www.chaffey.edu

Grossmont-Cuyamaca College
8800 Grossmont College Dr.
El Cajon, CA 92020
www.gcccd.edu

Loma Linda University
Department of Nutrition and
  Dietetics
School of Allied Health
  Professions
Loma Linda, CA 92350
www.llu.edu

Long Beach City College
Family and Consumer Studies
4901 E. Carson St.
Long Beach, CA 90808
www.lbcc.edu

Los Angeles City College
855 N. Vermont Ave.
Los Angeles, CA 90029
www.lacitycollege.edu

Merritt College
12500 Campus Drive
Oakland, CA 94619
www.merritt.edu

Orange Coast College
2701 Fairview Rd.
Costa Mesa, CA 92626
www.orangecoastcollege.edu

Santa Rosa Junior College
Consumers Department
1501 Mendocino Avenue
Santa Rosa, CA 95401
www.santarosa.edu

Colorado
Front Range Community College
3645 W. 112th Ave.
Westminster, CO 80031
www.frontrange.edu

Connecticut
Briarwood College
2279 Mount Vernon Rd.
Southington, CT 06489
www.briarwood.edu

Gateway Community College
88 Bassett Road
North Haven, CT 06473
www.gwctc.commnet.edu

Florida
Miami Dade College
300 NE 2nd Ave.
Miami, FL 33132
www.mdc.edu

Florida Community College at
  Jacksonville
North Campus
4501 Capper Road
Jacksonville, FL 32218
www.fccj.org

Hillsborough Community College
P.O. Box 30030
Tampa, FL 33630
www.hccfl.edu

Palm Beach Community College
4200 Congress Ave.
Lake Worth, FL 33461
www.pbcc.edu

Pensacola Junior College
1000 College Boulevard
Pensacola, FL 32504
www.pjc.edu

Illinois
Harper College
1200 W. Algonquin Rd.
Palatine, IL 60067
www.harpercollege.edu/

Malcolm X College
1900 W. Van Buren St.
Chicago, IL 60612
http://malcolmx.ccc.edu/

Parkland College
2400 W Bradley Avenue
Champaign, IL 61821
www.parkland.edu

Louisiana
Delgado Community College
615 City Park Ave.
New Orleans, LA 70119
www.dcc.edu

Maine
Southern Maine Community
  College
2 Fort Rd.
South Portland, ME 04106
www.smccme.edu

Maryland
Baltimore City Community College
2901 Liberty Heights Ave.
Baltimore, MD 21215
www.bccc.edu

Massachusetts
Caritas Laboure College
2120 Dorchester Avenue
Boston, MA 02124
www.laboure.edu

Michigan
Wayne County College District
Department of Food and Nutrition
8200 West Outer Drive
Detroit, MI 48219
www.wcccd.edu

Minnesota
Normandale Community College
9700 France Avenue South
Bloomington, MN 55431
www.normandale.edu

University Minnesota-Crookston
Dietetic Technology Program
2900 University Avenue
Crookston, MN 56716
www.crk.umn.edu

Missouri
St. Louis Community College
300 S. Broadway
St. Louis, MO 63102
www.stlcc.edu

Nebraska
Southeast Community College
8800 O St.
Lincoln, NE 68520
www.southeast.edu

Nevada
Truckee Meadows Community
  College
7000 Dandini Boulevard
RDMT 3341
Reno, NV 89512
www.tmcc.edu

New Hampshire
University of New Hampshire
Thompson School of Applied
  Science
15 Putnam Hall
Durham, NH 03824
www.unh.edu

New Jersey
Camden City College
P.O. Box 200 College Dr.
Blackwood, NJ 08012
www.camdencc.edu

Middlesex County College
2600 Woodbridge Ave.
Edison, NJ 08818
www.middlesexcc.edu

New York
Erie Community College
6205 Main St.
Williamsville, NY 14221
www.ecc.edu

LaGuardia Community College
31-10 Thomson Ave.
Long Island City, NY 11101
www.lagcc.cuny.edu

Morrisville State College
Brooks Hall
Morrisville, NY 13408
www.morrisville.edu

Rockland Community College
145 College Rd.
Suffern, NY 10901
www.sunyrockland.edu

Suffolk County Community College
Eastern Campus
20 East Main Street
Riverhead, NY 11901
www.sunysuffolk.edu

Westchester Community College
75 Grasslands Rd.
Valhalla, NY 10595
www.sunywcc.edu

North Carolina
Gaston College
Division of the David Belk Cannon
  Health Education Institute
Dietetic Technician Program
P.O. Box 600
Lincolnton. NC 28093
www.gaston.edu

Ohio
Cincinnati State Technical and
  Community College
Health Technology Center
3520 Central Pkwy.
Cincinnati, OH 45223
www.cincinnatistate.edu

Columbus State Community
  College
550 E. Spring St.
Columbus, OH 43125
www.cscc.edu

Cuyahoga Community College
2900 Community College Ave.
Cleveland, OH 44115
www.tri-c.edu

Hocking Technical College
3301 Hocking Pkwy.
Nelsonville, OH 45764
www.hocking.edu

Owens Community College
P.O. Box 10000
Toledo, OH 43699
www.owens.edu

Sinclair Community College
444 W. 3rd St.
Dayton, OH 45402
www.sinclair.edu

Youngstown State University
One University Plaza
Youngstown, OH 44555
www.ysu.edu

Oklahoma
Oklahoma State University–
  Okmulgee
1801 E. Fourth St.
Okmulgee, OK 74447
www.osuit.edu

Oregon
Portland Community College
12000 SW 49th Ave.
P.O. Box 19000
Portland, OR 97280
www.pcc.edu

Pennsylvania
The Pennsylvania State University
  School of Hospitality
  Management
201 Mateer Building
University Park, PA 16802
www.psu.edu

Community College of Allegheny
  County
808 Ridge Ave.
Pittsburgh, PA 15212
www.ccac.edu

Community College of
  Philadelphia
1700 Spring Garden St.
Philadelphia, PA 19130
www.ccp.edu

Westmoreland County Community
  College
Commissioners Hall
400 Armbrust Rd.
Youngwood, PA 15697
www.wccc.edu

South Carolina
Greenville Technical College
P.O. Box 5616
Greenville, SC 29606
www.greenvilletech.com

Tennessee
Southwest Tennessee Community
  College
5983 Macon Cove
Memphis, TN 38134
www.southwest.tn.edu

Texas
El Paso Community College
P.O. Box 20500
El Paso, TX 79998
www.epcc.edu

San Jacinto College Central
8060 Spencer Hwy.
Pasadena, TX 77505
www.sjcd.edu

St. Philip's College
1801 Martin Luther King Dr.
San Antonio, TX 78203
www.alamo.edu/spc/

Tarrant County College
1500 Houston St.
Ft. Worth, TX 76102
www.tccd.edu

Tarrant County College
Business and Technology Division
2100 Southeast Parkway
Arlington, TX 76018
www.tccd.net

Virginia
J. Sargeant Reynolds Community
  College
P.O. Box 85622
Richmond, VA 23285
www.jsr.cc.va.us

Northern Virginia Community
  College
4001 Wakefield Chapel Rd.
Annandale, VA 22003
www.nvcc.edu

Tidewater Community College
7000 College Dr.
Portsmouth, VA 23703
www.tcc.edu

Washington
Shoreline Community College
16101 Greenwood Ave. N.
Shoreline, WA 98133
www.shoreline.edu

Spokane Community College
1810 N. Greene St.
Spokane, WA 99217
www.scc.spokane.edu

Wisconsin
Madison Area Technical College
3550 Anderson St.
Madison, WI 53704
www.matcmadison.edu

Milwaukee Area Technical College
700 W. State St.
Milwaukee, WI 53233
www.matc.edu

Electroneurodiagnostic Technologists

Principal activity: Obtaining electro-encephalograms from patients

Work commitment: Full-time

Preprofessional education: High school diploma

Program length: 1 to 2 years

Work prerequisites: A formal or informal training program

Career opportunities: Favorable

Income range: $35,000 to $49,000

Scope

The human brain exhibits electrical activity that reflects its functional state. An encephalograph is an instrument that can sense and record the brain's minute electrical impulses. The brain wave record of electrical activity is called an encephalogram (EEG). Electroneurodiagnostic technologists (sometimes referred to as EEG technologists) are primarily responsible for obtaining these records from patients. Neurologists and other doctors use such a tracing to diagnose and evaluate strokes, head injuries, brain tumors, epilepsy, and even learning disabilities. The EEG identifies brain damage and reveals its site and extent. It also is used to determine whether a patient is clinically alive.

Activities

Initially the electroneurodiagnostic technologist must ensure that the equipment is in optimal operational condition. The technologist briefs the patient about the procedure and then applies electrodes to the patient's scalp. These electrodes are connected to the EEG machine. Using the optimal settings for that patient, the technologist makes the recording. During the procedure, the technologist also monitors the patient's condition and behavior.

Many electroneurodiagnostic technologists are trained to use other kinds of equipment, including evoked potential (used to record responses to specific stimuli) and polysomnography (used in sleep studies).

Work Settings

Most electroneurodiagnostic technologists work in medical centers, hospitals, the offices of neurologists and neurosurgeons, HMOs, free-standing emergency clinics, and psychiatric facilities.

Advancement

With experience, an electroneurodiagnostic technologist can move to a supervisory or instructional position.

Prerequisites

Those entering this field need a high school diploma and a demonstrated interest and abilities in the biological sciences.

Desirable personal attributes include skill with electronics, manual dexterity, good vision, strong communication skills, and a favorable personality. Compassion and tact are also valuable assets that facilitate working with very sick people and those who may be brain-damaged.

Experience/Training

There are two routes to becoming an electroneurodiagnostic technologist: graduating from a formal training program and securing on-the-job training. The latter usually entails two six-month educational phases that include didactic instruction and supervised practice. You can expect to receive a stipend during the training period.

A variety of institutions offer formal training programs, including community and senior colleges, universities, medical schools, and hospitals. Studies involve gross anatomy and neuroanatomy, physiology, neurology, neurophysiology, electronics, and instrumentation. The program usually lasts one to two years, and a certificate or associate degree may be awarded on completion.

Electroneurodiagnostic technologists learn to identify normal and abnormal brain activity shown on a tracing and how best to secure the desired information. They also become familiar with the diseases for which the EEG is a valuable diagnostic tool and with the equipment's operational characteristics.

Certification/Registration/Licensure

Currently there are no licensing requirements for electroneurodiagnostic technologists, but you can obtain the title of registered EEG technologist from the American Board of Registration for Electroencephalographic and Evoked Potential Technologists. This registration follows a one-year training program and examination.

Career Potential

The employment outlook is strong for those entering this field because of the aging U.S. population and greater use of EEGs in clinical medicine and research.

For More Information

The professional organization for this field is the American Society of Electroneurodiagnostic Technologists, Inc., 426 W. 42nd St., Kansas City, MO 64111 (www.aset.org).

You can get information on registration from the American Board of Registration of Electroencephalographic and Evoked Potential Technologists, 1904 Croydon Dr., Springfield IL 62703 (www.abret.org).

EEG Technologist Programs

California
Orange Coast College
2701 Fairview Rd.
Costa Mesa, CA 92626
www.orangecoastcollege.edu

Colorado
Community College of Denver
1111 W. Colfax Ave.
Denver, CO 80204
www.ccd.edu

Florida
Erwin Technical Center
2010 E. Hillsborough Ave.
Tampa, FL 33610
www.erwintech.org

Illinois
East-West University
816 S. Michigan Ave.
Chicago, IL 60605
www.eastwest.edu

Loyola University Health System
2160 S. First St.
Maywood, IL 60153
www.loyolamedicine.org

St. John's Hospital
800 E. Carpenter St.
Springfield, IL 62769
www.st-johns.org

Indiana
Clarian Health Partners–Methodist
21st St., White Hall
Indianapolis, IN 46206
www.clarian.org

Indiana University–Purdue
University Indianapolis
702 Barnhill Dr.
Indianapolis, IN 46202
www.iupui.edu

Iowa
Kirkwood Community College
6301 Kirkwood Blvd. SW
Cedar Rapids, IA 52404
www.kirkwood.edu

Scott Community College
500 Belmont Rd.
Bettendorf, IA 52722
www.eicc.edu

Maryland
Harford Community College
401 Thomas Run Rd.
Bel Air, MD 21015
www.harford.edu

Naval School of Health Sciences
8901 Wisconsin Ave.
Bethesda, MD 20889
http://nshs.med.navy.mil/

Massachusetts
Children's Hospital Boston
300 Longwood Ave.
Boston, MA 02115
www.childrenshospital.org

Laboure College
2120 Dorchester Ave.
Dorchester, MA 02124
www.laboure.edu

Michigan
Carnegie Institute
550 Stephenson Hwy., Ste. 100
Troy, MI 48083
www.carnegie-institute.edu

Oakland Community College
Children's Hospital of Michigan
3901 Beaubien
Detroit, MI 48201
www.oaklandcc.edu

Minnesota
Mayo Medical Center
Siebens 1016
200 1st St. SW
Rochester, MN 55905
www.mayo.edu

New York
Niagara County Community
  College
3111 Saunders Settlement Rd.
Sandborn, NY 14132
www.niagaracc.suny.edu

North Carolina
Pamlico Community College
P.O. Box 185
Grantsboro, NC 28529
www.pamlico.cc.edu

Southwestern Community College
447 College Dr.
Sylva, NC 28779
www.southwestern.edu

Ohio
Cuyahoga Community College
700 Carnegie Ave.
Cleveland, OH 44115
www.tri-c.edu

Pennsylvania
Carlow College
Children's Hospital of Pittsburgh
3705 Fifth Ave.
Pittsburgh, PA 15213
www.carlow.edu

Crozer-Keystone Health System
One Medical Center Blvd.
Upland, PA 19013
www.crozer.org

West Virginia
St. Joseph Hospital
1824 Murdoch Avenue
Parkersburg, WV 26101
www.stjosephs-hospital.com

Wisconsin
Western Wisconsin Technical
  College
304 6th St. N.
La Crosse, WI 54601
www.wwtc.edu

Canada
British Columbia Institute of
  Technology
3700 Willingdon Ave.
Burnaby, British Columbia
  V5G 3H2
www.bcit.ca

Children & Women's Health Centre
  of British Columbia
4500 Oak St.
Vancouver, British Columbia
  V6H 3N1
www.cw.bc.ca

Emergency Medical Technicians

Principal activity: Providing emergency medical care

Work commitment: Part- or full-time

Preprofessional education: High school diploma

Program length: 64 to 1,200 hours, depending on the level

Work prerequisites: Completion of an EMT course

Career opportunities: Stable

Income range: (level-dependent) $23,000 to $41,000

Scope

As the name indicates, emergency medical technicians (EMTs) respond to calls by or for people in medical distress. They are trained in a wide range of lifesaving techniques. They may respond to vehicle or industrial accidents, heart attacks, bodily injuries due to accidents or violence, cases of poisoning or drug overdose, childbirth, drownings, and situations involving emotionally disturbed individuals. EMTs are the first medical responders to traumatic injuries and acute illnesses.

Activities

EMTs are directed to the scenes of medical emergencies by a police or fire department, hospital, or emergency services dispatcher. They are given preliminary information about the medical problem(s) they will face so that they can prepare the necessary equipment.

Upon arriving at the scene, EMTs assess the situation, note the patient's vital signs, and determine whether hospitalization is required. If it is not, they prioritize the emergency treatment needed and initiate therapeutic activities.

If the situation is life-threatening, they may call for backup medical help or seek guidance from the local hospital emergency room physician. Following the physician's advice (and subject to the EMTs' level of competence and the state's legal guidelines), they may perform a wide variety of procedures, both on the scene and on the way to the hospital.

When appropriate, EMTs drive the patient to the emergency room. Once there, they report the patient's vital signs and the emergency treatment they provided. They may also remain to help the emergency staff treat the patient.

Work Settings

EMTs are employed by medical centers and hospitals, police and fire departments, rescue agencies, and private ambulance companies. They also serve with volunteer corps that address emergencies in their communities.

Advancement

Three levels of EMTs are recognized, based on the training they have received and the procedures they are permitted to perform:

- An EMT–basic is qualified to carry out fundamental procedures such as cardiovascular resuscitation, fracture care (bandaging and splinting), bleeding control, childbirth assistance, and treatment for shock. This category is also called EMT–ambulance.
- An EMT–intermediate is qualified to perform the fundamental procedures just described and to assess trauma, open an intravenous line, introduce fluids, provide airway management techniques, and use anti-shock garments.
- An EMT–paramedic is trained in advanced life support techniques, including interpreting electrocardiograms, administering medications, and providing defibrillation when a person's heart has stopped beating. Those especially qualified in the latter technique may also be designated as EMT–defibrillator.

With continuing education, training, experience, and qualifying examinations, an EMT can advance from one level to another.

Prerequisites

Those entering this field must be at least 18 years old and have a high school diploma and a valid driver's license.

Desirable personal attributes include good physical health and strength, good vision, manual dexterity, good judgment under stress, and a desire to help those in need.

Education/Training

EMT–Basic

The basic course requires 110 hours of training in emergency medical care techniques. Instruction covers handling emergencies associated with bleeding, fractures, shock, soft-tissue trauma, cardiac arrest, internal injuries, childbirth, and the ingestion of toxic substances. Trainees learn how to use standard emergency equipment, communication skills, and vehicle operation and maintenance. They also gain familiarity with the legal aspects of hospitalization.

EMT–Intermediate

Trainees take courses in patient assessment, shock management, advanced airway maintenance, and intravenous fluid provision.

EMT–Paramedic

Training for this level requires EMT–basic or higher status plus 700 to 1,000 hours of course work, as well as hospital clinical practice and a supervised field internship. The training program usually lasts about nine months.

Certification/Registration/Licensure

EMTs at every level can register with the National Registry of Emergency Medical Technicians if they meet the requirements for training, field experience, and examinations. Each state may have its own certifying agency. To maintain certification, EMTs must register every two years.

Career Potential

The job market for EMTs in the foreseeable future is average. The most attractive positions are those with police and fire departments and rescue squads. However, most of the opportunities in the future will be with hospitals and private ambulance services.

The demand for emergency medical assistance should increase somewhat due to the growing elderly population and the need to replace those workers who leave due to the modest pay and the stress of the job.

For More Information

The professional EMT organization is the National Association of Emergency Medical Technicians, P.O. Box 1400, Clinton, MS 39060 (www.naemt.org). For information on certification and licensure, contact the National Registry of Emergency Medical Technicians, Rocco V. Morando Building, 6610 Busch Blvd., P.O. Box 29233, Columbus, OH 43229 (www.nremt.org).

EMT–Paramedic Programs

Alabama

University of Alabama at
  Birmingham
1530 3rd Ave. S.
Birmingham, AL 35294
www.uab.edu

University of Alabama at
  Tuscaloosa
College of Community Health
  Services
Tuscaloosa, AL 35487
www.ua.edu

University of South Alabama
307 University Blvd. N.
Mobile, AL 36688
www.southalabama.edu

Wallace Community College
Department of Emergency Medical
  Services
1141 Wallace Dr.
Dothan, AL 36303
www.wallace.edu

Alaska

University of Alaska–Anchorage
3211 Providence Dr.
Anchorage, AK 99508
www.uaa.alaska.edu

Arizona

St. Mary's Hospital
1601 W. St. Mary's Rd.
Tucson, AZ 85745
www.carondelet.org

Arkansas

University of Arkansas for Medical
  Sciences
College of Health Related
  Professions
4301 W. Markham St.
Little Rock, AR 72205
www.uams.edu

California

Crafton Hills College
11711 Sand Canyon Rd.
Yucaipa, CA 92399
www.craftonhills.edu

Daniel Freeman Memorial Hospital
333 N. Prairie Ave.
Inglewood, CA 90301
www.danielfreemanmemorial
  hospital.com

Loma Linda University
School of Allied Health
  Professions
Loma Linda, CA 92350
www.llu.edu

San Francisco City College
Paramedics Training Programs
1860 Hayes Street
San Francisco, CA 94117
www.ccsf.edu

San Joaquin Valley College–
  Bakersfield
201 New Stine Rd.
Bakersfield, CA 93309
www.sjvc.edu

West Medical College
5300 Steven Creek Blvd.
San Jose, CA 95129
www.westmedcollege.edu

Colorado

St. Anthony Central Hospital
4231 W. 16th Ave.
Denver, CO 80204
www.stanthonycentral.org

Swedish Medical Center
501 E. Hampden Ave.
Englewood, CO 80110
www.swedishhospital.com

District of Columbia

The George Washington University
  Medical Center
School of Medicine and Health
  Sciences
2300 Eye St. NW
Washington, DC 20037
www.gwumc.edu

Florida

Brevard Community College
1519 Clearlake Rd.
Cocoa, FL 32922
www.brevard.edu

Broward Community College
111 E. Las Olas Blvd.
Ft. Lauderdale, FL 33301
www.broward.edu

Central Florida Community College
3001 SW College Rd.
Ocala, FL 34474
www.cfcc.cc.fl.us

Daytona Beach Community
  College
1200 W. International Speedway
  Blvd.
Daytona Beach, FL 32114
www.daytonastate.edu

Edison College
8099 College Pkwy. SW
Ft. Myers, FL 33919
www.edison.edu

Florida Community College at
  Jacksonville
501 W. State St.
Jacksonville, FL 32202
www.fccj.org

Gulf Coast Community College
5230 W. Hwy. 98
Panama City, FL 32401
www.gulfcoast.edu

Hillsborough Community College
Dale Mabry Campus
P.O. Box 30030
Tampa, FL 33630
www.hccfl.edu

Indian River Community College
3209 Virginia Ave.
Ft. Pierce, FL 34981
www.ircc.edu

Lake City Community College
149 SE Vocational Place
Lake City, FL 32025
www.lakecitycc.edu

Lake Technical Center
2001 Kurt St.
Eustis, FL 32726
http://laketech.org/

Manatee Technical Institute
5603 34th St. W.
Bradenton, FL 34210
www.manateetechnicalinstitute.
  org

Miami Dade Community College
Medical Center
950 NW 20th St.
Miami, FL 33127
www.mdc.edu

Palm Beach State College
4200 Congress Ave.
Lake Worth, FL 33461
www.palmbeachstate.edu

Pasco-Hernando Community
  College
36727 Blanton Rd.
Dade City, FL 33523
http://phcc.edu

Pensacola Junior College
1000 College Blvd.
Pensacola, FL 32504
www.pjc.edu

Polk Community College
999 Ave. H NE
Winter Haven, FL 33881
www.polk.edu

Santa Fe Community College
3000 NW 83rd St., P237
Gainesville, FL 32606
www.sfccnm.edu

Sarasota County Technical
  Institute
4748 Beneva Rd.
Sarasota, FL 34233
www.scti.edu

St. Petersburg College
P.O. Box 13489
Pinellas Park, FL 33733
www.spcollege.edu

Tallahassee Community College
444 Appleyard Dr.
Tallahassee, FL 32304
http://tcc.fl.edu/

Valencia Community College
190 S. Orange Ave.
Orlando, FL 32801
www.valenciacc.edu

Idaho
American Institute of Health
  Technology
1200 N. Liberty
Boise, Idaho 83704

Indiana
Methodist Hospital of Indiana
1701 N. Senate Blvd.
Indianapolis, IN 46206
www.clarian.org

Iowa
Mercy Medical Center Des Moines
1111 Sixth Ave.
Des Moines, IA 50314
www.mercydesmoines.org

Kansas
Johnson County Community
  College
12345 College Blvd.
Overland Park, KS 66210
www.jccc.edu

Kentucky
Eastern Kentucky University
521 Lancaster Ave.
Richmond, KY 40475
www.eku.edu

Massachusetts
Springfield Technical Community
  College
One Armory Square, Ste. 1
P.O. Box 9000
Springfield, MA 01102
www.stcc.edu

Michigan
Lansing Community College
P.O. Box 40010
Lansing, MI 48901
www.lcc.edu

Minnesota
Northeast Metro Career &
  Technical Center
3300 Century Ave. N.
White Bear Lake, MN 55110
www.nemetro.k12.mn.us

Nebraska
Creighton University
2500 California Plaza
Omaha, NE 68178
www.creighton.edu

New Hampshire
New Hampshire Technical
  Institute
31 College Dr.
Concord, NH 03301
www.nhti.edu

New Mexico
University of New Mexico
Health Sciences Center
Albuquerque, NM 87131
http://hsc.unm.edu/

North Carolina
Catawba Valley Community
  College
2550 Hwy. 70 SE
Hickory, NC 28602
www.cvcc.edu

Western Carolina University
Cullowhee, NC 28723
www.wcu.edu

Ohio
Columbus State Community
  College
550 E. Spring St.
P.O. Box 1609
Columbus, OH 43216
www.cscc.edu

Youngstown State University
One University Plaza
Youngstown, OH 44555
www.ysu.edu

Oregon
Oregon Health & Science
  University
3181 SW Sam Jackson Park Rd.
Portland, OR 97239
www.ohsu.edu

Pennsylvania
Harrisburg Area Community
  College
One HACC Dr.
Harrisburg, PA 17110
www.hacc.edu

St. Joseph Hospital & Health Care
Center
250 College Ave.
Lancaster, PA 17604

Williamsport Hospital & Medical
Center
Susquehanna Health System
777 Rural Ave.
Williamsport, PA 17701
www.shscares.org

South Carolina
Greenville Technical College
P.O. Box 5616
Greenville, SC 29606
www.gvltec.edu

Tennessee
Jackson State Community College
2046 North Pkwy.
Jackson, TN 38301
www.jscc.edu

Roane State Community College
276 Patton Ln.
Harriman, TN 37748
www.roanestate.edu

Southwest Tennessee Community
College
737 Union Ave.
P.O. Box 40568
Memphis, TN 38174
www.southwest.tn.edu

Volunteer State Community
College
1480 Nashville Pike
Gallatin, TN 37066
www.volstate.edu

Texas
Austin Community College
5930 Middle Fiskville Rd.
Austin, TX 78752
www.austincc.edu

Texas Tech University
Health Sciences Center
Lubbock, TX 79409
www.ttu.edu

University of Texas
Health Science Center at
San Antonio
7703 Floyd Curl Dr.
San Antonio, TX 78229
www.uthscsa.edu

University of Texas Southwestern
Medical Center at Dallas
5323 Harry Hines Blvd.
Dallas, TX 75390
www.utsouthwestern.edu

Utah
Weber State University
3850 University Circle
Ogden, UT 84408
www.weber.edu

Virginia
Jefferson College of Health
Sciences
Community Hospital of Roanoke
Valley
920 S. Jefferson St.
Roanoke, VA 24011
www.jfchs.edu

Northern Virginia Community
College
4001 Wakefield Chapel Rd.
Annandale, VA 22003
www.nvcc.edu

Washington
Bellingham Technical College
3028 Lindbergh Ave.
Bellingham, WA 98225
www.btc.ctc.edu

Central Washington University
Department of Health, Human
Performance, and Recreation
400 E. University Way
Ellensburg, WA 98926
www.cwu.edu

Harborview Medical Center
University of Washington
325 Ninth Ave.
Seattle, WA 98104
www.uwmedicine.washington.edu

Spokane Community College
1810 N. Greene St.
Spokane, WA 99217
www.scc.spokane.edu

Tacoma Community College
6501 S. 19th St.
Tacoma, WA 98466
www.tacomacc.edu

Food Technologists

Principal activity: Providing nourishing and safe food for public consumption

Work commitment: Full-time

Preprofessional education: High school diploma

Program length: 4 years

Work prerequisites: Bachelor's degree required; master's degree preferred

Career opportunities: Favorable

Income range: $44,000 to $81,000

Scope

Food technologists are involved in a wide variety of activities associated with providing the public with sanitary and nutritious food. They help select, process, package, preserve, and distribute food.

To achieve the goal of manufacturing food that is beneficial, tasty, attractive, and lasting, the food production industry employs technologists in food laboratories, food-testing kitchens, and production facilities. Technologists also help develop new products.

Activities

Food technologists are commonly employed in industrial settings. They work in research and development, pilot testing of new food processes and equipment, and packaging systems. They supervise plant safety, quality control, and waste disposal. Technologists also are responsible for the chemical analysis of food composition.

Work Settings

The major employers of food technologists are the three categories of companies that belong to the food industry:

- *Food processors,* which convert raw foods into food products
- *Food manufacturers,* including those that create entirely new food products
- *Food ingredient makers,* including those that produce spices, vitamins, and food supplements

Many food technologists work for the federal government, including the Food and Drug Administration, the Environmental Protection Agency, and NASA. State agencies that monitor the handling of foods in restaurants, hotels, and other retail food distribution businesses also are sources of employment. Technologists also are employed by such organizations as the United Nations and the World Health Organization, as well as by colleges, universities, and health foundations.

Advancement

Candidates with advanced degrees (such as a master's or doctorate) can secure professional advancement.

Prerequisites

Desirable personal attributes for those entering this field include a solid interest in science and food, an organized way of thinking and working, patience, and good communication and teamwork skills.

Education/Training

A bachelor's degree is the minimum requirement for employment in this field. The preferred major is food technology, but related areas such as nutrition may be acceptable. Course work should include food processing analysis and engineering, chemistry, microbiology, physics, mathematics, and statistics.

Those interested in the business aspects of the food industry should take economics and business administration courses. In addition, you should take the traditional humanities and social science courses.

Many schools with undergraduate food technology programs also offer advanced degrees. Almost half of food technologists employed in the United States have master's or doctorate degrees.

Junior colleges, community vocational schools, and technical training schools offer two-year programs and award associate degrees. Graduates of such programs are called *food technicians* and, with further education, may become technologists.

Certification/Registration/Licensure

No certification or licensure currently is available in this field. Those with at least a bachelor's degree in food technology and five years of professional experience can apply for professional membership in the Institute of Food Technology.

Career Potential

The employment outlook in this field is fairly positive. Job growth will be driven by advances in technology, as well as a heightened public awareness of diet, health, and food safety issues.

For More Information

The professional organization for this field is the Institute of Food Technologists, 525 W. Van Buren, Ste. 1000, Chicago, IL 60607 (www.ift.org).

Food Technologist Programs

Alabama
Alabama A&M University
4900 Meridian St.
Huntsville, AL 35811
www.aamu.edu

Auburn University
College of Human Sciences
210 Spidle Hall
Auburn, AL 36849
http://humsci.auburn.edu/

Arkansas
University of Arkansas
Fayetteville, AR 72701
www.uark.edu

California
California Polytechnic State
  University
San Luis Obispo, CA 93407
www.calpoly.edu

California State University, Fresno
5241 N. Maple Ave.
Fresno, CA 93740
www.csufresno.edu

Chapman University
One University Dr.
Orange, CA 92866
www.chapman.edu

San Jose State University
One Washington Square
San Jose, CA 95192
www.sjsu.edu

University of California, Davis
1 Shields Ave.
Davis, CA 95616
www.ucdavis.edu

Colorado
Colorado State University
Fort Collins, CO 80523
www.colostate.edu

Delaware
University of Delaware
College of Health & Nursing
  Sciences
Newark, DE 19717
www.udel.edu

Florida
University of Florida
Gainesville, FL 32611
www.ufl.edu

Georgia
University of Georgia
Food Science Building
Athens, GA 30602
www.uga.edu

Hawaii
University of Hawaii
2444 Dole St.
Honolulu, HI 96822
www.hawaii.edu

Idaho
University of Idaho
Holm Research Center
Moscow, ID 83844
www.uidaho.edu

Illinois
University of Illinois at
  Urbana-Champaign
1401 W. Green St.
Urbana, IL 61801
www.uiuc.edu

Indiana
Purdue University
745 Agriculture Mall Dr.
West Lafayette, IN 47906
www.purdue.edu

Iowa
Iowa State University
Ames, IA 50011
www.iastate.edu

Kansas
Kansas State University
Justin Hall 104
Manhattan, KS 66506
www.ksu.edu

Kentucky
University of Kentucky
210C Erikson Hall
Lexington, KY 40506
www.uky.edu

Louisiana
Louisiana State University
Food Science Building
Baton Rouge, LA 70803
www.lsu.edu

Maine
University of Maine
5735 Hitchner Hall
Orono, ME 04469
www.maine.edu

Maryland
University of Maryland
College Park, MD 20742
www.umd.edu

Massachusetts
University of Massachusetts
  Amherst
Amherst, MA 01003
www.umass.edu

Michigan
Michigan State University
East Lansing, MI 48824
www.msu.edu

Minnesota
University of Minnesota
College of Food, Agriculture, and
  Natural Resource Sciences
277 Coffey Hall
1420 Eckles Ave.
St. Paul, MN 55108
www.cfans.umn.edu

Mississippi
Mississippi State University
Mississippi State, MS 39762
www.msstate.edu

Missouri
University of Missouri–Columbia
Columbia, MO 65211
www.missouri.edu

Nebraska
University of Nebraska–Lincoln
Lincoln, NE 68588
www.unl.edu

New Jersey
Rutgers
65 Dudley Rd.
New Brunswick, NJ 08903
http://sebs.rutgers.edu/

New York
Cornell University
Department of Food Science
116 Stocking Hall
Ithaca, NY 14853
www.foodscience.cornell.edu

North Carolina
North Carolina State University
College of Agriculture and Life
  Sciences
115 Patterson Hall, Box 7642
Raleigh, NC 27695
http://harvest.cals.ncsu.edu/

North Dakota
North Dakota State University
1301 12th Ave. N.
Fargo, ND 58105
www.ndsu.nodak.edu

Ohio
Ohio State University
Columbus, OH 43210
www.osu.edu

Oklahoma
Oklahoma State University
Stillwater, OK 74078
http://osu.okstate.edu/

Oregon
Oregon State University
Corvallis, OR 97331
http://oregonstate.edu/

Pennsylvania
Delaware Valley College
Department of Food Science and
  Management
Culinary Technology
700 E. Butler Ave.
Doylestown, PA 18901
www.delval.edu

Pennsylvania State University
College of Agricultural Sciences
Department of Food Science
111 Borland Laboratory
University Park, PA 16802
http://foodscience.psu.edu/

Rhode Island
University of Rhode Island
College of the Environment and
  Life Sciences
Department of Nutrition and Food
  Sciences
106 Ranger Hall
Kingston, RI 02881
www.uri.edu

South Carolina
Clemson University
Department of Food Science and
  Human Nutrition
224 Poole Agricultural Center
P.O. Box 340371
Clemson, SC 29634
www.clemson.edu/cafls/depart-
  ments/foodscience/

Tennessee
University of Tennessee
Knoxville, TN 37996
www.utk.edu

Texas
Texas A&M University
College Station, TX 77843
www.tamu.edu

Utah
Brigham Young University
Provo, UT 84602
www.byu.edu

Utah State University
Logan, UT 84332
www.usu.edu

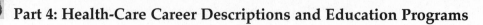

Virginia
Virginia Polytechnic Institute and
  State University
104 Burruss Hall
Blacksburg, VA 24061
www.vt.edu

Washington
University of Washington
Box 355680
Seattle, WA 98105
www.washington.edu

Washington State University
Department of Food Science
Pullman, WA 99164
www.wsu.edu

Wisconsin
University of Wisconsin–Madison
College of Agricultural & Life
  Sciences
Department of Food Science
Madison, WI 53706
www.foodsci.wisc.edu

University of Wisconsin–River
  Falls
410 S. Third St.
River Falls, WI 54022
www.uwrf.edu

Canada
Acadia University
Wolfville, Nova Scotia B4P 2R6
www.acadiau.ca

McGill University
845 Sherbrooke St. W.
Montreal, Quebec H3A 2T5
www.mcgill.ca

Université Laval
Québec G1K 7P4
www.ulaval.ca

University of Alberta
Department of Agricultural, Food
  & Nutritional Science
114th St. and 89th Ave.
Edmonton, Alberta T6G 2P5
www.afns.ualberta.ca

University of British Columbia
2329 W. Mall
Vancouver, British Columbia
  V6T 1Z4
www.ubc.ca

University of Guelph
Guelph, Ontario N1G 2W1
www.uoguelph.ca

University of Manitoba
Winnipeg, Manitoba R3T 2N2
www.umanitoba.ca

Histology Technicians

Principal activity: Preparing histological slides for microscopic examination by pathologists

Work commitment: Full-time

Preprofessional education: High school diploma

Program length: 6 months to 2 years

Work prerequisites: On-the-job training or formal education

Career opportunities: Stable

Income range: $42,000 to $63,000

Scope

Anatomy, which is one of the biomedical sciences, has many subdivisions. One of these is *histology*, or the microscopic study of tissues. For a technician to study tissues, the material must be specially prepared and suitable for analysis under a standard microscope. The tissues may be used for diagnostic, research, or educational purposes. Because of the critical nature of their work, these technicians and their supervisors, who are known as *histotechnologists*, are essential to the proper functioning of hospitals and research and teaching institutions.

Activities

For routine microscopic examination, histology technicians preserve and embed tissue samples in wax sections. The specimens are then mounted on glass slides. Next, they are dehydrated and stained. This reveals the internal structure, with different elements of the cells revealed in contrasting colors.

The procedure that is routinely used in tissue preparation is time-consuming, often taking several days. However, sometimes it is essential to obtain sections immediately for pathological evaluation. For example, when a biopsy is taken of suspected malignant tissue while a patient is on the operating table, the surgeon needs a pathologist's opinion and advice within minutes to determine how to proceed. In these cases a technician treats the biopsied material using a quick-freeze method and then sections it for prompt pathological review.

Work Settings

Most histology technicians work in medical centers and hospitals. Others work in research and teaching institutions.

Advancement

With experience, additional education, and evidence of managerial skills, advancement to histology technologist is possible.

Prerequisites

A high school diploma or its equivalent is essential for entry into this field. Studies in biology and chemistry are important.

Desirable personal attributes for workers in this field include an interest in the biomedical sciences, superior vision, manual dexterity, patience, the ability to do routine work in a responsible manner, and an exacting nature.

Education/Training

This field has two training routes: on-the-job training and formal preparation. The latter is becoming increasingly commonplace. Formal educational programs are offered by medical centers and hospitals as well as community and junior colleges. From the former, you can secure a certificate or diploma; from the latter, you can be granted an associate degree. These programs can extend from six months to two years, depending on where they are undertaken.

In accredited programs the curriculum usually consists of classroom instruction and practical laboratory work. Courses include anatomy, histology, histochemistry, chemistry, mathematics, processing techniques, and medical technology. Record keeping and administrative procedures are also taught.

Certification/Registration/Licensure

Certification in this field is available through the Board of Registry of the American Society of Clinical Pathology or other organizations (see the section "For More Information"). A variety of prerequisites for people with different backgrounds are available, and you must pass an examination. Histology technologists can obtain certification, but a bachelor's degree is required.

Career Potential

Demand for professionals in this field should remain stable for the foreseeable future. However, changing health-care reimbursement and coverage plans may significantly affect professional needs in this field.

For More Information

The professional organization for this field is the National Society for Histotechnology, 4201 Northview Dr., Ste. 502, Bowie, MD 20716 (www.nsh.org). Certification is available through the National Accrediting Agency for Clinical Laboratory Sciences, 8410 W. Bryn Mawr Ave., Ste. 670, Chicago, IL 60631 (www.naacls.org); the National Credentialing Agency for Laboratory Personnel, P.O. Box 15945-289, Lenexa, KS 66285 (www.nca-info.org); and the ASCP Board of Registry, P.O. Box 12277, Chicago, IL 60612.

Medical Assistants

Principal activity: Serving as an office assistant for health-care practitioners

Work commitment: Part- or full-time

Preprofessional education: High school diploma

Program length: 1 to 2 years

Work prerequisites: Diploma, certificate, or associate degree

Career opportunities: Highly favorable

Income range: $24,000 to $33,000

Scope

A medical assistant is a multiskilled professional who is qualified to function in both clinical and administrative areas. This person works under the supervision of a licensed health-care practitioner. The medical assistant also serves as a liaison between patient and doctor. He or she provides guidance and personal attention to the patient to relieve anxiety. The efficiency of a medical office depends, in large measure, on the ability and efficiency of the medical assistant.

Activities

The range of a medical assistant's clinical duties is determined by state law. These duties may include preparing the exam room, taking a preliminary medical history from patients, measuring their height and weight, recording their vital signs (such as pulse, blood pressure, and temperature), preparing patients for and assisting in examinations and treatment processes, applying dressings, drawing blood, performing routine blood tests and electrocardiograms, preparing and administering medications under the physician's direction, cleaning and sterilizing instruments, disposing of used supplies, maintaining the stock of standard supplies, and ordering replacements.

The administrative responsibilities of medical assistants involve secretarial, clerical, and receptionist duties along with bookkeeping and record keeping. These responsibilities include scheduling patient appointments, receiving patients upon their arrival, updating patient records, coding procedures and diagnoses, preparing correspondence, and arranging for pharmacy prescriptions or hospital admissions when necessary. Additional duties may involve responding to phone calls, maintaining accounts, and dealing with insurance carriers.

The ratio of clinical to administrative work usually is determined by the size of the practice. In a small office, the medical assistant typically handles both, but a larger office might separate these duties.

Medical assistants working for specialists are responsible for special procedures relevant to their specialty. Thus, each major specialty may have its own medical assistants. (See, for example, the discussion of ophthalmic assistants.)

Work Settings

The majority of medical assistants work in the offices of practicing physicians; for individual practitioners or medical groups; or for HMOs, hospitals, clinics, or nursing homes.

Advancement

Securing additional experience and training can enhance the status of a medical assistant, who can move into supervisory or specialty work areas.

Prerequisites

A high school diploma is needed both as a prerequisite for formal education and for on-the-job training. Courses in biology, computers, and bookkeeping are an asset.

Desirable personal attributes for a medical assistant include a pleasant personality and disposition, strong verbal and written communication skills, a service orientation, organized work habits, and a respect for individual privacy.

Education/Training

Some medical assistants secure on-the-job training, but most are graduates of formal educational programs. Such programs are offered by community and junior colleges and vocational schools. Programs include courses in biology, anatomy, physiology, medical terminology, computers, accounting, record keeping, transcription, and office management. Clinical aspects are covered in courses dealing with laboratory techniques, clinical procedures, and patient care.

Training programs vary in length. Most vocational school programs take one year, and those at community colleges take two years of course work and supervised clinical experience.

The two medical assistant program accrediting agencies are the Commission for the Accreditation of Allied Health Education Programs (CAAHEP) and the Accrediting Bureau of Health Education Schools (ABHES). Programs accredited by CAAHEP are listed in the section "Medical Assistant Programs."

Certification/Registration/Licensure

The two professional organizations in this field provide certification or registration to those who meet their requirements. Those meeting the standards set by the American Association of Medical Assistants are designated *certified medical assistants* (*CMAs*), and those meeting the standards set by the American Medical Technologists are designated *registered medical assistants* (*RMAs*).

Career Potential

Experts foresee a highly favorable outlook for employment in this field over the next decade. This is especially true for those having formal training. Both the size of the U.S. population and the number of physicians are increasing. Consequently, the demand for medical services is greater, and the need for medical assistants is accelerating.

For More Information

The two professional organizations in this field are the American Association of Medical Assistants, 20 N. Wacker Drive, Ste. 1575, Chicago, IL 60606 (www.aama-ntl.org), and the Registered Medical Assistants of the American Medical Technologists, 710 Higgins Rd., Park Ridge, IL 60068 (www.amt1.com).

Medical Assistant Programs

Alabama

H. Councill Trenholm State
  Technical College
1225 Air Base Blvd.
Montgomery, AL 36108
www.trenholmtech.cc.al.us

Remington College–Mobile
828 Downtowner Loop West
Mobile, AL 36609
www.remingtoncollege.edu

South University–Montgomery
5355 Vaughn Rd.
Montgomery, AL 36116
www.southuniversity.edu

Wallace Community College
1141 Wallace Dr.
Dothan, AL 36303
www.wallace.edu

Alaska

University of Alaska Anchorage
3211 Providence Dr.
Anchorage, AK 99508
www.uaa.alaska.edu

Arizona

Apollo College–Tucson
3550 N. Oracle Rd.
Tucson, AZ 85705
www.apollocollege.com

Arizona State University
Tempe Campus
1001 S Mill Avenue
Tempe, AZ 85281
www.asu.edu

College of America-Flagstaff
1800 South Milton Road
Flagstaff, AZ 86001
www.collegeamerica.edu/flag-
  staff-college.html

Phoenix College
1202 W. Thomas Rd.
Phoenix, AZ 85013
www.pc.maricopa.edu

Pima Medical Institute
957 S. Dobson Rd.
Mesa, AZ 85202
www.pima.edu

Remington College–Tempe
875 W. Elliott Rd., Ste. 126
Tempe, AZ 85284
www.remingtoncollege.edu

Arkansas

Capital City Junior College of
  Business
7723 Asher Ave., Box 4818
Little Rock, AR 72214

Remington College–Little Rock
19 Remington Rd.
Little Rock, AR 72204
www.remingtoncollege.edu

California

Academy of Professional Careers
8376 Hercules St.
La Mesa, CA 91942

Bryman College–Hayward
22336 Main St., 1st Floor
Hayward, CA 94541
www.bryman.edu

Bryman College–Reseda
18040 Sherman Way, Ste. 400
Reseda, CA 91335
www.bryman.edu

Empire College
3035 Cleveland Ave.
Santa Rosa, CA 95403
www.empcol.edu

Maric College
1360 S. Anaheim Blvd.
Anaheim, CA 92805
www.mariccollege.com

Maric College
4900 Rivergrade Rd., Ste. E-210
Irwindale, CA 91706
www.mariccollege.com

Maric College
3699 Wilshire Blvd., 4th Floor
Los Angeles, CA 90010
www.mariccollege.com

Maric College
14355 Roscoe Blvd.
Panorama City, CA 91402
www.mariccollege.com

Maric College
6160 Mission Gorge Rd., Ste. 108
San Diego, CA 92120
www.mariccollege.com

Colorado

Boulder Valley Area Vocational
  Technical Center
6600 E. Arapahoe
Boulder, CO 80303

Emily Griffith Opportunity School
1250 Welton St.
Denver, CO 80204
www.egos-school.com

Everest College
1815 Jet Wing Dr.
Colorado Springs, CO 80916
www.everest.edu

Remington College
11011 W. 6th Ave.
Lakewood, CO 80215
www.remingtoncollege.edu

Connecticut
Branford Hall Career Institute
995 Day Hill Rd.
Windsor, CT 06095
www.branfordhall.edu

Morse School of Business
275 Asylum St.
Hartford, CT 06103

Northwestern Connecticut
 Community College
Park Place East
Winstead, CT 06098
www.nwctc.commnet.edu

Stone Academy
1315 Dixwell Ave.
Hamden, CT 06514
www.stoneacademy.com

Florida
David G. Erwin Technical Center
2010 E. Hillsborough Ave.
Tampa, FL 33610
http://erwin.edu

Florida Technical College
12689 Challenger Pkwy.
Orlando, FL 32826
www.flatech.edu

Fortis College
1573 W. Fairbanks
Winter Park, FL 32789
www.fortis.edu

Pensacola Junior College
1000 College Blvd.
Pensacola, FL 32504
www.pjc.edu

Pinellas Technical Educational
 Center
901 34th St. S.
St. Petersburg, FL 33711
www.myptec.org

Remington College
7011 A.C. Skinner Pkwy., Ste. 140
Jacksonville, FL 32256
www.remingtoncollege.edu

Sarasota County Technical
 Institute
4748 Beneva Rd.
Sarasota, FL 34233
www.scti.edu

South University
1760 N. Congress Ave.
West Palm Beach, FL 33409
www.southuniversity.edu

United Education Institute
3563 Philips Hwy., Building C
Jacksonville, FL 32207
www.ueicareers.com

Georgia
Atlanta Technical College
1560 Metropolitan Pkwy. SW
Atlanta, GA 30310
www.atlantatech.org

Columbus Technical College
928 Manchester Expressway
Columbus, GA 31904
www.columbustech.edu

Medix School
2108 Cobb Pkwy.
Smyrna, GA 30080
www.medixschool.edu

Savannah Technical College
5717 White Bluff Rd.
Savannah, GA 31405
www.savannahtech.edu

South College
709 Mall Blvd.
Savannah, GA 31406
www.southcollege.edu

Southwest Georgia Technical
 College
15689 U.S. Hwy. 19 N.
Thomasville, GA 31792
www.southwestgatech.edu

United Education Institute
2 Executive Park W., Ste. 100
Atlanta, GA 30329
www.ueicareers.com

Valdosta Technical College
4089 Val Tech Rd.
P.O. Box 928
Valdosta, GA 31603
www.valdostatech.org

Idaho
College of Southern Idaho
315 Falls Ave.
Twin Falls, ID 83303
www.csi.edu

Illinois
Fox College
4201 W. 93rd St.
Oak Lawn, IL 60453
www.foxcollege.edu

Midstate College
411 W. Northmoor Rd.
Peoria, IL 61614
www.midstate.edu

Northwestern Business College
4811 N. Milwaukee Ave.
Chicago, IL 60630
www.northwesterncollege.edu

Indiana
Brown Mackie College
1000 E. 80th Place, Ste. 101N
Merrillville, IN 46410
www.brownmackie.edu

Brown Mackie College
1030 E. Jefferson Blvd.
South Bend, IN 46617
www.brownmackie.edu

International Business College
5699 Coventry Ln.
Ft. Wayne, IN 46804
www.ibcfortwayne.edu

International Business College
7205 Shadeland Station
Indianapolis, IN 46256
www.ibcindianapolis.edu

Ivy Tech State College–Columbus
4475 Central Ave.
Columbus, IN 47203
www.ivytech.edu/columbus/

Ivy Tech State College–Northwest
2401 Valley Dr.
Valparaiso, IN 46383
www.gary.ivytech.edu

Iowa
Iowa Lakes Community College
1900 N. Grand
Spencer, IA 51301
www.iowalakes.edu

Kaplan College
1801 E. Kimberley Rd.
Davenport, IA 52807
http://davenport.
 kaplanuniversity.edu/

Southeastern Iowa Community
 College
1500 W. Agency Rd.
P.O. Box 180
West Burlington, IA 52655
www.scciowa.edu

Kentucky
Jefferson Technical College
727 W. Chestnut St.
Louisville, KY 40203
www.kyhealthcareers.org

National College of Business &
 Technology–Danville
115 E. Lexington Ave.
Danville, KY 40422
www.ncbt.edu

National College of Business &
 Technology–Florence
7627 Ewing Blvd.
Florence, KY 41042
www.ncbt.edu

National College of Business &
 Technology–Lexington
628 E. Main St.
Lexington, KY 40508
www.ncbt.edu

National College of Business &
 Technology–Louisville
4205 Dixie Hwy.
Louisville, KY 40216
www.ncbt.edu

National College of Business &
 Technology–Pikeville
288 S. Mayo Trail, Ste. 2
Pikeville, KY 41501
www.ncbt.edu

National College of Business &
 Technology–Richmond
139 S. Killarney Ln.
Richmond, KY 40475
www.ncbt.edu

West Kentucky Community and
 Technical College
4810 Alben Barkley Dr.
P.O. Box 7380
Paducah, KY 42002
www.westkentucky.kctcs.edu

Louisiana
Bossier Parish Community College
2719 Airline Dr. N.
Bossier City, LA 71111
www.bpcc.edu

Bryman College–New Orleans
1201 Elmwood Park Blvd, Ste.
 600
New Orleans, LA 70123
www.bryman.edu

Massachusetts
Lincoln Technical Institute
5 Middlesex Ave.
Somerville, MA 02145
www.lincolnedu.com

Salter School
515 Woburn St.
Tewksbury, MA 01876
www.salterschool.com

Southeastern Technical Institute
250 Foundry St.
South Easton, MA 02375

Michigan
Baker College of Muskegon
1903 Marquette Ave.
Muskegon, MI 49442
www.baker.edu

Baker College of Owosso
1020 S. Washington St.
Owosso, MI 48867
www.baker.edu

Davenport College
415 E. Fulton St.
Grand Rapids, MI 49503
www.davenport.edu

Detroit Business Institute
19100 Fort St.
Riverview, MI 48192
www.dbidownriver.com

Henry Ford Community College
5101 Evergreen Rd.
Dearborn, MI 48128
www.hfcc.edu

Macomb Community College
14500 E. 12 Mile Rd.
Warren, MI 48088
www.macomb.edu

Oakland Community College
7350 Cooley Lake Rd.
Waterford, MI 48327
www.oaklandcc.edu

Minnesota
Anoka Technical College
1355 W. Hwy. 10
Anoka, MN 55303
www.anokatech.edu

Argosy University/Twin Cities
College of Health Sciences
1515 Central Pkwy.
Eagan, MN 55121
www.argosy.edu

Duluth Business University
4724 Mike Colalillo Dr.
Duluth, MN 55807
www.dbumn.edu

Herzing College–Minneapolis
5700 W. Broadway
Minneapolis, MN 55428
www.herzing.edu

Medical Institute of Minnesota
5503 Green Valley Dr.
Bloomington, MN 55437

Minneapolis Business College
1711 W. County Rd. B
Roseville, MN 55113

Northwest Technical College
905 Grant Ave. SE
Bemidji, MN 56601
www.ntcmn.edu

Rochester Community & Technical
College
851 30th Ave. SE
Rochester, MN 55904
www.rctc.edu

Mississippi
Hinds Community College
Rankin Campus
3805 Hwy. 80 E.
Pearl, MS 39208
www.hindscc.edu

Missouri
Metro Business College
1407 Southwest Blvd.
Jefferson City, MO 65109
www.metrobusinesscollege.edu

Springfield College
1010 W. Sunshine
Springfield, MO 65807
www.springfieldcollege.edu

Nebraska
Central Community College
E. Hwy. 6
P.O. Box 1024
Hastings, NE 68902
www.cccneb.edu

New Hampshire
New Hampshire Community
Technical College
One College Dr.
Claremont, NH 03743
www.ccsnh.edu

Seacoast Career School
670 N. Commercial St.
Manchester, NH 03101
http://seacoastcareerschools.
edu

New Jersey
Berdan Institute
265 Route 46 W.
Totowa, NJ 07512
www.berdaninstitute.edu

Fairleigh Dickinson University
1000 River Rd.
Teaneck, NJ 07666
www.fdu.edu

Health-Care Training Institute
1969 Morris Avenue
Union, NJ 07083
www.healthcaretraininginsti-
tute.edu

Hudson County Community
College
70 Sip Ave.
Jersey City, NJ 07306
www.hccc.edu

New Mexico
Apollo College–Albuquerque
5301 Central Ave. NE, Ste. 101
Albuquerque, NM 87108
www.apollocollege.com

New York
Medical Assisting Career
8 East 40th Street
Brooklyn, NY 11203
www.woodtobecoburn.edu

Bryant & Stratton
465 Main St., Ste. 400
Buffalo, NY 14203
www.bryantstratton.edu

Bryant & Stratton
953 James St.
Syracuse, NY 13203
www.bryantstratton.edu

Erie Community College
121 Ellicott St.
Buffalo, NY 14203
www.ecc.edu

North Carolina
Carteret Community College
3505 Arendell St.
Morehead City, NC 28557
www.carteret.edu

Gaston College
201 Hwy. 321 S.
Dallas, NC 28034
www.gaston.edu

Guilford Technical Community
College
P.O. Box 309
Jamestown, NC 27282
www.gtcc.edu

Haywood Community College
185 Freedlander Dr.
Clyde, NC 28721
www.haywood.edu

King's College
335 Lamar Ave.
Charlotte, NC 28204
www.kingscollegecharlotte.edu

Pitt Community College
P.O. Drawer 7007
Greenville, NC 27835
www.pittcc.edu

Wake Technical Community
College
9101 Fayetteville Rd.
Raleigh, NC 27603
www2.waketech.edu

Wingate University
P.O. Box 159
Wingate, NC 28174
www.wingate.edu

Ohio
Akron Institute
1625 Portage Trail
Cuyahoga Falls, OH 44223
www.akroninstitute.com

Belmont Technical College
120 Fox-Shannon Place
St. Clairsville, OH 43950
www.belmont.edu

Bradford School
6170 Busch Blvd.
Columbus, OH 43229
www.bradford.edu

Brown Mackie College–Akron
2791 Mogadore Rd.
Akron, OH 44312
www.brownmackie.edu

Davis College
4747 Monroe St.
Toledo, OH 43623
www.daviscollege.edu

Knox County Career Center
306 Martinsburg Rd.
Mt. Vernon, OH 43050
www.knoxcc.org

Medina County Career Center
1101 W. Liberty St.
Medina, OH 44256
www.mcjvs.org

National College of Business &
  Technology–Cincinnati
6871 Steger Dr.
Cincinnati, OH 45237
www.ncbt.edu

National College of Business &
  Technology–Dayton Area
1837 Woodman Center Dr.
Kettering, OH 45420
www.ncbt.edu

Remington College
14445 Broadway Ave.
Cleveland, OH 44125
www.remingtoncollege.edu

Oklahoma
Tulsa Community College
909 S. Boston Ave.
Tulsa, OK 74119
www.tulsacc.edu

Oregon
Apollo College–Portland
2004 Lloyd Center, 3rd Floor
Portland, OR 97232
www.apollocollege.com

Mt. Hood Community College
26000 SE Stark St.
Gresham, OR 97030
www.mhcc.edu

Oregon Health Sciences University
3181 Sam Jackson Park Road
UHSU-2
Portland, OR 97239
www.ohsu.edu

Pennsylvania
Bradford School–Pittsburgh
707 Grant St.
Pittsburgh, PA 15219
www.bradfordpittsburgh.edu

Delaware County Community
  College
901 S. Media Line Rd.
Media, PA 19063
www.dccc.edu

Everest
100 Forbes Ave., Ste. 1200
Pittsburgh, PA 15222
www.everest.edu

Harcum College
750 Montgomery Ave.
Bryn Mawr, PA 19010
www.harcum.edu

Mt. Aloysius College
7373 Admiral Peary Hwy.
Cresson, PA 16630
www.mtaloy.edu

South Carolina
Trident Technical College
P.O. Box 118067
Charleston, SC 29423
www.tridenttech.edu

South Dakota
Lake Area Technical Institute
230 11th St. NE
P.O. Box 730
Watertown, SD 57201
www.lakeareatech.edu

Tennessee
Knoxville Business College
720 N. Fifth Ave.
Knoxville, TN 37917
www.knoxvillebusinesscollege.
  com

Miller-Motte Technical Institute
1820 Business Park Dr.
Clarksville, TN 37040
www.miller-motte.com

National College of Business &
  Technology–Knoxville
8415 Kingston Pike
Knoxville, TN 37919
www.ncbt.edu

National College of Business &
  Technology–Nashville
3748 Nolensville Pike
Nashville, TN 37211
www.ncbt.edu

Remington College
2731 Nonconnah Blvd.
Memphis, TN 38132
www.remingtoncollege.edu

Texas
Brown Mackie College–Dallas
1500 Eastgate Dr.
Garland, TX 75041
www.brownmackie.edu

Utah
American Institute of Medical-
  Dental Technology
1675 N. Freedom Blvd.
Provo, UT 84604
www.americaninstitute.edu

Latter-Day Saints Business
  College
411 East South Temple
Salt Lake City, UT 84111
www.ldsbc.edu

Salt Lake City Community College
4600 S. Redwood Rd.
Salt Lake City, UT 84123
www.slcc.edu

Virginia
National College of Business &
  Technology–Bluefield
100 Logan St.
P.O. Box 629
Bluefield, VA 24605
www.ncbt.edu

National College of Business &
  Technology–Charlottesville
1819 Emmet St.
Charlottesville, VA 22901
www.ncbt.edu

National College of Business &
  Technology–Danville
734 Main St.
Danville, VA 24541
www.ncbt.edu

National College of Business &
  Technology–Harrisonburg
51 B Burgess Rd.
Harrisonburg, VA 22801
www.ncbt.edu

National College of Business &
  Technology–Lynchburg
104 Candlewood Court
Lynchburg, VA 24502
www.ncbt.edu

National College of Business &
  Technology–Martinsville
10 Church St.
Martinsville, VA 24114
www.ncbt.edu

National College of Business &
  Technology–Roanoke Valley
1813 E. Main St.
Salem, VA 24153
www.ncbt.edu

National College of Business &
  Technology–Tri-Cities
300 A Piedmont Ave.
Bristol, VA 24201
www.ncbt.edu

Washington
Apollo College–Spokane
10102 E. Knox, Ste. 200
Spokane, WA 99206
www.apollocollege.com

Wisconsin
Blackhawk Technical College
6004 Prairie Rd.
P.O. Box 5009
Janesville, WI 53547
www.blackhawk.edu

Bryant & Stratton
310 W. Wisconsin Ave., Ste. 500
Milwaukee, WI 53203
www.bryantstratton.edu

Mental Health Assistants

Principal activity: Helping care for the mentally disabled

Work commitment: Full-time

Preprofessional education: Usually a high school diploma

Program length: Several months to 2 years

Work prerequisites: On-the-job training possible; usually an associate degree is necessary

Career opportunities: Limited

Income range: $23,000 to $36,000

Scope

Mental health assistants perform a variety of services for those who are emotionally and mentally handicapped. They provide therapeutic, supportive, and preventive care. The population served is wide-ranging, extending from children to the aged, both acutely and chronically sick, and those suffering from mental retardation or alcohol or drug dependencies. These workers are supervised by psychiatrists, psychologists, social workers, and most directly by registered nurses.

Activities

Mental health assistants initially interview and evaluate clients, keep records, teach new skills, help motivate clients to learn, carry out therapeutic activities, provide behavior modification counseling, act as client advocates, help clients make the transition back to their homes, prepare their families for their care, follow up and report on client progress, and serve as a community resource for clients and their families.

    These workers also take vital signs and participate in physical treatments and personal care. Their general goal is to help clients reach their highest potential.

Work Settings

Mental health assistants work in state and private inpatient mental health facilities such as hospitals, schools for the mentally retarded, clinics, and community health centers. They also work in crisis and emergency centers, halfway houses, sheltered workshops, nursing homes, rehabilitation centers, and educational institutions.

Advancement

With increased experience and responsibilities, these workers can receive salary increases. Some advancement is possible for those who develop specialty capabilities, such as working with children, substance abuse clients, crisis intervention clients, or the developmentally disabled.

Prerequisites

A high school diploma or its equivalent is desirable. When an associate degree is sought, such a diploma is essential.

Desirable personal attributes for these workers include a strong sense of compassion, a great deal of patience, emotional stability, an outgoing and cheerful personality, tactfulness, and a genuine desire to help the emotionally ill.

Education/Training

Most openings in this field require an associate degree in mental health. Many community colleges offer programs in this field at this level. The curriculum in a mental health program involves courses in basic and psychiatric nursing, general and abnormal psychology, the theory of personality and social development, child development, group dynamics, and mental health technology.

Most training programs also offer the opportunity for students to perform supervised mental health work with clients.

Certification/Registration/Licensure

Only a few states require licensure, but their number is expected to increase.

Career Potential

Overall job growth will be minimal. The increased number of clients being located in community settings rather than inpatient facilities will have a direct impact on the need for mental health assistants. Job growth also could be affected by changes in government funding.

For More Information

Several hundred programs offer training in this field—far too many to list here.

Currently, this field has no professional organization. For more information, write to the Center for Mental Health Services, 1 Choke Cherry Rd., Ste. 6-1057, Rockville, MD 20857 (www.mentalhealth.samhsa.gov/cmhs).

Nuclear Medicine Technologists

Principal activity: Taking nuclear medicine images of patients for physicians

Work commitment: Full-time

Preprofessional education: High school diploma

Program length: 1 to 4 years

Work prerequisites: A certificate or degree/license

Career opportunities: Favorable

Income range: $57,000 to $78,000

Scope

Doctors use many diagnostic techniques to uncover the causes of disease. One especially useful approach is administering radioactive compounds, whose unstable atoms emit radiation spontaneously, and then to monitor their uptake in organs and tissues in which they localize. Abnormal areas show lower or higher concentrations of radioactivity than normal ones. To see these concentrations, a special camera is placed over the body area of interest, and the radioactivity concentrated there is translated into light spots that expose the camera's film. The developed film—or *scan*—can show doctors a variety of functional or structural abnormalities.

Under a doctor's supervision, nuclear medicine technologists carry out the procedures that provide the data required to form a diagnosis of a possible structural or functional abnormality.

Nuclear medicine is used to detect diseases of the brain, heart, liver, thyroid, and other organs.

Activities

Nuclear medicine technologists explain the procedure to patients, position them, and calculate the needed radioactive dose. Under a physician's supervision, they then administer the drugs for the test. Next, they operate the gamma ray-detecting equipment, check the image quality, and arrange to record the data and develop the film.

Nuclear medicine technologists also perform the laboratory procedure known as *radio assay.* This involves adding radioactive materials to specimens such as blood serum to determine hormone levels, for example.

Technologists also are responsible for ordering, handling, and properly disposing of radioactive drugs. They also maintain records of radionuclides and patient data.

Work Settings

Most nuclear medicine technologists work in hospitals, but some are employed in radiologists' offices, public health facilities, and research and teaching institutions.

Advancement

With experience and education, a nuclear medicine technologist can advance to a position as chief technologist, department administrator, or lab director.

Prerequisites

A high school diploma or its equivalent is necessary for admission into most training programs.

Desirable personal attributes for workers in this field include physical stamina, strong verbal and math skills, attention to detail, and the ability to work well with other professionals and patients.

Education/Training

This field has three kinds of training programs:

- **Certificate programs.** These one-year programs are designed for health professionals seeking to change careers. Typically, they are offered in hospitals and medical centers.

- **Associate degree programs.** These two-year programs usually are offered by community colleges.
- **Bachelor's degree programs.** These four-year programs are offered by colleges and universities.

In a formal program of studies, courses include statistics, instrumentation, biochemistry, immunology, radionuclide chemistry and therapy, radiopharmacy administration, radiology, clinical nuclear medicine, and computer application and operation.

Most formal training programs in this field are accredited by the Joint Review Committee on Education Programs in Nuclear Medicine Technology Certification Board.

Certification/Registration/Licensure

About half of all states require nuclear medicine technologists to be licensed, and most employers prefer to hire registered or certified technologists.

You become certified by meeting the requirements of the American Registry of Radiologic Technologists or the Nuclear Medicine Technology Certification Board.

Career Potential

The demand for nuclear medicine technologists is expected to be above-average in the coming years. As the U.S. population ages, the demand for this diagnostic technique will increase. However, the use of less-invasive diagnostic techniques may negatively affect this field.

For More Information

For more information, contact one of these agencies:

American Society of Radiologic
 Technologists
15000 Central Ave. SE
Albuquerque, NM 87123
www.asrt.org

Joint Review Committee on
 Educational Programs in Nuclear
 Medicine Technology
PMB 418
1 Second Ave. E., Ste. C
Polson, MT 59860
www.jrcnmt.org

Nuclear Medicine Technology
 Certification Board
2970 Clairmont Rd., Ste. 935
Atlanta, GA 30329
www.nmtcb.org

Society of Nuclear Medicine
1850 Samuel Morse Dr.
Reston, VA 20190
http://interactive.snm.org/

Nuclear Medicine Technologist Programs

Alabama
University of Alabama at
 Birmingham
School of Health-Related
 Professions
UAB Station, SHRP 214
Birmingham, AL 35294
www.uab.edu

Arizona
GateWay Community College
108 N. 40th St.
Phoenix, AZ 85034
www.gatewaycc.edu

Arkansas
Baptist Health Medical Center
 11900 Glen road
Little Rock, AR 722 10
www.baptist-health.org

St. Vincent Health System
2 St. Vincent Circle
Little Rock, AR 72205
www.stvincenthealth.com

University of Arkansas for Medical
Sciences
4301 W. Markam St.
Little Rock, AR 72205
www.uams.edu

California
California State University–
Dominguez Hills
1000 E. Victoria St.
Carson, CA 90747
www.csudh.edu

Cancer Foundation of Santa
Barbara
300 W. Pueblo St.
Santa Barbara, CA 93105
www.ccsb.org

Charles R. Drew University of
Medicine and Science
1731 E. 120th St.
Los Angeles, CA 90059
www.cdrewu.edu

Loma Linda University
School of Allied Health
Professions
Loma Linda, CA 92350
www.llu.edu

Los Angeles County USC Medical
Center
1200 N. State St.
Los Angeles, CA 90033
www.usc.edu

University of California,
San Francisco
San Francisco, CA 94143
www.ucsf.edu

West Los Angeles Ambulatory Care
Center
11301 Wilshire Blvd.
Los Angeles, CA 90073

Colorado
Community College of Denver
1111 W. Colfax Ave.
P.O. Box 173363
Campus Box 250
Denver, CO 80217
www.ccd.edu

Connecticut
Gateway Community College
88 Bassett Road
New Haven, CT 06473
www.gatewaycc.edu

Delaware
Delaware Technical & Community
College
333 Shipley St.
Wilmington, DE 19801
www.dtcc.edu

District of Columbia
George Washington University
Medical Center
2300 Eye St. NW
Washington, DC 20037
www.gwumc.edu

Florida
Barry University
School of Natural and Health
Sciences
11300 NE 2nd Ave.
Miami Shores, FL 33161
www.barry.edu

Broward Community College
1000 Coconut Creek Blvd.
Coconut Creek, FL 33066
www.broward.edu

Hillsborough Community College
Dale Mabry Campus
P.O. Box 30030
Tampa, FL 33630
www.hccfl.edu

Institute of Allied Medical
Professions
Nuclear Medicine Technology
5150 Linton Blvd.
Delray Beach, FL 33484
www.iamp.edu

Keiser University
Nuclear medicine Technology
8505 Mills Drive
Miami, FL 33183
www.keiseruniversity.edu

Mt. Sinai Medical Center of
Greater Miami
4300 Alton Rd.
Miami Beach, FL 33140
www.msmc.com

Santa Fe College
3000 NW 83rd St.
Gainesville, FL 32606
www.sfcollege.edu

University of Miami–Jackson
Memorial Medical Center
1611 NW 12th Ave.
Miami, FL 33136
www.miami.edu

Georgia
Armstrong Atlantic State
University
Nuclear Medicine Technology
Program
11935 Abecorn St.
Savannah, GA 31419
www.armstrong.edu

Medical College of Georgia
987 St. Sebastian Way
Augusta, GA 30912
www.mcg.edu

Illinois
College of DuPage
425 Fanwell Blvd.
Glen Ellyn, IL 60137
www.cod.edu

Edward Hines, Jr. Veterans
Administration Hospital
Fifth Ave. and Roosevelt Rd.
P.O. Box 5000
Hines, IL 60141
www.hines.va.gov

Northwestern Memorial Hospital
School of Nuclear Medicine
Technology
Galter-8
251 E Huron St.
Chicago, IL 60611
www.nmh.org

St. Francis Medical Center
530 NE Glen Oak Ave.
Peoria, IL 61637
www.osfsaintfrancis.org

Triton College
2000 Fifth Ave.
River Grove, IL 60171
www.triton.edu

Indiana

Ball State University
Methodist Hospital of Indiana
1701 N. Senate Blvd.
Indianapolis, IN 46202
www.clarian.org

Indiana University School of
  Medicine
1120 South Dr.
Fesler Hall 302
Indianapolis, IN 46202
http://medicine.iu.edu/

Indiana University Medical Center
Nuclear Medicine Technological
  Program
541 Clinical Drive
Indianapolis, IN 46202
www.indyrad.iupui.edu

Iowa

University of Iowa
Roy J. and Lucille A. Carver
  College of Medicine
200 CMAB
Iowa City, IA 52242
www.medicine.uiowa.edu/ccom/

University of Iowa Hospitals &
  Clinics
Division of Nuclear Medicine
200 Hawkings Drive
Iowa City, IA 52242
www.radiology.uiowa.edu

Kansas

University of Kansas
School of Allied Health
3901 Rainbow Blvd.
Kansas City, KS 66160
www.alliedhealth.kumc.edu

Kentucky

Bluegrass Community and
Technical College
470 Cooper Drive
Oswald Building 330-A
Lexington, KY 40506
www.bluegrass.ketts.edu

University of Louisville
Louisville, KY 40292
www.louisville.edu

Jefferson Community College
Nuclear Medicine Technological
  Program
109 E Broadway
Louisville, KY 40202
www.jcc.kctcs.edu

Louisiana

Delgado Community College
615 City Park Ave.
New Orleans, LA 70119
www.dcc.edu

Ochsner Clinic Foundation
1514 Jefferson Hwy.
New Orleans, LA 70121
www.ochsner.org

Overton Brooks Veterans
  Administration Medical Center
510 E. Stoner Ave.
Shreveport, LA 71101

Maine

Central Maine Medical Center
Nuclear Medicine Technology
  Program
300 Main Street
Lewiston, ME 04240
www.cmmc.org

Maryland

Community College of Baltimore
  County Essex
7201 Rossville Blvd.
Baltimore, MD 21237
www.ccbcmd.edu

Naval School of Health Sciences
8901 Wisconsin Ave.
Bethesda, MD 20889
http://nshs.med.navy.mil/

The Johns Hopkins Hospital
Nuclear Medicine Technology
  Program
8 Market Place
Baltimore, MD 21202
http://radiologycareers.rad.
  jhmi.edu/

Prince George's Community
  College
301 Largo Rd.
Largo, MD 20774
www.pgcc.edu

Massachusetts

Beth Israel Deaconess Medical
  Center
School of Nuclear Medicine
  Technology
330 Brookline Ave
Boston, MA 02215
www.bidmc.org

Bunker Hill Community College
250 New Rutherford Ave.
Boston, MA 02129
www.bhcc.mass.edu

Massachusetts College of
  Pharmacy and Health Sciences
179 Longwood Ave.
Boston, MA 02115
www.mcphs.edu

Salem State College
352 Lafayette St.
Salem, MA 01970
www.salemstate.edu

Springfield Technical Community
  College
One Armory Square
Springfield, MA 01102
www.stcc.edu

University of Massachusetts
  Medical Center
55 Lake Ave. N.
Worcester, MA 01655
www.umassmed.edu

Michigan

Ferris State University
  200 Ferris Dr.
Big Rapids, MI 49307
www.ferris.edu

St. John's Hospital & Medical
  Center
22101 Moross Rd.
Detroit, MI 48236
www.stjohn.org

William Beaumont Hospital
3601 W. Thirteen Mile Rd.
Royal Oak, MI 48073
www.beaumont.edu

Minnesota
Mayo Foundation
200 First St. SW
Rochester, MN 55905
www.mayo.edu

St. Mary's University of Minnesota
700 Terrace Heights
Winona, MN 55987
www.smumn.edu

Mississippi
University of Mississippi Medical
 Center
2500 N. State St.
Jackson, MS 39216
www.umc.edu

Missouri
Research Medical Center
2316 E. Meyer Blvd.
Kansas City, MO 64132
www.researchmedicalcenter.com

St. Louis University
School of Allied Health
 Professions
221 N. Grand Blvd.
St. Louis, MO 63103
www.slu.edu

St. Luke's Hospital of Kansas City
4400 Wornall Rd.
Kansas City, MO 64111
www.saintlukeshealthsystem.org

University of Missouri–Columbia
605 Lewis Hall
Columbia, MO 65211
www.umshp.org

Nebraska
University of Nebraska Medical
 Center
42nd and Emile
Omaha, NE 68198
www.unmc.edu

Nevada
University of Nevada
4505 Maryland Pkwy.
Las Vegas, NV 89154
www.unlv.edu

New Jersey
Gloucester County College
1400 Tanyard Rd.
Sewell, NJ 08080
www.gccnj.edu

John F. Kennedy Medical Center
65 James St.
Edison, NJ 08820
www.jfkmc.org

Muhlenberg Regional Medical
 Center
Nuclear Medicine Technology
 Program
Park Avenue& Randolph Road
Plainfield, NJ 07061
www.muhlenbergschools.org

Overlook Hospital
99 Beauvoir Ave.
Summit, NJ 07902
www.atlantichealth.org

University of Medicine &
 Dentistry of New Jersey
65 Bergen St.
Newark, NJ 07107
www.umdnj.edu

New Mexico
University of New Mexico
School of Medicine
Albuquerque, NM 87131
 www.hsc.unm.edu

New York
Bronx Community College
City University of New York
2155 University Ave. at W. 181st
 St.
Bronx, NY 10453
www.bcc.cuny.edu

Institute of Allied Medical
 Professions
405 Park Ave., Ste. 501
New York, NY 10022
www.iamp.edu

Manhattan College
Manhattan College Pkwy.
Nuclear Medicine Technology
 Program
Riverdale, NY 10471
www.manhattan.edu

Molloy College
Nuclear Medicine Technology
 program
1000 Hempstead Avenue
P.O. Box 5002
Rockville Center, NY 11571
www.molloy.edu

New York University Medical Center
550 First Ave.
New York, NY 10016
www.med.nyu.edu

Northport VA Medical Center
79 Middleville Rd.
Northport, NY 11768
www.northport.va.gov

Rochester Institute of Technology
One Lomb Memorial Dr.
Rochester, NY 14623
www.rit.edu

St. Vincent's Hospital and Medical
 Center of New York
153 W. 11th St.
New York, NY 10011
www.svmc.org

SUNY Downstate Medical Center
450 Clarkson Ave.
Brooklyn, NY 11203
www.downstate.edu

SUNY Health Science Center–
 Buffalo
105 Parker Hall
Buffalo, NY 14260
www.buffalo.edu

Wagner College
One Campus Rd.
Staten Island, NY 10301
www.wagner.edu

North Carolina
Caldwell Community College &
 Technical Institute
Nuclear Medicine Program
2855 Hickory Boulevard
Hudson, NC 28638
www.caldwell.cc.nc.us

Forsyth Technical Community
 College
2100 Silas Creek Pkwy.
Winston-Salem, NC 27103
www.forsythtech.edu

Pitt Community College
Nuclear Medicine Technology
  Program
P.O. Box 7007
Greenville, NC 27835
www-health.pitt.cc.nc.us

UNC Health Care
101 Manning Dr.
Chapel Hill, NC 27514
www.unchealthcare.org

Ohio
Aultman Hospital
2600 Sixth St. SW
Canton, OH 44710
www.aultman.com

Kettering College of Medical Arts
Division of Allied Health
3737 Southern Blvd.
Kettering, OH 45429
www.kcma.edu

Ohio State University Medical
  Center
389 GR 550 E Spring Street
Columbus, OH 43215
http://medicalcenter.osu.edu/

St. Elizabeth Hospital Medical
  Center
1044 Belmont Ave.
Youngstown, OH 44501
www.hmpartners.org

University Hospital
234 Goodman St.
Cincinnati, OH 45219
www.health-alliance.com

University of Cincinnati Medical
  Center
College of Allied Health Sciences
Medical Imaging Technology
P.O. Box 670394
Cincinnati, OH 45267
http://medcenter.uc.edu/

University of Findlay
1000 N. Main St.
Findlay, OH 45840
www.findlay.edu

Oklahoma
American Institute of Medical
  Technology
Nuclear Medicine Technology
7040 South Yale,
Tulsa, OK 74136
www.aimt-edu.com

University of Oklahoma
Health Sciences Center
1100 N. Lindsay
Oklahoma City, OK 73104
www.ouhsc.edu

Oregon
Oregon Institute of Technology
Nuclear Medicine Program
3201 Campus Drive SE
Klamath Falls, OR 97601
www.oit.edu

Portland VA Medical Center
P.O. Box 1034
3710 SW U.S. Veterans Hospital
  Rd.
Portland, OR 97207

Pennsylvania
Cedar Crest College
100 College Dr.
Allentown, PA 18104
www.cedarcrest.edu

Community College of Allegheny
  County
808 Ridge Ave.
Pittsburgh, PA 15212
www.ccac.edu

Harrisburg Hospital
111 S. Front St.
Harrisburg, PA 17101
www.pinnaclehealth.org

Lancaster General
410 N. Lime St.
Lancaster, PA 17602
www.lancastergeneralcollege.
  edu

Temple University
College of Health Professions
1801 N. Broad St.
Philadelphia, PA 19122
www.temple.edu

Thomas Jefferson University
Nuclear Medicine Technology
130 South 9th Street
Philadelphia, PA 19107
www.jefferson.edu

University of Pennsylvania Health
  System
3400 Spruce St.
Philadelphia, PA 19104
www.pennmedicine.org

Wilkes-Barre General Hospital
575 N. River St.
Wilkes-Barre, PA 18764
www.wvhcs.org

Rhode Island
Rhode Island Hospital
593 Eddy St.
Providence, RI 02902
www.brown.edu

South Carolina
Horry-Georgetown Technical
  College
Nuclear Medicine Technology
P.O. Box 261966
Conway, SC 29528
www.hgtc.edu

Midlands Technical College
P.O. Box 2408
Columbia, SC 29202
www.midlandstech.edu

Tennessee
Baptist Memorial College Health
  Sciences
 1003 Monroe Avenue
Memphis, TN 38104
www.bchs.edu

University of Tennessee Medical
  Center
1924 Alcoa Hwy.
Knoxville, TN 37920
www.utmck.edu

Vanderbilt University Medical
  Center
Radiology Department
Room R1317 MCN
21st Ave. S. and Garland Ave.
Nashville, TN 37232
www.mc.vanderbilt.edu

Texas

Amarillo College
Nuclear Medicine Department
P O Box 447
Amarillo, TX 79178
www.actx.edu

Baylor University Medical Center
Nuclear Medicine Technology
2625 Elm St.
Dallas, TX 75226
www.baylorhealth.edu

Houston Community College
 System
Eastwood Health Sciences Center
1300 Holman
Houston, TX 77004
www.hccs.edu

University of the Incarnate Word
4301 Broadway
San Antonio, TX 78209
www.uiw.edu

UTMB School of Allied Health
 Sciences
301 University Blvd.
Galveston, TX 77555
http://shp.utmb.edu/

Utah

University of Utah Health
 Sciences Center
50 N. Medical Dr.
Salt Lake City, UT 84132
http://healthcare.utah.edu/

Weber State University
3850 University Circle
Ogden, UT 84408
www.weber.edu

Vermont

University of Vermont
Nuclear Medicine Technology
Rowell Building
Burlington, VT 05405
www.uvm.edu

Virginia

Carilion Health System
Roanoke Memorial Hospital
1906 Belleview Ave.
P.O. Box 13367
Roanoke, VA 24033
www.carilionclinic.org

Old Dominion University
222 Spong Hall
Norfolk, VA 23529
www.odu.edu

University of Virginia Health
 Science Center
P.O. Box 400160
Charlottesville, VA 22904
www.virginia.edu

Virginia Commonwealth University
Department of Radiation Sciences
West Hospital, 701 W Grace St.
1200 E. Broad St.
Richmond, VA 232 84
www.vcu.edu

Washington

Bellevue Community College
3000 Landerholm Circle SE
Bellevue, WA 98007
http://bellevuecollege.edu

West Virginia

West Virginia State University
P.O. Box 1000
Institute, WV 25112
www.wvstateu.edu

West Virginia University
Robert C. Byrd Health Sciences
 Center
Box 8062
Morgantown, WV 26506
www.hsc.wvu.edu

Wheeling Jesuit University
316 Washington Ave.
Wheeling, WV 26003
www.wju.edu

Wisconsin

Milwaukee County Medical
 Complex
9455 W. Watertown Plank Rd.
Milwaukee, WI 53226

St. Joseph's Hospital
611 St. Joseph Ave.
Marshfield, WI 54449
www.ministryhealth.org

St. Luke's Medical Center
2900 W. Oklahoma Ave.
Milwaukee, WI 53215
www.aurorahealthcare.org

St. Mary's Hospital of Milwaukee
2320 N. Lake Dr.
Milwaukee, WI 53211
www.columbia-stmarys.org

Nurse's Aides

Principal activity: Assisting with routine patient care in medical and psychiatric hospitals

Work commitment: Usually full-time

Preprofessional education: High school diploma

Program length: 6 weeks to 3 months

Work prerequisites: On-the-job training

Career opportunities: Highly favorable

Income range: $18,000 to $27,000

Scope

Nurse's aides help with the routine daily care of ill patients in a variety of settings. Although it doesn't involve sophisticated equipment or cutting-edge procedures, their work is vital in helping people recover or at least remain physically stable and as comfortable as possible in an environment outside their homes.

Activities

Nurse's aides, also known as *nursing assistants* or *hospital attendants*, work under the direct supervision of the nursing staff to facilitate routine activities and enhance patients' well-being. They make beds; help patients eat, bathe, dress, and walk; take readings of vital signs (such as temperature, pulse, and respiration); help secure meals; provide massages (to maintain skin health); and respond to patients' calls for assistance. When necessary, they transport patients to specific sites for treatment, therapy, or recreation. They also help maintain the condition of their patients' rooms and report to their supervisors any significant changes in patients' conditions.

Work Settings

About half of all nurse's aides are employed in nursing homes, where they are frequently called *geriatric aides*. One-quarter work in acute-care or chronic-care hospitals, and the rest work in residential facilities or private households.

Advancement

Opportunities for advancement within this occupation are limited. To enter other health occupations, aides generally need additional formal training. Some employers and unions provide opportunities by simplifying the educational paths to advancement. Experience as an aide can also help individuals decide whether to pursue a career in the health-care field.

Prerequisites

No formal education is needed for this position, but a high school diploma is helpful.

Desirable personal attributes for this job include good physical and emotional health, the ability to follow instructions and use good judgment, dependability, and a strong sense of compassion.

Education/Training

Formal nurse's aide training, which varies in length and depth, is offered by some high schools, vocational-technical institutes, community colleges, and nursing homes. Courses cover body mechanics, nutrition, anatomy, physiology, infection control, communication skills, personal-care skills, and resident rights.

Many facilities rely exclusively on informal, on-the-job training provided by a nurse or experienced aide. This training may last several days or a few months.

Certification/Registration/Licensure

Professional accreditation is uncommon, but some nursing homes require aides to successfully complete state-mandated programs. Others require aides to take a minimum of 75 hours of training and pass a competency exam within four months. Successful candidates receive certificates and are placed on a State Registry of Nursing Aides.

Career Potential

Employment prospects for nurse's aides will be excellent over the next decade. The expanding older U.S. population will result in an increase of nursing homes and long-term care facilities. In fact, this occupation is expected to grow faster than most other occupations, even those in the health-care industry.

For More Information

This field has no professional organization. For more information, contact the American Health Care Association, 1201 L St. NW, Washington, DC 20005 (www.ahca.org). You can also visit the National Network of Career Nursing Assistants' Web site at www. cna-network.org.

Ophthalmic Assistants

Principal activity: Assisting ophthalmologists

Work commitment: Usually full-time

Preprofessional education: High school diploma

Program length: 1 to 2 years

Work prerequisites: Certification preferred

Career opportunities: Favorable

Income range: $20,000 to $30,000

Scope

The ophthalmic assistant is the lowest of three ranks of paraophthalmic personnel. These workers perform various support services to help eye doctors diagnose and treat their patients. The other two levels are ophthalmic technician (see p. 285) and ophthalmic technologist (see p. 287).

Activities

The major function of an ophthalmic assistant is to collect information about patients' overall medical conditions and specific details about their ocular history, as well as any current problems; to measure their visual acuity (both with and without glasses); to secure other ocular measurements; to administer medications; to handle minor adjustments of and repairs to eyeglasses; to maintain ophthalmologic equipment; and to sterilize the doctor's instruments.

Work Settings

Most ophthalmic assistants are employed in ophthalmologists' offices. Others secure positions in medical centers, hospitals, clinics, and research facilities.

Advancement

With additional experience and training, an ophthalmic assistant can become a technician or technologist.

Prerequisites

A high school diploma or its equivalent is necessary to enter this field.

Desirable personal attributes include excellent vision, a commitment to accuracy, manual dexterity, good communication skills, a pleasant personality, and a great deal of patience.

Education/Training

There are two routes to becoming an ophthalmic assistant. One is securing on-the-job training and experience. The other is an educational program completed at a hospital or teaching institution. Courses include anatomy (especially of the eye), physiology, psychology, medical terminology, microbiology, optics, eye testing, diagnostic treatment methods, and ophthalmic instruments.

Certification/Registration/Licensure

Certification is voluntary but does facilitate career advancement. Meeting certain educational requirements and having a set amount of experience qualify you to take the written certification exam.

Career Potential

The job outlook for this profession is favorable because of the increase in the U.S. population—especially of the elderly, who are most frequently in need of eye care.

For More Information

The certification organization for this field is the Joint Commission on Allied Health Personnel in Ophthalmology, 2025 Woodlane Dr., St. Paul, MN 55125 (www.jcahpo. org).

Ophthalmic Assistant Programs

Arizona
Pima Medical Institute
3350 E. Grant Rd., #200
Tucson, AZ 85716
www.pmi.edu

California
Jules Stein Eye Institute
100 Stein Plaza UCLA
Los Angeles, CA 90095
www.jsei.org

Colorado
Pima Medical Institute
1701 W. 72nd Ave., #130
Denver, CO 80221
www.pmi.edu

District of Columbia
Georgetown University Medical
  Center
4000 Reservoir Rd. NW
Ste. 120
Washington, DC 20007
http://gumc.georgetown.edu/

Louisiana
Delgado Community College
615 City Park Ave.
New Orleans, LA 70119
www.dcc.edu

Tulane University Medical Center
1430 Tulane Ave.
New Orleans, LA 70112
http://tulane.edu/som/

Massachusetts
Boston University School of
  Medicine
715 Albany St., L-124
Boston, MA 02118
www.bumc.bu.edu

Michigan
Detroit Institute of
  Ophthalmology
15415 E. Jefferson Ave.
Grosse Pointe Park, MI 48230
www.eyeson.org

New Jersey
University of Medicine &
   Dentistry
Ophthalmic Allied Health Program
90 Bergen St., Room 6157
Newark, NJ 07103
www.umdnj.edu

New York
Bronx Lebanon Hospital
Affiliated with the Albert Einstein
   College of Medicine
46 W. 86th St.
New York, NY 10024
www.bronx-leb.org

Lighthouse International
111 E. 59th St.
New York, NY 10022
www.lighthouse.org

Ohio
Stark State College of Technology
6200 Frank Ave. NW
Canton, OH 44720
www.starkstate.edu

Pennsylvania
Westmoreland County Community
   College
400 Armbrust Rd.
Youngwood, PA 15697
www.wccc.edu

Texas
U.S. Army Medical Department
   Center & School
2751 McIndoe Rd.
Fort Sam Houston, TX 78234
www.cs.amedd.army.mil

Utah
American Institute of Medical-
   Dental Technology
1675 N. Freedom Blvd.
Provo, UT 84604
www.americaninstitute.edu

West Virginia
Carver Career and Technical
   Educational Center
4700 Midland Dr.
Charleston, WV 25306
www.carvercareercenter.net

West Virginia University
University Eye Center
1 Stadium Dr.
Morgantown, WV 26506
www.wvu.edu

Canada
Centennial College
Box 631, Station A
Scarborough, Ontario M1K 5E9
www.cencol.on.ca

Ophthalmic Laboratory Technicians

Principal activity: Fabricating prescription eyeglasses

Work commitment: Full-time

Preprofessional education: On-the-job training

Program length: 6 to 18 months

Work prerequisites: High school diploma

Career opportunities: Favorable

Income range: $22,000 to $35,000

Scope

People often see an ophthalmologist or optometrist for routine eye examinations. They also do so because they are having difficulty with their vision. After an examination, the eye doctor is likely to prescribe eyeglasses for the first time or to replace existing lenses with a stronger set. Patients then go to their optometrist or dispensing optician to select frames and to be fitted for new lenses. Once these steps are accomplished, the optometrist or optician passes the prescription with instructions to an ophthalmic laboratory technician for processing. Don't confuse this position with an ophthalmic technician, who works directly with patients in an ophthalmologist's or optometrist's office (see p. 285).

Activities

The ophthalmic laboratory technician uses tools and machines to properly grind, edge, and polish each lens to meet the dimensions and specifications called for by the eye doctor and the shape of the frame selected by the patient.

To achieve these goals, the ophthalmic laboratory technician marks the lenses to identify where the curves should be ground. The unshaped lenses are then placed in a machine whose controls are set to the prescription's specifications. A different machine is used to smooth the rough edges and polish the lenses.

A check of the accuracy is the next step. This is done using a measuring device called a lensometer, which determines whether the degree and placement of the curve are exact. If satisfied, the technician cuts the edges of the lenses and brushes them off so that they fit into the frame. The technician then assembles the frame.

Work Settings

The technical activities associated with preparing lenses are performed at an optical laboratory or at an optometry facility equipped with the machinery needed to provide such services.

Advancement

In large laboratory facilities, with adequate experience you eventually can move up to a supervisory position and become a production manager. If you have the ambition and ability to move ahead, you can graduate from a college program and become an optician, which will enhance your status and earning potential.

Desirable personal attributes for this profession include excellent manual dexterity, an inclination toward precision work, and the ability to work well with others. Patience and being able to work in an organized, consistent fashion are essential.

Prerequisites

A high school diploma is essential. Graduating from a vocational institution can prove helpful in securing a position and meeting this job's requirements.

Education/Training

Training to become an ophthalmic laboratory technician usually occurs on the job. On-the-job training may last from 6 to 18 months. A training program may be offered by vocational or trade schools, which award you a certificate or diploma after you complete the program. This should prove quite helpful when you seek employment.

Certification/Registration/Licensure

None of these requirements are needed to work as an ophthalmic laboratory technician.

Career Potential

Contact lenses and laser surgery that reshapes the cornea have diminished the number of people who wear glasses. On the other hand, with the increase in life expectancy, more people are wearing glasses, especially those who cannot afford alternative measures. This should favorably affect the employment prospects for ophthalmic laboratory technicians.

For More Information

There is no specific organization for ophthalmic laboratory technicians. But you can obtain information from the Opticians Association of America, 441 Carlisle Dr., Herndon, VA 20170 (www.oaa.org), and the Commission on Opticianry Accreditation, P.O. Box 3073, Merrifield, VA 22116 (www.coaccreditation.com).

Ophthalmic Technicians

Principal activity: Assisting ophthalmologists

Work commitment: Usually full-time

Preprofessional education: High school diploma

Program length: 1 to 2 years

Work prerequisites: Certification preferred

Career opportunities: Very favorable

Income range: $22,000 to $27,000

Scope

Ophthalmic technicians are in the middle of the three ranks of paramedical eye care personnel. Their support services for ophthalmologists are more sophisticated than that of ophthalmic assistants and thus demand a higher degree of training and skill.

Activities

Ophthalmic technicians perform the same tasks as ophthalmic assistants (see p. 281). Additionally, they are qualified to evaluate ocular mobility, measure for contact lenses and instruct patients in their use and care, secure eye samples for cultures, ensure that optical instruments are aligned and calibrated, change dressings, and provide other direct patient care.

Work Settings

Most ophthalmic technicians work in the offices of ophthalmologists. Others work in patient treatment facilities such as medical centers, hospitals, and clinics.

Advancement

With experience and training, an ophthalmic technician can become an ophthalmic technologist. Supervisory responsibilities also are possible.

Prerequisites

A high school diploma or its equivalent is needed to work in this field.

Desirable personal attributes for people entering this field include good visual acuity, meticulous work habits, strong interpersonal skills, manual dexterity, and a strong sense of responsibility.

Education/Training

Both informal on-the-job training and formal training programs are available. Formal programs include courses in anatomy, physiology, pharmacology, microbiology, pathology, optics, eye diseases, visual field testing, and supervised clinical practice.

Certification/Registration/Licensure

Certification is not mandatory, but it can be helpful in advancing your career. With a certain amount of experience, you can take the certification exam.

Career Potential

The job potential for ophthalmic technicians is positive due to the increasing demands for ophthalmological services.

For More Information

The certifying body for this field is the Joint Commission on Allied Health Personnel in Ophthalmology, 2025 Woodlane Dr., St. Paul, MN 55125 (www.jcahpo.org).

Ophthalmic Technician Programs

Colorado
Pima Medical Institute
1701 W. 72nd Ave., #130
Denver, CO 80221
www.pmi.edu

Pueblo Community College
900 W. Orman Ave.
Pueblo, CO 81004
www.pueblocc.edu

District of Columbia
Georgetown University Medical
  Center
Department of Ophthalmology
4000 Reservoir Rd. NW
Washington, DC 20057
http://gumc.georgetown.edu/

Florida
University of Florida
P.O. Box 100284 JHMHC
Gainesville, FL 32610
www.ufl.edu

Georgia
Emory University
1365-B Clifton Rd. NE
Atlanta, GA 30322
www.emory.edu

Illinois
Triton College
2000 Fifth Ave.
River Grove, IL 60171
www.triton.edu

Massachusetts
Boston University Medical Center
Department of Ophthalmology
715 Albany St., L-124
Boston, MA 02118
www.bumc.bu.edu

Michigan
Detroit Institute of
  Ophthalmology
15415 E. Jefferson Ave.
Grosse Point Park, MI 48230
www.eyeson.org

Minnesota
Regions Hospital
School of Ophthalmic Technology
864 Terrace Court
St. Paul, MN 55130
www.regionshospital.com

North Carolina
Duke University School of Medicine
Ophthalmic Medical Technician
  Program
Box 3802
Durham, NC 27710
www.medschool.duke.edu

Ohio
Lakeland Community College
7700 Clocktower Dr.
Kirtland, OH 44094
www.lakelandcc.edu

Oregon
Portland Community College
705 N. Killingsworth St.
Portland, OR 97217
www.pcc.edu

Tennessee
Volunteer State Community
  College
1480 Nashville Pike
Gallatin, TN 37066
www.volstate.edu

Virginia
Eastern Virginia Medical School
600 Gresham Dr.
Norfolk, VA 23507
www.evms.edu

Ophthalmic Technologists

Principal activity: Assisting ophthalmologists

Work commitment: Usually full-time

Preprofessional education: High school diploma

Program length: 1 to 2 years

Work prerequisites: Certification preferred

Career opportunities: Favorable

Income range: $29,000 to $50,000

Scope

The ophthalmic technologist is the highest level of the three ranks of paraophthalmic personnel. Technologists are qualified to provide the most advanced type of assistance to ophthalmologists. They are involved in the widest array of activities, carry the greatest responsibilities, and receive the highest salaries.

Activities

Ophthalmic technologists provide a wide range of patient services. They take patient histories, perform routine tests and measurements, fit patients for contact lenses, and maintain sophisticated ophthalmological equipment. They also take vital measurements, perform tests, and assist in surgery (both in the doctor's office and in hospitals).

Work Settings

For the most part, ophthalmic technologists are employed in private-practice offices of ophthalmologists. They may also work in medical centers, hospitals, and clinics.

Advancement

An ophthalmic technologist may secure a supervisory position in a larger office.

Prerequisites

A high school diploma or its equivalent is necessary for this profession.

Desirable personal attributes for technologists include superior vision, the ability to perform highly detailed work, above-average manual dexterity, strong oral communication skills, a positive personality, strong organizational skills, and supervisory ability.

Education/Training

On-the-job training is available, but undergoing formal education will help you find a better position. Formal programs include courses in the basic biomedical sciences, ophthalmic pharmacology, toxicology, optics, eye diseases and their diagnoses and treatment, visual testing and measurements, optical instrument care, and ophthalmic surgical procedures. Supervised practice is required.

Certification/Registration/Licensure

Being certified enhances your employability. If you've completed a formal education program and have the required experience, you can take a written certification exam. You also must pass a hands-on test.

Career Potential

Job opportunities in this profession are very good. This is the result of the strong demand for the services of ophthalmologists, especially by the elderly. In addition, public awareness of the need for quality eye care is increasing.

For More Information

The certifying body for this field is the Joint Commission on Allied Health Personnel in Ophthalmology, 2025 Woodlane Dr., St. Paul, MN 55125 (www.jcahpo.org).

Ophthalmic Technologist Programs

Arkansas
University of Arkansas for Medical
  Sciences
Jones Eye Institute
4301 W. Markham
Little Rock, AR 72205
www.uams.edu

Colorado
Pima Medical Institute-Denver
7475 Dakin St.
Denver, CO. 80221
www.pmi.edu

District of Columbia
Georgetown University Medical
  Center
3800 Reservoir Rd. NW
Washington, DC 20007
http://gumc.georgetown.edu/

Florida
University of Florida
Box 100284
Gainesville, FL 32610
www.ufl.edu

Georgia
Emory University
Master of Medical Sciences in
  Ophthalmic Technology
1365B Clifton Rd. NE
Atlanta, GA 30322
www.emory.edu

Louisiana
Louisiana State University Health
  Sciences Center
2020 Gravier St.
New Orleans, LA 70112
www.lsu-eye.lsuhsc.edu

Massachusetts
Boston University Medical Center
715 Albany St.
Boston, MA 02118
www.bumc.bu.edu

Michigan
Detroit Institute of
  Ophthalmology
15415 E. Jefferson Ave.
Grosse Pointe, MI 48230
www.eyeson.org

Minnesota
Regions Hospital
School of Ophthalmic Technology
664 Terrace Ct.
St. Paul, MN 55130
www.regionshospital.com

Missouri
University of Missouri
Eye Foundation of Kansas City
2300 Holmes St.
Kansas City, MO 64108
www.eyefoundationkc.org

New York
New York Eye & Ear Infirmary
310 E. 14th St.
New York, NY 10003
www.nyee.edu

Tennessee
Volunteer State Community
  College
1480 Nashville Pike
Gallatin, TN 37066
www.volstate.edu

Virginia
Eastern Virginia Medical School
600 Gresham Dr.
Norfolk, VA 23507
www.evms.edu

Canada
Dalhousie Medical School
5859 University Ave.
Halifax, Nova Scotia B3H 4H7
www.dal.ca

Stanton Yellowknife Hospital
P.O. Box 10
Yellowknife, Ontario X1A 2N1
www.srhb.org

Opticians

Principal activity: Dispensing eyeglasses and contact lenses

Work commitment: Usually full-time, but part-time is possible

Preprofessional education: High school diploma

Program length: 2- to 4-year apprenticeship; 6-month to 2-year educational program

Work prerequisites: Completion of an apprenticeship or formal program with certificate or diploma

Career opportunities: Favorable

Income range: $26,000 to $42,000

Scope

Most people recognize the importance of proper eye care and periodically visit an ophthalmologist (a medical doctor specializing in eye diseases) or an optometrist. Children may have their eyes routinely checked in school, where some will find that they have problems such as nearsightedness.

Like optometrists, opticians fit, adjust, and dispense glasses and contact lenses—but they don't prescribe them. Many people, especially those at the onset of middle age, find that their vision no longer is sharp and that they need corrective lenses. They are given prescriptions for glasses or contact lenses to overcome this limitation. An alternative name for these professionals is *dispensing opticians*.

Activities

Opticians evaluate the prescriptions presented to them and measure the distance between the centers of the patient's pupils to determine the lenses' positioning. Then they help customers choose frames that accommodate the thickness and weight of their lenses and that complement their face.

Once the selection is made, the optician orders the frames and lenses. The latter usually are prepared by an ophthalmic laboratory technician (see p. 283), who receives a work order specifying the lens prescriptions, size, material, color, and style.

The optician may place the ground lenses in the selected frame, but often they are already inserted. The glasses are adjusted so that they are comfortable and properly positioned.

Opticians may also duplicate glasses. The prescription may be on file, obtained from an ophthalmologist, or determined by use of a lensometer. Opticians also repair broken lenses and frames.

Some opticians are also qualified to fit contact lenses. To do so, they must be trained to measure eye shape and size. Fitting contact lenses requires considerable care, skill, and patience. The selected lenses are checked to see if they fit, and the patient is taught how to avoid damaging the lens or infecting the eyes.

Some opticians also are skilled in fitting artificial eyes or dispensing cosmetic shells that conceal defects in the eye's appearance.

Work Settings

Opticians may work for ophthalmologists or optometrists or in hospital eye clinics. Most commonly they are employed by optical stores or chains. Many are self-employed.

Advancement

Opticians can advance by moving to a larger facility or by opening their own business. Others become managers in stores or sales representatives.

Prerequisites

A high school diploma or its equivalent is essential for this field. Recommended courses include basic anatomy, physics, algebra, geometry, and mechanical drawing.

Desirable personal attributes include the ability to deal with the public in a tactful and courteous manner, good communication skills, manual dexterity, superior vision, and a desire to help people.

Education/Training

Training usually is secured in an on-the-job apprenticeship, but formal programs do exist. Large employers generally offer structured training programs, and small employers provide more informal training that can last two to four years. Apprenticeship programs involve instruction in optical mathematics, optical physics, usage of precision instruments for measurement, usage of other equipment, office management, and sales.

Some community colleges offer two-year associate degree programs in optical fabrication and dispensing. Shorter formal educational programs are offered by vocational-technical institutes, trade schools, and manufacturers. These programs last six months to two years and award a diploma or certificate upon completion.

Certification/Registration/Licensure

Opticians may apply to the Commission on Optical Accreditation and the National Contact Lens Examiners for certification of their skills. Certification must be renewed every three years through continuing education.

Many states require a license to dispense eyeglasses. Candidates must meet certain educational standards and pass a written or practical examination.

Career Potential

Job opportunities in this field should be favorable due to the aging of the U.S. population. Improvements in lenses and changes in frame styles also enhance opticians' business.

For More Information

The professional organization for this field is the Opticians Association of America, 441 Carlisle Dr., Herndon, VA 20170 (www.oaa.org). An additional source of information is the National Academy of Opticianry, 8401 Corporate Dr., Ste. 605, Landover, MD 20785 (www.nao.org).

Optician Programs

Connecticut
Gateway Community College
New Haven, CT
www.gwctc.commnet.edu

Housatonic Community College
900 Lafayette Blvd
Bridgeport, CT 06134
www.hcc.commnet.edu

Middlesex Community College
100 Training Hill Rd.
Middletown, CT 06457
www.middlesex.mass.edu

Mt. Carmel Opticians
2301 State Street
Hamden, CT 06517
www.matchpoint.com

Florida
Hillsborough Community College
Dale Mabry Campus
4001 Tampa Bay Blvd.
P.O. Box 30030
Tampa, FL 33630
www.hccfl.edu

Miami Dade College
Medical Center
950 NW 20th St.
Miami, FL 33127
www.mdc.edu/medical/

Georgia
DeKalb Technical Institute
495 N. Indian Creek Dr.
Clarkston, GA 30021
www.dekalbtech.edu

Ogeechee Technical College
One Joe Kennedy Blvd.
Statesboro, GA 30458
www.ogeecheetech.edu

Indiana
Indiana University
School of Optometry
800 E. Atwater Ave.
Bloomington, IN 47405
www.opt.indiana.edu

Massachusetts
Holyoke Community College
303 Homestead Ave.
Holyoke, MA 01040
www.hcc.edu

Mount Ida College
777 Dedham St.
Newton, MA 02459
www.mountida.edu

Worcester Polytechnic Institute
100 Institute Rd.
Worcester, MA 01609
www.wpi.edu

Michigan
Ferris State University
901 S. State St.
Big Rapids, MI 49307
www.ferris.edu

Minnesota
Anoka Technical College
1355 W. Hwy. 10
Anoka, MN 55303
www.anokatech.edu

Nevada
College of Southern Nevada
6375 W. Charleston Blvd.
Las Vegas, NV 89146
www.csn.edu

New Hampshire
New Hampshire Community
 Technical College
505 Amherst St.
Nashua, NH 03063
www.ccsnh.edu

New Jersey
Camden County College
P.O. Box 200
College Dr.
Blackwood, NJ 08012
www.camdencc.edu

Essex County College
303 University Ave.
Newark, NJ 07102
www.essex.edu

Raritan Valley Community College
P.O. Box 3300
Somerville, NJ 08876
www.raritanval.edu

New Mexico
Southwestern Indian Polytechnic
 Institute
9169 Coors Rd. NW
P.O. Box 10146
Albuquerque, NM 87184
www.sipi.edu

New York
Erie Community College
6205 Main St.
Williamsville, NY 14221
www.ecc.edu

Interboro Institute
254 W. 54th St.
New York, NY 10019
www.interboro.edu

New York City College of
 Technology
300 Jay St.
Brooklyn, NY 11201
www.citytech.cuny.edu

North Carolina
Durham Technical Community
 College
1637 Lawson St.
Durham, NC 27703
www.durhamtech.edu

Tennessee
Roane State Community College
276 Patton Ln.
Harriman, TN 37748
www.roanestate.edu

Texas
El Paso Community College
P.O. Box 20500
El Paso, TX 79998
www.epcc.edu

Tyler Junior College Vision Care
  Technology
P.O. Box 9020
Tyler, TX 75711
www.tjc.edu/vision/

Virginia
J. Sargeant Reynolds Community
  College
P.O. Box 85622
Richmond, VA 23285
www.jsr.cc.va.us

Naval Ophthalmic Support &
  Training Activity
160 Main Rd., Ste. 350
Naval Weapons Station, Building
  1794
Yorktown, VA 23691
www.med.navy.mil/sites/
  nostra/

Thomas Nelson Community College
99 Thomas Nelson Dr.
P.O. Box 9407
Hampton, VA 23670
www.tncc.edu

Washington
Seattle Central Community
  College
1701 Broadway
Seattle, WA 98122
www.seattlecentral.edu

Wisconsin
Milwaukee Area Technical College
700 W. State St.
Milwaukee, WI 53233
www.milwaukee.tec.wi.us

Optometric Assistants

Principal activity: Assisting optometrists

Work commitment: Part- or full-time

Preprofessional education: High school diploma

Program length: 1 year

Work prerequisites: Registered status preferred

Career opportunities: Highly favorable

Income range: $20,000 to $29,000

Scope

Optometric assistants facilitate the professional activities of optometrists. They are categorized as paraoptometrists or eye care paramedics. Their various but routine activities are essential to the effective functioning of an optometrist's office.

Activities

Optometric assistants perform office and record-keeping duties and act as a patient receptionist. They take medical histories, prepare patients for eye examinations, order lenses prescribed by the optometrist, obtain facial and frame measurements, and help patients choose their frames. They also may record the data an optometrist obtains during an examination.

Work Settings

The usual work setting is an optometrist's office, which may be a private practice or part of a chain. HMOs, health-care clinics, and government agencies also employ optometric assistants.

Advancement

Becoming a registered assistant and working in a large establishment offer the possibility of a supervisory appointment. With additional training, an optometric assistant can become a technician.

Prerequisites

A high school diploma or its equivalent is required for work in this field.

Desirable personal attributes for optometric assistants include the ability to work well with people, organized work habits, and accuracy.

Education/Training

Most people seeking to become optometric assistants get on-the-job training. However, formal education is becoming increasingly common.

Vocational-technical schools and community colleges offer one-year courses. The program covers office procedures and secretarial skills in addition to courses in anatomy and physiology of the eye and other vision-related topics. Students do classroom and laboratory work as well as obtain supervised clinical experience.

Certification/Registration/Licensure

After completing a training program and gaining some experience, an optometric assistant can become registered by passing the Optometric Assistant Registry Examination. This lets you be designated as an Opt.A.R., an attribute that can increase your employment opportunities.

Career Potential

The job outlook for optometric assistants is excellent. Two major considerations lead to this positive forecast. The first is that the overall U.S. population is increasing—especially the elderly, who have the greatest need for optometric services. Second, today's graduating optometrists are trained to use the services of paraoptometric personnel, to whom they delegate many routine responsibilities in order to free up their time and help control costs.

For More Information

There is no professional organization for optometric assistants, but additional information is available from the American Optometric Association (AOA), Paraoptometric Section, 243 N. Lindbergh Blvd., St. Louis, MO 63141 (www.aoanet.org).

The following list of optometric assistant programs was prepared by the AOA.

Optometric Assistant Programs

California
Southern California College of
  Optometry
2575 Yorba Linda Blvd.
Fullerton, CA 92831
www.scco.edu

Florida
Erwin Technical Center
2010 E. Hillsborough Ave.
Tampa, FL 33610
http://erwin.edu

Manatee Technical Institute
Optometric Assistant Program
5540 Lakewood Ranch Blvd.
Brandenton, FL 34211
www.manateetechnicalinstitute.
  org

McFatter Technical Center
6500 Nova Dr.
Davie, FL 33317
www.mcfattertech.com

Nova Southeastern University
College of Optometry
3200 S University Dr.
Ft. Lauderdale, FL 33328
www.optimetry.nova.edu

Traviss Career Center
3225 Winter Lake Rd.
Lakeland, FL 33803
www.traviss.edu

Illinois
Illinois Wesleyan University
1312 Park Street
Bloomington, IL 61701
www.iwu.edu

Iowa
North Iowa Area Community
College
500 College Dr.
Mason City, IA 50401
www.niacc.cc.ia.us

Optometric Assistant Program
Hawkeye Community College
1501 E Orange Road
Waterloo, I050704
www.hawkeye.cc.ia

Maryland
National Eye Institute
2020 Vision Place
Bethesda, MD 20902
www.nei.nih.gov

Prince George's Community
College
301 Largo Road
Largo, MD 20774
www.pgcc.edu

Minnesota
Minnesota West Community &
Technical College
1593 11th Ave.
Granite Falls, MN 52641
www.mnwest.edu

St. Cloud Technical College
1540 Northway Dr.
St. Cloud, MN 56303
www.sctc.edu

Nebraska
Mid-Plains Community College
1101 Halligan Dr.
North Platte, NE 69101
www.mpcca.edu

Ohio
Ohio State University
College of Optometry
338 w 10th Avenue
Columbus, OH 43210
www.optometry.osu.edu

South Carolina
Greenville Technical College
P.O. Box 5616, Station B
Greenville, SC 29606
www.gvltec.edu

Washington
Optometric Assistant Program
Spokane Community College
1810 N Greene St.
Spokane, WA 99207
www.scc.spokane.edu

Wisconsin
Lakeshore Technical College
1290 North Ave.
Cleveland, WI 53015
www.gotoltc.edu

Madison Area Technical College
3550 Anderson St.
Madison, WI 53704
http://matcmadison.edu/

Optometric Technicians

Principal activity: Assisting optometrists

Work commitment: Part- or full-time

Preprofessional education: High school diploma

Program length: 2 years

Work prerequisites: Associate degree preferred

Career opportunities: Favorable

Income range: $24,000 to $33,000

Scope

Optometric technicians are also called paraoptometric workers or eye care paramedics. They facilitate the professional activities of the offices in which they work.

Activities

The activities of the optometric technician include those of the optometric assistant (see p. 292) but also incorporate more complex tasks that are vital to good eye care. The optometric technician may determine the power of lenses and perform vision tests to determine acuity in color discrimination and field pattern. They may even record ocular pressure. Their work is more sophisticated than that of other paraoptometrics.

Work Settings

The principal work setting for optometric technicians is the optometrist's office, but opportunities also exist in HMOs, health clinics, and government agencies. The armed forces also employ optometric technicians.

Advancement

Becoming registered and working for a large establishment offer the possibility of a supervisory appointment.

Prerequisites

A high school diploma or its equivalent is essential for entering this field.

Desirable personal attributes for optometric technicians include good communication skills; organized work habits; manual dexterity; a neat, presentable appearance; and a desire to help others.

Education/Training

You can acquire on-the-job training from optometrists and then get experience while working. Formal training programs are offered by hospitals, optometry colleges, and medical schools. These programs last two years and can lead to an associate degree. In addition to the basic ocular anatomy and physiology, courses are provided in vision training, contact lens theory and practice, and supervised field experience.

Certification/Registration/Licensure

After securing the necessary training and experience and passing the Optometric Technician Registry Examination, you become eligible for registration and use of the designation Oph.T.R. Your employment potential is significantly enhanced with these credentials.

Career Potential

The demand for optometric technicians is strong. Experts predict an increased need for their services as the U.S. population increases and ages. Becoming a registered technician improves your employability and advancement prospects.

For More Information

There is no professional organization for optometric technicians. For more information, contact the American Optometric Association, Paraoptometric Section, 243 N. Lindbergh Blvd., St. Louis, MO 63141 (www.aoanet.org).

Optometric Technician Programs

Florida
Florida Community College
4501 Caper Road
Jacksonville, FL 32218
www.fccj.org

Miami Dade College
950 NW 20th St.
Miami, FL 33127
www.mdc.edu

Indiana
Indiana University
800 East Atwater
Bloomington, IN 47405
www.opt.indiana.edu

Michigan
Ferris State University
901 S. State St.
Big Rapids, MI 49307
www.ferris.edu

Ohio
Owens Community College
Oregon Rd.
P.O. Box 10000
Toledo, OH 43699
www.owens.edu

Texas
Sheppard AFB
Optometric Technician Program
383 TRS/XUGF
939 Missile Road
Sheppard AFB, TX 76311
www.sheppard.edu

Washington
Spokane Community College
1810 N. Greene St.
Spokane, WA 99217
www.scc.spokane.edu

Wisconsin
Madison Area Technical College
3550 Anderson Street
Madison, WI 53704
http://matcmadison.edu

Orthoptists

Principal activity: Providing muscle therapy for eye-motion disorders

Work commitment: Part- or full-time

Preprofessional education: Bachelor's degree

Program length: 2 years

Work prerequisites: Certification after training

Career opportunities: Stable

Income range: $38,000 to $72,000

Scope

An orthoptist is a professional who, working under the supervision of an ophthalmologist, treats problems of eye movement and the inability to focus both eyes simultaneously. These problems are due to eye misalignment, a condition called strabismus, which occurs in about 3 percent of young children. If left untreated, it results in being cross-eyed. This situation may cause both physical and psychological discomfort.

Activities

There are three therapeutic approaches to correcting strabismus. Using prescribed eyeglasses to correct the misalignment is the most straightforward. If that is unsuccessful, another alternative is surgery, in which eye muscle is repaired. A third and noninvasive approach is orthoptic therapy, in which the patient is taught to perform special exercises that gradually improve eye movement. Orthoptists, many of whom are also ophthalmic technologists (see p. 287), may also be involved in carrying out special eye tests.

Work Settings

Orthoptists work in the offices of ophthalmologists as well as in hospitals, eye clinics, and teaching institutions.

Advancement

Salary increases come with experience and perhaps a move to a larger facility.

Prerequisites

A bachelor's degree is mandatory to undertake study in this field. Students should major in a relevant subject, such as biology or psychology, and should take courses in biology, chemistry, physics, anatomy, and psychology.

Desirable personal attributes include the ability to work with children, patience, a sense of humor, and an outgoing personality.

Education/Training

After completing a bachelor's degree, a candidate must complete a two-year training program in one of the centers approved by the American Orthoptic Council. Graduate-level programs also are offered in this field.

Certification/Registration/Licensure

Those who complete an accredited orthoptic program and who pass written, oral, and practical examinations are awarded certification. Certification is essential for employment in this field.

Career Potential

Opportunities in this profession are stable, with average growth projected over the next decade. More parents and teachers are taking note of children's eye-focusing difficulties. Thus, parents are more likely to seek professional help for this problem than in the past.

For More Information

The professional organization for this field is the American Orthoptic Council, 3914 Nakoma Rd., Madison, WI 53711 (www.orthoptics.org).

Orthoptic Programs

Florida
University of Florida
Health Science Center
Gainesville, FL 32608
www.hsc.ufl.edu

Iowa
University of Iowa Hospitals and
  Clinics
Center for Disabilities and
  Development
100 Hawkins Dr.
Iowa City, IA 52242
www.medicine.uiowa.edu/cdd/

Michigan
University of Michigan
W.K. Kellogg Eye Center
1000 Wall St.
Ann Arbor, MI 48105
www.kellogg.umich.edu

Minnesota
University of Minnesota
516 Delaware St. SE
P.O. Box 493
Minneapolis, MN 55455
www.umn.edu

Missouri
St. Louis University Medical
  Center
1755 Grand Blvd.
St. Louis, MO 63104
www.slu.edu

Washington University
College of Arts and Sciences
One Brookings Dr.
St. Louis, MO 63130
www.wustl.edu

New York
New York Eye & Ear Infirmary
310 E. 14th St.
New York, NY 10003
www.nyee.edu

The Ross Eye Institute
Orthoptic Program
1176 Main Street
Buffalo, NY 14209
www.smbs.buffalo.edu

Virginia
Eastern Virginia Medical School
600 Gresham Dr.
Norfolk, VA 23507
www.evms.edu

Wisconsin
University of Wisconsin Hospital
  and Clinics
600 Highland Ave.
Madison, WI 53705
www.uwhospital.org

Canada
Hospital for Sick Children
555 University Ave.
Toronto, Ontario M5G 1X8
www.sickkids.on.ca

University of Saskatchewan
Royal University Hospital
Saskatoon, Saskatchewan S7N 4L3
www.usask.ca

Orthotists and Prosthetists

Principal activity: Designing, fabricating, and fitting braces and artificial limbs for patients

Work commitment: Full-time

Preprofessional education: High school diploma

Program length: 2 years

Work prerequisites: Certificate or bachelor's degree

Career opportunities: Favorable

Income range: $44,000 to $71,000

Scope

A variety of medical problems can result in weakened limbs or a spinal column that needs artificial support. Stroke victims, those with spinal cord or bone damage, and patients with congenital musculoskeletal disorders such as muscular dystrophy belong to this group. They may need a device to support and help straighten their limbs or spine. Orthotists help these patients by designing, making, and fitting the braces or other supportive devices they need.

Patients who have lost one or more limbs due to illnesses such as diabetes, an accident, or a congenital defect need artificial limbs (prostheses) to help them cope with their handicaps. Prosthetists design, fabricate, and fit artificial limbs using a variety of materials.

The fields of orthotics and prosthetics are interrelated; professionals in one field also study the other, and many are skilled in both.

Activities

To make braces, orthotists use a wide variety of materials, including wood, plastic, metals, carbon, and leather. They make the necessary measurements and casts and then modify the model, perform fittings, and evaluate the finished product. They also must teach patients how to use and care for their braces. All the work is initiated on the basis of a prescription written by a physician, often after consultation with an orthotist.

Prosthetists design artificial limbs, select the most suitable material for them, take measurements, make casts and models, and perform adjustments. They also teach patients to use and care for the prostheses.

Artificial limbs are designed on the basis of a physician's prescription, often written in consultation with the prosthetist.

Prosthetists don't make only traditional artificial limbs. They may incorporate advanced microelectronics and computer technology into the design of electromechanical units. Thus, when electrodes detect a weak signal resulting from muscular contraction, the mechanism amplifies and processes the signal to stimulate a motor within the prosthesis, thereby activating a body part.

Computers are used to design and manufacture artificial limbs today. The measurements taken by a prosthetist are coded into a computer, which is programmed to develop a three-dimensional image of the most appropriate design. This image is then fed into the operating system of the manufacturing machine that produces the limb.

Orthotists and prosthetists also supervise the work of orthotic and prosthetic technicians. These professionals also work in laboratories, under the supervision of an orthotist or prosthetist, fabricating and maintaining braces, surgical supports, and artificial limbs. Such technicians also can be certified by obtaining a high school diploma, completing a formal program in either field (or both), and passing a technical examination. Many junior or community colleges offer training for such technicians.

Work Settings

Orthotists and prosthetists are employed in hospital laboratories, rehabilitation centers, privately owned facilities, and research agencies (both private and governmental).

Advancement

Advancement typically comes with certification and increased experience and education. Developing expertise in both fields improves your chances for advancement.

Prerequisites

A high school diploma or its equivalent is needed for entry into a training program. Courses in biology, chemistry, physics, and mathematics are helpful, as are workshops in metal, wood, and plastics.

Desirable personal attributes include mechanical ability, manual dexterity, patience, an ability to grasp and resolve manipulative problems, tact, solid communication skills, and a desire to help disabled people.

Education/Training

There are three educational routes for careers in these two fields:

- You can earn a bachelor's degree with a major in orthotics or prosthetics at an undergraduate school that has an accredited program. Undergraduate preparation involves courses in biology, chemistry, physics, anatomy, physiology, mathematics, biostatistics, mechanics, biomechanics, mechanical drawing, properties of materials, metal working, orthotic and prosthetic techniques, orthopedic and neuromuscular disorders, upper and lower limb orthotics and prosthetics, and spinal orthotics.

- If you have a bachelor's degree in a field other than orthotics or prosthetics, you can complete an accredited postgraduate certificate program that takes one to two years.

- You can obtain a combination of relevant educational background, clinical experience, and professional training that meets the requirements for certification.

Certification/Registration/Licensure

Those completing an accredited program in orthotics or prosthetics or an accredited certificate program, and those meeting the special requirements and who also have one year of clinical experience, are eligible to take the American Board for Certification in Orthotics and Prosthetics Practitioners Certification Examination. If you're qualified, you can become certified in both fields by passing the three-part exam given in each field.

Career Potential

Employment prospects are above average,; there is a growing demand for qualified personnel in this field. The introduction of new materials and fabrication techniques have made the work more interesting and challenging.

For More Information

The professional organizations for this field are the American Orthotic & Prosthetic Association, 330 John Carlyle St., Ste. 200, Alexandria, VA 22314 (www.aopanet.org) and the American Academy of Orthotists and Prosthetists, 526 King St., Ste. 201, Alexandria, VA 22314 (www.oandp.org).

Orthotics and Prosthetics Programs

California
California State University
1000 E. Victoria St.
Carson, CA 90747
www.csudh.edu/oandp/

Rancho Los Amigos National
  Rehabilitation Center
7601 E. Imperial Hwy.
Downey, CA 90242
www.rancho.org

Connecticut
Newington Certificate Program
181 Patricia M. Genova Dr.
Newington, CT 06111
www.hanger.com/ncp/

Georgia
Georgia Institute of Technology
281 Ferst Drive
Atlanta, GA 30332
www.gatech.edu

Illinois
Northwestern University
345 E. Superior St.
Chicago, IL 60611
www.nwu.edu

Eastern Michigan University
106 Welch Hall
Ypsilanti, MI 48197
www.emich.edu

Minnesota
Century College
3300 Century Ave. N.
White Bear Lake, MN 55110
www.century.edu

New Jersey
Rutgers
98 Brett Rd.
Piscataway, NJ 08854
www.rutgers.edu

Texas
University of Texas
Southwestern Medical Center at
  Dallas
 6011 Harry Hines Blvd.
Dallas, TX 75235
www.swmed.edu

Washington
University of Washington
School of Medicine
BB805C Health Sciences Building
Seattle, WA 98195
www.washington.edu

Perfusionists

Principal activity: Operating heart-lung bypass equipment during surgery

Work commitment: Full-time

Preprofessional education: Bachelor's degree

Program length: 1 to 2 years

Work prerequisites: Certification after formal education

Career opportunities: Highly favorable

Income range: $33,000 to $62,000

Scope

One of the major medical technological breakthroughs of the last 50 years is the development of the heart-lung machine. It was devised to maintain the human body in a living state when vital organs such as the heart and lungs are not functioning. Carbon dioxide is removed from the blood and oxygen is added as the blood passes through the machine and is then returned to the anesthetized patient. Thus, surgeons can make the necessary repairs.

The professional who operates the heart-lung machine during surgery is the perfusionist. These workers also acquire patients' blood for temporary storage before surgery. With coronary bypass surgery becoming commonplace, the current focus of advancement in this field involves organ transplantation.

Activities

Perfusionists are trained to carry out a complicated, challenging, and extremely responsible job. They use complex, specialized instruments and life-support techniques. Constant monitoring of vital signs is essential to properly manage the patient's physiologic functions. The perfusionist must be prepared to respond quickly and appropriately to instructions from the surgeon or anesthesiologist.

Work Settings

Most perfusionists work in medical centers and hospitals. They may be involved in securing and transporting organs for transplantation between institutions.

Advancement

Salary increases come with experience. You can enhance your status by developing expertise in a specialized area in this field.

Prerequisites

Most formal education programs require a bachelor's degree. Some also prefer applicants with a background in respiratory therapy, medical technology, or nursing.

Desirable personal attributes include superior intelligence, quick responsiveness, manual dexterity, mechanical ability, emotional stability, being able to work as part of a team, the ability to function well under stress over prolonged periods, a long attention span, and a strong desire to help people who are seriously ill.

Education/Training

Training is provided at community colleges and hospitals and increasingly at universities. Course work includes anatomy, physiology, chemistry, pharmacology, and pathology. Training is provided in the operation of heart-lung bypass equipment for adults, children, and even infants; long-term life support; and perfusion of transplant organs. Clinical experience covering a variety of procedures is an essential part of the program.

Certification/Registration/Licensure

You can become certified through the American Board of Cardiovascular Perfusion (www.abcp.org). To secure certification, you must have the stipulated educational and clinical experience and pass a demanding oral and written examination. Certification is essential for employment.

Career Potential

There is a shortage of perfusionists, so opportunities are good for those planning to enter this field. New technology and more attractive salaries enhance this field's appeal to those seeking a challenging and demanding career.

For More Information

The professional organization for this field is the American Society of Extra-Corporeal Technology, 503 Carlisle Dr., Ste. 125, Herndon, VA 20170 (www.amsect.org).

For more information, write to the American Academy of Cardiovascular Perfusion, P.O. Box 3596, Allentown, PA 18106.

For information on certification, contact the American Board of Cardiovascular Perfusion, 207 N. 25th Ave., Hattiesburg, MS 39401 (www.abcp.org), or the Accreditation Committee Perfusion Education, 6654 S. Sycamore St., Littleton, CO 80120 (www.ac-pe.org).

Perfusionist Programs

Arizona
University of Arizona
Gittings Building, Room 102
P.O. Box 210093
Tucson, AZ 85721
www.arizona.edu

Connecticut
Quinnipiac University
275 Mt. Carmel Ave.
Hamden, CT 06518
www.quinnipiac.edu

District of Columbia
Walter Reed Army Medical Center
6900 Georgia Ave. NW
Washington, DC 20307
www.wramc.amedd.army.mil

Florida
Barry University
11300 NE Second Ave.
Miami Shores, FL 33161
www.barry.edu

Illinois
Rush University Medical Center
1643 W. Congress Hwy.
Chicago, IL 60612
www.rush.edu

Iowa
University of Iowa
Iowa City, IA 52242
www.uiowa.edu

Kansas
Via Christi Regional Medical
  Center
St. Joseph Campus
3600 E. Harry
Wichita, KS 67218
www.via-christi.org

Maryland
Johns Hopkins Bayview Medical
  Center
4940 Eastern Ave.
Baltimore, MD 21224
www.johnshopkins.edu

Massachusetts
Northeastern University
360 Huntington Ave.
Boston, MA 02115
www.northeastern.edu

Minnesota
University of Minnesota Heart &
  Lung Institute
425 E. River Rd.
Minneapolis, MN 55455
www.mmf.umn.edu/heartlung/

Nebraska
University of Nebraska Medical
  Center
985150 Nebraska Medical Center
Omaha, NE 68198
www.unmc.edu

New Jersey
Cooper Health System
One Cooper Plaza
Camden, NJ 08103
www.cooperhealth.org

General Hospital Center at Passaic
350 Boulevard
Passaic, NJ 07055
www.atlantichealth.org

New York
State University of New York
Upstate Medical University
College of Health Professions
750 E. Adams St.
Syracuse, NY 13210
www.upstate.edu

Ohio
Christ Hospital
2139 Auburn Ave.
Cincinnati, OH 45219
www.health-alliance.com/
  christ/perfusion_science.html

Cleveland Clinic Foundation
9500 Euclid Ave.
Cleveland, OH 44195
www.clevelandclinic.org

Ohio State University
Columbus, OH 43210
www.osu.edu

Pennsylvania
Drexel University
3141 Chestnut St.
Philadelphia, PA 19104
www.drexel.edu

Duquesne University
600 Forbes Ave.
Pittsburgh, PA 15282
www.duq.edu

Milton S. Hershey Medical Center
Penn State University
College of Medicine
500 University Dr.
Hershey, PA 17033
www.pennstatehershey.org

University of Pittsburgh Medical
Center Health System
200 Lothrop St.
Pittsburgh, PA 15213
www.upmc.edu

South Carolina
Medical University of South
Carolina
1513 Rutledge Avenue
Charleston, SC 29425
www.musc.edu

Tennessee
Vanderbilt University Medical
Center
21st Ave. South and Garland Ave.
Nashville, TN 37232
www.mc.vanderbilt.edu

Texas
Texas Heart Institute
6770 Bertner Ave.
Houston, TX 77030
www.texasheartinstitute.org

Wisconsin
Milwaukee School of Engineering
1025 N. Broadway
Milwaukee, WI 53202
www.msoe.edu/grad/msp/

Pharmacy Technicians

Principal activity: Assisting pharmacists in a variety of profession-related activities

Work commitment: Full-time

Preprofessional education: High school diploma

Program length: 5 to 10 months

Work prerequisites: Prior experience or a certificate from a training program

Career opportunities: Highly favorable

Income range: $23,000 to $33,000

Scope

Working under the supervision of registered pharmacists, technicians help them meet their operational responsibilities in a wide variety of ways.

Activities

Among the varied duties of the pharmacy technician are filling routine prescriptions and mixing preparations. The pharmacy technician also fills orders for nonprescription drugs. He or she also might deliver completed prescriptions to those who are unable to pick them up themselves. Another significant activity is helping maintain the stock of nonprescription items on the pharmacy's display counters. These and other similar activities are carried out under the oversight of a supervising registered pharmacist.

Helping maintain delivery records of pharmaceutical and nonpharmaceutical items is another important responsibility. Pharmacy technicians know that some drugs cannot be kept at room temperature and need to be stored in the refrigerator. Proper storage of newly delivered products and restocking of items also fall under a pharmacy technician's responsibilities.

Technicians may be assigned to determine the cost of prescriptions and appropriate patient charges for them. They also may be placed in charge of maintaining the pharmacy's business records and, when requested, complete needed forms.

Pharmacy technicians who are employed in health-care facilities such as hospitals carry out functions similar to those working in a local pharmacy. They may also be called on to deliver completed prescriptions to nursing stations and pick up medication requisitions.

Pharmacy technicians generally work 40 hours a week. Technicians employed in local pharmacies may have somewhat variable daytime hours, but those in a hospital may need to work nights and weekends in order to meet patient needs, which are continuous.

Work Settings

Most commonly, pharmacy technicians are employed in neighborhood sites owned by individuals or pharmacy chains. They also are employed by hospitals, HMOs, extended-care institutions, and clinics.

Advancement

With additional experience and increased responsibilities, technicians can advance salary-wise. In a large establishment, pharmacy technicians may be appointed to a level of supervisory responsibility over others. Genuine advancement can come from returning to school and enrolling in and graduating from pharmacy school.

Prerequisites

A high school diploma is usually required. Some experience in dealing with the public, especially in a sales capacity, is useful.

Desirable personal attributes include willingness to follow orders from a supervisor, focusing on details when executing responsibilities, accepting serious responsibilities involving health issues, being conscientious and dedicated, enjoying working with people, and carrying out duties in an organized fashion.

Education/Training

Most entry-level positions provide on-the-job training. Graduating from a pharmacy training program offered at a community college is desirable.

Certification/Registration/Licensure

Generally certification or licensure is not required. However, in a few states pharmacy technicians need to be licensed, probably because they are involved in preparing prescriptions.

Career Potential

The job outlook for pharmacy technicians is expected to be excellent over the next decade, due, in large part, to the increasing number of prescription medications available on the market and the growing number of prescriptions held by the average American. Also, as pharmacists become more involved in patient care, pharmacy technicians will continue to see an expansion of their role in the pharmacy.

For More Information

The professional organization for pharmacy technicians is the American Association of Pharmacy Technicians, P.O. Box 1447, Greensboro, NC 27402 (www.pharmacytechnician.com). Another source of information is the Accreditation Council for Pharmacy Education, 20 N. Clark St., Ste. 2500, Chicago, IL 60602 (www.acpe-accredit.org).

Pharmacy Technician Programs

Alabama

Auburn University
Harrison School of Pharmacy
2316 Walker Bldg.
Auburn, AL 36849
www.pharmacy.auburn.edu

Remington College–Mobile
828 Downtowner Loop W.
Mobile, AL 36609
www.remingtoncollege.edu

Arizona

Apollo College–Mesa
630 W. Southern Ave.
Mesa, AZ 85210
www.apollocollege.com

Apollo College–Tucson
3550 N. Oracle Rd.
Tucson, AZ 85705
www.apollocollege.com

Pima Medical Institute–Mesa
957 S. Dobson Rd.
Mesa, AZ 85202
www.pmi.edu

Remington College–Little Rock
19 Remington Rd.
Little Rock, AR 72204
www.remingtoncollege.edu

Remington College–Tempe
875 W. Elliot Rd., Ste. 126
Tempe, AZ 85284
www.remingtoncollege.edu

California

American Career College–
  Los Angeles
4021 Rosewood Ave.
Los Angeles, CA 90004
www.americancareer.com

American Career College–Orange
  County
1200 N. Magnolia Ave.
Anaheim, CA 92801
www.americancareer.com

Cerritos College
11110 Alondra Blvd.
Norwalk, CA 90650
www.cerritos.edu

Everest College–San Francisco
814 Mission St., Ste. 500
San Francisco, CA 94103
www.everest.edu

Everest College–San Jose North
1245 S. Winchester Blvd., Ste. 102
San Jose, CA 95128
www.everest.edu

Everest College–Torrance
1231 Cabrillo Ave., Ste. 201
Torrance, CA 90501
www.everest.edu

Institute of Technology–Clovis
731 W. Shaw Ave.
Clovis, CA 93612
www.it-colleges.edu

Institute of Technology–Modesto
5737 Stoddard Rd.
Modesto, CA 95356
www.it-colleges.edu

Institute of Technology–Roseville
333 Sunrise Ave.
Roseville, CA 95661
www.it-colleges.edu

Institute of Technology–
  Sacramento
3695 Bleckely St.
Mather, CA 95655
www.it-colleges.edu

North-West College–Pomona
134 W. Holt Ave.
Pomona, CA 91768
www.northwestcollege.com

North-West College–West Covina
2121 W. Garvey Ave. N.
West Covina, CA 91790
www.northwestcollege.com

San Joaquin Valley College–
  Bakersfield
201 New Stine Rd.
Bakersfield, CA 93309
www.sjvc.edu

San Joaquin Valley College–Fresno
295 E. Sierra Ave.
Fresno, CA 93710
www.sjvc.edu

San Joaquin Valley College–
  Rancho Cucamonga
10641 Church St.
Rancho Cucamonga, CA 91730
www.sjvc.edu

San Joaquin Valley College–Visalia
8400 W. Mineral King
Visalia, CA 93291
www.sjvc.edu

Trinity College–Fairfield
934 Missouri St.
Fairfield, CA 94533
www.trinitycollege.com

United Education Institute–
  Chula Vista
310 3rd Ave., Ste. C6
Chula Vista, CA 91910
www.uei-edu.com

United Education Institute–
  Huntington Park
6812 Pacific Blvd.
Huntington Park, CA 90255
www.uei-edu.com

United Education Institute–
  Los Angeles
3727 W. 6th St.
Los Angeles, CA 90020
www.uei-edu.com

United Education Institute–
  Ontario
3380 Shelby St., #150
Ontario, CA 91764
www.uei-edu.com

United Education Institute–
  San Bernardino
295 E. Caroline St., Ste. E
San Bernardino, CA 92408
www.uei-edu.com

United Education Institute–
  San Diego
1323 6th Ave.
San Diego, CA 92101
www.uei-edu.com

United Education Institute–
  Van Nuys
7335 Van Nuys Blvd.
Van Nuys, CA 91405
www.uei-edu.com

Western Career College–Emeryville
1400 65th St., Ste. 200
Emeryville, CA 94608
http://westerncollege.edu/

Western Career College–Fremont
41350 Christy St.
Fremont, CA 94538
http://westerncollege.edu/

Western Career College–
  Pleasant Hill
380 Civic Dr., Ste. 300
Pleasant Hill, CA 94523
http://westerncollege.edu/

Western Career College–
  Sacramento
8909 Folsom Blvd.
Sacramento, CA 95826
http://westerncollege.edu/

Western Career College–San Jose
6201 San Ignacio Ave.
San Jose, CA 95119
http://westerncollege.edu/

Western Career College–
  San Leandro
170 Bayfair Mall
San Leandro, CA 94578
http://westerncollege.edu/

Western Career College–
  Walnut Creek
2800 Mitchell Dr.
Walnut Creek, CA 94598
http://westerncollege.edu/

Colorado
IBMC–Fort Collins
1609 Oakridge Dr.
Fort Collins, CO 80525
www.ibmc.edu

IntelliTec College–
  Colorado Springs
2315 E. Pikes Peak Ave.
Colorado Springs, CO 80909
www.intelliteccollege.edu

Pima Medical Institute–
  Colorado Springs
370 Printers Pkwy.
Colorado Springs, CO 80910
www.pmi.edu

Remington College–
  Colorado Springs
6050 Erin Park Dr.
Colorado Springs, CO 80918
www.remingtoncollege.edu

Remington College–Denver
11011 W. 6th Ave.
Lakewood, CO 80215
www.remingtoncollege.edu

Connecticut
University of Connecticut
School of Pharmacy
69 N Eagleville Road
Storrs, CT 06269
www.pharmacy.uconn.edu

Florida
Everest University–Brandon
3924 Coconut Palm Dr.
Tampa, FL 33619
www.everest.edu

Everest University–Ft. Lauderdale
1040 Bayview Dr.
Ft. Lauderdale, FL 33304
www.everest.edu

Everest University–Hialeah
4410 W. 16th Ave., Ste. 52
Hialeah, FL 33012
www.everest.edu

Everest University–Kendall
9020 SW 137th Ave.
Miami, FL 33186
www.everest.edu

Everest University–Lakeland
995 E. Memorial Blvd., Ste. 110
Lakeland, FL 33801
www.everest.edu

Everest University–Melbourne
2401 N. Harbor City Blvd.
Melbourne, FL 32935
www.everest.edu

Everest University–Miami
111 NW 183rd St., Second Floor
Miami, FL 33169
www.everest.edu

Remington College–Jacksonville
7011 A.C. Skinner Pkwy.
Jacksonville, FL 32256
www.remingtoncollege.edu

Remington College–Largo
8550 Ulmerton Rd., Unit 100
Largo, FL 33771
www.remingtoncollege.edu

Remington College–Tampa
2410 E. Busch Blvd.
Tampa, FL 33612
www.remingtoncollege.edu

Southwest Florida College–
  Fort Myers
1685 Medical Ln.
Fort Myers, FL 33907
www.swfc.edu

Southwest Florida College–Tampa
3910 Riga Blvd.
Tampa, FL 33619
www.swfc.edu

Georgia
Emory University
1380 Oxford Rd.
Atlanta, GA 30322
www.emory.edu

Idaho
Apollo College
1200 N. Liberty
Boise, ID 83704
www.apollocollege.du

Idaho State University
College of Pharmacy
970 S. 5th St.
Campus Box 8288
Pocatello, ID 83209
www.pharmacy.isu.edu

Illinois
South Suburban College
15800 S. State St.
South Holland, IL 60473
www.southsuburbancollege.edu

Kentucky
National College–Danville
115 E. Lexington Ave.
Danville, KY 40422
www.ncbt.edu

National College–Florence
7627 Ewing Blvd.
Florence, KY 41042
www.ncbt.edu

National College–Lexington
628 E. Main St.
Lexington, KY 40508
www.ncbt.edu

National College–Louisville
4205 Dixie Hwy.
Louisville, KY 40216
www.ncbt.edu

National College–Pikeville
288 S. Mayo Trail, Ste. 2
Pikeville, KY 41501
www.ncbt.edu

National College–Richmond
139 S. Killarney Ln.
Richmond, KY 40475
www.ncbt.edu

Louisiana
Everest University–New Orleans
1201 Elmwood Park Blvd.,
  Ste. 600
New Orleans, LA 70123
www.everest.edu

Remington College–Baton Rouge
1900 N. Lobdell
Baton Rouge, LA 70806
www.remingtoncollege.edu

Remington College–New Orleans
321 Veterans Memorial Blvd.
Metairie, LA 70005
www.remingtoncollege.edu

New Jersey
Lincoln Technical Institute–
  Edison
1697 Oak Tree Rd.
Edison, NJ 08820
www.lincolntech.com

Lincoln Technical Institute–Mount
  Laurel
1000 Howard Blvd.
Mt. Laurel, NJ 08054
www.lincolntech.com

Lincoln Technical Institute–
  Paramus
160 E. Route 4
Paramus, NJ 07652
www.lincolntech.com

New Mexico
Apollo College–Albuquerque
5301 Central Ave. NE, Ste. 101
Albuquerque, NM 87108
www.apollocollege.com

Pima Medical Institute–
  Albuquerque
2201 San Pedro NE
Building 3, Ste. 100
Albuquerque, NM 87110
www.pmi.edu

North Carolina
Caldwell Community College and
  Technical Institute
2855 Hickory Blvd.
Hudson, NC 28638
www.caldwell.cc.nc.us

North Dakota
North Dakota State College of
  Science
800 6th St. N.
Wahpeton, ND 58076
www.ndscs.edu

Ohio
National College–Cincinnati
6871 Steger Dr.
Cincinnati, OH 45237
www.ncbt.edu

National College–Dayton Area
1837 Woodman Center Dr.
Kettering, OH 45420
www.ncbt.edu

Remington College–Cleveland
14445 Broadway Ave.
Cleveland, OH 44125
www.remingtoncollege.edu

Remington College–Cleveland
  West
26350 Brookpark Rd.
North Olmstead, OH 44070
www.remingtoncollege.edu

Oregon
Apollo College–Portland
2004 Lloyd Center, 3rd Floor
Portland, OR 97232
www.apollocollege.com

Pennsylvania
Lincoln Technical Institute–
  Northeast
2180 Hornig Rd.
Philadelphia, PA 19116
www.lincolntech.com

Tennessee
National College–Knoxville
8415 Kingston Pike
Knoxville, TN 37919
www.ncbt.edu

National College–Nashville
3748 Nolensville Pike
Nashville, TN 37211
www.ncbt.edu

Remington College–Memphis
2731 Nonconnah Blvd., Ste. 160
Memphis, TN 38132
www.remingtoncollege.edu

Remington College–Nashville
441 Donelson Pike, Ste. 150
Nashville, TN 37214
www.remingtoncollege.edu

Texas
Remington College–Dallas
1800 Eastgate Dr.
Garland, TX 75041
www.remingtoncollege.edu

Remington College–Houston
3110 Hayes Rd., Ste. 380
Houston, TX 77082
www.remingtoncollege.edu

Remington College–Houston
  North
11310 Greens Crossing, Ste. 300
Houston, TX 77067
www.remingtoncollege.edu

Virginia
National College–Bluefield
100 Logan St.
P.O. Box 629
Bluefield, VA 24605
www.ncbt.edu

National College–Charlottesville
1819 Emmet St.
Charlottesville, VA 22901
www.ncbt.edu

National College–Danville
734 Main St.
Danville, VA 24541
www.ncbt.edu

National College–Harrisonburg
51 B Burgess Rd.
Harrisonburg, VA 22801
www.ncbt.edu

National College–Lynchburg
104 Candlewood Court
Lynchburg, VA 24502
www.ncbt.edu

National College–Martinsville
10 Church St.
Martinsville, VA 24114
www.ncbt.edu

National College–Roanoke Valley
1813 E. Main St.
Salem, VA 24153
www.ncbt.edu

National College–Tri-Cities
300 A Piedmont Ave.
Bristol, VA 24201
www.ncbt.edu

Washington
Apollo College–Spokane
10102 E. Knox, Ste. 200
Spokane, WA 99206
www.apollocollege.com

Everest University–Renton
981 Powell Ave. SW, Ste. 200
Renton, WA 98055
www.everest.edu

Everest University–Tacoma
2156 Pacific Ave.
Tacoma, WA 98402
www.everest.edu

West Virginia
Everest University–
  Cross Lanes
5514 Big Tyler Rd.
Cross Lanes, WV 25313
www.everest.edu

Wisconsin
Fox Valley Technical College
1825 N. Bluemond Dr.
P.O. Box 2277
Appleton, WI 54912
www.foxvalley.tec.wi.us

Phlebotomists

Principal activity: Drawing, collecting, and labeling blood samples for laboratory analysis

Work commitment: Full-time

Preprofessional education: High school diploma

Program length: Several weeks

Work prerequisites: Completion of a short training program

Career opportunities: Highly favorable

Income range: $24,000 to $33,000

Scope

To obtain samples of a patient's blood, phlebotomists draw the needed quantity, collect and label the vials, and deposit them for evaluation.

Activities

Phlebotomists are members of an institution's pathology laboratory staff. They secure patient blood specimens requisitioned by a physician. Obtaining blood samples usually involves venipuncture when large samples of blood are needed. When only droplets of blood are required, phlebotomists use finger-stick and needle-stick procedures.

It is the responsibility of the phlebotomist to draw blood antiseptically and as painlessly as possible. To meet the former requirement, the area where the blood will be drawn must be adequately cleaned with an antiseptic swab. For venipuncture the phlebotomist selects the most appropriate vein to draw from so that the extraction procedure will be successful on the first attempt. Each specimen then is properly labeled to ensure the lab reports' reliability. To achieve this goal, after the procedure is completed, the sample is logged in, either manually or by computer, so that a record of the proceedings is established. The specimen is brought to the assigned location so that processing can be initiated.

The principal function of phlebotomists is drawing blood from hospital patients, but they may also be called on to apply their skills at clinics and health fairs. In such cases they also are required to get the specimens back to the laboratory as soon as possible.

Because drawing blood is slightly painful, it is only natural that some patients might be somewhat anxious. The phlebotomist needs to reassure the patients, especially children, that they will experience only momentary and minor discomfort. This task can be made easier by explaining the procedure to the patient.

Work Settings

Employment opportunities for phlebotomists vary. The majority are employed by hospitals and medical centers, but many others work for HMOs, commercial labs, physicians' offices, and public health clinics. Most phlebotomists work a regular 40-hour week. Hospital employment, however, may require night or weekend hours.

Advancement

Phlebotomists can move up the career ladder by two paths. With additional experience they can secure a position at a more prestigious institution where their responsibilities and pay are greater. With additional education they can move up to become a laboratory technician or even a laboratory technologist. This opens up a broader range of work opportunities and a greater salary.

Prerequisites

Having a high school diploma or its equivalent is essential. Gaining exposure to a hospital atmosphere through volunteer work can prove very beneficial. Volunteer work also might give you an opportunity to "shadow" a phlebotomist and thus get exposure to his or her work activities.

Education/Training

You can secure the essential phlebotomy background by completing a course at a community or junior college or a vocational-technical school. Some hospitals offer such courses or provide on-the-job training.

Desirable personal attributes are an outgoing personality; good manual dexterity; being tactful and acting responsibly; working in an organized manner, even under pressure; being detail-oriented; and being computer-literate.

Certification/Registration/Licensure

Some states require certification, registration, or licensure.

Career Potential

Prospects for employment are excellent, with opportunities in a variety of facilities. Also, this work is essential to patients' basic medical diagnostic and treatment needs. You can find positions through classified ads and by applying to personnel departments at health-care facilities.

For More Information

Prospective phlebotomists can get information from the American Healthcare Association, 1201 L St. NW, Washington, DC 20005 (www.ahca.org) or from the American

Medical Technologists, 710 Higgins Rd., Park Ridge, IL 60068 (www.amt1.com). Phlebotomists usually are eligible for membership in the local health service workers' union at the facility where they work.

Pulmonary Function Technologists

Principal activity: Administering and evaluating pulmonary function tests

Work commitment: Usually full-time

Preprofessional education: High school diploma required; associate or bachelor's degree preferred

Program length: 6 months to 4 years

Work prerequisites: On-the-job training is possible; formal education is preferred

Career opportunities: Highly favorable

Income range: $35,000 to $60,000

Scope

Increasingly, the medical profession is stressing the importance of preventive health care. This approach involves maintaining a good diet, having a regular exercise regime, and undergoing periodic checkups by a physician. Some medical screenings have become a routine part of checkups. Patients with the potential for lung problems are encouraged to have pulmonary function tests. Pulmonary technologists operate these machines and evaluate their data.

Activities

Technologists help evaluate a patient's lung health by running several types of tests, including exercise tolerance, bronchial challenge studies, blood gas studies, gas diffusion studies, and sleep studies. The pulmonary function technologist selects and readies the test equipment and then explains the procedure to the patient. The technologist performs the test while monitoring the patient's response and then evaluates the results and their reliability. A composite of different test results provides the physician with the information needed to establish a diagnosis and, when necessary, to provide appropriate therapeutic management for problems.

Work Settings

Pulmonary technologists are employed by hospitals and clinics as well as in private-practice offices, rehabilitation facilities, and diagnostic centers.

Advancement

Advancement comes with experience and further education, such as a bachelor's degree. Specialization in specific diagnostic procedures enhances a technologist's status.

Prerequisites

A high school diploma is a minimum requirement, but to enroll in most programs an associate or bachelor's degree is necessary.

Desirable personal attributes include patience, good communication skills, dependability, and manual dexterity.

Education/Training

There are several ways to get training for this field:

- You can earn a bachelor's degree in pulmonary technology from a college or university with an accredited program.
- You can earn an associate degree in pulmonary technology from a community college with an accredited program.
- You can attend a post-college program in pulmonary technology offered at a medical center or hospital.
- You can obtain on-the-job training.

Certification/Registration/Licensure

Certification is offered by the National Board for Respiratory Care upon satisfactory completion of a written examination. To be eligible to take the exam, candidates must have graduated from an accredited pulmonary technology or respiratory therapy program and have at least six months of experience in the field. Alternatively, you can have a high school diploma and two years of experience.

At present, licensure is not required, and certification is voluntary but recommended.

Career Potential

Currently this field has a shortage of trained personnel. More openings are anticipated as more medical facilities establish cardiopulmonary laboratories. Thus, prospects for employment opportunities are quite good.

For More Information

The professional organization for this field is the National Society of Pulmonary Technology, 1101 14th St. NW, Ste. 1100, Washington, DC 20005.

For information on accredited educational programs, contact the Committee on Accreditation for Respiratory Care, 1248 Harwood Rd., Bedford, TX 76021 (www.coarc.com).

Radiation Therapy Technologists

Principal activity: Helping administer therapeutic radiation

Work commitment: Full-time

Preprofessional education: High school diploma

Program length: 1 to 4 years

Work prerequisites: Certificate or diploma; associate or bachelor's degree and certification

Career opportunities: Highly favorable

Income range: $48,000 to $77,000

Scope

One of the biggest killers in the United States is cancer. In treating those who have been diagnosed with this disease, three approaches typically are used: surgery, chemotherapy, and radiation. These treatments are used either alone or in combination. Depending on the nature of the tumor and how much it has spread, these techniques can extend and even save lives and reduce pain.

Radiation sources in use today include high-energy X rays, electron beams, and gamma rays. The goal is to pinpoint the tumor site so that it can be exclusively targeted by the radiation beam while minimizing as much as possible destruction of healthy cells. A variety of techniques are used to locate the position and extent of tumors. Once this is done, a physician, the radiation oncologist, determines the best treatment plan. Doctors often use computers for this process, which results in the preparation of a radiation prescription and treatment plan. The radiation therapy technologist puts this plan into effect.

Activities

Using sophisticated equipment, the radiation therapy technologist helps program the control panel so that exactly prescribed doses of radiation are omitted. Using lead shields, the technologist ensures that exposure is restricted to the exact body site being targeted. Working with the radiation physicist, technologists also help prepare, maintain, and calibrate the radiation equipment to ensure its safe and effective usage.

Technologists help prepare and handle the radioactive materials used in the tests. They must keep detailed, accurate records of radiation treatments. Throughout all activities, they must work to ensure the safety of patients and attending medical personnel. They also identify the location of any radiation hazards and take appropriate action. They must deal with their patients with sensitivity and tact during very stressful times.

Work Settings

Most radiation therapy technologists work in medical centers and hospitals. A few work in commercial sales and as educators, instructing new professionals.

Advancement

With increased experience and education, upward career movement is possible. At larger institutions, you may become a supervisor.

Prerequisites

A high school diploma or its equivalent is the minimum requirement for those seeking professional training.

Desirable personal attributes include detail-oriented work habits, strong mathematical ability, compassion, and a desire to help others.

Education/Training

This field has several training paths:

- You can attend a four-year bachelor's degree program.
- You can attend a two-year associate degree program.
- You can get a two-year certificate (or diploma) from a hospital program.
- You can earn a one-year certificate (or diploma) from a hospital program.

Education in this field involves classroom and laboratory work and supervised clinical experience. Courses include anatomy, physiology, mathematics, pathology, clinical radiation oncology, radiation physics, radiology, radiation protection, technical radiation oncology, medical imaging, introduction to computers, venipuncture, methods of patient care, and medical ethics.

Certification/Registration/Licensure

Certification is required for employment in this field and is provided by the American Registry of Radiologic Technologists (ARRT). To become certified, you must graduate from an accredited radiation therapy program and pass a four-hour competency examination. Some states accept ARRT certification in lieu of taking a state licensure exam.

Career Potential

The existing shortage of registered radiation therapy technologists is expected to continue through the next decade. This is due to the growing population, the increased number of senior citizens, and the expanded use of radiological technology.

For More Information

The professional organization for this field is the American Society of Radiologic Technologists, 15000 Central Ave. SE, Albuquerque, NM 87123 (www.asrt.org).

For information about certification, contact the American Registry of Radiologic Technologists, 1255 Northland Dr., St. Paul, MN 55120 (www.arrt.org).

Radiological Technologists

Principal activity: Securing radiographs using varied radiological instruments

Work commitment: Part- or full-time

Preprofessional education: High school diploma

Program length: 1 to 4 years

Work prerequisites: Certificate, diploma, associate degree, or bachelor's degree

Career opportunities: Favorable

Income range: $43,000 to $63,000

Scope

The use of X rays, or radiography, to reveal the body's internal organization has become much more common in the past few decades. It is now possible to study not only the state of bones and joints, but also organs, tissues, and vessels, as well as the digestive, circulatory, and urinary systems. This remarkable capacity results from the development of such sophisticated equipment as CT (computerized tomography) scanning, MRI (magnetic resonance imaging), and digital subtraction angiography.

Today, in addition to standard flat films, images are recorded on videotape and motion-picture film. The radiological technologist or radiographer is responsible for obtaining these images.

Activities

To obtain the standard radiographs that are commonly ordered, technologists prepare patients by explaining the procedure, ensuring that they are not carrying accessories that will be impervious to the X rays and properly positioning them to expose the correct area. Technologists shield sensitive areas of the patient's body with lead-containing covers so that he or she is not exposed to radiation. Then they focus the X-ray source at the proper height and angle for the body area being filmed, place the film holder in the correct position under the patient's body, and expose that part of the body to the beam. Finally, the radiographer sets the instrument's controls to make sure that the film is adequately exposed to provide an image with the right density, contrast, and detail. The film is then removed, quickly developed, checked, and passed on to the physician.

Experienced radiographers may carry out more complex imaging procedures, such as fluoroscopy. In this procedure, radiographs are taken while or shortly after a patient drinks or is infused with a contrast medium (usually containing barium), which provides images of different parts of the digestive tract. In addition to taking the X rays, the technologist prepares the contrast medium and makes sure that the required amount enters the body.

Some specialized radiographers, called CT scanners, are trained in the use of machines that produce cross-sectional views of a patient's body. Others may be called MRI technologists. They are trained to operate machines that use giant magnets and radio waves to create an image of both hard and soft body tissues.

Work Settings

Radiological technologists work primarily in hospitals, usually as members of a radiology department. They may use mobile X-ray units to take bedside, operating room, or emergency room X rays. Some radiographers are employed in private-practice settings, clinics, educational institutions, and industry.

Advancement

With experience and training, a staff technologist may be elevated to chief supervisor, chief technologist, or even department manager. Others may advance by specializing, becoming CT or MRI scanners or angiographers. Those who teach can advance through the academic ranks, while others may move up in a corporate sales setting.

Prerequisites

A high school diploma or its equivalent is required for entry into a training program. Recommended high school courses include biology, chemistry, physics, algebra, trigonometry, and psychology.

Desirable personal attributes include attention to detail, good communication skills, careful work habits (to avoid radiation exposure), a sense of compassion, and a desire to help people.

Education/Training

Radiography programs are offered by several kinds of institutions, so their awards upon completion are varied. Consequently, there are multiple routes to completing a radiography program:

- Hospitals account for more than 50 percent of accredited programs in the U.S. These are two-year certificate or diploma programs.
- Junior and community colleges offer 40 percent of accredited programs. These are two-year associate degree programs.
- Universities offer less than 5 percent of accredited programs. These are four-year bachelor's or two-year master's degree programs and are best for those who want teaching or supervisory positions.

- Some vocational-technical institutes offer one-year programs for those with a background in the allied health sciences, such as medical technologists or registered nurses. These provide certificates or diplomas at completion.

It should be noted that some institutions offer all three levels of educational preparation, leaving the option up to the individual. This is because employment opportunities are available to those who complete an accredited program at any level. The programs are both didactic and practical. Classroom-lab work and training include courses in anatomy, physiology, radiation physics, radiation protection, medical terminology, medical imaging and processing, positioning of patients, medical ethics, and the use of computers in radiological science.

Certification/Registration/Licensure

Certification is essential for work in this field. Graduates from accredited programs can take a four-hour examination administered by the American Registry of Radiologic Technologists to become certified.

Career Potential

The employment outlook is strong, with more openings than candidates in many places. With a growing demand for health care and an older population, opportunities should be plentiful for the foreseeable future. However, technologists willing to relocate may have the best job opportunities.

For More Information

The professional organization for this field is the American Society of Radiologic Technologists, 15000 Central Ave. SE, Albuquerque, NM 87123 (www.asrt.org).

For information on certification, contact the American Registry of Radiologic Technologists, 1255 Northland Dr., St. Paul, MN 55120 (www.arrt.org).

Almost all radiography students receive their education by attending programs accredited by the Joint Review Committee on Education in Radiologic Technology. There are at least 700 such programs in North America—far too many to list here.

For a complete list of accredited programs, contact the Joint Review Committee on Education in Radiologic Technology, 20 N. Wacker Dr., Ste. 900, Chicago, IL 60606 (www.jrcert.org).

Surgical Technologists

Principal activity: Performing vital operating-room services

Work commitment: Full-time

Preprofessional education: High school diploma

Program length: 9 months to 2 years

Work prerequisites: Certificate, diploma, or associate degree

Career opportunities: Highly favorable

Income range: $33,000 to $47,000

Scope

Surgical technologists used to be called operating room technicians. During surgical operations, they work under the direction of surgeons and the supervision of registered nurses to help maintain the sterile atmosphere and contribute to the operating room's efficiency. Their services facilitate a successful surgical outcome.

Activities

Before surgery, technologists prepare the sterile instruments to be used as well as sterile drapings and solutions. They may also ensure that necessary nonsterile equipment is available and in working order. Surgical technologists also see that patients are properly prepared. They help place patients on and secure them to the operating table and help the surgical team put on their gowns and gloves for the operation.

During surgery a scrub (sterile) technologist passes sterile instruments and other supplies to the surgeon or assistant surgeon. He or she may thread needles, hold retractors, cut sutures, and count sponges, and generally tries to anticipate the surgeons' needs during the procedure. A circulating (nonsterile) technologist stands by to provide needed supplies, adjust lighting, and bring in any necessary diagnostic machines. After the operation, this technologist arranges for excised specimens to be sent to the pathology lab and helps transport the patient to the recovery room. In the meantime, the scrub technologist cleans the area, ensuring that instruments are placed in the appropriate sites for sterilization. Technologists also make sure that the operating facility is adequately stocked with commonly used supplies.

Work Settings

Surgical technologists typically work in hospital surgical facilities (either inpatient or outpatient), delivery rooms, emergency rooms, and private specialized surgical centers. Some work for a physician or a group of physicians.

Advancement

With experience, certification, and supervisory skills, a surgical technologist can become an assistant operating room supervisor. In this position you direct the activities of other surgical technologists and report to the operating room supervisor, who is usually a registered nurse.

Alternatively, you can become an assistant operating room administrator, who orders supplies and helps arrange the work schedule.

You also can advance by specializing in such areas as open-heart surgery or neurosurgery, for which special skills are needed.

Prerequisites

A high school diploma is essential for entry into a surgical technologist training program.

Desirable personal qualities include intelligence, manual dexterity, stamina, and the capacity to work effectively with other professionals. Candidates should also be able to exercise quick, calm, sound judgment.

Education/Training

Formal training programs for surgical technologists are offered by vocational schools, junior and community colleges, universities, hospitals, and the military. Programs last from nine months to two years. The shorter programs award certificates or diplomas, and the two-year programs award associate degrees. More than 150 accredited programs are available nationwide.

Formal programs consist of classroom education and supervised clinical experience. Courses are offered in anatomy, physiology, microbiology, pharmacology, medical terminology, and professional ethics. Others cover the care of patients during surgery, aseptic techniques, and surgical procedures. During clinical training, which varies from 500 to 1,000 hours, students learn about common surgical procedures and those used in various specialties.

Another educational route is open to hospital personnel such as nurses' aides or licensed practical nurses. They can simply transfer to the surgery department, where they receive on-the-job training. This training may extend from six weeks to one year. Such technologists are ineligible for certification.

Certification/Registration/Licensure

Surgical technologists can apply for certification from the Liaison Council on Certification for Surgical Technologists, 7108-C South Alton Way, Englewood, CO 80112. Prerequisites include graduating from an accredited program and successfully completing a national certification exam. To retain certification, candidates must take continuing education and periodically retake the exam.

Career Potential

The employment outlook for surgical technologists is quite favorable because the number of surgical procedures is generally increasing as the population can better afford them and is living longer. Cost containment also favors the use of surgical technologists, especially where HMO coverage is a consideration.

For More Information

The professional organization for this field is the Association of Surgical Technologists (AST), 7108-C S. Alton Way, Centennial, CO 80112 (www.ast.org).

Surgical Technologist Programs

Hundreds of programs throughout the United States train people to become surgical technologists—far too many to list here. For information on an accredited training program in your area, contact the Association of Surgical Technologists or visit their Web site.

Veterinary Assistants

Principal activity: Helping veterinarians care for animals

Work commitment: Full-time

Preprofessional education: High school diploma

Program length: 3 months to 2 years

Work prerequisites: Adequate training and experience

Career opportunities: Highly favorable

Income range: $21,000 to $32,000

Scope

The activities of a veterinary assistant (or technician) are comparable to those of a primary-care nurse. They observe the status of animals placed in a veterinarian's care and help with facility operations.

Activities

Veterinary assistants ready animals for surgery, help anesthetize them, and watch them postoperatively. They ensure that medications are given on schedule and change dressings periodically. They also are responsible for maintaining sanitary conditions in the facility. They make sure that sterile instruments and adequate supplies are available. They also may be required to perform certain laboratory tests and obtain specimens. Record keeping and routinely weighing animals are additional responsibilities.

Work Settings

Veterinary assistants work in private offices, veterinary hospitals, boarding kennels, animal shelters, zoos, grooming shops, research centers, and private stables. Some are employed by various government agencies.

Advancement

In larger facilities, a veterinary assistant with the right training, experience, and management abilities can assume administrative responsibilities.

Prerequisites

A high school diploma is necessary for entry into this field.

Desirable personal attributes include a love of animals, good physical health and strength, patience, emotional stability, responsibility, and dependability.

Education/Training

Many veterinary assistants receive on-the-job training, while others get postsecondary education at trade schools and junior, technical, or community colleges. Those attending the latter receive associate degrees.

Certification/Registration/Licensure

These awards of recognition are not required, but you can earn them from one of the organizations listed in the section "For More Information."

Career Potential

Employment prospects for veterinary assistants are positive for the foreseeable future, though it is somewhat dependent on the economy. When the economy is strong, the number of pet owners increases. Consequently, more caretakers are needed to provide pet maintenance and medical treatment.

For More Information

This field has no professional organization, but information is available from the American Veterinary Medical Association, 1931 N. Meacham Rd., Ste. 100, Schaumburg, IL 60173 (www.avma.org), or the Humane Society of the United States, 2100 L St. NW, Washington, DC 20037 (www.humainesociety.org).

For information on certification, contact the American Association for Laboratory Animal Science, 9190 Crestwyn Hills Dr., Memphis, TN 38125 (www.aalas.org).

Rehabilitation Careers: Therapists, Therapy Assistants, and Aides

The health-care field includes many rehabilitation careers. The goal of these careers is to help individuals with impairments achieve a higher level of functioning and fulfillment. These careers require direct and often close contact with patients. Practice locations vary and include hospitals, nursing homes, outpatient facilities, and in-home services.

Therapists evaluate patients' levels of functioning. With other members of the treatment team, they plan therapeutic activities and exercise programs for patients with physical, emotional, social, or educational impairments.

An activities program may include creative skills (art, dance, music, poetry, or drama), manual skills (crafts or industrial arts), educational skills (writing, reading, or perceptual training), daily living skills (self-care or homemaking), functional skills (use of prostheses or adaptive equipment), or recreational skills (either individual or group).

When necessary, therapists design treatment plans involving more than one approach. They set goals in light of the existing problems and the patient's motivation and conduct periodic assessments to determine progress and see whether the established goals have been met. Then they modify the treatment plan accordingly. When a patient transfers home or to another facility, the therapist provides needed information to ensure continuity of therapy.

Art Therapists

Principal activity: Using art therapeutically to improve clients' physical and emotional states

Work commitment: Part- or full-time

Preprofessional education: High school diploma

Program length: 4 to 6 years

Work prerequisites: Bachelor's degree acceptable; master's degree preferred

Career opportunities: Favorable

Income range: $30,000 to $49,000

Scope

Art therapy is a means of communication for mentally and physically impaired people who are unable to communicate verbally. Such patients can express themselves by drawing, painting, and doing crafts, providing an opportunity to help improve their self-image and personal growth.

Activities

Art therapists encourage their patients to express their feelings about themselves, their families, and their homes. The therapist analyzes the content of the drawn material in terms of perspective, proportions, detail (or lack of it), technique, colors, nature of the subject selected, and general aesthetic quality. He or she then attempts to interpret the thoughts, feelings, fears, and hopes reflected in the drawing and seeks to uncover the meaning of the illustrations.

Commonly, the art therapist participates with others on the health-care team—psychiatrists, psychologists, and other therapists—to formulate a diagnosis and overall treatment plan. The therapist then designs specific art activities to be carried out in an individual or group context. Using various types of arts and crafts, the therapist provides instruction. Then he or she observes and notes what occurs during therapy sessions and reports the degree of progress to the health-care team so that the treatment plan can be modified to better meet the client's needs.

When provided in a group setting, art therapy can stimulate socialization among participants. Expressing themselves through art and other creative outlets also gives patients a sense of satisfaction, relaxes them, and enhances their self-esteem. Thus, art therapy can benefit victims of trauma and violence and those with learning or sensory disabilities.

Half of those treated by art therapists annually are adults, and the other half are adolescents and children. This profession makes a significant contribution to the rehabilitation of emotionally disabled and handicapped people.

Work Settings

Art therapists work in psychiatric clinics, community centers, nursing homes, schools, and group homes. Some work as private practitioners. The largest employment sites are short- and long-term psychiatric hospitals.

Advancement

You can advance in this career by securing a master's degree and certification.

Prerequisites

A high school diploma is a prerequisite for admission to college. In addition, natural art skills are essential.

Desirable personal attributes for art therapists include patience, a strong sense of compassion, an ability to communicate well, and emotional stability.

Education/Training

The educational backgrounds of art therapists vary, with programs offered by universities, hospitals, and art institutes. These may be entry-level undergraduate, certificate/

diploma, or master's degree programs. Most are not approved by the American Art Therapy Association (AATA), which has accredited more than 25 graduate programs.

At the undergraduate level, you should major or minor in creative or commercial art or art education. Preparing an art portfolio is also a good idea. Courses in the behavioral and social sciences are desirable.

While some job opportunities are open to those with a bachelor's degree and clinical experience, completing a one-year certificate/diploma program or a two-year master's degree program is very desirable. The latter forms the basis of securing certification.

Master's degree programs usually include art-related courses in normal and pathological art expression; art therapy for children, adolescents, and the aged; therapeutic ability through art; art therapy and communication; and art therapy for the disabled. Behaviorally oriented courses include normal and abnormal psychological development, dynamics and group practice, and diagnosis and treatment approaches. Experience in a variety of clinical settings is required.

Certification/Registration/Licensure

Certification may be secured through the American Art Therapy Association. To gain certification, you must satisfy the association's educational, internship, and paid-work experience requirements and provide letters of recommendation and a portfolio of slides. Securing registered status as an art therapist (ATR), while not essential, can help you find employment at higher salary levels. To work in public schools, you need state licensure.

Career Potential

Employment prospects are positive, reflected, in part, in the increasing number of graduate programs that now offer training in art therapy. Art therapy has gained federal recognition and support, and there has been a significant increase in the number of therapists seeking certification as registered art therapists. This bodes well for raising the status of the profession.

For More Information

The professional organization for this field is the American Art Therapy Association (AATA), 1202 Allanson Rd., Mundelein, IL 60060 (www.arttherapy.org).

Art Therapy Programs

The master's degree programs listed here are accredited by the AATA. Many more institutions offer bachelor's degrees or certificates/diplomas in the field.

Master's Degree Programs

California
Notre Dame of Namur University
1500 Ralston Ave.
Belmont, CA 94002
www.ndnu.edu

Loyola Marymount University
1 LMU Dr.
Los Angeles, CA 90045
www.lmu.edu/mft/

Phillips Graduate Institute
5445 Balboa Blvd.
Encino, CA 91316
www.pgi.edu

Sonoma State University
1801 E. Cotati Ave.
Rohnert Park, CA 94928
www.sonoma.edu

Colorado
Naropa University
2130 Arapahoe Ave.
Boulder, CO 80302
www.naropa.edu

Connecticut
Albertus Magnus College
700 Prospect St.
New Haven, CT 06511
www.albertus.edu

District of Columbia
George Washington University
2121 Eye St. NW
Washington, DC 20052
www.gwu.edu

Florida
Florida State University
126 Carothers Hall B-171
Tallahassee, FL 32306
www.fsu.edu

Georgia
Georgia College and State
  University
School of Health Sciences
Music Therapy
CBX 067
Miltegville, GA 31061
www.gcsu.edu/mtherapy/

Illinois
Adler School of Professional
  Psychology
65 E. Wacker Place
Suite 2100
Chicago, IL 60601
www.adler.edu

Art Institute of Chicago
37 S. Wabash
Chicago, IL 60603
www.saic.edu

Illinois State University
Normal, IL 61790
www.ilstu.edu

Southern Illinois University at
  Edwardsville
Edwardsville, IL 62026
www.siue.edu

University of Illinois at Chicago
935 W. Harrison St.
Chicago, IL 60607
www.uic.edu

Kansas
Emporia State University
1200 Commercial St.
Emporia, KS 66801
www.emporia.edu

Kentucky
University of Louisville
Louisville, KY 40292
www.louisville.edu

Massachusetts
Lesley University
29 Everett St.
Cambridge, MA 02138
www.lesley.edu

Springfield College
263 Alden St.
Springfield, MA 01109
www.spfldcol.edu

Michigan
Wayne State University
163 Community Arts Building
Detroit, MI 48202
www.wayne.edu

Missouri
St. Louis Institute of Art
  Psychotherapy
308-A N. Euclid Ave.
St. Louis, MO 63108

New Mexico
Southwestern College
P.O. Box 4788
Santa Fe, NM 87502
www.swc.edu

University of New Mexico
Albuquerque, NM 87131
www.unm.edu

New York
College of New Rochelle
29 Castle Place
New Rochelle, NY 10805
www.cnr.edu

Hillside Children's Center
1183 Monroe Ave.
Rochester, NY 14620
ww.hillside.com

Hofstra University
212 Mason Hall
Hempstead, NY 11550
www.hofstra.edu

Long Island University
700 Northern Blvd.
Brookville, NY 11548
www.liu.edu

Nazareth College of Rochester
4245 East Ave.
Rochester, NY 14618
www.naz.edu

New York University
34 Stuyvesant St.
New York, NY 10003
www.nyu.edu

Pratt Institute
200 Willoughby Ave.
Brooklyn, NY 11205
www.pratt.edu

Steinhardt School of Culture
  Education
82 Washington Square E
New York, NY 10003
www.steinhardt.nyu.edu

Ohio
Ursuline College
2550 Lander Rd.
Pepper Pike, OH 44124
www.ursuline.edu

Oregon
Marylhurst University
17600 Pacific Hwy. (Hwy. 43)
P.O. Box 261
Marylhurst, OR 97036
www.marylhurst.edu

Pennsylvania
Drexel University
3141 Chestnut St.
Philadelphia, PA 19104
www.drexel.edu

Marywood University
2300 Adams Ave.
Scranton, PA 18509
www.marywood.edu

Seton Hill University
One Seton Hill Dr.
Greensburg, PA 15601
www.setonhill.edu

Vermont
Vermont College
Norwich University
158 Harmon Dr.
Northfield, VT 05663
www.norwich.edu

Virginia
Eastern Virginia Medical School
P.O. Box 1980
Norfolk, VA 23501
www.evms.edu

Wisconsin
Mount Mary College
2900 N. Menomonee River Pkwy.
Milwaukee, WI 53222
www.mtmary.edu

University of Wisconsin–Superior
Belknap and Catlin
P.O. Box 2000
Superior, WI 54880
www.uwsuper.edu

Canada
Concordia University
1455 de Maisonneuve Blvd. W.
Montreal, Quebec H3G 1M8
www.concordia.ca

Certificate Programs

California
Notre Dame of Nadur University
1500 Ralston Ave.
Belmont, CA 94002
www.ndnu.edu

New York
New School University
66 W. 12th St.
New York, NY 10011
www.newschool.edu

Oklahoma
University of Oklahoma
1700 Asp Ave.
Norman, OK 73072
www.occe.ou.edu

Texas
University of Houston–Clear Lake
2700 Bay Area Blvd.
Houston, TX 77058
www.uhcl.edu

Canada
University of Western Ontario
1151 Richmond St.
Suite 2
London, Ontario N6A 5B8
www.uwo.ca

Bachelor's Degree Programs

Alabama
Spring Hill College
4000 Dauphin St.
Mobile, AL 36608
www.shc.edu

Illinois
Barat College
700 E. Westleigh Rd.
Lake Forest, IL 60045
www.barat.edu

Indiana
University of Indianapolis
1400 E. Hanna Ave.
Indianapolis, IN 46227
www.uindy.edu

Kansas
Pittsburgh State University
1701 S. Broadway
Pittsburgh, KS 66762
www.pittstate.edu

Massachusetts
Anna Maria College
50 Sunset Ln.
Paxton, MA 01612
www.annamaria.edu

Our Lady of the Elms College
291 Springfield St.
Chicopee, MA 01013
www.elms.edu

Springfield College
263 Alden St.
Springfield, MA 01109
www.spfldcol.edu

New Jersey
Caldwell College
9 Ryerson Ave.
Caldwell, NJ 07006
www.caldwell.edu

New York
St. Thomas Aquinas College
123 Route 340
Sparkill, NY 10976
www.stac.edu

Ohio
Bowling Green State University
Bowling Green, OH 43403
www.bgsu.edu

Pennsylvania
Mercyhurst College
501 E. 38th St.
Erie, PA 16546
www.mercyhurst.edu

University of the Arts
Philadelphia College of Arts
320 S. Broad St.
Philadelphia, PA 19102
www.uarts.edu

South Carolina
Converse College
580 E. Main St.
Spartanburg, SC 29302
www.converse.edu

Wisconsin
Alverno College
3400 S. 43rd St.
P.O. Box 343922
Milwaukee, WI 53234
www.alverno.edu

Edgewood College
1000 Edgewood College Dr.
Madison, WI 53711
www.edgewood.edu

Mt. Mary College
2900 N. Menomonee River Pkwy.
Milwaukee, WI 53222
www.mtmary.edu

University of Wisconsin–Superior
Belknap and Catlin
Superior, WI 54880
www.uwsuper.edu

Dance/Movement Therapists

Principal activity: Improving clients' mental and physical states

Work commitment: Part- or full-time

Preprofessional education: Bachelor's degree

Program length: 4 to 6 years

Work prerequisites: Master's degree

Career opportunities: Favorable

Income range: $30,000 to $52,000

Scope

Dance therapy uses movement to improve patients' emotional and physical condition. It facilitates the diagnosis and treatment of persons with such mental illnesses as schizophrenia and psychotic depression, and also those with personality disorders. People with brain damage and learning disabilities and those with hearing, visual, and physical disabilities also can benefit from this type of therapy. Others who can be helped are those who have suffered physical or emotional trauma.

The basic premise of dance therapy is that there is a constant interaction between the mind and the body. These two entities register both pain and pleasure. Emotional pain experienced during anxiety and depression can be expressed outwardly, involuntarily, through posture, movements, muscle tension, and breathing patterns. In other words, motion provides a pathway to express one's feelings. In addition, dance can divert patients' attention from their inner concerns and uplift their spirits.

Dance therapists work with physicians and other therapists to help restore the health of their patients.

Activities

Initially, the therapist observes and interprets the patient's outward physical expressions and seeks to establish meaningful contact. Then, using dance exercises either individually or in groups, the therapist seeks to improve communication and enhance patients' self-image and confidence.

Activities that require touching and rhythmic motion can help reconnect severely disturbed individuals with their social environments. Working through their feelings, even in a nonverbal form such as motion, can facilitate the recovery process.

Similarly, dance and movement can be applied to a wide variety of disabilities faced by both children and adults and can improve their ability to function.

Work Settings

Dance therapists are employed by short- and long-term residential facilities, nursing homes, and psychiatric institutions. Some are in private practice, contracting with such facilities to provide services on an hourly basis. Others teach, either full- or part-time, at dance studios or educational institutions.

Advancement

Because this is a relatively new profession, advancement opportunities are limited. They include entering the teaching profession to develop dance/motion training programs at educational institutions and promotion to supervisory appointments in a variety of settings.

Prerequisites

A person who wants to enter this field must first secure a bachelor's degree. Most applicants take courses or major in psychology, dance, or physical education as part of a broad liberal arts program. Experience as a dance instructor for youth and adults, in choreography, or in kinesiology (the study of human muscle movement) is also recommended.

Desirable personal attributes include a love of dance, good dance skills, physical strength, a great deal of patience, a strong sense of compassion, and a desire to work with disabled people.

Education/Training

A dance therapist must secure a master's degree from a college or university program that is accredited by the American Dance Therapy Association (ADTA). Graduate work includes courses in psychopathology, human development, dance/movement theory and practice, and observation and research skills, as well as a supervised internship in a clinical setting. The program usually takes two years. Two master's degrees are offered in this field: a Master of Arts in movement theory and a Master of Arts in creative arts therapy.

Certification/Registration/Licensure

At present there are no state licensing requirements for dance therapists, but professional competence is identified through registered status from the ADTA. Two different levels of registration exist. To be qualified to work in a professional treatment system, you need a master's degree plus 700 supervised clinical internship hours. Additional requirements and more experience are needed to be registered to teach, supervise, and engage in private practice.

Career Potential

Dance therapy is relatively new, but it has become accepted in its own right. This field (along with art and music therapy) has been recognized as beneficial in working with elderly citizens, and some government funding has been provided. With the growing pool of older Americans, the need for dance/movement therapists should increase.

For More Information

The professional organization for this field is the American Dance Therapy Association, Inc., 2000 Century Plaza, Suite 108, Columbia, MD 21044 (www.adta.org).

Dance/Movement Therapy Programs

Master's Degree Programs

Arizona
Arizona State University
Tempe, AZ 85287
www.asu.edu

California
California State University–
  East Bay
25800 Carlos Bee Blvd.
Hayward, CA 94542
http://www.csueastbay.edu

California Institute of Integral
  Studies
1453 Mission St.
San Francisco, CA 94103
www.ciis.edu

University of California,
  Los Angeles
P.O. Box 951369
Los Angeles, CA 90095
www.ucla.edu

Colorado
Naropa Institute
2130 Arapahoe Ave.
Boulder, CO 80302
www.naropa.edu

Connecticut
Wesleyan University
Wesleyan Station
Middletown, CT 06459
www.wesleyan.edu

Illinois
Columbia College–Chicago
600 S. Michigan Ave.
Chicago, IL 60605
www.colum.edu

Massachusetts
Lesley University
29 Everett St.
Cambridge, MA 02138
www.lesley.edu

New Hampshire
Antioch New England Graduate
  School
40 Avon St.
Keene, NH 03431
www.antiochne.edu

New Jersey
Dance Therapy Institute
Of Princeton
301 N Harrison Street
Princeton, NJ 08540
www.adta.org

New York
New York University
70 Washington Sq. S.
New York, NY 10012
www.nyu.edu

Pratt Institute
200 Willoughby Ave.
Brooklyn, NY 11205
www.pratt.edu

Southampton College
Long Island University
239 Montauk Hwy.
Southampton, NY 11968
www.southampton.liu.edu

State University of New York at
  Brockport
350 New Campus Dr.
Brockport, NY 14420
www.brockport.edu

Kinections
718 University Avenue
Rochester, NY 14607
www.kinections.com

Oregon
Marylhurst College
17600 Pacific Hwy. (Hwy. 43)
P.O. Box 261
Marylhurst, OR 97036
www.marylhurst.edu

Pennsylvania
Drexel University
3141 Chestnut St.
Philadelphia, PA 19104
www.drexel.edu

Bachelor's Degree Programs

California
Loyola Marymount University
1 LMU Dr.
Los Angeles, CA 90045
www.lmu.edu

Illinois
Barat College
700 Westleigh Rd.
Lake Forest, IL 60045
www.barat.edu

Maryland
Goucher College
1021 Dulaney Valley Rd.
Baltimore, MD 21204
www.goucher.edu

Michigan
Hope College
Dow Center
Holland, MI 49423
www.hope.edu

Minnesota
Metropolitan State University
700 E. 7th St.
St. Paul, MN 55106
www.metrostate.edu

New Jersey
Brookdale Community College
765 Newman Springs Rd.
Lincroft, NJ 07738
www.brookdale.cc.nj.us

New York
Hunter College
695 Park Ave.
New York, NY 10021
www.hunter.cuny.edu

Marymount College
Tarrytown, NY 10591
www.marymt.edu

Home Health Aides

Principal activity: Helping the elderly and disabled meet their daily needs

Work commitment: Part- or full-time

Preprofessional education: High school diploma

Program length: 75 hours recommended

Work prerequisites: Formal training recommended

Career opportunities: Highly favorable

Income range: $18,000 to $28,000

Scope

Most people can take care of themselves. However, a significant number of people are unable to meet their personal needs and require assistance. The underlying problem may be injury, illness, emotional problems, or a social disadvantage (such as language impairment). Frequently, however, the sole cause is the weakness that sometimes comes with old age. Home health aides help all these people meet their daily needs.

Activities

Home health aides provide a broad spectrum of personal care services. They may help with personal hygiene, walking and voluntary or prescribed exercises, shopping and preparing meals (while seeing that special dietary restrictions are met), and maintaining an orderly and clean home. They also make sure their clients take the proper medications on schedule, change surgical dressings, and check vital signs. These helpers also provide companionship for clients and report on their progress to the family or a supervisor (typically, a registered nurse or social worker). By providing these services, home health aides allow their clients to remain in their own homes, which is less costly and less traumatic than custodial care.

Work Settings

Home health aides are employed by many kinds of agencies to work in clients' homes. They may be referred by local welfare departments, hospitals, community agencies, or private health-care agencies. Some aides also find work helping clients in nursing homes.

Advancement

Working for more affluent clients over extended periods can result in gradual increases in salary (which is usually on an hourly basis).

The Home Care Aide Association of America has proposed a three-level career ladder for aides. If this plan is accepted, it will provide for formal advancement possibilities.

Prerequisites

A high school diploma or its equivalent is recommended for work in this field.

Desirable personal attributes include good health, physical stamina, maturity and good judgment, a desire to help others, a great deal of patience, and a positive, outgoing personality.

Education/Training

While definitive standards have not yet been established nationwide, two basic avenues are currently available to prepare for becoming an aide:

- Many employment agencies offer a very short training program, followed by on-the-job experience.
- Currently, about half the states require a formal program that involves about 60 hours of training, followed by 15 hours of practical experience.

Training programs are offered by community colleges, state programs for the aged, adult education programs, and private agencies. In these programs, a prospective aide is taught how to meet a client's personal hygiene needs, plan and prepare nutritious meals, ensure comfort, monitor the client's health, administer medications, and cope with the types of problems commonly faced in the job.

Certification/Registration/Licensure

The National Association for Home Care and Hospice (NAHC) offers national certification for aides. Certification requires the completion of 75 hours of training; observation and documentation of 17 skills for competency, assessed by a registered nurse; and the passing of a written exam developed by NAHC. No license is required to serve as a home health aide.

Career Potential

Excellent employment prospects in the home care field are the result of a rapidly growing population of elderly people. Many need only part-time assistance, but others are too feeble to care for themselves. In addition, many are chronically ill or disabled. Over time, specialization in this area should occur, which will only increase career potential and advancement possibilities.

For More Information

The professional organization for this field is the Home Care Aide Association of America, 519 C St. NE, Washington, DC 20002 (www.nahc.org).

Horticultural Therapists

Principal activity: Using gardening as therapy for appropriate patients

Work commitment: Part- or full-time

Preprofessional education: High school diploma

Program length: 4 years

Work prerequisites: Bachelor's degree in horticulture

Career opportunities: Favorable

Income range: $30,000 to $49,000

Scope

This unique profession uses nature for therapeutic purposes. Two premises serve as the basis of horticultural therapy, which seeks to improve the well-being of persons with mental, physical, and social disabilities. The first is that seeing the beauty of nature—expressed in the form of flowers, plants, and shrubs—generates inner pleasure. This seems to be an innate human response. For example, flowers are a common gift for those we seek to please. The colors and aroma of flowers stimulate happiness and contentment, which may be especially meaningful to those deprived of their full capabilities. The second premise is that the work associated with growing flowers, fruits, vegetables, and shrubs can be beneficial. Gathering the products of one's own labor from the soil can give the individual a unique sense of accomplishment.

Activities

Horticultural therapists encourage disabled clients to participate in all phases of gardening, from planting to selling their produce. They help their clients improve their self-esteem, confidence, attitudes, motor and problem-solving skills, sociability, and communication skills. In conjunction with other therapies, this kind of activity can generate a new sense of independence and purpose and helps prepare clients for a return to their homes.

Work Settings

Horticultural therapists are employed in hospitals (both general and psychiatric), convalescent centers, nursing homes, rehabilitation centers, and correctional facilities.

Advancement

With additional experience, therapists can move to a larger facility or go into private practice, offering their services on a contract basis.

Prerequisites

A high school diploma or its equivalent is essential for work in this field. It's also a good idea to get experience working for greenhouses, nurseries, or landscape companies during the summer. Volunteer work with disabled people also is helpful.

Desirable personal attributes include a desire to help the disabled, manual dexterity, a love of gardening, and patience.

Education/Training

A bachelor's degree in horticulture is the basic requirement for employment. Degree programs are offered by at least 15 colleges and universities in the U.S. Courses include agriculture, psychology, sociology, horticultural therapy, and a supervised internship.

Certification/Registration/Licensure

Currently this profession has no state licensing laws. However, horticultural therapists can voluntarily register with the American Horticultural Therapy Association. This organization has established two classifications for horticultural therapists based on education and experience. A registered horticultural therapist holds a bachelor's degree and has had at least one year of paid employment; a master horticultural therapist holds a master's degree and has had at least four years of paid employment.

Career Potential

This emerging health-care field has growth potential. Increased awareness of the therapeutic effects of gardening and the expanding population of senior citizens are generating a need for horticultural therapists.

For More Information

The professional organization for this field is the American Horticultural Therapy Association, 909 York St., Denver, CO 80206 (www.ahta.org).

Horticultural Therapy Programs

The following notations denote the type of program offered:

    a associate degree   e elective courses
    b bachelor's degree   m master's degree
    c certificate program   o one-year program

Arizona
Arizona State University (c)
Tempe, AZ 85287
www.asu.edu

California
Merritt College (e)
12500 Campus Dr.
Oakland, CA 94619
www.merritt.edu

Colorado
Horticultural Therapy Institute (o)
P.O. Box 461189
Denver, CO 80246
www.htinstitute.org

Illinois
College of DuPage (e)
425 Fawell Blvd.
Glen Ellyn, IL 60137
www.cod.edu

Iowa
Hawkeye Community College (a)
1501 E. Orange Rd.
Waterloo, IA 50701
www.hawkeye.cc.ia.us

Kansas
Kansas State University (e)
Division of Continuing Education
13 College Court Building
Manhattan, KS 66506
www.dce.k-state.edu

Kansas State University (b, m)
K-State Research and Extension
2021 Throckmorton Hall
Manhattan, KS 66506
www.oznet.k-state.edu

Massachusetts
University of Massachusetts (e)
French Hall
Amherst, MA 01002
www.umass.edu

New Jersey
Rutgers University (b, m)
59 Dudley Rd.
New Brunswick, NJ 08901
www.rutgers.edu

New York
New York Botanical Garden (c)
200th St. and Kazimiroff Blvd.
Bronx, NY 10458
www.nybg.org

SUNY Cobleskill (e)
Agriculture and Natural Resources
  Department
Cobleskill, NY 12043
www.cobleskill.edu

SUNY Rockland Community
  College (e)
145 College Rd.
Suffern, NY 10901
www.sunyrockland.edu

Oklahoma
Oklahoma State University–
  Oklahoma City (e)
400 N. Portland
Oklahoma City, OK 73107
www.okstate.edu

Tulsa Community College (a)
Tulsa, OK 74135
www.tulsacc.edu

Pennsylvania
Temple University–Ambler (e)
580 Meetinghouse Rd.
Ambler, PA 19002
www.temple.edu/ambler/

Rhode Island
University of Rhode Island (a)
Kingston, RI 02881
www.uri.edu

Tennessee
Tennessee Technological
  University (e)
Cookeville, TN 38505
www.tntech.edu

Texas
Texas A&M University (a)
College Station, TX 77843
www.tamu.edu

Virginia
Northern Virginia Community
  College (c)
1000 Harry Flood Byrd Hwy.
Sterling, VA 20164
www.nvcc.edu

Virginia Tech (a)
Department of Horticulture
Blacksburg, VA 24061
www.hort.vt.edu

Washington
Edmonds Community College (o)
20000 68th Ave. W.
Lynnwood, WA 98036
www.edcc.edu

Massage Therapists

Principal activity: To apply massage as a means of reducing pain, diminishing stress and relaxing from overwork.

Work commitments: Part or full-time

Preprofessional education: High school diploma or its equivalent.

Program length: Varies from several months to several years depending on the program.

Work prerequisites: Certification and or regulation by an accrediting agency and or state board.

Career Opportunities: Favorable

Salary range: Earnings vary considerably (from $19,000 to $54,000 annually)

Scope

The health benefits of massage were recognized by the early Greeks. It can be of benefit to patients with painful ailments, individuals suffering from stress and overworked muscles, as well as those being rehabilitated from injuries.

Activities

Massage is done by manipulating the soft tissue muscles of the body in order, to improve circulation and remove waste products from them. Massage therapy is used by many for relaxation purposes. There is a wide range of relaxation treatments available to meet this distinct needs. Massage therapy that simply aims to improve physical health, typically differs in technique and duration from massage that is intended to simply relax or rejuvenate clients.

There are many types of massage and practitioners will be specialized in a number of them.

Work Settings

Massage therapists work in an array of settings both private and public, studios, hospitals, nursing homes, fitness centers, sports medicine facilities, airports and shopping malls.

Advancement

Because of the nature of massage therapy, opportunities for advancement are limited. However, those who are well organized and have an entrepreneurial spirit may go into business themselves. Self-employed massage therapists with a large client base often have the largest incomes.

Prerequisites

A high school diploma is necessary as well as a strong interest in physical fitness and health care.

Desirable personal attributes include an outgoing and pleasant personality, flexible nature, and a genuine desire to help people.

Education/Training

Training programs are provided at postsecondary institutions of various types and require completing courses, in anatomy, physiology, kinesiology, studies of motion and biomechanics, as well as hands-on practice of massage techniques. Training programs also provide continuing educational services.

Both full-time and part-time education and training programs are available.

Certification/Registration/Licensure

Massage therapy programs vary in accreditation. They generally are approved by all-state boards and may also be accredited by an independent accrediting organization or agency. In states that regulate massage therapy, graduation from an approved school or training programs is required in order to practice. Some states require practitioners to keep their skills up-to-date by taking continuing education courses.

Career Potential

Employment of massage therapists is expected to increase substantially over the next decade. As individuals become more familiar with this form of therapy and medical insurance providers increasingly provide coverage for this service, demands for therapists will undoubtedly increase.

For More Information

Information on entering this profession can be secured from the Associated Bodywork & Massage Professionals, 1271 Surgarbush Drive, Evergreen, CO 80439 (www.massagetherapy.com/careers/) or The American Massage Therapy Association, 500 Davis Street, Suite 900, Evanston, IL 60201 (www.americanmassage.org).

For certification information, contact the National Certification Board for Therapeutic Massage and Bodywork, 1901 S. Meyers Rd. Suite 240, Overlook Terrace, IL 60181 (www.ncbtmb.org).

Music Therapists

Principal activity: Using music thera-peutically for a variety of disorders

Work commitment: Part- or full-time

Preprofessional education: High school diploma

Program length: 4 years

Work prerequisites: Bachelor's degree in music therapy

Career opportunities: Favorable

Income range: $30,000 to $45,000

Scope

Humans seem to have a natural positive reaction to music, whether vocal or instrumen-tal. Infants respond to lullabies by falling asleep; adolescents respond to hard rock by getting "pumped up." Music can change a person's mood, and this forms the basis of music therapy. This therapy is used as part of a treatment plan to help change patients' behavior. Music is helpful in treating a variety of behavioral, physical, and learning disorders. Music therapy can improve patients' self-control and self-image, enhance their attention span, reduce depression, and facilitate their integration into their sur-roundings.

Activities

Music therapists plan and execute musical activities as part of a rehabilitation program for disabled people. They coordinate their work with other health-care professionals such as physicians, nurses, teachers, social workers, psychiatrists, psychologists, and other therapists. They provide their services to emotionally and socially maladjusted or mentally disabled children, adolescents, and adults. Others who can benefit are those with learning disabilities, geriatric patients, and those with physical impairments such as vision or hearing loss. The activities can be done individually or in a group and may be used in combination with dance therapy. The therapist may teach patients new tunes or play music to help withdrawn patients recall their past, reminisce, and participate with others in social activities.

Work Settings

Music therapists work in a wide variety of settings, including hospitals (both general and psychiatric), rehabilitation centers, nursing homes, extended-care facilities, hos-pices, schools, and correctional facilities.

Advancement

Music therapists can advance by securing a master's or doctoral degree and obtain-ing an administrative or supervisory position. Teaching and private practice are other options.

Prerequisites

A high school diploma is required to gain admission to a college or university offering a music therapy program.

In addition to musical skills, desirable personal attributes include patience, emotional stability, creativity, compassion, and a desire to help people.

Education/Training

Those seeking to enter this field should earn a bachelor's degree in music theory. This program includes courses in music, music theory, voice, and instrument lessons. These classes are supplemented by courses in psychology, sociology, biology, and liberal arts. Those who want to work in a school also need education courses.

Most institutions with programs in this field offer bachelor's degrees, but a few offer master's and even doctoral programs.

Certification/Registration/Licensure

Certification is available from the Certification Board of Musical Therapists (www. cbmt.org). Those seeking certification must pass a standard exam and maintain continuing education requirements. Registration is available from the National Association of Music Therapists and the American Association for Music Therapy.

Career Potential

Music therapists will find positive employment prospects in the coming decade. In addition to public and medical acceptance of the field, the U.S. Congress has recognized its significance and has approved financial grants for the elderly in this area.

However, the state of the economy and the impact of health-care system changes will significantly influence employment prospects.

For More Information

The professional organization for this field is the American Music Therapy Association, Inc., 8455 Colesville Rd., Suite 1000, Silver Spring, MD 20910 (www.musictherapy. org).

Music Therapy Programs

Alabama
University of Alabama at
  Birmingham
1714 Ninth Ave. S.
Birmingham, AL 35294
www.uab.edu

Arizona
Arizona State University
School of Music
Tempe, AZ 85287
www.asu.edu

California
California State University–
  Northridge
18111 Nordhoff St.
Northridge, CA 91330
www.csun.edu

Chapman University
One University Dr.
Orange, CA 92866
www.chapman.edu

University of the Pacific
3601 Pacific Ave.
Stockton, CA 95211
www.pacific.edu

Colorado
Colorado State University
Fort Collins, CO 80523
www.colostate.edu

District of Columbia
Howard University
2400 6th St. NW
Washington, DC 20059
www.howard.edu

Florida
Florida State University
Department of Music
Tallahassee, FL 32306
www.fsu.edu

University of Miami
5801 Red Rd.
Coral Gables, FL 33124
www.miami.edu

Georgia
Georgia College & State
  University
P.O. Box 23
Milledgeville, GA 31061
www.gcsu.edu

Illinois
Illinois State University
Music Department
Normal, IL 61790
www.ilstu.edu

Western Illinois University
Department of Music
1 University Circle
Macomb, IL 61455
www.wiu.edu

Indiana
Indiana University–Purdue
  University Fort Wayne
2101 E. Coliseum Blvd.
Fort Wayne, IN 46805
www.ipfw.edu

University of Evansville
1800 Lincoln Ave.
Evansville, IN 47722
www.evansville.edu

Iowa
University of Iowa
Division of Music Education
Iowa City, IA 52242
www.uiowa.edu

Wartburg College
100 Wartburg Blvd.
Waverly, IA 50677
www.wartburg.edu

Kansas
University of Kansas
126 Strong Hall
Lawrence, KS 66045
www.ku.edu

Louisiana
Loyola University New Orleans
6363 St. Charles Ave.
New Orleans, LA 70118
www.loyno.edu

Massachusetts
Anna Maria College
50 Sunset Ln.
Paxton, MA 01612
www.annamaria.edu

Michigan
Eastern Michigan University
Department of Music
Ypsilanti, MI 48197
www.emich.edu

Michigan State University
Department of Music
East Lansing, MI 48824
www.msu.edu

Western Michigan University
1903 W. Michigan Ave.
Kalamazoo, MI 49008
www.wmich.edu

Minnesota
Augsburg College
2211 Riverside Ave. S.
Minneapolis, MN 55454
www.augsburg.edu

University of Minnesota–
  Twin Cities
240 Williamson
Minneapolis, MN 55455
www.umn.edu

Missouri
Maryville University, St. Louis
13550 Conway Rd.
St. Louis, MO 63141
www.maryville.edu

University of Missouri–Kansas City
650 E. 25th St.
Kansas City, MO 64108
www.umkc.edu

New Jersey
Montclair State University
1 Normal Ave.
Montclair, NJ 07043
www.montclair.edu

New Mexico
Eastern New Mexico University
1200 W. University
Portales, NM 88130
www.enmu.edu

New York
Nazareth College
4245 East Ave.
Rochester, NY 14618
www.naz.edu

State University of New York at
  Fredonia
280 Central Ave.
Fredonia, NY 14063
www.fredonia.edu

State University of New York at
  New Paltz
Music Department
75 S. Manheim Blvd.
New Paltz, NY 12561
www.newpaltz.edu

North Carolina
East Carolina University
E. 5th St.
Greenville, NC 27858
www.ecu.edu

Queens University of Charlotte
Department of Music
1900 Selwyn Ave.
Charlotte, NC 28274
www.queens.edu

Ohio
Baldwin Wallace College
Department of Music
275 Eastland Rd.
Berea, OH 44017
www.bw.edu

Cleveland Institute of Music
11021 East Blvd.
Cleveland, OH 44106
www.cim.edu

College of Mt. Saint Joseph
5701 Delhi Rd.
Cincinnati, OH 45233
www.msj.edu

College of Wooster
Department of Music
1189 Beall Ave.
Wooster, OH 44691
www.wooster.edu

Ohio University
416 Tower
Athens, OH 45701
www.ohio.edu

University of Dayton
300 College Park
Dayton, OH 45469
www.udayton.edu

Oklahoma
Southwestern Oklahoma State
  University
100 Campus Dr.
Weatherford, OK 73096
www.swosu.edu

Oregon
Willamette University
900 State St.
Salem, OR 97301
www.willamette.edu

Pennsylvania
Duquesne University
600 Forbes Ave.
Pittsburgh, PA 15282
www.duq.edu

Elizabethtown College
Department of Music
One Alpha Dr.
Elizabethtown, PA 17022
www.etown.edu

Mansfield University
Beecher House
Mansfield, PA 16933
www.mansfield.edu

Marywood University
2300 Adams Ave.
Scranton, PA 18509
www.marywood.edu

MCP Hahnemann University
905 Broad St.
Philadelphia, PA 19101
www.drexel.edu/hs/

Slippery Rock University
Department of Music
1 Morrow Way
Slippery Rock, PA 16057
www.sru.edu

Temple University
1801 N. Broad St.
Philadelphia, PA 19122
www.temple.edu

South Carolina
Charleston Southern University
Music Department
9200 University Blvd.
Charleston, SC 29423
www.csuniv.edu

Tennessee
Tennessee Technological
   University
Cookeville, TN 38505
www.tntech.edu

Texas
Sam Houston State University
Department of Music
Huntsville, TX 77341
www.shsu.edu

Southern Methodist University
Division of Music
Dallas, TX 75275
www.smu.edu

Texas Woman's University
P.O. Box 425589
Denton, TX 76204
www.twu.edu

West Texas A&M University
2501 Fourth Ave.
Canyon, TX 79016
www.wtamu.edu

Utah
Utah State University
University Hall
Logan, UT 84322
www.usu.edu

Virginia
Radford University
E. Main St.
Radford, VA 24142
www.radford.edu

Shenandoah University
Music Therapy Department
1460 University Dr.
Winchester, VA 22601
www.su.edu

Wisconsin
Alverno College
3400 S. 43rd St.
Milwaukee, WI 53234
www.alverno.edu

University of Wisconsin–Eau
   Claire
105 Garfield Ave.
Eau Claire, WI 54702
www.uwec.edu

University of Wisconsin–Oshkosh
Department of Music
800 Algoma Blvd.
Oshkosh, WI 54901
www.uwosh.edu

Occupational Therapists

Principal activity: Helping disabled people improve their quality of life

Work commitment: Part- or full-time

Preprofessional education: High school diploma

Program length: 4 years

Work requirements: Bachelor's degree, certification, and license

Career opportunities: Highly favorable

Income range: $55,000 to $81,000

Scope

Occupational therapists (OTs) use a variety of activities to improve the lives of their patients, who may have mental, emotional, developmental, or physical disabilities. These therapists use educational, vocational, and rehabilitation techniques to improve their clients' ability to carry out the daily tasks of living as well as to recover and maintain their work skills. They help patients improve their basic motor functions and reasoning capacities and teach them how to compensate for a permanent loss of function. The ultimate goal of the occupational therapist is to help a patient achieve the most independent, productive, and satisfying lifestyle possible.

Activities

Occupational therapists train temporarily or permanently disabled patients to perform a variety of activities. They may use physical exercises to increase strength and manual dexterity. They may use pencil-and-paper games, list-making games, and eye-hand coordination activities to help various patients gain coordination and memory abilities. They also use computer programs to help patients improve their decision making, abstract reasoning, and memory, as well as their perceptual, sequencing, and coordination skills.

Therapists teach those with permanent disabilities—such as spinal cord injuries, muscular dystrophy, or cerebral palsy—how to use adaptive equipment, including wheelchairs, splints, and devices that help with dressing and eating.

Work Settings

Occupational therapists provide services in a variety of settings. Most work in hospitals and nursing homes. Others work in rehabilitation centers, clinics, retirement communities, senior citizen centers, and special camps.

Advancement

With increased experience, an occupational therapist can become a senior therapist or specialized therapist. With a master's degree, you can be promoted to a supervisory or administrative position.

Prerequisites

A high school diploma or its equivalent is needed undertake a college program.

Desirable personal attributes include an abundance of patience, physical stamina, manual dexterity, compassion, the ability to improvise, and a genuine desire to help people.

Education/Training

There are several ways to get your education in this field; all involve completing an accredited program:

- You can complete two years of liberal arts and science and then enter an OT program for the last two years of your undergraduate studies.
- You can complete a four-year bachelor's degree program in occupational therapy.
- Those holding a bachelor's degree in another field can enroll in a graduate program and secure a certificate or master's degree in occupational therapy.

The standard OT curriculum includes courses in anatomy, neuroanatomy, physiology, neurophysiology, kinesiology, psychology, psychobiology, pediatrics, gerontology, and home economics. Manual and industrial arts, self-care activities, vocational skills, and rehabilitation skills are also included. Students must also obtain six to nine months of practical experience.

Certification/Registration/Licensure

Graduates of accredited occupational therapy programs can take a certification examination administered by the American Occupational Therapy Association. After passing it, you become a registered occupational therapist (OTR). Most states require therapists to be licensed as well.

Career Potential

Occupational therapists are in high demand and enjoy very favorable employment options because of the current interest in sports and a rapidly aging population.

For More Information

The professional organization for this field is the American Occupational Therapy Association, Inc., 4720 Montgomery Ln., P.O. Box 31220, Bethesda, MD 20824 (www. aota.org).

Occupational Therapy Programs

The following notations denote the type of program offered:

 b bachelor's degree
 b/m combined bachelor's and master's degrees
 m master's degree

Alabama
Alabama State University (b)
College of Health Sciences
915 S. Jackson St.
Montgomery, AL 36101
www.alasu.edu

Tuskegee University (b/m)
Basil O'Connor Hall
Tuskegee, AL 36088
www.tuskegee.edu

University of Alabama at
 Birmingham (m)
School of Health-Related
 Professions
1530 3rd Ave. S., RMSB 338
Birmingham, AL 35294
www.uab.edu

University of South Alabama
 (b/m, m)
Springhill Academic Campus
1504 Springhill Ave., Room 5108
Mobile, AL 36604
www.southalabama.edu

Arizona
Arizona School of Health
 Sciences (m)
5850 E. Still Circle
Mesa, AZ 85206
www.ashs.edu

Midwestern University–Glendale
 Campus (b, m)
19555 N. 59th Ave.
Glendale, AZ 85308
www.midwestern.edu

Arkansas
University of Central Arkansas
 (b/m, m)
201 Donaghey Ave.
Conway, AR 72035
www.uca.edu

California
California State University–
 Dominguez Hills (b)
1000 E. Victoria St.
Carson, CA 90747
www.csudh.edu

Dominican University of
 California (m)
50 Acacia Ave.
San Rafael, CA 94901
www.dominican.edu

Loma Linda University (b/m, m)
Nichol Hall, Room A901
Loma Linda, CA 92350
www.llu.edu

Samuel Merritt College (m)
450 30th Street
Oakland, CA 94609
www.samuelmerritt.edu

San Jose State University
 (b, b/m, m)
One Washington Square
San Jose, CA 95192
www.sjsu.edu

University of Southern California
 (b, m)
Department of Occupational
 Science and Occupational
 Therapy
1540 Alcazar St., CHP 133
Los Angeles, CA 90089
http://ot.usc.edu/

Colorado

Colorado State University (m)
Department of Occupational
 Therapy
219 Occupational Therapy
 Building
Fort Collins, CO 80523
www.ot.cahs.colostate.edu

Connecticut

Quinnipiac University (b/m)
School of Health Sciences
275 Mount Carmel Ave.
Hamden, CT 06518
www.quinnipiac.edu

Sacred Heart University (m)
5151 Park Avenue
Fairfield, CT 06825
www.sacredheart.edu

University of Hartford (b)
College of Education, Nursing
 and Health Professions
200 Bloomfield Ave.
West Hartford, CT 06117
www.hartford.edu

District of Columbia

Howard University (b)
Division of Allied Health
 Sciences
2400 6th St. NW
Washington, DC 20059
www.howard.edu

Florida

Barry University (m)
11300 NE Second Ave.
Miami Shores, FL 33161
www.barry.edu

Florida A&M University (b)
School of Allied Health Sciences
Tums Back Bldg.
Tallahassee, FL 32307
www.famu.edu

Florida Gulf Coast University
Occupational Therapy
10501 FGCU Boulevard South
Fort Myers, FL33965
www.fgcu.edu

Florida International University
Department of Occupational
 Therapy
11200 SW 8th Street
University Park Campus,HLS 248
Miami, FL 33199
www.fiu.edu

Nova Southeastern University (m)
Health Professions Division
3200 S. University Dr.
Ft. Lauderdale, FL 33328
www.nova.edu/ot/

University of Florida (m)
College of Public Health and
 Health Professions
Occupational Therapy
P.O. Box 100164
Gainesville, FL 32610
http://ot.phhp.ufl.edu/

University of St. Augustine for
 Health Sciences (m)
Institute of Occupational Therapy
1 University Blvd.
St. Augustine, FL 32086
www.usa.edu

Georgia

Brenau University (b/m)
School of Health and Science
Occupational Therapy Department
One Centennial Circle
Gainesville, GA 30501
www.brenau.edu

Medical College of Georgia (m)
Department of Occupational
 Therapy
1120 15th St.
Augusta, GA 30912
www.mcg.edu/sah/ot/

Medical College of Georgia at
 Columbus State University (m)
4225 University Ave.
Columbus, GA 31907
www.mcg.edu/sah/ot/

Idaho

Idaho State University (b/m, m)
Department of Physical and
 Occupational Therapy
Campus Box 8045
Pocatello, ID 83209
www.isu.edu

Illinois

Chicago State University
 (b/m, m)
College of Health Sciences
9501 S. King Dr.
Chicago, IL 60628
www.csu.edu

Governors State University (m)
Occupational Therapy Program
College of Health Professions
1 University Pkwy.
University Park, IL 60466
www.govst.edu

Midwestern University (m)
College of Health Sciences
555 31st St.
Downers Grove, IL 60515
www.midwestern.edu

Rush University (m)
Rush–Presbyterian–St. Luke's
 Medical Center
600 S. Paulina St., Ste. 440
Chicago, IL 60612
www.rush.edu

University of Illinois at Chicago
 (m)
College of Health and Human
 Development Sciences
Department of Occupational
 Therapy
1919 W. Taylor St., Room 560
 AHSB, MC 528
Chicago, IL 60612
www.uic.edu

Indiana

Indiana University (b)
School of Health & Rehabilitation
 Sciences
Coleman Hall 120
1140 W. Michigan St.
Indianapolis, IN 46202
www.shrs.iupui.edu

University of Indianapolis (m)
School of Occupational Therapy
1400 E. Hanna Ave.
Indianapolis, IN 46227
http://ot.uindy.edu/

University of Southern Indiana
 (b/m)
8600 University Blvd.
Evansville, IN 47712
www.usi.edu

Iowa
St. Ambrose University (m)
518 W. Locust St.
Davenport, IA 52803
http://web.sau.edu/ot/

Kansas
Newman University (b)
3100 McCormick Ave.
Wichita, KS 67213
www.newmanu.edu/ot/

University of Kansas Medical
 Center (b/m)
3901 Rainbow Blvd.
Kansas City, KS 66160
www.alliedhealth.kumc.edu

Kentucky
Eastern Kentucky University
 (b/m, m)
College of Health Sciences
Department of Occupational
 Therapy
521 Lancaster Ave.
Richmond, KY 40475
www.ot.eku.edu

Spalding University (b/m, m)
Auerbach School of Occupational
 Therapy
851 S. Fourth St.
Louisville, KY 40203
www.spalding.edu

Louisiana
Louisiana State University Health
 Sciences Center (m)
New Orleans Campus
School of Allied Health
 Professions
Department of Occupational
 Therapy
1900 Gravier St.
New Orleans, LA 70112
http://alliedhealth.lsuhsc.edu/
 occupationaltherapy/

Louisiana State University Health
 Sciences Center (m)
Shreveport Campus
Department of Rehabilitation
 Sciences
1501 Kings Hwy.
Shreveport, LA 71130
www.lsuhscshreveport.edu

University of Louisiana at
 Monroe (b)
College of Health Sciences
Department of Occupational
 Therapy
Monroe, LA 71209
www.ulm.edu/ot/

Maine
Husson University (m)
One College Circle
Bangor, ME 04401
www.husson.edu

University of New England
Occupational Therapy
716 Stevens Avenue
Biddeford, ME 04005
www.une.edu

University of Southern Maine (m)
Lewiston-Auburn College
51 Westminster St.
Lewiston, ME 04240
www.usm.maine.edu

Maryland
Towson University (b/m, m)
Department of Occupational
 Therapy & Occupational Science
8000 York Rd.
Towson, MD 21252
wwwnew.towson.edu/OT

Massachusetts
American International College
 (b/m, m)
1000 State St.
Springfield, MA 01109
www.aic.edu

Bay Path College (b/m, m)
588 Longmeadow St.
Longmeadow, MA 01106
www.baypath.edu

Boston University (b/m, m)
Sargent College of Health and
 Rehabilitation Sciences
635 Commonwealth Ave.
Boston, MA 02215
www.bu.edu/sargent/

Salem State College (b)
352 Lafayette St.
Salem, MA 01970
www.salemstate.edu

Springfield College (b/m, m)
Occupational Therapy Department
263 Alden St.
Springfield, MA 01109
www.springfieldcollege.edu/ot

Tufts University–Boston School of
 Occupational Therapy (m)
26 Winthrop St.
Medford, MA 02155
www.tufts.edu

Worcester State College (b/m, m)
486 Chandler St.
Worcester, MA 01602
www.worcester.edu

Michigan
Baker College of Flint (b)
G-1050 W. Bristol Rd.
Flint, MI 48507
www.baker.edu

Eastern Michigan University
 (b/m, m)
Department of Associated Health
 Professions
322 Everett Marshall Hall
Ypsilanti, MI 48197
www.emich.edu

Grand Valley State University (m)
School of Health Professions
Department of Occupational
 Therapy
301 Michigan St. NE
Suite 200
Grand Rapids, MI 49503
www.gvsu.edu/ot/

Saginaw Valley State
 University (b)
7400 Bay Rd.
University Center, MI 48710
www.svsu.edu

Wayne State University (m)
Eugene Applebaum College of
   Pharmacy and Health Sciences
Detroit, MI 48202
www.cphs.wayne.edu/ot/

Western Michigan University
   (b/m, m)
1903 W. Michigan Ave.
Kalamazoo, MI 49008
www.wmich.edu

Minnesota
College of St. Catherine (b/m, m)
Department of Occupational
   Science & Occupational Therapy
2004 Randolph Ave.
St. Paul, MN 55105
www.stkate.edu

College of St. Scholastica
   (b/m, m)
1200 Kenwood Ave.
Duluth, MN 55811
www.css.edu

University of Minnesota (m)
420 Delaware St. SE
Mayo Mail Code 388
Minneapolis, MN 55455
www.ot.umn.edu

Mississippi
The University of Mississippi
   Medical Center (b, b/m)
School of Health-Related
   Professions
2500 N. State St.
Jackson, MS 39216
www.umc.edu

Missouri
Maryville University (m)
650 Maryville University Drive
St. Louis, MO 63141
www.maryville.edu

Rockhurst University (m)
College of Arts and Sciences
1100 Rockhurst Rd.
Kansas City, MO 64110
www.rockhurst.edu/ot/

Saint Louis University (m)
Edward and Margaret Doisy School
   of Allied Health Professions
3437 Caroline St.
St. Louis, MO 63104
www.slu.edu

University of Missouri–
   Columbia (b)
School of Health-Related
   Professions
425 Lewis Hall
Columbia, MO 65211
www.umshp.org/ot/

Washington University (m)
School of Medicine
4444 Forest Park Ave.
St. Louis, MO 63108
www.ot.wustl.edu

Nebraska
College of Saint Mary (b)
7000 Mercy Road
Omaha, NE 68106
www.csm.edu

Creighton University (m)
School of Pharmacy and Health
   Professions
2500 California Plaza
Omaha, NE 68178
http://ot.creighton.edu/

Nevada
Touro University Nevada
School of Occupational Therapy
824 American Pacific Drive
Henderson, NV 89014
www.tu.edu

New Hampshire
University of New Hampshire
   (b/m, m)
School of Health and Human
   Services
217 Hewitt Hall
4 Library Way
Durham, NH 03824
www.shhs.unh.edu/ot/

New Jersey
Kean University (b, m)
Nathan Weiss Graduate College
Occupational Therapy Department
1000 Morris Ave.
Union, NJ 07083
www.kean.edu/~ot/

Richard Stockton College of New
   Jersey (m)
Occupational Therapy Program,
   Professional Studies Division
P.O. Box 195
Pomona, NJ 08240
www2.stockton.edu

Seton Hall University (b/m, m)
School of Graduate Medical
   Education
400 S. Orange Ave.
South Orange, NJ 07079
www.shu.edu

New Mexico
University of New Mexico (m)
Health Sciences Center
MSC 09 5240
1 University of New Mexico
Albuquerque, NM 87131
http://hsc.unm.edu/som/ot/

New York
The City University of New York
   (b/m)
York College
Department of Health Sciences
94-20 Guy R. Brewer Blvd.
Jamaica, NY 11451
www.york.cuny.edu

Columbia University (m)
Neurological Institute, 8th Floor
710 W. 168th St.
New York, NY 10032
www.columbiaot.org

Dominican College (b/m)
470 Western Hwy.
Orangeburg, NY 10962
www.dc.edu

D'Youville College (b/m, m)
320 Porter Ave.
Buffalo, NY 14201
www.dyc.edu

Ithaca College (b/m)
204-D Smiddy Hall
Ithaca, NY 14850
www.ithaca.edu/hshp/ot/

Keuka College (b/m)
141 Central Ave.
Keuka Park, NY 14478
www.keuka.edu

Long Island University, Brooklyn
Campus (b/m)
One University Plaza
Brooklyn, NY 11201
www.brooklyn.liu.edu

Mercy College (b/m, m)
555 Broadway
Dobbs Ferry, NY 10522
www.mercy.edu

New York Institute of Technology
(b/m, m)
Northern Blvd.
Old Westbury, NY 11568
www.nyit.edu

New York University (m)
The Steinhardt School of
Education
Department of Occupational
Therapy
35 W. 4th St., 11th Floor
New York, NY 10012
http://steinhardt.nyu.edu/ot/
index.php

The Sage Colleges (b/m, m)
45 Ferry St.
Troy, NY 12180
www.sage.edu

State University of New York
Downstate Medical Center (m)
Department of Occupational
Therapy
450 Clarkson Ave., Box 81
Brooklyn, NY 11203
www.downstate.edu/CHRP/ot/

Stony Brook University (b/m)
Health Sciences Center
School of Health Technology &
Management
Stony Brook, NY 11794
www.stonybrook.edu

Touro College (b/m)
27-33 W. 23rd St.
New York, NY 10010
www.touro.edu/shs/ot/

Touro College (b/m)
Occupational Therapy
1700 Union Boulevard
Bayshore, NY 11706
www.touro.edu/ shs/ot/

University at Buffalo (b)
State University of New York
Department of Rehabilitation
Science
Buffalo, NY 14214
www.phhp.buffalo.edu/rs/ot/

Utica College of Syracuse
University (m)
Division of Health and Human
Studies
1600 Burrstone Rd.
Utica, NY 13502
www.utica.edu

York College (b, m)
City University New York
94-20 Guy R. Breuer Blvd.
Jamaica, NY 11451
www.york.cnuy.edu

North Carolina
East Carolina University (m)
School of Allied Health Sciences
Occupational Therapy
306 Belk
Greenville, NC 27858
www.ecu.edu/ot/

Lenoir-Rhyne College (b, b/m, m)
7th Ave. and 8th St. NE
Hickory, NC 28601
www.lrc.edu/ot/

University of North Carolina at
Chapel Hill (m)
Division of Occupational Science
CB #7120, Medical School Wing E
Chapel Hill, NC 27599
www.alliedhealth.unc.edu/
ocsci/

Winston-Salem State
University (b)
601 Martin Luther King, Jr. Dr.
Winston-Salem, NC 27110
www.wssu.edu

North Dakota
University of Mary (m)
7500 University Dr.
Bismarck, ND 58504
www.umary.edu

University of North Dakota (m)
School of Medicine and Health
Sciences
Occupational Therapy Department
Hyslop Sports Center
Grand Forks, ND 58202
www.med.und.edu

Ohio
Cleveland State University (m)
2121 Euclid Ave.
HS 101
Cleveland, OH 44115
www.csuohio.edu

Medical College of Ohio at
Toledo (m)
School of Allied Health
3015 Arlington Ave.
Toledo, OH 43614
www.mco.edu

Ohio State University (b)
School of Allied Medical
Professions
Atwell Hall
453 W. 10th Ave.
Columbus, OH 43210
www.osu.edu

Shawnee State University (b)
940 Second St.
Portsmouth, OH 45662
www.shawnee.edu

University of Findlay (b/m)
1000 N. Main St.
Findlay, OH 45840
www.findlay.edu

Xavier University (m)
3800 Victory Pkwy.
Cincinnati, OH 45207
www.xavier.edu

Oklahoma
University of Oklahoma Health
Sciences Center (m)
College of Allied Health
4502 E 41 Street
Tulsa, OK 7413 5
www.ah.ouhsc.edu/rehab/

Oregon

Pacific University (m)
School of Occupational Therapy
222 SE 8th Avenue
Hillsboro, OR 97123
www.pacificu.edu

Pennsylvania

Alvernia College (b/m)
400 Saint Bernardine St.
Reading, PA 19607
www.alvernia.edu

Chatham University (b/m)
Occupational Therapy Program
Woodland Road
Pittsburgh, PA 15232
www.chatham.edu

Duquesne University (b/m, m)
John G. Rangos, Sr. School of
   Health Sciences
Room 234
Forbes Avenue
Pittsburgh, PA 15219
www.duq.edu/occupational-
   therapy/

Elizabethtown College (b/m)
One Alpha Dr.
Elizabethtown, PA 17022
www.etown.edu

Gannon University (b/m, m)
109 University Square
Erie, PA 16541
www.gannon.edu

Misercodia University
Occupational Therapy Program
301 Lake Street
Dallas, PA 18612
www.misercodia.edu

Mount Aloysius College (b, m)
BS Occupational Therapy Program
7373 Admiral Peary Hwy.
Cresson, PA 16630
www.mtaloy.edu

Philadelphia University (m)
School House Ln. and Henry Ave.
Philadelphia, PA 19144
www.philau.edu/ot/

Saint Francis University (b/m, m)
117 Evergreen Dr.
P.O. Box 600
Loretto, PA 15940
www.saintfrancisuniversity.edu

Temple University (m)
College of Health Professions
3307 N. Broad St.
Philadelphia, PA 19140
www.temple.edu/ot/

Thomas Jefferson University
   (b/m, m)
Jefferson College of Health
   Professions
Edison Building
130 S. 9th St.
Philadelphia, PA 19107
www.jefferson.edu

University of Pittsburgh (m)
School of Health and
   Rehabilitation Sciences
Pittsburgh, PA 15260
www.shrs.pitt.edu/ot/

University of Scranton (b, b/m)
Scranton, PA 18510
http://matrix.scranton.edu/

University of the Sciences in
   Philadelphia (b/m, m)
600 S. 43rd St.
Philadelphia, PA 19104
www.usip.edu

South Carolina

Medical University of South
   Carolina (m)
College of Health Professions
   1518 Rutledge Avenue
P.O. Box 250700
Charleston, SC 29425
www.musc.edu

South Dakota

University of South Dakota (m)
414 E. Clark St.
Vermillion, SD 57069
www.usd.edu

Tennessee

Belmont University (m)
1900 Belmont Blvd.
Nashville, TN 37212
www.belmont.edu/OT/

Milligan College (m)
P.O. Box 130
Milligan College, TN 37682
www.milligan.edu

Tennessee State University (b)
School of Allied Health
   Professions
3500 John Merritt Blvd.
Nashville, TN 37209
www.tnstate.edu/OT/

University of Tennessee Health
   Science Center (b)
College of Allied Health Sciences
Department of Occupational
   Therapy
930 Madison Ave., 6th Floor
Memphis, TN 38163
www.uthsc.edu

Texas

Texas Tech University Health
   Sciences Center (m)
3601 4th St.
Lubbock, TX 79430
www.ttuhsc.edu

Texas Woman's University
   (b/m, m)
P.O. Box 425589
Denton, TX 76204
www.twu.edu

University of Texas at El Paso (b)
College of Health Sciences
1101 N. Campbell St.
El Paso, TX 79902
www.utep.edu

University of Texas Health
   Science Center at Laredo (b/m)
Laredo, TX 78040
www.uthscsa.edu

University of Texas
Health Science Center at
   San Antonio (b/m)
7703 Floyd Curl Dr.
San Antonio, TX 78229
www.uthscsa.edu

University of Texas Medical
   Branch (b/m)
School of Allied Health Sciences
301 University Blvd.
Galveston, TX 77555
http://shp.utmb.edu/ot/

The University of Texas–
Pan American (b)
1201 W. University Dr.
Edinburg, TX 78541
www.panam.edu

Utah
University of Utah (m)
Health Sciences Center
Division of Occupational Therapy
520 Wakara Way
Salt Lake City, UT 84132
www.health.utah.edu/ot/

Virginia
James Madison University (b)
Department of Health Sciences
Harrisonburg, VA 22807
www.healthsci.jmu.edu

Jefferson College of Health
Sciences (b)
Community Hospital of Roanoke
Valley
920 S. Jefferson St.
Roanoke, VA 24016
www.jchs.edu

Shenandoah University (b/m, m)
Department of Occupational
Therapy
333 W. Cork St., 5th Floor
Winchester, VA 22601
www.su.edu

Virginia Commonwealth
University (m)
Department of Occupational
Therapy
1000 E. Marshall St.
P.O. Box 980008
Richmond, VA 23298
www.sahp.vcu.edu/occu/

Washington
Eastern Washington University (b)
Department of Occupational
Therapy
Health Sciences Building
310 N. Riverpoint Blvd., Box R
Spokane, WA 99202
www.ewu.edu

University of Puget Sound (m)
School of Occupational Therapy
1500 N. Warner
Tacoma, WA 98416
www.ups.edu/ot/

University of Washington (m)
Department of Rehabilitation
Medicine
1959 NE Pacific St., Box 356490
Seattle, WA 98195
http://rehab.washington.edu/

West Virginia
West Virginia University (m)
School of Medicine–Human
Performance
Division of Occupational Therapy
P.O. Box 9139
Morgantown, WV 26506
www.hsc.wvu.edu/som/ot/

Wisconsin
Concordia University
Wisconsin (m)
12800 N. Lake Shore Dr.
Mequon, WI 53092
www.cuw.edu

Mount Mary College (b/m, m)
2900 N. Menomonee River Pkwy.
Milwaukee, WI 53222
www.mtmary.edu

University of Wisconsin–
La Crosse (b)
Occupational Therapy Program
1725 State St., 4054 HSC
La Crosse, WI 54601
www.uwlax.edu/ot/

University of Wisconsin–
Madison (b)
2175 Medical Sciences Center
1300 University Ave.
Madison, WI 53706
www.wisc.edu

University of Wisconsin–
Milwaukee (b, b/m)
College of Health Sciences
P.O. Box 413
Milwaukee, WI 53201
www4.uwm.edu/chs

Wyoming
University of North Dakota at
Casper College
125 College Drive, LS102
Casper, WY 82601
www.med.und.edu/depts/ot/

Occupational Therapy Assistants

Principal activity: Helping occupational therapists

Work commitment: Full-time

Preprofessional education: High school diploma

Program length: 1 to 2 years

Work prerequisites: Certificate or associate degree

Career opportunities: Favorable

Income range: $39,000 to $47,000

Scope

Occupational therapy assistants carry out routine activities designed by occupational therapists, who supervise their activities.

Activities

Occupational therapy assistants select or construct equipment to help patients, individually and in groups, move toward independent living. They also help with the planning of and are major participants in implementing treatment programs. As part of their routine responsibilities, they lay out materials needed for treatment, make sure that adequate materials are on hand, and order them when necessary. They also see to it that equipment is properly maintained.

Work Settings

Nearly half of all occupational therapy assistants work in hospitals, and a small portion work in nursing homes. Other work settings include senior citizen residences and mental health facilities.

Advancement

With experience and professional success, a motivated assistant may return to school to become a fully trained therapist. However, it is preferable to follow the direct route to such a career.

Prerequisites

A high school diploma or its equivalent is needed to enroll in an occupational therapy assistant program.

Desirable personal attributes include manual dexterity, patience, maturity, an ability to work with and for people, and a sense of compassion.

Education/Training

There are two routes to getting the training for a position in this field:

- Many vocational and technical schools offer a one-year certificate program.
- Some community colleges offer a two-year associate degree program.

The curriculum includes anatomy, physiology, and occupational therapy theory and skills, plus several months of supervised practical experience.

Certification/Registration/Licensure

After completing an accredited program and passing the certification examination of the American Occupational Therapy Certification Board, you are entitled to be designated as a Certified Occupational Therapy Assistant (COTA).

Career Potential

The outlook for job opportunities in this field is excellent. This is consistent with the need for occupational therapists and the increasing population of elderly individuals needing such services.

For More Information

The American Occupational Therapy Association, Inc., 4720 Montgomery Ln., Bethesda, MD 20824 (www.aota.org), is the professional organization for both therapists and assistants.

Occupational Therapy Assistant Programs

Alabama

University of Alabama at
  Birmingham
University Station
Birmingham, AL 36088
www.uab.edu

Wallace State Community College
801 Main St.
P.O. Box 2000
Hanceville, AL 35077
www.wallacestate.edu

Arkansas

South Arkansas Community
  College
300 S. West Ave.
El Dorado, AR 71730
www.southark.edu

California

Grossmont College
8800 Grossmont College Dr.
El Cajon, CA 92020
www.grossmont.edu

Loma Linda University
School of Allied Health
  Professions
Nichol Hall
Loma Linda, CA 92350
www.llu.edu

Los Angeles City College
855 N. Vermont Ave.
Los Angeles, CA 90029
www.lacitycollege.edu

Sacramento City College
Science and Allied Health
  Division
3835 Freeport Blvd.
Sacramento, CA 95822
www.scc.losrios.edu

Santa Ana College
1530 W. 17th St.
Santa Ana, CA 92706
www.sac.edu

Colorado

Pueblo Community College
900 W. Orman Ave.
Pueblo, CO 81004
www.pueblocc.edu

Connecticut

Briarwood College
2279 Mount Vernon Rd.
Southington, CT 06489
www.briarwoodcollege.com

Housatonic Community College
900 Lafayette Blvd.
Bridgeport, CT 06604
www.hctc.commnet.edu

Manchester Community College
P.O. Box 1046
Manchester, CT 06045
www.mctc.commnet.edu

Delaware

Delaware Technical & Community
  College
Owens Campus
P.O. Box 610
Georgetown, DE 19947
www.dtcc.edu

Delaware Technical & Community
  College
Wilmington Campus
333 Shipley St.
Wilmington, DE 19801
www.dtcc.edu

Florida

Daytona Beach Community
  College
1200 W. International Speedway
  Blvd.
Daytona Beach, FL 32114
www.dbcc.cc.fl.us

Florida Hospital College of Health
  Sciences
800 Lake Estelle Dr.
Orlando, FL 32803
www.fhchs.edu

Keiser College, Ft. Lauderdale
  Campus
1500 NW 49th St.
Ft. Lauderdale, FL 33309
www.keisercollege.edu

Keiser College, Melbourne Campus
900 S. Babcock St.
Melbourne, FL 32901
www.keisercollege.edu

Manatee Community College
5840 26th St. W.
Bradenton, FL 34207
www.mccfl.edu

Palm Beach State College
4200 Congress Ave.
Lake Worth, FL 33461
www.pbcc.edu

Polk Community College
Math, Science and Health
  Division
999 Ave. H NE
Winter Haven, FL 33881
www.polk.edu

Georgia

Augusta Technical College
3200 Augusta Tech Dr.
Augusta, GA 30906
www.augustatech.edu

Darton College
2400 Gillionville Rd.
Albany, GA 31707
www.darton.edu

Middle Georgia College
1100 Second St. SE
Cochran, GA 31014
www.mgc.edu

Northwestern Technical College
265 Bicentennial Trail
P.O. Box 569
Rock Spring, GA 30739
www.northwesterntech.org

Hawaii
Kapi'olani Community College
4303 Diamond Head Rd.
Honolulu, HI 96816
www.kcc.hawaii.edu

Illinois
College of DuPage
425 Fawell Blvd.
Glen Ellyn, IL 60137
www.cod.edu

Illinois Central College
1 College Dr.
East Peoria, IL 61635
www.icc.edu

Lewis & Clark Community College
5800 Godfrey Rd.
Godfrey, IL 62035
www.lc.cc.il.us

Lincoln Land Community College
5250 Shepherd Rd.
P.O. Box 19256
Springfield, IL 62794
www.llcc.edu

Parkland College
2400 W. Bradley Ave.
Champaign, IL 61821
www.parkland.edu

Southern Illinois Collegiate
  Common Market
3213 S. Park Ave.
Herrin, IL 62948
www.siccm.com

Wilbur Wright College
4300 N. Narragansett Ave.
Chicago, IL 60634
http://wright.ccc.edu/

Indiana
Brown Mackie College
Fort Wayne Campus
4422 E. State Blvd.
Fort Wayne, IN 46815
www.brownmackie.edu

Brown Mackie College
South Bend Campus
1030 E. Jefferson Blvd.
South Bend, IN 46617
www.brownmackie.edu

University of Saint Francis
Department of Allied Health
2701 Spring St.
Fort Wayne, IN 46808
www.sf.edu

University of Southern Indiana
School of Nursing and Health
  Professions
8600 University Blvd.
Evansville, IN 47712
www.usi.edu

Iowa
Kirkwood Community College
6301 Kirkwood Blvd. SW
P.O. Box 2068
Cedar Rapids, IA 52404
www.kirkwood.edu

Kansas
Barton County Community College
245 NE 30 Road
Great Bend, KS 67530
www.barton.cc.ks.us

University of Kansas
318 Blake Hall
Lawrence, KS 66045
www.ku.edu

Kentucky
Jefferson Community College
109 E. Broadway
Louisville, KY 40202
www.jefferson.edu

Madisonville Community College
2000 College Dr.
Madisonville, KY 42431
www.madisonville.kctcs.edu

Louisiana
Delgado Community College
City Park Campus
615 City Park Ave.
New Orleans, LA 70119
www.dcc.edu

University of Louisiana at Monroe
College of Health Sciences
Monroe, LA 71209
www.ulm.edu

Maine
Kennebec Valley Community
  College
92 Western Ave.
Fairfield, ME 04937
www.kvcc.me.edu

Maryland
Allegany College of Maryland
12401 Willowbrook Rd. SE
Cumberland, MD 21502
www.allegany.edu

Community College of Baltimore
  County
800 S. Rolling Rd.
Baltimore, MD 21228
www.ccbcmd.edu

Massachusetts
Bay Path College
588 Longmeadow St.
Longmeadow, MA 01106
www.baypath.edu

Becker College
61 Sever St.
Worcester, MA 01609
www.beckercollege.edu

Bristol Community College
777 Elsbree St.
Fall River, MA 02720
www.bristolcc.edu

Massachusetts Bay Community
  College
Framingham Campus
19 Flagg Dr.
Framingham, MA 01702
www.massbay.edu

North Shore Community College
1 Ferncroft Rd.
Danvers, MA 01923
www.northshore.edu

Quinsigamond Community College
670 W. Boylston St.
Worcester, MA 01606
www.qcc.edu

Springfield Technical Community
College
One Armory Square
Springfield, MA 01102
www.stcc.edu

Kaplan Career Institute-Boston
540 Commonwealth Avenue
Boston, MA 02129
http://boston.
    kaplancareerinstitute.com

Michigan
Baker College of Muskegon
1903 Marquette Ave.
Muskegon, MI 49442
www.baker.edu

Grand Rapids Community College
143 Bostwick Ave. NE
Grand Rapids, MI 49503
www.grcc.cc.mi.us

Lake Michigan College
Bertrand Crossing Campus
1905 Foundation Dr.
Niles, MI 49120
www.lakemichigancollege.edu

Macomb Community College
14500 E. 12 Mile Rd.
Warren, MI 48088
www.macomb.edu

Mott Community College
1401 E. Court
Flint, MI 48503
www.mcc.edu

Schoolcraft College
18600 Haggerty Rd.
Livonia, MI 48152
www.schoolcraft.cc.mi.us

Wayne County Community College
District
1001 W. Fort St.
Detroit, MI 48226
www.wcccd.edu

Minnesota
Anoka Technical College
1355 W. Hwy. 10
Anoka, MN 55303
www.anokatech.edu

College of St. Catherine–
Minneapolis
601 25th Ave. S.
Minneapolis, MN 55454
www.stkate.edu

Northland Community and
Technical College
East Grand Forks
2022 Central Ave. NE
East Grand Forks, MN 56721
www.northlandcollege.edu

Mississippi
Holmes Community College
Ridgeland Campus
412 W. Ridgeland Ave.
Ridgeland, MS 39157
www.holmes.cc.ms.us

Pearl River Community College
5448 U.S. Hwy. 49 S.
Hattiesburg, MS 39401
www.prcc.edu

Missouri
Ozarks Technical Community
College
P.O. Box 5958
Springfield, MO 65801
www.otc.edu

St. Charles County Community
College
4601 Mid Rivers Mall Dr.
St. Peters, MO 63376
www.stchas.edu

St. Louis Community College at
Meramec
11333 Big Bend Blvd.
St. Louis, MO 63122
www.stlcc.edu

Nevada
Community College of Southern
Nevada
West Charleston Campus
6375 W. Charleston Blvd.
Las Vegas, NV 89146
www.csn.edu

New Hampshire
New Hampshire Community
Technical College–Claremont
One College Dr.
Claremont, NH 03743
www.claremont.nhctc.edu

New Jersey
Atlantic Cape Community College
5100 Black Horse Pike
Mays Landing, NJ 08330
www.atlantic.edu

Union County College
232 E. Second St.
Plainfield, NJ 07060
www.ucc.edu

New Mexico
Eastern New Mexico University
1200 W. University
Portales, NM 88130
www.enmu.edu

Western New Mexico University
1000 W. College Ave.
Silver City, NM 88061
www.wnmu.edu

New York
Erie Community College
6205 Main St.
Williamsville, NY 14221
www.ecc.edu

Genesee Community College
One College Rd.
Batavia, NY 14020
www.genesee.edu

Jamestown Community College
525 Falconer St.
P.O. Box 20
Jamestown, NY 14702
www.sunyjcc.edu

LaGuardia Community College/
CUNY
31-10 Thomson Ave.
Long Island City, NY 11101
www.lagcc.cuny.edu

Maria College
700 New Scotland Ave.
Albany, NY 12208
www.mariacollege.edu

Mercy College
555 Broadway
Dobbs Ferry, NY 10522
www.mercy.edu

Orange County Community College
115 South St.
Middletown, NY 10940
www.sunyorange.edu

Suffolk County Community College
Michael J. Grant Campus
Crooked Hill Road–MA 308
Brentwood, NY 11717
www.sunysuffolk.edu

SUNY Canton
College of Technology
34 Cornell Dr.
Canton, NY 13617
www.canton.edu

SUNY Rockland Community
College
145 College Rd.
Suffern, NY 10901
www.sunyrockland.edu

Touro College
1700 Union Blvd.
Bay Shore, NY 11706
www.touro.edu

North Carolina
Cabarrus College of Health
Sciences
401 Medical Park Dr.
Concord, NC 28025
www.cabarruscollege.edu

Caldwell Community College &
Technical Institute
2855 Hickory Blvd.
Hudson, NC 29638
www.cccti.edu

Cape Fear Community College
411 N. Front St.
Wilmington, NC 28401
http://cfcc.edu/

Durham Technical Community
College
1637 Lawson St.
Durham, NC 27703
www.durhamtech.edu

Pitt Community College
P.O. Drawer 7007
Hwy. 11 S.
Greenville, NC 27835
www.pittcc.edu

Stanly Community College
141 College Dr.
Albemarle, NC 28001
www.stanly.edu

North Dakota
North Dakota State College of
Science
800 6th St. N.
Wahpeton, ND 58076
www.ndscs.nodak.edu

Ohio
Cincinnati State Technical and
Community College
3520 Central Pkwy.
Cincinnati, OH 45223
www.cincinnatistate.edu

Cuyahoga Community College
700 Carnegie Ave.
Cleveland, OH 44115
www.tri-c.edu

James A. Rhodes State College
4240 Campus Dr.
Lima, OH 45804
www.rhodesstate.edu

Kent State University
East Liverpool Campus
400 E. Fourth St.
East Liverpool, OH 43920
www.kent.edu

Owens Community College
Toledo Campus
P.O. Box 10000
Toledo, OH 43699
www.owens.edu

Sanford-Brown College
Cleveland Ohio Campus
17535 Rosbough Drive
Middleburg Heights, OH 44130
www.sanfordbrown.edu

Shawnee State University
940 Second St.
Portsmouth, OH 45662
www.shawnee.edu

Sinclair Community College
444 W. Third St.
Dayton, OH 45402
www.sinclair.edu

Stark State College of Technology
6200 Frank Ave. NW
Canton, OH 44720
www.starkstate.edu

Zane State College
1555 Newark Rd.
Zanesville, OH 43701
www.zanestate.edu

Oklahoma
Caddo Kiowa Technology Center
P.O. Box 190
Fort Cobb, OK 73038
www.caddokiowa.com

Oklahoma City Community College
Division of Health Professions
7777 S. May Ave.
Oklahoma City, OK 73159
www.occc.edu

Tulsa Community College,
Metro Campus
909 S. Boston Ave.
Tulsa, OK 74119
www.tulsacc.edu

Oregon
Mt. Hood Community College
26000 SE Stark St.
Gresham, OR 97030
www.mhcc.edu

Pennsylvania
California University of
Pennsylvania
Department of Health Sciences
250 University Ave.
California, PA 15419
www.cup.edu

Community College of Allegheny
County
Boyce Campus
595 Beatty Rd.
Monroeville, PA 15146
www.ccac.edu

Harcum College
750 Montgomery Ave.
Bryn Mawr, PA 19010
www.harcum.edu

ICM School of Business & Medical
Careers
10 Wood St.
Pittsburgh, PA 15222
http://pittsburgh.
kaplancareerinstitute.com/

Lehigh Carbon Community College
4525 Education Park Dr.
Schnecksville, PA 18078
www.lccc.edu

Mount Aloysius College
7373 Admiral Peary Hwy.
Cresson, PA 16630
www.mtaloy.edu

Pennsylvania State University
Berks-Lehigh Valley College
8380 Mohr Ln.
Fogelsville, PA 18051
www.lv.psu.edu

Pennsylvania State University
DuBois Campus
College Place
DuBois, PA 15801
www.ds.psu.edu

Pennsylvania State University
Mont Alto Campus
One Campus Dr.
Mont Alto, PA 17237
www.ma.psu.edu

Rhode Island
Community College of Rhode
Island
Satellite Campus at Newport
Hospital
275 Broadway
Newport, RI 02840
www.ccri.edu

New England Institute of
Technology
2500 Post Rd.
Warwick, RI 02886
www.neit.edu

South Carolina
Greenville Technical College,
Greer Campus
506 S. Pleasantburg Dr.
Greenville, SC 29606
www.gvltec.edu

Trident Technical College
P.O. Box 118067
Charleston, SC 29423
www.tridenttech.edu

South Dakota
Lake Area Technical Institute
230 11th St. NE
P.O. Box 730
Watertown, SD 57201
www.lakeareatech.edu

Tennessee
Cleveland State Community
College
3535 Adkisson Dr.
Cleveland, TN 37320
www.clevelandstatecc.edu

Nashville State Technical
Institute
120 White Bridge Rd.
Nashville, TN 37209
www.nscc.edu

Roane State Community College
276 Patton Ln.
Harriman, TN 37748
www.roanestate.edu

South College
720 N. Fifth Ave.
Knoxville, TN 37917
www.southcollegetn.edu

Texas
Amarillo College
P.O. Box 447
Amarillo, TX 79178
www.actx.edu

Austin Community College
5930 Middle Fiskville Rd.
Austin, TX 78752
www.austincc.edu

Del Mar College
Department of Allied Health
101 Baldwin Blvd.
Corpus Christi, TX 78404
www.delmar.edu

Houston Community College
System
1900 Glen Dr.
Houston, TX 77030
www.hccs.edu

Kingwood College
North Harris Montgomery
Community College District
20000 Kingwood Dr.
Kingwood, TX 77339
www.kingwoodcollege.com

Laredo Community College
West End Washington St. and
5500 S. Zapata Hwy.
Laredo, TX 78045
www.laredo.edu

Navarro College
3200 W. 7th Ave.
Corsicana, TX 75110
www.navarrocollege.edu

Panola College
1109 W. Panola
Carthage, TX 75633
www.panola.edu

South Texas College
Nursing and Allied Health
Division
1101 E. Vermont
McAllen, TX 78501
www.southtexascollege.edu

St. Philip's College
1801 Martin Luther King Dr.
San Antonio, TX 78203
www.alamo.edu/spc/

Tomball College
North Harris Montgomery
Community College District
30555 Tomball Pkwy.
Tomball, TX 77375
http://tomball.lonestar.edu

Utah
Salt Lake Community College
4600 S. Redwood Rd.
Salt Lake City, UT 84123
www.slcc.edu

Virginia
Jefferson College of Health
  Sciences
Community Hospital of Roanoke
  Valley
920 S. Jefferson St.
Roanoke, VA 24016
www.jchs.edu

Southwest Virginia Community
  College
P.O. Box SVCC
Richlands, VA 24641
www.sw.edu

Tidewater Community College
1700 College Crescent
Virginia Beach, VA 23456
www.tcc.edu

Washington
Green River Community College
12401 SE 320th St.
Auburn, WA 98002
www.greenriver.edu

West Virginia
Mountain State University
School of Health Sciences
P.O. Box 9003
Beckley, WV 25802
www.mountainstate.edu

Wisconsin
Fox Valley Technical College
1825 N. Bluemound Dr.
P.O. Box 2277
Appleton, WI 54912
www.fvtc.edu

Madison Area Technical College
3550 Anderson St.
Madison, WI 53704
www.matcmadison.edu

Milwaukee Area Technical College
700 W. State St.
Milwaukee, WI 53233
www.matc.edu

Western Wisconsin Technical
  College
304 Sixth St. N.
La Crosse, WI 54601
www.wwtc.edu

Wisconsin Indianhead Technical
  College
Ashland Campus
2100 Beaser Ave.
Ashland, WI 54806
www.witc.edu

Wyoming
Casper College
125 College Dr.
Casper, WY 82601
www.caspercollege.edu

Patient Representatives

Principal activity: Helping resolve patients' problems while they are hospitalized

Work commitment: Part- or full-time

Preprofessional education: High school diploma

Program length: Varies

Work prerequisites: Bachelor's degree preferred

Career opportunities: Favorable

Income range: $25,000 to $38,000

Scope

Hospitalization results in major changes in an individual's lifestyle. People experience a loss of independence and are often uncertain about their options and rights. This unstable situation can lead to a sense of confusion, which is more profound for aged, disadvantaged, and language-limited individuals. To enhance the quality of patients' hospital stays and to facilitate their recovery, most hospitals employ a patient representative, who acts as the advocate for those who are hospitalized. This service goes a long way toward helping with the nonmedical stresses of a hospital stay.

Activities

Patient representatives help resolve problems between hospitals and patients. They must be attentive to patient concerns, even if they seem trivial, since they may be significant in the patient's mind. By ascertaining exactly what the problem is, determining whether it is genuine, giving clarification on hospital procedures, and explaining the need for certain actions, they can help resolve difficulties before they escalate into major problems.

Representatives may find information on a patient's treatment plan and then explain it to the patient's family. When a genuine complaint is voiced by a patient, representatives may intercede with the appropriate authorities to seek a solution.

Hospitals have a vested interest in their patients' satisfaction. In today's marketplace, they often must compete for patients. The efforts of the patient representative can contribute significantly to this goal.

Work Settings

Most patient representatives work in hospitals, but some are employed by HMOs, nursing homes, and health centers.

Advancement

With experience and education, a patient representative can move to a larger institution or gain supervisory status.

Prerequisites

A high school diploma or its equivalent is the minimum prerequisite. Employers establish their own educational and work experience requirements, so other requirements may vary.

Desirable personal attributes include sound judgment, an ability to view situations objectively, the capacity to work with a diverse group of people, a personality that generates a sense of trust, and an ability to work under emotionally stressful conditions.

Education/Training

Because no formal educational standards exist for this position, employers establish their own guidelines. These may include prior work in health-related areas and college courses in biology, medical terminology, social sciences, and a foreign language (especially Spanish).

Many employers now require a bachelor's degree, and one school offers a master's degree program in this field.

Certification/Registration/Licensure

At present, this field has no certification or licensing requirements.

Career Potential

The outlook for employment in this field is favorable, but this assessment is based on the assumption that positive factors outweigh negative ones. Thus, as health-care institutions realize the benefits of services in this field and as consumer advocates become more vocal, the pressure to appoint patient representatives increases. On the other hand, cost-cutting measures will serve as a deterrent to expansion of this field.

For More Information

For more information, write to the National Society for Patient Representation and Consumer Affairs of the American Hospital Association, 1 N. Franklin, Chicago, IL 60606.

Patient Representative Programs

New York
Sarah Lawrence College
1 Mead Way
Bronxville, NY 10708
www.slc.edu

Wisconsin
The Center for Patient Partnerships
University of Wisconsin-Madison
975 Bascom Mall, Suite 4311
Madison, WI 53706
www.patientpartnerships.org

Physical Therapists

Principal activity: Helping patients overcome physical limitations

Work commitment: Part- or full-time

Preprofessional education: High school diploma, plus 200 to 300 volunteer hours

Program length: 4 years for a bachelor's degree; 2 for a master's degree

Work prerequisites: Bachelor's degree plus certification and licensure required; master's degree preferred

Career opportunities: Highly favorable

Income range: $60,000 to $88,000

Scope

Physical therapists help relieve pain, restore function, promote healing, and prevent permanent disability. To achieve these goals, they may use a variety of treatments, including exercise, water, heat, cold, electricity, ultrasound, and massage. Physical therapy provides benefits to joints, bones, muscles, and nerves that have been impaired because of disease or injury. When healing or function restoration is not possible, physical therapists teach patients how to adapt to their limitations.

Physical therapy is applicable in a wide range of medical specialties, including orthopedics, neurology, neurosurgery, geriatrics, pediatrics, rheumatology, obstetrics-gynecology, sports medicine, internal medicine, and even psychiatry.

Patients who benefit most from physical therapy include victims of strokes and brain, spinal cord, burn, or sports injuries; postoperative patients; cerebral palsy and muscular dystrophy patients; arthritis sufferers; and newborns with physical defects.

Activities

Physical therapists evaluate a patient's status using various diagnostic procedures and then establish a treatment plan and arrange for its implementation.

A patient treatment plan depends on the nature of the illness or injury. Thus, for a paraplegic, the therapist might recommend exercises to maintain lower limb joint motion and strengthen the muscles of the shoulder and upper limb. He or she also teaches the patient to use a wheelchair or crutches. Physical therapists work with arthritis sufferers, burn victims, open-heart surgery patients, and even newborns. Because this field is growing, some therapists today specialize in one field, such as pediatrics or orthopedics.

Work Settings

Physical therapists work in many different settings. About a third work in hospitals. Others work in rehabilitation centers, institutions for the disabled, community centers, private offices, nursing homes, and even private residences. Some hold teaching or administrative positions at colleges and universities.

Advancement

With experience, a physical therapist can become a senior therapist, department supervisor, coordinator of rehabilitation services, or even facility administrator. Along with such increases in responsibility come substantial pay increases.

Prerequisites

A high school diploma or its equivalent is needed to begin a college program in physical therapy.

Desirable personal attributes include patience, manual dexterity, physical strength, strong communication skills, endurance, and an optimistic personality.

Education/Training

High school students who are interested in becoming physical therapists should take courses in biology, chemistry, physics, mathematics, and social studies. After securing a high school diploma or its equivalent, they should attend a bachelor's degree program in physical therapy (more than 100 are offered in the United States).

Those already holding a bachelor's degree in a different area can pursue one of two routes:

- They can earn an additional bachelor's degree in physical therapy (with advanced standing credits).
- They can apply to a master's degree program (after completing the required science and other course prerequisites). There are about 25 such programs in the United States, and most take two years to complete. (Many physical therapists secure master's degrees, and some even pursue doctorates to enhance their status.)

The typical program of studies includes basic courses in human anatomy, physiology, and neuroanatomy, and clinical courses in medicine, tests and measurements, and therapeutic exercises. Students then must have supervised clinical experience.

Certification/Registration/Licensure

All states require physical therapists to be licensed in order to practice. Some even require continuing education.

Career Potential

Because of the increase in the elderly population and the number of those participating in physical activities, the demand for physical therapists today is very high. In fact, physical therapy consistently ranks as one of the fastest-growing fields in the United States. Competition to gain admission to educational programs is also intense.

For More Information

The professional organization for this field is the American Physical Therapy Association, 1111 N. Fairfax St., Alexandria, VA 22314 (www.apta.org).

Physical Therapy Programs

Alabama
South University–Montgomery
5355 Vaughn Rd.
Montgomery, AL 36116
www.southuniversity.edu

University of Alabama at
 Birmingham
900 19th St.
UAB Station, AL 35294
www.uab.edu

University of South Alabama
1504 Spring Hill Ave.
Mobile, AL 36604
www.southalabama.edu

Arizona
Northern Arizona University
S. San Francisco St.
Flagstaff, AZ 86011
www.nau.edu

Arkansas
University of Central Arkansas
201 Donaghey Ave.
Conway, AR 72035
www.uca.edu

California
Azusa Pacific University
Department of Physical Therapy
901 E. Alosta Ave.
Azusa, CA 91702
www.apu.edu

California State University
Domingues Hills
1000 E Victoria Street
Carson, CA 90747
www.calstate.edu

California State University, Fresno
2345 E Ramon Avenue
Fresno, CA 93740
www.csufresno.edu

California State University,
 Long Beach
1250 Bellflower Blvd.
Long Beach, CA 90840
www.csulb.edu

California State University,
 Northridge
18111 Nordhoff St.
Northridge, CA 91330
www.csun.edu

California State University,
 Sacramento
6000 J St.
Sacramento, CA 95819
www.csus.edu

Chapman University
One University Dr.
Orange, CA 92866
www.chapman.edu

Loma Linda University
Loma Linda, CA 92350
www.llu.edu

Mount St. Mary's College
10 Chester Pl.
Los Angeles, CA 90007
www.msmc.edu

Samuel Merritt College
370 Hawthorne Ave.
Oakland, CA 94609
www.samuelmerritt.edu

San Francisco State University
1600 Holloway Ave.
San Francisco, CA 94132
www.sfsu.edu

University of the Pacific
3601 Pacific Ave.
Stockton, CA 95211
www.uop.edu

University of California–San
 Francisco
Physical Therapy
Box 0736
San Francisco, CA 94143
www.uscf.edu

University of Southern California
1540 E Alcazar Street
Los Angeles, CA 90033
www.usc.edu

Western University of Health
 Sciences
309 E. 2nd St.
Pomona, CA 91766
www.western.edu

Colorado
Regis University
3333 Regis Blvd.
Denver, CO 80221
www.regis.edu

University of Colorado at Denver
Campus Box 167
P.O. Box 173364
Denver, CO 80217
www.cudenver.edu

Connecticut
Quinnipiac University
School of Health Sciences
275 Mount Carmel Ave.
Hamden, CT 06518
www.quinnipiac.edu

Sacred Heart University
College of Education & Health
 Professions
5151 Park Ave.
Fairfield, CT 06825
www.sacredheart.edu

University of Connecticut
Storrs-Mansfield, CT 06269
www.uconn.edu

University of Hartford
200 Bloomfield Ave.
West Hartford, CT 06117
www.hartford.edu

Delaware
University of Delaware
Newark, DE 19716
www.udel.edu

District of Columbia
Howard University
2400 6th St. NW
Washington, DC 20059
www.howard.edu

Florida
Florida A&M University
Tallahassee, FL 32307
www.famu.edu

Florida International University
Miami, FL 33199
www.fiu.edu

Nova Southeastern University
3200 S. University Dr.
Ft. Lauderdale, FL 33328
www.nova.edu

South University–West Palm
  Beach
1760 N. Congress Ave.
West Palm Beach, FL 33409
www.southuniversity.edu

University of Central Florida
4000 Central Florida Blvd.
Orlando, FL 32816
www.ucf.edu

University of Florida
Gainesville, FL 32611
www.ufl.edu

University of Miami School of
  Medicine
Department of Physical Therapy
5915 Ponce de Leon Blvd.,
  5th Floor
Coral Gables, FL 33146
www.miami.edu

University of North Florida
4567 St. Johns Bluff Rd. S.
Jacksonville, FL 32224
www.unf.edu

University of St. Augustine for
  Health Sciences
1 University Blvd.
St. Augustine, FL 32086
www.usa.edu

Georgia
Armstrong Atlantic State
  University
11935 Abercorn St.
Savannah, GA 31419
www.armstrong.edu

Emory University
1380 Oxford Rd.
Atlanta, GA 30322
www.emory.edu

Georgia State University
33 Gilmer St. SE
Atlanta, GA 30303
www.gsu.edu

Medical College of Georgia
1120 15th St.
Augusta, GA 30912
www.mcg.edu

North Georgia College & State
  University
Dahlonega, GA 30597
www.ngcsu.edu

South University-Savannah
709 Mall Blvd.
Savannah, GA 31406
www.southuniversity.edu

Idaho
Idaho State University
921 S. 8th Ave.
Pocatello, ID 83209
www.isu.edu

Illinois
Bradley University
1501 W. Bradley Ave.
Peoria, IL 61625
www.bradley.edu

Governors State University
College of Health Professions
1 University Pkwy.
University Park, IL 60466
www.govst.edu

Midwestern University
555 31st St.
Downers Grove, IL 60515
www.midwestern.edu

Northern Illinois University
P.O. Box 3001
DeKalb, IL 60115
www.niu.edu

Northwestern University
Feinberg School of Medicine
Department of Physical Therapy
  and Human Movement Sciences
645 N. Michigan Ave.
Suite 1100
Chicago, IL 60611
www.feinberg.northwestern.edu

University of Chicago Medical
  School
3333 Green Bay Rd.
North Chicago, IL 60064
www.uchicago.edu

University of Illinois at Chicago
Chicago, IL 60612
www.uic.edu

Indiana
Indiana University
1226 W. Michigan St.
Indianapolis, IN 46202
www.shrs.iupui.edu/pt/

University of Evansville
1800 Lincoln Ave.
Evansville, IN 47722
www.evansville.edu

University of Indianapolis
1400 E. Hanna Ave.
Indianapolis, IN 46227
www.uindy.edu

University of St. Francis
Department of Allied Health
2701 Spring St.
Fort Wayne, IN 46808
www.sf.edu

Iowa
University of Iowa
2600 Steindler Building
Iowa City, IA 52242
www.uiowa.edu

University of Osteopathic
  Medicine & Health Sciences
3200 Grand Ave.
Des Moines, IA 50312
www.dmu.edu

Kansas
University of Kansas Medical
  Center
3901 Rainbow Blvd.
Kansas City, KS 66160
http://alliedhealth.kumc.edu/

Wichita State University
1845 N. Fairmount
Wichita, KS 67260
www.wichita.edu

Kentucky
University of Kentucky
121 Washington Ave.
Lexington, KY 40506
www.uky.edu

University of Louisville
Louisville, KY 40292
www.louisville.edu

Louisiana
Louisiana State University
One University Place
Shreveport, LA 71115
www.lsus.edu

Maine
University of New England
11 Hills Beach Rd.
Biddeford, ME 04005
www.une.edu

Maryland
University of Maryland,
  Eastern Shore
1 Backbone Rd.
Princess Anne, MD 21853
www.umes.edu

University of Maryland School of
  Medicine
655 W. Baltimore St.
Baltimore, MD 21201
http://medschool.umaryland.
  edu/

Massachusetts
Boston University
Sargent College of Health and
  Rehabilitation Sciences
635 Commonwealth Ave.
Boston, MA 02215
www.bu.edu

Northeastern University
360 Huntington Ave.
Boston, MA 02115
www.northeastern.edu

Simmons College
300 The Fenway
Boston, MA 02115
www.simmons.edu

Springfield College
263 Alden St.
Springfield, MA 01109
www.springfieldcollege.edu

University of Massachusetts
  Lowell
1 University Ave.
Lowell, MA 01854
www.uml.edu

Michigan
Andrews University
Berrien Springs, MI 49104
www.andrews.edu

Central Michigan University
134 Pearce Hall
Mt. Pleasant, MI 48859
www.cmich.edu

Grand Valley State University
1 Campus Dr.
Allendale, MI 49401
www.gvsu.edu

Oakland University
Rochester, MI 48309
www.oakland.edu

University of Michigan–Flint
303 E. Kearsley St.
Flint, MI 48502
www.umflint.edu

Wayne State University
439 Shapero Hall
Detroit, MI 48202
www.wayne.edu

Minnesota
College of St. Catherine
601 25th Ave. S.
Minneapolis, MN 55454
www.stkate.edu

College of St. Scholastica
1200 Kenwood Ave.
Duluth, MN 55811
www.css.edu

Mayo Clinic College of Medicine
Mayo School of Health Sciences
1104 Siebens Building
Rochester, MN 55905
www.mayo.edu

University of Minnesota
Box 388 UMHC
Minneapolis, MN 55455
www.umn.edu

Mississippi
University of Mississippi Medical
  Center
2500 N. State St.
Jackson, MS 39216
www.olemiss.edu

Missouri
Maryville University of St. Louis
13550 Conway Rd.
St. Louis, MO 63141
www.maryville.edu

Rockhurst University
1100 Rockhurst Rd.
Kansas City, MO 64110
www.rockhurst.edu

St. Louis University
221 N. Grand Blvd.
St. Louis, MO 63103
www.slu.edu

University of Missouri–Columbia
Columbia, MO 65211
www.missouri.edu

Washington University
School of Medicine
660 S. Euclid Ave.
St. Louis, MO 63110
http://medschool.wustl.edu/

Montana
University of Montana–Missoula
32 Campus Dr.
Missoula, MT 59812
www.umt.edu

Nebraska
Creighton University
2500 California Plaza
Omaha, NE 68178
www.creighton.edu

University of Nebraska Medical
  Center
600 S. 42nd
Omaha, NE 68198
www.unmc.edu

New Jersey
Kean University
1000 Morris Ave.
Union, NJ 07083
www.kean.edu

Richard Stockton College of
  New Jersey
P.O. Box 195
Pomona, NJ 08240
www.stockton.edu

Rutgers, The State University of
  New Jersey
40 E. Laurel Rd.
Stratford, NJ 08084
www.rutgers.edu

Seton Hall University
School of Graduate Medical
  Education
400 S. Orange Ave.
South Orange, NJ 07079
www.shu.edu

New Mexico
University of New Mexico
Albuquerque, NM 87131
www.unm.edu

New York
Clarkson University
College of Staten Island
The City University of New York
2800 Victory Blvd.
Staten Island, NY 10314
www.csi.cuny.edu

Columbia University
710 W. 168th St., 8th Floor
New York, NY 10032
www.columbia.edu

Daemen College
4380 Main St.
Amherst, NY 14226
www.daemen.edu

D'Youville College
320 Porter Ave.
Buffalo, NY 14201
www.dyc.edu

Hunter College
695 Park Ave.
New York, NY 10021
www.hunter.cuny.edu

Ithaca College
335 Smiddy Hall
Ithaca, NY 14850
www.ithaca.edu

Long Island University
One University Plaza
Brooklyn, NY 11201
www.brooklyn.liu.edu

New York Medical College
Valhalla, NY 10595
www.nymc.edu

New York University
345 E. 24th St.
Weissman Building
New York, NY 10010
www.nyu.edu

The Sage Colleges
45 Ferry St.
Troy, NY 12180
www.sage.edu

Stony Brook University
Health Sciences Center
School of Health Technology &
  Management
Stony Brook, NY 11794
www.stonybrook.edu

SUNY Downstate Medical Center
College of Health-Related
  Professions
450 Clarkson Ave.
Brooklyn, NY 11203
www.downstate.edu

SUNY Upstate Medical University
College of Health Professions
750 E. Adams St.
Syracuse, NY 13210
www.upstate.edu

Touro College
1700 Union Blvd.
Bay Shore, NY 11764
www.touro.edu

Touro College
27 W. 23rd St.
New York, NY 10010
www.touro.edu

University at Buffalo
The State University of New York
405 Kimball Tower
Buffalo, NY 14214
www.buffalo.edu

Utica College of Syracuse
  University
1600 Burrstone Rd.
Utica, NY 13502
www.utica.edu

North Carolina
Duke University
Durham, NC 27708
www.duke.edu

East Carolina University
E. Fifth St.
Greenville, NC 27858
www.ecu.edu

University of North Carolina at
  Chapel Hill
Medical School Wing CB #7135
Chapel Hill, NC 27599
www.unc.edu

Winston-Salem State University
601 Martin Luther King, Jr. Dr.
Winston-Salem, NC 27110
www.wssu.edu

North Dakota
University of North Dakota School
  of Medicine
Grand Forks, ND 58202
www.und.nodak.edu

Ohio
Cleveland State University
2121 Euclid Ave.
Cleveland, OH 44115
www.csuohio.edu

Ohio State University
Columbus, OH 43210
www.osu.edu

Ohio University
Athens, OH 45701
www.ohio.edu

University of Cincinnati
2624 Clifton Ave.
Cincinnati, OH 45221
www.uc.edu

University of Findlay
1000 N. Main St.
Findlay, OH 45840
www.findlay.edu

Oklahoma
Langston University
Langston, OK 73050
www.lunet.edu

University of Oklahoma
P.O. Box 26901
Oklahoma City, OK 73190
www.ou.edu

Oregon
Pacific University
School of Physical Therapy
2043 College Way
Forest Grove, OR 97116
www.pacificu.edu

Pennsylvania
Arcadia University
450 S. Easton Rd.
Glenside, PA 19038
www.arcadia.edu

Chatham College
Woodland Rd.
Pittsburgh, PA 15232
www.chatham.edu

College Misericordia
301 Lake St.
Dallas, PA 18612
www.misericordia.edu

Drexel University
College of Nursing and Health
  Professions
3141 Chestnut St.
Philadelphia, PA 19104
www.drexel.edu/cnhp/

Duquesne University
111 Health Science Building
Pittsburgh, PA 15282
www.duq.edu

Gannon University
109 University Square
Erie, PA 16541
www.gannon.edu

University of the Sciences in
  Philadelphia
600 S. 43rd St.
Philadelphia, PA 19104
www.pcps.edu

Slippery Rock University
1 Morrow Way
Slippery Rock, PA 16057
www.sru.edu

Temple University
College of Health Professions
3307 N. Broad St.
Philadelphia, PA 19140
www.temple.edu/pt/

Thomas Jefferson University
Jefferson College of Health
  Professions
Edison Building
130 S. 9th St.
Philadelphia, PA 19107
www.jefferson.edu/jchp/pt/

University of Pittsburgh
School of Health and
  Rehabilitation Sciences
Pittsburgh, PA 15260
www.shrs.pitt.edu/

University of Scranton
Scranton, PA 18510
http://matrix.scranton.edu/

Widener University
1 University Place
Chester, PA 19013
www.widener.edu

Rhode Island
University of Rhode Island
Kingston, RI 02881
www.uri.edu

South Carolina
Medical University of South
  Carolina
171 Ashley Ave.
Charleston, SC 29425
www.musc.edu

South Dakota
University of South Dakota
414 E. Clark St.
Vermillion, SD 57069
www.usd.edu

Tennessee
East Tennessee State University
P.O. Box 70267
Johnson City, TN 37601
www.etsu.edu

Tennessee State University
3500 John A. Merritt Blvd.
Nashville, TN 37209
www.tnstate.edu

University of Tennessee
Health Science Center
Memphis, TN 38163
www.uthsc.edu

University of Tennessee at
  Chattanooga
615 McCallie Ave.
Chattanooga, TN 37403
www.utc.edu

Texas
Baylor University
Army Medical Department Center
  and School
Ft. Sam Houston, TX 78234
www.baylor.edu/ompt/

Hardin-Simmons University
2200 Hickory
Abilene, TX 79601
www.hsutx.edu

Southwest Texas State University
Health Science Center
601 University Dr.
San Marcos, TX 78666
www.swt.edu

Texas Tech University
Health Science Center
3601 4th St.
Lubbock, TX 79430
www.ttu.edu

Texas Woman's University
P.O. Box 425589
Denton, TX 76204
www.twu.edu

University of Texas
Health Science Center at
  San Antonio
7703 Floyd Curl Dr.
San Antonio, TX 78229
www.uthscsa.edu

University of Texas Medical
  Branch–Galveston
301 University Blvd.
Galveston, TX 77555
www.utmb.edu

University of Texas
Southwestern Medical Center
  at Dallas
5323 Harry Hines Blvd.
Dallas, TX 75390
www.utsouthwestern.edu

Utah
University of Utah
Health Sciences Center
50 N. Medical Dr.
Salt Lake City, UT 84132
www.health.utah.edu/pt/

Vermont
University of Vermont
Burlington, VT 05405
www.uvm.edu

Virginia
Old Dominion University
Health Science Building
Norfolk, VA 23529
www.odu.edu

Shenandoah University
1460 University Dr.
Winchester, VA 22601
www.su.edu/pt/

Virginia Commonwealth University
Richmond, VA 23284
www.vcu.edu

Washington
Eastern Washington University
526 Fifth St.
Cheney, WA 99004
www.ewu.edu

University of Puget Sound
1500 N. Warner
Tacoma, WA 98416
www.ups.edu

University of Washington
1959 NE Pacific St., Box 356490
Seattle, WA 98195
www.washington.edu

West Virginia
West Virginia University School
  of Medicine
P.O. Box 6201
Morgantown, WV 26506
www.wvu.edu

Wheeling Jesuit University
316 Washington Ave.
Wheeling, WV 26003
www.wju.edu

Wisconsin
Concordia University Wisconsin
12800 N. Lake Shore Dr.
Mequon, WI 53097
www.cuw.edu

Marquette University
P.O. Box 1881
Milwaukee, WI 53201
www.mu.edu

University of Wisconsin–La Crosse
1725 State St.
La Crosse, WI 54601
www.uwlax.edu/pt/

University of Wisconsin–Madison
1300 University Ave.
Madison, WI 53706
www.wisc.edu

Canada
McGill University
845 Sherbrooke St. W.
Montreal, Quebec H3A 2T5
www.mcgill.ca

Queens University
Kingston, Ontario K7L 3N6
www.queensu.ca

Universite de Montreal
CP 6128-Succursale Centre-Ville
Montreal, Quebec H3C 3J7
www.umontreal.ca

University of Alberta
114th St. and 89th Ave.
Edmonton, Alberta T6G 2E1
www.ualberta.ca

University of British Columbia
2329 West Mall
Vancouver, British Columbia
  V6T 1Z4
www.ubc.ca

University of Manitoba
770 Bannatyne Ave.
Winnipeg, Manitoba R3T 2N2
www.umanitoba.ca

University of Saskatchewan
1121 College Dr.
Saskatoon, Saskatchewan
  S7N 0W3
www.usask.ca

University of Western Ontario
Elborn College
1151 Richmond St., Suite 2
London, Ontario N6A 5B8
www.uwo.ca

Physical Therapy Assistants

Principal activity: Helping physical therapists execute treatment plans

Work commitment: Usually full-time

Preprofessional education: High school diploma

Program length: 2 years

Work prerequisites: Associate degree

Career opportunities: Highly favorable

Income range: $37,000 to $55,000

Scope

Physical therapy assistants work under the direction of a licensed physical therapist to help treat patients. Their specific activities are regulated by state law and are determined by the policies of the facility at which they work and by their supervising therapist.

Activities

The guiding program for the physical therapy assistant is the treatment plan developed by the therapist. The assistant helps teach disabled patients to carry out daily life activities (such as dressing), assists in their prescribed exercises, carries out tests, administers treatments (such as heat and hydrotherapy), notes and reports on patient progress, teaches patients how to use and care for assisting devices, and helps with a variety of routine office chores.

Work Settings

Physical therapy assistants work in hospitals, rehabilitation centers, nursing homes, and offices of private practitioners.

Advancement

Some physical therapy assistants go back to school to pursue their physical therapy degree. Their prior experience is an asset in seeking a place in a program.

Prerequisites

A high school diploma is needed for admission into a physical therapy assistant program. Those seeking to enter the field should be physically strong and prepared to work closely with and under the supervision of others. They should also have a pleasant personality and a desire to help others.

Education/Training

Physical therapy assistants must complete an accredited two-year program, leading to an associate degree. The program includes classes in anatomy and physiology and a year of technical courses in treatment modalities (such as massage, exercises, heat, and ultrasound) and clinical experience.

Certification/Registration/Licensure

Licensure is required in some states. Where no licensure requirement exists, a specific educational background and exam may be specified by the state licensing board.

Career Potential

The field of physical therapy has become much in demand because of advances in orthopedics (such as knee and hip replacements), sports medicine, and personal fitness programs. Simultaneously, the pool of elderly citizens is steadily increasing. Thus, the demand for physical therapy assistants is high, and career prospects are very attractive.

For More Information

The professional organization for this field is the American Physical Therapy Association, 1111 N. Fairfax St., Alexandria, VA 22314 (www.apta.org).

Physical Therapy Assistant Programs

There are hundreds of physical therapy assistant programs in the United States—too many to include here. For a complete list of accredited programs, contact the American Physical Therapy Association at the address just listed.

Psychiatric Aides

Principal activity: Providing routine care for emotionally disturbed individuals

Work commitment: Full-time

Preprofessional education: A high school diploma is desirable

Program length: Several weeks to several months

Work prerequisites: Prior experience or on-the-job training

Career opportunities: Stable

Income range: $21,000 to $33,000

Scope

Psychiatric aides assist emotionally disturbed and mentally impaired individuals with daily living activities.

Activities

Psychiatric aides are also known as psychiatric nursing assistants or mental health assistants. They spend much of their time in the day-to-day care of patients. They help them bathe, dress, and groom themselves. During the day they are also expected to socialize with the patients who are assigned to their care. This activity is important, because it helps patients improve their interpersonal skills and maintain emotional stability.

Psychiatric aides may join their patients in leisure activities, thereby enhancing the level of social contact and the relationship with their patients. As part of their professional obligations, psychiatric aides need to be constantly alert and carefully monitor patient behavior. It is essential that they report any aberrations to their supervisors, who record all relevant information in the patient's record. Consequently, any emotional disturbance can be brought to the attention of the patient's physician.

Another task assigned to psychiatric aides is to accompany patients, both within a facility and off grounds, to a physician's office or for medical or other treatments. On occasion they may find it necessary to help restrain unruly patients.

The intimate contact that psychiatric aides have with their patients can potentially have a positive impact on their patient's emotions and can favorably influence their patient's behavior. This task, however, can prove challenging in view of potential wide fluctuations in the mood and temperament of emotionally impaired people, which can take place rapidly.

Work Settings

Most psychiatric aides render their services in hospitals (federal, state, county, private, and acute-care), residential care facilities, and community health centers. Some are also employed in nursing homes.

Advancement

While advancement opportunities are limited, with enhanced experience and education you can become a psychiatric technician or ward supervisor.

Prerequisites

No formal education is needed to work as a psychiatric aide, but having a high school diploma is very helpful. Some positions might require having one.

To do well at this job, you need considerable patience and tolerance for working with emotionally disturbed people. You should be physically strong, emotionally stable, and have an especially compassionate nature. You also should be friendly and outgoing, willing to follow directions, and able to assume responsibilities and recognize their importance relative to the well-being of dysfunctional individuals.

Education/Training

Formal training programs that prepare you for work as a psychiatric aide are offered in some high schools, vocational-technical institutes, community colleges, and psychiatric hospitals. Background training requirements vary from one position to another. Those that don't require experience usually provide essential on-the-job-training on a formal or informal basis.

Certification/Registration/Licensure

There is no need to meet any of these requirements for a psychiatric aide position.

Career Potential

Employment prospects for work in this field are average. You can find positions through personnel departments of mental-health facilities, psychiatric hospitals, and extended-care facilities. You also can check newspaper classified ads under the various relevant job headings.

For More Information

This field has no professional organization. For more information, contact the American Health Care Association, 1201 L St. NW, Washington, DC 20005 (www.ahca.org).

Recreational Therapists

Principal activity: Using recreational activities to enhance rehabilitation

Work commitment: Full-time

Preprofessional education: High school diploma

Program length: 4 years

Work prerequisites: Bachelor's degree

Career opportunities: Favorable

Income range: $30,000 to $49,000

Scope

Recreational therapists work with mentally, emotionally, and physically disabled patients, helping them recover from or adjust to illnesses, disabilities, or social problems. The therapist's observations of patients' physical, mental, and social progress contributes to a fuller understanding of their treatment goals.

Activities

Recreational therapists plan and carry out programs that may involve athletics, art, dancing, music, gardening, or camping. These activities help patients get needed exercise, develop social relationships, diminish anxiety and tension, and increase self-esteem. Recreational therapists also help their clients use the recreational activities their communities offer. They may train volunteers and help institutions develop courses in this field.

Work Settings

Recreational therapists are employed by a variety of public and private institutions, including mental and VA hospitals, residences for the mentally disabled, prisons, juvenile detention homes, senior citizen residences, and rehabilitation centers.

Advancement

Advancement comes with experience and education. For government positions, recreational therapists can take the civil service exam.

Moving from a certificate or associate degree to a bachelor's degree, or from a bachelor's degree to a master's degree, also facilitates your upward mobility.

Prerequisites

A high school diploma or its equivalent is necessary to enter a degree program.

Desirable personal attributes include patience, a pleasant personality, working well with others, creativity, and a desire to help people.

Education/Training

For some entry-level positions, a certificate or associate degree is sufficient. However, to get a professional appointment, you need a bachelor's degree in recreation, with an emphasis on rehabilitation or therapeutic recreation. Additionally, recreational therapists must complete 400 hours of training at a university- or college-affiliated hospital.

Certification/Registration/Licensure

You can secure registration through the American Association for Rehabilitation Therapy (AART). Although this isn't mandatory, being registered can help in your job search.

To become registered, you must be a member of the AART, get two years of experience in a health-care facility, and submit a transcript of your college records and two letters of recommendation.

Career Potential

Prospects for rehabilitation therapists entering the workforce are generally good. In nursing care facilities especially, employment will grow faster than average as the number of older adults continues to grow. In addition, schools will experience a greater need for therapists due to increased federal funding for programs for disabled students. The demand for recreational therapists is very much dependent on to what extent insurance companies are willing to reimburse for such services.

For More Information

The professional organization for this field is the National Recreation and Park Association, 22377 Belmont Ridge Rd., Ashburn, VA 20148 (www.nrpa.org).

Recreational Therapy Programs

California
California State University–
  Northridge
18111 Nordhoff St.
Northridge, CA 91330
www.csun.edu

Indiana
Indiana Tech
1600 E. Washington Blvd.
Fort Wayne, IN 46803
www.indianatech.edu

Indiana University
300 N. Jordan Ave.
Bloomington, IN 47405
www.indiana.edu

Iowa
University of Iowa
Recreational Therapy Department
Iowa City, IA 52242
www.uiowa.edu

Maine
University of Southern Maine
P.O. Box 9300
Portland, ME 04104
www.usm.maine.edu

Massachusetts
Northeastern University
360 Huntington Ave.
Boston, MA 02115
www.northeastern.edu

Springfield College
263 Alden St.
Springfield, MA 01109
www.springfieldcollege.edu

Michigan
Lake Superior State University
650 W. Easterday Ave.
Sault Sainte Marie, MI 49783
www.lssu.edu

New York
SUNY College at Cortland
P.O. Box 2000
Cortland, NY 13045
www.cortland.edu

Utica College of Syracuse
  University
1600 Burrstone Rd.
Utica, NY 13502
www.utica.edu

North Carolina
Belmont Abbey College
100 Belmont–Mt. Holly Rd.
Belmont, NC 28012
www.belmontabbeycollege.edu

Catawba College
2300 W. Innes St.
Salisbury, NC 28144
www.catawba.edu

East Carolina University
Recreational Therapy Degree
Belk Bldg. #2405
Greenville, NC 27858
www.edu.edu

Western Piedmont Community
  College
Recreational Therapy
1001 Burkemont Avenue
Morgantown, NC 26855
www.wpcc.edu

Ohio
Defiance College
701 N. Clinton St.
Defiance, OH 43512
www.defiance.edu

University of Toledo
College of Health Science and
   Human Services
Recreational Therapy
MS #119
Toledo, OH 43606
www.utoledo.edu

Oklahoma
Southwestern Oklahoma State
   University
100 Campus Dr.
Weatherford, OK 73096
www.swosu.edu

Pennsylvania
Lincoln University
Recreational Therapy Program
1570 Baltimore Pike
P.O. Box 179
Lincoln University, PA 19352
www.lincoln.edu

Vermont
Green Mountain College
One College Circle
Poultney, VT 05764
www.greenmtn.edu

Virginia
Virginia Wesleyan College
1584 Wesleyan Dr.
Norfolk, VA 23502
www.vwc.edu

Washington
Eastern Washington University
Cheney, WA 99004
www.ewu.edu

West Virginia
West Virginia State University
Institute, WV 25112
www.wvsc.edu

Wisconsin
University of Wisconsin–La Crosse
1725 State St.
La Crosse, WI 54601
www.uwlax.edu

Rehabilitation Counselors

Principal activity: Providing guidance to people with disabilities to help them manage their handicap and thus maximize their quality of life

Work commitment: Full-time

Preprofessional education: Bachelor's degree

Program length: 6 years

Work prerequisites: Master's degree

Career opportunities: Favorable

Income range: $24,000 to $64,000

Scope

Rehabilitation counselors advise individuals who are handicapped and who need guidance on dealing with their disability's personal, social, and occupational impact on their lives.

Activities

To provide meaningful guidance to the client, the rehabilitation counselor first must assess the extent of the person's handicap. This requires focusing attention not only on his disability, but also on his assets. Using this approach, the counselor is provided with a comprehensive view of the individual's abilities and potential that can be used to compensate for any deficiencies.

The rehabilitation counselor develops a program designed specifically for each disabled individual. This program allows the person to utilize his potential to live as independently as possible. This should provide him with an enhanced standard of living.

A special area of concern for rehabilitation counselors is helping handicapped individuals secure suitable employment. To do so, counselors need to bear in mind the extent of the client's physical and/or mental limitations, intellect, manual dexterity and other skills, interests, personality, and prior employment experience. In addition to matching the individual with suitable potential job openings, counselors can help clients find opportunities to obtain additional education and training.

The efforts of rehabilitation counselors not only help disabled clients, but also assist their families. This contact lets counselors make more realistic judgments about their clients' potential and how they can be successfully integrated into the family unit.

The rehabilitation counselor also may help clients overcome personal and social obstacles resulting from their disabilities. To achieve this, they may need to coordinate other services for their clients to enhance their overall well-being.

It is important for rehabilitation counselors to keep accurate records of their clients' progress and report periodically to their supervisors.

Work Settings

Work opportunities for rehabilitation counselors exist with vocational and rehabilitation agencies sponsored by federal, state, and local governments; schools; hospitals; not-for-profit and for-profit facilities; and industry.

Advancement

You can advance as a rehabilitation counselor by obtaining additional education and experience. You also can advance by moving up to administrative or supervisory positions. Opportunities also exist in private practice and consulting.

Prerequisites

The basic requirement is to secure a bachelor's degree, preferably with a major in psychology. This serves as a basis for the advanced degree that is necessary in this profession. Volunteer work in a hospital, especially in an occupational therapy department, can help you discover how you feel about working with handicapped individuals.

Desirable personal attributes for work in this field are having a genuine concern for people who are greatly in need of help and being able to work independently as well as part of a health-care rehabilitation team. You also need creativity to overcome obstacles to successful guidance and strong communication skills. You also need to be sensitive, patient, and tactful.

Education/Training

To secure a position as a rehabilitation counselor, you need a master's degree from an accredited program. You should major in rehabilitation counseling, counseling and guidance, or counseling psychology. You also need to complete a period of supervised clinical training.

Certification/Registration/Licensure

With many positions, it is desirable and in some cases even necessary to be certified. You can become certified through the Council on Rehabilitation Education (www.core-rehab.org). Gaining certification indicates that you graduated from an accredited program, completed an internship, and passed a written examination.

Career Potential

Opportunities for securing a position as a rehabilitation counselor are good. You can find positions through newspaper classified advertisements or by sending a resume and cover letter to personnel departments at facilities that employ rehabilitation counselors.

For More Information

The professional organization for this field is the National Rehabilitation Counseling Association, P.O. Box 4480, Manassas, VA 20108 (http://nrca-net.org).

Rehabilitation Counseling Programs

Alabama
Alabama A&M University
P.O. Box 500
Normal, AL 35762
www.aamu.edu

Auburn University
1228 Haley Center
Auburn, AL 36849
www.auburn.edu

Troy University
#10 McCartha Hall
Troy, AL 36082
www.troy.edu

University of Alabama
318 Graves Hall, P.O. Box 870231
Tuscaloosa, AL 35487
www.ua.edu

University of Alabama at
  Birmingham
901 S. 13th St.
Birmingham, AL 35294
www.ed.uab.edu/
  counseloreducation/

Arizona
University of Arizona
Tucson, AZ 85721
www.arizona.edu

Arkansas
Arkansas State University
P.O. Box 1560
State University, AR 72467
www.astate.edu

University of Arkansas
100 Graduate Education Bldg.
Fayetteville, AR 72701
www.uark.edu

University of Arkansas at
  Little Rock
Little Rock, AR 72204
www.ualr.edu

University of Arkansas–Pine Bluff
1200 N University Drive
Pine Bluff, AR 71601
www.uapb.edu

California
California State University, Fresno
5005 N. Maple Ave., MS 302
Fresno, CA 93740
www.csufresno.edu

California State University, LA
5151 State University Dr.,
  King Hall, C1065
Los Angeles, CA 90032
www.calstatela.edu

California State University,
  San Bernardino
5500 University Pkwy.
San Bernardino, CA 92407
www.csusb.edu

San Diego State University
3590 Camino del Rio, N.
San Diego, CA 92108
www.sdsu.edu

Colorado
University of Northern Colorado
Campus Box 132
Greeley, CO 80639
www.unco.edu

District of Columbia
George Washington University
Washington, DC 20052
www.gwu.edu

Florida
Florida State University
205 Stone Bldg.
Tallahassee, FL 32306
www.fsu.edu

University of Florida
P.O. Box 100175
Gainesville, FL 32610
www.ufrehabcounseling.com

University of North Florida
4567 St. Johns Bluff Rd., S.
Jacksonville, FL 32224
www.unf.edu

University of South Florida
4202 E. Fowler Ave.
Tampa, FL 33620
www.usf.edu

Georgia
Fort Valley State University
1005 State University Dr.
Fort Valley, GA 31030
www.fvsu.edu

Georgia State University
P.O. Box 3980
Atlanta, GA 30303
www.gsu.edu

Thomas University
1501 Millpond Rd.
Thomasville, GA 31792
www.thomasu.edu

Hawaii
University of Hawaii-Manoa
1776 University Ave.
Honolulu, HI 96822
www.uhm.hawaii.edu

Idaho
University of Idaho
Moscow, ID 83844
www.uidaho.edu

Illinois
Illinois Institute of Technology
3101 S. Dearborn St.
Chicago, IL 60616
www.iit.edu

Northern Illinois University
DeKalb, IL 60115
www.niu.edu

Southern Illinois University,
 Carbondale
Carbondale, IL 62901
www.siu.edu

University of Illinois at
 Urbana-Champaign
1206 S. Fourth St.
Champaign, IL 61820
www.uiuc.edu

Indiana
Ball State University
2000 W. University Ave.
Muncie, IN 47306
www.bsu.edu

Iowa
Drake University
 3206 University Ave.
Des Moines, IA 50311
www.drake.edu

The University of Iowa
N362 Lindquist Center N.
Iowa City, IA 52242
www.uiowa.edu

Kansas
Emporia State University
Campus Box 4036
1200 Commercial
Emporia, KS 66801
www.emporia.edu

Kentucky
University of Kentucky
224 Taylor Education Bldg.
Lexington, KY 40506
www.uky.edu

Louisiana
LSU Health Science Center
1900 Gravier St.
New Orleans, LA 70112
http://alliedhealth.lsuhsc.edu/

Southern University
229 Blanks Hall
Baton Rouge, LA 70813
www.subr.edu

University of Louisiana
Counselor Education
P.O. Box 40104
Lafayette, LA 70504
www.counseling.louisiana.edu

Maine
University of Southern Maine
400 Bailey Hall
Gorham, ME 04038
www.usm.maine.edu

Maryland
Coppin State College
2500 W. North Ave.
Baltimore, MD 21216
www.coppin.edu

University of Maryland
Benjamin Bldg., Room 3214
College Park, MD 20742
www.umd.edu

University of Maryland Eastern
 Shore
934-5 Backbone Rd.
Princess Anna, MD 21853
www.umes.edu

Massachusetts
Assumption College
500 Salisbury St.
Worcester, MA 01609
www.assumption.edu

Boston University
635 Commonwealth Ave.
Boston, MA 02215
www.bu.edu

University of Massachusetts at
 Boston
Boston, MA 02125
www.rehabilitation.umb.edu

Michigan
Michigan State University
237 Erickson Hall
East Lansing, MI 48824
www.msu.edu

Wayne State University
329 College of Education
Detroit, MI 48202
www.wayne.edu

Western Michigan University
3404 Sangren Hall
Mail Stop 5218
Kalamazoo, MI 49008
www.wmich.edu

Minnesota
Minnesota State University,
 Mankato
103 Armstrong Hall
Mankato, MN 56001
www.mnsu.edu

St. Cloud State University
720 Fourth Ave. S.
St. Cloud, MN 56301
www.stcloudstate.edu

Mississippi
Jackson State University
P.O. Box 17501
Jackson, MS 39217
www.jsums.edu

Mississippi State University
Mail Stop 9727
Mississippi State, MS 39762
www.msstate.edu

Missouri
Maryville University of St. Louis
St. Louis, MO 63141
www.maryville.edu

University of Missouri–Columbia
4B Hill Hall
Columbia, MO 65211
www.missouri.edu

Montana
Montana State University–Billings
1500 N. 30th St.
Billings, MT 59101
www.msubillings.edu

New York
Hofstra University
119 Hofstra University
160 Hagedorn
Hempstead, NY 11549
www.hofstra.edu

Hunter College of the City
  University of New York
695 Park Ave.
New York, NY 10021
www.hunter.cuny.edu

New York University
239 Greene St.
New York, NY 10063
www.nyu.edu

St. John's University
Marilac Hall
8000 Utopia Pkwy.
Jamaica, NY 11439
www.stjohns.edu

University at Albany, SUNY
1400 Washington Ave.
Albany, NY 12222
www.albany.edu

University at Buffalo, SUNY
409 Baldy Hall
Buffalo, NY 14260
http://gse.buffalo.edu/

Syracuse University
257 Huntington Hall
Syracuse, NY 13244
www.syr.edu

North Carolina
East Carolina University
Greenville, NC 27858
www.ecu.edu

University of North Carolina at
  Chapel Hill
117 Medical School Wing E
Chapel Hill, NC 27599
www.unc.edu

Ohio
Bowling Green State University
451 Education Bldg.
Bowling Green, OH 43403
www.bgsu.edu

Kent State University
405 White Hall
Kent, OH 44242
www.kent.edu

Ohio State University
356 Arps Hall, 1945 N. High St.
Columbus, OH 43210
www.osu.edu

Ohio University
201 McCracken Hall
Athens, OH 45701
www.ohio.edu

Wright State University
M052 Creative Arts Center
Dayton, OH 45435
www.wright.edu

Oklahoma
East Central University
Box C-1
Ada, OK 74820
www.ecok.edu

Langston University
4205 N. Lincoln Blvd.
Oklahoma City, OK 73105
www.lunet.edu

Oregon
Portland State University
P.O. Box 751
Portland, OR 97207
www.pdx.edu

Western Oregon University
Education Building 220
Monmouth, OR 97361
www.wou.edu

Pennsylvania
Edinboro University of
  Pennsylvania
318 Butterfield Hall
Edinboro, PA 16444
www.edinboro.edu

Pennsylvania State University
329 CEDAR Building
University Park, PA 16803
www.psu.edu

University of Pittsburgh
5044 Forbes Tower
3600 Forbes at Atwood St.
Pittsburgh, PA 15260
www.pitt.edu

University of Scranton
Scranton, PA 18510
www.scranton.edu

South Carolina
South Carolina State University
300 College St.
Orangeburg, SC 29117
www.scsu.edu

University of South Carolina
3555 Harden St.
Columbia, SC 29203
www.sc.edu

Tennessee
University of Memphis
Patterson Hall, Room 119
Memphis, TN 38152
www.memphis.edu

University of Tennessee
A207 Claxton Complex
Knoxville, TN 37996
www.utk.edu

Texas
Stephen F. Austin State
  University
P.O. Box 13019, SFA Station
Nacogdoches, TX 75962
www.sfasu.edu

Texas Tech University
3601 4th St.
Lubbock, TX 79430
www.ttu.edu

University of North Texas
P.O. Box 311456
Denton, TX 76203
www.unt.edu

University of Texas at Austin
1 University Station, D300
Austin, TX 78712
www.utexas.edu

University of Texas Pan American
1201 W. University Dr.
Edinburg, TX 78539
www.panam.edu

University of Texas Southwestern
  Medical Center
5323 Harry Hines Blvd.
Dallas, TX 75390
www.utsouthwestern.edu

Utah
Utah State University
Logan, UT 84322
www.usu.edu

Virginia
Virginia Commonwealth University
1112 E Clay St., Box 980330
Richmond, VA 23298
www.vcu.edu

Washington
Western Washington University
6912 220th St. SW
Mountlake Terrace, WA 98043
www.wwu.edu

West Virginia
West Virginia University
504-A Allen Hall, P.O. Box 6122
Morgantown, WV 26506
www.wvu.edu

Wisconsin
University of Wisconsin–Madison
432 N. Murray St.
Madison, WI 53706
www.wisc.edu

University of Wisconsin–Stout
227 Vocational Rehabilitation
Menomonee, WI 54751
www.uwstout.edu

Respiratory Therapists

Principal activity: Treating patients with breathing disorders

Work commitment: Full-time

Preprofessional education: High school diploma

Program length: 2 to 4 years

Work prerequisites: Associate or bachelor's degree

Career opportunities: Highly favorable

Income range: $44,000 to $62,000

Scope

Respiratory therapists provide treatment for patients suffering from cardiorespiratory problems, including asthma, bronchitis, emphysema, and pneumonia. They also treat postoperative patients, accident victims, and patients suffering from heart failure, drowning, electric shock, drug overdose, and stroke. Their patients range from premature babies to older people with chronic lung diseases.

Activities

Respiratory therapists participate in patients' evaluation and treatment. They may test patients' lung capacity and analyze the oxygen, carbon dioxide, and PH levels of patients' blood. These therapists work under a physician's supervision to administer therapy, monitor and record patient progress, and teach patients about respiratory exercises and equipment use. They also are responsible for maintaining equipment such as mechanical ventilators, resuscitators, and blood-gas analyzers.

Work Settings

Most respiratory therapists are employed by hospitals or medical centers, where they may work night or weekend hours. Others work in the offices of pulmonary medicine specialists, in nursing homes, or for companies that rent equipment to home-bound patients.

Advancement

One way to get a promotion is to move from caring for general patients to caring for critical patients. Those with a bachelor's degree may advance to supervisory or managerial positions at a hospital or commercial company.

Prerequisites

A high school diploma or its equivalent is necessary, because formal training for this field is offered at a post-secondary level.

Desirable personal attributes for this field include good judgment, mechanical ability, physical stamina, the capacity to function under stressful conditions, and a desire to help those who are gravely ill.

Education/Training

Two programs can prepare you for a career in this field:

- You can earn a two-year associate degree, offered by junior colleges and vocational technical institutes.
- You can pursue a four-year bachelor's degree, offered by colleges, universities, medical schools, and hospitals.

The standard educational program includes courses in anatomy, physiology (with special emphasis on the cardiopulmonary aspect), microbiology, pharmacology, respiratory and cardiovascular diseases, anesthesiology, patient psychology, and respiratory therapy techniques (such as airway management, blood-gas analysis, mechanical ventilation, cardiopulmonary resuscitation, and pulmonary function testing).

Certification/Registration/Licensure

To become a registered respiratory therapist, you must graduate from an accredited program and pass a three-hour certification exam, a two-part written exam, and a clinical exam.

Career Potential

The growing number of elderly people in the United States implies a strong demand for respiratory therapists. This makes for a favorable job outlook in this profession. Advances in medical treatment for heart attacks, premature births, accident victims, and AIDS patients will further increase the need for professionals in this field.

For More Information

The professional organization for this field is the American Association for Respiratory Care, 9425 N. McArthur Blvd., Ste. 100, Irving, TX 75063 (www.aarc.org). For more information on certification and registration, contact the National Board for Respiratory Care, 8310 Nieman Rd., Lenexa, KS 66214 (www.nbrc.org).

Respiratory Therapy Programs

Hundreds of colleges, community colleges, and technical institutes offer training for respiratory therapists—far too many to list here. For a list of educational programs in your area, contact the American Association for Respiratory Care or the National Board for Respiratory Care (see the addresses in the preceding section).

Respiratory Therapy Technicians

Principal activity: Helping treat patients with breathing disorders

Work commitment: Full-time

Preprofessional education: High school diploma

Program length: 2 years

Work prerequisites: Associate degree

Career opportunities: Limited

Income range: $35,000 to $44,000

Scope

Respiratory therapy technicians perform many of the same functions as respiratory therapists (see p. 372), but their education and training level is lower. Thus, they do not perform the more complex respiratory procedures.

Activities

See this section under Respiratory Therapists.

Work Settings

See this section under Respiratory Therapists.

Advancement

See this section under Respiratory Therapists.

Prerequisites

See this section under Respiratory Therapists.

Education/Training

Respiratory therapy technicians undergo the same kind of training as respiratory therapists, but in a shorter, less-intensive program.

Certification/Registration/Licensure

The National Board for Respiratory Care has established criteria for certified respiratory therapy technicians. Candidates must graduate from an accredited program and pass a three-hour examination.

Career Potential

Job prospects for respiratory therapy technicians are limited and the number of openings is projected to decrease over the next decade. This is due primarily to cost containment, as most work in respiratory care is being done by respiratory therapists, resulting in limited demand for respiratory therapy technicians.

For More Information

See this section under Respiratory Therapists.

Social Service Aides

Principal activity: Helping social workers secure needed services for clients

Work commitment: Part- or full-time

Preprofessional education: High school diploma

Program length: Several months

Work prerequisites: On-the-job training

Career opportunities: Highly favorable

Income range: $22,000 to $35,000

Scope

People in need can potentially secure services from a wide variety of social agencies. Working under the supervision of a social worker, the social service aide helps such individuals secure assistance.

A wide variety of duties fall within the domain of a social service aide. One of these is informing potential clients who seek assistance at an agency of the type of help they can anticipate receiving. This lets them know at the outset if they have come to a potential source of assistance. If they have, the social service aide can then help the clients obtain and fill out the appropriate forms. Some clients may need the aide's assistance in documenting essential information. After acquiring some knowledge of the client's background, the aide might be able to speak on the client's behalf when necessary in order to further his or her cause.

Social service aides also act as a client liaison to government and public agencies. At times, because of a variety of circumstances, clients may be unable to get to an agency. Should an emergency arise, the social service aide may be asked to arrange transportation for the client so that his or her needs can be met.

Activities

Social service aides fall into two categories: generalists and specialists. Generalists have a wide variety of duties, including assisting case workers. These individuals are also known as case aides. They may help clients secure medical care or affordable housing. Their work also can include helping unemployed people find work. Such aides may focus on more than just one personal issue. This can be done by providing clients with information on resources and agencies that provide specific help with other problems they may have. Thus, case aides have duties comparable to those of case workers.

Specializing social service aides are employed in community activities. They may be assigned by state or local agencies to investigate the nature of social problems in some neighborhoods. These problems may be the result of inherent disadvantage. The aide may be able to guide the people to the appropriate assistance agencies.

Work Settings

Social service aides may visit clients in their home or other locations. Many work primarily in offices. They usually have a standard 40-hour workweek. On occasion, weekend or evening work may be necessary.

Advancement

You can advance through further education and training, which result in increased responsibilities and pay. Enhanced qualifications can help you attain a position as a social service technician. With significant additional education and experience, you can achieve the rank of social worker (see p. 451).

Prerequisites

A high school education is mandatory for securing a position as a social service aide. Volunteer work involving interpersonal activities that treat others is especially useful.

Desirable personal attributes for this type of work are compassion, eagerness to help others, and tactfulness. Having good communication and computer skills are important assets.

Education/Training

Entry-level positions provide on-the-job training. Attending a junior or community college and taking sociology and psychology courses enhances your background and chances for advancement. Taking senior college-level courses and securing a bachelor's degree further advances your status and job benefits.

Certification/Registration/Licensure

The position of social service aide does not require any of these.

Career Potential

The prospects are very good for employment as a social service aide. These opportunities may be found in government at the federal, state, county, or municipal level. In addition, other facilities use the services of such aides, including hospitals of all sizes, nursing homes, social service agencies, and religious and community organizations. As the number of individuals needing help increases, the job opportunities for aides should multiply.

For More Information

This field has no professional organization, but you can contact the Council on Social Work Education, 1725 Duke St., Suite 500, Alexandria, VA 22314 (www.cswe.org) to obtain material on this field.

Speech-Language Pathologists

Principal activity: Helping people who have speech and hearing disorders

Work commitment: Part- or full-time

Preprofessional education: Bachelor's degree

Program length: 4 to 6 years

Work prerequisites: Master's degree

Career opportunities: Favorable

Income range: $50,000 to $80,000

Scope

Tens of millions of Americans have speech or hearing disorders. These problems may be due to hearing loss, brain damage, stroke, cleft palate, mental disability, or emotional difficulties. Speech pathologists evaluate and treat people with speech, language, voice, and fluency defects.

Activities

Speech-language pathologists evaluate and diagnose patients using instruments as well as written and oral examinations. This allows them to determine the nature and extent of impairments as well as record and analyze speech abnormalities. These professionals then plan and implement treatment programs to restore or improve communication skills. They teach patients how to make sounds, improve their voices, and increase their language skills. For clients with severe impairments, they may provide automated devices or offer sign language instruction.

Work Settings

Most professionals in this field are employed in medical centers, hospitals, rehabilitation centers, or schools.

Advancement

Speech-language pathologists can advance to administrative or teaching positions.

Prerequisites

You need a bachelor's degree in speech pathology. As part of such a program, you learn biology, anatomy, physiology, sociology, linguistics, semantics, phonetics, and psychology.

Desirable personal attributes include a friendly personality, a desire to help people, and patience.

Education/Training

A master's degree in speech pathology is necessary to practice in this field. Studies include advanced work in anatomy, physiology, physics, speech, language and hearing disorders, and psychology. Courses in the evaluation and treatment of disorders in this field are taught in clinical settings.

A master's degree permits you to be certified and makes you eligible for federal reimbursement (Medicare and Medicaid).

Certification/Registration/Licensure

Speech pathologists who hold a master's degree and have completed a one-year internship at an approved setting are eligible to take a certification examination administered by the American Speech-Language-Hearing Association. Certification is an asset in gaining advancement.

Many states require a Certificate of Clinical Competence (CCC), which allows you to work in public schools.

Career Potential

Opportunities are expected to be above average in this field. There is now a greater emphasis on detecting and remedying speech disorders at an early age resulting in more demand for speech pathology services.

For More Information

The professional organization for this field is the American Speech-Language-Hearing Association, 10801 Rockville Pike, Rockville, MD 20852 (www.asha.org).

Speech-Language Pathologist Programs

Alabama

Alabama A&M University
4900 Meridian St.
Huntsville, AL 35811
www.aamu.edu

Auburn University at Montgomery
1199 Haley Center
Auburn, AL 36849
www.auburn.edu

University of Alabama
Tuscaloosa, AL 35487
www.ua.edu

University of Montevallo
Station 6720
Montevallo, AL 35115
www.montevallo.edu

University of South Alabama
2000 University Commons
Mobile, AL 36688
www.southalabama.edu

Arizona

Arizona State University
326 E Orange Street
Tempe, AZ 85287
www.asu.edu

Northern Arizona University
307 W DuPont Avenue
Flagstaff, AZ 86011
www.nau.edu

University of Arizona
Tucson, AZ 85721
www.arizona.edu

Arkansas

Arkansas State University
P.O. Box 1450
State University, AR 72467
www.astate.edu

University of Arkansas at
Little Rock
2801 S. University Ave.
Little Rock, AR 72204
www.ualr.edu

University of Arkansas–
Fayetteville
Fayetteville, AR 72701
www.uark.edu

University of Central Arkansas
210 Donaghey Ave.
Conway, AR 72035
www.uca.edu

California

California State University, Chico
400 W. First St.
Chico, CA 95929
www.csuchico.edu

California State University, Fresno
5241 N. Maple Ave.
Fresno, CA 93740
www.csufresno.edu

California State University,
Fullerton
800 N State College Boulevard
Fullerton, CA 92834
www.fullerton.edu

California State University,
Hayward
25800 Carlos Bee Blvd.
Hayward, CA 94542
www.csuhayward.edu

California State University,
Long Beach
1250 Bellflower Blvd.
Long Beach, CA 90840
www.csulb.edu

California State University,
Los Angeles
5151 State University Dr.
Los Angeles, CA 90032
www.calstatela.edu

California State University,
Northridge
18111 Nordhoff St.
Northridge, CA 91330
www.csun.edu

California State University,
Sacramento
6000 J St.
Sacramento, CA 95819
www.csus.edu

Loma Linda University
Nicholl Hall
Loma Linda, CA 92350
www.llu.edu

San Diego State University
5500 Campanile Dr.
San Diego, CA 92182
www.sdsu.edu

San Francisco State University
1600 Holloway Ave.
San Francisco, CA 94132
www.sfsu.edu

University of the Pacific
3601 Pacific Ave.
Stockton, CA 95211
http://web.pacific.edu/

University of the Redlands
1200 E. Colton Ave.
P.O. Box 3080
Redlands, CA 92373
www.redlands.edu

Colorado

Metropolitan State College of
  Denver
P.O. Box 173362
Denver, CO 80217
www.mscd.edu

University of Colorado
Box 425
Boulder, CO 80309
www.colorado.edu

University of Northern Colorado
Gunter 1000, Box 134
Greeley, CO 80639
www.unco.edu

Connecticut

Southern Connecticut State
  University
501 Crescent St.
New Haven, CT 06515
www.southernct.edu

University of Connecticut
1392 Storrs
Storrs-Mansfield, CT 06269
www.uconn.edu

District of Columbia

Gallaudet University
800 Florida Ave. NE
Washington, DC 20002
www.gallaudet.edu

George Washington University
2121 1st Street
Washington, DC 20052
www.gwu.edu

Howard University
2400 6th St. NW
Washington, DC 20059
www.howard.edu

University of the District of
  Columbia
4200 Connecticut Ave. NW
Washington, DC 20008
www.udc.edu

Florida

Florida Atlantic University
777 Glades Rd.
P.O. Box 3091
Boca Raton, FL 33431
www.fau.edu

Florida State University
107 Regional Rehabilitation
  Center
Tallahassee, FL 32306
www.fsu.edu

Nova Southeastern University
3200 S. University Dr.
Fort Lauderdale, FL 33328
www.nova.edu

University of Central Florida
4000 Central Florida Blvd.
Orlando, FL 32816
www.ucf.edu

University of Florida
335 Dauer Hall
Gainesville, FL 32611
www.ufl.edu

University of South Florida
4202 E. Fowler Ave.
Tampa, FL 33620
www.usf.edu

Georgia

Georgia State University
33 Gilmer Street SE
University Plaza
Atlanta, GA 30303
www.gsu.edu

State University of West Georgia
1601 Maple St.
Carrollton, GA 30118
www.westga.edu

University of Georgia
Athens, GA 30602
www.uga.edu

Valdosta State University
1500 N. Patterson St.
Valdosta, GA 31698
www.valdosta.edu

Hawaii

University of Hawaii at Manoa
John A. Burns School of Medicine
2500 Lower Campus Rd.
Honolulu, HI 96822
www.hawaii.edu

Idaho

Idaho State University
921 S. 8th Ave.
Pocatello, ID 83209
www.isu.edu

Illinois

Eastern Illinois University
600 Lincoln Ave.
Charleston, IL 61920
www.eiu.edu

Governors State University
College of Health Professions
1 University Pkwy.
University Park, IL 60466
www.govst.edu

Northern Illinois University
Department of Communications
DeKalb, IL 60115
www.niu.edu

Northwestern University
633 Clark St.
Evanston, IL 60208
www.nwu.edu

Rush University Medical Center
College of Health Sciences
600 S. Paulina St., Suite 440
Chicago, IL 60612
www.rush.edu

Saint Xavier University
3700 W. 103rd St.
Chicago, IL 60655
www.sxu.edu

Southern Illinois University
  Carbondale
Carbondale, IL 62901
www.siuc.edu

Southern Illinois University
  Edwardsville
Box 1600
Edwardsville, IL 62026
www.siue.edu

University of Illinois
901 W. Illinois St.
Urbana, IL 61801
www.uiuc.edu

Western Illinois University
1 University Circle
Macomb, IL 61455
www.wiu.edu

Indiana

Ball State University
2000 W. University Ave.
Muncie, IN 47306
www.bsu.edu

Indiana University
107 S. Indiana Ave.
Bloomington, IN 47405
www.indiana.edu

Purdue University
West Lafayette, IN 47907
www.purdue.edu

Iowa

Iowa State University
228 Gray Avenue
Ames, IA 50011
www.iastate.edu

University of Iowa
Iowa City, IA 52242
www.uiowa.edu

University of Northern Iowa
1227 W. 27th St.
Cedar Falls, IA 50614
www.uni.edu

Kansas

Fort Hays State University
600 Park St.
Hays, KS 67601
www.fhsu.edu

Kansas State University
Manhattan, KS 66506
www.ksu.edu

University of Kansas
School of Allied Health
3901 Rainbow Blvd.
Kansas City, KS 66160
www.kumc.edu

University of Kansas
Lawrence, KS 66045
www.ku.edu

Wichita State University
1845 N. Fairmount
Wichita, KS 67260
www.wichita.edu

Kentucky

Eastern Kentucky University
521 Lancaster Ave.
Richmond, KY 40475
www.eku.edu

Murray State University
16th and Main Sts.
Murray, KY 42071
www.murraystate.edu

Spalding University
851 S. 4th St.
Louisville, KY 40203
www.spalding.edu

University of Kentucky
1028 S. Broadway, Ste. 3
Lexington, KY 40504
www.uky.edu

Western Kentucky University
1906 College Hts. Blvd.
Bowling Green, KY 42101
www.wku.edu

Louisiana

Grambling State University
100 Founder Street
Grambling, LA 71245
www.gram.edu

Louisiana State University
423 Main Street
Baton Rouge, LA 70803
www.lsu.edu

Louisiana State University Health
  Sciences Center
1900 Gravier St.
New Orleans, LA 70112
www.lsuhsc.edu

Louisiana Tech University
305 Wisteral St.
Ruston, LA 71272
www.latech.edu

Southeastern Louisiana University
University Station, P.O. Box 879
Hammond, LA 70402
www.selu.edu

Southern University
P.O. Box 9888
Baton Rouge, LA 70813
www.subr.edu

University of Louisiana at Monroe
College of Health Sciences
Department of Communicative
  Disorders
Brown Hall
Monroe, LA 71209
www.ulm.edu/codi/

Maryland

Loyola College
4501 N. Charles St.
Baltimore, MD 21210
www.loyola.edu

Towson University
8000 York Rd.
Towson, MD 21252
www.towson.edu

University of Maryland at
  College Park
College Park, MD 20742
www.umd.edu

Massachusetts

Boston University
Sargent College of Health and
  Rehabilitation Sciences
685 Commonwealth Ave.
Boston, MA 02215
www.bu.edu

Bridgewater State College
131 Summer Street
Bridgewater, MA 02325
www.bridgew.edu

Elms College
291 Springfield St.
Chicopee, MA 01013
www.elms.edu

Northeastern University
10 Speare Pl.
Boston, MA 02115
www.northeastern.edu

Worcester State College
486 Chandler St.
Worcester, MA 01602
www.worcester.edu

Michigan

Eastern Michigan University
300 W Michigan Avenue
Ypsilanti, MI 48197
www.emich.edu

Wayne State University
5700 Cass Avenue
Detroit, MI 48202
www.wayne.edu

Western Michigan University
1903 W. Michigan Ave.
Kalamazoo, MI 49008
www.wmich.edu

Minnesota
Minnesota State University–
Mankato
MSU 77-Elis and Stadium Rd.
Mankato, MN 56001
www.mnsu.edu

Minnesota State University–
Moorhead
1104 7th Ave. S.
Moorhead, MN 56563
www.mnstate.edu

St. Cloud State University
720 4th Ave. S.
St. Cloud, MN 56301
www.stcloudstate.edu

University of Minnesota
164 Pillsbury Dr. SE
Minneapolis, MN 55455
www.umn.edu

University of Minnesota–Duluth
1049 University Dr.
Duluth, MN 55812
www.d.umn.edu

Mississippi
Mississippi University for Women
1100 College St.
Columbus, MS 39701
www.muw.edu

University of Mississippi
University, MS 38677
www.olemiss.edu

University of Southern Mississippi
118 College Dr.
Hattiesburg, MS 39406
www.usm.edu

Missouri
Fontbonne College
6800 Wydown Blvd.
St. Louis, MO 63105
www.fontbonne.edu

Southeast Missouri State
University
One University Plaza
Cape Girardeau, MO 63701
www.semo.edu

Southwest Missouri State
University
901 S. National Ave.
Springfield, MO 65897
www.smsu.edu

St. Louis University
221 N. Grand Blvd.
St. Louis, MO 63103
www.slu.edu

Truman State University
100 E. Normal Street
Kirksville, MO 63501
www.truman.edu

University of Missouri–Columbia
Columbia, MO 65211
www.missouri.edu

Nebraska
University of Nebraska at Kearney
905 W. 25th St.
Kearney, NE 68849
www.unk.edu

University of Nebraska at Omaha
6001 Dodge St.
Omaha, NE 68182
www.unomaha.edu

University of Nebraska–Lincoln
Lincoln, NE 68588
www.unl.edu

Nevada
University of Nevada–Reno
1664 N. Virginia St.
Reno, NV 89557
www.unr.edu

New Hampshire
University of New Hampshire
Grant House, 4 Garrison Ave.
Durham, NH 03824
www.unh.edu

New Jersey
College of New Jersey
2000 Pennington Rd.
P.O. Box 7718
Ewing, NJ 08628
www.tcnj.edu

Kean University
1000 Morris Ave.
Union, NJ 07083
www.kean.edu

Montclair State University
1 Normal Ave.
Montclair, NJ 07043
www.montclair.edu

Seton Hall University
School of Graduate Medical
Education
400 S. Orange Ave.
South Orange, NJ 07079
http://gradmeded.shu.edu/

William Paterson University
300 Pompton Rd.
Wayne, NJ 07470
www.wpunj.edu

New Mexico
Eastern New Mexico University
1200 W. University
Portales, NM 88130
www.enmu.edu

New Mexico State University
P.O. Box 30001
Las Cruces, NM 88003
www.nmsu.edu

University of New Mexico
Albuquerque, NM 87131
www.unm.edu

New York
Adelphi University
P.O. Box 701
Garden City, NY 11530
www.adelphi.edu

Brooklyn College
The City University of New York
2900 Bedford Ave.
Brooklyn, NY 11210
www.brooklyn.cuny.edu

Buffalo State College
1300 Elmwood Ave.
Buffalo, NY 14222
www.buffalostate.edu

College of St. Rose
432 Western Ave.
Albany, NY 12203
www.strose.edu

The Graduate Center
365 Fifth Ave.
New York, NY 10016
www.gc.cuny.edu

Hunter College
695 Park Ave.
New York, NY 10021
www.hunter.cuny.edu

Ithaca College
201 Cerrache Center
Ithaca, NY 14850
www.ithaca.edu

Lehman College of CUNY
Bedford Park Blvd. W.
Bronx, NY 10468
www.lehman.cuny.edu

Long Island University
One University Plaza
Brooklyn, NY 11201
www.brooklyn.liu.edu

Long Island University
700 Northern Blvd.
Brookville, NY 11548
www.liu.edu

Marymount Manhattan College
221 E. 71st St.
New York, NY 10021
www.mmm.edu

Nazareth College of Rochester
4245 E. Ave.
Rochester, NY 14618
www.naz.edu

New York Medical College
School of Public Health
Valhalla, NY 10595
www.nymc.edu

New York University
The Steinhardt School of
   Education
82 Washington Sq. E.
New York, NY 10003
www.nyu.edu

Pace University
1 Pace Plaza
New York, NY 10038
www.pace.edu

Queens College
The City University of New York
65-30 Kissena Blvd.
Flushing, NY 11367
www.qc.edu

St. John's University
8000 Utopia Pkwy.
Jamaica, NY 11439
www.stjohns.edu

St. Joseph's College
155 W. Roe Blvd.
Patchogue, NY 11772
www.sjcny.edu

SUNY at Fredonia
280 Central Ave.
Fredonia, NY 14063
www.fredonia.edu

SUNY at Geneseo
One College Circle
Geneseo, NY 14454
www.geneseo.edu

SUNY at New Paltz
1 Hawk Drive
New Paltz, NY 12561
www.newpaltz.edu

SUNY Plattsburgh State
101 Broad St.
Plattsburgh, NY 12901
www.plattsburgh.edu

Syracuse University
Syracuse, NY 13244
www.syr.edu

Teachers College of Columbia
   University
525 W. 120th St.
New York, NY 10027
www.tc.columbia.edu

University at Buffalo
The State University of New York
17 Capen Hall
Buffalo, NY 14260
www.buffalo.edu

North Carolina
Appalachian State University
Boone, NC 28608
www.appstate.edu

East Carolina University
School of Allied Health Sciences
Carol Belk Building
Greenville, NC 27858
www.ecu.edu

Elizabeth City State University
1704 Weeksville Rd.
Elizabeth City, NC 27909
www.ecsu.edu

North Carolina Central University
1801 Fayetteville St.
Durham, NC 27707
www.nccu.edu

University of North Carolina at
   Chapel Hill
Chapel Hill, NC 27599
www.unc.edu

University of North Carolina at
   Greensboro
1000 Spring Garden St.
Greensboro, NC 27403
www.uncg.edu

Western Carolina University
Hwy. 107
Cullowhee, NC 28723
www.wcu.edu

North Dakota
Minot State University
500 University Ave. W.
Minot, ND 58707
www.minotstateu.edu

University of North Dakota
University Station
Grand Forks, ND 58202
www.und.nodak.edu

Ohio
Bowling Green State University
Bowling Green, OH 43403
www.bgsu.edu

Case Cleveland Western Reserve
University
10900 Euclid Ave.
Cleveland, OH 44106
www.cwru.edu

Cleveland State University
2121 Euclid Ave.
Cleveland, OH 44115
www.csuohio.edu

Kent State University
Kent, OH 44242
www.kent.edu

Miami University
College of Arts & Science
E. High Street
Oxford, OH 45056
www.muohio.edu

Ohio State University
460 W 10th Avenue
Columbus, OH 43210
www.osu.edu

Ohio University
Athens, OH 45701
www.ohio.edu

University of Akron
302 E. Buchtel Ave.
Akron, OH 44325
www.uakron.edu

University of Cincinnati
2600 Clifton Ave.
Cincinnati, OH 45221
www.uc.edu

Oklahoma
Northeastern State University
600 N. Grand Ave.
Tahlequah, OK 74464
www.nsuok.edu

Oklahoma State University
324 Student Union
Stillwater, OK 74078
www.okstate.edu

University of Central Oklahoma
100 N. University Dr.
Edmond, OK 73034
www.ucok.edu

University of Oklahoma
660 Parrington Oval
Norman, OK 73019
www.ou.edu

University of Tulsa
600 S. College Ave.
Tulsa, OK 74104
www.utulsa.edu

Oregon
Portland State University
P.O. Box 751
Portland, OR 97207
www.pdx.edu

University of Oregon
Eugene, OR 97403
www.uoregon.edu

Pennsylvania
Bloomsburg University
400 E. 2nd St.
Bloomsburg, PA 17815
www.bloomu.edu

California University of
Pennsylvania
250 University Ave.
California, PA 15419
www.cup.edu

Clarion University of Pennsylvania
Clarion, PA 16214
www.clarion.edu

East Stroudsburg University of
Pennsylvania
200 Prospect St.
East Stroudsburg, PA 18301
www.esu.edu

Edinboro University of
Pennsylvania
115A Compton Hall
Edinboro, PA 16444
www.edinboro.edu

Indiana University of
Pennsylvania
1011 South Dr.
Indiana, PA 15705
www.iup.edu

Marywood University
2300 Adams Ave.
Scranton, PA 18509
www.marywood.edu

Temple University
1801 Broad St. North
Philadelphia, PA 19122
www.temple.edu

University of Pittsburgh
School of Health and
Rehabilitation Sciences
4020 Forbes Tower
Pittsburgh, PA 15260
www.shrs.pitt.edu

West Chester University
Carter Drive
West Chester, PA 19383
www.wcupa.edu

Rhode Island
University of Rhode Island
Kingston, RI 02881
www.uri.edu

South Carolina
South Carolina State University
Taylor Hall
300 College St. NE
Orangeburg, SC 29117
www.scsu.edu

University of South Carolina
Columbia, SC 29208
www.sc.edu

South Dakota
University of South Dakota
414 E. Clark St.
Vermillion, SD 57069
www.usd.edu

Tennessee
University of Memphis
101 Wilder Tower
Memphis, TN 38152
www.memphis.edu

Vanderbilt University
2201 West End Ave.
Nashville, TN 37235
www.vanderbilt.edu

Texas
Baylor University
1311 S 5th Street
Waco, TX 76798
www.baylor.edu

Lamar University
4400 Martin Luther King Blvd.
P.O. Box 10009
Beaumont, TX 77705
www.lamar.edu

Our Lady of the Lake University
411 SW 24th St.
San Antonio, TX 78207
www.ollusa.edu

Stephen F. Austin State
  University
SFA Station
1936 North Street
Nacogdoches, TX 75962
www.sfasu.edu

Texas A&M University–Kingsville
700 University Blvd., MSC 114
Kingsville, TX 78363
www.tamuk.edu

Texas Christian University
2800 S. University Dr.
Fort Worth, TX 76129
www.tcu.edu

Texas Tech University
18th Street & Boston Ave
Lubbock, TX 79409
www.ttu.edu

Texas State University–San
  Marcos
601 University Dr.
San Marcos, TX 78666
www.txstate.edu

Texas Woman's University
P.O. Box 425589
Denton, TX 76204
www.twu.edu

University of Houston
4800 Calhoun Rd.
Houston, TX 77204
www.uh.edu

University of North Texas
P.O. Box 311277
Denton, TX 76203
www.unt.edu

University of Texas at Austin
Austin, TX 78712
www.utexas.edu

University of Texas at Dallas
1966 Inwood Rd.
Dallas, TX 75235
www.utdallas.edu

University of Texas at El Paso
500 W. University Ave.
El Paso, TX 79968
www.utep.edu

University of Texas–Pan American
1201 W. University Dr.
Edinburg, TX 78541
www.utpa.edu

Utah
Brigham Young University
Provo, UT 84601
www.byu.edu

University of Utah
201 S. Presidents Circle,
  Room 201
Salt Lake City, UT 84112
www.utah.edu

Utah State University
Logan, UT 84322
www.usu.edu

Vermont
University of Vermont
Burlington, VT 05405
www.uvm.edu

Virginia
Hampton University
Hampton, VA 23668
www.hamptonu.edu

James Madison University
800 S. Main St.
Harrisonburg, VA 22807
www.jmu.edu

Old Dominion University
202 Rollins Hall
Norfolk, VA 23529
www.odu.edu

Radford University
E. Main St.
Radford, VA 24142
www.radford.edu

University of Virginia
1300 Jefferson Park Avenue
Charlottesville, VA 22903
www.virginia.edu

Washington
Eastern Washington University
101 Sutton Hall
Cheney, WA 99004
www.ewu.edu

University of Washington
1959 NE Pacific St., Box 356490
Seattle, WA 98195
www.washington.edu

Washington State University
Lighty 307 Box 641269
Pullman, WA 99164
www.wsu.edu

Western Washington University
516 High St.
Bellingham, WA 98225
www.wwu.edu

West Virginia
Marshall University
One John Marshall Dr.
Huntington, WV 25755
www.marshall.edu

West Virginia University
P.O. Box 6201
Morgantown, WV 26506
www.wvu.edu

Wisconsin
Marquette University
P.O. Box 1881
Milwaukee, WI 53201
www.mu.edu

University of Wisconsin–Eau
  Claire
105 Garfield Ave.
P.O. Box 4004
Eau Claire, WI 54702
www.uwec.edu

University of Wisconsin–Madison
1975 Willow Dr.
Madison, WI 53706
www.wisc.edu

University of Wisconsin–
  Milwaukee
2200 E. Kenwood Blvd.
P.O. Box 413
Milwaukee, WI 53201
www.uwm.edu

University of Wisconsin–Oshkosh
800 Algoma Blvd.
Oshkosh, WI 54901
www.uwosh.edu

University of Wisconsin–
River Falls
410 S. Third St.
River Falls, WI 54022
www.uwrf.edu

University of Wisconsin–Stevens
Point
2100 Main St.
Stevens Point, WI 54481
www.uwsp.edu

University of Wisconsin–
Whitewater
800 W. Main St.
Whitewater, WI 53190
www.uww.edu

Wyoming
University of Wyoming
1000 E. University Ave.
Laramie, WY 82071
www.uwyo.edu

Substance Abuse Counselors

Principal activity: Providing guidance to and monitoring the progress of clients who are addicted to or abuse drugs or alcohol

Work commitment: Part- or full-time

Preprofessional education: High school diploma

Program length: From 1 to 6 years

Work prerequisites: Vary from a 1-year certificate to a master's degree

Career opportunities: Highly favorable

Income range: $29,000 to $47,000

Scope

Substance abuse counselors are professionals trained to evaluate, advise, and follow up on the progress of individuals who are excessively dependent on or addicted to alcohol or drugs.

Activities

In recent decades, drug abuse has taken on epidemic proportions. It has overtaken alcohol as the main addiction problem in the population. It affects a wide range of people, including children, pregnant women, and professionals in varying fields.

Dealing with people who abuse or are addicted to drugs or alcohol is a major challenge. The initial barrier that needs to be overcome is to get the client to accept that he or she has a problem. This admission is essential for the person to realize that outside help is needed. Working with people who have reached this stage can be difficult. To weaken and then eliminate the dependency on alcohol or drugs, counselors need to apply suitable motivational techniques that improve the therapy's chance of success.

The substance abuse counselor's responsibilities depend on the position. The counselor may service a broad range of individuals with a wide range of addiction problems or limit his or her practice to a specific group of people, such as teenagers or business executives.

The counselor's specialization may also be determined by the nature of the abused substance. Some may restrict their practice to cocaine, heroin, or another drug or to alcoholics. A treatment team for addicts may include physicians, psychiatrists, psychologists, social workers, psychiatric nurses, and substance abuse counselors.

When working with clients, the counselor first conducts an overall evaluation. This involves assessing the nature, extent, and pattern of the individual's substance abuse. It is also essential to become acquainted with the client's background, lifestyle, and personality to determine how he or she can best be helped.

Once a treatment plan is in place, counseling is provided on a one-to-one or group basis or both. Each client's progress (or lack thereof) needs to be carefully followed, and a written record should be kept. In addition, the counselor periodically submits reports on his or her clients.

Work Settings

Substance abuse counselors are employed by hospitals, educational institutions (at various levels), public or private substance abuse centers, mental health clinics, HMOs, government agencies (federal, state, and local), community service organizations, and even large corporations. The work schedule varies, depending on the nature of the employer. Counseling may take place during the day or in evening sessions and on weekends.

Advancement

You can advance by gaining additional education and/or experience. Either way, your enhanced background will help you obtain a better-paying and more responsible position with a more prestigious organization or gain a promotion to a supervisory or administrative post.

Prerequisites

The basic requirement is a high school diploma with a strong academic record. This gives you a good basis for securing the necessary higher levels of education for work in this field. Volunteer work at a hospital or substance abuse clinic can prove helpful in directing your career goals.

Desirable personal attributes for work in this field are sensitivity to people seriously in need of help, the objectivity to not prejudge people, strong interpersonal and communication skills, and emotional stability. It is important to be able to work as part of a team with other mental health professionals.

Education/Training

You can work as a substance abuse counselor with varied educational credentials. This may range from a one-year certificate program all the way to a master's degree. The appropriate major for work in this field is alcohol and drug technology.

Certification/Registration/Licensure

In many states, substance abuse counselors must be certified. This can be achieved through the National Association of Substance Abuse Counselors or by individual state certification. To attain certification, you must complete a substance abuse program at an accredited institution, pass written and oral examinations, complete supervised clinical training, and provide recorded samples of clinical work.

Career Potential

The very favorable employment prospects in this field stem from the wide range of work settings where substance abuse counselors are employed. You can find positions through classified newspaper ads or by applying directly to institutional personnel directors by sending them your resume and a cover letter.

For More Information

The professional organizations for this field are the National Association of Substance Abuse Trainers and Educators, 1521 Hillary St., New Orleans, LA 70118, and the National Association of Alcoholism and Drug Abuse Counselors, 1911 Fort Myer Dr., Suite 900, Arlington, VA 22209 (www.naadac.org).

Substance Abuse Counseling Programs

Alaska
University of Alaska at Anchorage
3211 Providence Dr.
Anchorage, AK 99508
www.uaa.alaska.edu

Arizona
Pima Community College
4905 E Broadway Blvd.
Tucson, AZ 85709
www.pima.edu

Rio Salado Community College
2323 W. 14th St.
Tempe, AZ 85281
www.rio.maricopa.edu

Arkansas
University of Arkansas for Medical
  Sciences
4310 W Markam St.
Little Rock, AR 72205
www.uams.edu

California
Alliant International University
10455 Pomerado Rd,
San Diego, CA 92131
www.alliant.edu

California State University at
  Fresno
5241 N. Maple Ave.
Fresno, CA 93740
www.csufresno.edu

John F. Kennedy University
370 Camino Pablo
Orinda, CA 94563
www.jfku.edu

Loyola Marymount University
Loyola Boulevard at W. 80th St.
Los Angeles, CA 90045
www.lmu.edu

Florida
Nova Southeastern University
3301 College Ave.
Fort Lauderdale, FL 33314
www.nova.edu

University of North Florida
4567 St. Johns Bluff Rd. S.
Jacksonville, FL 32224
www.unf.edu

Hawaii
Argosy University/Honolulu
3465 Waialae Ave. Ste. 300
Honolulu, HI 96816
www.argosyu.edu

Iowa
University of Iowa
N 338 Lindquist Center
Iowa City, IA 52242
www.uiowa.edu

Illinois
Adler School of Professional
  Psychology
65 E. Wacker Pl.
Chicago, IL 60601
www.adler.edu

Governors State University
University Park, IL 60466
www.govst.edu

National-Louis University
2840 Sheridan Rd.
Evanston, IL 60201
http://nlu.nl.edu/

Southern Illinois University
Mail Code 4609
Rehabilitation Institute
Carbondale, IL 62901
www.siu.edu

Louisiana
Southern University at
  New Orleans
6400 Press Dr.
New Orleans, LA 70126
www.suno.edu

University of Louisiana at Monroe
128 Strauss Hall
Monroe, LA 71209
www.nlu.edu

Massachusetts
Cambridge College
1000 Massachusetts Ave.
Cambridge, MA 02138
www.cambridge.edu

Fitchburg State College
160 Pearl St.
Fitchburg, MA 01420
www.fsc.edu

Northeastern University
Bouve College of Health Sciences
360 Huntington Ave.
Mugar Bldg. 134
Boston, MA 02115
www.neu.edu

Springfield College
263 Alden St.
Springfield, MA 01109
www.springfieldcollege.edu

Maryland
Johns Hopkins University
Department of Counseling and
  Human Services
Baltimore, MD 21218
www.jhu.edu

Maine
University of Southern Maine
400 Bailey Hall
Gorham, ME 04038
www.usm.maine.edu

Michigan
Siena Heights University
1247 Siena Heights Dr.
Adrian, MI 49221
www.sienahts.edu

University of Detroit Mercy
8200 W. Outer Dr.
Detroit, MI 48219
www.udmercy.edu

Wayne State University
Detroit, MI 48202
www.wayne.edu

Minnesota
Capella University
222 S. 8th St.
Minneapolis, MN 55404
www.capellauniversity.edu

Winona State University
Rochester Center, Box 5838
Winona, MN 55987
www.winona.edu

Missouri
University of Missouri at St. Louis
8001 Natural Bridge Rd.
St. Louis, MO 63121
www.umsl.edu

Montana
University of Great Falls
13101 20th St. S.
Great Falls, MT 59405
www.ugf.edu

North Carolina
Appalachian State University
B.B. Dougherty Administration
 Bldg.
P.O. Box 32068
Boone, NC 28608
www.appstate.edu

East Carolina University
Belk Building
Greenville, NC 27858
www.ecu.edu

University of North Carolina at
 Chapel Hill
Tate-Turner-Kuralt Bldg.
301 Pittsboro St., CB #3350
Chapel Hill, NC 27599
www.unc.edu

University of North Carolina at
 Charlotte
9201 University City Blvd.
Charlotte, NC 28223
www.uncc.edu

University of North Carolina at
 Wilmington
Wilmington, NC 28403
www.uncwil.edu

North Dakota
North Dakota State University
Education Department
Fargo, ND 58105
www.ndsu.nodak.edu

University of North Dakota
Box 8255
Grand Forks, ND 58202
www.und.nodak.edu

New Hampshire
Antioch New England Graduate
 School
40 Avon St.
Keene, NH 03431
www.antiochne.edu

New Jersey
College of New Jersey
Ewing, NJ 08628
www.tcnj.edu

Fairleigh Dickinson University
285 Madison Ave.
Madison, NJ 07940
www.fdu.edu

Kean University
Campus School East
Union, NJ 07083
www.kean.edu

Montclair State University
Chapin Hall, 1 Normal Ave.
Upper Montclair, NJ 07043
www.montclair.edu

Rutgers, The State University of
 New Jersey
536 George St.
New Brunswick, NJ 08901
www.rutgers.edu

Nevada
University of Nevada at Reno
Mail Stop 281
Reno, NV 89557
www.unr.edu

New York
City University of New York
Queens College
65-30 Kissena Blvd.
Flushing, NY 11367
www.qc.edu

College of Mt. Saint Vincent
6301 Riverdale Ave.
Riverdale, NY 10471
www.cmsv.edu

Fordham University
113 W. 60th St.
New York, NY 10023
www.fordham.edu

Iona College
715 North Ave.
New Rochelle, NY 10801
www.iona.edu

Long Island University
Brooklyn Campus
Brooklyn, NY 11201
www.brooklyn.liunet.edu

Manhattan College
MC Parkway
Riverdale, NY 10471
www.mancol.edu

New York University
New York, NY 10012
www.nyu.edu

Pace University
1 Martine Ave.
White Plains, NY 10606
www.pace.edu

Rochester Institute of Technology
One Lomb Memorial Dr.
Rochester, NY 14623
www.rit.edu

Sage College Graduate School
Troy, NY 12180
www.sage.edu

St. Johns University
8000 Utopia Pkwy.
Jamaica, NY 11439
www.stjohns.edu

State University of NY at
  Brockport
17B Hartwell Hall
Brockport, NY 14420
www.brockport.edu

State University of NY at Oneonta
503 Fitzelle Hall
Oneonta, NY 13820
www.oneonta.edu

State University of NY at
  Stonybrook
Rm. 902, Level 2
Stonybrook, NY 11794
www.sunysb.edu

Ohio
Methodist Theological School
  in Ohio
P.O. Box 8004
3081 Columbus Pike
Delaware, OH 43015
www.mtso.edu

Wright State University
E344 Student Union
3640 Colonel Glen Hwy.
Dayton, OH 43015
www.wright.edu

Oklahoma
University of Oklahoma
1000 Asp Ave.
Norman, OK 73019
www.ou.edu

Oregon
Chemeketa Community College
4000 Lancaster Dr. NE
P.O. Box 14007
Salem, OR 93709
www.chemeketa.edu

Lewis and Clark College
0615 SW Palatine Hill Rd.
Portland, OR 97219
www.lclark.edu

Pennsylvania
Chestnut Hill College
9601 Germantown Ave.
Philadelphia, PA 19118
www.chc.edu

Indiana University of
  Pennsylvania
Keith Hall
Indiana, PA 15705
www.iup.edu

La Salle University
1900 W. Olney Ave.
Philadelphia, PA 19141
www.lasalle.edu

Pennsylvania State University
327 Cedar Bldg.
University Park, PA 16802
www.psu.edu

Slippery Rock University of
  Pennsylvania
Slippery Rock, PA 16057
www.sru.edu

Villanova University
Villanova, PA 19085
www.villanova.edu

Rhode Island
Rhode Island College
600 Mt. Pleasant Ave.
Providence, RI 02908
www.ric.edu

South Carolina
Francis Marion University
Florence, SC 29501
www.fmarion.edu

University of South Carolina
Columbia, SC 29208
www.sc.edu

Texas
University of Texas
Health Science Center at Houston
P.O. Box 20036
Houston, TX 77225
www.uth.tmc.edu

Virginia
College of William and Mary
P.O. Box 8795
Williamsburg, VA 23187
www.wm.edu

Virginia Commonwealth University
921 W. Franklin St., Box 2030
Richmond, VA 23284
www.vcu.edu

Washington
Eastern Washington University
526 5th St., MS 18
Cheney, WA 99004
www.ewu.edu

Wisconsin
University of Wisconsin–Stout
225 Vocational Rehabilitation
  Bldg.
Menomonee, WI 54751
www.uwstout.edu

Wyoming
University of Wyoming
McWhinnie Hall, Box 3374
Laramie, WY 82071
www.uwyo.edu

Administrative Health-Care Careers

This chapter describes seven careers. Although the responsibilities for each are different, they all have in common the goal of facilitating a successful stay at a health-care institution. Each of these careers also has a significant administrative component, and many may include significant supervisory responsibilities. The educational background requirements for these positions vary, but they demand a strong sense of responsibility and empathy. Each of these positions has its own special challenges, but they all can provide a strong sense of satisfaction that results from a meaningful public service career.

Admitting Officers

Principal activity: Arranging admission to a health-care facility

Work commitment: Full-time

Preprofessional education: High school diploma or college degree

Program length: Several weeks

Work prerequisites: Prior experience preferable or on-the-job training

Career opportunities: Favorable

Income range: Varies considerably depending on level of responsibility (can range from $25,000 to $52,000)

Scope

Those who find it necessary to become an inpatient or resident of a hospital or other health-care facility must be appropriately processed for admission. The individual responsible for this task is known as an admitting officer or admitting clerk.

Activities

The function of an admitting officer is to walk the patient through the steps of becoming an inpatient. An admitting officer helps patients fill out the required forms and answer any questions they may have. Where a communication barrier exists, due to language or some other reason, the admitting officer communicates with a relative or friend of the patient to secure the necessary information. This may include the patient's name, address, age, any prior hospitalizations, the reason for admission, insurance information, emergency contact information, and the name of the attending physician. When a child is admitted, a parent or legal guardian needs to provide the information, fill out all the necessary forms, and authorize the transfer of the child to the institution's custody.

An important activity of the admitting officer is to make sure that the patient (or, in the case of a child, the family member) signs the hospital or health-care facility consent form. This authorizes the institution to provide routine health and medical care, such as lab tests and X rays.

Admitting officers usually are contacted by physicians' offices to schedule admissions for procedures, especially those of an elective surgical nature. They also frequently are contacted for emergency admissions. They need to alert the appropriate departments (such as obstetrics or surgery) about the admission. Another function is to mail or fax pre-admission forms and information to prospective patients.

It is essential to ensure that admitted patients receive their identification bracelets before being taken to their rooms. Arranging for an escort to take the admitted patient to his or her room is also a function of the admitting officer. The exact room and bed assignment is coordinated by the admission office with availability information provided by the nursing station.

Admitting personnel also complete relevant insurance documentation for each patient they process. Appropriate forms then need to be passed on to the institution's billing and other relevant departments.

Admitting officers may be delegated additional responsibilities, such as preparing birth certificate applications and maintaining records of deceased patients. The work schedule is usually 40 hours per week, but night and weekend shifts are common at hospitals, since admissions can take place at any time.

Work Settings

Admitting officers principally work in hospitals. However, some positions are also available in nursing homes and extended-care facilities.

Advancement

There are two basic advancement paths. You can earn a college degree and in time secure a promotion to chief admitting officer—or, if the position becomes available, even director of admissions. Alternatively, you may seek a comparable position at a more prestigious institution where you have greater responsibilities and thus receive a higher salary.

Prerequisites

Having a high school diploma is the minimum educational requirement, but having a college degree improves your advancement prospects.

Desirable personal attributes for this position are having a pleasant and outgoing personality, enjoying dealing with people on a one-to-one basis, and being courteous and polite. It's important to understand that in this position you deal with individuals who need reassurance and compassion. In addition, you need an ability to work in an organized, systematic fashion while being detail-oriented and computer-literate.

Education/Training

A high school diploma is the minimum prerequisite, and prior experience in office work is desirable. For entry-level positions, on-the-job training is usually provided. Securing an associate or college degree enhances your attractiveness to prospective employers.

Certification/Registration/Licensure

None of these requirements is applicable to this position.

Career Potential

Health-care facilities, especially hospitals, may have multiple admitting officers. Thus, entry-level positions are commonly available. To apply, send a resume with a cover letter to the personnel department of a health-care facility. You also can scan the newspaper classified ads for suitable openings.

For More Information

There is no specific organization for admitting officers. A source of information is the American Health Care Association, 1201 L St. NW, Washington, DC 20005 (www.ahca. org).

Coordinators of Health Wellness

Principal activity: Promoting wellness education in an institution and the community

Work commitment: Full-time

Preprofessional education: High school diploma

Program length: Variable

Work prerequisites: Bachelor's degree and relevant experience

Career opportunities: Highly favorable

Income range: $33,000 to $69,000

Scope

Coordinators of health wellness develop, implement, and coordinate a program emphasizing activities that further health wellness and education.

Activities

The coordinator of health wellness generally works with the director of public relations. Their goal is to use skills, knowledge, and awareness techniques to further the concept of health promotion among the hospital staff and members of the community served by the hospital or medical center.

Seeking to further health promotion requires determining community needs. When this is achieved, appropriate program development can begin. Once the program content is established, the details of implementing the plan and scheduling events can be worked out.

Various types of programs offered by the coordinator may be designed to create awareness and stimulate positive lifestyle changes. Thus, the coordinator may help create support groups for individuals with common health problems, such as alcoholism, asthma, or cancer. They meet regularly and discuss their problem and how they cope. Similarly, the coordinator may organize health fairs where individuals can have their vision, blood pressure, and weight monitored. This helps identify people with possible abnormal conditions, such as glaucoma, hypertension, and obesity. These evaluations may take place at the local health-care facility or community centers, schools, houses of worship, or even shopping centers. The coordinator may organize public lectures on health topics of general interest (such as arthritis, stroke, diabetes, and women's health) by staff specialists. The results of such outreach efforts need to be evaluated by means of surveys and questionnaires so that their effectiveness can be judged.

For continuing-education purposes, the coordinator is expected to participate in professional conferences and meetings on health wellness education. The coordinator usually reports on his or her activities to an institutional department head, such as the director of public relations, marketing, or fund-raising and development. Such a report furthers the overall efforts of such departments.

Work Settings

The principal sites of employment for a coordinator of health wellness are medical centers and large hospitals. Smaller institutions usually combine this function with that of the director of public relations. Other large health-care facilities occasionally employ someone in this position.

Advancement

There are two basic paths to advancing your career in this profession. You can secure a position in a more prestigious institution offering greater responsibilities as well as increased pay. Alternatively, with greater experience and education you can move into a higher-level position in public relations.

Prerequisites

Because you need a college degree for this position, first you must secure a high school diploma. While doing so, gaining exposure to health-care activities by volunteering at a hospital can help you become oriented to working in a health-care facility.

Desirable personal attributes for working in this position are superior verbal and written communication skills, having organized work habits (including being detail-oriented), and being outgoing. You also should be able to develop good interpersonal relations with both professionals and laypeople. In addition, you should be able to design and carry out large-scale projects involving both professionals and the public.

Education/Training

Having a bachelor's degree is a basic requirement for this position. A major in psychology, marketing, communications, public relations, or nursing is desirable. Experience in marketing, public relations, or health-care administration activities is very helpful.

Certification/Registration/Licensure

You do not need to be certified or licensed to serve in this position.

Career Potential

Employment prospects in this field are very good. Positions of this kind are found in medical centers and larger general hospitals. Smaller institutions use members of the public relations or fund-raising departments to carry out this function.

For More Information

Professionals serving as coordinators of health wellness may secure information from and ultimately membership in the American Society for Hospital Public Relations, 1 N. Franklin, Chicago, IL 60606, as well as the Society for Healthcare Strategy and Market Development (www.shsmd.org).

Directors of Hospital Public Relations

Principal activity: Promoting a favorable public image for the facility

Work commitment: Full-time

Preprofessional education: High school diploma

Program length: Variable

Work prerequisites: Bachelor's degree and experience

Career opportunities: Favorable

Income range: $40,000 to $98,000

Scope

Directors of hospital public relations enhance the facility's reputation by providing information in a manner that gives its activities the most positive image.

Activities

The specific nature of this position largely depends on the hospital's size. For small institutions, this is usually a one-person operation. Larger ones have a department with the director supervising the staff, which usually involves several individuals, each covering a specific area of responsibility. However, the director is responsible for all three aspects of the position—dealing with the press, promoting the facility's image, and public relations.

A hospital issues many nonscientific communications. These inform the community about the hospital's activities and services. They need to be written by or are put out under the oversight of the director of hospital public relations. In addition, as part of the public relations mission, special programs and activities are commonly planned, organized, and carried out. These may include general public health affairs, men's and women's health awareness events, infant and child wellness sessions, and support groups of various types. Making the public aware of such activities and securing hospital facilities and institutional personnel to participate all fall under the director's aegis.

To attract patients, it is important to bring to the public's attention special features and the unique aspects of the hospital staff and facilities. Press releases might cover physicians of prominence or those having special expertise, the start-up of new services, the acquisition of new equipment, or the enlarging of facilities. Similarly, if any staff members receive awards for their achievements, these also need to be publicized by the director.

To ensure adequate coverage of hospital activities by local newspapers and radio and TV stations, the director needs to establish personal contacts with appropriate personnel at such facilities to improve the chances of securing adequate coverage. The director needs to plan to have well-written releases, photographs, and relevant hospital personnel available for interviews. With adequate preparation and using cooperative contacts, the director can help ensure that the hospital can secure favorable coverage.

A director's success in large measure depends on the media to put the message it receives out to the public. The director must be alert to the possibility of newsworthy material being generated in the hospital. These may include performing rare and newsworthy surgery, treating a celebrity, or meeting an unusual community medical need such as treating victims of a tragedy.

While the aforementioned activities deal with external communications, the director of hospital public relations has significant responsibilities relative to in-house communications. These include producing an interhospital news bulletin to get staff to publicize their activities, preparing public relations materials for programs being sponsored by the facility, or developing material to publicize hospital activities. These actions promote health care in the community and give the director material for use by other departments, such as fund-raising, promotions, and marketing. Depending on the institution, the director is involved to varying degrees with placing ads in the media for the institution and its constituencies.

The director may be asked by the senior administration to represent the institution at public functions or at meetings with community groups and the hospital auxiliary. Supplementary activities at some institutions, particularly smaller ones, are to provide tours of the facilities to VIPs, as well as handle fund-raising, marketing, and development responsibilities.

Work Settings

Directors of hospital public relations, as the name indicates, are essentially employed in hospitals. However, other health-care institutions, such as rehabilitation centers and nursing homes, may also use their services. They perform their activities over a standard workweek but when the need arises may have to spend evenings or weekends on the job.

Advancement

There are two basic paths of advancing career in this profession. You can secure a position in a more prestigious institution offering greater responsibilities as well as increased pay. Alternatively, with greater experience and education, you can move into higher-level positions in public relations.

Prerequisites

For a career leading to a position of director of public relations, you need at the outset a high school diploma. In addition, gaining exposure to a hospital environment by working as a volunteer proves very useful.

Desirable personal attributes for working in this field are an outgoing personality, good verbal and written communication skills, and administrative knowledge of publications, layout, and graphics, including photography. Also valuable are organized work habits, attention to detail, and creative problem-solving ability.

Education/Training

At a minimum, a bachelor's degree is required to attain a director's position. It's helpful to major in communication journalism, public relations, business advertising, or English. Experience in public relations, especially at a hospital facility, is very helpful.

Certification/Registration/Licensure

None of these qualifications is necessary for this position.

Career Potential

Opportunities in this position are good overall, though prospects are obviously better in larger metropolitan areas with numerous medical facilities and media outlets.

For More Information

Several professional organizations provide information and opportunities for membership, such as the American Society for Hospital Public Relations, 1 N. Franklin, Chicago, IL 60606, the American Hospital Association (www.aha.org) and the Society for Healthcare Strategy and Market Development (www.shsmd.org).

Directors of Nursing Home Activities

Principal activity: Developing programs that enhance the quality of life of nursing home residents and those in similar long-term resident facilities

Work commitment: Full-time

Preprofessional education: High school diploma

Program length: Varies

Work prerequisites: Varies with position

Career opportunities: Favorable

Income range: $30,000 to $40,000

Scope

The goal of the director of nursing home activities is to develop and implement programs that stimulate residents' physical and mental well-being.

Activities

For the aged to be provided with a good quality of life at residential facilities, they need to occupy their time in a meaningful manner. It is the responsibility of the director of nursing home activities to develop a program to meet the clients' recreational, social, and cultural needs.

In formulating a program of activities, the director should be cognizant of the makeup of the resident population, including their capabilities and limitations. To create a realistic program, it's essential to coordinate the program with other institutional professionals, such as social workers and therapists. To meet the clients' needs, you need to know their personal interests, often learned by interviewing them and their families.

The clients' physical and mental conditions vary widely at a long-term residence facility. Many may suffer from a variety of physical and emotional ailments. Their impairment places limitations on their skills. These deficiencies result from such problems as memory loss, anxiety, depression, senility, and Alzheimer's disease. On the other hand, some people are fully alert mentally but suffer serious physical handicaps. Activities for them therefore must be designed with these limitations in mind. Creating a successful program for a diverse group of clients clearly is quite challenging. It demands creativity and planning.

To achieve this goal, the activities director needs to develop a personal rapport with each client. After a new client is admitted to the facility, the director needs to become acquainted with the person's background, interests, and physical and mental status and activities. When the evaluation is complete, a suitable program can be designed that lets the client pass the time at the facility in a pleasant manner.

In addition to generating programs for individual events, the activities director is responsible for organizing group activities. These may include lectures, entertainment, classes in painting or cooking, games, reading, and group exercises. Another important responsibility is arranging group trips. These may include visits to shopping malls, entertainment sites, parks, concerts, or shows. Additionally, the director uses client birthdays, holidays, and other auspicious dates to plan group celebrations.

By creating activities that occupy their clients' time, activity directors help maintain the clients' mental acuity. If the activity has a physical component, this is an additional benefit. Group activities also help facilitate socialization among clients at the institution. This can compensate partially for the loneliness of institutional life.

Activity directors should monitor clients' participation and note their adjustment to the facility and to fellow residents. Recording a client's level of participation is important information for other health-care providers associated with the client.

Another service frequently rendered by activity directors involves being responsible for coordinating volunteer efforts. Selecting suitable volunteers and assigning them appropriate tasks is an important function.

Work Settings

Directors of nursing home activities are essential staff members not only at nursing homes but also at other long-term facilities that care for the elderly, such as extended-care and assisted-living institutions.

Advancement

By seeking additional education and/or experience, you can attain a position at a more prestigious facility. This involves greater responsibility and remuneration.

Prerequisites

Having a high school diploma with attractive credentials is desirable for preparing to undertake advanced studies. Volunteering in a facility with a geriatric population is an asset. This includes senior centers, nursing homes, extended-care facilities, and hospitals.

Desirable personal attributes for this work are creativity, patience, tolerance, good communication skills, being eager to assist the elderly, and gaining personal satisfaction by doing so.

Education/Training

Requirements for an activities director vary. At the minimum, only a high school diploma and at least two years of experience working in a geriatric facility are required. Preferably, you should have an associate degree; ideally, a bachelor's degree is desirable. Individuals with backgrounds in social work, recreation, occupational therapy, or geriatrics are especially suited to be activities directors.

Certification/Registration/Licensure

Some states may require nursing home activities directors to be state-approved. You can seek accreditation through the National Council for Therapeutic Recreation Certification (www.nctrc.org).

Career Potential

While opportunities for employment are good, especially with the greater numbers of individuals entering such facilities, the more education and experience you have, the greater your chances of being placed.

For More Information

For additional information, contact the National Association of Activity Professionals, P.O. Box 5530, Sevierville, TN 37864 (www.thenaap.com); the National Therapeutic Recreation Society, 22377 Belmont Ridge Rd., Ashburn, VA 20148 (www.nrpa.org); or the National Council for Therapeutic Recreation Certification, 7 Elmwood Dr., New City, NY 10956 (www.nctrc.org).

Directors of Quality Assurance

Principal activity: Monitoring and enhancing institutional patient care

Work commitment: Full-time

Preprofessional education: High school diploma

Program length: Variable

Work prerequisites: Nursing or a medically related degree

Career opportunities: Favorable

Income range: Varies considerably (many earn $80,000 or more)

Scope

Directors of quality assurance monitor the quality of patient care. They also develop and implement programs that enhance patient care.

Activities

The goal of the director of quality assurance is to maximize patient care by eliminating or reducing factors that can put patients at risk. In planning an effective quality assurance program, the director must become cognizant of hospital assets and liabilities. It is essential to evaluate the effectiveness of the current quality assurance program before recommending alterations aimed at improving the level of patient care.

Quality assurance refers to a variety of tasks, including evaluating the level of medical care, the adequacy of services offered, the nature of risk management, and the adequacy of staff support. These evaluations help ensure quality patient care and thus favorable treatment outcomes. It is important to ensure that the mandated level of health-care service is maintained. Many hospital services must meet levels established by federal and state agencies. The Joint Commission on the Accreditation of Health Care Organizations and third-party payers also exert supervisory interest over the level of quality.

The director of quality assurance must remain informed about both existing and changing regulatory agency requirements relevant to health-care facilities. All agency changes sent to the institution should be brought to the director's attention. They should be evaluated and acted on. The director might need to develop new quality assurance programs or modify existing ones to ensure that the necessary standards are met. Another essential function is evaluating quality assurance programs, noting the results if any changes are made, and preparing a report of findings for senior management. The director also analyzes outside agency reviews of the institution's quality assurance programs and then institutes changes if necessary.

The director is supported by a staff and prepares and monitors the budget for departmental operations. For this position, regular weekday work hours are usual, but pressing needs such as report deadlines might necessitate overtime work.

Work Settings

The operations of health-care facilities are under the legal jurisdiction of both federal and state agencies. Thus, quality assurance personnel need to monitor compliance with current regulations. Therefore, positions as directors of quality assurance can be found in hospitals, extended-care facilities, and nursing homes.

Advancement

With increased education and/or experience, a director may become an attractive candidate for a similar position in a more prestigious institution. This involves greater responsibilities and a greater salary.

Prerequisites

To become a director of quality assurance, you need a high school diploma and some health-care service exposure as a volunteer or low-level staffer.

To work in this field, you should have good supervisory, management, and interpersonal skills, be detail-oriented, be knowledgeable about health-care facility operations, and be able to communicate well.

Education/Training

No specific educational background is required for the position of director of quality assurance, but a bachelor's degree is essential. Commonly the degree is in nursing, but it can be in some other medically related area, such as medical records. What is especially important is obtaining experience by securing an entry-level position as a staff member of a quality assurance department. Over time and with additional education, you can move up to the supervisory post of director.

Certification/Registration/Licensure

None of these requirements is mandated for this position.

Career Potential

A good number of opportunities are available in health-care facilities for directors of quality assurance. Smaller institutions may have a one-person operation rather than a fully staffed department, as large facilities such as medical centers do.

For More Information

No specific organizations exist for professionals in this field. However, for more information, write to the American Health Care Association, 1201 L St. NW, Washington, DC 20005 (www.ahca.org).

Directors of Volunteer Services

Principal activity: Coordinating the activities of institutional volunteers

Work commitment: Full-time

Preprofessional education: High school diploma

Program length: Variable

Work prerequisites: Bachelor's degree and appropriate experience

Career opportunities: Favorable

Income range: $34,000 to $49,000

Scope

Directors of volunteer services secure, train, and assign appropriate volunteers to the institution's various departments as needed.

Activities

Health-care facilities employ a wide variety of paid personnel to meet institutional needs. However, many nontechnical tasks can be ably performed by qualified volunteers. This removes some of the burden from the staff and also is financially beneficial for the institution. Such volunteers can serve in many areas and departments. Coordinating the activities of all these individuals is the responsibility of the director of volunteer services.

The range of service areas for volunteers is very broad. Among these are serving as a roving librarian, serving as a clerk in hospital admissions and other offices, and acting as a gift or coffee shop attendant. Volunteers can also be receptionists in emergency rooms, and they can reassure families of patients who are undergoing surgery and keep them updated.

The director ascertains the need for volunteers for the various segments of the institution and the nature of their responsibilities. The challenge then is to secure and place an adequate number of volunteers in the most suitable locations. To achieve such a match, the director of volunteer services needs to get to know the volunteers. This involves interviewing them to ascertain their skills, interests, backgrounds, and personalities. An in-depth evaluation is needed to be certain that a prospective volunteer is emotionally stable enough to function in a sensitive environment such as a medical facility and that he or she will act responsibly in dealing with patients and their families.

Finding the right people and properly utilizing them is one of the director's main challenges. However, before the director of volunteer services can place individuals in various institutional sites, they must be recruited and trained. Both these tasks are part of the director's responsibilities. The director needs to develop or continue an outreach program in the community that attracts suitable individuals for volunteer service. The hospital's auxiliary (if one exists) can further the recruitment effort. Another potential source of volunteers is teenagers. The director can enlist them by organizing special recruitment meetings and speaking at high schools and colleges, emphasizing the value of volunteer service as a maturing experience and possible career enhancement opportunity.

To fulfill his or her mission, the director must become familiar with the need for volunteers in all the institution's departments and service areas. In addition, the director needs to identify the specific duties and responsibilities that are assigned in each unit and the optimal number of individuals needed. The director also orients volunteers to their obligations and duties.

Work Settings

Directors of volunteer services are predominantly employed in hospitals and medical centers, but other health-care institutions such as large nursing homes and extended care facilities may also use volunteers. Directors can facilitate health-care efforts on behalf of their clients. Thus, positions for directors of volunteer services may be available in some non-hospital health-care institutions, enhancing employment possibilities.

Advancement

You can advance in this position by securing a job in a more prestigious health-care institution, where you will have greater responsibilities and increased pay.

Prerequisites

You should have a high school diploma and, if possible, an associate degree, with some prior work experience, preferably in a health-care field.

Desirable personal attributes for this type of position include having good organizational and communication skills. You should be personable, good with details, a good judge of character, and a natural problem solver. Being a good public speaker is also valuable.

Education/Training

While requirements may vary, holding a bachelor's degree is essential. Useful majors include psychology, sociology, and marketing. Experience working in a health-care facility and securing administrative and supervisory experience are desirable.

Certification/Registration/Licensure

There is no need to meet any of these requirements in this position.

Career Potential

Employment prospects for work in this field are good overall. With the rising cost of health care, many facilities will look to volunteer staff to fill crucial roles. Positions are available at medical centers, hospitals, mental health facilities, psychiatric hospitals, extended-care facilities, and nursing homes. To find positions, you can check newspaper classified ads and institutional personnel offices.

For More Information

This field has no professional organization. For more information, write to the American Health Care Association, 1201 L St. NW, Washington, DC 20005 (www.ahca.org).

Geriatric Care Managers

Principal activity: Facilitating daily living activities of elderly clients

Work commitment: Part- or full-time

Preprofessional education: High school diploma

Program length: 4 to 6 years

Work prerequisites: Bachelor's degree or higher

Career opportunities: Favorable

Income range: $37,000 to $61,000

Scope

Geriatric care managers provide a wide range of assistance to elderly clients in their daily lives so that they can maintain their physical and emotional well-being.

Activities

Geriatric care managers help fill the void in the lives of seniors having difficulty caring for themselves at home. Their responsibilities vary depending on the client's needs.

The activities of a geriatric care manager include checking up on clients at their homes on a regular basis to make sure that they are well and living properly. This includes seeing if they have and are taking their required medications, determining if they are regularly visiting their physician, finding out if they have adequate and suitable amounts of food, seeing if they are eating regularly and adequately, and are maintaining an orderly and sanitary home.

The elderly sometimes require the help of various health-care professionals to meet their needs. Thus, geriatric care managers may have to arrange for their clients' appointments with physicians, dentists, and therapists. Moreover, they also ensure that the client has suitable transportation to the appointment.

In addition, clients may need assistance from social service agencies. The geriatric care manager is responsible for determining which agency can fill a specific need. It may be necessary to secure and fill out forms for the client so that services may be obtained. Such services may include housekeeping assistance, transportation, and securing health-care coverage through Medicare or Medicaid.

Frequently, geriatric care managers need to make sure that routine household expenses are paid in order to maintain essential services. It is not uncommon for them to arrange for payment of personal, medical, and household bills. Occasionally the geriatric care manager may also need to accompany the client on shopping trips for food, clothing, and other essentials.

Work Settings

Support of elderly clients usually takes place in their homes. Geriatric care services may also be provided in nursing homes and extended-care facilities. Geriatric care managers are engaged by the client's adult children or another close relative who is concerned with the client's well-being but who cannot provide the assistance needed. When the geriatric care manager is self-employed, he or she is hired directly. Otherwise, the manager may be engaged through a home care agency, private geriatric care management company, hospital, or social service office.

Advancement

To advance your position and enhance your income, you can become self-employed and develop a large client base, or you can join a more prestigious home care organization to increase your employment potential.

Prerequisites

Having a college degree is a basic necessity. Majoring in business, psychology, gerontology, or social work is advisable.

Desirable personal attributes for work in this field include a strong sense of compassion (especially for the elderly), an ability to communicate, patience, tolerance, organizational skills, and attention to detail. Having some bookkeeping or accounting skills and creativity (to help you solve unexpected problems) is quite advantageous.

Education/Training

There are no established educational requirements for the position of geriatric care manager. A college degree is essential, however, and some positions require a master's degree. This advanced degree may be in business administration, gerontology, social work, or psychology. Where work involves dealing with wealthy clients, having a law or accounting degree is most useful. Experience working as a volunteer with the elderly in hospitals, nursing homes, or extended-care facilities is especially useful.

Certification/Registration/Licensure

Some states require that geriatric care managers be certified or licensed. Those who oversee their clients' financial assets may need to be bonded.

Career Potential

Employment growth for geriatric care managers is expected to be better than average over the next decade. Positions should be available at mental-health facilities, psychiatric hospitals, extended-care facilities, rehabilitation centers, and nursing homes. To find positions, you can check newspaper classifieds and institutional personnel offices.

For More Information

The professional organization for this field is the National Association of Professional Geriatric Care Managers, 1604 N. Country Club Rd., Tucson, AZ 85716 (www.caremanager.org).

Affiliated Health-Care Careers: Medical Scientists, Educators, and Information Workers

A wide variety of careers are affiliated with the health-care industry. These responsible and challenging positions are of great value to physicians, dentists, and other diagnosing and treating practitioners. The activities of affiliated health-care professionals have a direct impact on patients' lives and well-being. In some cases, these professions involve public health and preventive medicine, and in others they may be of direct benefit to sick patients. Some careers involve the continuing education of practitioners and furthering the study of health-related knowledge and information.

The wide-ranging nature of the professions discussed in this chapter is reflected in the significant differences in their educational requirements. The job prerequisites range from a high school diploma to a professional degree, and each career demands its own skills. The diversity of occupational opportunities makes this chapter especially valuable if you haven't found a suitable occupation in any of the other five major areas.

Biomedical Engineers

Principal activity: Designing and testing biomedical products for safety and effectiveness

Work commitment: Usually full-time

Preprofessional education: High school diploma or its equivalent

Program length: 4 to 8 years

Work prerequisites: Bachelor's degree; master's or doctorate preferred

Career opportunities: Highly favorable

Income range: $59,000 to $99,000

Scope

Biomedical engineers convert ideas into products and develop solutions to technical problems presented by physicians, dentists, scientists, and other health-care specialists. The problems may be mechanical, electrical, chemical, or a combination of these and thus are wide-ranging. The heart-lung bypass machine, pacemaker, laser, ultrasound, and nuclear imaging equipment are examples of products developed by biomedical engineers in collaboration with physicians. The consequences of their work have been enormous for both diagnostic and therapeutic aspects of medicine and dentistry. Efforts by bioengineers not only have been life-saving but also have improved the quality of people's lives.

Activities

Because biomedical problems are so variable, the nature of the engineer's work is multifaceted, encompassing divergent specialties. These generally fall into one of four groups:

- **General bioengineering** involves applying engineering principles to understanding the anatomy and physiology of the normal and diseased body. This area is concerned with enhancing the biological environment by ridding it of pollutants.
- **Clinical engineering** uses engineering principles and technological advances to enhance health-care delivery systems, including testing and upkeep of medical equipment and training staff in their proper use.
- **Medical engineering** involves developing biomaterials, diagnostic and therapeutic instruments, and devices needed in both patient care and research.
- **Rehabilitation engineering** concerns the design of devices for people with disabilities.

Work Settings

Bioengineers work at universities, research centers, industrial laboratories, and government facilities.

Advancement

Advancement comes from securing a graduate degree (master's or doctorate) or by demonstrating supervisory or management potential.

Prerequisites

A high school diploma or its equivalent is needed to enroll in a college bioengineering program. For many jobs, a master's or doctorate degree is necessary. Students who are considering this field should take classes in mathematics (including algebra, trigonometry, precalculus, and calculus), biology, chemistry, physics, computers, and a foreign language.

Desirable attributes include inventiveness, abstract thinking skills, analytical skills, and problem-solving ability. Personal qualities important for this field include patience, determination, a positive work attitude, and good verbal and written communication skills.

Education/Training

Entry-level positions in bioengineering require a bachelor's degree from an accredited program. Undergraduate courses that are commonly offered for majors in this field include biomedical engineering systems and design, biomedical computers, bioinstrumentation, engineering, biophysics, biothermodynamics, biotransport, and artificial organs and limbs.

Graduate-level programs are more numerous than undergraduate ones. A graduate degree is necessary for senior or teaching appointments. Those with traditional undergraduate engineering degrees have the option of securing a graduate degree in bioengineering and entering the field by this means.

Certification/Registration/Licensure

Certification is available for those in clinical engineering through the International Certification Commission for Clinical Engineering and Biomedical Technology. To become certified you need an engineering degree and three years of hospital-based experience in the specialty, and you must complete a five-hour written and oral exam.

Career Potential

The very favorable career opportunities in this field are expected to continue for next decade. In fact, it is expected to be one of the fastest growing professions in an already-in-demand market. In addition to the standard outlets needing their services, the demands for these specialists for work in the area of homeland security has significantly increased.

For More Information

The professional organization for this field is the Biomedical Engineering Society, 8401 Corporate Dr., Ste. 225, Landover, MD 20785 (www.bmes.org).

Program accreditation is provided by the Accreditation Board for Engineering and Technology, 111 Market Place, Ste. 1050, Baltimore, MD 21202 (www.abet.org).

Biomedical Engineering Programs

Alabama
University of Alabama at
  Birmingham
1530 3rd Ave. S.
Birmingham, AL 35294
ww.uab.edu

Arizona
Arizona State University
Tempe, AZ 85287
www.asu.edu

California
California State University
6000 J St.
Sacramento, CA 95819
www.csus.edu

University of California, Berkeley
Berkeley, CA 94720
www.berkeley.edu

University of California, Davis
One Shields Ave.
Davis, CA 95616
www.ucdavis.edu

University of California, San
  Diego
9500 Gilman Dr.
La Jolla, CA 92093
www.ucsd.edu

University of California, San Francisco
Graduate Program in Biological
  and Medical Informatics
Genentech Hall, Room 524
Mission Bay Campus
600 16th St.
San Francisco, CA 94143
www.bmi.ucsf.edu

University of Southern California
McClintock Avenue
Ollin Hall of Engineering
Los Angeles, CA 90089
www.usc.edu

Colorado
Colorado State University
Biomedical Engineering
1040 Campus Delivery
Fort Collins, CO 80423
www.colostate.edu

Connecticut
Trinity College
300 Summit St.
Hartford, CT 06106
www.trincoll.edu

University of Connecticut
Storrs, CT 06269
www.uconn.edu

District of Columbia
Catholic University of America
620 Michigan Ave. NE
Washington, DC 20064
www.cua.edu

Florida
Florida State University
College of Engineering
2525 Pottsdamer Street
Talahassee, FL 32310
www.eng.fsu.edu

University of Miami
Coral Gables, FL 33124
www.miami.edu

University of South Florida
4202 E. Fowler Ave., FAC 174
Tampa, FL 33620
www.eng.usf.edu

Georgia
Georgia Tech College of
  Engineering
Emory University School of
  Medicine
Atlanta, GA 30332
www.bme.gatech.edu

Mercer University
1400 Coleman Ave.
Macon, GA 31207
www.mercer.edu

Illinois
Northwestern University
633 Clark St.
Evanston, IL 60208
www.northwestern.edu

University of Illinois at Chicago
Chicago, IL 60612
www.uic.edu

Indiana
Purdue University
1146 ABE Building
West Lafayette, IN 47907
www.purdue.edu

Iowa
University of Iowa
Iowa City, IA 52242
www.uiowa.edu

Kentucky
University of Kentucky
Lexington, KY 40506
www.uky.edu

Louisiana
Louisiana Tech University
P.O. Box 3178
Ruston, LA 71272
www.latech.edu

Tulane University
New Orleans, LA 70118
www.eng.tulane.edu

Maine
University of Maine
5782 Winslow Hall
Orono, ME 04469
www.maine.edu

Maryland
Johns Hopkins University
School of Engineering
120 New Engineering Building
3400 N. Charles St.
Baltimore, MD 21218
www.jhu.edu

University of Maryland
College Park, MD 20742
www.umd.edu

Massachusetts
Boston University
One Sherborn St.
Boston, MA 02215
www.bu.edu

Massachusetts Institute of
  Technology
Cambridge, MA 02139
http://web.mit.edu/

Tufts University
Science and Technology Center
4 Colby St.
Medford, MA 02155
www.tufts.edu

University of Massachusetts
  Medical School
Graduate School of Biomedical
  Sciences
55 Lake Ave. N.
Worcester, MA 01655
www.umassmed.edu

Western New England College
1215 Wilbraham Rd.
Springfield, MA 01119
www.wnec.edu

Worcester Polytechnic Institute
100 Institute Rd.
Worcester, MA 01609
www.wpi.edu

Michigan
University of Michigan
Ann Arbor, MI 48109
www.umich.edu

Wayne State University
College of Engineering
5050 Anthony Wayne Dr.
Detroit, MI 48202
www.eng.wayne.edu

Minnesota
University of Minnesota
1117 University Dr.
Duluth, MN 55812
www.d.umn.edu

Mississippi
Mississippi State University
James Worth Bagley College of
Engineering
P O Box 9632
Mississippi, MS 39762
www.msstate.edu

Missouri
Washington University in
St. Louis
Campus Box 1097
1 Brookings Dr.
St. Louis, MO 63130
www.wustl.edu

Nevada
University of Nevada-Reno
Biomedical Engineering
Reno, NV 89667
www.unr.edu

New Jersey
Rutgers, The State University of
New Jersey
98 Brett Rd.
Piscataway, NJ 08854
www.rutgers.edu

New York
College of Staten Island
City University of New York
Department of Biology
2800 Victory Blvd.
Staten Island, NY 10314
www.csi.cuny.edu

Columbia University
Department of Biomedical
Engineering
351 Engineering Terrace,
Mail Code 8904
1210 Amsterdam Ave.
New York, NY 10027
www.bme.columbia.edu

Cornell University
College of Engineering
Carpenter Hall
Ithaca, NY 14853
www.engineering.cornell.edu

Hofstra University
Hempstead, NY 11549
www.hofstra.edu

Rensselaer Polytechnic Institute
110 8th St.
Troy, NY 12180
www.rpi.edu

Syracuse University
223 Link Hall
Syracuse, NY 13244
www.ecs.syr.edu

University of Rochester
Rochester, NY 14627
www.rochester.edu

North Carolina
Duke University
Durham, NC 27708
www.duke.edu

North Carolina State University
Raleigh, NC 27695
www.ncsu.edu

University of North Carolina at
Chapel Hill
Chapel Hill, NC 27599
www.unc.edu

North Dakota
North Dakota State University
1301 12th Ave. N.
Fargo, ND 58105
www.ndsu.nodak.edu

Ohio
Case Western Reserve University
10900 Euclid Ave.
Cleveland, OH 44106
www.cwru.edu

Ohio State University
Columbus, OH 43210
www.osu.edu

University of Cincinnati
2624 Clifton Ave.
Cincinnati, OH 45221
www.uc.edu

University of Toledo
College of Engineering
Toledo, OH 43606
www.eng.utoledo.edu

Wright State University
Fairborn, OH 45435
www.wright.edu

Pennsylvania
Allegheny College
520 N. Main
Meadville, PA 16335
www.allegheny.edu

Carnegie Mellon University
5000 Forbes Ave.
Pittsburgh, PA 15213
www.cmu.edu

Drexel University
3141 Chestnut St.
Philadelphia, PA 19104
www.drexel.edu

Pennsylvania State University
College of Medicine
Biomedical Engineering
Institute
500 University Dr.
Hershey, PA 17033
www.psu.edu

Pennsylvania State University
University Park Campus
University Park, PA 16802
www.psu.edu

University of Pennsylvania
3451 Walnut St.
Philadelphia, PA 19104
www.upenn.edu

University of Pittsburgh at
Johnstown
450 School House Rd.
Johnstown, PA 15904
www.pitt.edu

South Carolina
Clemson University
Clemson, SC 29634
www.clemson.edu

Tennessee
University of Memphis
Herff College of Engineering
Biomedical Engineering
Rm 330, Engineering Technology
Memphis, TN 38152
www.memphis.edu

Vanderbilt University
2201 West End Ave.
Nashville, TN 37235
www.vanderbilt.edu

Texas
Baylor College of Medicine
One Baylor Plaza
Houston, TX 77030
www.bcm.edu

Rice University
Bioengineering
6100 Main St.
Houston, TX 77005
www.rice.edu

Texas A&M University
College Station, TX 77843
www.tamu.edu

University of Texas at Arlington
701 S. Nedderman Dr.
Arlington, TX 76019
www.uta.edu

University of Texas at Austin
Austin, TX 78712
www.utexas.edu

Utah
University of Utah
50 So. Central Campus Dr.
Salt Lake City, UT 84112
www.utah.edu

Vermont
University of Vermont
Burlington, VT 05405
www.uvm.edu

Virginia
College of William and Mary
Applied Science
P.O. Box 8795
Williamsburg, VA 23187
www.wm.edu

University of Virginia
Charlottesville, VA 22906
www.virginia.edu

Virginia Commonwealth University
Richmond, VA 23284
www.vcu.edu

Virginia Tech
308 Seitz Hall
Blacksburg, VA 24061
www.vt.edu

Washington
University of Washington
309 HHL, Box 357962
Seattle, WA 98195
www.washington.edu

Wisconsin
Marquette University
P.O. Box 1881
Milwaukee, WI 53201
www.mu.edu

Milwaukee School of Engineering
1025 N. Broadway
Milwaukee, WI 53202
www.msoe.edu

Wyoming
University of Wyoming
1000 E. University Ave.
Laramie, WY 82071
www.uwyo.edu

Biomedical Equipment Technicians

Principal activity: Maintaining biomedical equipment

Work commitment: Full-time

Preprofessional education: High school diploma

Program length: 1 to 4 years; usually 2 years

Work prerequisites: Associate degree

Career opportunities: Favorable

Income range: $31,000 to $60,000

Scope

One of the most significant medical events in the past several decades was the introduction of a continuous stream of innovative instruments and devices that have had a profound impact on improving medical care. Biomedical engineers have used technologies such as lasers, ultrasound, computers, and nuclear science to develop sophisticated diagnostic and treatment equipment. Consequently, a wide range of instruments are in use at medical centers, hospitals, and even small clinics. These include advanced EKG machines, dialysis units, complex incubators for premature infants, and mammoth computerized axial tomography (CAT) scanners. To be effective, instruments must be safe to use, accurate in their operation and readings, and properly employed to produce reliable and optimal benefits. The people who maintain the equipment at medical facilities are biomedical equipment technicians (BMETs).

Activities

Biomedical equipment technicians have many different responsibilities at the facilities they serve. They install the equipment, calibrate it so that its readings and operation are reliable, train the personnel who will be working with it, and do preventive maintenance and repairs when necessary. They may also be called on to evaluate equipment that is being considered for purchase.

Work Settings

These skilled technicians are employed by medical centers, large hospitals, medical schools, research institutions, biomedical equipment manufacturers, service maintenance companies, and government agencies.

Advancement

Being promoted through the four levels of biomedical equipment technician ranks (BMET 1–4) enhances your status:

- A BMET-1 is an entry-level worker who does supervised routine maintenance, safety checks, and repairs.
- A BMET-2 has several years of experience and works independently, doing maintenance and repair work.
- A BMET-3 has significant education and training and can perform challenging assignments requiring great skill.
- A BMET supervisor works under a department head or hospital supervisor and oversees the activities of the lower-grade technicians.

Prerequisites

A high school diploma or its equivalent is necessary to enter this field. Course work should include algebra, trigonometry, physics, biology, and chemistry. Computer, electronics, and shop courses are especially helpful.

Desirable personal attributes include a strong interest in technology, superior eye-hand coordination and vision, aptitude for precise and meticulous work, patience, and the ability to respond quickly to unforeseen problems.

Education/Training

Two educational routes are available to those entering this field:

- Formal biomedical equipment technician programs are offered by vocational-technical schools, community colleges, and even universities. Most award an associate degree after two years, and some offer a bachelor's degree. These programs provide practical experience at assigned hospitals or labs. A typical program includes courses in biology, chemistry, anatomy, physiology, medical terminology, mathematics, electronics, and computers.
- You can earn an associate degree from a college offering an A.S. in electronics and then secure on-the-job training. However, you are at a disadvantage when attaining a position using this alternative route.

Certification/Registration/Licensure

Before taking the General Biomedical Equipment Certification Examination, candidates must have four years of experience, or three years of experience and an associate degree in electronic technology, or two years of experience and an associate degree in biomedical technology. Specialty examinations for certification in the areas of clinical laboratory equipment and radiology equipment also are possible.

Career Potential

With the rapid increase in the use of biomedical equipment, the need for technicians is strong, so the employment outlook is favorable for the foreseeable future.

For More Information

The professional organization for this field is the Junior Engineering Technology Society, 1420 King St., Ste. 405, Alexandria, VA 22314 (www.jets.org).

For more information, contact the Association for the Advancement of Medical Instrumentation, 1110 N. Glebe Rd., Ste. 220, Arlington, VA 22201 (www.aami.org).

Biomedical Equipment Technician Programs

Alabama
Community College of the Air
  Force
Maxwell Air Force Base
130 W. Maxwell Blvd.
Montgomery, AL 36112
www.au.af.mil/au/ccaf/

Faulkner State Community College
1900 Hwy. 31 S.
Bay Minette, AL 36507
www.faulknerstate.edu

Jefferson State Community
  College
2601 Carson Rd.
Birmingham, AL 35215
www.jscc.cc.al.us

University of Alabama
Kirklin Clinic
2000 6th Ave. S.
Birmingham, AL 35233
www.uab.edu

Wallace Community College
3000 Earl Goodwin Pkwy.
Selma, AL 36707
www.wccs.edu

Arkansas
Arkansas State University–Beebe
P.O. Box 1000
Beebe, AR 72012
www.asub.edu

California
Cerritos College
11110 Alondra Blvd.
Norwalk, CA 90650
www.cerritos.edu

Napa Valley College
2277 Napa-Vallejo Hwy.
Napa, CA 94558
www/napavalley.edu

Santa Barbara City College
721 Cliff Dr.
Santa Barbara, CA 93109
www.sbcc.edu

Colorado
Aims Community College
5401 W 20 Street
Greeley, CO 80634
www.aims.edu

Colorado College
14 E. Cache La Poudre St.
Colorado Springs, CO 80903
www.coloradocollege.edu

Connecticut
Connecticut AHEC Program
University of Connecticut School
  of Medicine
263 Farmington Avenue
MC 2928
Farmington, CT. 06030
www.uchc.edu

Gateway Community College
60 Sargeant Drive
New Haven, CT. 06511
www.gwtc.commnet.edu

Delaware
Delaware Technical & Community
  College
400 Stanton-Christiana Rd.
Newark, DE 19713
www.dtcc.edu

Florida
Florida Community College at
  Jacksonville
501 W. State St.
Jacksonville, FL 32202
www.fccj.edu

MedVance Institute
Biomedical Technician
W Palm Beach Campus
1630 South Congress Avenue
Palm Springs, FL 33461
www.medvance.edu

Georgia
Dekalb Technical College
495 N. Indian Creek Dr.
Clarkston, GA 30021
www.dekalb.edu

Illinois
Oakton Community College
1600 E. Golf Rd.
Des Plaines, IL 60016
www.oakton.edu

South Suburban College
15800 S. State St.
South Holland, IL 60473
www.southsuburbancollege.edu

Indiana
Ivy Tech Community College
4301 S. Cowan Rd.
Muncie, IN 47302
www.ivytech.edu

Iowa
Des Moines Area Community
 College
2006 S. Ankeny Blvd.
Ankeny, IA 50021
www.dmacc.edu

Kansas
Johnson County Community
 College
12345 College Blvd.
Overland Park, KS 66210
www.jccc.edu

Kansas City Community College
7250 State Ave.
Kansas City, KS 66112
www.kckcc.edu

Kentucky
Madisonville Community College
2000 College Dr.
Madisonville, KY 42431
www.madcc.kctcs.edu

Louisiana
Delgado Community College
615 City Park Ave.
New Orleans, LA 70119
www.dcc.edu

Maryland
Howard University
10901 Little Patuxent Pkwy.
Columbia, MD 21044
www.howard.edu

Massachusetts
Berkshire Community College
1350 West St.
Pittsfield, MA 01201
www.berkshirecc.edu

Springfield Technical Community
 College
1 Armory Square
Springfield, MA 01102
www.stcc.edu

Michigan
Lansing Community College
P.O. Box 40010
Lansing, MI 48901
www.lcc.edu

Muskegon Community College
221 S. Quarterline Rd.
Muskegon, MI 49442
www.muskegoncc.edu

Schoolcraft College
18600 Hagerty Rd.
Livonia, MI 48152
www.schoolcraft.edu

Minnesota
Anoka Technical College
1355 W. Hwy. 10
Anoka, MN 55303
www.anoka.edu

Missouri
St. Louis Community College
Forest Park
5600 Oakland
St. Louis, MO 63110
www.stlcc.edu

New Jersey
County College of Morris
214 Center Grove Rd.
Randolph, NJ 07869
www.ccm.edu

New Jersey Institute of
 Technology
University Heights
Newark, NJ 07102
www.njit.edu

New York
Erie Community College
4041 Southwestern Blvd.
Orchard Park, NY 14127
www.ecc.edu

Farmingdale State University of
 New York
Route 110
2350 Broadhollow Rd.
Farmingdale, NY 11735
www.farmingdale.edu

North Carolina
Alamance Community College
1247 Jimmie Kerr Rd.
I-85/I-40 Exit 150
P.O. Box 8000
Graham, NC 27253
www.alamance.edu

Caldwell Community College &
 Technical Institute
2855 Hickory Blvd.
Hudson, NC 28638
www.cccti.edu

Stanly Community College
141 College Dr.
Albemarle, NC 28001
www.stanly.edu

Ohio
Air Force Institute of Technology
Wright Patterson AFB
2950 P St.
Dayton, OH 45433
www.afit.edu

Cincinnati State Technical &
 Community College
3520 Central Pkwy.
Cincinnati, OH 45223
www.cincinnatistate.edu

Cuyahoga Community College
700 Carnegie Ave.
Cleveland, OH 44115
www.tri-c.edu

Kettering College of Medical Arts
3737 Southern Blvd.
Kettering, OH 45429
www.kcma.edu

North Central State College
2441 Kenwood Circle
Mansfield, OH 44906
www.ncstatecollege.edu

Owens Community College
P.O. Box 10000
Toledo, OH 43699
www.owens.edu

Pennsylvania
Delaware County Community
  College
901 S. Media Line Rd.
Media, PA 19063
www.dccc.edu

Johnson College
3427 N. Main Ave.
Scranton, PA 18508
www.johnsoncollege.com

Lehigh Carbon Community College
4525 Education Park Dr.
Schnecksville, PA 18078
www.lccc.edu

Penn State University–DuBois
College Place
DuBois, PA 15801
www.ds.psu.edu

Penn State University–Greater
  Allegheny
University Drive
McKeesport, PA 15132
www.mk.psu.edu

Penn State University–
  New Kensington
3550 7th St. Rd.
New Kensington, PA 15068
www.nk.psu.edu

Tennessee
East Tennessee State University
Box 70267
Johnson City, TN 37614
www.etsu.edu

Texas
Houston Community College
3100 Main
Houston, TX 77002
www.hccs.edu

Southwestern Medical Center
At Dallas
5323 Harry Hines Blvd.
Dallas, TX 75390
www.utsouthwestern.edu

St. Philip's College
1801 Martin Luther King Dr.
San Antonio, TX 78203
www.alamo.edu/spc/

Texas A & M University
233 Zachry Engineering Center
3120 Tamu
College Station, TX 77843
www.tamu.edu

Texas State Technical College–
  Harlingen
1902 North Loop 499
Harlingen, TX 78550
www.harlingen.tstc.edu

Texas State Technical College–
  Marshall
2650 East End Blvd. South
Marshall, TX 75671
www. marsahll.tstc.edu

Texas State Technical College–
  Waco
3801 Campus Dr.
Waco, TX 76705
www.waco.tstc.edu

University of Texas–Austin
ENS 610
Austin, TX 78712
www.utexas.edu

Virginia
ECPI College of Technology
5555 Greenwich Rd.
Virginia Beach, VA 23462
www.ecpi.edu

Washington
North Seattle Community College
9600 College Way N.
Seattle, WA 98103
www.northseattle.edu

Spokane Community College
1810 N. Greene St.
Spokane, WA 99217
www.scc.spokane.edu

Wisconsin
Milwaukee Area Technical College
700 W. State St.
Milwaukee, WI 53233
www.milwaukee.tec.wi.us

Western Wisconsin Technical
  College
304 6th St. N.
La Crosse, WI 54601
www.western.tec.wi.us

Biomedical Photographers

Principal activity: Preparing photographs for medical records, educational, and research purposes

Work commitment: Full-time

Preprofessional education: High school diploma

Program length: 2 to 4 years

Work prerequisites: Associate or bachelor's degree

Career opportunities: Favorable

Income range: $28,000 to $55,000

Scope

Biomedical photographers are skilled professionals who help biologists, researchers, and others establish documentary records of their work. They must be skilled in all aspects of photography.

Activities

Biomedical photographers must be prepared to work with both living and nonliving subjects. They may be called on to make simple prints of charts, graphs, and transparencies or to carry out more complex tasks, such as producing motion pictures of complex activities, making videotapes or digitized images for teaching, or making presentations at scientific meetings. The work of these specialists may involve photorecording a patient's medical condition over an extended period to keep track of changes. They may take motion pictures during operations or autopsies. At other times, they might be asked to make images of tissues seen under a microscope.

With the capacity of computers to enhance the quality of images, biomedical photographers have a host of new tools at their disposal. Understanding changing technology is essential for those in this profession.

Work Settings

Biomedical photographers work in medical centers, medical schools, and research institutes. Some also work for dental and veterinary schools, pharmaceutical companies, museums, and government agencies. Some biomedical photographers are self-employed, offering their services on a freelance basis.

Advancement

In a large department, a photographer can move into a supervisory post. Advancement also comes through specializing in such areas as cinematography, microphotography, pathological photography, or ophthalmic photography.

Prerequisites

A high school diploma or its equivalent is necessary to enter an educational program in this field.

Desirable personal attributes include patience, manual dexterity, a strong interest in photography, good communication skills, and the ability to work under pressure and time constraints.

Education/Training

In the past, on-the-job training at a teaching hospital was the standard route to an entry-level position as a photographic technician. Today, however, candidates should complete at least a two-year associate degree program at a school that offers a biological photography program. Another approach is to combine a two-year college program with two years of commercial photography education or on-the-job training.

The Biological Photographic Association offers several short training programs.

Certification/Registration/Licensure

Biomedical photographers can attain certification by passing written, practical, and oral examinations. Certified professionals are called registered biological photographers

(RBPs), which is accepted as evidence of competency in the field. Certification is useful but not essential for securing employment.

Career Potential

The overall employment prospects in this field are positive due to the enormous growth of the health-care industry. The demands of educational and research institutions are growing, as are the needs of museums, publishers, and related industries. Technological advances have created a greater need for specialized personnel.

For More Information

The professional organization for this field is the Biocommunications Association, 220 Southwind Ln., Hillsborough, NC 27278 (www.bca.org).

Biomedical Writers

Principal activity: Preparing written materials on health-related issues

Work commitment: Part- or full-time

Preprofessional education: High school diploma or its equivalent

Program length: 4 years

Work prerequisites: Bachelor's degree

Career opportunities: Favorable

Income range: $47,000 to $79,000

Scope

Biomedical communications is a broad field, covering health materials in print, on the radio, and on television. A biomedical writer may spend the day writing advertising copy, a script for a radio program, or a TV documentary. These writers convey complex information to people in a simple format they can understand.

Activities

Biomedical writers have the challenging job of writing about medical matters so that people outside the medical field can comprehend them. To do this, they must understand, analyze, interpret, and accurately write about some very complex subjects.

They may prepare sales brochures or instruction manuals for new diagnostic and treatment equipment, write announcements of new medical findings by pharmaceutical companies, draft scripts for radio and television shows on health issues, or write articles for newspapers, magazines, or exhibits. The most successful medical writers have their own regular or syndicated columns.

Work Settings

Biomedical writers are employed by publishers of newspapers, magazines, and textbooks; pharmaceutical and medical equipment companies; medical centers and major hospitals; professional health-care organizations and volunteer health agencies; advertising agencies; and radio and TV stations.

Advancement

Advancement in this field comes from moving to specialty areas, where salaries are higher, or by joining the staff of a larger organization. Earning a master's degree or an advanced certificate from the American Medical Writers' Association also can be helpful.

Prerequisites

A high school diploma or its equivalent is needed to begin studies in this field.

Desirable personal attributes include an interest in writing and in the medical field; good interviewing, research, and interpersonal skills; and the ability to work under deadline pressure.

Education/Training

The basic requirement for entering this field is a bachelor's degree with the appropriate courses and skills. Some positions require a master's degree. Undergraduates should major in English or journalism and minor in the biological sciences. Computer proficiency is mandatory.

Certification/Registration/Licensure

The American Medical Writers' Association offers continuing-education courses at its annual conference and at regional and chapter workshop meetings. These courses are based on a core curriculum to improve skills in six relevant areas: editing, writing, audiovisual work, public relations and advertising, freelancing, and teaching. A certificate is awarded on completion of each of these courses. An advanced certificate is offered to eligible candidates who complete eight in-depth courses.

Career Potential

The overall employment outlook in this field is better than average. In recent decades people have become much more health-conscious, requiring access to more medical information. In addition, radio and TV now devote more time to health-related issues. Pharmaceutical and research companies also actively seek talented research writers. Nevertheless, competition for high-paying positions is quite stiff.

For More Information

The professional organization for this field is the American Medical Writers Association, 40 W. Gude Dr., Ste. 101, Rockville, MD 20850 (www.amwa.org).

Biomedical Writing Programs

Many colleges and universities offer courses in biomedical or technical communications—far too many to list here. A few also offer master's degree programs. For a list of programs in your area, contact the American Medical Writers Association at the address just listed or visit their Web site.

Certified Athletic Trainers

Principal activity: Supervising athletes' physical well-being

Work commitment: Part- or full-time

Preprofessional education: High school diploma

Program length: 4 years

Work prerequisites: Bachelor's degree and certification

Career opportunities: Highly favorable

Income range: $32,000 to $49,000

Scope

Specialists in this field are educated and trained to identify and evaluate sports injuries, provide prompt treatment to injured athletes, and determine whether further medical care is needed. They also develop and implement injury-prevention programs, teach about health care, and supervise athletic training programs.

Activities

Athletic trainers provide initial care for injured athletes, protect them from further trauma, and ensure that appropriate medical treatment is provided when necessary. They work in collaboration with and under the direction of the supervising institutional physician. Trainers ensure that the athletes understand and follow the physician's instructions and wear appropriate protective gear during team activities. They also work with coaches to make sure that athletes are in shape or have adequately recovered from injuries before returning to limited or full sports activities.

Work Settings

Certified athletic trainers are employed at physical-fitness centers, at gyms, at health-club facilities, and by professional sports organizations and clubs as well as private individuals seeking to improve their athletic performance or physical fitness.

Advancement

A trainer can advance by earning a higher degree and by gaining additional professional experience.

Prerequisites

A high school diploma or its equivalent is essential for entering a training program. Students should take biology, chemistry, and physics as well as first aid. If possible, they should secure some experience as coaches or team captains.

Desirable personal attributes include an interest in both athletics and health care, good hygiene, good communication skills, and an understanding of and tolerance for human limitations. Trainers also must be able to relate well to people and inspire them.

Education/Training

Trainers must earn a college degree in an accredited program. This includes courses in human anatomy and physiology, kinesiology, physiology of exercise, psychology, nutrition, personal and community health, first aid (including CPR), physical education, coaching, and athletic training. A mandatory part of the program is gaining extensive field experience.

A limited number of graduate programs lead to a master's or doctoral degree. These require advanced-level courses in the subjects just listed.

Certification/Registration/Licensure

Certification is a requirement for professional success in this field. To be certified by the National Athletic Trainers' Association, candidates must earn a college degree with the appropriate course of studies and secure 800 hours of experience. In addition, they must pass a three-part exam that evaluates basic knowledge, clinical skills, and decision-making abilities. Continuing-education courses are required to maintain accredited status. Some states also require a license for trainers.

Career Potential

Strong employment opportunities are anticipated in this field. The increased interest in athletics is stimulating opportunities, the majority of them at high schools, where athletic trainers frequently combine teaching with their training activities.

For More Information

The professional organization for this field is the National Athletic Trainers' Association, 2952 Stemmons Freeway, Dallas, TX 75247 (www.nata.org).

For information on certification, contact the NATA Board of Certification, 4223 S. 143rd Circle, Omaha, NE 68137 (www.bocatc.org).

Athletic Training Programs

Alabama
University of Alabama
Tuscaloosa, AL 35487
www.ua.edu

Arkansas
Arkansas State University
P.O. Box 1450
Jonesboro, AR 72467
www.astate.edu

California
Azusa Pacific University
901 E. Alosta Ave.
Azusa, CA 91702
www.apu.edu

California State University, Fresno
5241 N. Maple Ave.
Fresno, CA 93740
www.csufresno.edu

California State University, Fullerton
P.O. Box 34080
Fullerton, CA 92834
www.fullerton.edu

California State University, Long Beach
Long Beach, CA 90840
www.csulb.edu

California State University, Northridge
18111 Nordhoff St.
Northridge, CA 91330
www.csun.edu

California State University, Sacramento
6000 J St.
Sacramento, CA 95819
www.csus.edu

Chapman University
One University Dr.
Orange, CA 92866
www.chapman.edu

University of La Verne
1950 Third St.
La Verne, CA 91750
www.ulv.edu

Point Loma Nazarene University
3900 Lomaland Dr.
San Diego, CA 92106
www.ptloma.edu

San Diego State University
Department of Exercise and Nutritional Science
5500 Campanile Dr.
San Diego, CA 92182
www.sdsu.edu

San Jose State University
One Washington Square
San Jose, CA 95192
www.sjsu.edu

University of the Pacific
Department of Sport Sciences
3601 Pacific Ave.
Stockton, CA 95211
www.pacific.edu

Vanguard University
55 Fair Dr.
Costa Mesa, CA 92626
www.vanguard.edu

Colorado
Colorado State University–Pueblo
2200 Bonforte Blvd.
Pueblo, CO 81001
www.colostate-pueblo.edu

Fort Lewis College
1000 Rim Dr.
Durango, CO 81301
www.fortlewis.edu

Mesa State College
1100 North Ave.
Grand Junction, CO 81501
www.mesastate.edu

University of Northern Colorado
School of Kinesiology and
 Physical Education
Greeley, CO 80639
www.unco.edu

Connecticut
Central Connecticut State
 University
1615 Stanley St.
New Britain, CT 06050
www.ccsu.edu

Quinnipiac University
275 Mount Carmel Ave.
Hamden, CT 06518
www.quinnipiac.edu

Sacred Heart University
5151 Park Ave.
Fairfield, CT 06825
www.sacredheart.edu

Southern Connecticut State
 University
501 Crescent St.
New Haven, CT 06515
www.southernct.edu

University of Connecticut
Storrs-Mansfield, CT 06269
www.uconn.edu

Delaware
University of Delaware
Newark, DE 19716
www.udel.edu

District of Columbia
George Washington University
2121 Eye St. NW
Washington, DC 20052
www.gwu.edu

Florida
Barry University
11300 NE 2nd Ave.
Miami Shores, FL 33161
www.barry.edu

Florida Southern College
111 Lake Hollingsworth Dr.
Lakeland, FL 33801
www.flsouthern.edu

Florida State University
Nutrition, Food, and Exercise
 Sciences
Tallahassee, FL 32306
www.fsu.edu

University of Central Florida
4000 Central Florida Blvd.
Orlando, FL 32816
www.ucf.edu

University of Florida
Gainesville, FL 32611
www.ufl.edu

University of Miami
Coral Gables, FL 33124
www.miami.edu

University of North Florida
4567 St. Johns Bluff Rd.
Jacksonville, FL 32224
www.unf.edu

University of South Florida
School of Physical Education,
 Wellness & Sports Studies
4202 E. Fowler Ave.
Tampa, FL 33620
www.usf.edu

University of Tampa
401 W. Kennedy Blvd.
Tampa, FL 33606
www.ut.edu

University of West Florida
11000 University Pkwy.
Pensacola, FL 32514
www.uwf.edu

Georgia
Georgia College & State
 University
Campus Box 65
Milledgeville, GA 31061
www.gcsu.edu

Georgia Southern University
P.O. Box 8024
Statesboro, GA 30460
www.georgiasouthern.edu

North Georgia College & State
 University
82 College Circle
Dahlonega, GA 30597
www.ngcsu.edu

University of Georgia
College of Education
G-3 Aderhold Hall
Athens, GA 30602
www.uga.edu

Valdosta State University
1500 N. Patterson St.
Valdosta, GA 31698
www.valdosta.edu

Idaho
Boise State University
1910 University Dr.
Boise, ID 83725
www.boisestate.edu

University of Idaho
Division of Health, Physical
  Education, Recreation and
  Dance
P.O. Box 442401
Moscow, ID 83844
www.uidaho.edu

Illinois
Aurora University
347 S. Gladstone Ave.
Aurora, IL 60506
www.aurora.edu

Eastern Illinois University
600 Lincoln Ave.
Charleston, IL 61920
www.eiu.edu

Illinois State University
Normal, IL 61790
www.ilstu.edu

Lewis University
One University Pkwy.
Romeoville, IL 60446
www.lewisu.edu

McKendree College
701 College Rd.
Lebanon, IL 62254
www.mckendree.edu

Millikin University
1184 W. Main St.
Decatur, IL 62522
www.millikin.edu

North Central College
30 N. Brainard St.
Naperville, IL 60540
www.noctrl.edu

North Park University
3225 W. Foster Ave.
Chicago, IL 60625
www.northpark.edu

Northern Illinois University
Dept. of Kinesiology and Physical
  Education
P.O. Box 3001
DeKalb, IL 60115
www.niu.edu

Olivet Nazarene University
One University Ave.
Bourbonnais, IL 60914
www.olivet.edu

Southern Illinois University
  Carbondale
Carbondale, IL 62901
www.siuc.edu

University of Illinois
1401 W. Green St.
Urbana, IL 61801
www.uiuc.edu

Western Illinois University
1 University Circle
Macomb, IL 61455
www.wiu.edu

Indiana
Ball State University
2000 W. University Ave.
Muncie, IN 47306
www.bsu.edu

DePauw University
313 S. Locust
Greencastle, IN 46135
www.depauw.edu

Franklin College
101 Branigin Blvd.
Franklin, IN 46131
www.franklincollege.edu

Indiana State University
200 N. 7th St.
Terre Haute, IN 47809
www.indstate.edu

Indiana University
300 N. Jordan Ave.
Bloomington, IN 47405
www.indiana.edu

Indiana Wesleyan University
4201 S. Washington St.
Marion, IN 46953
www.indwes.edu

Manchester College
604 E. College Ave.
North Manchester, IN 46962
www.manchester.edu

Purdue University
West Lafayette, IN 47907
www.purdue.edu

University of Evansville
1800 Lincoln Ave.
Evansville, IN 47722
www.evansville.edu

University of Indianapolis
1400 E. Hanna Ave.
Indianapolis, IN 46227
www.uindy.edu

Iowa
Buena Vista University
610 W. Fourth St.
Storm Lake, IA 50588
www.bvu.edu

Clarke College
1550 Clarke Dr.
Dubuque, IA 52001
www.clarke.edu

Coe College
1220 First Ave. NE
Cedar Rapids, IA 52402
www.coe.edu

Iowa State University
Ames, IA 50011
www.iastate.edu

Loras College
1450 Alta Vista
P.O. Box 178
Dubuque, IA 52004
www.loras.edu

Simpson College
701 N. C St.
Indianola, IA 50125
www.simpson.edu

University of Iowa
Iowa City, IA 52242
www.uiowa.edu

University of Northern Iowa
1227 W. 27th St.
Cedar Falls, IA 50614
www.uni.edu

Upper Iowa University
605 Washington St.
P.O. Box 1857
Fayette, IA 52142
www.uiu.edu

Kansas
Fort Hays State University
600 Park St.
Hays, KS 67601
www.fhsu.edu

Kansas State University
241 Justin Hall
1100 Mid-Campus Dr.
Manhattan, KS 66506
www.ksu.edu

University of Kansas
Lawrence, KS 66160
www.ku.edu

Kentucky
Eastern Kentucky University
521 Lancaster Ave.
Richmond, KY 40475
www.eku.edu

Louisiana
Louisiana State University
110 Thomas Boyd Hall
Baton Rouge, LA 70803
www.lsu.edu

Nicholls State University
P.O. Box 2004
Thibodeaux, LA 70310
www.nicholls.edu

Southeastern Louisiana University
SLU 10752
Hammond, LA 70402
www.selu.edu

University of Louisiana at
  Lafayette
104 University Circle
Lafayette, LA 70504
www.louisiana.edu

Maine
University of Maine at
  Presque Isle
181 Main St.
Presque Isle, ME 04769
www.umpi.maine.edu

University of New England
Department of Exercise and
  Sport Performance
11 Hills Beach Rd.
Biddeford, ME 04005
www.une.edu

University of Southern Maine
37 College Ave.
Gorham, ME 04038
www.usm.maine.edu

Maryland
Salisbury University
1101 Camden Ave.
Salisbury, MD 21801
www.salisbury.edu

Towson University
8000 York Rd.
Towson, MD 21252
www.towson.edu

Massachusetts
Boston University
635 Commonwealth Ave.
Boston, MA 02215
www.bu.edu

Bridgewater State College
Bridgewater, MA 02325
www.bridgew.edu

Endicott College
376 Hale St.
Beverly, MA 01915
www.endicott.edu

Lasell College
1844 Commonwealth Ave.
Newton, MA 02466
www.lasell.edu

Northeastern University
360 Huntington Ave.
Boston, MA 02115
www.northeastern.edu

Salem State College
352 Lafayette St.
Salem, MA 01970
www.salemstate.edu

Springfield College
Allied Health Science Center
263 Alden St.
Springfield, MA 01109
www.spfldcol.edu

Westfield State College
Department of Movement Science
577 Western Ave.
P.O. Box 1630
Westfield, MA 01086
www.wsc.ma.edu

Michigan
Albion College
611 E. Porter St.
Albion, MI 49224
www.albion.edu

Central Michigan University
Mount Pleasant, MI 48859
www.cmich.edu

Eastern Michigan University
318P John W. Porter Building
Ypsilanti, MI 48197
www.emich.edu

Grand Valley State University
Movement Science Department
192 Fieldhouse
Allendale, MI 49401
www.gvsu.edu

Hope College
168 E. 13th St.
Holland, MI 49422
www.hope.edu

Lake Superior State University
Athletic Training Program
650 W. Easterday Ave.
Sault Ste. Marie; MI 49783
www.lssu.edu

Michigan State University
East Lansing, MI 48824
www.msu.edu

Northern Michigan University
Department of Health, Physical
  Education and Recreation
1401 Presque Isle Ave.
Marquette, MI 49855
www.nmu.edu

Saginaw Valley State University
7400 Bay Rd.
University Center, MI 48710
www.svsu.edu

University of Michigan
401 Washtenaw Ave.
4745 Kinesiology Building
Ann Arbor, MI 48109
www.umich.edu

Western Michigan University
1903 W Michigan Avenue
Kalamazoo, MI 49008
www.wmich.edu

Minnesota

Bethel College
3900 Bethel Dr.
St. Paul, MN 55112
www.bethel.edu

Gustavus Adolphus College
800 W. College Ave.
St. Peter, MN 56082
www.gac.edu

Minnesota State University,
 Mankato
1400 Highland Center
Mankato, MN 56001
www.mnsu.edu

Minnesota State University
 Moorhead
106D Alex Nemzek Hall
1104 Seventh Ave. S.
Moorhead, MN 56563
www.mnstate.edu

Winona State University
Department of Health and
 Human Performance
117 Memorial Hall
P.O. Box 5838
Winona, MN 55987
www.winona.edu

Mississippi

University of Southern Mississippi
118 College Dr.
Hattiesburg, MS 39406
www.usm.edu

Missouri

Central Methodist College
411 Central Methodist Square
Fayette, MO 65248
www.cmc.edu

Lindenwood University
209 S. Kingshighway
St. Charles, MO 63301
www.lindenwood.edu

Park University
8700 NW River Park Dr.
Parkville, MO 64152
www.park.edu

Southeast Missouri State
 University
One University Plaza
Cape Girardeau, MO 63701
www.semo.edu

Southwest Missouri State
 University
901 S. National Ave.
Springfield, MO 65804
www.smsu.edu

Truman State University
100 E. Normal
Kirksville, MO 63501
www.truman.edu

William Woods University
One University Ave.
Fulton, MO 65251
www.williamwoods.edu

Montana

University of Montana–Missoula
32 Campus Dr.
Missoula, MT 59812
www.umt.edu

Nebraska

Creighton University
2500 California Plaza
Omaha, NE 68178
www.creighton.edu

Nebraska Wesleyan University
5000 St. Paul Ave.
Lincoln, NE 68504
www.nebrwesleyan.edu

University of Nebraska at Kearney
905 W. 25th St.
Kearney, NE 68849
www.unk.edu

University of Nebraska at Omaha
6001 Dodge St.
HPER 207
Omaha, NE 68182
www.unomaha.edu

Nevada

University of Nevada, Las Vegas
4505 Maryland Pkwy.
Box 453034
Las Vegas, NV 89154
www.unlv.edu

New Hampshire

Colby-Sawyer College
541 Main St.
New London, NH 03257
www.colby-sawyer.edu

Keene State College
229 Main St.
Keene, NH 03435
www.keene.edu

Plymouth State College
17 High St.
Plymouth, NH 03264
www.plymouth.edu

University of New Hampshire
Department of Kinesiology
145 Main St./Field House
Durham, NH 03824
www.unh.edu

New Jersey

Kean University
1000 Morris Ave.
Union, NJ 07083
www.kean.edu

Montclair State University
1 Normal Ave.
Montclair, NJ 07043
www.montclair.edu

Rowan University
201 Mullica Hill Rd.
Glassboro, NJ 08028
www.rowan.edu

Seton Hall University
400 S. Orange Ave.
South Orange, NJ 07079
www.shu.edu

William Paterson University
300 Pompton Rd.
Wayne, NJ 07470
www.wpunj.edu

New Mexico

New Mexico State University
P.O. Box 30001
Las Cruces, NM 88003
www.nmsu.edu

University of New Mexico
Albuquerque, NM 87131
www.unm.edu

New York

Canisius College
2001 Main St.
Buffalo, NY 14208
www.canisius.edu

Dominican College
470 Western Hwy.
Orangeburg, NY 10962
www.dc.edu

Hofstra University
Hempstead, NY 11550
www.hofstra.edu

Ithaca College
Department of Exercise and
  Sports Science
10 Hill Center
Ithaca, NY 14850
www.ithaca.edu

Marist College
3399 North Rd.
Poughkeepsie, NY 12601
www.marist.edu

State University of New York at
  Brockport
350 New Campus Dr.
Brockport, NY 14420
www.brockport.edu

SUNY College at Cortland
Exercise Science and Sport
  Studies Department
P.O. Box 2000
Cortland, NY 13045
www.cortland.edu

The Sage Colleges
45 Ferry St.
Troy, NY 12180
www.sage.edu

University at Buffalo
State University of New York
Department of Exercise and
  Nutrition Sciences
Buffalo, NY 14214
www.buffalo.edu

North Carolina

Appalachian State University
Health, Leisure and Exercise
  Science
Boone, NC 28608
www.appstate.edu

Barton College
Department of Physical Education
  and Sports Studies
P.O. Box 5000
Wilson, NC 27893
www.barton.edu

Campbell University
P.O. Box 488
Buies Creek, NC 27506
www.campbell.edu

Catawba College
2300 W. Innes St.
Salisbury, NC 28144
www.catawba.edu

East Carolina University
Sports Medicine Division
245 Ward Sports Medicine
  Building
Greenville, NC 27858
www.ecu.edu

Elon University
2700 Campus Box
Elon, NC 27244
www.elon.edu

Gardner-Webb University
Department of Physical Education
Wellness & Sports Studies
Campus 7257
Boiling Springs, NC 28017
www.gardner-webb.edu

Greensboro College
815 W. Market St.
Greensboro, NC 27401
www.greensborocollege.edu

High Point University
833 Montlieu Ave.
High Point, NC 27262
www.highpoint.edu

Lenoir-Rhyne College
Department of Healthful Living
  and Sports
625 7th Ave. NE
Hickory, NC 28601
www.lrc.edu

Mars Hill College
100 Athletic St.
Mars Hill, NC 28754
www.mhc.edu

Methodist College
5400 Ramsey St.
Fayetteville, NC 28311
www.methodist.edu

University of North Carolina at
  Chapel Hill
Chapel Hill, NC 27599
www.unc.edu

University of North Carolina at
  Charlotte
Department of Kinesiology
9201 University City Blvd.
Charlotte, NC 28223
www.uncc.edu

University of North Carolina at
  Greensboro
1000 Spring Garden St.
Greensboro, NC 27403
www.uncg.edu

University of North Carolina at
  Wilmington
Department of Health, Physical
  Education and Recreation
601 S. College Rd.
Wilmington, NC 28403
www.uncwil.edu

Wingate University
P.O. Box 159
Wingate, NC 28174
www.wingate.edu

North Dakota

North Dakota State University
Bentson Bunker Fieldhouse 1G
1301 12th Ave. N.
Fargo, ND 58105
www.ndsu.nodak.edu

University of Mary
7500 University Dr.
Bismarck, ND 58504
www.umary.edu

University of North Dakota
Division of Sports Medicine
P.O. Box 9013
Grand Forks, ND 58202
www.und.edu

Ohio

Baldwin-Wallace College
275 Eastland Rd.
Berea, OH 44017
www.bw.edu

Bowling Green State University
Bowling Green, OH 43403
www.bgsu.edu

Capital University
1 College and Main
Columbus, OH 43209
www.capital.edu

College of Mount St. Joseph
Department of Health Sciences
5701 Delhi Rd.
Cincinnati, OH 45233
www.msj.edu

Denison University
Department of Physical Education
Granville, OH 43023
www.denison.edu

Kent State University
School of Exercise, Leisure and
  Sport
Kent, OH 44242
www.kent.edu

Marietta College
215 Fifth St.
Marietta, OH 45750
www.marietta.edu

Miami University
Department of Physical Education, Health and Sport Studies
Oxford, OH 45056
www.muohio.edu

Mount Union College
1972 Clark Ave.
Alliance, OH 44601
www.muc.edu

Ohio Northern University
Department of Human
  Performance and Sport Sciences
525 S. Main St.
Ada, OH 45810
www.onu.edu

Ohio State University
Columbus, OH 43210
www.osu.edu

Ohio University
Athens, OH 45701
www.ohio.edu

Otterbein College
180 Center St.
Roush Hall 320
Westerville, OH 43081
www.otterbein.edu

University of Akron
302 Buchtel Mall
Akron, OH 44325
www.uakron.edu

University of Cincinnati
2624 Clifton Ave.
Cincinnati, OH 45221
www.uc.edu

University of Toledo
College of Health and Human
  Services
Department of Kinesiology
Toledo, OH 43606
www.utoledo.edu

Urbana University
579 College Way
Urbana, OH 43078
www.urbana.edu

Wilmington College
251 Ludovic St.
Wilmington, OH 45177
www.wilmington.edu

Wright State University
Health & Physical Education
  Department
316 Nutter Center
Dayton, OH 45435
www.wright.edu

Xavier University
3800 Victory Pkwy.
Cincinnati, OH 45207
www.xavier.edu

Oklahoma

East Central University
Ada, OK 74820
www.ecok.edu

Oklahoma State University
427 Willard Hall
Stillwater, OK 74078
www.okstate.edu

Southwestern Oklahoma State
  University
100 Campus Dr.
Weatherford, OK 73096
www.swosu.edu

University of Tulsa
600 S. College Ave.
Tulsa, OK 74104
www.utulsa.edu

Oregon

Linfield College
900 SE Baker St.
McMinnville, OR 97128
www.linfield.edu

University of Oregon
Certified Athletic Trainers
  Program
Eugene, OR 97403
www.uoregon.edu

Oregon State University
Corvallis, OR 97331
http://oregonstate.edu/

Pennsylvania

Alvernia College
400 Saint Bernardine St.
Reading, PA 19607
www.alvernia.edu

California University of
  Pennsylvania
250 University Ave.
California, PA 15419
www.cup.edu

Duquesne University
122 Health Sciences Building
Pittsburgh, PA 15282
www.duq.edu

East Stroudsburg University
200 Prospect St.
East Stroudsburg, PA 18301
www.esu.edu

Indiana University of
  Pennsylvania
1011 South Dr.
Indiana, PA 15705
www.iup.edu

King's College
133 N. River St.
Wilkes-Barre, PA 18711
www.kings.edu

Lock Haven University
401 N. Fairview St.
Lock Haven, PA 17745
www.lhup.edu

Marywood University
2300 Adams Ave.
Scranton, PA 18509
www.marywood.edu

Mercyhurst College
Sports Medicine Department
501 E. 38th St.
Erie, PA 16546
www.mercyhurst.edu

Pennsylvania State University
Kinesiology Department
University Park, PA 16802
www.psu.edu

Slippery Rock University
School of Allied Health
1 Morrow Way
Slippery Rock, PA 16057
www.sru.edu

Temple University
127 Pearson Hall
Philadelphia, PA 19122
www.temple.edu

University of Pittsburgh
School of Health and
  Rehabilitation Sciences
Pittsburgh, PA 15260
www.shrs.pitt.edu

Waynesburg College
51 W. College St.
Waynesburg, PA 15370
www.waynesburg.edu

West Chester University
West Chester, PA 19383
www.wcupa.edu

South Carolina
College of Charleston
66 George St.
Charleston, SC 29424
www.cofc.edu

Erskine College
Two Washington St.
Due West, SC 29639
www.erskine.edu

Lander University
320 Stanley Ave.
Greenwood, SC 29649
www.lander.edu

University of South Carolina
Columbia, SC 29208
www.sc.edu

South Dakota
Augustana College
2001 S. Summit Ave.
Sioux Falls, SD 57197
www.augustana.edu

Dakota Wesleyan University
1200 W. University Ave.
Mitchell, SD 57301
www.dwu.edu

National American University
321 Kansas City St.
Rapid City, SD 57701
www.national.edu

Si Tanka University
333 9th St. SW
Huron, SD 57350
www.sitanka.edu

South Dakota State University
Department of Health, Physical
  Education and Recreation
Brookings, SD 57007
www.sdstate.edu

Tennessee
David Lipscomb University
Department of Kinesiology
3901 Granny White Pike
Nashville, TN 37204
www.lipscomb.edu

East Tennessee State University
P.O. Box 70267
Johnson City, TN 37601
www.etsu.edu

Lincoln Memorial University
6965 Cumberland Gap Pkwy.
Harrogate, TN 37752
www.lmunet.edu

Middle Tennessee State University
Department of Health,
  Physical Education, Recreation
  and Safety
1301 E. Main St.
Murfreesboro, TN 37132
www.mtsu.edu

Tusculum College
60 Shiloh Rd.
Greeneville, TN 37743
www.tusculum.edu

Union University
1050 Union University Dr.
Jackson, TN 38305
www.uu.edu

University of Tennessee at
  Chattanooga
615 McCallie Ave.
Chattanooga, TN 37403
www.utc.edu

Texas
Southwestern University
1001 E. University Ave.
Georgetown, TX 78626
www.southwestern.edu

Texas Christian University
2800 S. University Dr.
Fort Worth, TX 76129
www.tcu.edu

Texas State University–San
  Marcos
601 University Dr.
San Marcos, TX 78666
www.txstate.edu

Texas Tech University
Health Sciences Center
3601 4th St.
Lubbock, TX 79430
www.ttu.edu

University of Texas at Arlington
Department of Kinesiology
701 S. Nedderman Dr.
Arlington, TX 76019
www.uta.edu

Utah

Brigham Young University
College of Health and Human
  Performance
Provo, UT 84602
www.byu.edu

University of Utah
201 S. Presidents Circle, Room
  201
Salt Lake City, UT 84112
www.utah.edu

Weber State University
3850 University Circle
Ogden, UT 84408
www.weber.edu

Vermont

Castleton State University
86 Seminary St.
Castleton, VT 05735
www.castleton.edu

University of Vermont
Burlington, VT 05405
www.uvm.edu

Virginia

Averett University
420 W. Main St.
Danville, VA 24541
www.averett.edu

Bridgewater College
Bridgewater, VA 22812
www.bridgewater.edu

Emory & Henry College
P.O. Box 947
Emory, VA 24327
www.ehc.edu

George Mason University
4400 University Dr.
Fairfax, VA 22030
www.gmu.edu

James Madison University
Department of Health Sciences
800 S. Main St.
Harrisonburg, VA 22807
www.jmu.edu

Jefferson College of Health
  Sciences
920 S. Jefferson St.
P.O. Box 13186
Roanoke, VA 24016
www.jchs.edu

Liberty University
Department of Health Sciences &
  Kinesiology
1971 University Blvd.
Lynchburg, VA 24502
www.liberty.edu

Longwood University
201 High St.
Farmville, VA 23909
www.longwood.edu

Lynchburg College
1501 Lakeside Dr.
Lynchburg, VA 24501
www.lynchburg.edu

Old Dominion University
Norfolk, VA 23529
www.odu.edu

Roanoke College
221 College Ln.
Salem, VA 24153
www.roanoke.edu

Shenandoah University
1460 University Dr.
Winchester, VA 22601
www.su.edu

University of Virginia
P.O. Box 400407
210 Emmet Street. South
Charlottesville, VA 22904
www.virginia.edu

Virginia Commonwealth University
Richmond, VA 23284
www.vcu.edu

Washington

Eastern Washington University
Athletic Department
207 Physical Education Building
Cheney, WA 99004
www.ewu.edu

Washington State University
Department of Kinesiology
Pullman, WA 99164
www.wsu.edu

Whitworth College
300 W. Hawthorne Rd.
Spokane, WA 99251
www.whitworth.edu

West Virginia

Alderson-Broaddus College
College Hill Rd.
Philippi, WV 26416
www.ab.edu

Concord College
P.O. Box 1000
Athens, WV 24712
www.concord.edu

Marshall University
College of Education & Human
  Services
One John Marshall Dr.
Huntington, WV 25755
www.marshall.edu

University of Charleston
2300 MacCorkle Ave. SE
Charleston, WV 25304
www.ucwv.edu

West Virginia University
P.O. Box 6201
Morgantown, WV 26506
www.wvu.edu

West Virginia Wesleyan College
59 College Ave.
Buckhannon, WV 26201
www.wvwc.edu

Wisconsin

Carroll College
100 N. East Ave.
Waukesha, WI 53186
www.cc.edu

Carthage College
2001 Alford Park Dr.
Kenosha, WI 53140
www.carthage.edu

University of Wisconsin–
  La Crosse
1725 State St.
La Crosse, WI 54601
www.uwlax.edu

University of Wisconsin–Madison
2000 Observatory Dr.
Madison, WI 53706
www.wisc.edu

University of Wisconsin–
Milwaukee
Department of Human Movement Sciences
Milwaukee, WI 53201
www.uwm.edu

University of Wisconsin–Oshkosh
169A Robert E. Kolf Physical
Education Center
800 Algoma Blvd.
Oshkosh, WI 54901
www.uwosh.edu

Child Life Specialists

Principal activity: Addressing the social and psychological needs of hospitalized children

Work commitment: Part- or full-time

Preprofessional education: High school diploma

Program length: 4 years

Work prerequisites: Bachelor's degree

Career opportunities: Stable

Income range: $35,000 to $49,000

Scope

Hospitalization means a complete break in the patient's life, separation from family and friends, and facing unfamiliar (and sometimes painful) tests and treatments. The potential for intense psychological stress is quite high, especially for children. Child life specialists help children deal with that stress.

Activities

Child life specialists use play therapy to help children deal with the stress of hospitalization. They may have children use dolls to act out their emotions and reveal their fears and distress. These specialists also provide young patients with needed reassurance and emotional support, explain what is happening, and prepare the children for what comes next.

Child life specialists act as storytellers and sometimes active listeners. Many times they act as a liaison between children and their nurses, physicians, dietitians, and other therapists.

Work Settings

Child life specialists work at medical centers and hospitals, where their involvement may come as early as the time of admission and extend until discharge. Some also are employed by outpatient facilities. The use of these specialists is not widespread, so this profession is growing slowly.

Advancement

Salary increases and tenure are available at hospitals with larger programs. With experience, a child life specialist may become director of the program at a large institution.

Prerequisites

A high school diploma or its equivalent is necessary to train for this profession.

Desirable personal attributes include common sense and judgment, superior communication skills, compassion, an optimistic and outgoing personality, a sense of humor, a caring and giving nature, and the emotional resilience to deal with critically ill children. Above all, child life specialists must love children.

Education/Training

Three routes are open to those who want to enter this field:

- You can earn a bachelor's degree at one of the few colleges offering a major in child life.
- You can earn a bachelor's degree in education, recreational therapy, or child psychology and then complete a practicum in child life as part of the program.
- If you have a degree in a related field, you can get on-the-job training as a child life assistant.

Undergraduate training usually involves courses in English, speech, biology, education, psychology, medical terminology, and pediatric illnesses. Field work provides practical experience in dealing with issues associated with the field, such as family dynamics, emotional trauma, and professional interaction with health-care providers.

Certification/Registration/Licensure

Certification is voluntary and can be secured through the Child Life Council. Ultimately, states may require licensure in this field.

Career Potential

This field is growing, though slowly. Employment growth in this field may be limited by future budget cuts to health-care providers.

For More Information

The professional organization for this field is the Child Life Council, 11820 Parklawn Dr., Ste. 240, Rockville, MD 20852 (www.childlife.org).

Child Life Programs

Most people entering this field major in psychology, education, or recreational therapy. Few schools offer a program in child life. For a list of schools that do, contact the Child Life Council at the address just listed or visit its Web site.

Dietary Managers

Principal activity: Supervising food service operations

Work commitment: Full-time

Preprofessional education: High school diploma

Program length: 1 year

Work prerequisites: Certification

Career opportunities: Stable

Income range: $41,000 to $62,000

Scope

Dietary managers supervise other workers who are involved in food service operations at hospitals, schools, hotels, prisons, nursing homes, and large companies.

Activities

The job responsibilities of dietary managers vary widely, depending on the size and nature of the institution that employs them. They hire and supervise other staff members, order and purchase supplies, and oversee meal preparation and cleanup. To carry out these duties, they work closely with registered dietitians to ensure that their clients' nutritional needs are met.

Work Settings

Dietary managers are employed by hospitals, long-term care facilities, educational institutions, hotels, prisons, and large corporations with in-house food service.

Advancement

Dietary managers can advance by moving to larger facilities. Some go into teaching.

Prerequisites

A high school diploma is necessary to train for this field. Students should take courses in biology, home economics, and business management.

Desirable personal attributes include a strong interest in food preparation, good business skills, and the ability to supervise others.

Education/Training

Dietary management programs, which typically last one year, are offered by many vocational-technical schools and community colleges. They offer courses in nutrition, food service management, quantity food production, and business practices.

Certification/Registration/Licensure

Graduates of accredited dietary management programs can take an examination to be certified by the Dietary Managers Association. This qualifies them as certified dietary managers.

Career Potential

With the United States' rapidly aging population and a continuing focus on diet as a means to maintaining good health, prospects are decent for long-term growth in this field. However, these positions are often at the mercy of institutional budget cuts

For More Information

The professional organization for this field is the Dietary Managers Association, 406 Surrey Woods Dr., St. Charles, IL 60174 (www.dmaonline.org).

Dietary Manager Training Programs

Alabama
Auburn University
Auburn, AL 36849
www.auburn.edu

Alaska
University of Alaska Anchorage
3211 Providence Dr.
Culinary Arts & Hospitality
Anchorage, AK 99508
www.uaa.alaska.edu

Arizona
Arizona Western College
2020 S. Ave. 8 E.
P.O. Box 929
Yuma, AZ 85366
www.azwestern.edu

Central Arizona College
8470 Overfield Road
Coolidge, AZ 85228
www.centralaz.edu

Arkansas
University of Arkansas–Ft. Smith
5210 Grand Ave.
P.O. Box 3649
Ft. Smith, AR 72913
www.uafortsmith.edu

California
Merritt College
12500 Campus Dr.
Oakland, CA 94619
www.merritt.edu

Florida
Erwin Technical Center
2010 E. Hillsborough Ave.
Tampa, FL 33610
www.erwintech.org

Florida Community College at
  Jacksonville
501 W. State St.
Jacksonville, FL 32202
www.fccj.org

Indian River Community College
3209 Virginia Ave.
Ft. Pierce, FL 34981
www.ircc.edu

Lindsey Hopkins Technical
  Education Center
750 NW 20th St.
Miami, FL 33127
http://lindsey.dadeschools.net/

Orlando Tech Center
301 W. Amelia St.
Orlando, FL 32801
www.orlandotech.ocps.net

Sarasota County Technical
  Institute
4748 Beneva Rd.
Sarasota, FL 34233
www.scti.edu

University of Florida
2209 NW 13th Street
Gainesville, FL 32609
www.ufl.edu

Georgia
University of Georgia
576 Aderhold Hall
Athens, GA 30602
www.uga.edu

Hawaii
Kapi'olani Community College
4303 Diamond Head Rd.
Honolulu, HI 96816
www.kcc.hawaii.edu

Idaho
Boise State University
1910 University Dr.
Boise, ID 83725
www.boisestate.edu

Illinois
John Wood Community College
1301 S. 48th St.
Quincy, IL 62305
www.jwcc.edu

Kaskaskia Community College
Dietary Department
27210 College Rd.
Centralia, IL 62801
www.kaskaskia.edu

Lincoln Land Community College
5250 Shepard Rd.
P.O. Box 19256
Springfield, IL 62794
www.llcc.edu

Rock Valley College
3301 N. Mulford Rd.
Rockford, IL 61111
www.rockvalleycollege.edu

Shawnee Community College
8364 College Rd.
Ullin, IL 62992
www.shawneecc.edu

Indiana
Ivy Tech State College
220 Dean Johnson Blvd.
South Bend, IN 46601
www.ivytech.edu/southbend/

Ivy Tech State College Northeast
3800 N. Anthony Blvd.
Ft. Wayne, IN 46805
www.ivytech.edu/fortwayne/

J. Everett Light Career Center
1901 E. 86th St.
Indianapolis, IN 46240
www.jelcc.com

Vincennes University
1002 N. 1st St.
Vincennes, IN 47591
www.vinu.edu

Iowa
Des Moines Area Community
  College
2006 S. Ankeny Blvd.
Ankeny, IA 50021
www.dmacc.org

Eastern Iowa Community College
  District
306 W. River Dr.
Davenport, IA 52801
www.eicc.edu

Iowa Lakes Community College
3200 College Dr.
Emmetsburg, IA 50536
www.iowalakes.edu

Kansas

Barton County Community College
245 NE 30 Rd.
Great Bend, KS 67530
www.barton.cc.ks.us

Coffeyville Community College
400 W. 11th St.
Coffeyville, KS 67337
www.ccc.cc.ks.us

Washburn University of Topeka
1700 SW College Ave.
Topeka, KS 66621
www.washburn.edu

Wichita Area Technical College
301 S. Grove
Wichita, KS 67211
www.wichitatech.com

Kentucky

Bellarmine University
2001 Newburg Rd.
Louisville, KY 40205
www.bellarmine.edu

Louisiana

Sowela Technical Community
   College
3820 J. Bennett Johnston Ave.
Lake Charles, LA 70616
www.sowela.edu

Maine

Washington County Community
   College
One College Dr.
Calais, ME 04619
www.wccc.me.edu

Michigan

Lansing Community College
419 N. Capitol Ave.
P.O. Box 40010
Lansing, MI 48901
www.lcc.edu

Marygrove College
8425 W. McNichols Rd.
Detroit, MI 48221
www.marygrove.edu

Minnesota

Alexandria Technical College
1601 Jefferson St.
Alexandria, MN 56308
www.atc.tec.mn.us

South Central Technical College
1920 Lee Blvd
North Mankato, MN 56003
www.southcentral.edu

St. Paul College
235 Marshall Ave.
St. Paul, MN 55102
www.saintpaul.edu

Missouri

Columbia Career Center
4203 S. Providence Rd.
Columbia, MO 65203
www.career-center.org

Herndon Career Center
11501 E. 350 Hwy.
Raytown, MO 64138
www.herndoncareercenter.com

Nebraska

Mid-Plains Community College
North Platte Community College
601 W. State Farm Rd.
North Platte, NE 69101
www.mpcc.edu

Northeast Community College
801 E. Benjamin Ave.
P.O. Box 469
Norfolk, NE 68702
www.northeast.edu

New Jersey

JAS Dietetic Assistant School
17 N. Essex Ave.
Livingston, NJ 07039

Passaic County Technical
   Institute
45 Reinhardt Rd.
Wayne, NJ 07470
www.pcti.tec.nj.us

Warren City Community College
475 Route 57 W.
Washington, NJ 07882
www.warren.edu

New York

Broome Community College
State University of New York
P.O. Box 1017
Binghamton, NY 13902
www.sunybroome.edu

Dutchess Community College
53 Pendell Rd.
Poughkeepsie, NY 12601
www.sunydutchess.edu

Erie Community College
6205 Main St.
Williamsville, NY 14221
www.ecc.edu

Senior Healthcare Alternatives
103 Head of Neck Rd.
P.O. Box 927
Bellport, NY 11713

Suffolk County Community College
533 College Rd.
Selden, NY 11784
www.sunysuffolk.edu

Westchester Community College
75 Grasslands Rd.
Valhalla, NY 10595
www.sunywcc.edu

North Carolina

Asheville-Buncombe Technical
   Community College
340 Victoria Rd.
Asheville, NC 28801
www.abtech.edu

Catawba Valley Community
   College
2550 Hwy. 70 SE
Hickory, NC 28602
www.cvcc.edu

Central Piedmont Community
   College
P.O. Box 35009
Charlotte, NC 28235
www.cpcc.edu

North Dakota

University of North Dakota
Grand Forks, ND 58202
www.und.nodak.edu

Pennsylvania
Pennsylvania State University
201 Mateer Building
University Park, PA 16802
www.psu.edu

South Carolina
Marion City Technical Education
  Center
2697 E. Hwy. 76
P.O. Box 890
Marion, SC 29571
www.mctec.org

Midlands Technical College
P.O. Box 2408
Columbia, SC 29202
www.midlandstech.edu

Orangeburg Calhoun Technical
  College
3250 St. Matthews Rd.
Orangeburg, SC 29118
www.octech.edu

Texas
Collin County Community College
9700 Wade Blvd.
Frisco, TX 75035
www.ccccd.edu

Del Mar College
101 Baldwin Blvd.
Corpus Christi, TX 78404
www.delmar.edu

Tarrant County College
Southeast Campus
2100 Southeast Pkwy.
Arlington, TX 76018
www.tccd.edu

Texas Health Care Association
P.O. Box 4554
Austin, TX 78765
www.txhca.org

Texas State Technical College
3801 Campus Dr.
Waco, TX 76705
www.waco.tstc.edu

Vernon College
Century City Center
4105 Maplewood
Wichita Falls, TX 76308
www.vernoncollege.edu

The Victoria College
2200 E. Red River
Victoria, TX 77901
www.victoriacollege.edu

Wisconsin
Nicolet Area Technical College
Lake Julia Campus
County Hwy. G
Rhinelander, WI 54501
www.nicoletcollege.edu

Southwest Wisconsin Technical
  College
1800 Bronson Blvd.
Fennimore, WI 53809
www.swtc.edu

Western Wisconsin Technical
  College
304 6th St. N.
La Crosse, WI 54601
www.wwtc.edu

Wisconsin Indianhead Technical
  College
1900 College Dr.
Rice Lake, WI 54868
www.witc.edu

Environmental Health Scientists

Principal activity: Helping reduce the threat to public health caused by environmental hazards

Work commitment: Full-time

Preprofessional education: High school diploma

Program length: 4 years

Work prerequisites: Bachelor's degree

Career opportunities: Favorable

Income range: $39,000 to $72,000

Scope

Environmental health scientists work to reduce health hazards caused by unsafe food and water or waste and sewage disposal. They also are concerned with atmospheric pollution and radioactive contamination.

Those working in this field play a vital role in maintaining public health in the United States. The efforts of the government to promote health and prevent disease have enhanced interest in this field.

Activities

Entry-level scientists usually act as inspectors, checking restaurants, schools, daycare centers, summer camps, hospitals, bakeries, and grocery stores. In addition, they check water supplies, sewage treatment facilities, and swimming pools.

More-experienced workers, in addition to inspection duties, provide education and consultation in this field.

Highly experienced environmental health scientists help organize training programs. Some sanitarians specialize in industrial hygiene, institutional hygiene, or radiation protection.

Work Settings

Most environmental health scientists are employed by public-health agencies at the local level and therefore are civil-service employees.

Advancement

After a few years of work experience, an environmental health scientists may advance to a supervisory position. Such a position might involve planning, organizing, and evaluating activities. Those with graduate degrees may conduct research, teach, or specialize.

Prerequisites

A high school diploma or its equivalent is the minimum requirement to train for work in this field.

Desirable personal attributes include good health and vision, superior communication skills, an interest in science and health care, and a desire to be in an active and responsible profession.

Education/Training

A bachelor's degree with a basic science background is needed to secure an entry-level position. Many accredited programs in environmental health exist in the U.S. These encompass biology, chemistry, physics, microbiology, mathematics, epidemiology, biostatistics, environmental health factors, communication, and behavioral sciences. Field training is also incorporated into the programs.

Many new openings in this field require a master's degree.

Certification/Registration/Licensure

Most states have their own standards for registration or licensure.

Career Potential

Employment prospects for environmental health scientists should be good in the foreseeable future. In recent years, the public has become more concerned with health hazards and a clean environment. This forces government agencies to be more cognizant of their responsibilities and more concerned with these issues. However, much of the demand for environmental health scientists is dependent upon government funding.

For More Information

The professional association for this field is the National Environmental Health Association, 720 S. Colorado Blvd., Ste. 970-S, Denver, CO 80246 (www.neha.org).

For information on certification, contact the National Environmental Health Science and Protection Accreditation Council at P.O. Box 15266, Portland, OR 97293 (www.eha-coffice.org).

Environmental Health Science Programs

Arkansas
University of Arkansas at Little
  Rock
2801 S. University Ave.
Little Rock, AR 72204
www.ualr.edu

California
California State University, Fresno
5241 N. Maple Ave.
Fresno, CA 93740
www.csufresno.edu

California State University,
  Northridge
18111 Nordhoff St.
Northridge, CA 91330
www.csun.edu

California State University,
  Sacramento
6000 J St.
Sacramento, CA 95819
www.csus.edu

Orange Coast College
Environmental Health Science
2701 Fairview Rd. Costa Mesa, CA
  92626
www.orangecoastcollege.edu

San Diego State University
5500 Campanile Dr.
San Diego, CA 92182
www.sdsu.edu

San Jose State University
1 Washington Square
San Jose, CA 95192
www.sjsu.edu

Colorado
Colorado State University
Fort Collins, CO 80523
www.colostate.edu

Connecticut
University of Hartford
200 Bloomfield Ave.
West Hartford, CT 06117
www.hartford.edu

Delaware
Delaware State University
1200 N. DuPont Hwy.
Dover, DE 19901
www.dsc.edu

Georgia
University of Georgia
576 Aderhold Hall
Athens, GA 30602
www.uga.edu

Idaho
Boise State University
1910 University Dr.
Boise, ID 83725
www.boisestate.edu

Illinois
Illinois State University
Normal, IL 61790
www.ilstu.edu

Indiana
Indiana State University
200 N. 7th St.
Terre Haute, IN 47809
www.indstate.edu

Purdue University
Schleman Hall
West Lafayette, IN 47907
www.purdue.edu

Kentucky
Eastern Kentucky University
521 Lancaster Ave.
Richmond, KY 40475
www.eku.edu

Maryland
Salisbury University
1101 Camden Ave.
Salisbury, MD 21801
www.salisbury.edu

Massachusetts
Anna Maria College
Environmental Health
50 Sunset Ln.
Paxton, MA 01612
www.annamaria.edu

Hampshire College
893 West St.
Amherst, MA 01002
www.hampshire.edu

Massachusetts Institute of
  Technology
77 Massachusetts Ave.
Cambridge, MA 02139
www.mit.edu

Springfield College
263 Alden St.
Springfield, MA 01109
www.spfldcol.edu

Michigan
Ferris State University
151 Fountain St. NE
Grand Rapids, MI 49503
www.ferris.edu

Oakland University
Rochester, MI 48309
www.oakland.edu

University of Michigan–Flint
303 E. Kearsley St.
Flint, MI 48502
www.flint.umich.edu

Missouri
Missouri Southern State
  University
3950 E. Newman Rd.
Joplin, MO 64801
www.mssu.edu

New Jersey
Rutgers, The State University of
  New Jersey
Cook College
New Brunswick, NJ 08903
www.rutgers.edu

New Mexico
Eastern New Mexico University
1200 W. University
Portales, NM 88130
www.enmu.edu

UNM Health Science Center
Albequerque, NM 87131
www.unm.edu

New York
Clarkson University
Environmental and Occupational
  Health
P.O. Box 5605
Potsdam, NY 13699
www.clarkson.edu/eoh/

SUNY College at Cortland
P.O. Box 2000
Cortland, NY 13045
www.cortland.edu

North Carolina
East Carolina University
E. 5th St.
Greenville, NC 27858
www.ecu.edu

Western Carolina University
Hwy. 107
Cullowhee, NC 28723
www.wcu.edu

Ohio
Bowling Green State University
Bowling Green, OH 43403
www.bgsu.edu

Ohio University
416 Tower
Athens, OH 45701
www.ohio.edu

Wright State University
Dayton, OH 45435
www.wright.edu

Oklahoma
East Central University
Ada, OK 74820
www.ecok.edu

Oregon
Oregon State University
Corvallis, OR 97331
www.oregonstate.edu

Pennsylvania
California University of
  Pennsylvania
250 University Ave.
California, PA 15419
www.cup.edu

Indiana University of
  Pennsylvania
1011 South Dr.
Indiana, PA 15705
www.iup.edu

West Chester University
West Chester, PA 19383
www.wcupa.edu

Tennessee
East Tennessee State University
P.O. Box 70267
Johnson City, TN 37601
www.etsu.edu

Texas
Texas Southern University
3100 Cleburne St.
Houston, TX 77004
www.tsu.edu

Virginia
Old Dominion University
Norfolk, VA 23529
www.odu.edu

Washington
University of Washington
1959 NE Pacific St., Box 356490
Seattle, WA 98195
www.washington.edu

Wisconsin
University of Wisconsin–Eau
  Claire
105 Garfield Ave.
Eau Claire, WI 54702
www.uwec.edu

Geriatric Social Workers

Principal activity: Helping elderly clients cope with life's problems

Work commitment: Full-time

Preprofessional education: High school diploma

Program length: 4 to 6 years

Work prerequisites: Bachelor's degree or higher

Career opportunities: Favorable

Income range: $31,000 to $52,000

Scope

Geriatric social workers help to secure a variety of services for individuals older than 70 who face serious challenges to maintaining their quality of life.

Activities

Many of today's elderly have special needs. These may include such basics as having nourishing meals three times daily as well as proper and sanitary housing facilities. Even finding a suitable apartment can be a source of concern for an elderly individual if he or she is living on an upper floor in a house that lacks an elevator. In addition, the elderly may have one or more health problems or may be caring for a spouse who has these problems. Emotional problems of varying types may exist, especially among those living alone. Compounding the situation is the fact that many of the elderly cannot get any or significant assistance from their children or relatives. Under the aforementioned circumstances, geriatric social workers can provide valuable sources of help that can result in improved quality of life for their clients.

An available option is placing elderly individuals into assisted-living facilities, extended-care institutions, or nursing homes. This is costly and not necessarily the best choice. In many situations such a placement may even be counterproductive. Perhaps the individual or couple wants to keep living in their long-time home. Achieving this aim may require the geriatric social worker to arrange for help, possibly in the form of a home health aide or live-in caretaker. Such an arrangement can be less costly than institutionalization and more psychologically appropriate for the client.

To be of help to elderly clients, the geriatric social worker has to evaluate their specific needs and problems. This makes it possible to provide guidance and arrange for suitable resources that will facilitate their having more fulfilling and meaningful lives. Any advice offered may be provided directly to the clients and/or their families. The issues raised in discussions with geriatric social workers may be acute, concerning medical care, housing, or transportation, or potential. The client ultimately might need to be relocated to a facility that can provide a suitable level of personal care. Geriatric social workers can be of significant assistance for both types of situations.

Geriatric social workers, as part of their responsibilities, keep records of their meetings with clients (and their families), whether in their offices or their clients' homes. When called for, periodic reports on the status of clients must be submitted to superiors.

To resolve client problems, geriatric social workers need to communicate with the appropriate agencies to secure assistance. They can obtain help for clients from caregiver organizations such as those providing therapists, visiting nurses, and home health aides; day care facilities; Meals on Wheels; outpatient medical clinics; and the local Office on Aging.

It is also essential for geriatric social workers to investigate any suspicion of neglect or abuse at the hands of family members or an institution's staff. Such conditions may be evidenced by poor sanitary conditions, inadequate food, or unsatisfactory medical or dental care. It is important to follow up to make sure that any negative situation is rectified.

Work Settings

Geriatric social workers service clients from their offices and also may visit homes and facilities caring for the elderly. Their employers can be federal, state, county, or municipal governments, as well as hospitals, hospices, nursing homes, extended-care facilities, and social service agencies. They usually work a standard 40-hour week. When special circumstances arise, weekend or evening work may prove necessary.

Advancement

You can move up the career ladder by obtaining a master's degree in social work (MSW). This could make it easier for you to find a more prestigious position with a more prominent or larger organization, leading to increased responsibilities and salary. Acquiring an administrative or supervisory position or entering college-level teaching or private practice are other options. Such positions may also result in increased pay.

Prerequisites

Having a high school diploma with credentials that will facilitate college admission is essential. Volunteer work with the elderly at senior centers and nursing homes or hospitals provides insight into issues associated with caring for the elderly.

You need at least a bachelor's degree to work in this field. If you obtain a master's degree, it preferably should be in gerontology. For a teaching career, a Ph.D. is desirable.

Education/Training

For your bachelor's degree, a major in sociology, psychology, or social work is most advisable. Other majors may be acceptable when supplemented with experience in the field. Obtaining a master's in social work or gerontology will help you obtain an attractive position.

Certification/Registration/Licensure

A bachelor's or master's degree is the only documentation required for work in this field.

Career Potential

Employment prospects in this field are good. You can obtain a position by sending your resume to personnel directors at facilities that hire geriatric social workers. You also can check the employment want ads. Government positions may be secured by taking civil-service exams, for which you can prepare by taking courses. Those with only a general social work background should gain gerontology experience by participating in workshops or seminars in the field.

For More Information

For more information on this field, contact the Council on Social Work Education, 1725 Duke St., Ste. 500, Alexandria, VA 22314 (www.cswe.org); the National Association of Social Workers, 750 First St. NE, Ste. 700, Washington, DC 20002 (www.socialworkers. org); or the Association for Gerontology in Higher Education, 1030 15th St. NW, Ste. 240, Washington, DC 20005 (www.aghe.org).

Health Educators

Principal activity: Helping improve people's lifestyles through education

Work commitment: Usually full-time

Preprofessional education: High school diploma

Program length: 4 years; 6 years for public-health educator

Work prerequisites: Bachelor's degree; master's degree for public-health educator

Career opportunities: Favorable

Income range: $33,000 to $61,000

Scope

Health education is performed by people in school, community, and public-health agencies. The goal is to teach people how to improve their health and prevent disease. By persuading people to practice healthy lifestyles, these educators have a profound impact not only on individual lives but on society in general. This is reflected, for example, by the education campaigns against smoking, alcohol and substance abuse, and AIDS.

Activities

School health educators must hold a teaching license and have expertise in health education. They teach about the importance of personal hygiene and emphasize the destructive impact of smoking, alcohol, and drugs. Greater emphasis in this area is anticipated, because it is so important to our society's future.

Community health educators reach out to the adult population through workplaces and the media. They use exhibits, public meetings, health runs, and smoking withdrawal clinics to encourage healthier lifestyles.

Public-health educators collect information on public-health issues and serve as liaisons between government agencies and community groups.

Work Settings

Health educators seek contact with the public in a variety of settings, in order to encourage people to improve the quality of their health. Thus, health educators visit schools at various educational levels, community groups, religious and social organizations, and community forums. They are sponsored by hospitals, civic organizations, and governmental agencies.

Advancement

Advancement in this field comes with experience and additional education (such as a master's degree).

Prerequisites

A high school diploma or its equivalent is needed to enter a training program. Public-health educators must hold at least a bachelor's degree. Some positions require a master's degree.

Desirable personal attributes include good communication skills, a desire to teach, the ability to interact in a group setting, and good health habits.

Education/Training

Those planning careers as school or community health educators must earn a bachelor's degree in education. Most colleges offer teacher training programs.

Public-health educators must earn a degree in public health, which is offered by many universities.

Certification/Registration/Licensure

Most health educators are not licensed. However, those teaching in schools must have a teaching license from their state education department.

Career Potential

Most school health educators work in public schools. Those holding a master's degree can teach at the college level.

Many health organizations hire health educators as administrative personnel. Educators also work in hospitals, clinics, HMOs, and government agencies. Overall prospects for employment in most organizations is good.

For More Information

The professional organization for this field is the American Public Health Association, 800 I St. NW, Washington, DC 20001 (www.apha.org).

Health Education Programs

Hundreds of colleges and universities offer teaching programs—far too many to list here. Contact your state university for more information on programs in your area.

Health Information Technicians

Principal activity: Maintaining medical records

Work commitment: Usually full-time

Preprofessional education: High school diploma

Program length: 2 to 4 years

Work prerequisites: Associate degree

Career opportunities: Highly favorable

Income range: $24,000 to $39,000

Scope

A major responsibility of hospitals and other health-care facilities is maintaining complete and accurate records for all their patients. These records are essential for insurance or Medicare payments, for example. Moreover, doctors use records to evaluate treatments, and government agencies use them to determine whether facilities are being managed in accordance with legal requirements.

Activities

Health information (medical record) technicians must determine whether patient records are complete, including the attending physician's name, admission date, history, symptoms, physical exam records, test results, diagnoses, physician notes, and discharge date. They also must translate diseases and procedures into coding symbols. They are responsible for maintaining all patient records in an organized fashion so that they can be easily retrieved. The work must be processed accurately and efficiently so that reimbursement is correct and expedited.

These workers find information for doctors and administrators and therefore must interact with health professionals, insurance companies, lawyers, administrators, and patients.

Work Settings

Most health information technicians work in hospitals. Others work in HMOs, nursing homes, health clinics, and physicians' offices.

Advancement

With experience and education, a health information technician may advance to a supervisory or managerial position.

Prerequisites

A high school diploma or its equivalent is necessary for admission to college-level programs in this field.

Desirable personal attributes include dependability, a concern for detail, good computer and communication skills, the ability to maintain confidentiality, and organized work habits.

Education/Training

Most people in this field complete a two-year course in medical record technology, leading to an associate degree. An alternative approach is to graduate from an independent study program offered by the American Medical Record Association.

Certification/Registration/Licensure

Meeting the educational requirements and passing a written examination sponsored by the American Medical Record Association ensures certification. This status is helpful in finding employment.

Career Potential

Employment prospects for health information technicians are excellent. The increasing numbers of elderly people in the United States will require more hospitalization and increased use of other health-care facilities, with a corresponding rise in the workload for health information technicians.

For More Information

The professional organization for this field is the American Health Information Management Association, 233 N. Michigan Ave., Ste. 2150, Chicago, IL 60611 (www.ahima. org).

Health Information Technician Programs

Alabama

University of Alabama at
  Birmingham
UAB Station
Birmingham, AL 35294
www.uab.edu

University of West Alabama
Livingston, AL 35470
www.uwa.edu

Arizona

Apollo College–Phoenix Westside
2701 W. Bethany Home Rd.
Phoenix, AZ 85017
www.apollocollege.com

Apollo College–Tucson
3550 N. Oracle Rd.
Tucson, AZ 85705
www.apollocollege.com

California

Cabrillo College
6500 Soquel Drive
Aptos, CA 95003
www.cabrillo.edu

Charles R. Drew University of
  Medicine and Science
1731 E. 120th St.
Los Angeles, CA 90059
www.cdrewu.edu

City College of San Francisco
Ocean Campus
50 Phelan Avenue
San Francisco, CA 94112
www.ccsf.edu

Fresno City College
1101 E University Avenue
Fresno, CA 93741
www.fresnocitycollege.edu

Loma Linda University
School of Allied Health
  Professions
Loma Linda, CA 92350
www.llu.com

San Diego Mesa College
7250 Mesa College Drive
San Diego, CA 92111
www.sdmesa.edu

Colorado

Regis University
School of Health Care
  Professions
3333 Regis Blvd.
Denver, CO 80221
www.regis.edu

Florida

Central Florida College
1573 W. Fairbanks
Winter Park, FL 32789
www.central-florida-college.com

Florida A&M University
Tallahassee, FL 32307
www.famu.edu

Florida International University
University Park Campus
11200 SW 8th St.
Miami, FL 33199
www.fiu.edu

North Florida Institute
530 Wells Rd.
Orange Park, FL 32073
www.northflorida-institute.com

Southwest Florida College
1685 Medical Ln.
Fort Myers, FL 33907
www.swfc.edu

University of Central Florida
4000 Central Florida Blvd.
Orlando, FL 32816
www.ucf.edu

Georgia

Clark Atlanta University
223 James P. Brawley Dr. SW
Atlanta, GA 30314
www.cau.edu

Columbus State University
4225 University Ave.
Columbus, GA 31907
www.colstate.edu

Medical College of Georgia
1120 15th St.
Augusta, GA 30912
www.mcg.edu

Idaho

Boise State University
1910 University Dr.
Boise, ID 83725
www.boisestate.edu

Illinois

Chicago State University
9501 S. King Dr.
Chicago, IL 60628
www.csu.edu

Illinois State University
Normal, IL 61790
www.ilstu.edu

University of Illinois at Chicago
935 W. Harrison St.
Chicago, IL 60607
www.uic.edu

Indiana

Indiana University
300 N. Jordan Ave.
Bloomington, IN 47405
www.indiana.edu

Indiana University Northwest
3400 Broadway
Gary, IN 46408
www.iun.edu

Indiana University–Purdue
  University Indianapolis
Cavanaugh Hall
Indianapolis, IN 46202
www.iupui.edu

Kansas

University of Kansas
School of Allied Health
3901 Rainbow Blvd.
Kansas City, KS 66160
http://alliedhealth.kumc.edu/

University of Kansas
126 Strong Hall
Lawrence, KS 66045
www.ukans.edu

Washburn University of Topeka
1700 SW College Ave.
Topeka, KS 66621
www.washburn.edu

Wichita State University
1845 N. Fairmount
Wichita, KS 67260
www.wichita.edu

Kentucky
Eastern Kentucky University
521 Lancaster Ave.
Richmond, KY 40475
www.eku.edu

National College of Business &
Technology–Louisville
4205 Dixie Hwy.
Louisville, KY 40216
www.ncbt.edu

Western Kentucky University
1 Big Red Way
Bowling Green, KY 42101
www.wku.edu

Louisiana
Louisiana Tech University
P.O. Box 3178
Ruston, LA 71272
www.latech.edu

University of Louisiana at
Lafayette
104 University Circle
Lafayette, LA 70504
www.louisiana.edu

Maine
University of Maine
Orono, ME 04469
www.umaine.edu

Massachusetts
Springfield College
263 Alden St.
Springfield, MA 01109
www.spfldcol.edu

Michigan
Baker College of Auburn Hills
1500 University Dr.
Auburn Hills, MI 48326
www.baker.edu

Baker College of Mt. Clemens
34950 Little Mack
Clinton Township, MI 48035
www.baker.edu

Baker College of Muskegon
123 E. Apple Ave.
Muskegon, MI 49442
www.baker.edu

Baker College of Owosso
Owosso, MI 48867
www.baker.edu

Baker College of Port Huron
3403 Lapeer Rd.
Port Huron, MI 48060
www.baker.edu

Davenport College
4123 W. Main St.
Kalamazoo, MI 49006
www.davenport.edu

Ferris State University
Applied Technology Center
151 Fountain St. NE
Grand Rapids, MI 49503
www.ferris.edu

Minnesota
College of St. Scholastica
1200 Kenwood Ave.
Duluth, MN 55811
www.css.edu

Minnesota State University
Moorhead
1104 7th Ave. S.
Moorhead, MN 56563
www.mnstate.edu

Mississippi
Alcorn State University
1000 ASU Dr.
Alcorn State, MS 39096
www.alcorn.edu

Jackson State University
1400 John R. Lynch St.
Jackson, MS 39217
www.jsums.edu

University of Mississippi Medical
Center
School of Health-Related
Professions
2500 N. State St.
Jackson, MS 39216
http://shrp.umc.edu/

Missouri
Sanford-Brown College
1203 Smizer Mill Rd.
Fenton, MO 63026
http://sanford-brown.edu/

Sanford-Brown College
3555 Franks Dr.
St. Charles, MO 63301
wwwsanfordbrown.edu

St. Louis University
221 N. Grand Blvd.
St. Louis, MO 63103
www.slu.edu

Nebraska
College of St. Mary
1901 S. 72nd St.
Omaha, NE 68124
www.csm.edu

New Jersey
Harris School of Business
1 Cherry Hill
Cherry Hill, NJ 08002
www.harrisschool.com

Kean University
1000 Morris Ave.
Union, NJ 07083
www.kean.edu

New Mexico
Apollo College–Albuquerque
5301 Central Ave. NE
Ste. 101
Albuquerque, NM 87108
www.apollocollege.com

New York
Ithaca College
Ithaca, NY 14850
www.ithaca.edu

Long Island University
700 Northern Blvd.
Brookville, NY 11548
www.liu.edu

New York Medical College
School of Public Health
Valhalla, NY 10595
www.nymc.edu

Pace University
1 Pace Plaza
New York, NY 10038
www.pace.edu

Rochester Institute of Technology
One Lomb Memorial Dr.
Rochester, NY 14623
www.rit.edu

St. Francis College
180 Remsen St.
Brooklyn Heights, NY 11201
www.stfranciscollege.edu

State University of New York
 Institute of Technology
P.O. Box 3050
Utica, NY 13504
www.sunyit.edu

SUNY Downstate Medical Center
450 Clarkson Ave.
Brooklyn, NY 11203
www.hscbklyn.edu

Touro College
27-33 W. 23rd St.
New York, NY 10010
www.touro.edu

North Carolina
East Carolina University
E. 5th St.
Greenville, NC 27858
www.ecu.edu

Western Carolina University
Hwy. 107
Cullowhee, NC 28723
www.wcu.edu

Ohio
Ohio State University
Columbus, OH 43210
www.osu.edu

University of Toledo
Toledo, OH 43606
www.utoledo.edu

Oklahoma
East Central University
Ada, OK 74820
www.ecok.edu

Southwestern Oklahoma State
 University
100 Campus Dr.
Weatherford, OK 73096
www.swosu.edu

Pennsylvania
Duquesne University
600 Forbes Ave.
Pittsburgh, PA 15282
www.duq.edu

Gwynedd-Mercy College
School of Allied Health
 Professions
1325 Sumneytown Pike
P.O. Box 901
Gwynedd Valley, PA 19437
www.gmc.edu

Temple University
1801 N. Broad St.
Philadelphia, PA 19122
www.temple.edu

University of Pittsburgh
Pittsburgh, PA 15260
www.pitt.edu

South Dakota
Dakota State University
820 N. Washington Ave.
Madison, SD 57042
www.dsu.edu

Tennessee
Tennessee State University
3500 John A. Merritt Blvd.
Nashville, TN 37209
www.tnstate.edu

University of Tennessee at
 Knoxville
Knoxville, TN 37996
www.utk.edu

University of Tennessee
Health Science Center
Memphis, TN 38163
www.utmem.edu

Texas
Southwest Texas State University
Health Science Center
601 University Dr.
San Marcos, TX 78666
www.swt.edu

Texas Southern University
3100 Cleburne St.
Houston, TX 77004
www.tsu.edu

University of Texas Medical
 Branch
301 University Blvd.
Galveston, TX 77555
www.utmb.edu

Utah
Weber State University
3850 University Circle
Ogden, UT 84408
www.weber.edu

Virginia
Norfolk State University
700 Park Ave.
Norfolk, VA 23504
www.nsu.edu

Washington
Apollo College–Spokane
1101 N. Francher Rd.
Spokane, WA 99212
www.apollocollege.com

West Virginia
Fairmont State College
1201 Locust Ave.
Fairmont, WV 26554
www.fairmontstate.edu

Marshall University
One John Marshall Dr.
Huntington, WV 25755
www.marshall.edu

Wisconsin
University of Wisconsin–
 Milwaukee
2200 E. Kenwood Blvd.
P.O. Box 413
Milwaukee, WI 53201
www.uwm.edu

Health Sciences Librarians

Principal activity: Collecting and compiling biomedical information	**Program length:** 1 to 2 years
Work commitment: Usually full-time	**Work prerequisites:** Master of library science degree
Preprofessional education: Bachelor's degree	**Career opportunities:** Stable
	Income range: $35,000 to $62,000

Scope

An essential component of any health education institution is its medical library. This is where information is kept—information vital to the teaching and research activities of faculty, staff, and students. With the major technological advances in medicine over the past decades, there has been an explosion of knowledge. Today, in addition to housing books and journals, libraries are linked by computers to a worldwide network that permits unlimited access to information.

Activities

Health sciences librarians are information specialists trained in the health sciences. They are responsible for securing the most suitable books, journals, and other materials for their institutions and then cataloging them so that they can be readily retrieved. Librarians help library users find the information they need for their work or studies. They teach users about the library's organization, acquire materials requested by users from other libraries, and update computer databases with bibliographic information. Thus, librarians at a medical school or hospital have access to MEDLINE, the general medical retrieval system operated by the National Library of Medicine, and to specialized databases focused on major diseases or subjects. Some hospital librarians also bring reading materials to patients.

Work Settings

Health sciences librarians work in a wide variety of health sciences institutions, including schools of medicine, dentistry, veterinary medicine, nursing, pharmacy, and allied health. Some work in medical centers, hospitals, research institutes, pharmaceutical companies, and professional health-care associations.

Advancement

With experience and certification, a librarian can gain additional responsibilities and manage a specialized area of library operations.

Prerequisites

A Master's degree in library science (MLS) is necessary for positions in most academic and specialty libraries. Supplementary knowledge of the area of medicine is necessary and may be secured by on-the-job training and or by additional courses in the relevant sciences.

Education/Training

A bachelor's degree is the basic prerequisite for undertaking an education in library science. Master's degree programs are accredited by the American Library Association and last one to two years. Courses deal with scientific literature, biomedical communication, use of bibliographic and informational resources, library organization and management, and standard cataloging systems.

Certification/Registration/Licensure

The Medical Library Association offers four levels of accreditation for librarians. Getting higher-level accreditation can help a librarian advance to a more responsible or management position.

Career Potential

Prospects for employment in this field are stable for the immediate future because of the enormous quantity of biomedical information being published. Because the number of librarians coming into the profession is significant, however, competition for more attractive positions is intense.

For More Information

The professional organization for this field is the Medical Library Association, 65 E. Wacker Place, Ste. 1900, Chicago, IL 60601 (www.mlanet.org).

Health Sciences Librarian Programs

Alabama
University of Alabama
Tuscaloosa, AL 35487
www.ua.edu

Arizona
University of Arizona
Tucson, AZ 85721
www.arizona.edu

California
San Jose State University
1 Washington Square
San Jose, CA 95192
www.sjsu.edu

University of California–
  Los Angeles
405 Hilgard Ave.
Los Angeles, CA 90024
www.ucla.edu

Connecticut
Southern Connecticut State
  University
501 Crescent St.
New Haven, CT 06515
www.southernct.edu

District of Columbia
Catholic University of America
620 Michigan Ave. NE
Washington, DC 20064
www.cua.edu

Florida
University of South Florida
4202 E. Fowler Ave.
Tampa, FL 33620
www.usf.edu

Georgia
Clark Atlanta University
223 James P. Brawley Dr. SW
Atlanta, GA 30314
www.cau.edu

Hawaii
University of Hawaii
2530 Dole St., C-200
Honolulu, HI 96822
www.uhwo.hawaii.edu

Illinois
Dominican University
7900 W. Division St.
River Forest, IL 60305
www.dom.edu

University of Illinois at Chicago
Chicago, IL 60612
www.uic.edu

Indiana
Indiana University
300 N. Jordan Ave.
Bloomington, IN 47405
www.indiana.edu

Iowa
University of Iowa
Iowa City, IA 52242
www.uiowa.edu

Kansas
Emporia State University
1200 Commercial St.
Emporia, KS 66801
www.emporia.edu

Kentucky
University of Kentucky
Lexington, KY 40506
www.uky.edu

Maryland
University of Maryland
Baltimore, MD 21228
www.umaryland.edu

Massachusetts
Simmons College
300 The Fenway
Boston, MA 02115
www.simmons.edu

Michigan
University of Michigan
Dearborn, MI 48128
www.umich.edu

Wayne State University
Detroit, MI 48202
www.wayne.edu

Mississippi
University of Southern Mississippi
118 College Dr.
Hattiesburg, MS 39406
www.usm.edu

Missouri
University of Missouri–Columbia
Columbia, MO 65211
www.missouri.edu

New York
Long Island University
One University Plaza
Brooklyn, NY 11201
www.brooklyn.liu.edu

Pratt Institute
Information Science Studies
200 Willoughby Ave.
Brooklyn, NY 11205
www.pratt.edu

Queens College
The City University of New York
65-30 Kissena Blvd.
Flushing, NY 11367
www.qc.edu

St. John's University
8000 Utopia Pkwy.
Jamaica, NY 11439
www.stjohns.edu

Syracuse University
Syracuse, NY 13244
www.syr.edu

University at Albany
The State University of New York
1400 Washington Ave.
Albany, NY 12222
www.albany.edu

University at Buffalo
The State University of New York
501 Capen Hall
Buffalo, NY 14260
www.buffalo.edu

North Carolina
North Carolina Central University
1801 Fayetteville St.
Durham, NC 27707
www.nccu.edu

University of North Carolina
One University Heights
Asheville, NC 28804
www.unca.edu

University of North Carolina at
  Greensboro
1000 Spring Garden St.
Greensboro, NC 27403
www.uncg.edu

Ohio
Kent University
Kent, OH 44242
www.kent.edu

Oklahoma
University of Oklahoma
407 W. Boyd
Norman, OK 73019
www.ou.edu

Pennsylvania
Clarion University of Pennsylvania
Clarion, PA 16214
www.clarion.edu

Drexel University
3141 Chestnut St.
Philadelphia, PA 19104
www.drexel.edu

University of Pittsburgh
Pittsburgh, PA 15260
www.pitt.edu

Rhode Island
University of Rhode Island
Kingston, RI 02881
www.uri.edu

Texas
Texas Woman's University
P.O. Box 425589
Denton, TX 76204
www.twu.edu

University of North Texas
P.O. Box 311277
Denton, TX 76203
www.unt.edu

University of Texas at Austin
Austin, TX 78712
www.utexas.edu

Washington
University of Washington
1959 NE Pacific St., Box 356490
Seattle, WA 98195
www.washington.edu

Wisconsin
University of Wisconsin–Madison
1300 University Ave.
Madison, WI 53706
www.wisc.edu

University of Wisconsin–
  Milwaukee
P.O. Box 413
Milwaukee, WI 53201
www.uwm.edu

Health Services Administrators

Principal activity: Overseeing operations at a health-care facility

Work commitment: Full-time

Preprofessional education: Bachelor's degree

Program length: 4 to 6 years

Work prerequisites: Bachelor's degree; master's degree is preferred

Career opportunities: Favorable

Income range: $44,000 to $88,000 (depending on the organization, salaries can be much higher)

Scope

Health services administrators manage medical centers, hospitals, HMOs, and clinics. Their principal responsibility is ensuring that all hospital activities function in a coordinated, efficient way. The chief administrator is the senior nonmedical officer and is responsible for executing policies set by the institution's board of trustees and for the facility's day-to-day activities. The administrator also acts as a liaison between the board and medical staff. Lower-level administrators have more limited and specialized responsibilities over routine institutional operations.

Activities

Senior health administrators usually function by delegating responsibilities to middle- and lower-level administrators. This includes purchasing, maintenance, admissions, business personnel, security, public relations, and other vital nonmedical jobs. The senior administrator is ultimately responsible for developing the operating budget that is submitted to the trustees or corporate officials for approval each year.

Work Settings

Health services administrators work in medical centers, hospitals, HMOs, public-health agencies, clinics, and other facilities that provide outpatient or inpatient health care.

Advancement

Advancement comes with experience and increased education. Lower-level administrators are called administrative assistants or assistant administrators.

Prerequisites

A high school diploma or its equivalent is necessary to undertake studies for a bachelor's degree in hospital administration. This major is not necessary for graduate work, because a broad liberal arts background can also serve as the basis for graduate work.

Desirable personal attributes include superior verbal and written communication skills, the ability to interact with colleagues and supervisors, a strong interest in following up on details, and good business and leadership skills.

Education/Training

Graduate-level work includes courses in medicine, public health, and business. The program lasts two years, including a summer internship at a health facility.

An alternative program involves a full year of academic work followed by a second year of residency as a health services administration intern.

Certification/Registration/Licensure

You can become certified by meeting the educational and experience requirements of the American College of Hospital Administrators, 840 N. Lake Shore Dr., Chicago, IL 60611.

Career Potential

The changing health-care industry, and especially the evolution of HMOs, has increased the demand for administrators. This, together with an increasing population of senior citizens, suggests favorable employment opportunities in this field for the foreseeable future.

For More Information

The professional organizations for this field are the American College of Health Care Administrators, 300 N. Lee St., Ste. 301, Alexandria, VA 22314 (www.achca.org), and the American College of Healthcare Executives, One N. Franklin St., Chicago, IL 60606 (www.ache.org).

Health Sociologists

Principal activity: Securing sociological data relevant to health care

Work commitment: Full-time

Preprofessional education: Bachelor's degree

Program length: 2 to 4 years

Work prerequisites: Master's or doctoral degree

Career opportunities: Favorable

Income range: $38,000 to $71,000

Scope

Since the last century, doctors have discovered treatments for many diseases, using antibiotics and other medicines and such preventive measures as inoculations.

There is another aspect to health care, however: Social factors also influence the incidence and course of disease. Health sociologists track who gets sick and why and collect information on how people respond to different treatment options. Armed with this information, they can advise medical professionals on how to choose the best treatments for a widespread disease.

Activities

Health sociologists seek information on a wide variety of issues. They study the underlying social factors that motivate people to seek medical attention, the interactions of health-care providers with patients and with each other, people's reactions to technological advances, and community responses to the danger of infectious diseases. An emerging area of specialization is health issues of the elderly.

Work Settings

Health sociologists are employed by federal agencies, state health departments, research institutes, and universities.

Advancement

With experience a health sociologist can be promoted to higher levels of authority and responsibility. Earning a Ph.D. enhances one's employment and advancement opportunities.

Prerequisites

A bachelor's degree with a major in sociology or a closely related field is the basis for the advanced degree required to enter this profession.

Desirable personal attributes include sound judgment, superior communication skills, computer literacy, patience, and perseverance.

Education/Training

Candidates should obtain a master's degree in sociology, which requires two years of full-time graduate work and completion of a thesis.

Earning a Ph.D. greatly enhances your marketability. A doctorate degree usually takes about four years and requires you to write a thesis.

Certification/Registration/Licensure

Certification is offered by the American Sociological Association and the Association for Applied and Clinical Sociology. No license is needed to work in this field.

Career Potential

It is difficult to make a definitive projection for this field, but it appears that employment opportunities will increase. The health-care industry will need much more information on elder-care issues as the population ages.

For More Information

The professional organizations for this field are the American Sociological Association, 1307 New York Ave. NW, Ste. 700, Washington, DC 20005 (www.asanet.org), and the Association for Applied and Clinical Sociology (www.aacsnet.org).

Instructors for the Blind

Principal activity: Teaching visually impaired people to be as mobile and independent as possible

Work commitment: Part- or full-time

Preprofessional education: High school diploma

Program length: 4 to 6 years

Work prerequisites: Bachelor's degree required; master's degree preferred

Career opportunities: Favorable

Income range: $41,000 to $64,000

Scope

The loss of vision, unfortunately, is not a rare occurrence. It can be caused by congenital factors, ophthalmologic disease, or injury. While devastating, the impact of blindness can be somewhat diminished by teaching the patient skills that give him or her greater mobility. This gives the visually impaired person a greater sense of independence and enhances his or her self-worth. Instructors for the blind provide this training.

Activities

Instructors first evaluate their clients to determine the nature and extent of their visual impairments. Then they form a plan for each individual and outline a schedule to implement it. They teach clients to become physically oriented to their surroundings by using their senses of hearing and touch. The initial goal is mobility within the client's neighborhood, but then the goals are broadened as much as possible. Mobility skills usually are taught on an individual basis, but other skills may be presented in a group setting.

Work Settings

These instructors work in private homes, VA hospitals, schools, rehabilitation centers, and community centers for the blind.

Advancement

With experience and a master's degree, an instructor's earning potential increases significantly.

Prerequisites

A high school diploma or its equivalent is required before you undertake studies for a bachelor's degree.

Because a master's degree is the preferred educational level, students should plan on completing a bachelor's degree first and then applying to an accredited master's program.

Desirable personal attributes include patience and perseverance, strong verbal communication skills, compassion, and a desire to help the visually handicapped.

Education/Training

The standard educational requirement is a master's degree. This two-year program involves both classroom and clinical experience, including an internship. More than 15 colleges and universities offer master's degrees in this field.

Because currently there is a shortage of instructors, individuals holding a bachelor's degree can often easily secure employment.

Certification/Registration/Licensure

Currently there are no state licensing requirements. Those who meet the educational and experience requirements can be certified by the Association for the Education and Rehabilitation of the Blind and Visually Impaired.

Career Potential

Employment prospects are positive overall due to shortage of instructors in some places. As the older population increases in this country, many will experience vision problems, so the need for instructors should remain strong.

For More Information

The professional organization for this field is the Foundation for the Blind, 11 Penn Plaza, Ste. 300, New York, NY 10001 (www.afb.org).

The accrediting agency is the Association for the Education and Rehabilitation of the Blind and Visually Impaired, 1703 N. Beauregard St., Ste. 440, Alexandria, VA 22311 (www.aerbvi.org).

Instructor for the Blind Programs

For a complete list of schools offering a master's degree in this field, contact the Association for the Education and Rehabilitation of the Blind and Visually Impaired at the address just listed.

Medical and Psychiatric Social Workers

Principal activity: Helping patients adjust to life's circumstances

Work commitment: Full-time

Preprofessional education: High school diploma

Program length: 4 to 6 years

Work prerequisites: Bachelor's degree required; master's degree preferred

Career opportunities: Highly favorable

Income range: $31,000 to $52,000

Scope

Medical social workers help patients (and their families) who are recovering from illness and those who are chronically ill or disabled cope with the varied stresses generated by their conditions. *Psychiatric social workers* focus on the needs of those with emotional problems, helping them adjust to home life and their community with a minimum of anxiety. These social workers are important members of the therapeutic professional community.

Activities

The duties of a medical social worker may include finding home care for a senior citizen, arranging placement for a patient in a convalescent home, securing help for the parents of a newborn with congenital medical problems, or helping a family cope with a parent who is seriously ill. Medical social workers are often called on to explain to family members the nature of a patient's illness and its short- and long-term impact on all aspects of their lives. Their duties vary daily as they play a significant role in the health-care team.

Psychiatric social workers similarly have varied responsibilities. They may serve as a liaison between patient, family, and staff; explain the nature of a patient's illness to the family in understandable terms; write reports on patient progress; help patients transition back into society; maintain contact to monitor their progress; and arrange for them to receive additional services.

Work Settings

These social workers are employed by all kinds of hospitals, nursing homes, long-term care facilities, clinics, home health agencies, crisis centers, public-health departments, and residence homes for the mentally disabled.

Advancement

Advancement to a supervisory position may come with increased education, certification, and experience.

Prerequisites

A high school diploma or its equivalent is necessary to undertake college studies for a bachelor's degree in social work.

Desirable personal attributes include concern for the well-being of others, emotional maturity, sound judgment, the ability to work with people from all social strata, good decision-making skills, patience, and the fortitude for working with people in crisis situations.

Education/Training

The minimum level of education necessary is a bachelor's degree in social work. Hundreds of colleges and universities offer programs accredited by the Council on Social Work Education. Such programs include courses in human behavior and the social environment, social welfare policy and services, methods of social work, and field experience.

A master's degree is advisable for medical social work. It takes two years of study, but it is required for many positions. More than 100 institutions offer such a program, which mandates a bachelor's as a prerequisite.

Those seeking teaching appointments should enroll in a doctoral program, which requires additional course work and a thesis. About 50 institutions currently offer degrees at this level.

Certification/Registration/Licensure

You can obtain certification from the Academy of Certified Social Workers. This certification requires a master's degree, two years of experience, membership in the National Association of Social Workers, and passing a written examination.

All states require that social workers be certified, registered, or licensed.

Career Potential

The employment outlook for social workers is very strong for the foreseeable future. Employment opportunities for those with backgrounds in gerontology should be excellent, particularly in the growing numbers of assisted-living and senior-living communities. In addition, advances in medical technology, an increased focus on community care for the emotionally disturbed, and an emphasis on substance abuse treatment will increase the need for social workers in the U.S.

For More Information

The professional organization for this field is the National Association of Social Workers, 750 First St. NE, Washington, DC 20002 (www.naswdc.org).

Medical Illustrators

Principal activity: Providing illustrations for medical materials

Work commitment: Part- or full-time

Preprofessional education: Bachelor's degree

Program length: 2 to 3 years

Work prerequisites: Master's degree

Career opportunities: Stable

Income range: $33,000 to $75,000

Scope

Medical illustrators provide the visual elements for the textbooks and journals used to train other medical professionals. They also provide illustrations for the journals and magazines that bring medical findings to the attention of the larger community. These illustrations enhance the readability and clarity of sometimes-complicated materials. Thus, illustrators are important contributors to health education.

Activities

Medical illustrators are artists who use their creative talents to produce illustrations, charts, and graphs for textbooks, journals, magazines, and exhibit displays. They may graphically represent the steps of an operation or re-create what can be seen under a microscope. Given the wide variety of assignments they may receive, illustrators need to be knowledgeable in a variety of techniques and media, including diagramming, drawing, painting, preparing models, and creating audiovisual aids.

Advancement

Advancement comes with experience and by specializing in different areas of medicine or in different media.

Prerequisites

The standard requirement is a bachelor's degree in art. Courses include drawing, life drawing, painting, design, theory of color, illustration techniques, photography, and layout. Students also should have a solid background in the sciences, including chemistry, biology, anatomy, developmental biology, physiology, histology, and microbiology. Developing an attractive portfolio of illustrative materials is essential.

Besides an interest in art and science, desirable attributes include creativity, an ability to translate scientific information into a clear and attractive format, patience, and the ability to work with demanding professionals under the pressure of deadlines.

Education/Training

A master's degree in medical illustration is offered by a few institutions, whose programs are accredited by the Association of Medical Illustrators. Most programs include gross anatomy, histology, physiology, human embryology, neuroanatomy, pathology, illustration in print and nonprint media, anatomical and surgical illustration, three-dimensional modeling, graph and chart design, exhibit construction, and cinematography.

Certification/Registration/Licensure

You can become certified through the Association of Medical Illustrators.

Career Potential

The employment outlook in this field is decent overall, though it is best for those holding a master's degree from an accredited program.

For More Information

The professional organization for this field is the Association of Medical Illustrators, 245 1st St., Ste. 1800, Cambridge, MA 02142 (www.ami.org).

Medical Illustrator Programs

Georgia
Medical College of Georgia
Department of Medical
 Illustration
1120 15th St., CJ1101
Augusta, GA 30912
www.mcg.edu/medart/

Illinois
University of Illinois at Chicago
1919 W. Taylor St.
Chicago, IL 60612
www.ahc.uic.edu/bhis/

Maryland
Johns Hopkins University
School of Medicine
1830 E. Monument St.
Ste. 7000
Baltimore, MD 21205
www.hopkinsmedicine.org

Michigan
University of Michigan
2000 Bonisteel Blvd.
Ann Arbor, MI 48109
www.umich.edu

Texas
University of Texas
Southwestern Medical Center at
 Dallas
5323 Harry Hines Blvd.
Dallas, TX 75390
www.utsouthwestern.edu

Canada
University of Toronto
1 King's College Circle
Toronto, Ontario M5S 1A8
www.bmc.med.utoronto.ca

Medical Scientists

Principal activity: Engaging in medical research either directly or in a supervisory capacity

Work commitment: Usually full-time; part-time if also teaching

Preprofessional education: Bachelor's degree

Program length: 4 to 8 years

Work prerequisites: Ph.D. in science, or MD plus medical research training on a postdoctoral level

Career opportunities: Highly favorable

Income range: $70,000 to $125,000

Scope

Medical scientists research human diseases and conditions. Their work results in advances in diagnosis, treatment, and prevention of many diseases, building the foundation for new vaccines, drugs, and procedures. They are often involved in clinical investigations, teaching, and technical writing.

Activities

Medical scientists study biological systems to understand the cause of disease. For example, some try to identify changes in cells or chromosomes. They then use this knowledge to develop treatments and design new research tools. They often collaborate with physicians to administer treatments, monitoring reactions and recording results for future use. The results of their work provide the basis for most of the advances we see in health care today.

Work Settings

Medical scientists find employment in a wide range of settings. These include universities, where they are usually also engaged in teaching and supervising the research activities of undergraduate and graduate students. They also work in the laboratories of independent research institutes, biotechnology companies, and pharmaceutical companies.

Advancement

Advancement comes with experience and increased responsibility. At universities, researchers can move up the ranks to become the head of a department. Many medical scientists are elevated to more of a management role.

Prerequisites

Work as a medical scientist usually requires having a Ph.D. in biological science, or an MD with a significant background in research, though some medical scientists get started with only a master's degree.

Desirable personal attributes include inventiveness, abstract thinking skills, analytical skills, and problem-solving ability. Also useful are patience, determination, and good verbal and written communication skills.

Education/Training

Graduate-level courses and research work leading to a Ph.D. in biological science is essential. Those with a medical degree and an interest and background in research often transfer to medical science as well.

Certification/Registration/Licensure

Medical scientists who are involved in administering drugs, drawing blood, or excising tissue need to be licensed and preferably board certified.

Career Potential

The demand for better treatment options and the constant innovation in the health-care field provides an exceptionally strong market for those interested in a career in medical science research. While the educational requirements are steep, the career provides numerous rewards, both material and non-material.

For More Information

There is no single professional organization that governs the work of medical scientists. For more information, however, contact the Federation of American Societies for Experimental Biology, 9650 Rockville Pike, Bethesda, MD 20814 (www.faseb.org).

Medical Secretaries

Principal activity: Performing office duties in a physician's practice

Work commitment: Full-time

Preprofessional education: High school diploma

Program length: 2 to 3 years

Work prerequisites: High school diploma required; college or business courses preferred

Career opportunities: Highly favorable

Income range: $27,000 to $38,000

Scope

Secretaries are the communication center of an office. They are largely responsible for the facility's efficient functioning. Medical secretaries are employed by physicians or by institutions where physicians work.

Activities

Medical secretaries type letters, transcribe dictation, set appointments, arrange for hospitalizations, and order supplies. They operate different types of equipment that facilitate communication and optimize office efficiency.

Work Settings

Medical secretaries are employed by private-practice physicians or by groups of physicians. Some work for hospitals, clinics, HMOs, insurance companies, and other agencies.

Advancement

Opportunities for advancement come with experience and training and with the demonstration of organizational and managerial talent. It also helps to increase your knowledge of the medical field. You can move up by being appointed an administrative assistant or office manager.

Prerequisites

A high school diploma or its equivalent is necessary for work in this field.

Desirable personal attributes include a neat appearance, a pleasant personality, attention to detail, and the ability to be discreet and to maintain confidentiality.

Education/Training

Training is offered at many business high schools, but college preparation is preferred. Candidates should take courses in English, data entry, computers, and business practices. A course in medical vocabulary also is desirable.

Secretaries must be able to operate various pieces of office equipment, such as a computer, fax machine, photocopier, and multiline phone. Training in word processing, database management, spreadsheets, desktop publishing, and computer graphics is desirable.

Certification/Registration/Licensure

Highly trained and experienced secretaries who pass a series of examinations offered by the National Secretaries' Association may qualify for the designation of certified professional secretary. This recognition carries weight with prospective employers.

Career Potential

With the continued growth of the health-care industry, there will be a continuing demand for medical secretaries. Thus, the job outlook for this field is excellent.

For More Information

Medical secretaries have no professional organization.

Medical Secretary Programs

California
La Sierra University
4500 Riverwalk Pkwy.
Riverside, CA 92515
www.lasierra.edu

Colorado
Denver Technical College
925 S. Niagara St.
Denver, CO 80224

Idaho
Boise State University
1910 University Dr.
Boise, ID 83725
www.boisestate.edu

Illinois
Moraine Valley Community College
9000 W College Pkwy
Palos Hills, IL 60465
www.morainevalley.edu

Indiana
Indiana University Northwest
3400 Broadway
Gary, IN 46408
www.iun.edu

Kansas
Washburn University of Topeka
1700 SW College Ave.
Topeka, KS 66621
www.washburn.edu

Maryland
Villa Julie College
1525 Greenspring Valley Rd.
Stevenson, MD 21153
www.vjc.edu

Michigan
Baker College of Auburn Hills
1500 University Dr.
Auburn Hills, MI 48326
www.baker.edu

Baker College of Flint
1050 W. Bristol Rd.
Flint, MI 48507
www.baker.edu

Baker College of Mt. Clemens
34950 Little Mack
Clinton Township, MI 48035
www.baker.edu

Baker College of Muskegon
123 E. Apple Ave.
Muskegon, MI 49442
www.baker.edu

Baker College of Owosso
1020 S. Washington St.
Owosso, MI 48667
www.baker.edu

Baker College of Port Huron
3403 Lapeer Rd.
Port Huron, MI 48060
www.baker.edu

Cleary College
3601 Plymouth Rd.
Ann Arbor, MI 48105
www.cleary.edu

Davenport College
415 E. Fulton
Grand Rapids, MI 49503
www.davenport.edu

Davenport College
4123 W. Main St.
Kalamazoo, MI 49006
www.davenport.edu

Northern Michigan University
1401 Presque Isle Ave.
Marquette, MI 49855
www.nmu.edu

Minnesota
Northland Community & Technical
College
2020 Central Avenue NE
East Grand Forks, MN 56721
www.northlandcollege.edu

Nebraska
Midland Lutheran College
900 N. Clarkson
Fremont, NE 68025
www.mlc.edu

New Jersey
Medical Career Training
New Jersey
www.cicollege.edu

New Mexico
Eastern New Mexico University
1200 W. University
Portales, NM 88130
www.enmu.edu

Western New Mexico University
1000 W. College Ave.
Silver City, NM 88061
www.wnmu.edu

North Dakota
Minot State University
500 University Ave. W.
Minot, ND 58707
http://warp6.cs.misu.nodak.
  edu/

Ohio
University of Akron
302 Buchtel Mall
Akron, OH 44325
www.uakron.edu

University of Cincinnati
2624 Clifton Ave.
Cincinnati, OH 45221
www.uc.edu

University of Toledo
Toledo, OH 43606
www.utoledo.edu

Wright State University
3640 Colonel Glenn Hwy.
Dayton, OH 45435
www.wright.edu

Oregon
Oregon Institute of Technology
3201 Campus Dr.
Klamath Falls, OR 97601
www.oit.edu

Pennsylvania
Waynesburg College
51 W. College St.
Waynesburg, PA 15370
www.waynesburg.edu

York College of Pennsylvania
York, PA 17405
www.ycp.edu

Rhode Island
Johnson & Wales University
8 Abbott Park Place
Providence, RI 02903
www.jwu.edu

Tennessee
Martin Methodist College
433 W. Madison St.
Pulaski, TN 38478
www.martinmethodist.edu

Middle Tennessee State University
1301 E. Main St.
Murfreesboro, TN 37132
www.mtsu.edu

Trevecca Nazarene University
333 Murfreesboro Rd.
Nashville, TN 37210
www.trevecca.edu

Texas
Lamar University–Beaumont
4400 Martin Luther King Blvd.
P.O. Box 10009
Beaumont, TX 77710
www.lamar.edu

Utah
Weber State University
3850 University Circle
Ogden, UT 84408
www.weber.edu

Washington
Walla Walla College
204 S. College Ave.
College Place, WA 99324
www.wwc.edu

West Virginia
Mountain State University
P.O. Box 9003
Beckley, WV 25802
www.mountainstate.edu

Marshall University
One John Marshall Dr.
Huntington, WV 25755
www.marshall.edu

West Virginia University Institute
  of Technology
405 Fayette Pike
Montgomery, WV 25136
www.wvutech.edu

Wisconsin
Concordia University Wisconsin
12800 N. Lake Shore Dr.
Mequon, WI 53097
www.cuw.edu

Mental Health Workers

Principal activity: Helping care for emotionally or developmentally disabled people

Work commitment: Full-time

Preprofessional education: High school diploma

Program length: 2 years

Work prerequisites: High school diploma required; associate degree preferred

Career opportunities: Stable

Income range: $25,000 to $40,000

Scope

Mental health workers are responsible for providing a wide variety of therapeutic, supportive, and protective services. They deal with mentally handicapped people of all ages, emotionally ill individuals, and those suffering from addiction. These mental health workers are important members of the health-care team.

Activities

Mental health workers motivate their clients to use their skills and acquire new ones, help them carry out therapeutic exercises, administer medications and treatments, take vital signs, provide behavior modification and counseling, serve as patient advocates, and act as a resource for patients and their families during the transition to an outside home. All these activities are carried out under the supervision of a registered nurse or social worker.

Work Settings

Mental health workers are employed by mental health facilities such as state and private hospitals, community health centers, mental health clinics, schools for the mentally disabled, crisis centers, nursing homes, child guidance clinics, and private psychiatric offices.

Prerequisites

Currently, no standard prerequisites for this field exist. Although it is not always required, a high school diploma or its equivalent is highly desirable.

The more common route to employment in this field is to take some post-high school courses in mental health—perhaps leading to an associate degree, which usually takes two years.

Desirable personal attributes include emotional stability, a strong sense of compassion, good health and stamina, strong verbal communication skills, patience, a sense of humor, and dependability.

Education/Training

Many community colleges offer programs in mental health and human services, leading to an associate degree. These programs include courses in basic and psychiatric nursing, general and abnormal psychology, mental health technology, theory of personality and social development, child development and growth, group dynamics, and sociology. As part of the program, students have the opportunity to get experience working with clients in a mental health setting.

Certification/Registration/Licensure

Certification does not as yet exist, but several states have instituted a licensure requirement for mental health workers. Other states are expected to follow suit and institute their own requirements.

Career Potential

Employment opportunities are expected to increase somewhat in this field as the health industry continues to recognize and accept that mental health workers provide cost-effective services to individuals who are in transition or who have been placed in community settings.

For More Information

This field has no professional organization, but for more information you can contact the National Association of Social Workers, 750 First St. NE, Washington, DC 20002 (www.naswdc.org), or the Council on Social Work Education, 1725 Duke St., Ste. 500, Alexandria, VA 22314 (www.cswe.org).

Mental Health Worker Programs

Arkansas
University of Central Arkansas
201 Donaghey Ave.
Conway, AR 72035
www.uca.edu

California
California State University
5151 State University Dr.
Los Angeles, CA 90032
www.calstatela.edu/

Illinois
Governors State University
1 University Pkwy.
University Park, IL 60466
www.govst.edu

National-Louis University
2840 Sheridan Rd.
Evanston, IL 60201
http://nlu.nl.edu/

Northern Illinois University
DeKalb, IL 60115
www.niu.edu

Indiana
Indiana University–Purdue
  University Fort Wayne
2101 E. Coliseum Blvd.
Ft. Wayne, IN 46805
www.ipfw.edu

Indiana Wesleyan University
4201 S. Washington St.
Marion, IN 46953
www.indwes.edu

Kansas
Emporia State University
1200 Commercial St.
Emporia, KS 66801
www.emporia.edu

Newman University
3100 McCormick Ave.
Wichita, KS 67213
www.newmanu.edu

Pittsburgh State University
1701 S. Broadway
Pittsburgh, KS 66762
www.pittstate.edu

Washburn University
1700 SW College Ave.
Topeka, KS 66621
www.washburn.edu

Kentucky
Northern Kentucky University
Highland Heights, KY 41099
www.nku.edu

Louisiana
Louisiana State University Health
  Sciences Center
433 Bolivar St.
New Orleans, LA 70112
www.lsuhsc.edu/no/

Maine
University of Maine at Farmington
246 Main St.
Farmington, ME 04938
www.umf.maine.edu

University of New England
11 Hills Beach Rd.
Biddeford, ME 04005
www.une.edu

Maryland
Morgan State University
1700 E. Cold Spring Ln.
Baltimore, MD 21251
www.morgan.edu

Massachusetts
Boston University
One Sherborn St.
Boston, MA 02215
www.bu.edu

Emmanuel College
400 The Fenway
Boston, MA 02115
www.emmanuel.edu

Springfield College
263 Alden St.
Springfield, MA 01109
www.spfldcol.edu

Michigan
Lake Superior State University
650 W. Easterday Ave.
Sault Sainte Marie, MI 49783
www.lssu.edu

Minnesota
St. Cloud State University
720 4th Ave. S.
St. Cloud, MN 56301
www.stcloudstate.edu

New Jersey
Thomas Edison State College
101 W. State St.
Trenton, NJ 08608
www.tesc.edu

New York
Elmira College
One Park Place
Elmira, NY 14901
www.elmira.edu

New York Institute of Technology
Northern Blvd.
Old Westbury, NY 11568
www.nyit.edu

North Carolina
Western Carolina University
Cullowhee, NC 28723
www.wcu.edu

Ohio
Franciscan University of
  Steubenville
1235 University Blvd.
Steubenville, OH 43952
www.franciscan.edu

University of Toledo
Toledo, OH 43606
www.utoledo.edu

Wright State University
3640 Colonel Glenn Hwy.
Dayton, OH 45435
www.wright.edu

Pennsylvania
Gannon University
109 University Square
Erie, PA 16541
www.gannon.edu

MCP Hahnemann University
245 N. 15th St.
Philadelphia, PA 19102
www.drexel.edu

Texas
University of North Texas
P.O. Box 311277
Denton, TX 76203
www.unt.edu

West Texas A&M University
P.O. Box 907
Canyon, TX 79016
www.wtamu.edu

Virginia
Virginia Commonwealth University
Richmond, VA 23284
www.vcu.edu

West Virginia
Marshall University
One John Marshall Dr.
Huntington, WV 25755
www.marshall.edu

Appendices

These appendices provide supplemental information to assist you in your job search.

Appendix A: Health-Care Education Admissions Tests
- A summary of the various admissions tests needed for admission into various health-care education programs.

Appendix B: Health-Care Professional Organizations
- Contact information for various health-care professional associations.

Appendix C: Job Search Resources
- An encyclopedia of job search resources in books, in magazines and journals, and online.

Health-Care Education Admissions Tests

The admissions tests described here are the ones you are most likely to face as a health-care student:

- **Medical College Admission Test (MCAT)** for admission to medical, veterinary, and podiatry schools.
- **Pharmacy College Admission Test (PCAT)** for pharmacy schools.
- **Optometry Admission Test (OAT)** for optometry schools.
- **Graduate Record Examination (GRE)** for admission to some graduate programs, such as Veterinary Medical Schools or master's degree programs for some allied-health programs.
- **Graduate Management Admission Test (GMAT)** or **Miller Analogies Test (MAT)** for admission to a graduate school of management, for careers such as health-care administration.
- **Dental Admission Test (DAT)** for admission to dental schools.

This appendix briefly discusses each of these tests, outlining their fees, content, and where to register.

Medical College Admission Test (MCAT)

The Medical College Admission Test (MCAT) is required for admission to most medical, many veterinary, and all podiatry schools. The extent to which test scores are used in the screening process varies from school to school. Generally, the admissions officer looks at your test scores, your undergraduate records, your references, and your interview performance in making the decision.

The MCAT is administered and scored by the MCAT Program. For an application or more information, contact

MCAT Program
P.O. Box 4056
Iowa City, IA 52243
(319) 337-1357
www.aamc.org/mcat

Contents

The MCAT consists of four separate sections:

1. **Verbal reasoning:** 40 questions (60 minutes)
2. **Physical sciences:** 52 questions (70 minutes)
3. **Writing sample:** 2 questions (60 minutes)
4. **Biological sciences:** 52 questions (70) minutes

Test Fees

Fee: $230; **Late Registration/Date Reschedule:** $55

Dental Admission Test (DAT)

Most dental schools require applicants to take the DAT. It is conducted two times a year (October and April).

For more information, contact

Division of Education Measurements
American Dental Association
212 E. Chicago Ave.
Chicago, IL 60611
(312) 440-2500
www.ada.org/dat.aspx/

Contents

The DAT consists of four parts (all multiple choice):

1. **Survey of Natural Sciences:** 100 questions (90 minutes)
2. **Reading Comprehension:** 50 questions (60 minutes)
3. **Quantitative Reasoning:** 40 questions (45 minutes)
4. **Perceptual Ability:** 40 questions (60 minutes)

Test Fees

Fee: $225 (includes 5 score reports); additional score report $25

Pharmacy College Admission Test (PCAT)

The PCAT measures general academic ability and scientific knowledge. The test is prepared and administered by the Psychological Corporation. For an application packet containing sample questions, contact

Pearson Assessments
195500 Bulverde Rd.
San Antonio, TX 78259
www.pcatweb.info

Contents

The PCAT consists of 240 multiple-choice questions and two writing prompts. The test lasts 4 hours, with one break.

There are six content areas, and you are allowed to work on each area only during the fixed time allotted for it. You cannot go back to earlier sections.

1. **Writing:** 2 writing topics (60 minutes)
2. **Verbal ability:** 48 questions (30 minutes)
3. **Biology:** 48 questions (30 minutes)
4. **Chemistry:** 48 questions (30 minutes)
5. **Quantitative ability**: 48 questions (40 minutes)
6. **Reading comprehension**: 48 questions (50 minutes)

Test Fees

Fee: $150; late registration and special location testing fees apply

Optometry Admission Test (OAT)

The OAT measures academic ability and comprehension of scientific information.

The test is administered by the Association of Schools and Colleges of Optometry. For an application packet containing sample questions, contact

Optometry Admission Testing Program
211 E. Chicago Ave., 6th Floor
Chicago, IL 60611
(312) 440-2693
www.ada.org/oat/

Contents

The OAT consists of 220 multiple-choice questions. Each question has 4 answer choices, only one of which is correct. The test lasts about 4 hours, with an optional 15-minute rest period.

There are 4 sections, and you are allowed to work on each area only during the fixed time allotted for it. You cannot go back to earlier sections.

1. **Survey of Natural Sciences:** 100 questions (90 minutes)
2. **Reading Comprehension:** 40 questions (50 minutes)
3. **Quantitative Reasoning:** 40 questions (45 minutes)
4. **Physics:** 40 questions (50 minutes)

Test Fees

Fee: $213

Graduate Record Examination

The GRE is taken by people applying to graduate schools for a post-baccalaureate degree. The test is offered in both computer- and paper-based formats. In addition, the

GRE is offered as a general test or as specific subject tests. Most allied health programs that require a GRE score expect the applicant to take the general test.

The test is administered by the Educational Testing Service. For an application packet and a sample general practice test, contact

Educational Testing Service
15 Rozedale Rd.
Princeton, NJ 08540
(609) 452-2209
www.ets.org/gre/

Contents

The GRE general test takes about 3 hours to complete. This test measures verbal, quantitative, and analytical reasoning and writing skills not necessarily related to any particular field of study.

You must work on the different sections sequentially, and you cannot return to a section you have completed. Here's a sample format of a general test (be aware that the formats of computer-based and paper-based tests are different):

- **Analytical Writing:** 2 prompts (75 minutes)
- **Verbal Reasoning:** 30 questions (30 minutes)
- **Quantitative Reasoning:** 28 questions (45 minutes)
- **Unscored section:** Varies
- **Research:** Varies

Test Fees

General test fee: $160; **subject test fee:** $140

Graduate Management Admission Test (GMAT)

This test is required for most students seeking an MBA degree from a graduate school of management. It is designed to help the graduate school assess the qualifications of applicants for advanced study in business and management (such as hospital administration).

For more information, contact

Graduate Management Admission Council
Educational Testing Service
P.O. Box 6103
Princeton, NJ 08541
www.mba.com

Contents

1. **Quantative:** 37 questions (75 minutes)
2. **Verbal:** 41 questions (75 minutes)
3. **Analytical writing:** 2 topics (30 minutes each)

Data-sufficiency and problem-solving questions will be mingled within the quantitative section; sentence correction, reading comprehension, and critical reasoning questions will be mingled within the verbal section.

Test Fees

Fee: $250; **rescheduling fee** $50

Miller Analogies Test (MAT)

The MAT is used to identify candidates for graduate school who are logical thinkers. It seeks to determine whether individuals have the ability to analyze information, rather than merely memorize and repeat it. This test is frequently used by institutions involved in hiring executives. The test seeks to measure your ability to recognize relationships between ideas, fluency in English, as well as general knowledge of literature, philosophy, history, science, mathematics, and the fine arts. The MAT is administered in both computer-based and paper versions.

For more information, contact

Pearson Assessment
19550 Bulverde Rd.
San Antonio, TX 78259
www.milleranalogies.com

Contents

An analogy is a statement that suggests two things are related to each other in the same way that two other things are related to each other. In each MAT analogy item, one term in the analogy is missing and has been replaced with four options, only one of which completes the analogy. This test consists of 120 partial analogies to be completed in 60 minutes. From these test items, 100 count toward the score and 20 are experimental for future test use.

Test Fees

Fee: This is set by each Controlled Testing Center.

Health-Care Professional Organizations

Alliance of Cardiovascular Professionals
Thalia Landing Offices, Building 2
4356 Bonney Rd., #103
Virginia Beach, VA 23452
www.acp-online.org

American Academy of Anesthesiologist Assistants
P.O. Box 13978
Tallahassee, FL 32317
www.anesthetist.org

American Academy of Cardiovascular Perfusion
P.O. Box 3596
Allentown, PA 18106
http://theaacp.addr.com/

American Academy of Orthotists and Prosthetists
526 King St.
Ste. 201
Alexandria, VA 22314
www.oandp.org

American Academy of Physician Assistants
950 N. Washington St.
Alexandria, VA 22314
www.aapa.org

American Art Therapy Association, Inc.
1202 Allanson Rd.
Mundelein, IL 60060
www.arttherapy.org

American Association for Respiratory Care
9425 N. McArthur Blvd.
Ste. 100
Irving, TX 75063
www.aarc.org

American Association of Blood Banks
8101 Glenbrook Rd.
Bethesda, MD 20814
www.aabb.org

American Association of Colleges of Osteopathic Medicine
5550 Friendship Blvd.
Ste. 310
Chevy Chase, MD 20815
www.aacom.org

American Association of Colleges of Pharmacy
1426 Prince St.
Alexandria, VA 22314
www.aacp.org

American Association of Colleges of Podiatric Medicine
15850 Crabbs Branch Way
Ste. 320
Rockville, MD 20855
www.aacpm.org

American Association of Critical-Care Nurses
101 Columbia
Aliso Viejo, CA 92656
www.aacn.org

American Association of Medical Assistants
20 N. Wacker Dr.
Ste. 1575
Chicago, IL 60606
www.aama-ntl.org

American Association of Nurse Anesthetists
222 S. Prospect Ave.
Park Ridge, IL 60068
www.aana.com

American Association of Pharmacy Technicians
P.O. Box 1447
Greensboro, NC 27402
www.pharmacytechnician.com

American Chiropractic Association
1701 Clarendon Blvd.
Arlington, VA 22209
www.amerchiro.org

American College of Health Care Administrators
300 N. Lee St.
Ste. 301
Alexandria, VA 22314
www.achca.org

American College of Healthcare Executives
One N. Franklin St.
Chicago, IL 60606
www.ache.org

American College of Nurse-Midwives
8403 Colesville Rd.
Silver Spring, MD 20910
www.midwife.org

American College of Nurse Practitioners
1111 19th St. NW
Ste. 404
Washington, DC 20036
www.acnpweb.org

American Dance Therapy Association, Inc.
2000 Century Plaza
Ste. 108
Columbia, MD 21044
www.adta.org

American Dental Assistants Association
35 E. Wacker Dr.
Ste. 1730
Chicago, IL 60601
www.dentalassistant.org

American Dental Association
211 E. Chicago Ave.
Chicago, IL 60611
www.ada.org

American Dental Hygienists' Association
444 N. Michigan Ave.
Ste. 3400
Chicago, IL 60611
www.adha.org

American Dietetic Association
120 S. Riverside Plaza
Ste. 2000
Chicago, IL 60606
www.eatright.org

American Health Care Association
1201 L St. NW
Washington, DC 20005
www.ahca.org

American Health Information Management Association
233 N. Michigan Ave.
Ste. 2150
Chicago, IL 60611
www.ahima.org

American Horticultural Therapy Association
909 York St.
Denver, CO 80206
www.ahta.org

American Hospital Association
1 N. Franklin
Chicago, IL 60606
www.aha.org

American Medical Association
515 N. State St.
Chicago, IL 60610
www.ama-assn.org

American Medical Student Association
1902 Association Dr.
Reston, VA 20191
www.amsa.org

American Medical Technologists
710 Higgins Rd.
Park Ridge, IL 60068
www.amt1.com

American Medical Women's Association
801 N. Fairfax St.
Alexandria, VA 22314
www.amwa-doc.org

American Medical Writers Association
40 W. Gude Dr.
Ste. 101
Rockville, MD 20850
www.amwa.org

American Music Therapy Association, Inc.
8455 Colesville Rd.
Ste. 1000
Silver Spring, MD 20910
www.musictherapy.org

American Nurses' Association
8515 Georgia Ave.
Ste. 400
Silver Spring, MD 20910
www.nursingworld.org

American Occupational Therapy Association, Inc.
4720 Montgomery Ln.
P.O. Box 31220
Bethesda, MD 20824
www.aota.org

American Optometric Association
243 N. Lindbergh Blvd.
St. Louis, MO 63141
www.aoanet.org

American Orthoptic Council
3914 Nakoma Rd.
Madison, WI 53711
www.orthoptics.org

American Orthotic & Prosthetic Association
330 John Carlyle St.
Ste. 200
Alexandria, VA 22314
www.aopanet.org

American Osteopathic Association
142 E. Ontario St.
Chicago, IL 60611
www.osteopathic.org

American Pharmacists Association
2215 Constitution Ave. NW
Washington, DC 20037
www.pharmacist.com

American Physical Therapy Association
1111 N. Fairfax St.
Alexandria, VA 22314
www.apta.org

American Podiatric Medical Association
9312 Old Georgetown Rd.
Bethesda, MD 20814
www.apma.org

American Public Health Association
800 I St. NW
Washington, DC 20001
www.apha.org

American Society for Clinical Laboratory Science
6701 Democracy Blvd.
Ste. 300
Bethesda, MD 20817
www.ascls.org

American Society for Clinical Pathology
2100 W. Harrison St.
Chicago, IL 60612
www.ascp.org

American Society for Hospital Public Relations
1 N. Franklin
Chicago, IL 60606
www.aha.org

American Society of Cytopathology
400 W. Ninth St.
Ste. 201
Wilmington, DE 19801
www.cytopathology.org

American Society of Echocardiography
1500 Sunday Dr., Ste. 102
Raleigh, NC 27607
www.asecho.org

American Society of Electroneurodiagnostic Technologists, Inc.
426 W. 42nd St.
Kansas City, MO 64111
www.aset.org

American Society of Extra-Corporeal Technology
503 Carlisle Dr.
Ste. 125
Herndon, VA 20170
www.amsect.org

American Society of Radiologic Technologists
15000 Central Ave. SE
Albuquerque, NM 87123
www.asrt.org

American Sociological Association
1307 New York Ave. NW
Ste. 700
Washington, DC 20005
www.asanet.org

American Speech-Language-Hearing Association
10801 Rockville Pike
Rockville, MD 20852
www.asha.org

American Veterinary Medical Association
1931 N. Meacham Rd.
Ste. 100
Schaumburg, IL 60173
www.avma.org

Association for Gerontology in Higher Education
1030 15th St. NW
Ste. 240
Washington, DC 20005
www.aghe.org

Association for the Advancement of Medical Instrumentation
1110 N. Glebe Rd.
Ste. 220
Arlington, VA 22201
www.aami.org

Association for the Education and Rehabilitation of the Blind and Visually Impaired
1703 N. Beauregard St.
Ste. 440
Alexandria, VA 22311
www.aerbvi.org

Association of American Medical Colleges
2450 N St. NW
Washington, DC 20037
www.aamc.org

Association of American Veterinary Medical Colleges
1101 Vermont Ave. NW
Washington, DC 20005
www.aavmc.org

Association of Medical Illustrators
245 1st St.
Ste. 1800
Cambridge, MA 02142
www.ami.org

Association of Schools and Colleges of Optometry
6110 Executive Blvd.
Ste. 510
Rockville, MD 20852
www.opted.org

Association of Surgical Technologists
7108-C S. Alton Way
Englewood, CO 80112
www.ast.org

Biocommunications Association
220 Southwind Ln.
Hillsborough, NC 27278
www.bca.org

Biomedical Engineering Society
8401 Corporate Dr.
Ste. 225
Landover, MD 20785
www.bmes.org

Child Life Council, Inc.
11820 Parklawn Dr.
Ste. 240
Rockville, MD 20852
www.childlife.org

Council on Chiropractic Education
8049 N. 85th Way
Scottsdale, AZ 85258
www.cce-usa.org

Council on Social Work Education
1725 Duke St.
Ste. 500
Alexandria, VA 22314
www.cswe.org

Dietary Managers Association
406 Surrey Woods Dr.
St. Charles, IL 60174
www.dmaonline.org

Foundation for the Blind
11 Penn Plaza
Ste. 300
New York, NY 10001
www.afb.org

Institute of Food Technologists
525 W. Van Buren
Ste. 1000
Chicago, IL 60607
www.ift.org

Joint Commission on Allied Health Personnel in Ophthalmology
2025 Woodlane Dr.
St. Paul, MN 55125
www.jcahpo.org

Junior Engineering Technology Society
1420 King St.
Ste. 405
Alexandria, VA 22314
www.jets.org

Medical Library Association
65 E. Wacker Place
Ste. 1900
Chicago, IL 60601
www.mlanet.org

National Academy of Opticianry
8401 Corporate Dr.
Ste. 605
Landover, MD 20785
www.nao.org

**National Association for Practical Nurse
Education and Service, Inc.**
P.O. Box 25647
Alexandria, VA 22313
www.napnes.org

National Association of Activity Professionals
P.O. Box 5530
Sevierville, TN 37864
www.thenaap.com

**National Association of Alcoholism and Drug
Abuse Counselors**
1911 Fort Myer Dr.
Ste. 900
Arlington, VA 22209
www.naadac.org

National Association of Dental Laboratories
1530 Metropolitan Blvd.
Tallahassee, FL 32308
www.nadl.org

**National Association of Emergency Medical
Technicians**
P.O. Box 1400
Clinton, MS 39060
www.naemt.org

National Association of Home Care and Hospice
228 Seventh St. SE
Washington, DC 20003
www.nahc.org

**National Association of Professional Geriatric
Care Managers**
1604 N. Country Club Rd.
Tucson, AZ 85716
www.caremanager.org

National Association of Social Workers
750 1st St. NE
Washington, DC 20002
www.socialworkers.org

National Athletic Trainers' Association
2952 Stemmons Freeway
Dallas, TX 75247
www.nata.org

**National Council for Therapeutic Recreation
Certification**
7 Elmwood Dr.
New City, NY 10956
www.nctrc.org

National Environmental Health Association
720 S. Colorado Blvd.
Ste. 970-S
Denver, CO 80246
www.neha.org

**National Federation of Licensed Practical
Nurses, Inc.**
605 Poole Dr.
Garner, NC 27529
www.nflpn.org

National League for Nursing
61 Broadway
New York, NY 10006
www.nln.org

National Recreation and Park Association
22377 Belmont Ridge Rd.
Ashburn, VA 20148
www.nrpa.org

National Rehabilitation Counseling Association
P.O. Box 4480
Manassas, VA 20108
http://nrca-net.org/

National Society for Histotechnology
4201 Northview Dr.
Ste. 502
Bowie, MD 20716
www.nsh.org

National Society of Genetic Counselors
233 Canterbury Dr.
Wallingford, PA 19086
www.nsgc.org

Opticians Association of America
441 Carlisle Dr.
Herndon, VA 20170
www.oaa.org

**Registered Medical Assistants of the American
Medical Technologists**
710 Higgins Rd.
Park Ridge, IL 60068
www.amt1.com

Society for Vascular Ultrasound
4601 Presidents Dr.
Ste. 260
Lanham, MD 20706
www.svunet.org

Society of Diagnostic Medical Sonographers
2745 Dallas Pkwy.
Plano, TX 75093
www.sdms.org

Society of Invasive Cardiovascular Professionals
1500 Sunday Dr.
Ste. 102
Raleigh, NC 27607
www.sicp.com

Society of Nuclear Medicine
1830 Samuel Morse Dr.
Reston, VA 20190
www.snm.org

Sociological Practice Association
Department of Sociology and Anthropology
St. Cloud State University
St. Cloud, MN 56301
www.socpractice.org

Appendix C

Job Search Resources

There are thousands of job search resources available, many of them specifically geared toward those interested in working in health care. To secure the job that's right for you, you should make use of general sources, journals, and the Internet to learn what positions are available and most appropriate for your needs.

General Sources

This section lists a variety of general reference sources, such as handbooks and directories, in several fields. They are organized alphabetically.

ALA Handbook of Organization and Membership Directory
American Library Association
50 E. Huron St.
Chicago, IL 60611
www.ala.org/ala/aboutala/governance/
  handbook/

American Library Directory
R.R. Bowker Co.
121 Chanlon Rd.
New Providence, NJ 07904
www.americanlibrarydirectory.com

AMO Directory
Group Health Association of America
1129 20th St. NW
Washington, DC 20036

Billan's Hospital Blue Book
2100 Powers Ferry Rd.
Atlanta, GA 30339
www.billianshealthdata.com

Blue Book Digest of HMOs
National Association of Employers on Health Care
  Action
420 Clandon Blvd.
Suite 110
P.O. Box 220
Key Biscayne, FL 33149

Directory of Accredited Laboratories
American Association for Laboratory Accreditation
656 Quince Orchard Rd.
Gaithersburg, MD 20878
www.a2la.org

Directory of Community Blood Bank Centers
The American Association of Blood Banks
8101 Glenbrook Rd.
Bethesda, MD 20814
www.aabb.org

Directory of Medical Library Associates
Medical Library Association
6 N. Michigan Ave.
Chicago, IL 60602
www.mlanet.org

Directory of Nursing Homes
Oryx Press
4041 N. Central 700
Phoenix, AZ 85012
www.greenwood.com

Encyclopedia of Medical Organizations and Agencies
Gale Research, Inc.
835 Penobscot Building
Detroit, MI 48226
www.gale.com

Federal Career Opportunities
Federal Research Services, Inc.
243 Church St.
New York, NY
www.fedjobs.com

Federal Jobs Digest
325 Pennsylvania Ave. SE
Washington, DC 20003
www.jobsfed.com

Freestanding Outpatient Surgery Career Directory
SMG Marketing Group, Inc.
1342 N. La Salle Dr.
Chicago, IL 60610
www.employerhealth.com

Hospitals Directory
American Business Directories, Inc.
5711 S. 86th Circle
Omaha, NE 68127
www.infousa.com

International Cytogenetic Laboratory Directory
Association of Genetic Technologists
616 S. Orchard Dr.
Burbank, CA 91506
www.agt-info.org

Laboratories—Medical Directories
American Business Information, Inc.
5711 S. 86th Circle
Omaha, NE 68127
www.infousa.com

Medical Laboratory Directory
U.S. Directory Service Publishers
655 128th St. NW
P.O. Box 68-1700
Miami, FL 33168

NMTCB Directory
Nuclear Medicine Technology Certification Board
2970 Clairmont Rd.
Atlanta, GA 30329
www.nmtcb.org

Occupational Handbook Outlook, 2010-2011
JIST Publishing
www.jist.com

Organization of Medical Record Departments in Hospitals
American Hospital Publishing, Inc.
737 N. Michigan Ave.
Chicago, IL 60611
www.ahaonlinestore.com

The City-County Recruiter and The State Recruiter
P.O. Box 2400, Station B
Lincoln, NE 68502

Web Sources

The following are some Web sites devoted to health-care careers (thanks to Wendy Enelow and Louise Kursmark, who compiled this list for their book *Expert Resumes for Health Care Careers*):

Site Name	URL
Absolutely Health Care	www.healthjobsUSA.com
Allhealthcarejobs.com	www.allhealthcarejobs.com
All Nurses	www.allnurses.com
Alliance of Medical Recruiters	www.physicianrecruiters.com
AlliedHealthCareers.com	www.alliedhealthcareers.com
American Medical Association (JAMA)	www.ama-assn.org/cgi-bin/webad/

(continued)

(continued)

Site Name	URL
Aureus Medical	www.aureusmed.com
CareerBuilder Health Jobs	www.healthopps.com
CompHealth	www.comphealth.com
Emergency Medicine and Primary Care Home Page	www.embbs.com
Healthcare Consultants (pharmacy staffing)	www.pharmacy-staffing.com
Health Care Job Store	www.healthcarejobstore.com
HealthcareSource	https://jobs.healthcaresource.com/
HealthCareerWeb	www.healthcareerweb.com
HealthJobSite.com	www.healthjobsite.com
Hospital Jobs OnLine	www.hospitaljobsonline.com/ jobsearch.aspx
HospitalLink	www.hospitallink.com
LocumTenens.com	www.locumtenens.com
MedCareers	www.medcareers.com
MedHunters.com	www.medhunters.com
MedicalJobSpot	www.medicaljobspot.com
Medzilla	www.medzilla.com/
Monster Health Care	http://healthcare.monster.com
NP Jobs (jobs for Nurse Practitioners)	www.npjobs.com
Nurse.com	www.nurse.com
Nurse Recruiter.com	www.nurse-recruiter.com
NurseVillage.com	www.nursevillage.com
Pharmaceutical Company Database	www.coreynahman.com/ pharmaceutical_company_ database.html
Physicians Employment	www.physemp.com
PracticeChoice	www.practicechoice.com
RehabJobsOnline	www.rehabjobs.com
RTjobs.com	www.rtjobs.com
Rx Career Center	www.rxcareercenter.com

Journals

Many journals carry help-wanted ads. Listed here are several such journals, arranged alphabetically. You can find journals like these in the libraries of most medical schools and universities.

AABB News

Acta Cytology

Aium Newsletter

American Clinical Laboratory

American Clinical Laboratory News

American Heart Journal

American Journal of Health Promotion

American Journal of Public Health

American Journal of Surgery

American Libraries

American Society of Extra-Corporal Technology

Annals of Surgery

Applied Cyto-Genetics

Applied Radiology

Archives of Pathology and Laboratory Medicine

Archives of Surgery

ASHA

Biomedical Engineering

Blood Banking

Cardiovascular & Pulmonary Technology

Clinical EEG

Clinical Imaging

Clinical Medical Laboratories

Clinical Nuclear Medicine

Computerized Medical Imaging and Graphics

CP Digest

Cyto-Technology & Histotechnology

Cytotenetry

Emergency Medicine

Emergency Medicine Services

Health and Social Work

Health Education

Information Manager

Information Science–Medical Records

Information Today

Journal of Clinical Endocrinology & Metabolism

Journal of Computer Assisted Topography

Journal of Histotechnology

Journal of Nuclear Medical Technology

Journal of Nuclear Medicine

Journal of the American Record Association

Journal of the American Society of Eco-Cardiography

Journal of Ultrasound Medicine

Laboratory Medicine

Magnetic Resonance Medicine

Medical Electronic Equipment News

Medical Electronic Products

Medical Imaging & Therapy

MLA News

Nursing

Nursing Economics

Optometry

Perfusion Life

Perfusionist

Pharmacy

Pharmacy Times

Radiological Technology

Radiology

Radiology and Nuclear Medicine

Review of Optometry

Sonography

Speech & Hearing

Surgery

Surgical Rounds

Surgical Technologist

Transfusion

Vision Monday

Index